# THE COMPLETE GUIDE TO
# ROCKS & MINERALS

# THE COMPLETE GUIDE TO
# ROCKS & MINERALS

How to find, identify and collect the world's most fascinating
specimens, featuring over 800 stunning photographs and artworks

## JOHN FARNDON

CONSULTANT: DR ALEC LIVINGSTONE,
X-RAY MINERALOGIST AND FORMER KEEPER OF MINERALS
AT THE NATIONAL MUSEUMS OF SCOTLAND, EDINBURGH

HERMES
HOUSE

This edition is published by Hermes House

Hermes House is an imprint of Anness Publishing Ltd
Hermes House, 88–89 Blackfriars Road, London SE1 8HA
tel. 020 7401 2077; fax 020 7633 9499

**www.hermeshouse.com; www.annesspublishing.com**

If you like the images in this book and would like to investigate using
them for publishing, promotions or advertising, please visit our website
**www.practicalpictures.com** for more information.

Publisher: Joanna Lorenz
Managing Director: Helen Sudell
Project Editor: Catherine Stuart
Production Manager: Steve Lang
Consultants: Dr Alec Livingstone and Dr John Schumacher (Department
of Earth Sciences, University of Bristol, England)
Editorial Readers: Alison Bolus and Jay Thundercliffe
Cover and Book Design: Nigel Partridge

ETHICAL TRADING POLICY
Because of our ongoing ecological investment programme, you, as our
customer, can have the pleasure and reassurance of knowing that a tree
is being cultivated on your behalf to naturally replace the materials used
to make the book you are holding. For further information about this
scheme, go to www.annesspublishing.com/trees

**NOTE**
The author and publishers have made every effort to ensure that all
instructions contained within this book are accurate and safe. Persons
handling and collecting rocks and mineral specimens do so at their own
risk. This book offers guidance on the basic safety precautions to take
when handling, identifying or collecting rock and mineral specimens;
however, we cannot accept any responsibility for any injury, loss or
damage to persons and property that may arise as a result of these
activities. It is especially important that collectors observe the protective
laws applied to a particular geological site before entering the site or
removing rock and mineral specimens, and note that these may vary
from region to region, and from country to country. Useful information
can, and should, be obtained from local government and environmental
agencies before visiting any geological site.

**PICTURE ACKNOWLEDGEMENTS**
Note: T = top; B = bottom; M = middle; L = left; R = right

The publishers would like to thank Richard Tayler, who provided the
majority of specimens photographed for this book from his own
collection, with additional material from his friends and associates.
The specimens were photographed by Martyn Milner. In addition, the
Department of Earth Sciences, University of Bristol, supplied the
specimen photographs of greensand (101B), doloritic limestone (111T),
fulgurite (131B), star sapphire (161B) and purpurite (191B). The School of
Earth, Atmospheric and Environmental Sciences, University of
Manchester, supplied the specimen photographs of boninite (67T), lapilli
(76T), tephra (76B), breadcrust bomb (77T), melilitite (79B), monzonite
(83B), monzodiorite (88B), charnockite (117B), greenschist (118T),
platinum (141B), diamond in kimberlite (145T), greenockite (148T),
jouravskite (185B) and vanadinite (201B). The Natural History Museum
provided the specimen photographs of bentonite (99T), thenardite
(187B), pearl (227T) and whewellite (227B).

Peter Bull drew all colour geological artworks included in the book,
except for p57 (Silicate shapes) which was drawn by Anthony Duke.
Anthony Duke also supplied the crystal structure diagrams appearing
throughout the *Directory of Minerals*.

Geological photographs were provided by the following:
2 (Granite rock exposed at Tarn (Midi-Pyrénées), France), Nature Picture
Library; 7TL, Natural History Museum.
*Understanding Rocks and Minerals:* 19BR, 27TR & 38–9, British
Geological Survey; 52BL, David Huston, Geoscience Australia; 17TR,
Marli Miller; 23TR, 48 (in Optical Effects panel: chatoyancy, play of
colour, pleochroism), 50BL & 51TR, Natural History Museum; 8–9, 32BL,
Nature Picture Library; 13BR, NHPA; 10BL, 18, 22, 25TR, 27B, 29T,
30BL, 32TL, 36TR, 36BL, 40T, 40B, 42T, 51TL & 51BR, Oxford Scientific;
13TL, Science Photo Library; 8–9, 34TR & 52T, Still Pictures; 27TL, 28M
& 59TL, Department of Earth Sciences, University of Bristol; 53B,
Andrew Wygralak, Northern Territory Geological Survey.
*Directory of Rocks:* 117, 123 & 129, British Geological Survey; 89,
Peter Frank © 2005 Canadian Museum of Nature, Ottawa, Canada;
113, Earth Observatory, NASA; 71, Nature Picture Library; 77 & 107,
Natural History Museum; 111 & 125, Oxford Scientific; 93, Anthony G
Taranto Jr, Palisades Interstate Park; 67 & 131, Science Photo Library;
69, Still Pictures; 91, David L Reid, Department of Geological Science,
University of Cape Town, South Africa; 65 & 127, Ian Coulson, University
of Regina, Canada.
*Directory of Minerals:* 211, British Geological Survey; 223, China Clay
Museum, Cornwall; 189, Shane Dohnt; 193, by permission of the Illinois
State Museum and the artist, Robert G Larson; 183, Jet Propulsion
Laboratory, NASA; 159, 197, 203, 205, 213, 215 & 231, Natural History
Museum; 167 & 175, Nature Picture Library; 141, 171, 177, 181, 199,
233, 237 & 247, Oxford Scientific; 187, Ted Rieger; 151, Science Photo
Library; 135, 201 & 249, Still Pictures Ltd; 165, Els Slots; 155, United
States Geological Survey; 149 & 191, Department of Earth Sciences,
University of Bristol; 235, Ian Coulson, University of Regina,
Saskatchewan, Canada.

# CONTENTS

# INTRODUCTION

Back in the early 19th century, when the whole idea of rock and mineral collecting was just getting under way, the famous Scottish poet Sir Walter Scott (1771–1832) described geologists thus, "Some rin uphill and down dale, knappin' the chucky stones to pieces like sa' many roadmakers run daft. They say it is to see how the warld was made!" Even today many people consider hunting rocks and minerals a rather strange activity.

Yet go to a beach or any stream where the water has exposed sand and gravel banks. You will see stone upon

*Below: Beautiful mineral specimens like these are rare treasures much sought after by rock hunters. Here are 'daisy' gypsum (top), 'dogtooth spar' calcite (left centre), 'blue john' fluorite (right centre) and pyrite (bottom), also known for obvious reasons as 'fool's gold'.*

stone lying there. To start with, they probably all look dull and grey. But look closer and you begin to see subtle differences in colour. One might be pale cream. Another mottled brown. A third slightly stripy. To the untrained eye, they're still just stones, but to an experienced rock hunter, each has its own fascinating story to tell.

The pale cream stone could be limestone. Look at it through a magnifying glass, and you begin to see it is made from tiny grains with shiny surfaces, each a crystal of calcite precipitated out of tropical oceans hundreds of millions of years ago. Here and there in the stone you may actually see fossils of the sea creatures that swam in these ancient oceans.

Your rock hunter might go on to tell you that the mottled brown stone is granite – then show how through the magnifying glass you can see three different minerals. There are tiny black flecks of mica, glassy grains of quartz, and yellow feldspar – all forged in the fiery heat of the earth's deep interior millions of years ago. The stripy stone could be a schist, a rock formed when other rocks came under such intense pressure from earth movements that the crystals in them broke down and were made anew in different forms – squeezed into stripes by the pressure. A magnifying glass might reveal tiny red spots embedded in the rock. A rock hunter might identify these as garnets or even rubies, tiny versions of the beautiful gems that kings have fought and died for.

*Above: Some specimens only reveal their true beauty when ground and polished like these specimens. At the top is the rock orbicular, a special variety of granite. Below are stones of the mineral onyx.*

With all this and much more in just three stones picked up on a beach, it is not surprising that many people have become hooked on rock and mineral collecting. Many stones are collectable for their sheer beauty and rarity – not just the well-known gems such as rubies and diamonds, but also non-gem minerals such as crocoite and rose quartz. Many rocks and minerals are sources of the ores that provide us with metals, or of building materials. Yet even when neither beautiful nor valuable, stones have a fascination because of the story they have to tell.

## Rocks through the ages

Rocks have long played a part in human history. Long ago, our ancestors were chipping the edges off hand-sized pebbles, perhaps to use as weapons. At least two million years ago, hominids began to use flints to make two-sided hand-axes, which is why the first age of humanity is known as the Stone Age. Finding good flints required a

*Above: Insects from tens of thousands of years ago can be perfectly preserved in amber, a stone formed from ancient tree sap.*

considerable practical knowledge of geology. Few people today would have a clue where to look for flints – yet these Stone Age people knew, and even dug mines to get at them underground.

Copper and gold were first used at least 10,000 years ago. They occur naturally as metals, and their distinctive colour makes them easy to see. Again, though, it required a real knowledge of geology to know where to look. Copper and gold were both too soft to make tools from, but the discovery that tin could be added to copper to make

*Below: None of these stones is especially beautiful but each has a story to tell. Top left is a dripstone formed in caverns from minerals dissolved in rainwater. Top right is a limestone rich in fossils of bryozoans, sea creatures that lived hundreds of millions years ago. At the bottom is a limestone imprinted by ancient corals.*

the tough alloy bronze about 5000 years ago initiated the first great age of metal use, the Bronze Age – and also the first great civilizations, such as that of Ancient Egypt. Tin only occurs in any quantity in the ore cassiterite, which has to be melted to extract the tin. Some cassiterite was found in river gravels where it often collects – but only in areas near granite. Some cassiterite was mined from veins deep underground, such as those in the Austrian Tyrol and in Cornwall. Again, locating these sources required a good knowledge of rocks and minerals.

Over the next 4000 years, miners acquired a wealth of hands-on practical geological skill as they hunted and exploited a range of metal ores and other materials. It is no accident that the word 'minerals' comes from miners. In the 1500s, the German mining engineer Georgius Agricola published the first great geology book, *De Re Metallica* (On things metallic).

## The rock hunters

All the same, it was not until the late 18th century that geology emerged as a science, pioneered by the great Scottish geologist James Hutton (1726–97). In Hutton's day, most people still believed the Earth was just a few thousand years old. Hutton realized it is much, much older – it is now thought to be 4.5 billion years old – and that the slow processes we see acting on the landscape today were quite enough to shape it without invoking great catastrophes, as others did. Hutton demonstrated that landscapes are worn away by rivers and that sediment washed into the sea forms new sedimentary rocks. He also saw how the Earth's heat could transform rocks, lifting and twisting them to

*Above and left: Very occasionally, the rock hunter is rewarded by the discovery of a gemstone, such as ruby (left) or even a diamond (above). Even if they are not especially valuable forms of the gems, the thrill of discovery is quite enough.*

create new mountains. So the world is shaped by countless cycles of erosion, sedimentation and uplift – each new beginning often clearly marked by breaks in the rock sequence called unconformities (see Reading the Landscape, Understanding Rocks and Minerals).

Inspired by Hutton's ideas, more and more geologists ventured out into the field to explore rocks and the story they tell. Geology became a popular pastime for many Victorian gentlemen, who ventured out in stout boots with just a hammer and a strong bag for specimens. They included Charles Darwin, who brought his knowledge of geological history to bear in formulating his theory of evolution. A huge proportion of the rock and mineral species we know today were first identified and named by Victorian specimen hunters.

As the following pages show, our knowledge of geological processes has developed tremendously since those early days, and professional geologists are aided by a range of sophisticated equipment. Yet the amateur armed with a few basic tools and a sharp eye can find fantastic specimens. It is the aim of this book to help in this search.

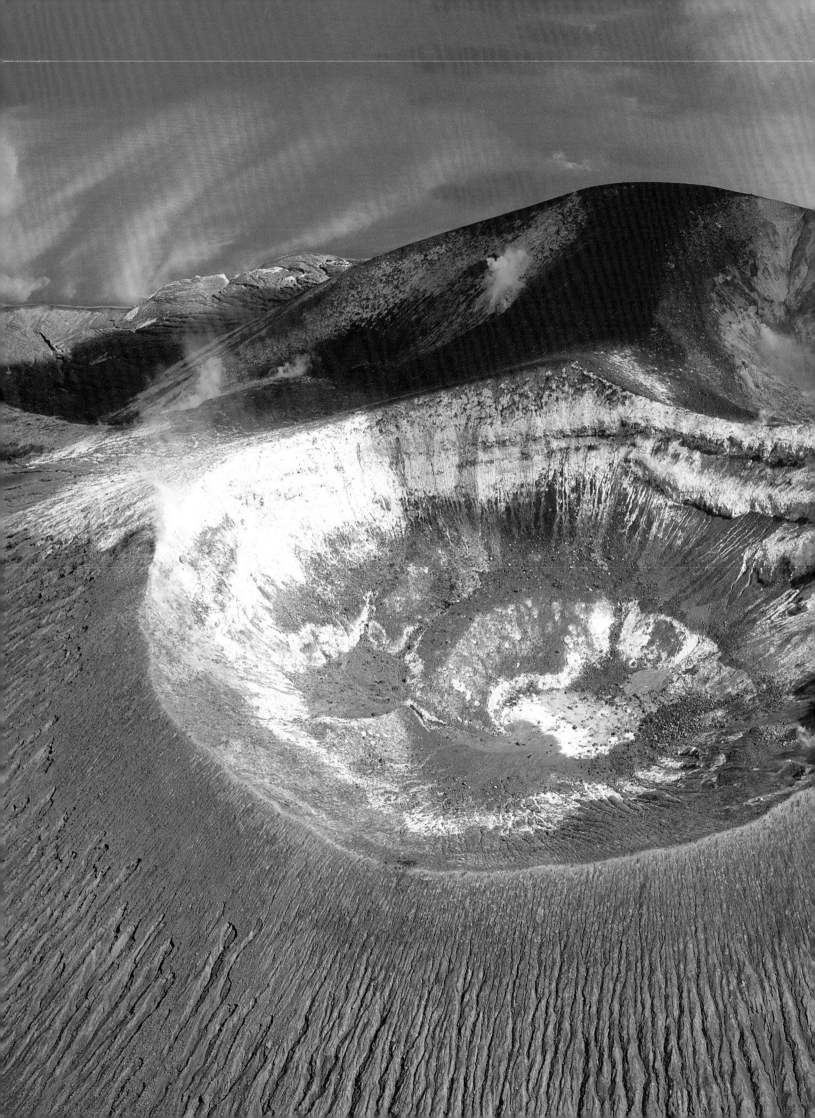

# UNDERSTANDING ROCKS AND MINERALS

Rocks and minerals are the raw materials of the landscape. Every valley, hill and mountain peak is made entirely of rocks and minerals. Yet every rock and mineral is also a clue to the Earth's history, for the characteristics of each depend on how and where it formed – whether forged in the heat of Earth's interior, transformed by volcanic activity and the crush of moving continents, or laid down in gently settling layers on the sea bed.

Climb any mountain away from the city and gaze out on the landscape, and you see rivers winding down to the sea, hills and valleys, forests and fields. It seems a timeless landscape, but in terms of the Earth's history it is very young. The fields may be no more than a few centuries old, the forests a few thousand years old, and even the hills and valleys no more than tens of thousands of years old. Yet the history of the Earth's surface and the rocks which make it dates back over four and a half billion years. In geological terms, then, the landscape we see today is just a fleeting moment.

Geologists first began to understand the ever-changing nature of the Earth's surface about 200 years ago, as they started to realize just how old it was, and how it was shaped and reshaped continuously by the power of such forces as water, earthquakes and volcanoes, which have worn mountains down and risen new ones up. Yet it is only in the last half century that they have learned just how dynamic the Earth's geology really is, with the discovery that the entire surface of the planet is on the move – broken into 20 or so giant, ever-shifting slabs called tectonic plates. The movement of these plates is slow in human terms – barely faster than a fingernail growing – yet over the vastness of geological time, it is momentous: able to shift continents and oceans right around the globe. Tectonic plate theory has revolutionized geologists' understanding of how rocks are made and remade over again, how mountains are built and knocked down, why volcanoes erupt, why earthquakes happen and much more besides.

*Left: Sulphurous vapour rises from the crater of the active Sierra Negra volcano on Isabela Island, one of the Galapagos Islands. Volcanoes are among the world's most important mineral factories, forever bringing materials to the surface to form new minerals.*

# INSIDE THE EARTH

*The Earth under your feet may seem solid, but recent research has shown that its interior is far more dynamic and complex than anyone ever thought. Beneath the thin rocky shell called the crust, the Earth is churning and bubbling like thick soup.*

Half a century ago, scientists' picture of the Earth's interior was simple. In some ways, they thought, it seems like an egg. The outside is just a thin shell of rock called the crust. Immediately beneath, no more than a few dozen kilometres down, is the deep 'mantle' were the rock is hot and soft. Then beneath that, some 2,900km/1,800 miles down is the yolk or 'core' of metal, mainly iron and nickel. The outer core is so ferociously hot that it is always molten, reaching temperatures as high as the Sun's surface. The inner core, at the centre of the Earth, is solid because pressures there are gigantic.

The key to this structure is density. The theory is that when the Earth was young, it was hot and semi-molten. Dense elements such as iron sank towards the centre to form the core. Lighter elements such as oxygen and silicon drifted to the surface like scum on water and eventually chilled enough to harden into a crust.

*Above: Meteorites big enough to cause a crater like this one, the famous Meteor Crater in Arizona, strike the Earth so hard they vaporize on impact. But some small meteorites survive and provide vital clues to the composition of the Earth's interior.*

*Below: Blacksmiths know that iron only melts at very high temperatures, and scientists have deduced that the temperatures of the molten iron in the Earth's outer core, where it is under intense pressure, may rise to 4,500K/7,600°F. The solid core could even reach 7,500K/13,000°F!*

Some heavy elements such as uranium ended up in the crust despite their density because they unite readily with oxygen to make oxides and with oxygen and silicon to make silicates. Substances like these are called 'lithophiles' and include potassium.

Blobs of 'chalcophile' substances – substances like zinc and lead that join readily with sulphur to form sulphides – spread up and out to add to the mantle. Dense globs of 'siderophile' substances – substances such as nickel and gold that combine readily with iron – sank towards the core.

The only real complications to this picture seemed to be on the surface, where the crust is divided into continental and oceanic portions. The crust in continents can be very ancient – some rocks are nearly four billion years old – and quite thick. Although it is just 20km/12 miles beneath California's Central Valley, it is 90km/54 miles thick under the Himalayas. The oceanic crust, on the other hand, is entirely made of young rocks – none older than 200 million years and some brand new – and is rarely more than 10km/6 miles thick.

## Listening in

Discoveries in the last few decades have forced scientists to re-evaluate this fairly simple picture. The problem has been to see inside the Earth. A Japanese ship launched in 2005 is now beginning to drill the deepest hole ever, through the oceanic crust, hoping to reach the mantle, but this is barely scratching the surface. Yet there are other ways of telling. Astronomical calculations based on gravity tell us Earth's mass and show that the interior must be denser than the crust. Meteorites tell us a little about the mineral make-up of the interior, with the two kinds of meteorite, stony and iron, reflecting Earth's stony mantle and iron core (see Space Rocks, Directory of Rocks). Similarly, volcanoes throw up materials like olivine and eclogite from deep in the mantle. Yet the main clues come from earthquake (seismic) waves.

Long after an earthquake, its reverberations shudder through the Earth. Sensitive seismographs can pick them up on the far side of the world. Just as you can hear the difference between wood and metal when tapped with a spoon, so scientists can 'hear' from seismic waves what the Earth's interior is made of. Seismic waves are refracted (bent) as they pass through different materials. They also travel at varying speeds, shimmering faster through the cold hard rocks of the crust, for instance, than the warmer, soft rocks of the mantle.

## Density and speed

One thing seismology has revealed is that there is another way of looking at the crust and upper mantle. Although they may be chemically different, their 'rheology' is not – that is, they distort and flow in much the same way. Fast seismic waves show the top 100km/ 60miles of the mantle is as stiff as the crust, and together upper mantle and crust form a rigid layer called the lithosphere. Below the lithosphere, slower waves show that heat softens the mantle to form a layer called the asthenosphere. Tectonic plates are huge chunks of lithosphere that float on the asthenosphere like ice floes on a pond.

About 220km/140 miles down pressure stiffens the mantle again to form the mesosphere. Farther down, pressure forces minerals with the same chemical composition through a phase change (like ice melting) into a denser structure. So below 420km/260 miles olivine and pyroxene are replaced by spinel and garnet. Deeper down still, beyond 670km/420 miles, even higher pressure changes mineral structure again or maybe the composition, this time to give perovskite minerals, from which the bulk of the mantle is made.

## The core boundary

Down through the mantle, seismic waves move ever faster. Yet at the Gutenberg discontinuity 2,900km/ 1,800 miles down, there is a drop in speed, marking the transition to the core along the Core-Mantle Boundary (CMB). The change is dramatic. In just a few hundred kilometres temperatures soar 1,500°C/2,732°F, and the contrast in density between mantle and core is even more marked than that between air and rock.

The transition zone in the mantle down to the CMB is called the D" (pronounced D double prime) layer, and has attracted a lot of attention. The outer surface of this layer is marked by valleys and ridges, and lab tests have shown that it may be made of a unique form of perovskite dubbed post-perovskite. In 2005, scientists detected an increase in speed below the D", suggesting that the outer rim of the core may actually be solid.

Research into this whole CMB zone may have key implications for our understanding of how continents move and volcanoes erupt, because these could be tied in with deep circulation of material in the mantle.

*The Earth's interior*
*This globe reveals scientists' idea of the Earth's interior layers (not to scale), including the crust, mantle and core.*

**The crust** *0–40 km/0–25 miles down is Earth's thin topmost layer, made mostly of silicate-rich rocks like basalt and granite. It is thinnest under the oceans and thickest under the continents. It is attached to the mantle's rigid upper layers, which floats in slabs on the soft mantle below.*

**The lower mantle** *is 670–2,900km/420–1,800 miles down. Here, huge pressures turn the lighter silicate minerals of the upper mantle into dense perovskite and pyroxene. Perovskite is the most abundant mineral in the mantle, and so in the Earth, since the mantle makes up four-fifths of the Earth's volume.*

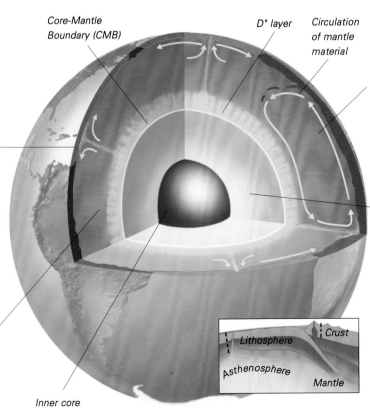

Core-Mantle Boundary (CMB)

D" layer

*Circulation of mantle material*

Inner core

Lithosphere

Asthenosphere

Crust

Mantle

**The upper mantle** *16–670km/10–420 miles down is so warm it is soft enough to flow. In the asthenosphere layer, below the lithosphere, pockets often melt to form the magma that bubbles up through the crust to erupt in volcanoes. The upper mantle is made mainly of the dense rock called peridotite.*

**The Earth's core** *2,900–6,370km/ 1,800–3,960 miles down is a dense ball of iron and nickel. The outer core is so hot, reaching temperatures of over 4,500K/ 7,600°F, that the metal is molten. The inner core is even hotter, up to 7,500K/13,000°F, but the pressures here are so great that the iron simply cannot melt.*

**Lithosphere** *(left) is the rigid outer layer of the Earth, broken into the tectonic plates that make up the surface. It consists of the crust and the stiff, cool upper portion of the mantle.*

# CONTINENTS AND PLATES

*The division of the world into land and sea seems so natural and so timeless that it is difficult to imagine how it could be any other way. Yet the very existence of continents is remarkable and Earth is the only planet we know to have them. Their foundations are even more astounding.*

Like Earth, Venus and many other planets and moons in the solar system have rocky crusts. But the crusts on these other worlds are made almost entirely of basalt, and are very stable and ancient, barely changed since they formed billions of years ago. Earth has a basalt crust, too. The crust under the oceans is basalt, for instance. But Earth's crust is mostly neither stable nor ancient. In fact, nowhere is the ocean crust older than 200 million years, and much is forming even now.

Even more unusually, the Earth has giant chunks of crust made from granite-like rocks such as granodiorite. It is these chunks of granitic crust that form our continents, light enough to ride high above the surface and form landmasses on partially molten matter.

## Making continents

No one knows for sure exactly how or why these chunks formed, but their formation is clearly a very slow process. The oldest pieces are almost four billion years old (the Earth is about 4.6 billion years old). Yet even now, granite crust still forms barely a quarter of the world's surface.

Basalt crust forms when magma (molten rock) from Earth's warm mantle cools and solidifies at the surface. Granite cannot form directly from mantle melts like this – only when basalt remelts, changing its chemistry and mixing in other substances met at the surface.

Geologists think this happens in two ways. The first is when hot, molten basalt magma wells up under the crust from the mantle, melting the crust to form granite magma. Less dense than basalt crust, the granite magma rises to the top before solidifying. The second process is when movement of the Earth's crust draws basalt crust back towards the mantle, remelting it and forming a new granite magma, which rises to form new continental crust.

This process initiated the evolution of the great continents that would support so much of Earth's living matter.

So just how does the Earth's crust move? The answer lies in the most powerful geological concept of the last century: plate tectonics. This is the idea that the Earth's rigid surface – all the lithosphere including the crust – is broken into 20 or so giant pieces of tectonic plates. These plates move slowly around the planet, carrying the continents and oceans with them.

## Continental drift

The seeds for plate tectonic theory were planted in the early 20th century by a German meteorologist called Alfred Wegener. He had noticed the extraordinary way the west coast of Africa mirrored the east coast of South America. He also noticed amazing matches between widely separated continents of things such as geological strata and ancient animal and plant

### The moving continents

*Over the last 500 million years, Earth's continents have merged together then split and drifted apart. About 225 mya (million years ago) at the end of the Permian, all land was joined in one supercontinent geologists named Pangaea. Pangaea began to rift apart about the time dinosaurs appeared on Earth, so different kinds of dinosaur evolved in newly separated parts of the world. The maps here show the current continental shapes to help identify them, but in fact their shapes varied as low areas were flooded and mountain ranges rose up.*

**Permian 225 mya** *During the Permian period all the world's landmasses moved together to form the giant continent Pangaea.*

**Late Triassic 205 mya** *During the Triassic, a wedge of ocean called the Tethys Seaway grew wider, elbowing into the east of Pangaea.*

**Jurassic 150 mya** *In the Jurassic, Pangaea began to split in various places, including the Tethys Seaway. South-western North America was flooded by the Sundance Sea.*

**Cretaceous 80 mya** *By the Cretaceous even southern Pangaea, called Gondwana, had split up to form today's southern continents. India began drifting northwards towards Asia.*

**Present day** *Over the last 50 million years, the North Atlantic has opened up to separate Europe and America, and India has crashed into Asia, throwing up the Himalayas.*

*Above: In recent years, dramatic evidence of tectonic activity has been found deep under the sea. Fissures like this one in the East Pacific seabed, some 2,600m (8,500ft) below the surface, indicate the spreading of the oceans. Volcanic activity along these fissures warms the water and produces a rich mixture of chemicals, which creates a unique habitat for these white crabs, as well as other marine life.*

fossils – especially from the Permian Period some 230 million years ago. Signs of ancient tropical species as far north as the Arctic circle only added to the impression.

Wegener guessed this was not mere coincidence. He realized that these matches might occur because today's separate continents were once actually joined together. He suggested that in Permian times they all formed one giant supercontinent which he called Pangaea, surrounded by a single giant ocean, which he called Panthalassa. At some time, perhaps some 200 million years ago Wegener thought, Pangaea split into several fragments and these have since drifted apart to form our present continental lands.

To many geologists of Wegener's time, the idea that continents drift around the world was ridiculous. The crust seems far too solid for this to happen. But over the next half century, the weight of evidence piled up. A key element was the discovery of grains of

*Right: Looking at this bleak tundra on the Arctic island of Spitsbergen, it is hard to believe that lush tropical vegetation ever grew here. Yet fossils show that it did – not because the whole world had a tropical climate, but because Spitsbergen was once in the tropics, before continental drift took it way out into the chilly polar regions.*

magnetite – a magnetic mineral – in ancient rock. These grains behaved like tiny compasses, lining up with the North Pole at the time when the rock formed. To geologists' surprise, these grains do not all point in the same direction. At first, geologists thought this must be because the magnetic North Pole had moved over time. Then they realized it was not the Pole that had moved, but the continents in which these grains were embedded, twisting this way and that. Geologists realized that with the aid of these ancient compasses or 'palaeomagnets' they could trace the entire path of a continent's movement through time – and this is how the maps below left were worked out.

## Spreading oceans

A second key element was the realization that it was not just the continents moving but the entire surface of the Earth, including the oceans. Indeed, the continents are just passengers aboard the great, slowly sliding tectonic plates that make up Earth's surface. The breakthrough came in 1960 when American geologist Harry Hess suggested that the ocean floors are not permanent. Instead, he suggested, they are spreading rapidly out from a ridge down the middle of the sea bed, as hot material wells up through a central rift, pushing the halves of the ocean bed apart. This does not make the crust bigger, because as quickly as new crust is created along the ridge, old crust is dragged down into the mantle and destroyed along deep trenches at the ocean's edge, in a process known by geologists as subduction.

Many were initially sceptical of Hess's idea, but evidence soon came when bands of magnetite were found in rocks on the sea floor in exactly matching patterns either side of the mid-ocean ridge. These bore witness to the spread of the ocean floor as truly as rings in a tree. Before long, the ideas of sea-floor spreading and continental drift were combined in the all-encompassing theory of plate tectonics.

It soon became clear that plate tectonics explained much more than coincidences of rocks and fossils. Earthquakes happen where plates shudder past each other. Volcanoes erupt where plates split asunder or dive into the mantle. Mountain ranges are thrown up where plates collide and crumple the edges of continents. In fact, the full implications of this revolutionary theory are only just beginning to be explored.

# THE MOVING EARTH

*Like a broken eggshell, Earth's surface is cracked into giant slabs of rock called tectonic plates. There are seven huge plates and a dozen or so smaller ones. The plates are not fixed, but ever shifting, breaking up and being made anew – almost imperceptibly slow in human terms, but dramatic geologically.*

Tectonic plates are fragments of the lithosphere – the cool, rigid outer layer of the Earth, topped by the crust. The scale of some of these plates is staggering. They may be no more than 100km/60 miles thick, but some plates encompass entire oceans or continents.

The biggest is the Pacific plate, which underlies most of the Pacific Ocean. Interestingly, this is the only major plate that is entirely oceanic. All the others – in size order, the African, Eurasian, Indo-Australian, North American, Antarctic and South American – carry continents, like cargo on a raft. The remaining dozen or so plates are much smaller. But even the smallest of them, like North America's Juan de Fuca, is bigger than a country such as Spain.

It seems almost unimaginable that slabs of rock as gigantic as these could move. Yet they are moving, all the

### The world's major plates
*On this map showing the world's major plates, red arrows indicate the direction of movement.*

time. Typically, they are shifting at about the pace of a fingernail growing – about a 1cm/0.4in a year, although the Nazca plate in the Pacific is moving 20 times as fast. Yet even a fingernail's pace has been fast enough to carry Europe and North America apart and create the entire North Atlantic in just 40 million years, which is a short time in geological terms. Accurate laser measurements can even detect the movements in a single month.

## Why plates move
Scientists are not yet certain what it is that drives the plates, but most theories focus on the idea of convection in the Earth's mantle.

Inside the mantle, material is continuously churning around, driven up by the ferocious heat of the core, then cooling and sinking back. It was once thought that all these 'convection' currents moved in vast cells as big as the plates, and the plates simply rode on top of them like packages on

conveyor belts. Now more scientists are focusing on hot currents called mantle plumes that bubble up from the deep mantle, and in places lift the crust like a pie crust in an oven.

This may tie in better with other theories that suggest the driving force is the weight of the plates alone. Mid-ocean ridges are 2–3km/1–2 miles higher than ocean rims, so plates could be sliding downhill away from them.

Another idea is that plates are like a cloth sliding off a table. Hot new rock formed at the mid-ocean ridge cools as it slides away to the ocean rim. As it cools, it gets denser and heavier and sinks into the mantle again. It then pulls the rest of the plate down with it, just as the weight of a table cloth hanging over the edge can be enough to pull the rest off. It may be that all these mechanisms play a part.

## Plate boundaries
Working out where one plate ends and another begins is far from easy. Seismic

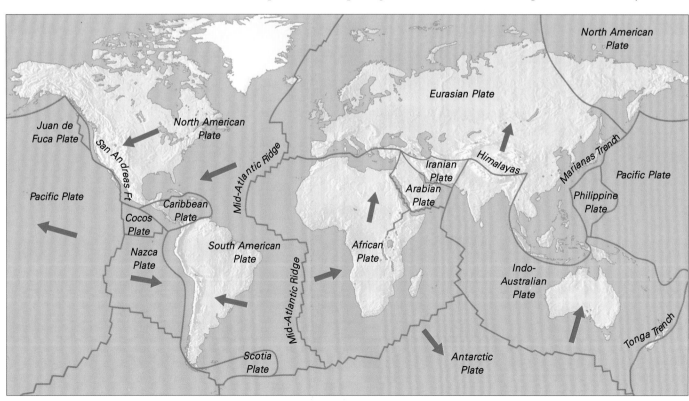

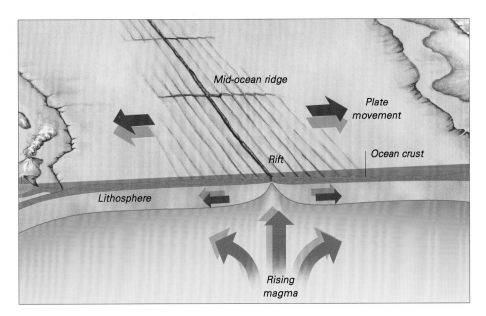

Mid-ocean ridge

Plate movement

Rift

Ocean crust

Lithosphere

Rising magma

*Divergent boundaries* typically occur in mid-ocean. Right down the middle of the Atlantic Ocean, for instance, there is a ridge about 2km/1.2 miles down on the sea bed, forming a jagged line where plates meet. In the middle of this ridge is a trough some 500m/1,640ft deep and no more than 10km/6 miles wide. This trough is where the plates are moving apart, spreading the ocean wider and wider. Beneath this trough, magma is welling up from the asthenosphere. Some solidifies on the underside of the crust, creating rocks like gabbro. Some oozes up into vertical cracks created by the pressure of the magma to form wall-like sheets of basalt rock called dykes. Some magma spills out on the sea bed and freezes in the cold water into blobs called pillow lavas. As soon as it forms, new oceanic crust moves away from the ridge, more magma wells up and new crust forms.

profiling using earthquake waves helps build a picture but it is often vague.

One of the best indicators of a plate boundary is where earthquakes start. Plates generate earthquakes as they judder past each other so nearly all major quakes occur in belts that follow plate boundaries. In May 2005, a Japanese geologist discovered a previously unknown plate under Japan's Kanto just by tracing the origin of over 150,000 small earthquakes.

Other features that identify a plate boundary include long chains of volcanoes, ranges of fold mountains, curving lines of islands and deep ocean trenches. Some plates meet along the coasts of continents, like the west coast of South America. Coasts like these are called active margins. Other plates meet in mid-ocean. The continental crust is actually attached to the oceanic crust, and so its margin is passive.

## Moving boundaries

All plates are on the move, some slow, some fast, and geologists identify three kinds of boundary, each with its own features. Divergent boundaries (see above) are where plates are pulling apart. Convergent boundaries (see below) are where they push together. Transforms are where they slide sideways past each other. Most transforms are short, linking segments of mid-ocean ridge. But some, like the Alpine Fault in New Zealand, link ocean trenches. The famous San Andreas fault in California lies along the boundary where the Pacific Plate is rotating slowly past the North American plate.

Plate boundaries can be quite short-lived geologically. Some ancient continental plates, for instance, were thrust together so hard they welded into one solid piece. There was once a plate boundary in Asia, north of Tibet, for example. Geologists detected evidence of this via a seismological image of the edge of one of the plates involved thrust far down into the mantle beneath the boundary.

*Convergent boundaries* typically occur along the edges of oceans. Here, as plates crunch together, the lighter continental plate rides up over the denser ocean plate, forcing it down into the mantle in a process called subduction. Deep ocean trenches open up where the descending plate plunges into the asthenosphere. As it goes down, the plate starts to melt, releasing hot, volatile materials, water and even molten rock, creating magma. Plumes of magma rise through the often shattered, faulted edge of the overlying plate, and may erupt to create an arc of volcanoes along the edge, or maybe even volcanic islands. The over-riding plate often acts like a giant mudscraper, scraping material off the sea floor on the subducted plate and piling it high in a wedge called an accretionary prism. As the subducted plate shudders down, the vibration can set off earthquakes, creating what is called a Wadati-Benioff zone, after seismologists Kiyoo Wadati and Hugo Benioff.

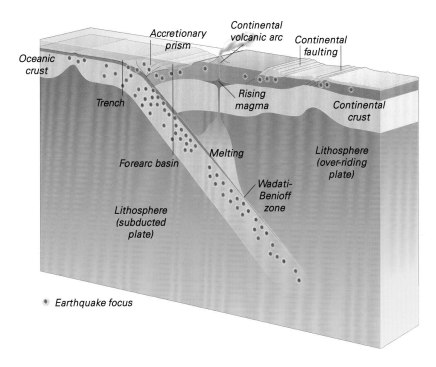

Oceanic crust

Accretionary prism

Continental volcanic arc

Continental faulting

Trench

Rising magma

Continental crust

Forearc basin

Melting

Lithosphere (over-riding plate)

Lithosphere (subducted plate)

Wadati-Benioff zone

• Earthquake focus

# MOUNTAIN BUILDING

*There are no more dramatic demonstrations of the dynamic power of the Earth's surface than mountains. Lifting the vast bulk of rock tens of thousands of metres upwards into towering ranges such as the Himalayas involves huge forces. Yet such forces have been deployed repeatedly in the Earth's history.*

The remarkable thing about the world's biggest mountain ranges is just how young they are in geological terms. The Himalayas, the Andes, the Rockies and the Alps have all appeared within the last 50 million years. In other words, the dinosaurs were long dead before these so timeless-seeming mountain ranges began to rise up from the plain.

Until the coming of plate tectonics theory, geologists had no real idea of how these mountains came to be. They realized that major mountain belts or 'orogens' are created in mountain-building events or 'orogenies' that last tens of millions of years then stop. They also realized that when orogeny ceases, erosion can wear mountains back to sea level in only a little longer.

*Below: The world's great mountain ranges, with lofty, snow-capped peaks like these in the Rockies, Colorado, were thrown up where tectonic plates crunch together, crumpling and fracturing rock in the collision zone. Mountains like these are called fold mountains. But isolated high mountain peaks, like Kenya's Mount Kilimanjaro – some 5895m (19,340 ft) high – are created by volcanoes.*

In 1899, the famous geologist William Morris Davis developed a beautifully simple life history for mountains, called the Cycle of Erosion. This envisaged the creation of mountains in a brief and violent spasm of uplift in the landscape then a gradual decline through 'youth', 'maturity' and 'old age' as forces of erosion such as rivers and the weather did their slow, steady work. Once the mountains were worn flat, another spasm of uplift started the cycle again. It did not explain how uplift took place, but Davis's model seemed so elegant that it was widely accepted – until the development of plate tectonics in the 1960s began to reveal an entirely new picture.

### Tectonic mountain-building

Mountains can be built in a number of ways (see below-right), but it now seems clear that most great ranges form along plate boundaries.

The world's longest range is actually the mid-ocean ridge that forms where plates are moving apart under the sea.

It winds all through the Atlantic and up into the Indian Ocean. All the high ranges on land, however, occur where plates are moving together. Like a rug rumpled against a wall, converging plates crumple the rocks in between, forcing them upwards and creating long folds all along the boundary.

When an oceanic plate slides under a continental plate, offshore volcanic arcs and other debris are swept against the continent. Too buoyant to subduct, they become welded to the edge of the continent as an 'accreted terrane'. As the oceanic plate goes on pushing under the continent, these terranes pile up higher and higher in fractured and folded mountain belts. The North American Cordillera formed like this.

Eventually, all the oceanic plate may slide into the mantle, leaving the two continents to collide head-on. The enormous force of their collision crumples up their edges to build the greatest mountain ranges of all.

In the distant past this happened when Africa and North America collided to throw up the Appalachians,

*Right: Mountains are also created where plates are pulling apart or 'rifting'. As the plates separate, magma wells up under the rift, stretching the crust and cracking it. Blocks of rock can then drop away down these 'faults' to open up a rift valley, flanked by mountains formed from blocks that didn't drop. The Basin and Range Province of the south-west USA (right) formed in this way.*

and also when what are now called Europe and North America collided to throw up the Caledonian mountains of Scotland and Norway. Both ranges are now worn down to a fraction of their former height. Now the same process is happening as India ploughs into Asia to build the Himalayas (see below).

## A more complex picture

In recent years, however, geologists have begun to realize that this basic scenario is only half the story. One complication comes from the discovery that crustal rocks are not simply rigid and brittle, but actually flow, albeit slowly. So the Himalayas, for instance, are more like a ship's bow wave in front of India than a rumpled carpet.

Moreover, other factors are involved in the process besides plate movement. When British scientist George Airy was surveying India in the 19th century, deviations of his plumbline revealed that the mass of the Himalayas extends far below the surface. In fact, we now know that all mountains have deep 'roots' that protrude far down into the mantle. This is because mountains, like

all the crust, float on the mantle. But because they are so big and heavy, mountains sink farther.

As mountain ranges are worn away by erosion, however, they get lighter and so actually float up. This phenomenon is called isostasy. When recent precise surveys showed the Appalachian Mountains are gaining a few centimetres in height each century, geologists were at first convinced the figures must be wrong, since the Appalachians are far from any plate boundary. In fact, it seems the Appalachians are rising isostatically – because erosion of rock in the valleys

so lightens them that the entire range is floating upward.

Erosion is slow, but it can wear mountain ranges flat in much the same time it takes to build them tectonically. So the process of uplift can actually be assisted by erosion.

Moreover, erosion can be sped up or slowed by changes in climate which can be altered by the way continents move, and even by mountains themselves. So geologists now realize that mountain building involves a complex interaction between erosion, climate, tectonic movements and isostatic adjustment.

---

**Himalayan Mountains**

**Kunlun Mountains**

**Continental crust**

**Tibetan Plateau**

**Continental crust**

**Complex thrust faults and folds**

**Strike-slip faults**

**Indian plate**

**Asian plate**

**Thin lithospheric bridge**

**Lithospheric mantle**

**Lithospheric mantle**

**Indian plate subducting beneath Asian plate**

*The Himalayas, the world's highest mountain range, began to form when the Indian plate crashed into southern Asia 55 million years ago. At the time Asia was made of softer, younger rock than India, and was powerless to resist the Indian advance. Long after the continents first crunched together, India has ploughed north at about 5cm/2in a year, pushing almost 2,000km/1,200 miles into the Asian plate. The Himalayas were thrown up as the crust doubled in thickness in the crumple zone. Because the Asian plate is warmer and lighter than the Indian plate, it is starting to ride over it, creating complex faults. But the creation of such high mountains interrupted the air flow over Asia, initiating India's famous monsoons. This intensifies erosion and is actually accelerating the ongoing uplift of the Himalayas as they are buoyed up isostatically by the weight of rock removed.*

# EARTHQUAKES AND FAULTS

*The relentless movement of the Earth's tectonic plates can put the brittle rocks of the crust under such stress that every now and then they crack altogether, and great blocks slide past each other along fractures called faults, sending out shock waves that make the ground quake far around.*

There is an earthquake somewhere in the world almost every day. Most are so tiny they are only detectable on the most sensitive of equipment. But a few are big enough to cause devastation, especially when they occur near major cities, or trigger giant waves called tsunami. Every year there are 20 quakes of the size that caused so much damage in the Turkish town of Izmit in 1999. Giant quakes such as that which triggered the tsunami that struck the coastal regions of Southern Asia on 26 December 2004 occur once every decade or so.

All kinds of things can trigger an earthquake, from a landslide or a volcanic eruption to the passing of a heavy vehicle, and they can occur almost anywhere. But most earthquakes – and nearly all major quakes – occur only in 'earthquake zones' which coincide with the edges of tectonic plates. In fact, an estimated 80 per cent of big quakes happen on the edges of the plates around the Pacific, and nearly all the rest happen on the boundary between the Eurasian and the Indo-Australian or Arabian plates. The mid-ocean rifts often send out tremors, but these are usually mild.

## What causes earthquakes

Most quakes occur because of the immense forces generated as two plates grind past each other – either in subduction zones where one plate dives beneath another or along transforms where two plates slide sideways past each other. When one plate passes another, the rock either side of the crack may bend and stretch a little, but sooner or later the stress builds up to such a level that the rock suddenly snaps. The sudden rupture sends shock waves (seismic waves) shuddering out through the ground in all directions from the focus or hypocentre – the point where the rock snaps.

Above: Slicing right down through the state of California, the San Andreas is one of the world's most famous faults. Tremors set off by bursts of movement along the fault shake the cities of San Francisco and Los Angeles again and again. Seismologists feel it is only a matter of time before one of these cities is struck again with a quake as big or bigger than the one that devastated San Francisco in 1906. The San Andreas is not actually a single crack but a series of strike-slip faults (see

Types of Fault, above right) that run along the transform boundary between two tectonic plates. To the west is the huge Pacific plate which runs right under the Pacific Ocean. To the east is the North American plate which makes up most of the continent of North America. Over the last 20 million years the Pacific plate has moved 560km/350 miles north – about 1cm/0.4in a year – but, disturbingly, the pace seems to have accelerated fivefold in the last century.

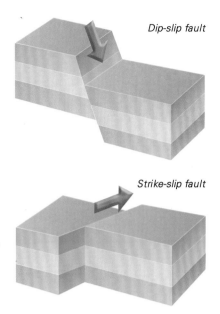

Dip-slip fault

Strike-slip fault

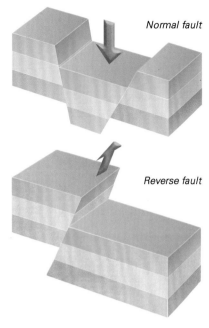

Normal fault

Reverse fault

### Types of fault

*Geologists classify faults by how the rock moves. A 'dip-slip' fault is one in which the rock slips up or down. A 'strike-slip' fault is one in which the rock moves sideways. Big strike-slip faults are called transcurrent faults, and typically lie along transform plate boundaries, where tectonic plates are sliding sideways. Dip-slip faults, on the other hand, occur where the crust is being squeezed or stretched horizontally. 'Normal' faults occur where tension pulls rocks apart, so that one block slips down. Rift valleys form where parallel sets of normal faults open up as the crust is stretched by upwelling magma. Where rock is squeezed – maybe by converging plates – a block may slide over another to create a 'reverse' fault. A thrust is a reverse fault that slides up at a shallow angle.*

The rupture spreads along the plate boundary like a crack spreading through glass. The longer the crack, the bigger the quake.

In the southern Asia quake of 2004, the rupture ripped 1,000km/620 miles along the Indo-Australian plate boundary. The massive Alaskan earthquake of 1964 moved entire mountains up 12m/40ft.

Most earthquakes only move the ground a few centimetres or so. Yet the cumulative effect of successive earthquakes has a bigger impact on the landscape. If the rocks either side of the crack or fault move just 10cm/4in a century, over a million years they can move up or down 1km/0.6 miles.

### Earthquake waves

There is no chance of running from an earthquake. There are four kinds of shock wave – P or Primary and S or Secondary waves underground, and Love and Rayleigh waves on the surface. All move very fast. P-waves, which shake the ground up and down, are the fastest, roaring along at 5km/ 3 miles per second. S-waves, which snake from side to side, travel only a little slower. Surface waves are slower but these are what do the damage when an earthquake strikes cities. In solid rock, the waves move too fast for the eye to see. But they can turn loose sediments – in, for example, vulnerable areas such as landfill sites – into fluids so that waves can be seen rippling

across them like waves in the sea. These waves can capsize buildings. In both the Kobe (Japan) quake of 1995, and the San Francisco tremor of 1989, the worst damage was to buildings built on landfill sites.

### Quake danger

Many of the world's cities – Los Angeles, Mexico City, Tokyo – are sitting on timebombs, because they are right in the middle of earthquake zones. People in these cities have learned to live with minor tremors. But sooner or later, one may be hit by a devastating quake that does terrible damage. For these people, learning to predict a quake is a race against time.

*Below: The quake which devastated Marmara and Izmit in Turkey in 1999 seems to be one of a series moving west along the North Anatolian Fault and may reach the capital, just 50 miles (80km) away.*

One approach is to look at the historical record. If there has not been a quake in an earthquake zone for some time, the chances are there will be one soon. The longer it has been quiet, the bigger the quake will be, as strain has been building in the rocks.

Most seismologists believe the key is to watch for strain building in rocks. In many earthquake zones, high-precision surveys monitor the ground for signs of deformation. Laser ranging from satellites such as the Japanese Keystone system can make acutely fine measurements. There is now some evidence that earthquakes occur in clusters, as one quake sets up stress further along a fault that will be in turn released as a quake. So a moving succession of quakes may be triggered off, as seems to be happening westwards along the North Anatolian Fault in Turkey, towards Istanbul.

# VOLCANOES

*Few sights are more awesome than a volcano erupting in a huge explosion of gas, ash and lava, and their effect on the landscape is immediate and dramatic. Volcanic activity is also going on beneath the Earth's surface. The combination of all this vulcanicity has a profound effect on the Earth's geology.*

Volcanoes are places where red-hot magma (molten rock) wells up through the Earth's crust and erupts on to the surface. They are not randomly located around the world but clustered in certain places – where there is a ready supply of magma. Despite the inferno of heat in the Earth's interior, immense pressure keeps most rock in the mantle beneath the surface solid. But along the margins between the great tectonic plates that make up the Earth's surface, mantle rock melts into magma in huge volumes, and buoyed by its relatively low density wells up to the surface to erupt as volcanoes.

All but a few of the world's active volcanoes lie close to plate margins – mostly where plates are converging – and especially in a ring around the Pacific Ocean known as the 'Ring of Fire'. The exceptions are so-called 'hot-spot' volcanoes, such as Mauna Loa in Hawaii, which well up over fountain-like concentrations of magma called mantle plumes.

*Above: Lava is the name for magma that has erupted on to the surface. It is so hot – over 1,100°C/2,000°F – the rock flows like a river.*

*Below: Most explosive eruptions begin with the blasting of a massive cloud of gas, ash and steam high into the atmosphere.*

Volcanic eruptions vary widely in character. Along the ocean bed ridges where plates are moving apart – and over hotspots – runny, silica-poor 'basaltic' magma wells up through cracks that ooze red-hot lava almost continuously in gentle spouts. Some volcanoes belch ash and steam. Others eject showers of pulverized rock. Some unleash devastating mudflows as the heat melts ice, and some spew glowing avalanches of cinders and hot gas.

## Explosive eruptions

The most terrifying and least predictable volcanoes of all tend to be those along the margins where plates are crunching together during subduction. Here, magma melting its way up through the thick plate margins becomes so contaminated with silica that it becomes 'dacitic' – so thick and viscous that it frequently clogs up the volcano vent. It seems as if the volcano is sleeping or even dead – until, almost without warning, the pent-up pressure bursts through the plug in a cataclysmic explosion that hurls out shattered fragments of the plug (called pyroclasts), huge jets of steam and clouds of ash and cinder, as well as streams of lava.

The driving force in explosive eruptions is the boiling off of carbon dioxide gas and steam trapped within the reservoir of magma beneath the volcano called the magma chamber. The more gas and water present in the magma, the more explosive a volcano becomes. Magma near subduction zones often contains ten times as much gas as elsewhere. Gas in magma can expand to hundreds of times the volume of molten rock in a matter of seconds.

## Types of eruption

No two volcanos are quite the same, but vulcanologists identify a number of distinctive styles of eruption. 'Effusive' eruptions occur when fluid basaltic lavas ooze from fissures and vents and flood far out over the landscape to form a plateau or a shallow dome. In some, lakes of lava pool up around the vent, while others shoot sprays of lava into the air. These sprays or fire fountains are driven by bubbles of gas in the lava, just like the droplets sprayed from a fizzy drink.

The explosive eruptions that occur with more viscous magmas are much more variable in character. Among the mildest are 'Strombolian' eruptions named after the island of Stromboli off the west coast of Italy. Gas escapes sporadically and the volcano repeatedly spits out sizzling clots of lava, but there is rarely a really violent explosion. 'Vulcanian' eruptions, named after Vulcano in the Italian Lipari islands, are much more ferocious. Here the magma is so viscous that the vent frequently clogs, in between roaring, cannon-like blasts that eject ash-clouds and fragments of magma followed by thick lava flows.

'Pelean' eruptions blast out glowing clouds of gas and ash called *nuées ardentes*, such as Mount Pelée, Martinique, in 1902. 'Plinian' eruptions are the most explosive of all, named after the Roman author Pliny, who witnessed the eruption of Vesuvius that buried Pompeii. Boiling gases blast clouds of ash and volcanic fragments high into the stratosphere.

*Right: Hawaiian volcanoes like Kilauea – one of the most active on Earth – are famous for their spectacular jet-like sprays of liquid lava called fire fountains. They can occur in short spurts or last for hours on end. Occasionally they can shoot hundreds of yards into the air, and in 1958 one shot up to almost 610m/2,000ft. However, this was dwarfed by a fire fountain on the Island of Oshima, Japan, in 1986, which reached 1,524m/5,000ft!*

## Types of volcano

Volcanoes can also be classified by the kind of cone they create. The instantly recognizable cone-shaped volcanoes like Japan's Mt Fuji are composite or 'stratovolcanoes' created where sticky magma erupts explosively from a single vent. Successive eruptions build the cone from alternate layers of lava and the ash that rains down on it. Some cones, though, are built entirely of cinders and ash, such as Mexico's Paricutin. Shield volcanoes such as Hawaii's Mauna Loa are shallow, dome-shaped volcanoes formed where fluid lava spreads far out from a single vent. Fissure volcanoes are ridges created when runny lava oozes from a long crack. Large scale fissures occur along the mid-ocean ridges. Smaller ones burst through on the flanks of larger volcanoes.

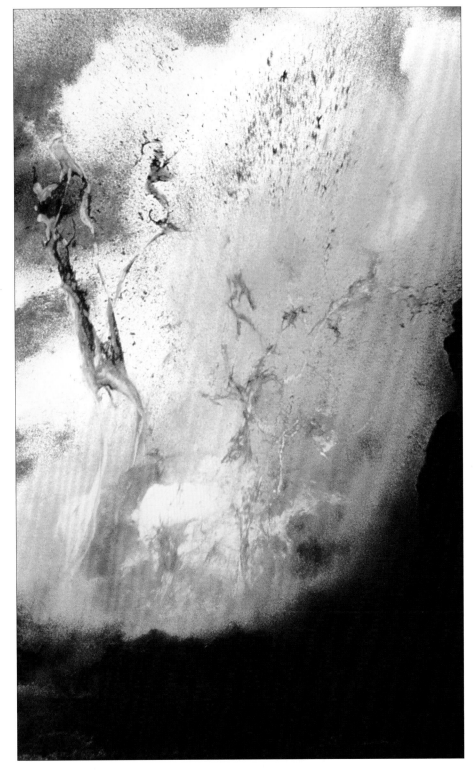

# IGNEOUS FEATURES

*Although eruptions are brief, volcanic activity leaves a lasting legacy as magma, lava and volcanic ash harden to form rock. Volcanic peaks and ash deposits are clearly visible on the surface, but much of the molten magma that wells up from the Earth's interior remains trapped underground, solidifying in situ.*

Rock features formed by volcanoes above ground and magma underground are together termed igneous features. Features formed from magma trapped underground are termed intrusive igneous features. Those formed above ground are called extrusive features.

Intrusions underlie all the world's major continents, and in many places they have been exposed on the surface after erosion of the surrounding 'country rock'. Intrusive igneous rock, which includes granite and gabbro, is almost invariably very tough and crystalline, and endures the weather to stand proud long after the surrounding softer rocks have been worn away.

## Massive intrusions

As seen in Types of Intrusion, opposite, the large intrusions forming deep underground are called plutons, and typically made of granite. Sometimes scores of plutons can coalesce over time to form monsters called batholiths (from the Greek for 'deep stone'), which lie like giant whale carcasses under most of the world's great mountain ranges. North America's Coast Range batholith extends 1,500km/932 miles under British Columbia and Washington. Batholiths mostly form as the convergence of two of the world's great tectonic plates generates huge quantities of magma underground. Sometimes, batholiths are topped by smaller protuberances called stocks and bosses. Erosion may expose several bosses on the surface, as at Dartmoor and Bodmin Moor in south-west England, which are linked underground to a single batholith.

## Minor intrusions

Nearer the surface, smaller intrusions often occur as sheetlike formations called dykes and sills. Dykes are anything from a few centimetres to

*Above: In California's Yosemite Park, spectacular cliffs of grey rock rear up where erosion has stripped naked the ironhard granite batholith that underlies much of the Sierra Nevada mountains. The Half Dome, seen above, is the most impressive example.*

hundreds of metres thick, and form as magma is injected into cracks in the rock. They are typically near vertical, but any sheet intrusion that cuts right across layers of country rock may be described as a dyke. Because they cut across existing structures, dykes are described as 'discordant'. Often, dykes form as the pressure of upwelling magma fractures overlying rock, opening cracks that fill with magma. A single intrusion may breed dozens of dykes like this in a 'dyke swarm'. Occasionally, these form in concentric downward-pointing cones or cone sheets crowning the intrusion, as famously on Mull in Scotland.

Ring dykes form like the sides of an upturned pan or cauldron as a round block of country rock drops away,

leaving a gap to fill with magma. Classic ring dykes like this are seen in Glencoe in Scotland and Mount Holmes in Yellowstone Park.

Sills are typically horizontal or gently sloping sheets, forming as magma seeps between existing bedding planes. Because they follow existing structures, they are described as 'concordant' structures. Sometimes the magma arches up between rock beds to form dome-shaped laccoliths or warps the rock downward to form dish-shaped lopoliths.

## Massive extrusions

Geologists have long debated over how vast intrusions form (see The Granite Problem under Granite, Directory of Rocks), but extrusions did not seem to pose the same problems, because volcanoes on land produce only small volumes of lava. Yet not only is the entire ocean floor made of extrusions of basalt erupted from mid-ocean fissures, but in places around the world there are solidified remains of gigantic lava flows.

Flood basalts are the solidified remains of huge floods of basalt lava that erupted in the past. The most spectacular is the Deccan Traps of India. Over 2km/1.2 miles thick and covering 500,000sq km/200,000sq miles, the Deccan Traps include half a million cubic km/120,000 cubic miles of lava – half a million times as much as erupted at Washington's Mount St Helens, USA, in 1980! The Traps' basalts erupted about 65 million years ago in a gigantic outpouring that has been blamed by some palaeontologists for the death of the dinosaurs.

Another huge flood basalt is the Columbia River plateau of north-western USA, which erupted 175,000 cubic km/42,000 cubic miles of lava about 16 million years ago. Others include southern Africa's Karoo and the Faroe Islands, North Atlantic.

## Undersea floods

These flood basalts were originally thought to be rare exceptions. Then in the late 1980s, seismic surveys of the sea floor began to reveal even more spectacular examples of what came to be called Large Igneous Provinces or LIPs under the oceans.

The largest of these, called the Ontong Java Plateau, lies under the Pacific to the east of Borneo and covers nearly 5 million sq km/2 million sq miles, an area bigger than the whole of the USA. This enormous Igneous Province erupted less than three million years ago.

*Above: India's Deccan Traps were the site of one of the greatest eruptions of lava in the Earth's history, about 65 million years ago. Traps is Dutch for staircase, referring to the steplike shape of the eroded layers of lava.*

Geologists believe 'mantle plumes' cause these massive eruptions. These are fountains of hot matter that rise through the Earth's mantle, perhaps all the way from the D" layer on the core boundary (see Inside the Earth, this section). The theory is that as they rise, the resulting heat melts mantle rock to create huge quantities of molten magma which burns through the crust and floods on to the surface.

### Types of intrusion

*Intrusions vary widely in size and shape. Deep underground, diapirs (rising blobs of magma) open up huge spaces in the country rock to form lumps of igneous rock called plutons. These include drum-shaped stocks a few kilometres across and gigantic batholiths made from scores of plutons and stretching thousands of kilometres. Nearer the surface, magma intrudes into cracks in the rock to create igneous rocks in thin sheets (dykes and sills) or lens shapes (lopoliths and laccoliths). Where these minor intrusions cut across existing structures, as dykes often do, they are said to be discordant; where they follow existing structures, like sills, they are said to be concordant. Minor near-surface intrusions are often exposed on the surface by subsequent erosion of the surrounding country rock, but even deep-forming plutons may be exposed this way over a considerable period of time.*

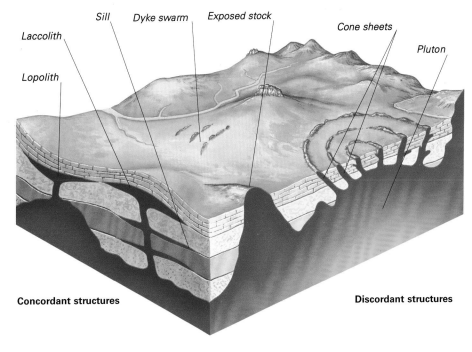

Laccolith · Sill · Dyke swarm · Exposed stock · Cone sheets · Pluton · Lopolith

**Concordant structures**          **Discordant structures**

# THE ROCK CYCLE

*Mountains and hills look so solid, it's hard to imagine they could ever change. Yet all the Earth's landscapes are being continually remodelled as rocks are attacked by the weather and worn away by running water, moving ice, waves, wind, and other 'agents of erosion'.*

Occasionally, the landscape is reshaped suddenly and dramatically – by an avalanche or landslide. Yet most of the time it is remoulded slowly but relentlessly. One cold night does little damage. A single shower of rain seems to run straight off. Yet night after freezing night, shower after shower, repeated over millions of years, takes its toll. Research into rates of erosion has shown it to average at least 0.5mm/0.04 inches a year on land. At that rate, even a mountain range as high as the Himalayas can be worn entirely flat in just over 20 millions of years.

Some new landforms are created from old as rock is denuded or stripped away by weathering and erosion. Some are created by steady accumulation or deposition of the rock debris. Most hills and valleys are formed by a combination of both denudation and deposition.

*Below. On coasts, shorelines are battered by waves packed with energy by wind blowing far over the ocean. Waves hurl tons of water filled with shingle against coastal rocks and ram air into cracks so that rocks are forced apart.*

## Weathering

As soon as rock is exposed to the weather, it gradually starts to break down under the assault of wind and rain, frost and sun. Sometimes the rock is corroded by chemical reactions caused by moisture in the air, or water trickling over it. Sometimes they are attacked by micro-organisms and lichens or chemicals released by plants. Sometimes they are broken down physically by, for instance, the effects of heat and cold. Water in cracks can expand so forcefully as it freezes that it can shatter rock. At -22°C/-7.6°F, ice can exert a pressure of 3,000kg/6,600lb on an area the size of a coin. This is called frost-shattering.

Geologists argue about the relative importance of chemical and physical weathering. Some limestone regions – known as 'karst' – show all the signs of chemical weathering which opens up potholes and spectacular caverns (see Rock Landscapes in this section). Other regions show strong signs of physical weathering. Frost-shattering

creates the jagged peaks in high mountain regions – as well as the piles of debris called scree below. In most places both chemical and physical processes are at work.

## Erosion and deposition

All the debris created by weathering is gradually carried away by agents of erosion – the most important of which is water. Without running water to mould it, the landscape would be as jagged as the surface of the Moon. Rivers and streams slowly soften contours – wearing away material here, depositing it there. Over millions of years, a river can carve a deep canyon or spread out a vast plain of sediment as it flows towards the sea.

In deserts, however, running water is scarce. Intermittent streams carve out valleys, but the landscape is angular, and some landforms are carved into weird shapes by the blast of windblown sand. On coasts, it is the waves which are the dominant agents of erosion, and their continuous

*Right: In many parts of the world, the landscape is shaped by water running over the land. Rivers can carve out deep valleys as they run down to the sea. A river's steady torrent washes small grains loose and grinds away solid rock with the stones it carries. Arizona's Grand Canyon (pictured here) was carved out as the Colorado river cut its way through a rising landscape over many millions of years.*

pounding on the shore creates a distinctive range of coastal landforms, including steep cliffs where waves cut into hillsides, platforms of rock sliced out as the waves wear back into the cliff and stacks of rock left behind as the waves erode the cliff.

It is far from certain how much of today's landscape has been created by the processes we see operating today – and how much by more dramatic events in the past. Some geologists argue that some river-eroded features in deserts were carved out during especially wet periods in the past called pluvials. There is also no doubt that cold periods in the past known as ice ages were crucial in shaping the land in Europe and North America. Giant U-shaped valleys in the mountains of north-west USA and Scotland, fjords in Norway and Canada and vast deposits of 'till' (rock debris) covering the USA's Midwest can only have been created by moving ice.

## Rocks remade

Just as erosion relentlessly destroys rock wherever it is exposed on the surface, so new rocks are created all the time. These new rocks are often forged from remnants of the old, so that rock is continually recycled in a process called the rock cycle (below).

Not all material moves through the cycle at the same rate. Some material in rocks in continental interiors may sit virtually unchanged for billions of years, while material in rocks near the active margins of continents – those

near coasts and near to subduction zones – has been through the mill again and again.

Some material eroded from rocks is taken back down into the mantle on subducted sea-beds. So too is rock forming oceanic plates. Some may melt as it descends and rise with magmas to form new igneous rocks. Some will be carried right down into mantle. Even there it is not necessarily lost forever. Convection makes material circulate right through the mantle, so it may re-emerge, eventually, as molten magma – even if the process takes hundreds of millions of years. Studies have shown that most of the atoms in rocks in the continental crust came up from the mantle over 2.5 billion years ago. Yet the rocks they are in are usually much, much younger, since these atoms have been recycled many times.

### Rock breaking

*New rock material is sometimes brought up from the mantle in magmas, but most surface rocks are made from ingredients that are continually recycled as rocks are made and remade. The ingredients can be large outcrops of rock, or small chunks, grains or even atoms, and geologists call the recycling process the rock cycle. There are many paths through the cycle. Igneous rock formed by the freezing of molten magma, for instance, might be broken up by the weather into fragments that are washed in rivers into the sea. There fragments pile up on the sea bed and eventually turn to sedimentary stone. This sedimentary rock may, in turn, be buried and squeezed or heated to form metamorphic rock. This too can be broken down and made into sedimentary rock.*

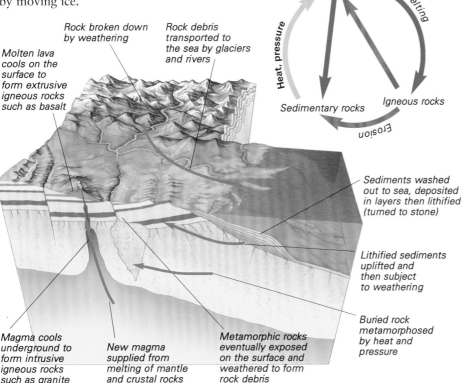

Rock broken down by weathering

Rock debris transported to the sea by glaciers and rivers

Molten lava cools on the surface to form extrusive igneous rocks such as basalt

Magma cools underground to form intrusive igneous rocks such as granite

New magma supplied from melting of mantle and crustal rocks

Metamorphic rocks eventually exposed on the surface and weathered to form rock debris

Sediments washed out to sea, deposited in layers then lithified (turned to stone)

Lithified sediments uplifted and then subject to weathering

Buried rock metamorphosed by heat and pressure

Metamorphic rocks — Melting — Igneous rocks — Erosion — Sedimentary rocks — Heat, pressure

# HOW IGNEOUS ROCKS FORM

*No rocks undergo quite such a change as they form as igneous rocks, the rocks that form almost all the ocean crust and a great deal of the continental crust. Before they solidified into their current form, these extraordinarily tough, crystalline rocks were glowing, searing hot liquid magma.*

Igneous rocks are quite literally frozen magma, hot molten rock from the Earth's interior. Magma may be quite thick and sticky, but it is quite genuinely a fluid and flows like one. The process that turns it to solid rock is exactly the same that turns water to ice when the temperature drops to 0°C/32°F. The difference is that magma freezes at much higher temperatures than water – anywhere between 650°C/1,200°F and 1,100°C/ 2,000°F. Magma also contains a complicated mix of substances, each with its own freezing point, so magma does not freeze in one go like water but bit by bit.

In magma, elements such as silicon, iron, sodium, potassium, magnesium and so on occur in pure form, or as simple compounds. Yet as the magma cools, these elements and compounds join to form crystals of various minerals. The commonest minerals to form are quartz, feldspars, micas, amphiboles, pyroxenes and olivine. Magma also contains gases such as water vapour, sulphur dioxide and carbon dioxide, but these are driven off during cooling.

As magma solidifies, molecules which were vibrating wildly when it was liquid begin to calm down enough to form clusters. These clusters soon begin to grow and form crystals here and there in the melt. They grow especially quickly near the surfaces, which cool fastest. This is why a solid crust can form on the surface of lava which is hot and fluid on the inside.

## Coarse and fine

The slower magma cools, the larger crystals grow. In intrusions below ground, cooling can take thousands, if not millions, of years, and crystals grow big enough to see with the naked eye. Rocks with such crystals are said to be phaneritic, or coarse-grained.

Cooling is usually much quicker in lavas – that is, magmas which erupt on the surface to form extrusive rocks. Cooling takes a matter of weeks or even days. Crystals have little time to grow and so are often only visible under a microscope. Rocks with such crystals are said to be aphanitic, or fine-grained. Sometimes a fine-grained rock may contain larger crystals that formed earlier, while the magma was still underground. These large crystals are called phenocrysts and the rock is said to be porphyritic.

Where lava is ejected in small blobs, it can cool in a matter of hours – so quickly that crystals cannot form at all. The result is a glass, like obsidian, in which there are no crystals at all.

## How igneous rocks evolve

Each mineral crystallizes at a different temperature. Olivine and pyroxene set at over 1,000°C/1,832°F. Silicate minerals such as quartz don't freeze until temperatures are as low as 650°C/1,200°F. So magmas crystallize progressively, with some minerals forming earlier than others.

In the 1920s, laboratory tests conducted by Norman Bowen showed how minerals crystallize in a sequence (Bowen's Reaction Series), from high to low temperature: olivine, pyroxene, amphibole, biotite mica, quartz,

*Left: There can be no more dramatic demonstration of the toughness of granite than these peaks in Torres del Paine, Chile. The softer country rock into which the granite magma was intruded has been stripped away by millions of years of erosion.*

*Above: Granite magmas cool slowly underground and crystals grow large enough to be seen with the naked eye, as in this specimen of Cornish granite. The white crystals are quartz, the black ones biotite mica and the pink ones potassium feldspar.*

muscovite mica, potassium-feldspar and plagioclase feldspar.

This sequence shows how igneous rocks form and how each kind develops its own mineral make-up, according to the circumstances in which it forms. It also provides a mechanism for igneous rocks to evolve. Without such a mechanism, the granitic magmas that form our continents could never have developed.

The idea is that when it formed, the Earth was much like the Moon, made mostly of just a simple parent rock – a 'mafic' or 'ultramafic' rock low in

silica like basalt and peridotite, but unlike granite (which is silica-rich). From this basic start all the many other kinds of igneous rocks evolved by a process called fractionation. This is the way the composition changes during either melting or freezing of the rock, as different minerals melt or freeze first.

When a mafic rock melts, for instance, it splits into two fractions as low temperature minerals such as quartz and feldspar melt first and flow away, leaving high temperature minerals behind. Low temperature minerals are all silicates. So the melt is much richer in silicate minerals than the original rock. Successive refreezing and melting further boosts the silica-content to create silica-rich granite. Which of the many kinds of igneous rock that ultimately forms depends on a variety of factors, including the depth at which the magma is generated and its history of fractionation.

## Where igneous rocks are found

Igneous rocks form only in certain places. Fractionation occurs mostly where tectonic plates are either moving apart at mid-ocean ridges, or pushing together at subduction zones. At mid-ocean ridges, fractionation of the parent magma from the mantle creates

*Above: Clearly visible under a microscope in this fine-grained igneous rock are larger crystals or phenocrysts that crystallized slowly underground before the lava erupted to the surface.*

basalt lava at the surface and gabbro deeper down. At subduction zones, partial melting of the subducted plate fractionates to create intermediate rocks such as diorite in island arcs. Further melting and remelting, especially beneath continents, creates granite. Granite only forms underground, but it can also melt to create the silica-rich lava rhyolite.

*Below: All igneous rocks form when red-hot molten magma like this freezes, either on the surface or underground. The temperature at which the magma freezes, and the kind of rock that forms, depends on the balance of the various chemical elements in the magma.*

# HOW SEDIMENTARY ROCKS FORM

*Over 90 per cent of the Earth's crust is made from igneous rock, but on land, 75 per cent of it is hidden beneath a veneer of sedimentary rock, rock formed from sediments laid down in places such as the sea-bed, buried and turned into stone over millions of years.*

Sedimentary rocks start to form wherever sediments settle on the beds of oceans, lakes and rivers, or are piled up by moving sheets of ice or the wind in the desert. As sediments build up, layers are buried ever deeper, drying and hardening as water is squeezed out. Over millions of years, the pressure of overlying layers and the heat of the Earth's interior turns layers of sediment to solid rock in a process called lithifaction.

When sediments are powdery and soft and contain few hard sand grains, compaction alone is enough to turn them to stone. Very sandy sediments, however, are too hard to be compacted so easily. To turn to stone, sandy sediments must be glued together by cements made from materials dissolved in the water from which the debris settled. The most common cements are silicate minerals, calcite and iron compounds which give rocks a rusty red look.

## Beds and joints

Because sediments settle layer upon layer, outcrops of sedimentary rocks are usually marked by a distinctive layered or 'stratified' look. Where the rock has been undisturbed since turning into stone, these layers appear horizontal. You are not very likely to

*Above: This ammonite fossil, preserved in chalk, once inhabited shallow waters.*

see such uniform layering, however, as the movements of the Earth's crust twists them into contorted shapes.

The thinnest layers or beds are marked out by lines called 'bedding planes'. Beds may be the sediments laid down in just a single season. Yet the thickest layers or strata may have taken millions of years to build up. Sedimentary rocks may also be marked by 'joints', cracks across layers formed as the rock dried out and shrank.

Sedimentary rocks usually contain another distinctive feature – fossils, the remains of living things turned to

### Enduring sand

Of the three major ingredients of clastic rocks, quartz is by far the most durable, surviving the destruction of its parent rock again and again. Once freed from igneous rocks by weathering, quartz accumulates in layers. Grains are then cemented together into sandstones (right) like the de Chelly beds of the buttes in Utah's famous Monument Valley (below). Tough though these rocks are, they too are broken down in time. Yet it is not the sand that is destroyed but just the cement. The liberated sand now scattered on the desert floor will, in time, form new sandstones.

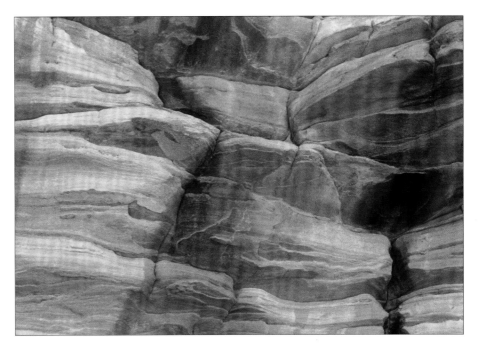

*Right: Sedimentation is very rarely continuous, but occurs in fits and starts. The result is that many sedimentary rocks, like these sandstones in Utah's famous Zion Canyon, are marked by countless bedding planes marking a brief pause in sedimentation.*

stone. Fossils help geologists to determine the conditions in which certain rocks formed. They can tell chalks formed in shallow tropical seas, for instance, because they are studded with fossils of sea creatures that live only in such conditions. Moreover, different creatures and plants lived at various times in Earth's history. So geologists can also work out the relative ages of sedimentary rocks from the range of fossils they contain, a process known as biostratigraphy.

## Kinds of sedimentary rock

Indeed, some sedimentary rocks, like limestone, are made almost entirely from the remains of living organisms, or else by chemicals created by them. Such rocks are described as organic. Chemical sediments such as evaporites are made from minerals precipitated directly from water. Most sedimentary rocks, however, are 'clastic' or 'detrital' which means they are made from fragments or clasts of rock broken down by the weather.

## Rocks from debris

When rocks such as granite are weathered, they eventually crumble to form clasts. The different minerals crumble in different ways. Quartz crystals, for instance, are so hard they are left as distinct sand grains, while orthoclase feldspar breaks down into clay and plagioclase forms calcite. Although this debris all starts off together, the different kinds of clast are gradually separated as they are washed down by rivers into seas and lakes.

Moving water is like a natural sieve, sorting the rock fragments into small and large by carrying smaller grains farther and faster. The farther from the source they are carried, the more they

*Right: Few rocks are so distinctive as white chalk, seen here in cliffs at Normandy, France. It is made of calcite-rich remains of countless marine plankton that floated in ancient seas.*

become sorted. So typically only rocks that form fairly near the source, such as some conglomerates, contain a full range of particle or grain sizes. Most rocks contain particles predominantly of a particular size of grain.

The result is that clastic sedimentary rocks can be divided into three groups according to grain size: large-grained 'rudites' such as conglomerates and breccias; medium-grained 'arenites' such as sandstones; and fine-grained 'lutites' such as shale and clay.

As a river washes into the sea, or into a lake, the heaviest quartz grains are dropped nearest the shore, forming sandstones. Finer clay particles are

washed farther out, forming shales. Dissolved calcite is washed farther out still, and only finally settles to form limestone rocks. This only happens once the particles are taken from the water by living things which use them for building shells and bones. When they die, they take the calcite down to the sea floor in their remains.

In some rocks, such as wackes, there is a mix of grain sizes. However, even wackes may be banded into layers, with a gradation of grain size from fine at the top to coarse at the bottom. This 'graded bedding' develops because the largest, heaviest grains settle out of the water first.

# HOW METAMORPHIC ROCKS FORM

*When rocks are seared by the heat of molten magma or crushed by the enormous forces involved in the movement of tectonic plates, they can be altered beyond recognition. The crystals they are made from re-form so completely that they become new rocks, called metamorphic rocks.*

Early geologists soon appreciated that igneous rocks formed from melts and sedimentary rocks from sediments. Yet there was a third very common kind which they could not quite pin down.

Slate used for roofs, for instance, has a colour and texture like shale. Yet it is much harder than shale and splits into sheets that are completely unrelated to bedding. An even harder rock called gneiss found in the Alps has strange swirls and bands. Beautiful white marble seems to be made of calcite like limestone, yet contains no fossils and has a dense crystalline structure not unlike granite.

Marble seemed to represent a cross between sedimentary and igneous rock and geologists began to realize that this could provide the clue to its origin. Marble was indeed once limestone but it has been altered by heat. The calcite it is made of has been cooked and its crystals reformed in a way that looks more like an igneous rock. Marble, like many other rocks, is metamorphosed or re-formed by heat, or pressure, or both. The word metamorphic comes from the Greek for 'change form'.

## Cooking and crushing

It is now clear that just about any rock – igneous, sedimentary and metamorphic – can be metamorphosed into new rock. To create a metamorphic rock, the heat and pressure were extreme enough to completely alter the original rock or 'protolith', but not so extreme as to melt it or break it down altogether. Heat intense enough to melt it would have created an igneous rock.

Rocks are subjected to heat and pressure either by being buried deep in the crust, or being crushed beneath converging tectonic plates. They are subjected to heat alone by proximity to hot magma.

Heat and pressure metamorphoses rocks in two ways. First, it changes the mineral content, by making minerals react together to form new ones. Some minerals are unique to metamorphic rock. When shale is metamorphosed to slate, for instance, its clay is changed to chlorite, a mineral only found in metamorphic rock.

Second, it changes the size, shape and alignment of crystals, breaking down old crystals and forming new ones in a process called recrystallization. The original rock might be made of just a single mineral. When this is metamorphosed the mineral recrystallizes in a different form. Pure quartz sandstone becomes quartzite. Pure calcite limestone becomes marble.

## Metamorphic environments

Each kind of metamorphic rock has its own particular protolith or set of protoliths. Marble is only formed from pure calcite limestone. However, mylonite can form from practically any rock. Each kind of rock also forms only in specific conditions. Mild metamorphism turns shale to slate. Yet if the heat and pressure become more intense, it turns first to phyllite, then to schist and finally to gneiss.

*Left: Like so much of the Canadian shield, the mountains of Churchill are made from ancient, very tough metamorphic rock. This quartzite landscape formed when sandstones were metamorphosed by intense heat and pressure, some two billion years ago.*

It has become clear that particular combinations of conditions are likely to create particular metamorphic rocks. So geologists talk about environments of metamorphism. They also focus on sets of conditions that form particular combinations or facies of metamorphic minerals (see Metamorphic facies under Schists, Directory of Rocks). One of the most important environments is next to hot igneous intrusions. An intrusion may have a temperature of 900°C/1652°F, and literally cooks the rock it comes into contact with. This is called 'contact metamorphism' and involves heat alone without significant pressure.

In fault zones, rock is ripped apart by tectonic movements. Near the surface, this shatters rock to form a breccia or crushes it to a powder. Deeper down, rock is so warm that it smears out rather than breaks. As it does it is subjected to 'dynamic metamorphism' which creates the rock mylonite.

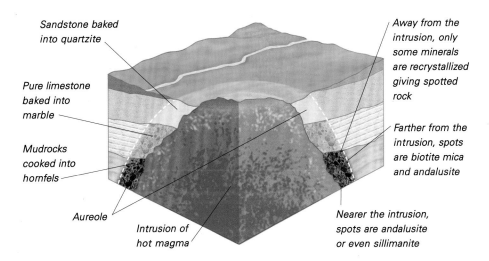

Sandstone baked into quartzite

Pure limestone baked into marble

Mudrocks cooked into hornfels

Aureole

Intrusion of hot magma

Away from the intrusion, only some minerals are recrystallized giving spotted rock

Farther from the intrusion, spots are biotite mica and andalusite

Nearer the intrusion, spots are andalusite or even sillimanite

### Regional metamorphism
*The huge forces involved when continents collide and throw up mountain ranges can crush and cook rocks over large areas. Near the fringes, this regional metamorphism can be mild, and mudrocks are altered to low-grade metamorphic rocks such as slate and phyllite. Towards the heart of the mountain belt heat and pressure gradually increase. Under moderate heat and pressure, slate and phyllite are metamorphosed to schist. Intense heat and pressure (high-grade metamorphism) creates gneiss. Even more extreme conditions can partially melt the rock to create migmatite.*

## Metamorphic grading
The most widespread metamorphic environment is where tectonic plates converge with the force to throw up mountains. Beneath the mountains, rocks are crushed and sheared, and heated by rising magma and their proximity to the Earth's mantle. The scale of this is enormous and is called 'regional metamorphism'. The intensity of regional metamorphism is described in terms of grades. Low-grade metamorphism means low temperature (below 320°C/608°F) and pressure. High-grade metamorphism means high temperature (above 500°C/932°F) and pressure. These different grades of metamorphism create different minerals and different structures.

Metamorphic rocks that form where plates converge have a very distinctive characteristic. Squeezed between the plates, new crystals are forced to grow flat, at right angles to the pressure. The

### Contact metamorphism
*When rocks are cooked by the heat of an intrusion, the result is contact metamorphism. Around the intrusion is a ring or 'aureole' of affected rock. The way in which particular rocks are affected depends on how close they are to the intrusion and the intrusion's size.*

crystals are so intensely aligned that the rocks have layered structure, like the leaves of a book and so called foliation. Foliation means slate breaks easily into flat sheets, it gives schist a stripey look, called schistosity, and gneiss even more dramatic swirling bands, as the minerals are separated out into layers. Foliation is such a distinctive characteristic of regionally metamorphosed rocks that all metamorphic rocks – not just regionally metamorphosed rocks – are divided into foliated rocks (such as slate, phyllite, schist and gneiss) and non-foliated rocks (such as hornfels, quartzite and amphibolite).

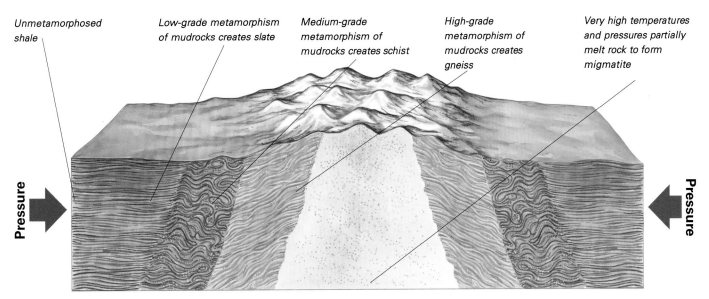

Unmetamorphosed shale

Low-grade metamorphism of mudrocks creates slate

Medium-grade metamorphism of mudrocks creates schist

High-grade metamorphism of mudrocks creates gneiss

Very high temperatures and pressures partially melt rock to form migmatite

Pressure

Pressure

# ROCK LANDSCAPES

*Every kind of rock and geological formation produces its own distinctive kind of landscape, from the jagged ice-capped peaks of young fold mountains and the spectacular gorges and caverns of some limestone regions to the gently rolling landscapes of chalk downland.*

The relationship between rocks and landscapes is a complex one, and geologists have been trying to unravel it for centuries. Yet an experienced geologist can tell a great deal about the nature of the rocks and the rock formations simply by studying the shape of the land.

Some landforms give an instant clue to the kind of rock involved. Gorges with pale rock faces, spectacular caverns and deep potholes cannot be anything but limestone (see opposite page). Granite tors are also easy to spot. Similarly, long mountain ranges with soaring, jagged peaks are clearly fold mountains, created by the convergence of two tectonic plates.

## Hills and vales

Most of the time, however, the relationship is more subtle. On the whole, the hardest rocks, such as granites, gneisses, sandstones and limestones tend to resist erosion and form hills. Softer rocks like clays and

*Above: Spitzkoppe in Namibia is one of many steep-sided granite monoliths in the tropics called inselbergs. It was once thought only deep weathering in ancient climatic conditions could have produced such outcrops. Now it is believed that the shape simply reflects the way ordinary weathering attacks the structure of the original intrusion.*

mudstones are worn away into valleys. There can also be valleys in hard rock, and tectonic movements can uplift soft rock to create hills or even mountains. Clay very rarely forms hills, however, because it is so quickly worn away.

In south-east England, and places in the Appalachians, gentle folding has tilted layers of sedimentary rock to create a distinctive 'belted' landscape of parallel ridges and valleys. Layers of softer rock, such as clay, are eroded faster to create valleys, while the harder rocks such as sandstones and chalk resist erosion to form ridges.

One side of the ridge is a steep 'scarp' slope where erosion has cut right across the strata. The other side, however, slopes gently down the top surface of the rock layer and is called the 'dip' slope. A ridge shaped like this, with one steep scarp and a gentle

dip slope, is called a cuesta. The angle of the dip slope gives an instant clue to the angle of the strata in the region.

## Underground water

Often the landscape that forms from a particular kind of rock depends on the way water moves through it or over it. Sandstone, for instance, is a permeable rock. This means that it allows water to seep through it easily. This is not the same as being porous, though the terms are often confused. Porosity is the capacity of a rock to hold water in

*Below: Salt Cellar Tor in England's Peak District is one of several tors in this region. They are made of the tough sandstone and shale rock series millstone grit. These tors probably formed when rock was weathered underground by water seeping into joints – perhaps during the ice ages. Weathered rock was then stripped away to reveal the tor.*

spaces in the rock – in other words, how full of holes it is. A rock like slate is barely 1 per cent porous; gravel is over 30 per cent porous. A rock that is porous is likely to be permeable – though not always – but a rock that is permeable is not necessarily porous.

Since sandstone is permeable, most water in sandstone landscapes soaks into the ground rather than flowing overland. This often makes sandstone landscapes quite angular because they are not rounded by water flowing over the land, except in times of flood. In wet regions, there may be too much water for the rock to soak up, so water erosion can do its work anyway.

Clays and shales, on the other hand, tend to be impermeable. They are often even more porous than gravel, but the pores are so small that water gets trapped. This means that the rocks easily become waterlogged and water remains on the surface to wear the rocks away, and round off contours.

## Chalk and limestone

Like clay, chalk is not at all porous, and often contains clays which make it even harder for water to seep through. The same is true of limestone. Yet both these rocks are permeable. In particular, limestone usually has joints (cracks) so big that water can filter into the formation even if it can't penetrate the rock directly. It is a particular feature of limestone that the infiltrating water, called groundwater, corrodes away the rock to open up potholes and caverns.

Chalk has far fewer joints and is much less permeable than limestone and is not so susceptible to corrosion. So it rarely develops anything more dramatic than the occasional cavern. All the same, the chalk downlands of southern England do have their own special features including dry valleys called bournes. Bournes look like river valleys but contain no river. They may have formed in times when the climate was wetter. Large hollows called combes may have been formed either by springs in these wetter times, or by frozen surface debris melting after the ice ages.

## Granite

Like limestone, granite is tough enough to form mountains. In cold regions, granite intrusions are often left standing proud as dramatic monoliths when exposed on the surface. Yet in warmer regions, granite's feldspar content makes it prone to chemical weathering. Feldspar corrodes quickly in warm water. As with limestone, joints in granite allow water to penetrate deep into the rock, so tropical granite is corroded underground. When the weathered rock is stripped away, it leaves outcrops called kopjes. Similar features called tors form in cooler regions, such as in England's Dartmoor. It's thought that these are the result of climate change.

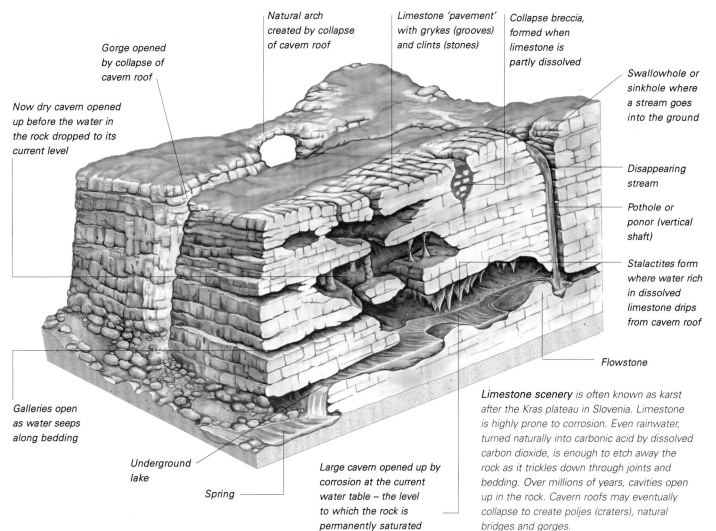

Gorge opened by collapse of cavern roof

Natural arch created by collapse of cavern roof

Limestone 'pavement' with grykes (grooves) and clints (stones)

Collapse breccia, formed when limestone is partly dissolved

Now dry cavern opened up before the water in the rock dropped to its current level

Swallowhole or sinkhole where a stream goes into the ground

Disappearing stream

Pothole or ponor (vertical shaft)

Stalactites form where water rich in dissolved limestone drips from cavern roof

Flowstone

Galleries open as water seeps along bedding

Underground lake

Spring

Large cavern opened up by corrosion at the current water table – the level to which the rock is permanently saturated

*Limestone scenery* is often known as karst after the Kras plateau in Slovenia. Limestone is highly prone to corrosion. Even rainwater, turned naturally into carbonic acid by dissolved carbon dioxide, is enough to etch away the rock as it trickles down through joints and bedding. Over millions of years, cavities open up in the rock. Cavern roofs may eventually collapse to create poljes (craters), natural bridges and gorges.

# THE AGES OF THE EARTH

*Written in the rocks of the crust is the entire history of the Earth's surface. The record is blurred in some places and lost in others. Nonetheless, by studying rocks in detail geologists have been able to piece together the remarkable story of how the Earth has changed through the ages.*

Barely two centuries ago, most people thought the Earth was just a few thousand years old and little changed since it was created. But in the 19th century, geologists began to realize its age is immense. It is now thought to be nearly 4,600 million years old, and has undergone huge changes during its life. Its remarkable history is recorded in the rocks, if you know how to read it.

## Pioneers of deep time

The great pioneers in the study of the Earth's distant past were James Hutton (1726–97) and William Smith (1769–1839). It was Scottish geologist Hutton who first suggested that the Earth is very, very old, and that the landscape has been shaped gradually by countless cycles of erosion and uplift.

Soon after, English surveyor William Smith was surveying routes for canals, and noticed that each layer of sedimentary rock contains its own range of fossils. He realized that all layers containing the same range of fossils must be of the same age. What's more, the 'principle of superposition' made it

possible to work out which layers are old and which young. In the 1600s, Danish geologist priest Nicolas Steno had realized that all sedimentary rocks were originally laid in flat beds, even if they've been tilted and broken since. Steno also realized beds were laid one on top of the other, so the oldest beds are always at the bottom and the

*Above: Earth's rocks have been traced back over 3,800 million years. Rocks of this age are found exposed in western Greenland, like Sondre Strom fjord on the south-west coast.*

youngest at the top. This is the principle of superposition.

Using this principle in conjunction with fossils, 'biostratigraphers' have built a detailed history of the Earth

## Geologic time

This illustration gives a simplified picture of the major periods of Earth's history since the Cambrian Period 545 million years ago (mya) – the time when complex life forms first flourished.

*4560–545 mya Precambrian The oceans formed and the first single-celled life forms appeared including algae which gave oxygen to the air. Later on, multi-celled animals like sponges and jellyfish appeared.*

Blue-green algae (early life)

Trilobite (segmented creature)

Orthonybyoceras (marine animals)

*545–495 mya Cambrian Period An explosion of life in the sea including small invertebrates and the first animals with hard shells easily preserved as fossils.*

Cooksonia (land plant)

*495–443 mya Ordovician Period Melting of the polar ice caps flooded much of the land. Crustaceans (like crabs), early marine animals and coral reefs appear.*

Ichthyostega (amphibian)

Giant tree fern (first forest)

*354–290 mya Carboniferous Period The sea level was high and large areas were covered in tree-filled swamps. Lime-stones laid down. Amphibians and insects spread, and possibly the first reptiles.*

*443–417 mya Silurian Period The Caledonian Orogeny threw up mountains in what became N America and NW Europe. Fish with jaws and river fish appeared, and the first land plants.*

*417–354 mya Devonian Period Continents and mountains grew. Old Red Sandstones laid down. Forests of club mosses and tree ferns spread. Vertebrates dominant. The first sharks. Animals began to live on land.*

*PALAEOZOIC*

stretching back half a billion years. If rock sediments remained undisturbed forever, it would be possible in theory to slice through them to reveal most of the sequence of Earth's history. If you could take a column through the sequence, you could read Earth's history like a book.

## The geologic time scale

Although such a column exists nowhere on Earth, a detailed geologic time scale based on it is now widely used. This timescale is constantly updated as geologists make new discoveries. It is detailed only back to the start of the Cambrian Period, 545 million years ago. Only since this time have shelly and bony life forms been common enough to leave a good fossil record. We once knew very little about the four billion years of Earth history before that, known as Precambrian time. In recent years, discoveries have begun to fill in the picture.

Just as day is divided into hours, minutes and seconds, so geological time is divided into units. The longest are Eons, lasting at least half a billion years. Eons are divided into Eras, Eras into Periods, Periods into Epochs, Epochs into Ages and Ages into Chrons. Each unit in the timescale is given a name,

usually derived from the area where rocks of the period were first studied. The Devonian Period, for instance, was named after Devon in England where rocks of the age were first studied.

Biostratigraphy now provides a detailed system for matching rock sequences around the world. Yet it has its limitations. It can show one rock is older than another, but not exactly how old. In other words, it gives a relative, not absolute, date. By working out how fast sediments might have been deposited and other clues, geologists established rough dates for the geologic timescale. But it is only with the development of radioactive dating in the last 50 years we can be confident dates are fairly accurate.

## Radiometric dating

Atoms of elements can occur in alternative varieties or isotopes, each with a different number of particles in its nucleus. The number of particles is given in the isotope's name, such as uranium-235. Radioactive or radiometric dating uses the way certain isotopes 'decay' naturally through time – that is, break down to become isotopes of different elements. This

decay begins from the moment a rock is formed. It happens at such a steady rate that it is possible to work out how long it has been going on by counting the relevant 'daughter' isotopes in the rock compared to those of the original 'parent' isotope. The steady rate is known as the half-life, the time it takes for half the parent isotopes to break down. The widely used rubidium-87 isotope (which breaks down to strontium-87) has a half-life of 47.5 billion years. Rubidium is a rare element, but is often found with potassium in minerals such as feldspars and micas, and rubidium-strontium dating is used to date granites and gneisses.

Different isotopes are used to date rocks of different ages. Potassium-40, which decays to argon-40, is used to date rocks under a million years. Uranium-235 is used for the oldest rocks. Traces of uranium-235 decay products are found in zircon, one of the few minerals that survives for billions of years unchanged. So geologists studying ancient rocks look for zircon. Zircon found in the Jack Hills of Western Australia dates back 4300 million years, almost to the Earth's birth.

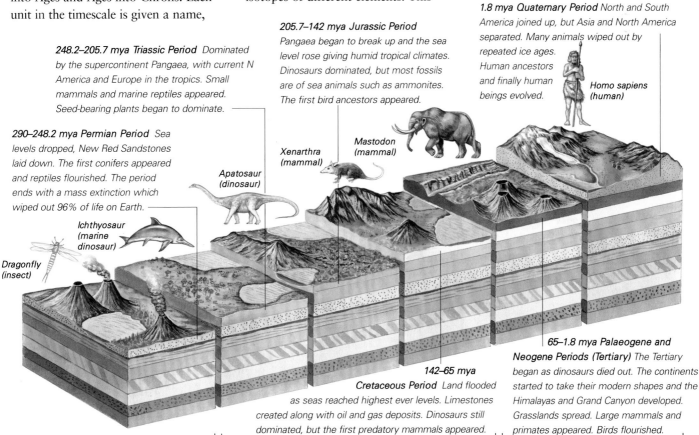

*1.8 mya Quaternary Period* North and South America joined up, but Asia and North America separated. Many animals wiped out by repeated ice ages. Human ancestors and finally human beings evolved.

Homo sapiens (human)

*205.7–142 mya Jurassic Period* Pangaea began to break up and the sea level rose giving humid tropical climates. Dinosaurs dominated, but most fossils are of sea animals such as ammonites. The first bird ancestors appeared.

*248.2–205.7 mya Triassic Period* Dominated by the supercontinent Pangaea, with current N America and Europe in the tropics. Small mammals and marine reptiles appeared. Seed-bearing plants began to dominate.

*290–248.2 mya Permian Period* Sea levels dropped, New Red Sandstones laid down. The first conifers appeared and reptiles flourished. The period ends with a mass extinction which wiped out 96% of life on Earth.

Mastodon (mammal)

Xenarthra (mammal)

Apatosaur (dinosaur)

Ichthyosaur (marine dinosaur)

Dragonfly (insect)

*142–65 mya Cretaceous Period* Land flooded as seas reached highest ever levels. Limestones created along with oil and gas deposits. Dinosaurs still dominated, but the first predatory mammals appeared.

*65–1.8 mya Palaeogene and Neogene Periods (Tertiary)* The Tertiary began as dinosaurs died out. The continents started to take their modern shapes and the Himalayas and Grand Canyon developed. Grasslands spread. Large mammals and primates appeared. Birds flourished.

*MESOZOIC*

*CENOZOIC*

# ROCKS AND FOSSILS

*The fossils that are found in most sedimentary rocks are one of the geologist's most valuable clues to Earth's history. Fossils not only help a geologist tell the age of a rock, but work out the conditions under which the rock formed – and track the occurrence of different strata right across the world.*

Fossils are time capsules buried within almost every sedimentary rock. By identifying fossils and comparing them with creatures alive today, geologists can trace the way plants and animals have changed through time and use this knowledge to learn about the rocks they are found in.

The fossil record from the time before the Cambrian Period, beginning 545 million years ago, is sparse. Since then, however, millions upon millions of species have come and gone – many, many times more than are alive on Earth today. Probably only a tiny minority of these species have been preserved as fossils. But there are enough to provide a rich source of information.

'Fossil correlation' is one of the central techniques for geologists studying the history of rocks. Fossil correlation means tracing the occurrence of particular rock

*Below: These arietitid ammonite fossils, in large pebbles washed ashore at Lyme Regis in Dorset, England, give very precise rock dating. They are an estimated 180 million years old.*

formations over wide areas by looking for repeat occurrences of the same range of fossils. Sedimentary rock formations can be widely separated, but if they contain the same range of fossils, a geologist can be confident that they formed at the same time.

Moreover, since species change with time, many only appear in a particular part of the sequence of rock layers. So geologists look for the level where particular species first appear in the rock sequence, and for the point where they finally disappear. That way they can tell the relative ages of rock strata from the fossils they contain. Rock strata containing fossils of species that became extinct 300 million years ago are clearly older than strata containing fossils of species that first appeared about 250 million years ago.

## Index fossils

Palaeontologists get excited if they find a rare dinosaur skeleton, but it is different for geologists. A fossil is little use for dating if it occurs in only a few rocks, if it is hard to identify, or if it

*Above: If a sediment has only been buried at a shallow depth and little disturbed since this time, fossils like this bivalve may be preserved so intact that they look as if they have just fallen into the sand.*

changed so little over time that it appears the same in rocks of all ages. So geologists actually look for certain very commonplace kinds of fossil, which they call 'index' fossils. If they spot one of these index fossils in a rock layer, they can often pinpoint its age instantly.

For a fossil to be used as an index, it must be widely distributed and easy to identify. It must also be small and have evolved rapidly, showing clear changes through time. All index fossils are small sea creatures – shellfish in

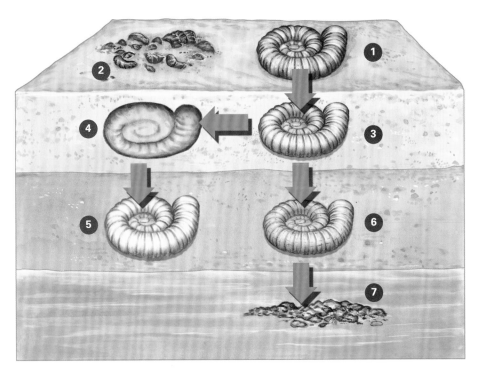

## The fossilization process

*Most fossils are shells or isolated bones. Complete skeletons are rare, and the soft body parts are almost never preserved. The vast majority of fossils are shellfish that lived in shallow seas. Fossils of land creatures are rare because they rotted away before they were preserved. When a creature such as a shellfish dies and falls to the sea floor, its soft body parts quickly rot away (1). However, its hard shell may be either broken (2) or buried intact (3). Over millions of years, the shell, made mostly of the mineral aragonite, may be dissolved away by water seeping through the sediments. Sometimes this leaves an empty cast or mould (4). The dissolved aragonite often recrystallizes in the cavity instead, creating a perfect replica of the shell in silicate or iron sulphide minerals (5). Occasionally, the shell is preserved almost intact (6). Nearly all fossils are destroyed if buried too deep or the rock undergoes metamorphism (7).*

particular – whose remains are easily preserved in the sea-bed sediments that form most sedimentary rocks.

## Fossil zones

Using these index fossils, geologists try to divide local sequences of rock into 'zones', each containing a particular range of index fossils. The acme zone is where the index fossil is especially abundant – either because the species thrived at the time the sediments were laid down, or because they happened to be especially well preserved. The full range of strata through which the

fossil is found is called the range zone. When two or more species of index fossils overlap in the sequence, they are said to form a concurrent range zone. Where one of the index fossils is not available, geologists rely on fossil assemblages. These are groups of fossils known to have lived at the same time, for example dinosaurs, redwoods and dragonflies.

## Zonal schemes

Because most creatures can only survive in a particular range of environments, most appear only in particular kinds of

rock. So each kind or 'facies' must have its own zonal scheme. This takes into account the range of creatures living at that particular time in each rock-forming environment. In Devonian rocks in Europe, for instance, there are three main facies, each with its own zonal scheme. Old Red Sandstone, which formed in lakes and estuaries, is zoned or indexed by fossil fish. Rhenish rock which formed on warm, shallow sandy sea-beds is zoned by brachiopods and corals. Hercynian rocks, which formed on deep muddy sea-beds, are zoned using ammonites.

### Index fossils

*The illustration shows some of the most widely used index fossils around the world. Below are listed the key marine fossils used in North America, two for each period. ID pictures can be found in a good fossil guide. Note that the Carboniferous Period is divided into the Mississippian and Pennsylvanian in North America.*

| | | |
|---|---|---|
| Quaternary | Pecten gibbus | Neptunea tabulata |
| Tertiary | Calyptraphorus velatus | Venericardia planicosta |
| Cretaceous | Scaphites hippocrepis | Inoceramus labiatus |
| Jurassic | Perisphinctes tiziani | Nerinea trinodosa |
| Triassic | Trophetes subbuliates | Monotis subcircularis |
| Permian | Leptodus americanus | Parafusulina bosei |
| Pennsylvanian | Dictyoclostus americanus | Lophophyllidium proliferum |
| Mississippian | Cactocrinus multibrachiatus | Prolecanites gurleyi |
| Devonian | Mucrospirifer mucronatus | Palmatolepus unicornia |
| Silurian | Cystiphyllum niagarense | Hexameroceras hertzeri |
| Ordovician | Bathyurus extans | Tetragraptus fructicosus |
| Cambrian | Paradoxides pinus | Billingsella corrugata |

*Ammonites were squidlike shellfish that make good index fossils for the Jurassic and Cretaceous Periods.*

*Trilobites were one of the first creatures with a body split into segments. They are index fossils for the Cambrian.*

*Echinoderms are very common fossils but have changed so little through the ages that they are of little use as indexes.*

*Corals are very common fossils but have changed so little through the ages that they are of little use as index fossils.*

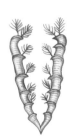

*Graptolites were sea creatures that make good index fossils for the Ordovician and Silurian Periods.*

# GEOLOGICAL MAPS

*A good geological map is probably the geologist's single most valuable tool. It displays what rocks appear where in the landscape and the major geological features. This not only helps the geologist identify rocks on the ground but provides a good indication of where to find particular minerals.*

For the experienced geologist, a geological map does not simply show where rocks appear. With skilful interpretation, it is possible to work out the three-dimensional structure of rock formations, the way they relate to each other, and even some of their history and the way that the landscape has developed.

Most conventional geological maps are known as 'solid' maps, because they show the solid rocks under the surface. They help geologists to find the rock structures most likely to yield mineral ores and oil and gas deposits.

Geological maps can also show loose surface deposits, such as the sediment deposited by rivers in flood

### Mapping the landscape
*The same area can be mapped by geologists in four different ways. A satellite image (left) shows the landscape very clearly, allowing the geologist to interpret ground features relating to the underlying geology before surveying in the field. A step on from the satellite image is the digital terrain model (below), which combines satellite and ground survey data to build a 3D computer model. This gives an even clearer picture of the landscape and clues to the underlying geology.*

or by glaciers. Maps like these are called 'drift' maps and are valuable for the construction industry since they reveal just how solid the ground on which they plan to build is likely to be. They are invaluable in the initial plotting of the course of a railway tunnel, for instance, before detailed survey work on the ground begins.

## Colours and symbols
Geological maps usually use areas of different colours to represent the different kinds of rock or drift. Igneous rocks, for instance, are usually shown in various shades of purple and magenta, depending on whether they are intrusive or extrusive. Metamorphic rocks are typically shown in shades of pink and grey-green. Sedimentary rocks are usually shown, appropriately, in sandy colours – shades of brown and yellow, plus green – except for limestones, which are typically blue-grey.

Besides colours, maps often use types of shading or pattern called ornament. Each rock type is also given a set of letters to symbolize it on the map. This usually begins with a capital letter to show the age of the rock – for example J for Jurassic, K for Cretaceous, T for Tertiary and Q for Quaternary. The smaller letters indicate either the name of the particular formation or rock type.

## Geology underground
Geological maps only actually show surface geology. Even solid maps only show outcrops – that is, where a solid rock of a particular kind reaches the surface, even if it is actually hidden beneath sheets of deposits. Outcrops that are not covered with deposits are called exposures. All the same, many maps have cross-sections showing a vertical slice through the rock formations, revealing how they are

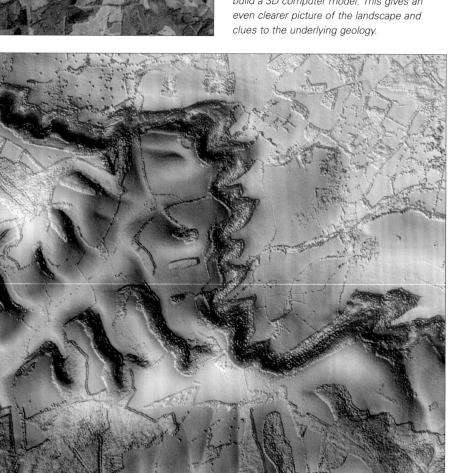

arranged beneath the surface. Often these incorporate results from boreholes and seismic surveys. Yet an experienced geologist can construct a cross-section directly from the map.

Where there are a series of roughly parallel bands of sedimentary rocks, for instance, it is highly likely that they are simply where gently dipping (tilted) sedimentary strata reach the surface. Contours on the map reveal the shape of the land surface. If these reveal an escarpment with a gentle dip slope (see Rock Landscapes in this section), the angle of the dip (tilt) is easy to guess.

## Geology in 3D

Cross-sections only show the structure of rocks in the landscape in two dimensions – as a thin slice – but

*A third map (below) shows the rock underlying the same terrain, with different rocks indicated by coloured bands. A professional geologist can use this map to construct a cross-section (right) of the landscape from, say, A to B, plotting the height given by contours, then interpreting how the rock beds lie from their surface configuration.*

geologists often want to know the whole structure of the area in three dimensions. In the past, they often constructed models called fence diagrams. These were made by constructing a series of cross-sections at right angles, interlocking like the fences of a square field. Sometimes these were created with card, and sometimes they were simply drawn.

## Computer modelling

With the spread of computers, however, geologists are able to construct complete 3D models of the ground. These can be manipulated and

projected to reveal the subsurface structure in any way the geologist wants. Many geologists hunting for minerals now use these computer models instead of conventional maps wherever they exist.

Until recently, it was solid geology, not drift geology that received the attention from computer modellers. Now, however, organizations such as the British Geological Survey (BGS) use GSID (Geological Surveying and Investigation in 3D) software to create 3D models that show not only outcrops in their entirety but the surface deposits as well.

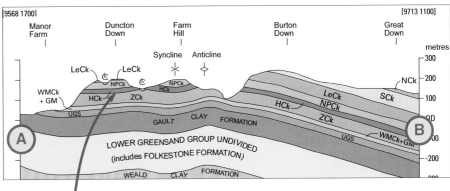

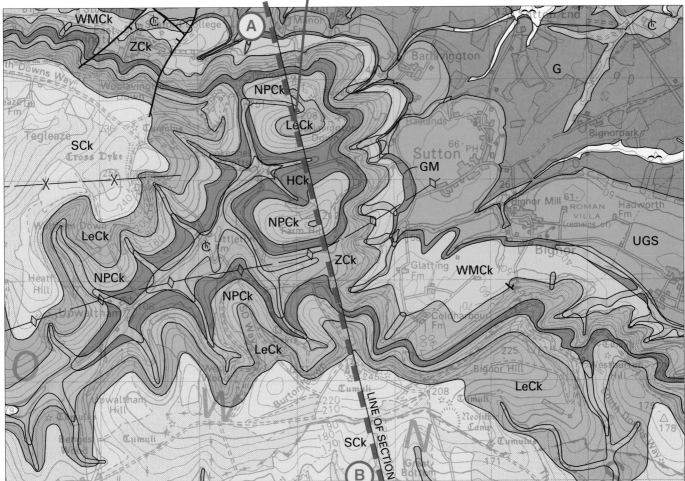

# READING THE LANDSCAPE

*Every bit of rock has a story to tell. Look at a craggy cliff face or pick up a stone on the shore, and if you know what to look for, you can read in it a great deal of its past, from scratches revealing episodes of glaciation to rock boundaries marking cataclysmic earthquakes.*

In some ways, the geologist is like a detective. The idea is to look for clues, study the evidence and work out just what has happened. Sometimes the clues are so small they are visible only under a powerful microscope. Sometimes they are so big they are visible only from space. Fortunately most can be identified with no more specialist equipment than basic common sense.

If you find a stone, see what you can work out about its history. At first it might seem baffling and dull, but with a little thought you can often piece together some of its long story. Obviously it helps to identify the stone, and the Directory of Rocks later in the book should help you here. Yet even without a strong positive identification, you can often work out quite a bit about it.

First of all, you can probably guess whether the stone arrived naturally where you found it – or whether there was a human hand involved. If you see other similar stones nearby in a natural setting, the chances are it got there naturally. Exotic stones that look very different can arrive in their resting

*Below: Cliffs and chasms, such as this feature of the Blue Mountains in NSW, Australia, are one of the best places to see rock strata.*

### The Great Unconformity
*One of the world's most famous unconformities is North America's Great Unconformity. This dramatic gap in the geological sequence stretches all the way from Arizona to Alberta in Canada. Perhaps the best place to see this is in the Grand Canyon National Park (the Canyon's west rim is shown above), where the Colorado River has cut down through the strata over five million years to reveal the Unconformity at the canyon's foot. Here young Tapeats sandstone sits so directly on top of ancient, two-billion-year-old Vishnu schist that it is possible to touch them both with the span of a hand. The schists began life some two billion years ago as sediments. These sediments were metamorphosed to schist about 1.7 billion years ago as they were penetrated by a magma intrusion and squeezed by tectonic movement. Slowly, over more than a billion years, this schist was worn flat, then sank beneath the sea. About 500 million years ago, the sediments that formed the Tapeats sandstone began to pile up on the sea floor. The sea floor began to subside under the weight of sediments, and sedimentation continued over hundreds of millions of years with little or no tilting, Eventually some 1,220 m/4,000 ft of level sedimentary beds were laid down. Since then the whole area has been uplifted, and the path of the Colorado river has exposed the whole sequence to reveal the Tapeats sandstone and the Great Unconformity at its base.*

place naturally. Glaciers, for instance, carry entire giant boulders, called erratics, into areas of different rock. Flash floods and avalanches can carry quite large stones. Yet exotics like these are rarities. Most loose stones in a natural setting are not only similar to each other; they are often similar to the rocks nearby. If they resemble the solid rock around, you can be sure the stones were eroded from it.

Often, you can see where the stones came from immediately. Reasonably large stones are rarely carried far from their origin. Often, stones simply fall down a mountain slope to gather in a scree at the foot. Stones and pebbles can fall from a sea cliff on to the beach below. There is often a marked difference between stones in a scree and stones on a beach. Scree stones are almost invariably sharp-edged and chunky, reflecting the way they were shattered from the mountain above by frost, often within the past few months. Beach stones, however, are often rounded pebbles. They are rounded because they have been rolled over and over in water laden with abrasive sand again and again. To get so rounded, they must have been in the water many thousands of years. Waves are powerful enough to carry stones some distance, so the pebbles on a beach have not necessarily come from the cliffs above.

## How an angular unconformity forms

*Sediments are usually laid down in a continual sequence but sometimes a break or unconformity develops. Shown below are the stages in the creation of an angular unconformity. It begins with the laying down of a sequence of sediments (1) which are then uplifted and folded into mountains (2). The mountains are worn down to a plain over a long period (3). The sea level rises, submerging the plain (4). New layers are laid down horizontally in the sea, over the contorted layers of the original sediments (5).*

*1 First sediments*

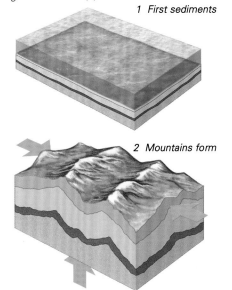

*2 Mountains form*

*3 Erosion*

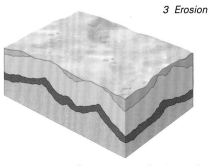

*4 Sea levels rise*

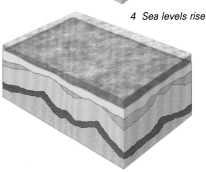

*5 New sediments*

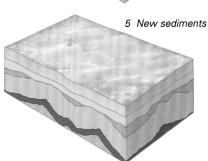

## Using rock layers

On a larger scale, you can tell a great deal about the history of rocks, especially sedimentary rocks, by stratigraphy – the study of rock layers and their contents. Earlier pages have shown how if rocks contain the same assemblage of key fossils they must be the same age. The law of superposition also shows how the uppermost layers are likely to have formed later in Earth's history. Another valuable rule of thumb is that the more contorted strata is, the older it is likely to be. Similarly, the law of cross-cutting relationships shows that whenever a geological feature like an igneous intrusion cuts across a sequence of rock layers, it is certain to be more recent than the rock layers.

## Breaks in the sequence

One feature geologists look for in particular is an unconformity. On the whole, sediments are laid down one on top of the other in sequence, but every now and then you find a gap or even a dramatic break in the sequence. A young rock may overlay an old rock, with no intervening 'middle-aged' rocks, or a sedimentary sequence may overlay metamorphic rock. This gap or break is the unconformity, and it can be very revealing.

One kind of unconformity, easily seen in the field, is an angular unconformity. In this case, younger sediments sit on top of older sediments that have been tilted and deformed and then eroded to form a flat plain.

There are other kinds too. If the older sequence remains both level and undeformed, then the only sign of the unconformity may be the great age difference between rock layers, indicated by a significant gap in the fossil record. This is known as a parallel unconformity.

A disconformity is formed where the eroded surface of the older sequence is not a flat plain but has hills and valleys. In this instance the break in the sequence is marked by a corresponding wavy line. A non-conformity occurs where the sedimentary rock sequence has been interrupted by either igneous or metamorphic rock.

### Stratification

*When a geologist sees a sequence of rocks exposed in a cliff, he can examine the layers and build up a picture of their history, using familiar clues. The nature of the rock gives a clue to the environment in which they formed. Fossils in the rock layers may give a clue to their relative age. So too can their position within the sequence, while unconformities bear witness to dramatic breaks in the sequence, and past geological events.*

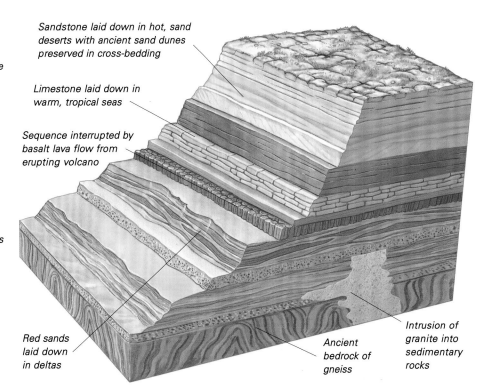

Sandstone laid down in hot, sand deserts with ancient sand dunes preserved in cross-bedding

Limestone laid down in warm, tropical seas

Sequence interrupted by basalt lava flow from erupting volcano

Red sands laid down in deltas

Ancient bedrock of gneiss

Intrusion of granite into sedimentary rocks

# HOW MINERALS FORM

*Minerals are the natural substances the world's rocks are made of. All of them are solid crystals with a particular chemical composition – some so tiny they can only be seen under a powerful microscope, others as big as tree trunks. Each kind forms under particular conditions in particular places.*

There are 4,000 to 5,000 different minerals in the Earth's crust. Yet only 30 or so are very widespread. Most of the rest are present in rocks only in minute traces, and are only easy to see when they become concentrated in certain places by geological processes. It is concentrations like these that give us the ores from which many metals are extracted.

Furthermore, large crystals of minerals like those that illustrate this book, even common minerals, are so rare that a mineral hunter feels understandably excited to find one. Big, spectacular crystals need both time and space to grow – and a steady supply of exactly the right ingredients. Such a perfect combination is extraordinarily rare.

Mineral crystals form in four main ways. Some form as hot, molten magma cools and crystallizes. Some form from chemicals dissolved in watery liquids. Some form as existing minerals are altered chemically, and some form as existing minerals are squeezed or heated as rocks are subjected to metamorphism.

*Below: The best crystals need space to grow, so they are often found in cavities, such as geodes. Geodes can look like dull round stones on the outside, but a tap with a hammer gives a tell-tale hollow sound. When cracked open, they reveal a glittering interior.*

*Above: This woman is inside the world's biggest geode – most are no bigger than a fist. Geodes are cavities that probably form from gas bubbles in lava (or limestone). The bubbles later fill with hydrothermal fluids in which large crystals such as amethyst grow.*

## Minerals from magma

As magmas cool, groups of atoms begin to come together in the chaotic mix and form crystals. The crystals grow as more atoms attach themselves to the initial structure – just as icicles grow as more water freezes on to them. Minerals with the highest melting points form first, and as they crystallize out the composition of the remaining melt changes (see How Igneous Rocks Form, this section).

Chemicals that slot easily into crystal structures are removed from the melt first, and it is bigger, more unusual atoms that are left behind. It is these 'late-stage' magmas, the last portion of the melt to crystallize, that give the most varied and interesting minerals.

Just what these minerals are depends on the original ingredients in the magma, and the way it cools. Large crystals tend to form in magmas that have cooled slowly. The biggest and most interesting often form in what are called pegmatites, which form from the fraction of melt left over after the rest has crystallized. Pegmatites typically collect in cracks in an intrusion or ooze into joints in the country rock, forming sheets of rock called dykes. The residual fluids in these late-stage magmas are rich in exotic elements such as fluorine, boron, lithium, beryllium, niobium and tantalum. These can combine to form giant crystals of tourmaline, topaz, beryl, and other rarer minerals. When the fluids are rich in boron and lithium, tourmaline is formed. When fluids are rich in fluorine, topaz is formed. When fluids are beryllium-rich, beryl forms.

## Minerals from water

Water can only hold so much dissolved chemicals. When the water becomes 'saturated' (fully loaded), the chemicals precipitate out – they come out of the water as solids. Typically this happens when water evaporates, or cools down.

When sodium, chlorine, borax and calcium are dissolved from rocks, they may be carried by rivers to inland seas and lakes, which then evaporate, leaving mineral deposits of minerals such as salt, gypsum and borax.

Many other minerals form from the cooling of hydrothermal solutions – hot water rich in dissolved chemicals. Sometimes the water is rainwater that seeps down through the ground (meteoric water) and is then heated by proximity to either the mantle or a hot igneous intrusion.

Hydrothermal solutions also come from late-stage magmas, and so are rich in unusual chemicals. Such solutions ooze up through cracks in the intrusion and cool to form thin, branching veins.

## Alteration minerals

Although some minerals such as diamond or gold seem to last forever, most have a limited life span. As soon as they are formed, they begin to react with their environment – some very slowly, some quite quickly. As they react, they form different minerals.

Metal minerals are often oxidized when exposed to the air, or oxygen-rich water. Iron minerals rust, like iron nails, turning to red and brown iron oxide. When water containing dissolved oxygen seeps down through the ground into rocks and veins containing metals, it creates an oxidation zone in the upper layers as the metals are altered. Cuprite, goethite, anglesite, chalcanthite, azurite and many other minerals form this way. Some sulphide minerals are oxidized to sulphates that dissolve in water. These sulphates may be washed down through the rock to be deposited lower down as different minerals which become often valuable ores such as chalcocite.

## Minerals remade

Many minerals become unstable when exposed to heat and pressure and respond by altering their chemistry to become different minerals. This is known as recrystallization and is typically linked to metamorphism. When a rock is remade by metamorphism, its mineral ingredients are recrystallized.

While it takes hot magma or tectonic movements to metamorphose rocks, simple burial is often enough to alter minerals, since heat and pressure rise as depth increases. Minerals can also be recrystallized by contact with hydrothermal fluids.

In the simplest recrystallizations, the resulting minerals depend merely on the combination of heat and pressure, and the minerals in the original rock. However, new ingredients may seep in to alter the picture. Where magma intrudes into a limestone, for instance, the magma 'cooks' the limestone but also introduces new chemicals to create a complex mix. The limestone supplies calcium, magnesium and carbon dioxide, while the magma brings silicon, aluminium, iron, sodium, potassium and various other ingredients. The result is a 'skarn' rich in a huge variety of interesting silicate minerals.

*Above: Topaz is one of many rare minerals that form when the last rare-mineral-rich residue of a magma finally crystallizes, particularly in dykes called granitic pegmatites. Topaz forms from residues rich in fluorine. Crystals formed in voids in the pegmatite, called miarolitic cavities, can occasionally grow very large.*

*Above: Fluorite is one of many minerals that form as hot hydrothermal solutions cool and precipitate some of their dissolved chemicals. Natural pipes carrying hydrothermal veins eventually completely crystallize to form veins.*

*Above: Cuprite is one of many minerals that form by oxidation reactions, caused by exposure to air, or oxygen-rich water. Cuprite forms a bright green crust on oxidized copper minerals.*

*Left: Rubies are among a number of rare and precious gem minerals that form when certain oxides are crystallized by the heat and pressure of metamorphism.*

# MINERAL CRYSTALS

*Although mineral crystals found in the ground are often chunky, they rarely have the beautiful, regular geometric shapes you see in drawings. All the same, crystals grow in certain ways, and have particular symmetrical forms.*

Mineral crystals all grow from countless tiny building blocks called unit cells. Every unit cell of a mineral is an identical arrangement of atoms, and it is the way these identical cells combine that gives the crystal its shape. If you could break up cubic salt crystals, for instance, you'd find they break into cubic grains, and the grains into tiny cubic unit cells.

The unit cells in crystals stack together to form an atomic 'lattice', a regular internal framework. This is what gives a crystal its essentially geometric shape or 'symmetry'.

All crystals are symmetrical in some way or other and crystallographers group crystals according to the manner of their symmetry. There are six basic crystal systems, each with a characteristic shape, further divided into classes. The simple, most symmetrical system is the isometric or cubic system. The other five in order of decreasing symmetry are hexagonal (including trigonal), tetragonal, orthorhombic, monoclinic and triclinic. Crystals in each system appear in many different 'forms' (see below and right).

The symmetry of a crystal can be described in various ways. One way is in terms of axial symmetry. An 'axis of symmetry' is an imaginary line drawn through the crystal's centre from the

## Crystal systems (with some possible forms)

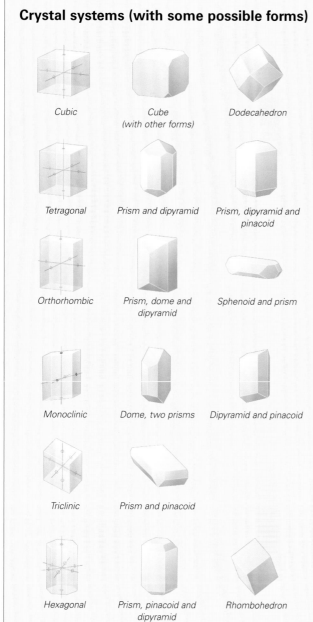

*Cubic*

*Cube (with other forms)*

*Dodecahedron*

*Tetragonal*

*Prism and dipyramid*

*Prism, dipyramid and pinacoid*

*Orthorhombic*

*Prism, dome and dipyramid*

*Sphenoid and prism*

*Monoclinic*

*Dome, two prisms*

*Dipyramid and pinacoid*

*Triclinic*

*Prism and pinacoid*

*Hexagonal*

*Prism, pinacoid and dipyramid*

*Rhombohedron*

**Cubic or isometric**
This is the most symmetrical possible, with three equal axes at right-angles; four-fold symmetry all round. The main forms are cubes, octahedron and rhombic dodecahedrons. E.g. Galena, halite, silver, gold, fluorite, pyrite (shown), garnet, spinel, magnetite, copper.

**Tetragonal**
Least common system, with three axes at right angles, two equal and one longer or shorter. One main four-fold axis of symmetry. E.g. vesuvianite (shown), chalcopyrite, zircon, cassiterite, rutile, wulfenite, scheelite.

**Orthorhombic**
Typically stubby matchbox or prisms maybe with pinacoid (see Crystal habit and form, opposite). Three unequal axes at right angles. Three axes of two-fold symmetry. E.g. barite (shown), olivine, topaz, sulphur, marcasite, aragonite, celestine, cerussite.

**Monoclinic**
Typically tabular. Three unequal axes, only two crossing at right angles. One two-fold axis of symmetry. E.g. selenite gypsum (shown), mica, orthoclase, manganite, hornblende, borax, azurite, orpiment, augite, diopside.

**Triclinic**
This is the least symmetrical system, with three unequal axes, none crossing at right angles. E.g. microcline feldspar (shown), plagioclases such as albite and anorthite, turquoise, kaolinite, serpentine, amblygonite.

**Hexagonal (and trigonal)**
Crystals in this system have three equal axes crossing at 60°, plus an unequal axis crossing at 90°. Hexagonal crystals have up to six-fold symmetry; trigonal crystals (sometimes considered a separate system) have up to three-fold symmetry. E.g. beryl (shown), quartz.

middle of opposite faces. Turn a crystal around one of its axes of symmetry and it always looks the same shape. Cubes are the most symmetrical of all shapes; you can draw an axis of symmetry through a cube in 13 ways.

Another way to think of symmetry is in planes or mirror images. Slice a crystal along a certain plane and each half forms a mirror image of the other. A perfect cube has nine planes of symmetry, which means that there are nine ways to slice it in half to create matching pairs. As you turn a crystal, matching images appear twice, three, four or six times, depending on the system. A slab-shaped crystal, for instance, may have to be turned 180 degrees to give a match. So the crystal is said to have two-fold symmetry. A cube needs only be turned 90 degrees for a match, so has four-fold symmetry. A hexagonal shape has to turn 60 degrees, so has six-fold symmetry.

One crucial feature of all crystals is the angles between the faces. These are always the same for each mineral, a feature called the Law of Constancy of Angle. It is so reliable that you can use the angle between faces to identify a mineral. Mineralogists measure it with an instrument called a goniometer, but you can make a home-made one with a protractor and a transparent ruler.

## Crystal habit

Of course, crystals never achieve their perfect form in nature. Growing in cracks in rocks, hemmed in on all sides, their natural shape is distorted. Even crystals grown in the laboratory are distorted by gravity. Only in the zero gravity conditions of the International Space Station have scientists grown near-perfect crystals.

Though never perfect, crystals of each mineral tend to grow, or grow together (as an aggregate), in distinctive ways, or habits. Hematite, for instance, tends to grow in kidney-shaped masses, a habit called 'reniform' after its Latin name.

On the whole, each kind of mineral tends to form in particular conditions, and its habit reflects the conditions in which it forms. Some minerals, such as quartz, form in a variety of conditions so have several different habits.

## Crystal form

### WHOLE CRYSTAL (CLOSED FORM)

**Isometric forms** have various numbers of matching faces; e.g. tetrahedron (4 faces); cube (6 faces); octahedron (8 faces), dodecahedron (12 faces).

**Non-isometric forms** have non-matching faces; e.g. rhombohedron, dipyramid and scalenohedron. A rhombohedron is like a box squashed on one side e.g. rhodochrosite. A dipyramid is like two pyramids stuck base-to-base, with a variable number of faces. A scalenohedron has triangular faces, with unequal sides, e.g. calcite.

## Crystal habit

**Acicular** Needlelike clusters of crystals, e.g. ulexite (left).

**Arborescent** Clusters of crystals in treelike branches, like native copper and silver. Similar to dendritic but chunkier.

**Bladed** Thin, flat crystals with a curved edge, like a butter knife blade. Barite crystals are often bladed.

**Botryoidal** Comes from the Latin for grapes, and means small, rounded masses, like a bunch of grapes, e.g. azurite, hemimorphite (above). Like reniform and mamilliform habits, but smaller.

**Capillary** Thin rods like hairs, like acicular but finer.

**Columnar** Clusters of columns or rods, e.g. aragonite (right). Usually parallel, but can be radiating.

**Crusty** Like a bread crust, e.g. limonite.

**Cryptocrystalline** Crystals too small to see without a microscope, e.g. chalcedony.

**Dendritic** Clusters of crystals in fernlike branches, like arborescent but finer, e.g. pyrolusite (left), psilomelane, copper and gold.

**Drusy** Thin layer of upright crystals coating a rocky surface like the pile of a carpet.

**Fibrous** Thin, fibrelike crystals, e.g. asbestos, sillimanite and strontianite. The crystals may point in all directions, but can be parallel bundles or radiating.

### PART OF CRYSTAL (OPEN FORM)

**Dome and sphenoid** With two angled faces, like a ridge-tent.

**Pedion** Single flat face

**Pinacoid** A pair of parallel faces, like the top and bottom ends of a column.

**Prism** Multiple faces running parallel to the axis, like a faceted column e.g. beryl (left) and orthoclase feldspar.

**Pyramid** Like a pyramid, with 3 to 16 faces.

**Foliated** In thin leaves, e.g. mica (right).

**Globular** In ball shapes, e.g. prehnite.

**Hopper** Faces indented like the hopper trucks in mines, e.g. halite.

**Lamellar** Thin plates, e.g. chlorite.

**Mamilliform** Clusters of large rounded blobs, e.g. malachite. Bigger than botryoidal but smaller than reniform.

**Massive** Solid, without any obvious structure.

**Nodular** Growing in round lumps or nodules, e.g. chert and chalcedony (left).

**Oolitic** Like tiny fish-eggs, e.g. chamosite. Smaller than pisolitic.

**Radial** Spreading out like the spokes of a wheel or a fan, e.g. marcasite, stibnite and stilbite.

**Reniform** Shaped like kidneys, such as hematite (right). Bigger than botryoidal or mamilliform.

**Reticulated** Criss-crossing net or lattice of crystals, e.g. cerussite.

**Rutilated** Needlelike inclusions (tiny internal crystals) of rutile, e.g. rutilated quartz.

**Stellated** Cluster of long narrow crystals radiating in a star-shape, e.g. pectolite (right) and snowflake crystals.

**Tabular** Crystals form flat slabs, similar in shape to lamellar, but much thicker. E.g. barite, linarite.

# MINERAL PROPERTIES: PHYSICAL

*Every mineral has a particular range of characteristics that distinguish it from other minerals and help mineralogists to identify it. Many of these properties are physical, including its hardness, its density, and the way it bends or breaks.*

Like all substances, minerals have a wide range of physical properties, from their melting points to their ability to conduct heat or electricity and reflect or absorb light. Mineralogists, however, concentrate mostly on those properties that help them distinguish various minerals in a practical way, particularly those that help them identify minerals in the field.

Perhaps the two most useful properties for a mineralogist are hardness and density. In the Identifying Minerals chart, which precedes the Directory of Minerals, minerals are grouped according to their hardness and density to assist with quick identification.

Hardness can be established very easily in the field and gives an instant clue to a mineral's identity. Density can only be estimated in the field, but it is very easy to measure at home (in terms of specific gravity), and narrows down the possibilities even further.

The ways a mineral bends and breaks are also useful distinguishing characteristics – particularly cleavage, fracture and tenacity, explained in the panel on the right.

One other property, useful for identifying a few minerals, is reaction to acids, given in the acid test.

## Hardness and the Mohs Scale

When mineralogists talk of hardness, they usually mean scratch hardness – the mineral's resistance to being scratched. The simplest way to measure this is on the Mohs scale, devised by German mineralogist Friedrich Mohs in 1812. He selected ten standard minerals and arranged them on a scale of 1 to 10, with each one slightly harder than the preceding one. The softest on the scale (1) is talc; the hardest is diamond (10), the world's hardest mineral. All other minerals can be rated on this scale by working which they will scratch, and which not. Each will scratch a softer mineral but be scratched by a harder one.

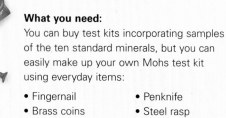

**What you need:**
You can buy test kits incorporating samples of the ten standard minerals, but you can easily make up your own Mohs test kit using everyday items:

- Fingernail
- Brass coins
- Iron nail
- Glass
- Penknife
- Steel rasp
- Sandpaper
- Knife sharpener

*To find the hardness of a material, scratch with each of the testers in turn, starting with the softest, a fingernail.*

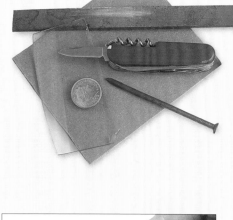

*If it can't be scratched with a fingernail, try a brass coin. If the coin scratches it, it must be 2 or below on the scale.*

*If it can't be scratched with a coin, work through the harder testers in turn to find out exactly where it lies on the scale.*

1 Talc
Fingernail

2 Gypsum

3 Calcite
Bronze coin

4 Fluorite
Iron nail

5 Apatite
Glass

6 Orthoclase
Penknife

7 Quartz
Steel rasp

8 Topaz
Emery
sandpaper

9 Corundum
Knife
sharpener

10 Diamond

## Bending and breaking: Cleavage

Cleavage is a mineral's tendency to break along lines of weakness. Because of the way crystals are built up from lattices of atoms, these lines of weakness tend to be flat planes. The majority of minerals have these characteristic planes of weakness, called cleavage planes. Most minerals tend to cleave in a certain number of directions. Mica, for instance, tends to break in just one direction, forming flakes. Fluorite, however, tends to break in four directions, forming octahedral (eight-sided) chunks.

Not all minerals break equally easily and cleanly. Mineralogists describe the cleavage as: good, distinct, poor and absent; very perfect, perfect, imperfect and none; or perfect, good, poor and indistinct. Fluorite has very good cleavage; quartz has none. Some minerals, like scheelite, cleave well in one direction and poorly in two others.

*Cleavage in one plane only, like flat sheets: example muscovite mica.*

*Cleavage in two planes, like a squarish rod: example orthoclase feldspar.*

*Cleavage in three planes, like a block: example halite.*

*In former times, miners used to describe minerals that split into rhombic shapes like calcite as 'spars'.*

*Cleavage in three planes at an angle to each other, like a three-dimensional diamond shape: example fluorite.*

## Bending and breaking: Fracture

When struck with a hammer, minerals sometimes break roughly and in no particular direction, rather than along flat cleavage planes. This is called fracture, and can sometimes help identify the mineral. The fragments or fractured surface may be conchoidal (shell-like), hackly (jagged), splintery, fibrous or earthy.

*Quartz varieties such as amethyst do not cleave but fracture into shell-like conchoidal fragments. So too do olivine, flint and glass.*

## Bending and breaking: Tenacity

When minerals are crushed, cut, bent or hit, they react in different ways. The way a mineral reacts is known as its 'tenacity' and is described by several terms. Most minerals are 'brittle', which means they crumble, break or powder when struck hard enough. Some are 'flexible' like molybdenite and talc (above) which means they bend. Some are 'elastic' like mica (above right), which means they bend and spring back.

'Malleable' minerals like native copper, gold and acanthite (below) can be hammered into sheets. 'Sectile' minerals like chlorargyrite can be sliced. 'Ductile' minerals can be drawn out or stretched into a wire.

## Simple tests: Specific gravity

Although values vary slightly because of impurities, minerals can often be very precisely identified by their density. Yet it is hard to measure the density of an irregular chunk, so geologists use the mineral's specific gravity (SG), its density relative to water. You can measure this using a sensitive spring balance.

*1 (left): To measure a sample's specific gravity, tie a thread around it and hang it from a spring balance to weigh it. Note the weight and call it A.*

*2 (right): Fully immerse the sample in a mug of water, and note the weight shown on the spring balance. Call this B. This should be less than A, as the water provides buoyancy. Subtract B from A, then divide A by the result. This gives the SG.*

## Simple tests: Acid test

One way of identifying minerals like calcite is with the 'fizz test'. If a little acid is dropped on a chip of carbonate mineral, for instance, it fizzes as it reacts with the acid. The fizzing is the carbon dioxide released as the carbonate dissolves. Sulphides such as galena and greenockite give the bad-egg smell of hydrogen sulphide gas. Powdered copper minerals such as covellite and bornite turn the acid greenish or bluish. Geologists use dilute hydrochloric acid, but strong household vinegar is safer. Vinegar (acetic acid) is weaker, so to get a reaction you need to either grind a sample of the mineral to powder, or warm the vinegar gently. If you wish to use hydrochloric acid, always wear rubber gloves and goggles to protect your eyes against splashes.

*Use a dropper to drop a little acid on to the solid or powdered mineral.*

# MINERAL PROPERTIES: OPTICAL

*Although it is not always possible to identify a mineral simply by the way it looks, every mineral has its own distinctive appearance – from the rich blue of azurite to the shimmering rainbow colours of opal – and these optical properties are often what gives a mineral its distinctive appeal.*

The first thing most people notice about a mineral is its colour. A mineral gets its colour from the colours it reflects or transmits. These colours depend in turn on the bonds between atoms in the mineral.

Despite the rainbow array of colours you see in minerals, most are actually white or colourless in their pure state. Indeed, very few chemical elements are naturally strongly coloured. The colour in minerals tends to come almost entirely from what are called transition metals, such as cobalt, copper and manganese. Copper tends to give blue or green colours and iron red or yellow, but this is not always so.

The few minerals which are highly coloured in their pure state are called idiochromatic minerals. These minerals usually have one of the transition metals as a major constituent. Cobalt in erythrite turns it violet-red, for instance. Chromium makes crocoite orange. Copper makes azurite blue. Manganese makes rhodochrosite pink. Nickel makes annabergite green.

Most other minerals, however, tend to get their colour from traces of impurities. These minerals are called

---

## Optical Effects

### Adularescence
The bluish-white schiller effect on the surface of adularia moonstone.

### Asterism
From the Greek word for star, asterism is a star-shaped sparkle in gems such as star sapphires, star rubies and star rose quartz, usually caused by minute needlelike rutile crystals included in the gem.

### Aventurism
Glistening reflections of leaflike inclusions in minerals such as aventurine feldspar.

### Birefringence
The way light is split as it passes through minerals like calcite, giving a double image as you look through it.

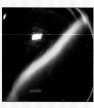

### Chatoyancy
From the French for cat's eye, this is the cat's eye effect in stones such as andalusite, a shimmering band across the middle caused by the inclusion of minute crystals in the stone.

### Dispersion
The degree to which minerals refract some colours more than others, dispersing the colours and creating the flashes of colour called fire in cut gems such as diamond, demantoid garnet and sphene.

**Fire** See Dispersion.

### Iridescence
Shimmering rainbow colours produced by interference between waves of light in the surface layers of a mineral.

### Labradorescence
Play of colours from blues to violets to greens and oranges in labradorite caused by twinning of sheets within the crystal.

### Moonstone

Alkali feldspar gemstone with silvery or bluish iridescence, or opalescent variety of adularia.

### Opalescence
Milky, lustrous shimmer on the surface of potch opal.

### Phosphorescence
The way some minerals store light and glow some time after the activating ultraviolet light source has gone.

### Play of colour
Shimmering rainbow colours that appear as a mineral is turned in the light. Effects include iridescence, schiller, labradorescence and adularescence. The play of colour on the surface of gem opal (left) is sometimes called opalescence. Strictly speaking, though, opalescence should refer only to the milky lustre in white, 'potch' opal.

### Pleochroism

The way some minerals show different colours, depending on the angle you look at them, because of how different colours of light are absorbed in different directions in the crystal. A three colour change is trichoic, a two colour change is dichroic. Pleochroism is strong in minerals such as andalusite, elbaite, zoisite and iolite (shown from two directions, above left).

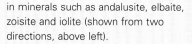

### Refraction
The way light passing through a transparent substance is bent.

### Schiller
Bronze metallic lustre in orthopyroxenes such as enstatite caused by interference between light rays reflecting off internal mineral plates.

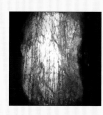

### Sunstone
A kind of aventurine feldspar that gives a golden shimmer, caused by reflection off tiny platelike inclusions of hematite.

### Thermoluminescence
The way some minerals glow when heated, e.g. apatite, calcite, fluorite, lepidolite and some feldspars.

*Above: The variety of colours of quartz alone show just how unreliable a guide to identity colour can be.*

allochromatic. Nearly all the famous coloured gems are allochromatic and get their colours from impurities. Beryl is turned into green emerald, for instance, by traces of chromium and vanadium. Corundum is turned to blue sapphire by titanium oxide and red ruby by chromium. Impurities can turn quartz almost any colour in the rainbow. Fluorite, too, can be many colours, but this is due to its special chemical structure, not impurities.

Many minerals are distinctively coloured. Some, like green malachite and blue azurite, are recognizable from their colour alone. Yet the fact that most get their colour from impurities means minerals are highly variable in colour, and colour alone is rarely a reliable guide to identity.

*Above: The streak given by rubbing a mineral on unglazed porcelain gives a consistent colour identity. Clockwise from top: cuprite, pyrite, hematite, azurite and malachite.*

The only way to be sure of mineral's colour is through its streak. This is a powdered version of the mineral. It is called a streak because it involves rubbing the mineral across the unglazed side of a white porcelain tile so that it leaves a distinctive streak. Hematite is often grey like galena, and often various other colours. Its streak though is always blood-red, while galena's is a lead-grey. So the streak test is very clear. Unfortunately, only

about a fifth of minerals have distinctive streak. Most translucent minerals have a white streak; most opaque minerals have a black streak.

Whatever their colour, minerals differ in the way they transmit light, a quality called diaphaneity. Some minerals are clear almost as glass in their pure state and let light shine clean through them. Minerals like these are said to be transparent. Tiny impurities make them less clear. Some minerals, like moonstone, are semi-transparent so that things seen through them look blurred. When a mineral lets light glow through but only obscurely, it is said to be translucent, like chrysoprase. Minerals that block off light completely like azurite, pyrite and galena are said to be opaque.

*Above, left to right: The mineral barite can be transparent, translucent or opaque.*

When some minerals are exposed to ultraviolet light, they glow in totally different colours than their normal daylight colour. This glow is called fluorescence, from the mineral fluorite, which varies tremendously in colour in daylight, but always glows blue or green in UV light. Other fluorescent minerals include willemite, benitoite, scheelite, adamite, sodalite and scapolite.

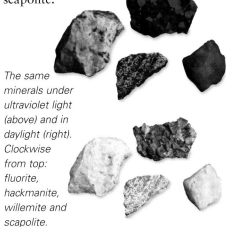

*The same minerals under ultraviolet light (above) and in daylight (right). Clockwise from top: fluorite, hackmanite, willemite and scapolite.*

## Lustre

Lustre is the way the surface of crystal looks – shiny, dull, metallic, pearly and so on. The terms used to described lustre are not scientific, but useful, subjective guides and are mostly self-explanatory.

### Adamantine
Brilliant and shiny like diamond and other gem crystals, e.g. cassiterite (right).

### Dull
Any non-reflective surface, e.g. glauconite.

### Earthy
Like dried mud, e.g. kaolinite.

### Greasy
Like grease. The surface would be adamantine but for slight irregularities on the mineral's surface, e.g. nepheline (left).

### Metallic
Gleaming like metal. Native metals have a metallic lustre. So to do most sulphides, e.g. stibnite (right).

### Pearly
Milky shimmer like pearl, e.g. talc (left).

### Resinous
Like sap or glue. Most minerals with a resinous lustre are yellow or brown, e.g. sulphur (right).

### Silky
Subtle shimmer like silk because of small parallel fibres as in asbestos, e.g. gypsum variety satin spar (left).

### Vitreous
The most common lustre, rather like glass, e.g. quartz (right).

### Waxy
Like wax, e.g. serpentine.

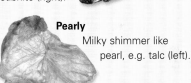

# MINERAL GEMS

*Most mineral crystals are dull and quite small, but a few are so richly coloured and sparkling that they almost take the breath away. When such beautiful stones are hard enough to cut and fashion into jewellery, they are called gemstones and are the most sought-after mineral specimens of all.*

Gemstones are incredibly rare. There are over 4,000 different minerals, yet only 130 are considered gemstones, and of these less than 50 are frequently used as gems. The rarest and most valuable of all are diamond, emerald (green beryl), ruby (red corundum) and sapphire (blue corundum). Slightly less

*Below: No gem comes in such a huge range of colours as tourmaline, which the Ancient Egyptians called rainbow rock. Traces of different chemicals can give it over a hundred different colours of which just a handful are shown here.*

rare stones, known as semi-precious stones, include aquamarine (blue beryl), chrysoberyl, sunstone, moonstone, garnet, topaz, tourmaline, peridot (gem olivine), opal (chalcedony), pearl (aragonite), jadeite, turquoise and lapis lazuli (lazurite).

Unusual geological conditions are required to create gemstones such as these, which is why they are so rare. They might form in volcanic pipes – or simply be found in them like diamonds in kimberlite and lamproite pipes. Gems are also often found in

*Above: Like pearl, opal and jet, amber is one of several gemstones that is not crystalline. Indeed, these gems are not strictly minerals since they form by organic processes. Amber is hardened droplets of sap from ancient pine trees that lived millions of years ago. When ground and polished, it makes one of the most beautiful of gemstones.*

pegmatites. In the last stages of magma intrusion, pegmatites concentrate rare minerals to form gems such as beryls, rubies, sapphires, tourmalines, topazes and many others. Intense metamorphism may create garnets, emeralds, jades and lapis lazuli.

## What defines a gem?

Gemstones are prized for their beauty, their durability and their rarity. Dealers often assess them in terms of what are called the four Cs: clarity, colour, cut and carat.

Clarity is the quality most prized in gems. A perfect gem is a flawless transparent crystal that sparkles brilliantly as it reflects light internally. Diamond, the most precious of all stones, is at its best when clear and colourless. Yet the best diamonds hide within them a rainbow of colours that flash with what is called 'fire' as light rays are 'dispersed' or split into colours inside the crystal. This fire cannot be seen in rough diamonds, and is only revealed once the stone is properly cut and faceted.

Opal gains a beautiful rainbow shimmer as light is reflected and split into colours by the tiny spheres of

*Above: Most of the world's diamonds come from mines like these, which plumb the pipes of volcanic rock, such as the kimberlites of South Africa and the lamproites of Australia.*

*Above: Diamonds look unremarkable when rough from the ground. It takes careful cutting with 57 or 58 triangular faces to bring out their hidden brilliance and sparkle.*

silica from which it is made. In some stones, particular flaws can enhance their beauty, such as the inclusions that create asterism in star sapphire and chatoyancy in chrysoberyl (see Mineral properties: Optical, in this section).

## Gem colours

A vivid colour is also prized. Jade, turquoise and lapis lazuli are completely opaque, but their rich greens and blues make them as sought after as many clear gems. With most clear gems, except for diamond, colour is highly valued. Colourless beryl is only moderately valued, but emerald (green beryl) is one of the world's most valued stones.

Many gems are given a wide range of colours by trace elements. Peridot (gem olivine) is commonly green, but can vary from pale lemon to dark olive. Often the different colour varieties of a gem mineral have their own name, as with sapphire and ruby which are simply different-coloured varieties of corundum.

## Cut and carat

For the collector, colour and sparkle are quite enough to make a stone attractive. Yet for a crystal to be a gemstone, it must also be tough enough to use in jewellery. All the major gemstones are at least as hard as quartz – over 7 on the Mohs scale – and diamond is the world's hardest mineral. A gemstone must be tough

enough to be cut to bring out all its sparkle and colour (see Olivine and Garnets: Gemstone cuts, Directory of Minerals).

On the whole, it is the largest stones that are the most highly prized. In the ancient world, gems were weighed with the seeds of the carob tree, which are remarkably constant in weight. Later, the carob seed became the basis of a standard weight called the carat, which is about a fifth of a gram.

A 632-carat Emerald known as the Patricia Emerald was found in the 1920s in Colombia. An 875 carat topaz was found in Ouro Preto in Brazil. Often the largest stones, though, contain flaws, so they are cut down to make smaller, flawless gems.

The world's largest cut diamond, called the Golden Jubilee, weighs 545.67 carats – a little over a hundred grams or about four ounces. It just beats the Great Star of Africa set in the British Royal Sceptre, which was one of several large diamonds cut from the gigantic 3,106 carat Cullinan Diamond found by Thomas Cullinan in 1905 at the Premier Mine, South Africa.

## Famous gems

All the biggest and most famous gems have their own names and their own stories. St Edward's Sapphire in the British Imperial State Crown was reputedly worn by Edward the Confessor almost 1,000 years ago. Another stone in this crown is the

Black Prince's Ruby given to Edward the Black Prince in 1366 by Pedro the Cruel of Spain. It is actually thought to be a red spinel, not a ruby. The 109-carat Koh-i-Noor diamond was found in India seven centuries ago.

## The Hope Diamond

Perhaps the most infamous of gems is the Hope Diamond, now in the Smithsonian Museum in Washington, DC. Found in India, this magnificent diamond weighed 112 carats when given to King Louis XIV in 1668. A few years later it was cut to a 67 carat heart-shape. Stolen during the French revolution in 1792, it resurfaced as a 45.5 carat gem in 1812, then mysteriously vanished again only to reappear in 1820 when it was bought by British King George IV. When George IV died it was bought by banker Henry Hope, after whom it was named. Over the next century it gained a reputation for bringing bad luck. One owner, an actress, was shot on stage while wearing it and another, a Russian prince, was stabbed to death by revolutionaries.

*Below: Diamonds are tough enough to survive weathering to end up in river gravels, where they can occasionally be found by laboriously sorting the river gravels by panning.*

# MINERAL ORES

*Our modern society could not function without metals extracted from rocks, yet even aluminium and iron, the most abundant metals, make up just a few per cent of rocks by weight. Fortunately, these and many other useful metals are concentrated by geologic processes in a few places as 'ore' minerals.*

The first metals people used were native metals – copper, silver and gold – which occur as chunks of metal in the ground and could be fashioned into jewellery and knives. Then some unsung genius realized that there are minerals that while not actually metallic contain metals that can be extracted by heating until the metal melts out. This smelting process has provided us with metals ever since.

Minerals which contain enough metal for it to be easily extracted are called ore minerals. Galena contains a very high percentage of lead, so is a major lead ore. Iron comes mainly from hematite and magnetite. Pyrite is also rich in iron, but because it is bound so tightly to sulphur in the mineral it cannot be extracted, so pyrite is rarely an ore of iron.

To form an ore, the metal must be sufficiently concentrated in the mineral, and the mineral sufficiently concentrated in the ground for it to be worth extracting. Fortunately, geological processes ensure that such concentrations, known as ore deposits, do occur in certain places.

*Below: Valuable minerals such as gold may sometimes be concentrated in iron-bearing ore deposits called gossans. They get their name from the Cornish for 'blood' because of their rusty red colour from the oxidized iron.*

*Above: Most ores are extracted from near-surface deposits in vast opencast mines like this copper mine in Bisbee, Arizona. Huge quantities of rock have to be dug out, much of which is later discarded.*

## Hot deposits

Many important ore deposits are linked to magma chambers, where melted rock collects. As the magma cools and begins to solidify, heavier minerals begin to sink to the bottom of the chamber. So when the magma finally freezes solid, heavy ore minerals may be concentrated at the base, especially sulphides ores, creating what are called magmatic sulphide ore deposits. Deposits like these tend to form only in relatively runny magmas such as komatiite basalt and gabbro. Famous sulphide deposits of this kind include South Africa's Bushveld Complex, Noril'sk in Russia, Jinchuan in China and Sudbury in Canada. Although their origins are not entirely understood, massive sulphide deposits can also occur in rock beds metamorphosed in the granulite facies (see Schists: Metamorphic facies in the Directory of Rocks). Australia's Broken Hill has superb lead, silver and zinc ores like this.

Rich ore deposits are also created by hydrothermal (hot-water) solutions circulating through magma or the rocks surrounding an intrusion. These fluids are typically rich in dissolved metals, which they deposit in fractures and pores, creating hydrothermal deposits.

If a hydrothermal deposit is dispersed throughout the intrusion, it forms a 'disseminated' deposit. If it follows cracks in the rock, filling them in with deposited minerals, it forms a hydrothermal vein deposit. Vein minerals include sulphide, oxide and silicate ores, as well as native metals such as gold, silver and platinum. Gold often appears as flakes in white quartz veins. Copper ores are often concentrated in porphyritic intrusions, forming porphyry copper deposits.

Some of the most valuable deposits are created when hydrothermal solutions percolate into limestone. When solutions seep into limestones and marbles around an intrusion, they create skarns, such as the tungsten skarns of Sangdong, Korea, King Island, Tasmania and Pine Creek in California.

The same process creates Mississippi Valley Type (MVT) deposits, which occur around the edge of sedimentary basins, deep down at the base of limestone beds. MVTs formed as hot solutions seeping through underlying rocks reacted with the limestone. North America's Tristate zinc district is the best known MVT, but there are also well known MVTs in Cumbria, England and Trepca, Serbia.

The hot waters flushed out of submarine volcanoes along the mid-ocean ridge are often rich in dissolved metals and sulphur. When the hot water meets the cold ocean, these dissolved chemicals often combine to form deposits of metal sulphides, which may be recovered in places where tectonic movements have lifted up ancient sea floor to much more accessible places.

## Cool deposits

It is not just hot water that concentrates minerals. Even cool groundwater can dissolve metal ores as it seeps through rocks. The metal ores may have been widely scattered through the rock, but when the water re-deposits them, it may deposit them together in a concentrated deposit – a

*Right: Lode gold is often found associated with quartz in veins like this one in siltstone in the Tanami desert of Australia's Northern Territory. This region is known for its gold and has recently become the target of seismic profiling, designed to reveal its geological structures and reveal likely sites for gold from the pattern of powerful vibrations sent through the ground by machines.*

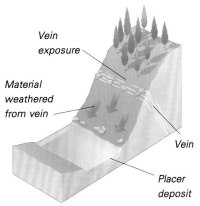

*Placer deposits As veins are exposed at the surface, valuable minerals such as gold may be tumbled or washed down slope to collect in stream beds, forming placer deposits. Prospectors may sometimes recover these placer golds by panning the stream gravel.*

process called secondary enrichment. This often happens when water seeping down through the ground reaches the water table, the level to which the ground is saturated.

In the opposite way, rainwater sinking into the ground may leach (dissolve) away particular chemicals, leaving behind concentrations of metals such as iron and aluminium. In the tropics where rainfall is heavy, the concentrations in these 'residual deposits' can become so intense that the soil itself becomes an ore, like bauxite aluminium ore.

Water can even help concentrate ore deposits without dissolving anything. After weathering has broken rocks up, rivers and streams carry away mineral grains. Heavier, more durable grains are dropped first by the water, and can accumulate in riverbed deposits. Gold, tin, diamonds and emeralds are among the minerals found in 'placer' deposits.

Some of the world's most important cold water ores formed in seawater. These include deep-sea manganese ores (see Aluminium and Manganese, Directory of Minerals) and the remarkable Banded Iron Formations (BIFs – see Iron Ores, Directory of Minerals) formed by bacteria almost two billion years ago, and now one of the world's major sources of iron.

## Finding ores

In the old days, prospectors would scour the landscape hoping to stumble on 'shows' – exposures of ores on the surface, with little to guide them other than a knowledge of what geologic features they are often found in association with. Nowadays, geologists still read the landscape but have an array of sophisticated technology to help them, including aerial and satellite photographs. Kimberlite pipes that might yield diamonds often show as pale discs on the surface, for instance.

Once a potential site has been identified, the extent and richness of a deposit can be assessed by testing the ground's electrical conductivity and its magnetism. An instrument called a magnetometer may be used to locate deposits of magnetic ores like magnetite and ilmenite. Since ore minerals tend to be denser than average, measuring the local pull of gravity can also be revealing. Radio-active minerals and elements such as uranium and thorium might be detected with a Geiger counter. Since plants absorb traces of metals through their roots, it can even be worth analysing the plants in the area.

# COLLECTING ROCKS AND MINERALS

*You need very little special equipment to start building a rock and mineral collection – just sharp eyes for loose specimens when you're out walking. All the same, it helps to know where to look, and to acquire a few basic tools and storage systems for extracting good specimens and looking after them.*

You can see rocks and minerals in many places. Office blocks often have polished granite faces. Houses might be built in sandstone and roofed with slate. Statues may be carved from marble. People wear precious gems made from mineral crystals. Many enthusiastic geologists get satisfaction from spotting such occurrences and identifying the rock.

Some enthusiasts build up a collection by looking for samples at rock shops and on the internet. But there is nothing to beat building up your own collection, by going out into the 'field', as geologists call it, to find your own samples.

Good, collectable specimens are not evenly spread around the Earth, but are concentrated in particular sites.

Some sites yield one or two kinds of mineral; others several hundred. The more you get to know local geology, the more likely you are to find good specimens. Good crystals are found in cavities and fissures, gemstones in pegmatites, gold in milky quartz veins and so on. Often minerals on the surface may be signposts to the real treasure beneath, like green copper.

## What you need

### Hammer

The key item in the geologist's toolbag is a good hammer. You can manage with an ordinary bricklayer's hammer, but it is really worth investing in a proper geological hammer. This typically has a square striking face and tapered tail (7). In the most common 'chisel' hammers, the tail is a flat edge at right angles to the handle, useful for levering samples out. In 'pick' hammers, the tail is a long, curved cutting edge, and is good for splitting rocks (6).

### Chisel

There are three kinds of chisel. Cold chisels have a long, narrow handle and wedge, ideal for extracting crystals from cavities (8). Gad-point chisels are shorter and thicker, with a tapered point good for splitting, prising and wedging rocks apart. Broad-bladed chisels, bolsters and 'pitching tools' (10) are short and thick with a wide blade, good for splitting and trimming rock samples. If you only have one chisel, get a gad-point.

### Safety equipment

Rocks can splinter when hit, so it is vital to wear good goggles when hammering. Goggles should have clear, hard plastic windows and flexible plastic sides (5). Avoid goggles without sides. Strong leather gloves are also useful protection and if you are visiting cliffs or quarries a safety helmet to protect the head is essential equipment (1).

### Magnifying lens

A good magnifying glass or hand lens (3) not only helps you spot small crystals in the field but also helps you identify minerals and rocks you have found. A 3-times magnification lens is too weak to be of much help, but don't make the mistake of getting too powerful a lens. A 20-times gives too restricted a view to be useful in the field. The best compromise is a 5- or 10-times lens. Lenses are easy to lose, so tie your lens on a cord and attach it to your belt or collecting bag, or hang it round your neck.

### Note-taking and recording

A notebook (2) and pen (9) are still the best way of noting down your finds. Sticky labels and markers (4) are good for labelling them on the spot. A small camera is useful for recording the site, and sometimes saves digging out a sample unnecessarily.

### Way-finding

You need good local maps and perhaps geological maps to help you find your collecting site. A handheld Global Positioning System (GPS) is also useful for finding your way if you're straying far from the beaten track, and for recording precise locations and details of finds. A compass is a useful alternative – and enables you to test minerals for magnetism.

### Collecting equipment

You need a strong bag for your samples. A small rucksack is ideal, leaving your hands free to pick up samples. Take bubble wrap and freezer bags to wrap samples.

### Extra tools

In terms of additional portable items, a multi-purpose penknife and a small shovel are useful but not essential items. Shovels should have a shallow, pointed blade.

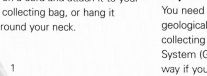

## Finding and cleaning specimens

There are two kinds of site to look for specimens: rock outcrops and deposits. Rock outcrops include cliffs, crags, quarries and cuttings. Deposits are where loose rock fragments have accumulated, including river beds, beaches, fields and even backyards. They include placer deposits where gold and gems such as diamonds have come to rest in stream sand and gravel (see Gold: Striking gold, in the Directory of Minerals).

Specimens taken from the ground are often filthy and should be cleaned before you stow them away. Make sure you have identified the mineral first, however, as some minerals, like halite, are soluble in plain water! For soluble specimens, scrub with a toothbrush, or dab with pure alcohol. If the sample is very soft, just use a blower brush like photographers use to clean lenses.

*Below: The geologist's rule is to hammer as little as possible. Hammering promotes erosion and leaves a scar in the rock. You should never use a hammer for knocking out samples – only for breaking specimens up. Always wear goggles to protect your eyes from splinters.*

With most minerals, fortunately, you can brush off loose dirt with a soft toothbrush, then rinse in warm (not hot) water. For greasy marks and stains, add a drop of household detergent to the water. If the specimen is encrusted with mud and grit, don't try to chip it off. Leave it to soak overnight to soften. It is fine to attack hard specimens like quartz with a nailbrush, but delicate specimens like calcite are all too easily damaged.

You can use vinegar to dissolve away unwanted calcite and limey deposits on most insoluble minerals. Iron stains can be removed with oxalic acid. You can get this from chemists, but it is poisonous so should be handled with care. It dissolves some minerals so test it on a fragment first.

Once your specimen is clean, you need to put it away in a cool, dry, dark place to keep it at its best. Don't store different minerals touching each other. Rocks and minerals 'breathe' and absorb and emit gases over time, and may alter accordingly. Keep your collection away from windows, room heaters, humid places such as bathrooms, and car exhaust, and try to keep conditions as stable as possible.

Some minerals, such as native copper and silver, oxidize and tarnish, especially in polluted city air. Some minerals, like borax, dry out, so store them in air-tight containers. Halite absorbs water from the air and gradually dissolves unless you keep it in an air-tight container with a little silica-gel to absorb any moisture.

Proper sample display drawers are expensive. Shallow drawers, wooden trays in cupboards, or glass and plastic boxes will do as alternatives. Identify every specimen with a number either on a sticky label or on a dab of white paint on an inconspicuous part of it. Enter this number, with the specimen profile, in your catalogue, which can be a computer file, cardfile or a notebook. You can group specimens by location or colour, but most geologists prefer to group by type: rocks into igneous, sedimentary and metamorphic types; minerals into chemical groups such as silicates and carbonates.

## Cataloguing a collection

The minimum data for a catalogue is your own catalogue number, the mineral or rock name and for minerals a Dana number (see Classifying minerals in this section). But it is better to put as much data as you can. These are the details you should have:
1. Personal catalogue number
2. Dana number for minerals
3. Mineral or rock name
4. Chemical or mineral composition
5. Mineral or rock class
6. Exactly where you found it
7. Name of rock formation or kind of site where you found it
8. Date you found it
9. The collector's name (you)
10. Any other details, such as its history if you bought it, unusual characteristics of the specimen, and so on

# CLASSIFYING ROCKS

*Most geologists agree on the basic grouping of rocks into igneous, sedimentary and metamorphic rocks, but when it comes to classifying rock species within those three broad groups, there is a great deal of controversy and there is no definitive system.*

Classifying rocks is not simply a matter of identifying rocks and sorting them. Each classification system depends on a theory of how rocks are made. As ideas of how rocks are made change with new discoveries, so too do rock classification systems.

Over the last half century, for instance, there have been over 50 different classification schemes suggested for sandstone alone – and sandstone is by no means the most contentious and complex of rocks. The debate over igneous rocks has been, if anything, more heated. So the classifications presented here are essentially just a snapshot.

## Igneous rocks

Rocks of this type are perhaps the most complex of all rocks to classify. Yet there is a surprisingly simple and easy-to-use basic classification that works well in the field. This is one based on colour and texture.

The texture or average grain size of an igneous rock depends largely on how long the melt from which it formed took to cool. So rocks that developed deep in the earth such as granite are coarse-textured or phaneritic, while rocks that formed on the surface such as basalt are fine-grained or aphanitic. Rocks which are basically fine-grained but contain large crystals (phenocrysts) are termed porphyries. Using texture, it is, on one level, easy to group igneous rocks according to their origin, into coarse-grained 'plutonic' rocks formed at great depth, mixed and porphyritic 'hypabyssal' rocks formed at shallow depths, and fine-grained 'volcanic' rocks formed from lava on the surface.

Colour provides the other means of basic classification. For reasons that are not entirely clear, minerals at the top of Bowen's Reaction Series (see How Igneous Rocks Form in this section) like pyroxenes and amphiboles tend to be dark in colour while those at the bottom like quartz and plagioclase

## Classifying igneous rocks

Colour and texture provide a good basic classification of igneous rocks, but geologists often need a more detailed system based on composition since colour and texture are not always enough to distinguish rocks. The Streckheisen system groups rocks according to the proportion of four minerals they contain: quartz, alkali feldspar, plagioclase feldspar and feldspathoids (foids). The percentages of each can be plotted on the diamond shaped diagrams. The corners represent 100% of the appropriate mineral.

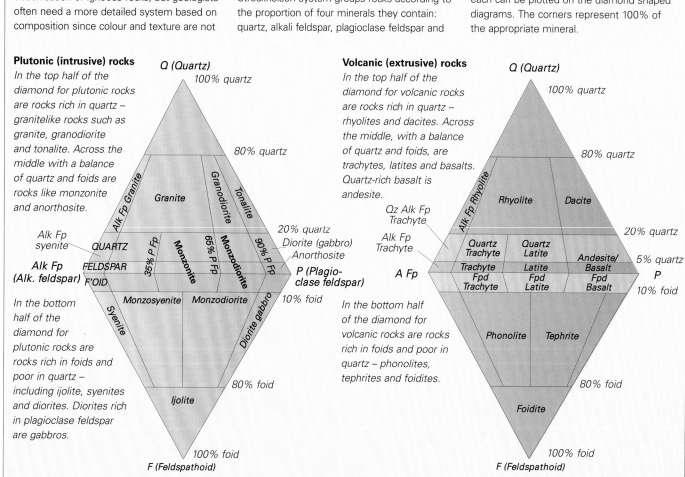

**Plutonic (intrusive) rocks**
*In the top half of the diamond for plutonic rocks are rocks rich in quartz – granitelike rocks such as granite, granodiorite and tonalite. Across the middle with a balance of quartz and foids are rocks like monzonite and anorthosite.*

*In the bottom half of the diamond for plutonic rocks are rocks rich in foids and poor in quartz – including ijolite, syenites and diorites. Diorites rich in plagioclase feldspar are gabbros.*

**Volcanic (extrusive) rocks**
*In the top half of the diamond for volcanic rocks are rocks rich in quartz – rhyolites and dacites. Across the middle, with a balance of quartz and foids, are trachytes, latites and basalts. Quartz-rich basalt is andesite.*

*In the bottom half of the diamond for volcanic rocks are rocks rich in foids and poor in quartz – phonolites, tephrites and foidites.*

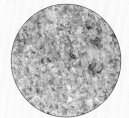

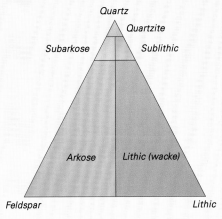

*Lutite (fine-grained): shale*

*Arenite (medium-grained): sandstone*

*Rudite (coarse-grained): breccia*

*QFL composition triangle for sandstone rocks*

**Classifying clastic sediments: texture**
Above: The simplest way of classifying clastic sediments is by texture into three groups: lutites, arenites and rudites. Lutites are mainly silt and clay particles; arenites mainly sand; and rudites gravel, pebbles, cobbles and boulders.

**Classifying clastic sediments: composition**
Right: They can also be divided according to composition in terms of quartz, feldspar and lithics, QFL. Various percentages of QFL can be plotted on a triangular graph as for sandstones. The main division is between feldspar-rich arkoses and lithic-rich wackes.

feldspar tend to be light. The dark minerals separate out into what are called mafic magmas, because they are rich in MAgnesium and FerrIC (iron) compounds. The light minerals are concentrated in felsic magmas which are rich in FELdspar and SIliCa minerals. So mafic igneous rocks are dark in colour; felsic rocks are light. Because they are rich in silica, light-coloured rocks are also said to be silicic or acidic, while mafic rocks, which are low in silica, like basalt, are said to be basic.

## Sedimentary rocks

This type of rock can form either from fragments of weathered rock or from minerals dissolved in water. Rocks made from rock fragments or 'clasts' are called clastic rocks. Rocks made from minerals dissolved in water are called chemical rocks, or biochemical rocks if they are made from chemicals derived from living things, such as the shells of shellfish.

Clastic rocks include sandstones and shales. They are made from fragments of rock that don't dissolve in water; those that do dissolve go on to form chemical rocks. Insoluble fragments are mostly silica-based minerals so clastic rocks are sometimes called siliclastic rocks.

Siliclastic rocks are typically classified according to the size of particle they are mostly made of. They mostly fall into three broad groups:

fine-grained lutites such as shale and clay; medium-grained arenites including many sandstones; and coarse-grained rudites such as breccia and conglomerate. But there are rocks that don't fit so neatly into these groups, such as wackes, sandstones made from a mix of grains. So some geologists prefer to classify according to the proportion of the three main grain types they contain – quartz sand, feldspar and lithics (rock fragments), sometimes known as QFL, plus the fine 'matrix' material. Using QFL, rocks such as sandstone are split into feldspar-rich arkose sandstones and lithic sandstones.

Chemical and biochemical rocks form into several groups. The biggest is the carbonates, including limestones and dolomite, made from calcium and magnesium carbonate. Others are chert, chalk, tufas and coal.

## Metamorphic rocks

On a broad level, metamorphic rocks are divided into granular or non-foliated rocks and foliated rocks. With the exception of hornfels, granular rocks are made mostly from a single mineral, such as marble from calcite and quartzite from quartz. They are formed mostly by the heat of close contact with hot magma. Foliated rocks are more complex. They are characterized by their layered texture, the result of the intense compressional pressure brought about by regional scale

metamorphism. They are divided into low-grade metamorphic rocks such as slate; medium-grade rocks such as schist and high-grade rocks such as gneiss and granulite.

This works as a basic classification, but the composition of regionally metamorphosed rocks is especially complex and varied, so some geologists look at metamorphic rocks in terms of facies, conditions in which particular assemblages of minerals are formed (see Schists: Metamorphic facies in the Directory of Rocks). Or they might work in terms of the zones, such as the Barrovian and Buchan zones, in which particular rocks and minerals are formed (see Gneiss and Granulite: Mineral identifiers, also in the Directory of Rocks).

*Below: Gneiss's dark and light zebra stripes of different minerals mark it out clearly as a foliated metamorphic rock. Non-foliated rocks show no such layered markings.*

# CLASSIFYING MINERALS

*There are over 4,000 different kinds of mineral, and dozens more are being discovered and verified every year. Since each mineral has its own unique chemical identity, this huge array of minerals is usually divided into groups on the basis of chemical composition and internal structure.*

Unlike rocks, minerals cannot be classified by any obvious visual characteristic. In fact, you usually have to identify a mineral first before you can slot it into any class. This is because although each mineral has its own chemical identity, it often appears in many guises, such as gypsum, or looks similar to another mineral that is totally different chemically. Indeed some minerals can be 'pseudomorphs', taking the same crystal shape as another mineral.

## The Dana system

The only sure way to classify a mineral is by its chemical composition and its internal structure. J J Berzelius made the first chemical classification in 1824, but the system used today has its origins in the system devised by Yale University mineralogy professor James Dwight Dana in 1854. Chemically, all minerals are either elements, such as gold, or compounds (combinations of elements such as lead and sulphur in lead sulphide). So after making natural or 'native' elements one group and organic minerals another, Dana arranged the remaining minerals into seven groups of chemical compounds (see Main mineral groups, below).

## Anion groups

In chemical compounds, elements typically occur not as atoms, but as ions. Ions are atoms that have either gained or lost electrons, which are tiny particles with a negative electrical charge. Certain elements, such as metals, tend to lose electrons to become positively charged ions or 'cations'. Other elements, such as oxygen, lose them to become negatively charged ions or 'anions'.

Just as opposite magnet poles attract each other, so do ions with an opposite electrical charge. So cations stick to anions. Most minerals are built up from unions of groups of cations with one or more anions. Chemically, halite, like table salt, is a compound of sodium and chloride. Sodium is the cation and chlorine is the anion.

All Dana's groups are anions or anion groups (unknown to Dana at the time). There is a good reason for this. Many minerals have a particular metal as a cation, such as the silver chloride (chlorargyrite). So you might think you could group minerals by the kind of metal they have as a cation. Yet silver chloride has very little in common with silver sulphide (acanthite) apart from its silver content. However, it has a lot in common with other minerals with the same anion, chlorine, such as sodium chloride (halite) and potassium chloride (sylvite).

All chlorides tend to form under similar geological conditions, for instance. So do many other anions. Sulphides tend to occur in vein or replacement deposits, for example, while silicates are major rock-formers. So it is logical to classify the major mineral groups according to their common anion.

## Main mineral groups

The following groups are based on the old Dana classification that split minerals into nine groups. A newer Dana system divides minerals in 78 classes, all of which fall within the original nine groups. These new classes are indicated in brackets. In this system, every mineral is given a number which consists of the class number, followed by a subclass number and finally a species number. Thus pyrite is numbered 2.12.1.1 (2 for sulphides, 12 for its subclass and 1.1 for its species).

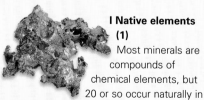

### I Native elements (1)

Most minerals are compounds of chemical elements, but 20 or so occur naturally in pure or at least uncombined form. These native elements are divided into three groups: metals, semi-metals and non-metals. The main native metals are gold, silver and copper, plus platinum and iridosmine, and very rarely iron and nickel. The semi-metals include antimony, arsenic and bismuth. Non-metals are sulphur, and carbon as diamond and graphite.

### II Sulphides and sulphosalts (2, 3)

Sulphides and sulphosalts are made from sulphur combined with a metal or metal-like substance and include some of the most important metal ores such as galena (lead ore), chalcopyrite (copper ore) and cinnabar (mercury ore). They are generally heavy and brittle. They form as primary minerals – that is, directly from melts or solutions rather than by alteration of other minerals. As soon as they are exposed to the weather, many are quickly altered to oxides.

### III Oxides and hydroxides (4–8)

Oxides are a combination of metal with oxygen. They have the most varied physical character of any of the mineral groups, ranging from dull earths such as bauxite to rare gems such as rubies and sapphires. Hard primary oxides typically form deep in the Earth's crust. Softer earths tend to form near the surface as sulphides and silicates are broken down by exposure to the air.

### IV Halides (9–12)

Halides are minerals that form when metals combine with halogen elements – chlorine, bromine, fluorine and iodine. They are very soft and dissolve easily in water. Yet they are so abundant that halide minerals such as halite (e.g. table salt) and fluorite are common world-wide.

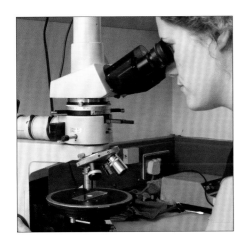

## Adding structure

Dana's system still provides the core of most mineral classifications, but it has been greatly revised and extended. It is now clear that chemical composition alone is not enough to determine a mineral's identity and classify it; its internal crystal structure is also crucial. A key breakthrough was the discovery in 1913 by British physicist Lawrence Bragg that X-rays could be used to look inside crystals and identify the arrangement of atoms. Bragg and Norwegian mineralogist Victor Goldschmidt went on to divide up the giant silicates group according to their internal structure (see Silicate shapes). X-ray crystallography remains a key way of confirming a mineral's identity.

### Scientific testing

Although many minerals can be identified in the field or by some of the simple home tests described earlier, the only way to be absolutely sure of a mineral's identity is to subject it to a series of sophisticated laboratory tests and in particular X-ray crystallography. In this, X-rays are beamed through the specimen. Because every crystal has its own unique chemical structure, its identity is revealed by the way it diffracts (breaks up) the rays. Other tests that a lab can do include spectroscopy (testing which colours of light are absorbed) and the way the crystal polarizes and refracts (bends) light.

## The Strunz system

The addition of crystallography to chemical composition was summed up by Hugo Strunz in 1941, and many mineral classifications today are based on Strunz, rather than Dana.

Strunz's classification system arranges minerals into ten groups: Elements; Sulphides and Sulphosalts; Halides; Oxides; Carbonates; Borates; Sulphates; Phosphates, Arsenates and Vanadates; Silicates; and Organic compounds. Within each group, minerals are split first into families according to their internal structure. Families are then subdivided into groups of minerals that are 'isostructural' – that is, have a similar internal structure.

## Silicate shapes

The vast silicate group is divided into six groups by their internal atomic structure. All silicates are built from basic silicate units – a silicon atom ringed by four oxygen atoms in a tetrahedron (a three-sided pyramid; see below). The way these units join determines the class of silicate.

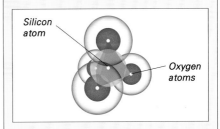

- **Nesosilicate (island)** – the simplest structure, made of just separate tetrahedrons, e.g. olivine and garnet.
- **Sorosilicate (group)** – the smallest class, made with pairs of tetrahedrons linked by an oxygen ion in an hour-glass-shape, e.g. epidote.
- **Inosilicate (chain)** – either single chains like pyroxene, or double chains linked by oxygen ions like amphiboles.
- **Cyclosilicate (ring)** – three, four or six tetrahedrons joined to form a ring, e.g. tourmaline.
- **Phyllosilicates (sheet)** – rings of tetrahedrons joined together in sheets, e.g. clay and mica.
- **Tectosilicate (framework)** – tetrahedrons interconnected like the framework of a building, e.g. feldspars, feldspathoids, quartz and zeolites.

### V Carbonates, Nitrates, Borates (13–27)

Carbonates are minerals that form when metals combine with a carbonate group (carbon and oxygen). The most abundant, calcite, is the major ingredient of limestone rocks. They are all soft, pale-coloured or even transparent. Most are secondary minerals, formed by the alteration of other minerals, though some form in carbonatite magmas, and in hydrothermal solutions or on the ocean bed.

### VI Sulphates, Chromates, Molybdates (28–36)

Sulphates are minerals that form when metals combine with a sulphate group (sulphur and oxygen). They are all soft, translucent or transparent, and pale in colour. Sulphates such as gypsum, barite and anhydrite are very common.

### VII Phosphates, Arsenates, Vanadates (37–49)

Phosphates are metals combined with a phosphate group (phosphorus and oxygen). This is the second largest group after silicates, but many of them are rare. They are usually secondary minerals that form when other minerals are altered., but they often have vivid colours, like bright blue-green turquoise.

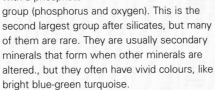

### VIII Silicates (51–78)

Silicates are metals combined with a silicate group (silicon and oxygen) and are the most common of all minerals. There are more silicates than all other minerals put together, both in mass and number. Almost a third of all minerals are silicates, and they make up 90 per cent of the Earth's crust. Quartz and feldspar alone make up a huge proportion of most rocks. They are divided into subgroups according to their internal structure (see Silicate shapes, above).

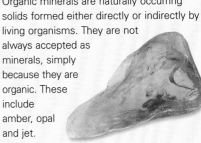

### IX Organic Minerals (50)

Organic minerals are naturally occurring solids formed either directly or indirectly by living organisms. They are not always accepted as minerals, simply because they are organic. These include amber, opal and jet.

# DIRECTORY OF ROCKS

*The Directory of Rocks gives detailed profiles of over 100 species of rock from around the world. Using the identification tips in the following pages, you can begin to gauge the type of rock you have recovered from the field, then follow up these clues in the Directory to draw a more acccurate conclusion.*

Rocks are made of countless grains packed together – that is, they are aggregates. Sometimes the grains are as least as big as sugar crystals and clearly visible to the naked eye. Others are too tiny to see except under a microscope. A few, like obsidian, have no grains at all.

A few rocks (such as the conglomerates and breccias) are made from large fragments of other rocks. More often, though, the grains in rocks are mineral crystals. Some rocks are made from just a single mineral. Marbles, for instance, can be almost pure calcite. Most, however, are made of at least two or three different minerals such as eclogite which is garnet and augite, and granite which is mica, quartz and feldspar. Most rocks

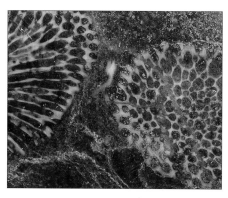

*Above: A high fossil content often points to the sedimentary rock limestone, which forms from the remains of ancient marine creatures.*

also contain a large number of 'accessory' minerals which are present in the rock but not in sufficient quantities to make a significant difference to its nature.

Rocks are typically divided into three major groups according to how they formed: igneous (from molten rock), sedimentary (from layers of sediment) and metamorphic (altered by extreme heat and pressure). This is how the specimens have been organized in the Directory.

Igneous rocks are further divided into extrusive (those that solidify from magma on the surface) and intrusive (those that solidify underground). Very loosely, the Directory section on Igneous rocks moves first through extrusive rocks from acidic, silica-rich or 'felsic' rocks like rhyolite, through intermediate rocks such as andesite to basic, silica-poor ('mafic' and 'ultramafic') rocks such as picrite. It then moves through intrusive rocks

## IGNEOUS ROCKS

**Rock name**: may be plural if several varieties are profiled.

**Identification**: Notes the typical techniques used to identify specimens recovered from the field.

**Data panel**: Quick reference tool summarizing standard rock characteristics.

### Norite

Norite is a similar rock to gabbro, based on a mix of plagioclase, pyroxene and olivine, and the two often form in the same large, layered intrusions as the mix separates during crystallization. Norite contains very slightly less plagioclase than gabbro, but the real difference is that gabbro's pyroxene is a clinopyroxene such as augite, while norite's is an orthopyroxene such as hypersthene. Unfortunately, the two can look so alike that they are impossible to distinguish without a microscope. Norite typically occurs in small, separate intrusions, or as layers along with other mafic igneous rocks such as gabbro. Norite also formed in association with ancient basalt intrusions, beneath huge basalt dyke swarms. One famous norite intrusion is at Sudbury in Ontario. Here a cavity 30m/98ft deep has been excavated from solid norite to house the Neutrino Observatory to detect neutrinos, minute particles streaming from the stars. Norite is unusually low in natural radioactivity and acts as a shield to allow scientists to block out unwanted background radiation.

**Identification**: Norite is a dark grey rock with a slightly matted look dominated by quite long, prismatic black hypersthene or enstatite crystals. It looks very like gabbro, but the plagioclase feldspar tends to be sandy coloured, while in gabbro it is whiter.

**Grain size**: Phaneritic (coarse-grained), occasionally pegmatitic
**Texture**: Even-grained or porphyritic
**Structure**: Layering and xenoliths are common
**Colour**: Dark grey, bronze
**Composition**: Silica (58%), Alumina (17%), Calcium and sodium oxides (10.5%), Iron and magnesium oxides (11%), Potassium oxides (2%)
**Minerals**: Plagioclase feldspar (labradorite or bytownite); Pyroxene (hypersthene); Olivine; A little hornblende, biotite mica, quartz and alkali feldspar
**Accessories**: Magnetite, apatite, ilmenite, picotite
**Phenocrysts**: Plagioclase feldspar, hornblende
**Formation**: Intrusive: dykes, stocks, bosses, often with gabbro
**Notable occurrences**: Aberdeen, Banff, Scotland; Norway; Great Dyke, Zimbabwe; Bushveld complex, S Africa; Sudbury, Ontario

**Grain size; Texture**: Grain size is the first step to identifying igneous rocks. Are grains visible to the naked eye? Texture is variations in grain size and shape.

**Structure**: Large-scale structures such as layers.

**Colour**: Overall colour impression.

**Composition**: This is the overall chemical content. Silica-rich rocks are generally lighter in colour.

**Minerals**: The major minerals that define the character of the rock.

**Accessories**: Any mineral not essential to the rock's character.

**Phenocrysts**: Unusually large crystal.

**Formation**: Where the magma solidifies to form the rock.

**Notable occurrences**: Entries are country by country except for Canada and the USA which are listed last, state by state. Each site in a country is separated by a comma. Additional location information is given in brackets.

**Profile**: The main features of the rock, its formation and characteristics.

**Specimen photograph**: Some important features may be annotated.

that form large intrusions such as granite, to those that form small intrusions such as pegmatites.

Sedimentary rocks are divided into clastic (formed from rock fragments), biogenic (formed by living things) and chemical (formed from once-dissolved chemicals). Clastic rocks are ordered from fine-grained lutites such as shale and clay through medium-grained arenites (sandstones) to coarse-grained rudites (conglomerates and breccias).

Metamorphic rocks are divided according to whether they display any pressure flaking, banding or striping into non-foliated and foliated, but there is considerable overlap, partly because some rocks, such as amphibolite, can be either foliated or non-foliated. Foliated rocks are ordered, very loosely, from those that are formed under least pressure (low-grade rocks such as slate and phyllite) to the most (high-grade rocks such as schist and gneiss). Rocks formed from meteorites such as tektites and suevites make an additional category.

# SEDIMENTARY ROCKS

## Breccias

Sometimes called sharpstone, breccia is basically rubble turned into stone. The stones in breccia are jagged, caught up before there was time to round off any rough edges. Unlike conglomerates, breccias can form from almost any rock, soft and hard alike. But they almost always form near to their source and are said to be 'intraformational'. If the stones are washed any further away, they tend to get sorted and so do not form breccias. In mountain areas, breccias often form when screes are cemented together by finer sediment accumulating between the stones. Many breccias are formed rapidly by dramatic events – as when landslides and avalanches come to rest, or when flash floods or storm waves sweep masses of sediment into a beach or bar. Breccias also form when the roofs of limestone caves collapse, burying the floor in rubble. Coral reefs often contain extensive limestone breccias made of fragments broken off the reef. A few breccias are 'extraformational,' swept far from their source before consolidating and so have a very mixed composition.

**Identification**: Breccias are easily recognized by the large, angular stones they contain. It is not so easy to identify what the stones are or where they came from. The best place to start is a comparison with nearby rocks.

**Grain size**: Over 2mm/ 0.079in
**Texture**: Large angular stones in a finer matrix
**Structure**: Breccias are generally small, poorly stratified deposits
**Colour**: The colours are as varied as their source rocks
**Composition**: The stones are usually rock fragments – of almost any rock, including softer rocks such as marble
**Formation**: Some form in fast-flowing rivers, or on storm beaches. Others form from landslides and avalanches, both on land and under the sea.
**Notable occurrences**: Thessaly, Greece; Mexico; Vancouver Island, Midway, British Columbia; Platte Co, Wyoming; San Bernardino Co, California; Makinac Island, Michigan; Zopilote, Texas

**Grain size and texture**: Grain size is the first step to identifying sedimentary rocks. Are they clay-, sand- or pebble-sized? Texture is variations in grain size and shape.

**Structure**: Large-scale structures such as bedding planes.

**Colour**: Overall colour impression.

**Composition**: The balance of minerals making up the grains.

**Formation**: Where and how the sediments were laid down.

**Notable occurrences**: Entries are country by country except for Canada and the USA which are listed last, state by state. US states may be given in standard abbreviations where space is limited.

# METAMORPHIC ROCKS

**Inset detail**: Illustrations of related species and special features.

## Mica schists

The most common schists are mica schists. Flakes of mica give them the most marked schistosity, and a real shine. The flakes are typically about 0.5mm/0.02in thick and can often be prised off with a knife. There is plenty of quartz in mica schist too, often concentrated in mica-poor layers, and a fair amount of albite feldspar. Sometimes red garnet or green chlorite crystals are visible. The mica in mica schists can be muscovite, sericite or biotite. Biotite is usually brown; muscovite and sericite are pale coloured and called white mica. If a white mica is fine-grained, it is called sericite; if it is coarser it is called muscovite. Most mica schists contain all three, but one usually predominates. Muscovite and sericite schists develop where metamorphism is of moderate intensity, and are often associated with greenschists and phyllites. Biotite develops partly at the expense of muscovite (and chlorite) when metamorphism becomes more intense. Even more intense metamorphism edges the schist towards garnet schists.

**Biotite schist**: Biotite schist is brown and dark, but still has the mica gleam.

**Muscovite schist**: Muscovite schists, with sericite schists, are the lightest-coloured schists, coloured by white mica. Unlike sericite schist, the grains of mica in muscovite schist are clearly visible to the naked eye.

**Mica (muscovite, sericite or biotite) schist**
**Rock type**: Foliated, regional metamorphic
**Texture**: Medium to coarse-grained, sometimes with porphyroblasts. Thin schistose layering of mica flakes always marked.
**Structure**: Typically folded, on a small or large scale
**Colour**: Light grey, greenish (biotite schist is browner)
**Composition**: Quartz and mica (usually muscovite), plus kyanite, sillimanite, chlorite, graphite, garnet, staurolite
**Protolith**: Mainly mudrocks such as shale
**Temperature**: Moderate
**Pressure**: Moderate
**Notable occurrences**: Connemara, Ireland; Scotland; Scandinavia; Alps, Switzerland; Black Forest, Germany; Quebec; Duchess Co, NY; New Hampshire

**Rock type**: The degree of metamorphic banding and the mode of formation.

**Texture**: Overall grain size and variation.

**Structure**: Large-scale structures such as layers.

**Colour**: Overall colour impression.

**Composition**: The balance of minerals making up the grains.

**Protolith**: The original rock from which it was metamorphosed.

**Temperature; Pressure**: The conditions under which the rock was metamorphosed: low, medium or high-grade.

**Notable occurrences**: Entries are country by country except for Canada and the USA which are listed last, state by state.

# IDENTIFYING ROCKS

*Often dull greys, browns and blacks, rocks all look much the same at first glance. Yet they are as individual and distinctive as people, and once you know what to look for you will find it is quite easy to identify most of them and put them into their family groups.*

Often the biggest clue to a rock's identity is where you found it. If you found it in an area of sandstone, it is likely to be sandstone. Before you begin to examine the specimen closely, see if you can spot formations of similar rock nearby that may yield useful clues. In cliffs and rock faces, the clear layering and beds of sedimentary rocks are usually unmistakable. Other rocks also create distinctive landscapes and landforms (see Rock Landscapes in Understanding Rocks and Minerals).

When you begin to examine your specimen in detail, the first task is to decide whether it is igneous, sedimentary or metamorphic.

Above: With a good eyeglass, you can often identify individual minerals within the rock, especially in medium- and coarse-grained igneous rocks such as granites.

Sedimentary rocks are pale in colour and tend to have similar grains, often held together by a cement. They may crumble as you rub them. Look for bedding planes and fossils.

Igneous rocks are identified by a harder, often shiny more compact look with a tightly packed interlocking mix of crystals. There should never be any layers or bands, except occasionally in layered granites and gabbros.

Some metamorphic rocks can look quite similar to igneous rocks, but foliation (layering and banding) is never found in igneous rocks. Granular metamorphic rocks tend to have a hard, shiny, sugary look and are more evenly dark or light, unlike igneous rocks which are quite often mottled.

The guides to identity given here are intended as a starting point, and should be used in conjunction with the clues given in the Directory.

## Igneous rocks
### COLOUR AND TEXTURE

| | Light-coloured (silica-rich, acidic, felsic) | Medium-coloured (intermediate) | Medium-coloured (intermediate, feldspathic) | Dark-coloured (silica-poor, basic, mafic) |
|---|---|---|---|---|
| **Fine-grained (aphanitic, volcanic, extrusive)** | Rhyolite: White, grey, pink | Andesite: Salt and pepper (black and white) | Trachyte: Brownish-grey | Basalt: Dark grey to black |
| **Medium-grained and porphyritic (hypabyssal, dyke, sill)** | Quartz porphyry: White, grey, pink with light spots | Andesite porphyry: Dark grey, black with white spots | Monzonite: Dark grey with pale spots | Dolerite: Dark grey to black |
| **Coarse-grained (phaneritic, plutonic, intrusive)** | Granite: White, grey, pink; pinkish or whitish (tonalite`) | Diorite: Salt and pepper (black and white) | Syenite: White, grey, pink; pinkish | Gabbro: Dark grey to black |

### OTHER TEXTURES AND COMPOSITIONS

| | | | | |
|---|---|---|---|---|
| **Foam-like (vesicular) and glassy** | Pumice: Whitish with fibrous look; very light | Scoria: Black to brown; very light | Vesicular basalt: Black to brown; heavy | Obsidian: Black, red, brown; glassy |
| **Medium-to-coarse-grained carbonate and ultramafic rocks** | Carbonatite: White with small grey spots | Dunite: Pale khaki to brown; ultramafic | Lamprophyre: Dark grey, with dark, shiny phenocrysts | Peridotite: Light to dark green; ultramafic |

## Metamorphic rocks

| GRANULAR (NON-FOLIATED) ROCKS with no obvious layers, bands or stripes | | FOLIATED ROCKS with obvious layers, bands or stripes | |
|---|---|---|---|
| **Won't scratch glass** | **Will scratch glass** | **Grains often too small to see** | **Grains visible to the naked eye** |
| Marble: Smooth feel; fizzes in dilute hydrochloric acid | Hornfels: Dark grey and black, dull, massive, conchoidal fracture | Slate: Dull grey, black, green, rings when struck; splits in thin sheets | Schist: Stripy bands or schistosity, platy cleavage |
| Dolomite marble: Smooth; powder fizzes in dilute hydrochloric acid | Metaquartzite: Pale translucent colours; fused quartz grains | Phyllite: Shiny grey, black, green; splits in thin sheets; may be striped | Biotite mica schist: dark; pale schist is muscovite mica |
| Greenstone: Greenish; harder than a fingernail unlike soapstone | Eclogite: Pale green pyroxene with red garnet | Mylonite: Streaky, smeared out texture | Gneiss: Tough, minerals separated into light and dark bands |
| Serpentinite: Greasy feel; green, yellow, brown or black | Amphibolite: Black, shiny crystals of amphiboles; also foliated | Glaucophane/Blue schist: Bluish colour, slender fibrous crystals | Granulite: No black mica, lenses of pale quartz and feldspar |

## Sedimentary rocks

| No visible grains | Sand-size, visible grains | At least gravel-sized grains | Biochemical rocks that react with vinegar if powdered |
|---|---|---|---|
| Siltstone: Gritty feel; hard enough to scratch glass | Sandstone: Even, sand-sized grains; may be yellow, brown or red | Breccia: Large angular fragments set in mudlike mix | Chalk: White, powdery, leaves white mark, feels gritty |
| Claystone: Smooth feel; too soft to scratch glass | Ironstone: Even, sand-sized grains; very dark brown, red | Conglomerate: Large round pebbles set in mudlike mix | Oolitic limestone: Buff-coloured, tiny spheres like fish roe |
| Shale: Smooth feel; too soft to scratch glass | Greensand: Even, sand-sized grains; greenish colour | Boulder clay: Huge mix of stones set in muddy clay | Pisolitic limestone: Sand-coloured, tiny spheres like small peas |
| Marl: Earthy, slimy feel; too soft to scratch glass | Arkose: Even, sand-sized grains; won't crumble; pinkish, red | | Fossil limestone: Pale grey, packed with fossils |
| Chert: Smooth, hard and glassy appearance | Greywacke: Mix of sand and fragments of rock | | Dolomite: Dull grey; weathers pink or brown |

# VOLCANIC ROCKS: SILICA-RICH ROCKS

*Volcanic rocks are formed mainly when lava erupting from volcanoes cools and solidifies, but any material ejected from a volcano can form volcanic rock if it turns to stone, including ash, blobs of molten rock and froth. Because exposure to the air cools lava quickly, before crystals have time to grow, volcanic rocks are usually aphanatic (fine-grained) or even glassy. Volcanic rocks that are rich in silica (at least 55 per cent) are light in colour and include rhyolite, quartz porphyry and dacite.*

## Rhyolite

One of the most widespread volcanic rocks, rhyolite forms from the same silica-rich (70–78 per cent) magma that forms granite when it solidifies underground. This is the magma that melts its way up through the continental crust, so rhyolite is a continental rock. Rhyolite has been found on islands far from land, but such oceanic occurrences are rare. Rhyolite is the fine-grained, extrusive equivalent of granite, but there are subtle differences in chemistry. The mica in rhyolite is black biotite, not the brown muscovite seen in granite, and its potassium feldspar is sanidine while that of granite is orthoclase.

The high quartz content of rhyolite magmas means they are relatively cool and very viscous, and this sticky magma tends to clog up the volcanic vent. Sometimes, a plug is left behind long after the volcano has died, leaving a spire of rhyolite as it is gradually exposed by weathering. More often, the plug is blasted away in a mighty explosive eruption, which is why rhyolite is linked to some of the world's most explosive volcanoes, especially caldera complexes such as Tambora in Indonesia. Explosive eruptions are fuelled by the sudden expansion of steam and carbon dioxide in the magma. The explosion blasts away fragments of the plug in huge clouds of ash and deadly avalanches of pyroclasts. Gas bubbles turn parts of the lava to a froth that later solidifies as pumice. So rhyolite rock often forms from ash and pyroclasts rather than lava. Only once there is less gas in the magma can the rhyolite flow on to the surface as lava. Rhyolite lava piles up thickly in domes or coulées (tongues) around the vent – too sluggish to flow far. Rhyolite flows have broken, blocky surfaces, because the rind shatters as the inner mass creeps forward. Ancient rhyolites may have flowed farther, though, if, as some geologists argue, they were superheated and made less viscous by hotspots.

Because they erupt on the surface and cool rapidly, rhyolites are basically fine-grained. Indeed, where they have been quenched (cooled ultra-quickly), they are mostly glassy. Glassy rhyolites include obsidian, pitchstone and perlite. Yet because rhyolites are so viscous, they usually contain phenocrysts – large crystals that formed while the magma lingered in the volcano's magma chamber. Sometimes phenocrysts dominate so much that rhyolite can look like granite, with the microcrystalline groundmass visible only under a microscope. Rocks like these are called nevadites.

Banded rhyolite (below): When rhyolitic lava erupts on the surface, smaller crystals often respond to the flow by aligning themselves in bands, an effect called flow-banding. Banded rhyolite is sometimes called wonderstone, and valued by collectors – especially when it contains cavities filled with silica precipitates such as agate.

**Spherulitic rhyolite (above)**: Sticky, rhyolitic lava often traps pockets of volatile vapours. In quickly cooled glassy rhyolites, some gas pockets develop into spherulites – balls of radiating needle-like crystals of quartz and feldspar – forming spherulitic rhyolite. Spherulites are typically a few millimetres across, but can be up to a metre.

**Grain size**: Aphanitic (fine-grained)
**Texture**: Phenocrysts common; alternating layers of grains common; flow-banding common (Banded rhyolite)
**Structure**: Vesicles and other remnant bubbles common; may contain spherules (Spherulitic rhyolite)
**Colour**: Usually light-coloured – pinkish or reddish brown, but also white, greenish, grey
**Composition**: As for granite: Silica (74% average), Alumina (13.5%), Calcium and sodium oxides (less than 5%), Iron and magnesium oxides (less than 3.5%)
**Minerals**: Quartz; Potassium feldspar (sanidine) and plagioclase feldspar (oligoclase); Biotite mica
**Accessories**: Aegerine, zircon, apatite, magnetite, amphibole or pyroxene
**Phenocrysts**: Quartz, orthoclase and oligoclase feldspar, hornblende, biotite mica, augite
**Formation**: Lava flows, dykes, volcanic plugs in continents
**Notable occurrences**: Lake District, Shropshire, England; Snowdonia, Wales; Vosges, France; Black Forest, Saxony, Germany; Carpathian Mountains, Austria; Siebenbürgen, Romania; Tuscany, Italy; Iceland; Caucasus, Georgia; Rocky Mountains including Yellowstone; Arizona.

Rhyolite volcanoes include: Tambora, Indonesia; Mount Kilimanjaro, Kenya/Tanzania; Yellowstone, Wyoming; Crater Lake, Oregon.

# Quartz porphyry

Quartz porphyry is a loose term for a rock with a similar chemical composition to granite and rhyolite that contains phenocrysts of white quartz (or, less often, orthoclase feldspar) that spot the rock like chunks of fat in a burger. The basic matrix of crystals around the phenocrysts is usually fine-grained, like rhyolite, because the melt containing the phenocrysts was fed into narrow dykes where it cooled and solidified quickly. So the average grain size is akin to granite. More recent quartz porphyries are dyke rocks, but ancient formations that formed in the Palaeozoic age of Earth's history – over 550 million years ago – were lava flows. So some geologists prefer to call ancient quartz porphyries palaeorhyolite. Many of these ancient quartz porphyries have been crushed and sheared by earth movements in their long history, giving them a striped look like schists. When the phenocrysts have been preserved, these rocks are called porphyry schists, and American geologists sometimes call them aporhyolite. They are well known from the Swiss Alps and from England's Charnwood Forest. The supposedly metamorphic halleflintas of Scandinavia may also have been formed like this.

**Identification**: Quartz porphyry is easily identified by the large white or grey blobs of quartz and feldspar in the reddish brown matrix of a rhyolitic mix of fine-grained crystals or even glass.

Rhyolite

Quartz phenocrysts

**Grain size**: Mixed
**Texture**: Phenocrysts in fine-grained, microcrystalline or glassy matrix
**Structure**: Vesicles rare
**Colour**: Usually light-coloured – red, brown, greenish
**Composition**: As for granite: Silica (74% average), Alumina (13.5%), Calcium and sodium oxides (< 5%), Iron and magnesium oxides (< 4%)
**Minerals**: Quartz; Potassium feldspar (sanidine) and plagioclase feldspar (oligoclase); Biotite mica
**Accessories**: Hornblende, augite, bronzite, garnet, cordierite, muscovite
**Phenocrysts**: Quartz, orthoclase feldspar
**Formation**: Dykes, or ancient lavas in continents
**Notable occurrences**: Devon, Cornwall, Charnwood Forest (Leics), England; Westphalia, Germany; Alps, Switzerland; San Bernardino Co, CA; Lake and St. Louis Co, MN; Green Lake Co, Wisconsin Pennsylvania

**Porphyries**
Porphyries are igneous rocks that contain large, conspicuous crystals in a groundmass of finer crystals. The phenocrysts, as the larger crystals are called, formed early on in the middle of the molten magma; the finer crystals formed later, typically after the magma containing them erupted or was injected into a dyke. In the micrograph of trachybasalt shown above, for example, large phenocrysts of olivine, clino-pyroxene (the large twinned crystal) and plagioclase feldspar are set in a fine-grained groundmass of the same crystals. The word porphyry now applies to any igneous rock with phenocrysts, but originally it referred to the beautiful red porphyries used by the Ancient Egyptians and the Romans in the time of the emperor Claudius. This rock, which the Romans called *porfido rosso antico*, was taken from a dyke 30m/98ft 5in thick on the Red Sea at Jebel Dhokan, and contained white or rose red pheno-crysts of plagioclase, dark black hornblende and plates of iron oxide, all in a dark red groundmass.

# Dacite

Named after the Roman province of Dacia in modern Romania, dacite can be a beautiful rock when polished, but is commonly used for road-chippings. It forms from fairly viscous lava (55–65 per cent silica) in lava flows and dykes. It can also form massive intrusions in the heart of old volcanoes, creating lava domes such as Mount St Helens in Washington. It contains less quartz than rhyolite and so is intermediate in composition between rhyolite and the basic lava andesite. The quartz is often in the form of rounded phenocrysts in the groundmass, a little like quartz porphyry. Dacite also has andesine and labradorite as its feldspars rather than sanidine as rhyolite.

Biotite, hornblende

Feldspar

**Grain size**: Aphanitic (fine-grained) or even glassy
**Texture**: Phenocrysts, alternating layers of grains and flow-banding common
**Structure**: Vesicles and other remnant bubbles common
**Colour**: Usually light-coloured – reddish or greenish
**Composition**: Silica (65% av), Alumina (16%), Calcium & sodium oxides (8%), Iron & magnesium oxides (6.5%)
**Minerals**: Quartz; Potassium feldspar (andesine and labradorine) and plagioclase feldspar; Biotite; Hornblende
**Accessories**: Pyroxene (augite and enstatite), hornblende, biotite, zircon, apatite, magnetite
**Phenocrysts**: Quartz, feldspar, hornblende, biotite
**Formation**: Lava flows, dykes
**Notable occurrences**: Argyll, Scotland; Massif C, France; Saar-Nahe, Germany; Hungary; Siebenbürgen, Romania; Almeria, Spain; New Zealand; Martinique; Andes, Peru; Rocky Mountains; Nevada.

**Identification**: Dacite's rich hornblende and biotite are grey or yellowish, with white specks of feldspar like this. Augite and enstatite-rich dacites are darker.

# ANDESITES

*Midway between rhyolite and basalt in silica content, andesites are the most common volcanic rocks after basalt and are found all around the world near subduction zones. They get their name from the Andes in South America, and are associated with all the classic cone-shaped volcanoes, such as Mount Fuji in Japan and Mount Edgecumbe in New Zealand.*

## Andesite

**Identification**: Most andesite has a classic 'salt and pepper' look with white tablet-shaped grains of plagioclase feldspar visible to the naked eye set in a dark, often almost black, groundmass of fine-grained, occasionally glassy, minerals – mainly biotite mica, hornblende and pyroxene. Typically the dark minerals make up about 40 per cent of the rock by volume, much less than in basalt.

Andesites are found pretty much anywhere that an oceanic plate is subducted beneath a continent. Here they create a string of volcanoes along the continental margin, or an arc of volcanic islands along the edge of the continental shelf. Andesites are especially common in areas of recent mountain building. Not only the Andes, but the entire cordillera of mountains running from the Andes to the Rockies is predominantly andesite. In fact, wherever there are volcanoes in the 'Ring of Fire' around the Pacific, there is likely to be andesite.

Continental and island arc volcanoes spew out mainly andesite, dacite or rhyolite, depending on their silica content, while oceanic volcanoes emit basic lavas such as olivine, basalt and trachyte. Geologists call the line separating the two the andesite line. It runs roughly down the west coast of the Americas, and down from Japan to New Zealand via the Marianas, the Palaus, the Bismarcks, Fiji and Tonga. Although not as silica-rich as rhyolite, is still fairly viscous and often gets clogged up in the vent of the volcano. Consequently, andesite generates some of the world's most dramatic eruptions, as pressure builds up high enough to blast through the plug.

Andesitic volcanoes frequently produce devastating pyroclastic volcanoes, and most andesite volcanoes are stratovolcanoes – the classic cone-shaped peaks in which layers of lava alternate with layers of ash and pyroclasts, as lava pours out after the ash in each eruption.

Andesite lava flows better than rhyolite, but still sluggishly. When erupted, it first forms a mound around the vent. This creeps down the flanks of the volcano, advancing barely a few metres a day. The lava moves so slowly that the outside of the flow cools and solidifies. So, as it moves, the surface of the flow breaks up into a jumble of angular blocks that look like rubble. Even the hottest, most fluid andesites rarely flow farther than 10km/6 miles from the vent.

**Porphyritic andesite**: Many andesites are porphyritic – that is, they are spattered with large grains, clearly visible to the naked eye, that formed before the lava erupted. When these phenocrysts are especially large, the rock is called porphyritic andesite. The phenocrysts are typically plagioclase feldspar (white), but can be pyroxenes and amphiboles (usually greenish black).

**Grain size**: Aphanitic (fine-grained), occasionally glassy
**Texture**: Often porphyritic
**Structure**: Often displays flow structure; occasional vesicles
**Colour**: Grey, purplish, brown, green, almost black
**Composition**: Silica (59% average), Alumina (17%), Calcium and sodium oxides (10%), Iron and magnesium oxides (11%)
**Minerals**: Quartz; Feldspar: plagioclase feldspar (andesine) plus small amounts of potassium feldspar (oligoclase, sanidine); Biotite mica; Amphibole (hornblende); Pyroxene (augite)
**Accessories**: Magnetite, apatite, zircon, olivine
**Phenocrysts**: Plagioclase feldspar, pyroxenes such as augite, amphibole, hornblende
**Formation**: Extrusive lavas, ashes and tuffs in subduction zones and areas of mountain building
**Notable occurrences**: Glencoe, Scotland; Lake District, England; Snowdonia, Wales; Vosges, Auvergnes, France; Rhineland, Germany; Siebenbürgen, Romania; Caucasus, Georgia; Andes; Rocky Mountains.
Andesite volcanoes include: Mount Fuji, Bandai-san, Japan; Krakatoa, Indonesia; Pinatubo, Philippines; Ngauruhoe, Mount Edgecumbe, Ruapehe, New Zealand; Citlaltépetl, Popocatépetl, Mexico; Mount Pelée, Martinique; Soufriere, St Vincent; Mount Shasta, California; Mount Hood, Oregon; Mount Adams, Washington.

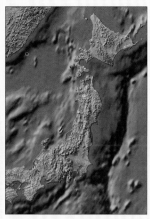

the plate may reflect the curvature of the Earth. There are many of these island arcs in the Pacific, including the Aleutians, the islands of Japan, the Marianas, Tonga and the Solomon Islands. The Antilles in the Caribbean also form an island arc. All these islands are volcanic and form when the subducted plate plunges down into the mantle, creating deep ocean trenches all along the margins of the plate. This satellite image of Japan (above) shows the Japan Trench, the dark area to the right of the islands, which forms part of the boundary between the Pacific and Eurasian plates. As the subducted plate sinks into the mantle, it melts and, in a complex process, forms magmas, including andesite, basalt and boninite. These hot magmas punch through the edge of the overriding plate like a needle stitching a hem, and as they penetrate, they erupt on the surface as volcanoes.

# Boninite

This rarity takes its name from the Izu-Bonin-Mariana chain of islands south of Japan in the Pacific. Most of the boninites formed here between about 30 and 50 million years ago, but boninites are still forming today. They are associated almost exclusively with island arcs, and seem to require particular conditions for their formation. They are formed when an ocean tectonic plate is subducted beneath another oceanic plate. The subducted plate carries sea water down into the mantle with it as it plunges into the Earth, and the water alters the chemistry of the magma formed as the plate melts in the heat of the mantle. Geologists suggest that boninites form only if high temperatures are reached fairly quickly as the plate is subducted – otherwise, andesites will form. They may be linked to the early stage of subduction.

**Grain size**: Glassy
**Texture**: Often porphyritic
**Structure**: Often displays flow structure; occasional vesicles
**Colour**: Dark grey, often black
**Composition**: Silica (59% average), Alumina (17%), Calcium and sodium oxides (10%), Iron and magnesium oxides (11%)
**Minerals**: Quartz; Feldspar: plagioclase feldspar; Pyroxene (augite, bronzite); Amphibole (hornblende)
**Accessories**: Pentlandite, spinel
**Phenocrysts (small)**: Pyroxenes: augite, bronzite
**Formation**: Extrusive lavas, dykes and sills in island arcs
**Notable occurrences**: Crimea, Ukraine; Izu-Bonin-Marianas island chain, Pacific; North Tonga Ridge, New Hebrides; Setouchi, Japan. Possible continental margin occurrences: Isua, Greenland; Yukon, Canada; Glenelg, South Australia: Antilles, Caribbean.

**Identification**: Boninite is dark in colour, with small black phenocrysts set against a dark glassy groundmass.

# Pyroxene andesite

**Biotite andesite**: Biotite andesite is typically yellow, pinkish or grey, often with black phenocrysts of amphibole or pyroxene.

There are actually several different kinds of andesite: the quartz-containing andesites normally thought of as dacite; the hornblende- or biotite-rich andesites; and the pyroxene andesites. Hornblende and biotite andesites are rich in feldspar and coloured pale pink, yellow or grey. The pyroxene andesites are by far the most common of the andesites and occur almost as widely as basalt, and often come from the same magma source. The pyroxene in pyroxene andesite is usually augite – giving augite andesite – but can be olivine. The augite gives these andesites a sparkle when the rock is broken, but they are frequently altered to hornblende. Sometimes, good-sized augite crystals can be found in pyroxene andesite tuffs – that is, deposits of ash and pyroclasts.

**Identification**: Pyroxene andesite can look quite like basalt, and its high pyroxene content means that it is chemically closer too. But pyroxene andesite usually contains phenocrysts and is usually slightly lighter in colour, with traces of white feldspar.

**Grain size**: Aphanitic (fine-grained), occasionally glassy
**Texture**: Often porphyritic
**Structure**: Often displays flow structure; occasional vesicles
**Colour**: Grey, green, almost black
**Composition**: Silica (59% average), Alumina (17%), Calcium and sodium oxides (10%), Iron and magnesium oxides (11%)
**Minerals**: Quartz; Feldspar: plagioclase feldspar (andesine) plus small amounts of potassium feldspar (oligoclase, sanidine); Biotite mica; Amphibole (hornblende) or Pyroxene
**Accessories**: Magnetite, apatite, zircon, olivine
**Phenocrysts**: Pyroxenes such as augite and olivine, amphibole, hornblende
**Formation**: Extrusive lavas, ashes and tuffs in subduction zones and areas of mountain building
**Notable occurrences**: See andesite

# TRACHYTES and SPILLITE

*Trachytes and phonolites are medium-coloured, fine-grained volcanic rocks that flow easily enough to form lavas. They occur in many of the same places as basalts, including rifts, but contain more lighter-coloured minerals, and a modicum of quartz. They are all alkaline rocks, containing sodium and potassium feldspars. Trachyte is the mildest alkaline, phonolite is the strongest.*

## Trachyte

This volcanic rock is medium-coloured and very fine-grained. It is the volcanic equivalent of syenite, and erupts along rifts, in oceanic settings, above hot spots and in back arc basins between island arcs and the continental land mass. Trachytes are often associated with basalt, and are sometimes thought to be characteristic of a volcano past its prime. The parasitic cones of the Hawaiian shield volcanoes often ooze trachyte lava, for instance. Yet trachytes can also form quite extensive lava flows in their own right, as they do in Saudi Arabia.

Trachyte is fine-grained, but unlike andesite and rhyolite, very rarely glassy. It seems that crystals nearly always form, even though they may be microscopically small. Remarkably, rectangular phenocrysts of white sanidine are often already formed in the lava when it erupts. These tend to line up with the direction of the lava flow, and through a microscope you can often see that the smaller crystals form flow patterns around them. This texture is described as trachytic, and is sometimes found in other lavas, such as Hawaiite.

Although they are too small to see, trachyte is full of tiny cavities left by gas bubbles. It is these that give the rock the slightly rough feel to which it owes its name, from *trachys*, the Greek for 'rough'. These cavities sometimes fill with tiny crystals of the silica minerals tridymite, cristobalite, opal and chalcedony. The bulk of trachyte, though, is mostly alkali (sodium- and potassium-rich) feldspars, notably sanidine (in rodlike microcrystals as well as phenocrysts), along with dark-coloured minerals such as biotite, amphiboles (hornblende) or pyroxenes such as aegerine and diopside. An increase in the silica content takes trachyte towards rhyolite; a decrease, with a corresponding increase in feldspathoids such as leucite, nepheline and sodalite, takes it towards phonolite.

**Identification**: Trachyte is a brownish grey, medium-coloured rock, which is microcrystalline but almost never glassy. The dark groundmass is usually spotted with thin white phenocrysts of sanidine. A tell-tale clue to its identity is the rough feel created by tiny gas bubbles.

**Grain size**: Aphanitic (fine-grained), can occasionally be glassy
**Texture**: Even, but often porphyritic
**Structure**: Often displays flow structure called trachytic visible only under a microscope in which crystals of groundmass appear to flow around phenocrysts. Some specimens also have minute steam cavities, making the surface of the rock feel rough.
**Colour**: Usually grey, but can be white, pink or yellowish
**Composition**: Silica (62% average), Alumina (17%), Calcium and sodium oxides (8%), Iron and magnesium oxides (6%)
**Minerals**: Quartz; Feldspar: potassium feldspar (sanidine) and plagioclase feldspar (oligoclase); Biotite mica; Amphibole (hornblende, often altered to magnetite and augite); Pyroxene (aegerine, diopside)
**Accessories**: Apatite, zircon, magnetite, leucite, nepheline, sodalite, analcime. Plus in cavities: tridymite, cristobalite, opal, chalcedony.
**Phenocrysts**: Tablet-shaped sanidine, often aligned with the flow
**Formation**: Extrusive lavas, dykes and sills often in association with basalt
**Notable occurrences**: Skye, Midland Valley, Scotland; Lundy Island, Devon, England; Eifel, Thuringia, Saar, Berkum, Drachenfels (Rhineland), Germany; Auvergne, France; Naples, Ischia, Sardinia, Italy; Iceland; Azores; Saudi Arabia; Ethiopia; Madagascar; Cambewarra (New South Wales), Australia; Hawaii; Black Hills, South Dakota; Colorado

Sanidine

**Porphyritic trachyte**: Trachyte is basically a medium-coloured rock, with a groundmass of dark minerals such as biotite, hornblende and pyroxenes, and light-coloured sanidine feldspar. Interestingly, the sanidine forms in two stages, and the rock may be spotted with large long white sanidine phenocrysts that formed early in the magma. Under a microscope, trachytic flow patterns are visible in the small crystals around them.

# Phonolite

Phonolites are mostly quite recent rocks, all forming within the Tertiary Age – that is, in the last 66 million years. They are medium-coloured, fine-grained volcanic rocks. They split into thin slabs and have such a compact structure that the slabs ring when struck with a hammer, which is why they were once called clinkstone. Phonolites are quite similar to trachyte, and the two occur in similar places. But phonolites are richer in alkaline minerals. Their lower silica content favours the formation of feldspathoids such as nepheline, leucite and sodalite, rather than the potassium feldspars of trachyte. So phonolites are the extrusive equivalent of nepheline syenite, rather than plain syenite. Like trachyte, they contain two generations of crystals. The first generation are the large, flattened tablet-shaped crystals of sanidine and nepheline, which form slowly in the magma. These become phenocrysts when the lava is erupted, and smaller crystals quickly form around them, often with a microscopic trachytic flow structure. Sometimes, leucite replaces nepheline to create leucite phonolite, as found near Naples, which is often studded with blue hauyne crystals, and sphene.

**Identification**: Phonolite is usually a mottled grey, but tiny needles of pyroxene can turn it greenish. The way phonolite breaks into flat slabs is often a real clue to identity, especially if the slabs give a metallic clink when hit with a hammer.

**Grain size**: Aphanitic (fine-grained), occasionally glassy
**Texture**: Dense, porphyritic
**Structure**: Platy structure, so breaks into slabs
**Colour**: Dark green, grey
**Composition**: Silica (57.5% av), Alumina (19.5%), Calcium & sodium oxides (11%), Iron & magnesium oxides (6%)
**Minerals**: Alkali feldspar (sanidine, anorthoclase); Foids (nepheline, leucite, sodalite, hauyne, nosean); Pyroxene (aegerine, diopside); Amphibole (barkevikite hornbl'd, riebeckite)
**Accessories**: Apatite, zircon, magnetite, sphene, garnet
**Phenocrysts**: Sanidine, nepheline, aegerine
**Formation**: Extrusive lavas, dykes and sills often with trachyte and nepheline syenite
**Notable occurrences**: Wolf Rock (Cornwall), England; Eildon, Scotland; Auvergne, France; Eifel, Laacher S, Germany; Bohemia, Czech Rep; Naples, Sardinia, Italy; Canary I; Cape Verde I; NSW; Cripple Creek, CO; Black Hills, SD; Devil's Tower, WY; Mt Erebus, Antarctica

**Great East African Rift Valley**
In few places is the power of tectonic plate movement more striking than in Africa's Great Rift Valley. The Valley is part of a huge set of fissures in Earth's crust called the East African Rift system, which threatens to split Africa in two. It started to open up about 100 million years ago, as plates on either side began to pull apart. As the crust stretched, volcanoes repeatedly burst through, and now dot the whole valley, including Erte Ale in Ethiopia and Ol Doinyo Lengai in Tanzania. Initially there were floods of basalt, then shield volcanoes emitting rhyolites and basanites, and finally volcanoes erupting trachyte and phonolite. The valley that formed is now over 6,000km/3,728 miles long and 50km/31 miles wide on average. The walls typically rise 900m/2,953ft above the valley floor, but at Mau in Kenya, cliffs soar to a height of 2,700m/8,858ft. Geologists believe that the Afar Triangle in Ethiopia, where the branches of the rift system meet, is the start of the world's next great ocean.

# Spillite

Spillite is a medium-dark greenish black volcanic rock made from a groundmass of dark amphiboles such as actinolite and riebeckite, with occasionally bright cream phenocrysts of albite. It erupts mainly in oceanic locations, along with basalt, though it can often be found in ancient locations on land. It is one of the main kinds of magma that form pillow lavas. Pillow lavas are balls or tubes of lava that form where lava erupts slowly on the ocean bed. As the lava oozes up, contact with cold sea water quickly chills it to form a thin crust, and as the lava goes on pushing up it solidifies into a ball or tube, just like blobs of toothpaste squeezed from a tube.

**Grain size**: Aphanitic (very fine-grained)
**Texture**: Often porphyritic
**Structure**: Platy structure, so breaks into slabs
**Colour**: Dark green, black
**Composition**: Silica (50% average), Alumina (16%), Calcium and sodium oxides (13%), Iron and magnesium oxides (18%)
**Minerals**: Plagioclase feldspar (albite); Amphibole (actinolite, riebeckite); Chlorite; Epidote
**Accessories**: Apatite, zircon, magnetite
**Phenocrysts**: Albite, actinolite
**Formation**: Pillow lavas and tuffs
**Notable occurrences**: Oceanic crust (worldwide); Cornwall, England; Alaska; California

**Identification**: Spillite is dark, fine-grained volcanic rock quite similar to basalt. It can sometimes be identified by the way it breaks into slabs or by its formation as pillow lavas.

# BASALTS

*Black and fine-grained, basalt is the classic 'mafic' volcanic rock – rich in iron and magnesium minerals, and very low in silica. It is one of the earliest lavas to erupt from any volcano, coming straight up from the mantle in huge quantities, very hot and very fluid, and uncontaminated by the silicas that make other lavas much more viscous (less fluid).*

## Basalt

**Alkali olivine basalt**: The typical basalt rock is dark in colour with no visible grain structure. It tends to be black when freshly exposed, but turns reddish or greenish when weathered. Alkali or olivine basalt contains lots of olivine and augite in the groundmass (not as phenocrysts).

**Ankaramite**: This basalt gets its name from Ankara in Turkey where it has been found. It is an alkaline basalt, with lots of phenocrysts of both dark green olivine and black augite. Although basalt often has olivine phenocrysts, augite phenocrysts are rare because augite crystallizes late. All the same, augite forms up to half basalt's groundmass. Ankaramite is closely related to picrite.

Basalt is the most common rock on Earth. Much of it, though, is hidden away under the sea, for it forms the bulk of the ocean floor, which itself makes up 70 per cent of the Earth's surface. Basalt lava wells up through fissures in the ocean floor at the mid-ocean ridge as the two halves of the ocean floor pull apart. The lava freezes on to the receding edges of the two halves and ensures new rock is added as the ocean spreads away. It often forms pillow lavas here, as hot lava is suddenly chilled by the cold sea water to create countless cushion-like knobs of solid rock.

Basalt lava also wells up where hot spots penetrate the ocean floor to create island volcanoes such as Mauna Loa and Kilauea in Hawaii. Sometimes the hot basalt lava flows straight into the sea and is shattered as it suddenly freezes, and the fragments create black beach sands like those of Hawaii. Not all basalt is oceanic, though. Some basalt can erupt in continental fissures in a process no one quite understands. For example, huge floods of basalt have poured from fissures on to the surface to form gigantic plateaux, such as India's Deccan and North America's Columbia River Plateau. When it erupts, basalt lava is so hot and fluid that it can flow for tens of kilometres from the vent. When particularly hot it can even flow 500km/ 310 miles or so. This is why basalt habitually forms broad shield volcanoes, or flood basalt plateaux.

The shape the lava takes as it freezes depends on its temperature and its speed. When it is quite warm and fluid, surfaces wrinkle into rope-like ridges known by their Hawaiian name of *pahoehoe* (pronounced 'pa-hoy-hoy'). If they are a little more viscous or cooler, the surface tends to freeze and then break up into a jumble of rubble, a flow known as *aa* (pronounced 'ah-ah').

**Grain size**: Aphanitic (very fine-grained) or tachylytic (glassy)
**Texture**: Usually dense, with no visible mineral grains
**Structure**: Often porphyritic, and tends to include xenoliths (large lumps of other minerals) of olivine and pyroxene. Frequently spongy with vesicles or amygdaloidal cavities. Large masses of basalt may be cracked into hexagonal columns, like the Giant's Causeway (N. Ireland)
**Colour**: Black or blackish grey when fresh, may weather to reddish or greenish crust
**Composition**: Silica (50% average), Alumina (16%), Calcium and sodium oxides (13%), Iron and magnesium oxides (18%)
**Minerals**: Plagioclase feldspar (labradorite); Pyroxene; Olivine; Magnetite; Ilmenite. Tholeitic basalts (low in olivine): Plagioclase, pyroxene (hypersthene, pigeonite); Magnetite. Alkali basalts; (olivine-rich): Olivine, Pyroxene (augite); Magnetite.
**Accessories**: Countless
**Phenocrysts**: Green glassy olivine or black shiny pyroxene, or occasionally white tabular plagioclase feldspar
**Amygdales**: Zeolites, carbonates, and silica in the form of chalcedony and agate
**Formation**: Extrusive lavas, dykes and sills. Most basalts occur as lava flows from volcanoes or as sheets building up lava plateaux in flood basalts. Surfaces are either smooth, ropey pahoehoe or clinkery aa. Under the ocean basalt is often in balloon-like masses of pillow lava
**Notable occurences:** See opposite page

## Vesicular and amygdaloidal basalt

The grains in basalt are usually so fine, they are invisible to the naked eye, and the impression of the rock is a black mass, created by a mix of dark minerals – essentially labradorite (plagioclase), pyroxene and olivine, with magnetite and ilmenite. But it can be porphyritic, or contain cavities called vesicles that form as gas bubbles expanded in the solidifying lava. Larger vesicles seem to form more commonly in basalt pahoehoe than any other lava. It may be because the lava is so hot and fluid enough for the bubbles to expand easily. Unlike vesicles in other, more viscous lavas, those in pahoehoe are pretty much round rather than long. Rock with lots of empty vesicles like these is called vesicular basalt. Once the lava is set, water percolating through the lava often begins to fill many of these cavities with mineral crystals. These infillings are called amygdales, from the Greek for almond for their typical shape. They can be anything from 1mm to 30cm/0.04 to 12in across and typically contain quartz, carbonates and zeolites. Basalt full of amygdales is called amygdaloidal basalt.

**Vesicular basalt**: Basalt is often filled with countless vesicles, which make it look as if some insects have been at it. Other igneous rocks do have vesicles, but they are especially numerous and rounded in basalt. A dark black groundmass indicates that a rock full of little holes like these is vesicular basalt.

Typical rounded vesicles

**The Giant's Causeway**
In the last stages of cooling, basalt lava flows often contract and fracture into extraordinary hexagonal columns. The most famous example of these is the Giant's Causeway in Antrim, Northern Ireland. Legend has it the stones were laid by the giant Finn MacCool to reach his lover in Scotland, but in fact they are a natural feature of basalt rock. About 65 million years ago, North America began to split apart from Europe, and basalt lavas welled up into the rift created. Here in Antrim, tholeitic lavas erupted over hundreds of thousands of years then stopped – only to start again abruptly. The lava poured into valleys and became so deeply ponded at the site of the Causeway that it formed a lava lake so deep that it cooled only slowly. As it slowly solidified and contracted, it developed regular hexagonal stress patterns. Soon six-sided columns 30–40cm/12–16in across permeated the whole cooling mass. Further eruptions followed, but this was the one that left its distinctive legacy.

## Alkali and tholeitic basalt

There is a wide spectrum of basalt rocks, but they can be divided into two broad groups according to their chemistry – the tholeitic basalts and alkali basalts. Tholeitic basalts are low in olivine and rich in calcium-poor pyroxenes such as hypersthene and pigeonite. Most basalts that ooze up from rifts and mid-ocean fissures are tholeitic. So ocean floors are tholeitic basalt. Flood basalts are tholeitic too. Alkali basalts contain more sodium and potassium and are rich in olivine, the feldspathoid nepheline and calcium-rich pyroxenes such as augite. Geologists believe they are more alkaline because minerals in the magma have been less divided by partial melting. In the Hawaiian hotspot volcanoes, lavas that build the initial undersea cone are alkali basalts, cooled quickly by seawater. But as the cone rises above the sea, streams of fluid tholeitic lava spew out to create a huge shield, cooling slower in the air and more affected by partial melting. As the volcano dies down again, spurts of alkali lavas resume, creating a cap of alkali basalt rock. In the million-year life cycle of Mauna Kea, Hawaii's biggest volcano, this last subdued alkaline stage has gone on for 40,000 years, and may yet last another 60,000 years.

**Notable occurrences**:
*Tholeitic basalts*: Deccan, India; Red Sea; Paraná Basin, South America; Palisades, New Jersey; Rio Grande Rift, Mexico; Columbia River Plateau, Washington-Oregon; Mauna Loa, Kilauea, Hawaii

*Alkali basalts*: Ocean floors; Inner Hebrides, Scotland; Antrim, Northern Ireland; Iceland; Faroe Islands; Mauna Kea, Mauna Loa, Kilauea, Hawaii

*Leucite basalts*: Italy; Germany; East Africa; Montana; Wyoming; Arizona

*Nepheline basalts*: Libya; Turkey; New Mexico

**Amygdaloidal basalt**: This kind of basalt with its white amygdale spots is easy to identify. Other igneous rocks do have amygdales, but they are rarely as large as in basalt. The black microscopically grained groundmass confirms its identity.

# GLASSY ROCKS

*When lava (or magma) cools quickly, there is no time for crystals to form within the mix, so the result is a glassy rock. Glassy rocks not only look like glass, though darker and cloudier, but they also shatter like it when struck with a hammer, giving sharp fragments. The main glassy rocks are obsidian, perlite and pitchstone, which are all inter-related and merge into each other, largely according to their water content.*

## Obsidian

Like rhyolite, obsidian forms from the same magma that solidifies as granite deep underground. When rhyolite magma approaches the surface, the reduction in pressure means that some of its water is lost as steam. This de-watered rhyolite magma becomes very thick and viscous. Indeed, it becomes so thick that crystals do not get a chance to grow before the erupted lava is chilled and frozen solid. The result is a rock that is just like solid glass except slightly harder, and often jet black. Obsidian lava is so thick that it advances at a snail's pace, and outcrops are usually quite small. It typically forms near the end of the volcanic cycle and creates just a small plug, a thin coating on rhyolite lava flows or a lining for rhyolite sills and dykes. Yet occasionally there are large flows of obsidian, as at Glass Buttes in Oregon and Valles Caldera in New Mexico, where there are layers of obsidian a few hundred metres thick. Such a flow occurred just 1,300 years ago at the Newberry volcano in Oregon.

Obsidian shatters like glass into sharp, conchoidal (curved) fragments. It quickly dulls with exposure, but when freshly broken obsidian gleams like polished glass. It is typically jet black, coloured by titanium oxide minerals, but streaks and swirls can make broken surfaces look like colour-flowed marbles, as in brown- and black-streaked 'mahogany' obsidian and 'midnight lace' obsidian, with its contorted streaks formed as the cooling lava rolled over and over. Iron oxides turn obsidian reddish or brownish, while gas bubbles and microcrystals make 'golden sheen' obsidians that shimmer iridescently in sunlight. Because it fractures with a beautifully curved glass-sharp edge, obsidian can easily be fashioned to make knife and axe blades, even better than flint. It can also take a high polish. As a result it was highly prized among early cultures. The Ancient Egyptians, the Aztecs and Mayans all used obsidian knives and arrowheads. So too did Native Americans. Because obsidian absorbs water once it is broken, some of these ancient obsidian artefacts can be accurately dated by measuring just how much water their surface layers have absorbed. Obsidian is rarely older than 20 million years, because it starts to alter as soon as it forms. In a process known as 'devitrification', the glass absorbs moisture and begins to form crystals and go cloudy.

**Identification**: Jet black obsidian, which looks like a lump of solid glass, is hard to mistake for any other rock, especially if it fractures conchoidally. But it can contain phenocrysts of quartz and microscopic crystals of feldspar.

Conchoidal fracture

**Snowflake obsidian**: Snowflake obsidian has white snowflake patches of the mineral christobalite. Sometimes, 'snowflakes' can form through devitrification, as moisture alters silica in the obsidian.

**Grain size**: None, obsidian is glassy

**Texture**: Occasional small phenocrysts or microlites (tiny crystals)

**Structure**: Breaks conchoidally; occasional spherulites (tiny radiating clusters of needlelike crystals); flow banding with alternating glassy and devitrified layers. Contortion of flowbands in unset lava creates 'midnight lace' obsidian.

**Colour**: Usually jet black, but presence of iron oxides turns it reddish and brownish, and inclusion of tiny gas bubbles gives it a golden sheen. Dark banding and mottled grey, green and yellow. Microscopic feldspar crystals create 'rainbow obsidian'.

**Composition**: As for rhyolite: Silica (74% average), Alumina (13.5%), Calcium and sodium oxides (less than 5%), Iron and magnesium oxides (less than 3.5%). Obsidian always includes a certain amount of water, often in the form of minute bubbles of water vapour trapped in the glass. These bubbles are usually visible under a magnifying glass.

**Minerals**: Quartz; Potassium feldspar (sanidine) and plagioclase feldspar (oligoclase); Biotite mica

**Phenocrysts**: Quartz; Christobalite

**Microlites**: Feldspar

**Formation**: Lava flows, dykes and sills

**Notable occurrences**: Scotland; Eolie Island, Italy; Mount Hekla, Iceland; Mexico; Obsidian Cliff (Yellowstone), Wyoming; Arizona; Colorado; Valles Caldera, New Mexico; Big Obsidian Flow (Newberry), Glass Buttes, Oregon

# Perlite

Like obsidian, perlite is a natural glass that forms from rhyolite lava, but rather than being shiny black, perlite is grey like dirty snow. Also while obsidian contains very little water, perlite gets its name because it contains concentric cracks that make the rock break into tiny pearl-like balls. Unlike obsidian, perlite contains water (2–5 per cent) because it cools so quickly that water has no time to escape. Once formed, it goes on absorbing water from its surroundings. Each little pearl is like a balloon full of water, and this is what makes perlite a rather amazing material. When heated to 871°C/1,600°F, the water evaporates, and the steam turns each pearl into a bubble, inflating the perlite like popcorn up to 20 times its original volume. This creates an incredibly light, gas-filled material, which is used for all kinds of insulation, for both heat and sound. Many roofing tiles contain perlite as does pipe insulation. It is also used instead of sand to make lightweight concrete. Horticulturalists often grow plants in a perlite mix instead of soil because of its good aeration and water retention.

**Identification**: Perlite looks a bit like dirty ice, and lumps of it can look rather like old snowballs. It has a glassy texture, with no crystalline structure, but is often dotted with phenocrysts, much more so than obsidian.

*Perlite pebble*

**Grain size**: None, perlite is glassy
**Texture**: Occasional small phenocrysts; when there are a lot of phenocrysts, the rock becomes 'vitrophyre'
**Structure**: Concentric cracks, which mean the rock breaks into pearl-shaped balls
**Colour**: Grey or greenish, but may be brown, blue or red
**Composition**: As for rhyolite: Silica (74% average), Alumina (13.5%), Calcium and sodium oxides (<5%), Iron and magnesium oxides (<3.5%)
**Minerals**: Quartz; Potassium feldspar (sanidine) and plagioclase feldspar (oligoclase); Biotite mica
**Phenocrysts**: Quartz, sanidine, oligoclase or, rarely, biotite or hornblende
**Formation**: Lava flows, dykes
**Notable occurrences**: Greece; Turkey; New Mexico; Sierra Nevada, California; Utah; Oregon

## Apache tears

Sometimes obsidian alters to perlite when it absorbs water during or after cooling. The water is gradually absorbed along cracks caused by the cooling process, turning more and more of the obsidian to balls of perlite. As more water is absorbed, these spread out in concentric circles through the obsidian. Eventually, all that is left is a small core of obsidian embedded in a mass of perlite. As the process goes on, the perlite is broken by weathering, leaving just a few isolated nodules of obsidian, rounded by wind and water into natural marbles, called 'Apache tears'. They got their name from the stones at Apache Leap Mountain near Superior in Arizona. Legend has it that in the 1800s Apache warriors were trapped at the top of a cliff on this mountain by pursuing US cavalry. Rather than surrendering to their enemies, the apaches leaped to their death. The tears of their wives and children are said to have fallen to the ground here and the Great Spirit, looking down, turned them into the Apache tears so that the courage of the warriors might be remembered forever.

# Pitchstone

Pitchstone is a glassy volcanic rock occurring famously in the Hebridean islands of Scotland, where it was used in the Stone Age to make blades. Some pitchstone is high in silica and forms from the same granite-like magma as rhyolite. Other pitchstones are lower in silica and more akin to trachyte or even andesite. Unlike obsidian, pitchstone contains a lot of water (up to 10 per cent) and is dull in lustre – especially older pitchstones that have become almost completely devitrified (lost their glassiness) and look pretty much like rhyolite. Many pitchstones contain phenocrysts arranged in wavy tracks reflecting the flow of the magma. Pitchstones are often mixed in with crystalline volcanic rocks, and may have formed when water driven out of the crystallizing rock was taken up by the glassy pitchstone.

**Grain size**: Glassy, or cryptocrystalline
**Texture**: Abundant phenocrysts; when phenocrysts dominate, the rock becomes 'vitrophyre' or pitchstone porphyry
**Structure**: Wavy flow streaks. Breaks to poorly defined conchoidal fracture
**Colour**: Streaked, mottled, or uniform black, brown, red, green
**Composition**: Quartz (variable), Potassium feldspar and plagioclase feldspar, Biotite mica
**Phenocrysts**: Quartz, potassium feldspar, plagioclase, or, rarely, pyroxene or hornblende
**Formation**: Dykes and sills
**Notable occurrences**: Arran, Eigg, Skye (Hebrides), Scotland; Chemnitz, Meissen, Germany; Lipari, Italy; Urals, Russia; Japan; New Zealand; Oregon; Colorado; Utah; California

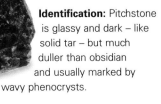

**Identification**: Pitchstone is glassy and dark – like solid tar – but much duller than obsidian and usually marked by wavy phenocrysts.

# VOLCANIC FROTH AND ASH

*Not all volcanic rocks are formed from molten lava. Pumices form from glassy lava so filled with gas bubbles that it becomes a froth. Tuffs form from ash and pyroclasts – fragments of solid magma and rock shattered by an explosive eruption. Some falls to the ground and only gradually consolidates into rock. Some rushes out in flows so hot that material is literally welded together, creating solid ignimbrite.*

## Pumice

**Floating rock**: Pumice will float for several months before becoming waterlogged and sinking.

Pumice is the only rock that floats. It is solidified lumps of rhyolitic or dacitic lava froth so full of holes that it is less dense than water. When the lava erupted, the release of pressure made gases dissolved in it effervesce – like unscrewing a shaken fizzy drink bottle – and form bubbles that blew the lava up into a froth. Had it stayed under pressure it would have formed obsidian. Basalt and andesite lavas form froth rocks, too, called scoria, but because these lavas are so fluid, gases can escape. So scoria contains fewer holes than pumice and won't float. A basalt pumice does form in Hawaii, however – and it is even lighter than rhyolite pumice, and black! As volcanoes have erupted through time, tiny fragments of pumice have been scattered all over the world, and now coat the deep ocean floor. Some has come from undersea eruptions, but much came from fragments falling on the ocean after big eruptions, then floating for months before becoming waterlogged and sinking. Ground up, pumice is the abrasive used to 'stonewash' jeans among other things. Commercially the word pumice refers only to large stones; grains are called pumicite. Pozzolan is a pumicite mixed with lime to make cement.

**Identification**: Fresh pumice is very easy to identify since it is whitish, full of holes and so light that it actually floats, until it becomes waterlogged. However, pumice retains this lightness for only a short time geologically. Soon enough all the holes are infilled with secondary minerals and it is no longer buoyant, and the glassy solid material becomes devitrified.

*Pumice is often full of air holes like this*

**Grain size**: None, it is glassy
**Texture**: Like a foam
**Structure**: The solid glass forms threads and fibres surrounding rounded or elongated holes depending on the flow of the lava. Cavities may be infilled when percolating water deposits secondary minerals.
**Colour**: Usually white or light grey; scoria is black or brown
**Composition**: The same as for rhyolite: Silica (74% average); Alumina (13.5%), Calcium and sodium oxides (<5%); Iron and magnesium oxides (2%)
**Minerals**: Quartz; Potassium feldspar (sanidine) and plagioclase feldspar (oligoclase); Biotite mica
**Formation**: Lava flows and pyroclasts
**Notable occurrences**: Pozzola, Italy; Greece; Spain; Turkey; Chile; Arizona; California; New Mexico; Oregon

## Banded tuff

**Identification**: Banded tuff is streaked with dark glass and welded ash.

Tuff is rock formed from consolidated volcanic ash. It typically shows layering as larger heavier particles land first in each eruption (unlike ignimbrite). But every now and then it can show a much more distinctive banded pattern. This is sometimes due to patterns created when hot ash is welded, and sometimes a result of last-minute mixing of magma from different sources. The two never mix perfectly, and the result is that when the pyroclasts finally settle, they accumulate in layers reflecting the different mixes of magma. Such banded tuffs were found after the cataclysmic 1912 eruption of Novarupta in the Valley of 10,000 Smokes in Katmai, Alaska.

**Grain size**: Welded into glassy or amorphous mass
**Texture**: Said to be eutaxitic when it contains flammes (glassy pancakes of pumice)
**Structure**: Welding and mixing creates other bands
**Colour**: Grey to black, may be turned pink by weathering
**Composition**: Variable – usually from rhyolite or tachyte glass
**Formation**: Ashfalls and pyroclastic flows
**Notable occurrences**: Charnwood Forest (Leics), England; Mato Grosso, Brazil; Santa Cruz, California; Cripple Creek, Colorado; Katmai, Alaska

**Vesuvius and Pompeii**
Mount Vesuvius is one of the world's most famous volcanoes. There have been eight major eruptions so far, the most recent in 1906 and 1944. Vesuvius is a composite volcano typical of subduction zones, supplied by trachyte and andesite magma. Its explosive, Plinian-type eruptions send up towering columns of ash, pumice and bombs, which smother the surrounding area, or collapse to push out devastating pyroclastic flows. In the terrible eruption of AD79, witnessed by the Roman writer Pliny, pyroclastic surges incinerated the mountainside town of Herculaneum (original settlement shown in the foreground, above), while ashfall completely buried Pompeii, killing the inhabitants, but preserving their homes perfectly. The eruption was catastrophic, but Vesuvius is a small cone sitting in the caldera of Monte Somma, a giant volcano that erupted 35,000 years ago with a force that would make the Pompeii eruption seem a mere puff. Over 30,000km²/11,583 sq miles of the land around the Bay of Naples is Campanian ignimbrite, created in a vast pyroclastic flow in this eruption.

# Ignimbrite

No rock is created in such a rapid and dramatic way as ignimbrite. It is the rock that forms when pyroclastic flows and surges finally come to rest. Its name is Latin for 'fire cloud', and is very apt. Pyroclastic flows are clouds of glowing ash, cinders and hot gases that roar down from an eruption at jet plane speeds and temperatures of 450°C/842°F or more. Many flows are still so hot when they come to a halt and settle that volcanic fragments within them are instantly welded together. Towards the base of flows, the heat can squeeze pumice fragments flat to create pancake shapes called *flamme* (flames).

**Grain size**: Varied, mostly less than 2mm/0.08in
**Texture**: Like a fruitcake. Said to be eutaxitic when it contains flammes (glassy pancakes of pumice).
**Structure**: Large pebbles of pumice in finer mass of glass fragments. Sometimes shows flowbanding and layering; welding creates other bands.
**Colour**: Grey to bluish grey, may be turned pink by weathering
**Composition**: Variable – usually from rhyolite or tachyte glass
**Phenocrysts**: Feldspar
**Formation**: Pyroclastic flows
**Notable occurrences**: Widespread; Mount Vesuvius, Italy; Hunter Valley (New South Wales), Australia; Coromandel, New Zealand; Ria Loa, Chile; Mount St Helens, Washington

**Identification:** Ignimbrite has a distinctive dark fruitcake look, with its isolated phenocrysts and flammes of pumice, but can easily be mistaken for lava flow rock.

# Lithic tuff

Ash thrown out by volcanoes settles on the ground like falling snow, building up in drifts. At first, ash-fall is just loose dust. But in time, it packs down and becomes consolidated into a soft, porous solid rock called tuff. Sometimes lithification (turning to stone) is helped by the way glass in the ash is turned by the weather into clay and zeolite cement. Tuffs vary widely in texture and composition, and older tuffs have lost most of their original texture through recrystallization. They can be classified into three kinds according to the predominant fragments in the ash: 'lithic' tuffs, made mostly of chunks of broken rock; 'vitric' tuff, made mostly of shards of volcanic glass; and 'crystal' tuff, made mostly of small crystals such as feldspar, augite and hornblende. Most ash grains in tuff are less than 2mm/0.08in across, but tuff can also contain pebble-sized fragments called lapilli. Wind can scatter ash over huge distances, but lapilli land close to the volcano. Those falling close enough may be still hot enough to weld ash together, forming welded tuff.

**Identification**: Tuff is much softer than any other volcanic rock, easy to scratch with a knife. Although there may be visible crystals in new tuffs, they are very unevenly distributed and rather shapeless.

**Grain size**: Varied, mostly less than 2mm/0.08in
**Texture**: Like a dense sponge cake
**Structure**: Tuffs are usually layered, rather like sedimentary rocks with the heaviest particles that drop first in each ashfall at the base of each layer
**Colour**: Grey, black, very variable – older basaltic tuffs may be turned green as original minerals are altered to chlorite
**Composition**: Variable
**Minerals**: Variable
**Formation**: Ashfall and pyroclasts
**Notable occurrences**: Widespread, including Santorini, Greece

# VOLCANIC DEBRIS

*When explosive volcanoes erupt, 90 per cent of the solid material ejected is not lava but pyroclastic material. The word 'pyroclastic' means 'fire-broken'. Pyroclasts are fragments of old magma, fresh magma and basement rock shattered into ash, lapilli (stones) and bombs (boulders) – collectively called tephra – by the explosive force of the eruption and scattered far and wide around the volcano.*

## Lapilli

Lapilli are pyroclasts usually thrown out by explosive volcanic eruptions. Lapilli is Italian for 'little stones' and geologists define them as pyroclasts 4–64mm/0.17–2.5in across – in other words, between the size of a pea and that of a walnut. Anything larger is classified as a bomb; anything smaller is ash. Some lapilli are globules of fresh, liquid magma. Some are fragments of exploded magma. Some are fragments chipped off basement rock by the eruption. Globules of magma can sometimes cool and solidify into a teardrop shape as they fly through the air. Lapilli like these are called 'Pelée's tears', after the Hawaiian goddess of volcanoes. Pelée's tears often trail a thread of liquid lava that chills in midair into a golden brown hair-like filament called Pelée's hair. Occasionally, nut-sized pellets called accretionary lapilli build up like hailstones in a thundercloud, as layers of ash cling to a drop of water. Froth in felsic lavas like rhyolite makes pumice lapilli that bob on water for months. Basaltic lava froth makes heavier scoria cinders, but occasionally forms reticulites. Reticulites are 98 per cent air bubbles – even lighter than pumice but so fragile they sink as the bubbles break and take in water.

**Identification**: Lapilli are little, light, cinder-like stones, often found in layers of ash or scattered around the foot of volcanoes. They may be glassy like these.

**Size**: 4–64mm/0.17–2.5in
**Texture**: Usually glassy and vesicular – that is, containing gas bubbles. Silicic magmas typically produce pumiceous (pumice-like) lapilli. Basalt typically produces scoria lapilli or, occasionally, light air-filled reticulite.
**Colour**: Black, grey or brown
**Composition**: Varies according to parent lava
**Formation**: Pyroclasts from fresh magma
**Notable occurrences**: Cumbria, England; Stromboli, Mount Etna, Mount Vesuvius, Mount Vulture, Italy; Santorini, Greece; Toba, Tambora, Krakatoa, Indonesia; Citlaltépetl, Popocatépetl, Mexico; Kilauea Volcano, Mauna Loa, Hawaii; Yellowstone, Wyoming; Alamo, Texas

## Tephra

This name was coined by Icelandic vulcanologist Sigurdur Thorarinsson in the 1950s. It comes from the Ancient Greek for 'ash', but is a general word used to describe all pyroclastic material thrown into the air by a volcano, including ash, lapilli and bombs of all kinds. The term is used only for material that falls from the air, but excludes pyroclastic flow material. Unlike tuff, tephra is loose material and turns into solid rock tuff only when cemented together. It varies in composition from scoria-fall (cinder) deposits to pumice-fall deposits. Scoria-falls are erupted in Strombolian-type eruptions and consist of basaltic to andesitic pyroclasts falling fairly close to the volcanic vent. These Strombolian scoria falls are typically dark in colour. Pumice-falls are blasted out in Plinian-type eruptions and consist of dacitic to rhyolitic pyroclasts often scattered over vast areas. Plinian-type pumice-falls are typically light in colour.

**Identification**: Tephra is a blanket term to describe any fragment thrown out by a volcano. It can be cinders like these, or ash and pumice, glass beads, and reticulite, to huge bombs and blocks.

**Size**: Full range of sizes
**Texture**: Usually glassy and vesicular – that is, containing gas bubbles
**Structure**: Mixture of ash, lapilli and bombs, usually sorted into layers with largest particles at the base and finest at the top
**Colour**: Black, brown or grey
**Composition**: Varies according to parent lava
**Formation**: From falling pyroclasts
**Notable occurrences**: Many locations including: Surtsey, Hekla, Iceland; Stromboli, Mount Etna, Mount Vesuvius, Italy; Santorini, Greece; Toba, Tambora, Krakatoa, Indonesia; Citlaltépetl, Popocatépetl, Mexico; Yellowstone, Wyoming

## Blocks and bombs

Blocks and bombs are large fragments of pyroclastic material. Blocks are chunks of broken magma. Bombs are large blobs of molten magma. Big eruptions can hurl blocks heavier than a truck 1km/0.6 miles from the vent. They can fling smaller bombs 20km/12 miles or even 80km/50 miles – at speeds approaching 75–200m/s (250–650ft/s), faster than a bullet. Most land close to the volcano, though. Bombs and blocks are not as heavy as they look, because they are usually full of holes. Volcanic bombs are fluid as they fly through the air and take on various, quite diverse shapes, according to just how fluid they are. Some end up as long, flat ribbon bombs. Some are so fluid that they are streamlined by force of motion as they fly into spindle bombs. Viscous lava bombs solidify at the surface to create breadcrust bombs as gas bubbles in the liquid interior expand and crack the surface like (very) crusty bread. 'Cow-dung' bombs hit the ground still molten and spread out in pancakes. Bombs can form various kinds of rock when they land, including tuff breccia, made from 25–75 per cent bombs, pyroclastic breccia (over 75 per cent bombs and blocks), agglomerates (over 75 per cent bombs) and agglutinate (made from spatters of basaltic lava still molten when it hits the ground).

**Breadcrust bomb**: Breadcrust bombs are made from blobs of viscous lava that crack on the surface to look like crusty bread. They earn their bomb name by occasionally exploding in mid-air as internal gas bubbles expand.

**Grain size**: Greater than 64mm/2.5in
**Texture**: Usually glassy and vesicular – that is, containing gas bubbles
**Structure**: Varies according to the way it cools in the air or on the ground, from the gas expansion cracks on the surface of breadcrust bombs to the long hair-like trails of Pelée's hair
**Colour**: Black or brown
**Composition**: Varies according to parent lava
**Formation**: Pyroclasts from fresh magma form into tuff breccia, pyroclastic breccia, agglomerate and agglutinate
**Notable occurrences**: Stromboli, Mount Etna, Italy; Kluchevskoy, Tolbachinksky (Kamchatka), Russia; Mauna Loa, Hawaii; Vanuatu; Mount Lassen, California; Yellowstone, Wyoming; Craters of the Moon, Idaho; Red Bomb Crater, Oregon

**Perilous volcanic snow**
Glowing streams of molten lava can be awe-inspiring, but tephra is also very dangerous. Ash quickly chokes people to death and buries vast areas under deep deposits. Rooftops covered in ash may collapse, crushing anyone beneath. Ash can also be a hazard to aircraft, as seen in 1982 when Java's Gallungang erupted, nearly bringing down two jet airliners as ash clogged their engines. Ash has also caused famine as it destroys vegetation. In 1815, Indonesia's Tambora sent ash up to 1,300km/808 miles away, and 80,000 people died of famine. The distance that ash travels depends on the height of the eruption column, the air temperature, and the wind direction and strength. The Krakatoa eruption of 1883 (Indonesia, above) spread 800,000km²/308,882 sq miles of ash, and burned the clothes of people 80km/50 miles away. The Toba (Indonesia) eruption of 75,000 years ago deposited 10cm/4in of ash 3,000km/ 1,864 miles away in India!

## Block lava

Basalt lavas produce very fluid pahoehoe lava, which slurps along to freeze in rope-like coils, or more brittle, chunky *aa* lava. But more silicic lavas such as andesite and dacite produce a 'blocky' lava. Blocky lava is usually linked to stratovolcanoes with alternating layers of lava and pyroclasts. Lava flows from these volcanoes are very slow indeed, and the flow surface quickly congeals into a large rubble-like mass of blocks on top and at the front of the flow. The flow often follows narrow tongues called 'coulées' down the volcano, channelled by embankments or 'levées' of lava blocks either side. Rhyolite lavas are chunkier still and often develop dam-like ridges of blocks called ogives on the surface.

**Pahoehoe lava**: This fluid lava solidifies in rope-like coils from the hottest, most fluid basalt lava.

**Texture**: Chunky, angular blocks
**Structure**: Biggest, most angular chunks occur on the edges of the flow
**Colour**: Black, brown or grey
**Composition**: When andesitic: Silica (59% average), Iron and magnesium oxides (7.5%)
**Formation**: Andesite, dacite and rhyolite lava flows

**Block lava**: The surface of more viscous, silicic lava like andesite and dacite breaks into block-like chunks.

# ULTRAMAFIC ROCKS

*Ultramafic rocks are dark-coloured igneous rocks with even less silica than basalt, a lot of magnesium and iron, and made mostly of dark green or black olivines and pyroxenes. They form deep in the Earth's mantle and are usually brought to the surface in small quantities, often in masses no smaller than a fist or as large as a house, swept up as lumps in other magmas, or as the entire crust is uplifted by tectonic movements.*

## Picrite

**Identification**: Picrite is best identified by its setting, its dark green to black colour, its slightly shiny, sugary look and its even texture – not mottled like peridotite nor with plagioclase feldspar laths like dolerite (diabase), which are both often found with picrite.

Picrites are dark, heavy rocks rather similar to peridotite. Both form deep in the Earth's mantle, and both are rich in dark green olivine and brown augite. But while peridotite is often carried up into large intrusive masses, along with gabbro, norite and pyroxenite, picrite tends to be found in sills and intrusive sheets. Although picrite magma forms only under extreme pressures deep in the mantle, it is the one ultramafic rock that normally erupts on the surface as lava, as it did in the 1959 eruption of Kilauea in Hawaii. In this eruption, gigantic fire fountains shot out picrite lavas containing as much as 30 per cent olivine. Yet for picrite to erupt as lava like this, temperatures must be very high indeed – which is why it is often linked to hotspot volcanoes such as those in Hawaii.

Picrite is also often found in association with basalt as part of the ocean floor, which is why many of the best known occurrences of picrite are in ophiolites – chunks of the ocean floor brought to the surface by massive tectonic movements.

Occasionally, picrite can occur in substantial quantities in flood basalts, as it does in India's Deccan and South Africa's Karoo, but most flood basalts have a fairly low picrite content.

Picrite is very rich in magnesium and iron. Indeed, one definition of picrite is that it has at least 18 per cent magnesium oxide by weight. Komatiite is similar but has even less sodium and potassium oxide. Picrite's iron content can be so high that it is actually slightly magnetic. Some picrites, though, are especially rich in hornblende (see right). Others are especially rich in augite, like a few of those of Devon and Cornwall in England, which are sometimes called palaeopicrites because they formed well over half a billion years ago in the Palaeozoic era. Most picrites in this part of the world date more specifically to the Devonian period, 408–360 million years ago.

**Grain size**: Moderately fine-grained (salt-sized)
**Texture**: Granular
**Structure**: Evenly textured
**Colour**: Dark green to black
**Composition**: Silica (47% average), Alumina (10%), Calcium and sodium oxides (10%), Iron and magnesium oxides (31%)
**Minerals**: Olivine; Clinopyroxene (augite); Orthopyroxene (enstatite); Biotite mica; Hornblende; Plagioclase feldspar
**Accessories**: Apatite, melilite, sphene, biotite, spinel, hornblende
**Phenocrysts**: Green olivine or red brown augite
**Formation**: In extrusive lavas at mid-ocean ridges and hotspots, dykes and sills. Appears in ophiolites and flood basalt lava plateaux.
**Notable occurrences**: Rhum (Hebrides), Inchcolm Island, Midland Valley, Scotland; Devon, Cornwall, Sark (Channel Islands), England; Wicklow, Ireland; Nassau, Fichtelberg, Germany; Troodos, Cyprus; Gran Canaria; Oman; Madagascar; Karoo, South Africa; Deccan, India; Dongwhazi, Kunlun, China; Tasmania; Hawaii; Yellowstone, Wyoming; Klamath Mts, California; Oregon; Hudson River; Alabama; Montana

**Hornblende picrite**: The minerals in picrite often decompose quite quickly. Olivine is replaced by green, yellow and red fibres of serpentine, while augite is replaced by chlorite or hornblende. Only hornblende remains unaltered, creating hornblende picrite. Many ancient picrites are like this, such as those found in Gwynedd and Anglesey in Wales and on Sark in the English Channel Islands.

# Pyroxenite

Like picrite and peridotite, pyroxenite is an ultramafic rock formed from magmas that develop deep in the Earth's mantle. What makes pyroxenite different from these rocks – though similar to wehrlite and clinopyroxenite – is that it contains a high proportion of clinopyroxene (usually the mineral augite, clinopyroxenite) or orthopyroxene (enstatite or hypersthene, orthopyroxenite), at the expense of olivine. Sometimes, pyroxenites are inclusions in other magmas, and look rather like obsidian: shiny black and fracturing into the same sharp, conchoidal (curved) fragments. Pyroxenites rarely occur alone. Very often, they form layered complexes with other plutonic (deep-forming) igneous rocks such as gabbro and norite. In the Bushveld complex of South Africa, for instance, gabbro, norite and pyroxenite layers are interwoven, with more pyroxenite layers at the base and more gabbro layers at the top. Occasionally pyroxenite-like rocks may form when certain limestones are altered by contact with hot magma, but these are more properly called pyroxene hornfels.

**Identification**: Pyroxenites are very much plutonic, which means they are almost entirely coarse-grained, often containing individual crystals several centimetres long. They are hard to distinguish from similar dunites, hornblendites, and melilitites, except by laboratory tests.

**Grain size**: Medium to coarse
**Texture**: Granular
**Structure**: May be layered
**Colour**: Green to black
**Composition**: Silica (47% average), Alumina (10%), Calcium and sodium oxides (10%), Iron and magnesium oxides (31%)
**Minerals**: Clinopyroxene (augite); Orthopyroxene (enstatite, bronzite, hypersthene); Olivine; Biotite mica; Chromite; Hornblende
**Accessories**: Plagioclase, chromite, spinel, garnet, iron oxides, rutile, scapolite
**Phenocrysts**: Green olivine or red brown augite, orthopyroxene
**Formation**: Small intrusions such as stocks and dykes and in bands in layered gabbro
**Notable occurrences**: Shetland Islands, Scotland; Saxony, Germany; Bushveld complex, S Africa; New Zealand; Cortlandt (Hudson River), North Carolina

## Ophiolites

The problem with learning about the oceanic crust is that it is so inaccessible. But in places segments of the crust have been heaved up by tectonic movements and incorporated into mountains. These segments are called ophiolites, and although rarely complete they afford a rich opportunity to study the ocean crust and its material. They are quite literally a slice through the ocean crust, and always tend to have the same layers. At the top is a blanket of sediment less than 1km/0.6 mile thick, composed of clay grains and dead plankton. Beneath this is a layer of basalt pillow lavas, sitting on sheets of gabbro dykes. Further down are more gabbros along with norite and olivine-rich gabbro. Further down still (3–4.75km/2–3 miles) are layers of chromite-rich dunite, wehrlite, peridotite and pyroxenite. At the base is an unlayered agglomeration of serpentinized peridotite with dunite, harzburgite and olivine pyroxenite. There are famous ophiolites at Troodos in Cyprus. Others are at Josephine County in Oregon.

Pelagic sediments
Basalt pillow lavas
Gabbro sheeted dikes and sills
Serpentinite
Harzburgite
Lherzolite

# Melilitite and nephelinite

These deep-forming ultramafic rocks are often linked to hot spots and rifts, where material from deep down is brought to the surface. They are typically 'coughed up' from the mantle as xenoliths, masses in other magmas, and probably form when mafic magmas mix with peridotite. Although they are rare, they are found all over the world. They are both highly alkaline, like carbonatite, lamprophyre and kimberlite. Nephelinite is essentially nepheline and clinopyroxene, plus olivine and iron and titanium oxides. Melilitite is basically the same and there is a gradation between the two, but melilitite has the mineral melilite instead of nepheline.

**Grain size**: Medium to coarse
**Texture**: Granular
**Structure**: May be layered
**Colour**: Green, dark green to black
**Composition**: Silica (less than 42% average), Alumina (15%), Calcium and sodium oxides (17.5%), Iron and magnesium oxides (18.5%)
**Minerals**: Feldspathoid (nepheline or melilite); Clinopyroxene (augite); Olivine; Perovskite
**Phenocrysts**: Green olivine or red-brown augite
**Formation**: Both intrusive and extrusive, forming xenoliths, lava or pyroclasts at hot spot and rift volcanoes
**Notable occurrences**: Umbria, Italy; Rhine, Germany; East Greenland; Ol Doinyo Lengai, Tanzania; Western Cape, S Africa; Tasmania; Amazon; Sword Mount (Washington Co), Maryland

**Identification**: Melilitite is almost as evenly dark as basalt, but the grains are coarse enough to be visible. It is often found in kimberlites or with carbonatites.

# OLIVINE-RICH ROCKS and CARBONATITE

*Some igneous rocks formed deep in the mantle are especially rich in the green mineral olivine, which is one of the most common minerals on Earth, though most of it is in the mantle rather than in the crust. These rocks are brought up as xenoliths in other magmas, or form in lower parts of the sea floor or near the surface in small quantities as they separate from hot magmas, like those over hotspots and at rifts.*

## Peridotite

Peridotite is one of the main materials of the upper mantle, and both basaltic and gabbroic magma are thought to be produced by the melting of peridotite in the mantle. So ultimately, mantle peridotite is the source of most of the material that makes up the rocks of the Earth's crust. Laboratory tests have shown that if peridotite is heated to melting point, the melt is basalt. Partial melting seems to give picrites and komatiites.

Some peridotites appear low down in ophiolite complexes, layered along with pyroxenite. Others seem to accumulate at the bottom of gabbro intrusions when olivines crystallize and settle out. A few peridotites are squeezed upwards in deep volcanic pipes. Rare chunks of peridotite reach the surface as solid lumps, swept up as xenoliths in liquid magma – spinel peridotites in basalt, basanite, nephelinite and occasionally andesite, and garnet peridotites in kimberlites and lamproites.

Peridotite is the least siliceous of all the igneous rocks, with less than 46 per cent silica by weight, and contains almost no feldspar. So it is a very dark coloured rock, with small pale green crystals of olivine set in a mass of dark pyroxene and hornblende. There are actually several varieties of peridotite. Besides olivine, lherzolite contains both clinopyroxene (augite) and orthopyroxene (enstatite); wehrlite contains only clinopyroxene; harzburgite contains only orthopyroxene.

A special form of peridotite called kimberlite is, with related lamproite, the world's only primary source of diamonds (see Kimberlites and lamproites, right). But other peridotites are major sources of nickel and chromium minerals, platinum and talc, and chrysotile asbestos, too. In warm, humid places, peridotite has weathered to soils rich in iron, nickel, cobalt and chromium, which may one day be exploited as ores on a large scale.

**Identification**: Peridotite is a dark green to black, medium to coarse grained rock that looks rather like sugar stained with a dark green engine oil. Often it is studded with small pale green balls of olivine, or more rarely with red garnets.

**Grain size**: Medium to coarse (sugar-sized)
**Texture**: Granular. Frequently poikilitic, which means small round crystals (of pale green olivine) embedded in large irregular masses (of pyroxene and hornblende). Rarely porphyritic.
**Structure**: May be layered
**Colour**: Dull green to black
**Composition**: Silica (44–45.5%), Alumina (2–4%), Calcium and sodium oxides (4–6%), Iron and magnesium oxides (41–49%)
**Minerals**: *Wehrlite*: Olivine; Clinopyroxene (augite); *Lherzolite*: Olivine; Clinopyroxene (augite); Orthopyroxene (enstatite) *Harzburgite*: Olivine; Orthopyroxene (enstatite)
**Minor and accessory minerals**: Biotite mica, hornblende, chromite, garnet, picotite, corundum, platinum, awaruite
**Formation**: Interlayered with other ultramafic rocks in ophiolite complexes; settled out of gabbroic intrusions; in volcanic pipes, dykes and other small intrusions; and as xenoliths in basalt
**Notable occurrences**: Lizard (Cornwall), England; Anglesey, Wales; Skye, Ayrshire, Scotland; Harzburg, Odenwald, Silesia, Germany; Lherz (Pyrenees), France; Hungary; Norway; Finland; New Zealand; New York; Maryland

Garnet

**Garnet peridotite**: Most peridotite has traces of garnet or spinel, but sometimes, especially in lherzolite, small crystals can form like cherries in a bun. Some are big enough to chip out as gems. Garnet and spinel peridotites, or rather lherzolites, are found as xenoliths in basaltic rocks and kimberlites, and are thought to form in the upper mantle.

## Dunite

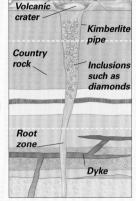

This rock is a kind of peridotite that is almost pure olivine. When freshly exposed it is olive green like olivine. But it gets its name from Mount Dun, the dun-coloured mountain in New Zealand, because dunite turns brown when weathered. Although some is formed in the mantle and appears in ophiolite complexes, much of it forms when olivine crystallizes out and sinks to the bottom of an intrusion of basic magma like gabbro. It is rich in a number of rare minerals, and is the world's major source of chromium ore.

**Identification**: Dunite is almost pure olivine, so when fresh it has a distinctive green colour as well as sugary texture. More usually though it is a tan brown, the colour it turns when exposed to the air.

**Grain size**: Medium to coarse (sugar-sized)
**Texture**: Granular
**Structure**: May be layered
**Colour**: Dull green, weathering to brown
**Composition**: Silica (41%), Alumina (2%), Calcium and sodium oxides (1%), Iron and magnesium oxides (54.5%)
**Minerals**: Olivine; Clinopyroxene (augite); Orthopyroxene (enstatite)
**Minor minerals**: Chromite, magnetite, ilmenite, pyrrhotite, pyroxene
**Formation**: At the base of gabbro intrusions or in the mantle
**Notable occurrences**: Lizard (Cornwall), England; Anglesey, Wales; Skye, Ayrshire, Scotland; Harzburg, Odenwald, Silesia, Germany; Lherz (Pyrenees), France; Hungary; Norway; Finland; New Zealand; New York; Maryland

## Carbonatite

Almost all volcanic activity involves magmas based on silicates, so the existence of igneous rocks containing over 50 per cent carbonates is surprising. When first discovered in the early 20th century, these carbonate rocks, called carbonatites, were thought by geologists to be simply limestones moulded by the heat of silicate magmas, especially as many carbonatites occur interleaved with silicate rocks in volcanic structures called complexes. In fact, carbonatites originate as magmas in the mantle, just like other magmas. They are the coolest of all magmas, melting at just 540°C/1,004°F (compared to over 1,100°C/2,012°F for basalt), and carbonatite lavas look like liquid mud. Carbonatites are forcing geologists to rethink their understanding of mantle processes and magma production. There are 350 or so known carbonatite intrusions, over half of them in Africa. Most are quite small and occur beneath volcanoes, interweaving with formations of other magmas to create complexes. Even more surprisingly, there are a few places in the East African Rift Valley, and at Kaiserstuhl in the Rhine, where carbonatites have erupted on the surface. In 1960, it was realized that Oldoinyo Lengai in Tanzania is actually a carbonatite volcano.

**Identification**: Carbonatite often looks just like marble. It is the only white or even light grey igneous rock, and it is often possible to distinguish it from marble only by the place where it occurs and by complex laboratory tests.

**Grain size**: Medium to fine
**Texture**: Granular
**Colour**: White to grey (Sövite), cream/yellow (Beforsite), yellow-brown (Ferro-carbonatite)
**Composition**: Over 50% carbonates (<3% silicates)
**Minerals**: Calcite (Sövite carbonatite); Dolomite (Beforsite carbonatite) or Ankerite (Ferro-carbonatite). Plus apatite, phlogopite, aegerine, magnetite
**Accessory minerals**: Many
**Trace elements**: Includes barium, zircon, niobium, molybdenum, yttrium
**Formation**: Intrusions in complexes with ijolites, syenites, fenites; eruptions of lava and ash with nephelinites
**Notable occurrences**: *Intrusions*: Fen, Norway; Kola, Russia; Loolekop, S Africa; Okurusu, Namibia; Ambar Dongar, India; Bayan Obo, Mongolia; Jacupiranga, Brazil; Oka, Quebec; Mountain P, CA *Volcanoes*: Kaiserstuhl (Rhine), Germany; Kerimasi, Mosonik, Shombole, Oldoinyo Lengai, East African Rift Valley

# SYENITES

*Unlike granites and their cousins, the syenites contain little or no quartz, but neither do they have large amounts of mafic minerals like peridotite and gabbro. Together, the syenites and their cousins make up a group called the alkaline igneous rocks, many of which are rich in feldspathoids, or 'foids', such as nepheline. The small amounts of mafic minerals they do contain are often in beautiful blues or greens.*

## Syenite

The name syenite was originally coined by the famous Roman scholar Pliny to describe the beautiful granite-like rocks quarried by the Ancient Egyptians at Syene (Aswan) on the Nile. In fact, these rocks are granite, and not syenite. But in the 18th century, the great German mineralogist A G Werner applied the term to some similar-looking rocks he found near Dresden, and the name now applies to igneous rocks like these.

The syenites are plutonic rocks that form massive intrusions rather like granite and, unlike the 'foid' syenites, are similarly rich in potassium feldspars. But syenites contain very much less quartz than granite. In fact, as the quartz content goes up they merge into granites, and since granites and syenites often form in the same places, quartz-rich syenites are hard to distinguish from quartz-poor granites.

Syenites are the underground equivalent of trachyte and are rich in alkali feldspars such as microcline and orthoclase. The orthoclase is white or pink and forms half the rock. So syenites, like the other alkaline igneous rocks, are all very light in colour – unlike mafic rocks that are low in quartz, such as basalt and peridotite, which are all dark.

Other minerals within syenites can make them among the most colourful and beautiful of igneous rocks, often displaying a shimmering iridescence when cut and polished. This is why they are such popular ornamental stones. Sodalite gives a lavender-blue tinge to soda syenite, while green aegerine can make aegerine syenite green. Syenites can sometimes be distinguished from granites because they contain dark blue needles of amphibole, while granite contains black prism-shaped amphiboles or micas.

Syenites are divided into three main kinds, according to which dark, ferromagnesian (iron and magnesium) mineral predominates – augite, hornblende or biotite mica. The Larvik area of southern Norway is famous for its beautiful rainbow-sheened red or grey augite syenites called larvikites or 'blue pearl granite', which are often used for pillars and facades. Similar rocks are found in the Sawtooth Mountains of Texas.

**Sodalite syenite**: Like granites, syenites can be divided into those in which the feldspars are mainly potash (potassium) or soda (sodium). Sodalite syenites such as pulaskite and nordmarkite are often perthitic, which means the sodium feldspar, mainly albite, intergrows with potash feldspar and gradually replaces it. Sodalite syenite can often be identified by lavender-blue specks of the feldspathoid sodalite.

**Cancrinite syenite**: This contains more of the feldspathoid mineral cancrinite than other syenites.

**Grain size**: Phaneritic (coarse- to medium-grained). Can be pegmatitic.
**Texture**: Usually even grains, but can often be porphyritic
**Structure**: Often contains drusy cavities. Feldspars are can be perthitic – that is, they have intergrowths of potassium and sodium feldspar. May have veins of white albite.
**Colour**: Light red, pink, grey or white
**Composition**: Silica (59.5% average), Alumina (17%), Calcium and sodium oxides (11%), Iron and magnesium oxides (8%), Potassium oxides (5%).
**Minerals**: Potassium feldspar (microcline, orthoclase); Plagioclase feldspar (albite, oligoclase, andesine); Biotite mica; Amphibole (hornblende); Pyroxene (augite). Can contain up to 10% quartz before it becomes granite.
**Accessories**: Sphene, apatite, zircon, magnetite, pyrites, plus feldspathoids nepheline, sodalite, cancrinite, feklichevite and leucite. Larger quantities of these grade the rocks towards 'foid' syenites.
**Phenocrysts**: Potassium feldspar, diopside, plagioclase
**Formation**: Stocks, dykes and small intrusions, or interwoven with granites in large intrusions
**Notable occurrences**: Larvik, Norway; Saxony, Germany; Alps, Switzerland; Piedmont, Italy; Azores; Kovdor Massif (Kola Peninsula), Russia; Ilmaussaq, Greenland; Pilanesburg (Bushveld complex), South Africa; Alaska; Dharwar, India; Montregian Hills, Quebec; White Mountains, Vermont; Sawtooth Mountains, Texas; Arkansas; Montana

# Nepheline or 'foid' syenites

Unlike ordinary syenites, the nepheline syenites contain no quartz whatsoever. Instead, they contain nepheline or another feldspathoid, or 'foid', such as sodalite or leucite – and the presence of quartz and these feldspathoids is mutually exclusive. Nepheline syenites are the intrusive equivalent of phonolite.

**Foyaite**: Grey, green or red nepheline syenite with a lot of microcline.

They are actually quite rare, and may form when soda-rich syenites and granites are altered in the melt, rather than forming distinct magmas. They often occur in ring dykes, and where granite magmas come into contact with limestones. There are many varieties of nepheline syenite, each with its own characteristics, including pink laurdalites from Laurdal in Norway, black mica-speckled miaskite from Miask in the Russian Urals, and nepheline-rich litchfieldite from Litchfield in Maine. But most come under the heading foyaites, after Foya in southern Portugal. The foyaites' odd chemistry means many rare minerals have been found in them, including eudialyte, eukolite, mosandrite, rinkite and lavenite.

**Identification**: Nepheline is often grey and can look like quartz, so it's easy to mistake nepheline syenite for granite or ordinary syenite. But nepheline syenite may have flow streaks and clots of dark minerals. And while quartz stays smooth on weathered surfaces, nepheline is pitted. The more nepheline there is, the greener it becomes. Blue sodalite and yellow cancrinite traces help to confirm the identity.

**Grain size**: Phaneritic (coarse). Can be pegmatitic.
**Texture**: Usually even grains, but often porphyritic
**Structure**: Flow streaks and clots of dark minerals
**Colour**: Usually grey, pink or yellow but can be greenish
**Composition**: Silica (42% av), Alumina (15%), Calcium & sodium oxides (17%), Iron & magnesium oxides (18.5%), Potassium oxides (5%)
**Minerals**: Potassium feldspar (orthoclase, microcline); Plagioclase (albite, oligoclase); Nepheline; Biotite; Hornblende; Pyroxene (augite, aegerine)
**Accessories**: Sphene, apatite, zircon, magnetite, pyrites, plus sodalite, cancrinite & leucite
**Phenocrysts**: Nepheline, albite
**Formation**: Stocks, ring dykes and small intrusions, with granites and syenites
**Notable occurrences**: Fen, Laurdal, Norway; Alnd I, Sweden; Foya, Portugal; Turkmenistan; Ilomba, Ulundi, Junguni, Malawi; Tasmania; Sierra de Tingua, Brazil; Quebec; White Mts, VT; Beemerville, NJ; Magnet C, AR

---

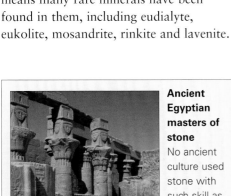

**Ancient Egyptian masters of stone**

No ancient culture used stone with such skill as the Ancient Egyptians. The land is blessed with many superb stones for construction and carving, including monzonite, black and red granite, quartzite, limestone, sandstone and graywacke (siltstone). Red granite quarried at Syeneh Aswan (pictured above) was cut in single giant blocks for obelisks. Quartzite quarried at Gebelein was used for the famous Colossi of Memnon. Limestone from Tura, Beni Hassan and Ma'asa was used for the first pyramid, Djoser's. The Egyptians had a knowledge of geology and geological strata well beyond any culture of the time – and unmatched until recently. They were also amazingly skilled at cutting and shaping the stones. No-one knows quite how they did, since, strangely, stone-working does not appear in hieroglyphics. Some think they cut stones with copper saws, or bronze wire held in a bow. Others think they used emery stone.

# Monzonite

Monzonite gets its name from Monzoni in the Italian Tyrol. Like syenite, it is a plutonic rock that contains some, but not a lot of, quartz, and lies between the foids and the granites. In fact, it is actually what some geologists describe as the 'average' igneous rock, containing equal amounts of potassium and plagioclase feldspar, and lying halfway between the most acid and the most basic rocks in composition. Although by no means a rare rock, it only occurs in small masses, associated with and perhaps blending into gabbro and, at the margins of an intrusion, pyroxenite. There are three kinds of monzonite, depending on the presence of quartz, nepheline or olivine. Quartz monzonite is found in many mountain belts, and because it is such a tough rock often forms dramatic landforms.

**Identification**: Monzonite is light coloured like granite but contains less quartz.

**Grain size**: Medium
**Texture**: Irregular plates of orthoclase embedded in plagioclase
**Structure**: Crystals often have zones of different chemical composition
**Colour**: Dark grey
**Composition**: Silica (58.5% av), Alumina (17%), Calcium & sodium oxides (11%), Iron & magnesium oxides (9%), Potassium oxides (3%)
**Minerals**: Potassium feldspar (orthoclase); Plagioclase feldspar (labradorite, oligoclase); Pyroxene (augite, hypersthene, bronzite); Hornblende; Quartz, Nepheline or olivine; Biotite
**Accessories**: Apatite, zircon, magnetite, pyrites
**Phenocrysts**: Apatite, augite, orthoclase
**Formation**: Stocks, dykes and intrusions
**Notable occurrences**: Kentallen (Argyll), Scotland; Norway; Monzoni, Italy; Sakhalin Is, Russia; Yogo Peak (yogoite), Beaver Crk, Montana; Black Canyon, Colorado (quartz monzonite)

# PLUTONIC ROCKS: GRANITE

*Granites are by far the most common of all the plutonic rocks, rocks that form deep underground as giant batholiths, tens or even thousands of kilometres across. Although granites form only deep underground, they are often seen on the surface because their high quartz content makes them so tough they may survive long after softer rock around them has been worn away by weathering.*

## Granite

Granite lasts. Long after other rocks have crumbled away, intrusions of granite stand proud, like islands above the sea. The pointing finger of Rio's Sugar Loaf mountain, the sheer cliffs of Yosemite's El Capitan and the wild wastes of England's Dartmoor all stand testament to granite's ability to endure. For all these eminences are batholiths – huge intrusions of magma that formed entirely underground, and have simply been exposed through erosion of overlying rocks. The moors of Cornwall and Devon are all just knobs on a single large batholith that will, in 100 million years' time, be thoroughly denuded just as the moors are now.

Granite batholith complexes can be huge. The Patagonian batholith underlying the southern Andes is 1,900km/935 miles long and up to 65km/40 miles wide. That underlying the Sierra Nevada is almost as vast. In fact, there are giant granite batholiths underlying most of the world's great mountain ranges, both ancient, such as the Appalachians of North America, and recent, such as the Himalayas. Indeed, granite is always closely linked to mountain building, and the margins of continents where subduction is going on.

Although the bulk of granite is in batholiths, it can also form dykes and sills, and veins and intrusions of one granite can cut across another. Granite intrusions frequently interweave with country rocks, changing them where they come into contact. In many places, granite blends imperceptibly into metamorphic granite gneisses. Granite intrusions engulf lumps of country rock, which become xenoliths, often partly altering them on the surface at least.

Granite is a light-coloured, speckled rock and is very 'acidic' – that is, it has a high silica content (at least 70 per cent), and a high proportion of quartz (at least 20 per cent). It is essentially a mix of white or pink feldspar, pale quartz and small specks of black muscovite mica. Because it forms by cooling slowly deep underground, crystals in granite are almost invariably large enough to be visible to the naked eye. Most are at least a few millimetres. The largest white feldspar crystals can be prisms up to 20cm/8in long.

*Feldspar*

**White granite**: Granites all have soft black flakes of mica, the first to crumble from weathered surfaces. They all have pale crystals of quartz, too, and this never crumbles. It is the large feldspar crystals that typically give the colour varieties.

**Pink granite**: Most granites are light grey or pinkish in colour, but can also be dark grey or red. They are light grey if they are dominated by a white alkali feldspar, but pink or red if their alkali feldspar is pink or red. If there are both white and pink feldspars, the pink one is likely to be alkali feldspar and the white one is likely to be plagioclase.

**Grain size**: Phaneritic (coarse-grained); often pegmatitic
**Texture**: Normally granular, with large visible crystals and often porphyritic with large phenocrysts
**Structure**: Typically uniform, but may be banded. Xenoliths are common. Near the crown of batholiths, may be cracked into massive rectangular blocks.
**Colour**: Usually light coloured – mottled white, grey, pink or red, with black specks
**Chemical composition**: Silica (72% average), Alumina (14.5%), Calcium and sodium oxides (4.5%), Iron and magnesium oxides (less than 3.5%)
**Minerals**: Quartz; Potassium feldspar (microcline) and plagioclase feldspar (oligoclase); Mica; Hornblende
**Accessories**: Aegerine, zircon, apatite, magnetite, amphibole or pyroxene
**Phenocrysts**: Quartz, orthoclase and oligoclase feldspar, hornblende, biotite mica, augite
**Formation**: Intrusive: batholiths, stocks, bosses, sills, dykes
**Notable occurrences**: Syenogranite: Donegal, Ireland; Cairngorms, Scotland; northern Nigeria; Réunion Islands; Azores Islands; Canary Islands; Sugar Loaf Mountain (Rio de Janeiro), Brazil; Appalachian Mountains. Monzogranite: Cornwall, Devon, Lake District, England; Baltic shield, Finland and Sweden; Massif Central, France; Spain; Tatra Mts, Slovakia; Barrens, Newfoundland. Granodiorite: Andes; Rocky Mountains. Leucogranites: Himalayan Mountains.

**The granite problem**

Just how the world's giant granite batholiths formed has been the subject of fierce debate since the 18th century. The great Austrian geologist Eduard Suess could see they formed after the surrounding country rocks but, if so, how was such an enormous volume of granite accommodated? This 'room' problem has been at the heart of the controversy ever since.

In the mid-20th century, thinking developed into two opposing camps – the granitizers and the magmatists. The granitizers, like Doris Reynolds, believed that granite was formed when existing country rock is granitized (changed to granite) by 'metasomatic' processes. It all involved gases or fluids which came to be called 'ichor' after the lifeblood of the Greek gods. The idea was that country rock was metasomatized (altered) to granite by ichor emanating through it. That way, there was no 'room' problem. Magmatists, such as Norman Bowen, on the other hand, believed that granite formed from magma, not altered country rock. The magma was created at depth by the partial melting or 'anatexis' of the country rocks above.

Gradually, field observation of rock formations and laboratory experiments with melting rocks came down firmly on the side of the magmatists, and it is now widely accepted that most granites do indeed form by partial melting.

The theory is that it all takes place in the later stages of mountain building, as two tectonic plates crunch together. The collision not only buckles the plate edges to throw up mountain ranges, but also eventually creates such extreme pressures and temperatures that huge volumes of the mountain roots partially melt to create granite magma.

These hot granite melts are lighter than the rocks above, and so well up into them, like a blob of hot oil in a lava lamp, creating their own space. As they ascend they begin to cool and solidify, eventually turning to solid rock again.

Although the magmatists appear to have won this particular round of The Granite Problem, the controversy is by no means over. If granites do form by partial melting, for instance, then just which rocks have melted to form granite? Moreover, even among those who believed granite was a

magma, there were always those who believed that it formed not directly by melting of other rocks, but from basalt magmas changed gradually to granite as some chemicals crystallized and others didn't, a process known as fractional crystallization.

The evidence is that most continental granites – the great batholiths under mountains – do form by partial melting. But fractional crystallization may play a part in granites such as tonalites, which form in oceanic locations such as island arcs.

## Granite varieties

**Granophyre or porphyric microgranite**: At the edges of intrusions, in thin intrusions and pegmatite, granite grains can be small. These microgranites often have phenocrysts of feldspar formed earlier and are related to graphic granites.

Granite and granite-like rocks, called granitoids, come in so many subtly different varieties they have proved a nightmare to classify. One method is according to the balance of Quartz, Alkali Feldspar and Plagioclase feldspar (QAP) in their make-up. In the middle lies monzogranite in which alkali and plagioclase feldspar are fairly even. Syenogranite has more alkali feldspar, granodiorite has less. The extremes are alkali-rich alkali feldspar granite and plagioclase-rich tonalite. After the discovery that magmas making granites in eastern Australia came from both sedimentary and igneous rocks, and contained xenoliths of either type, geologists developed an 'alphabetic' way of dividing granites. I-type granites, rich in biotite mica and maybe hornblende, have a chemical make-up that implies they were formed from mafic igneous rocks. S-types, rich in both biotite and muscovite mica (plus garnet, cordierite and sillimanite), have a make-up that implies a sedimentary origin. M-types have a make-up implying they came from Earth's mantle. A-types have a make-up implying they are anorogenic – that is, they formed not in areas of mountain building but near hot spots and rifts.

**Graphic granite**: Graphic granite is an extraordinary kind of granite that occurs in pegmatites. The entire rock is one large crystal of pale feldspar, typically microcline. Embedded in the feldspar are thin wedge-shaped growths of quartz, giving an effect that looks like the cuneiform writing of Ancient Sumeria. It is thought that both the feldspar and the quartz formed at the same time.

*Quartz*    *Feldspar*

**GRANITE VARIETIES**

**Alkali feldspar granite**: Granite with a very high proportion of alkali feldspar and almost no plagioclase

**Biotite granite**: Granite containing up to 20% biotite mica

**Flaser granite**: Granite-like gneiss, which has flattened feldspar crystals giving it a foliated look

**Augite granite**: Granite rich in dark augite

**Tourmaline granite**: Granite rich in black tourmaline

**Leucogranite**: Light-coloured granite with less than 30% of the norm for mafic minerals

**Melanogranite**: Dark-coloured granite with more than 30% of the norm for mafic minerals

**Granite gneiss**: Gneiss formed from a sedimentary or metamorphic rock and with the same mineral composition as granite

**Peralkaline granite**: Granite rich in alkaline feldspars and also alkaline amphiboles and pyroxenes such as aegerine and riebeckite

# GRANITOIDS

*There are many varieties of granite and granitoids (granite-like rocks). Some form only small patches within other granite outcrops, such as rapakivi granite and orbicular granite, with their highly distinctive round markings. Others, such as granodiorite and tonalite, have their own particular chemical and mineral make-ups and are individual rock types in their own right.*

## Rapakivi granites

Rapakivi granites get their name from the Finnish for 'rotten rock' because they weather easily. They are granites – usually syenogranites – with an unusual grain pattern called rapakivi texture. In rapakivi texture, large, oval crystals of alkali feldspar such as sanidine are encased in a plagioclase feldspar such as albite. The alkali feldspar forms first, then is enveloped by a 'reaction rim' of plagioclase as it reacts with the surrounding magma. One theory is that alkali feldspars from rhyolite magma react with plagioclase from basaltic magma as the two magmas mix. Another is that the effect occurs as pressure drops in a rising magma. Some geologists believe that the conditions for rapakivis occurred along continental rifts that never quite developed. Rapakivi granites dating back 1,100 to 1,800 million years are found in a belt stretching right across Finland, Sweden and the Baltic to Labrador and the American south-west. They also occur in Brazil and Venezuela, and small pockets of more recent rapakivis are widely scattered.

**Identification**: Rapakivi granite is distinctive, with its pale rounds of feldspar embedded in a dark groundmass of mica, hornblende and quartz. When cut and polished, as here, rapakivi makes a popular decorative stone.

**Grain size**: Mixed
**Texture**: Oval feldspar phenocrysts up to 2cm/0.8in across embedded in a groundmass of small crystals
**Structure**: Typically uniform
**Colour**: Pink or tan K feldspar crystals rimmed with white albite in a dark groundmass
**Chemical composition**: Silica (72% average), Alumina (14.5%), Calcium and sodium oxides (4.5%), Iron and magnesium oxides (3.5%)
**Minerals**: Quartz; Potassium feldspar (sanidine) and plagioclase feldspar (albite); Mica
**Phenocrysts**: Usually alkali feldspar, but can be quartz or plagioclase feldspar
**Formation**: In syenogranites
**Notable occurrences**: S Finland; SE Sweden; St Petersburg, Russia; Estonia; Poland; Brazil; Venezuela; Labrador; Ontario; Maine; US mid-west and south-west

## Orbicular granite

Occasionally, granites may contain small patches with an unusual texture called orbicular granite. This looks a little like rapakivi, but the balls, or 'orbicules', are bigger and they are not phenocrysts, but formations that develop around cores of foreign material in the magma. Each core may be a grain of another igneous rock (a small xenolith), but could also be a grain of granite. Alternating layers of pale feldspar and dark biotite or hornblende grow around the core, a process called 'rhythmic crystallization' in which first one mineral crystallizes then another as conditions change in the magma.

**Identification**: Orbicular granites are masses only a few metres across, and are easy to identify with their black and white rounds.

**Grain size**: Mixed
**Texture**: Large round orbicules 2–15cm/0.8–6in across embedded in a groundmass of small crystals
**Structure**: Typically uniform
**Colour**: Black and white layered phenocrysts in a light grey groundmass
**Chemical composition**: Silica (72% average), Alumina (14.5%), Calcium and sodium oxides (4.5%), Iron and magnesium oxides (3.5%)
**Minerals**: Quartz; Potassium feldspar (microcline) and plagioclase feldspar (oligoclase); Mica
**Notable occurrences**: Finland; Sweden; Waldviertel, Austria; Riesengebirge, Poland; Japan; New Zealand; Peru; Vermont

# Granodiorite

Granodiorite is the intrusive equivalent of dacite and is the most abundant of all the granitoid rocks. It is very similar to granite but contains more plagioclase feldspar, and more mafic minerals (usually biotite and hornblende). In fact, granodiorite and granite often occur together, along with diorite, which contains even more plagioclase. In large batholiths, for instance, a single granodiorite magma may develop a granite heart and a skin of diorite or even tonalite, as minerals separate out in a particular way from the magma. This kind of process tends to happen only in large batholiths though. Where granite, granodiorite and diorite are all found in a smaller intrusion, the chances are they all came from separate magmas. Granitoid rocks such as granodiorite often occur in 'suites' – repeated associations of particular similar rocks. Granodiorite, for instance, is found in ancient, Archean formations along with tonalite and trondheimite. These TTG suites are among the world's oldest rocks, dating back more than two billion years, and are found all around the world, in places such as Lapland in Scandinavia, and the Big Horn Mountains of Wyoming.

**Identification**: Granodiorite is generally grey, and looks quite like granite, but it contains a higher proportion of dark minerals such as biotite mica and hornblende. Granite looks basically light grey with black specks. In granodiorite the grey and the black are more evenly balanced, giving a 'salt-and-pepper' look.

**Grain size**: Phaneritic (coarse)
**Texture**: Even texture; often porphyritic
**Structure**: Typically uniform
**Colour**: Black and white with pink potassium feldspar
**Chemical composition**: Silica (67%), Alumina (16%), Calcium & sodium oxides (7.5%), Iron & magnesium oxides (6%)
**Minerals**: Quartz; Plagioclase feldspar (oligoclase); Potassium feldspar (sanidine); Biotite mica; Hornblende
**Accessories**: Zircon, apatite, magnetite, ilmenite, sphene
**Phenocrysts**: Quartz or plagioclase feldspar
**Formation**: Intrusive: stocks, bosses, batholiths, sills, dykes
**Notable occurrences**: As for granite but also Aleutian Islands; Sonora, Mexico; Peninsular Mts, Baja California; Sierra Nevada, California.
*TTG suites*: Lapland, Finland; Barberton Mtn Land, S Africa; Pilbara, Yilgarn, Australia; Big Horn Mts, Wyoming

**Tors**
Granite-like rocks form underground, but are so tough they are often left standing proud after softer rocks are worn away. In some places, granite

gives huge bare-rock cliffs. In others it gives rounded hills topped by outcrops of bare rock the size of a house, usually called by the ancient Cornish name 'tors'. Tors are a distinctive feature of the moors of England's south-west, but occur in many other places such as Scotland's Cairngorms and in South Africa, where they are called 'castle koppies'. There are several theories on how Cornish tors formed, but all are connected with the pattern of cracks, or 'joints', that develops parallel to the surface of the rock. Tors are tough clumps of rock that have survived after weaker surrounding granite was stripped away. One theory is that the softer granite was weathered in an earlier tropically warm age by natural chemicals seeping into the joints deep below ground. Another is that it was weathered by frost in the Ice Ages. The debris was, in both cases, probably swept away at the end of the Ice Ages by a process called solifluction, in which the water in frozen ground melts, turning the soil into a liquid mush that flows easily away.

# Tonalite

This rock takes its name from Tonale in the Italian Alps near Monte Adamello. It is the quartz-rich, granitoid equivalent of diorite. It has the least potassium feldspar and the most plagioclase of any of the granite-like rocks, and also the most of the dark mafic minerals such as hornblende and biotite. The hornblende is often greenish rather than brown, while the biotite is pleochroic – that is, shows different colours from different directions. Tonalite is actually quite like granodiorite, and the two frequently occur together in TTG suites (see Granodiorite above). They have the same black and light grey 'salt-and-pepper' look, and can be hard to tell apart – tonalite has more black pepper.

**Identification**: Tonalites look very like granite, but are slightly darker and browner.

**Grain size**: Phaneritic (coarse)
**Texture**: Even texture; often porphyritic
**Structure**: Often threaded by veins of quartz and feldspar (aplites)
**Colour**: Pink or tan potassium feldspar crystals rimmed with white albite in a dark groundmass
**Chemical composition**: Silica (58%), Alumina (17%), Calcium and sodium oxides (10%), Iron and magnesium oxides (11%)
**Minerals**: Quartz; Plagioclase feldspar (oligoclase); Biotite mica; Hornblende
**Accessories**: Zircon, apatite, magnetite, orthite, sphene
**Phenocrysts**: Quartz or plagioclase feldspar
**Formation**: Intrusive: stocks, bosses, batholiths, sills, dykes
**Notable occurrences**: Galloway, Cairngorms, Scotland; Ireland; Rieserferner and Traversella (Tyrol), Austria/Italy; Andes, Patagonia; Sierra Nevada, California; Alaska.
*TTG suites*: Lapland, Finland; Barberton Mtn Land, S Africa; Pilbara, Yilgarn, Australia; Big Horn Mts, Wyoming.

# GABBRO AND DIORITE

*Gabbro and diorite occupy the middle ground of intrusive igneous rocks as far as the mineral balance goes. On the one hand, they contain only a little quartz and alkali feldspar – markedly less than the granitoid rocks. On the other, they contain only moderate amounts of olivine – much less than the ultramafics such as peridotite. Instead, they are made predominantly of plagioclase feldspar.*

## Diorite

**Dark diorite:** Sometimes dark minerals can predominate over light in diorite.

Diorite is the coarse-grained, plutonic equivalent of andesite. It is darker than granitoids and contains heavier minerals, but it has a similar grain structure and forms in a similar way. Diorite is one of the igneous rocks that make their presence felt along continental margins where subduction of tectonic plates is throwing up mountain chains like the Andes. With granite, it forms the great long batholiths that underlie so many of these mountain chains. There is much less diorite than granite, and it often forms when rocks are caught up in a granite intrusion. Diorite contains much less quartz and alkali feldspar than granite, but more plagioclase feldspar than any other rock except anorthosite – over 75 per cent, even more than gabbro. The rest is mainly dark minerals such as hornblende and biotite. Diorite is similar to gabbro, but diorite's plagioclase tends to be oligoclase and andesine, whereas in gabbro much more of it is anorthite, bytownite and labradorite.

**Identification:** Diorite looks very similar to gabbro and it can be quite hard to tell them apart. Yet even though it contains very little quartz, its high plagioclase feldspar content means that light minerals are usually more prominent in diorite than gabbro. Essentially, diorite is light grey with patches of black, while gabbro is black with patches of light grey, but this is by no means a hard and fast rule.

**Grain size:** Phaneritic (coarse-grained), occasionally pegmatitic
**Texture:** Even-grained or porphyritic – often close together in the same rock
**Structure:** Foliation and xenoliths common
**Colour:** Speckled black and white, occasionally dark greenish or pinkish
**Composition:** Diorite: Silica (58.5% average), Alumina (17%), Calcium and sodium oxides (10.5%), Iron and magnesium oxides (11%), Potassium oxides (2%). Monzodiorite: Silica (58% average), Alumina (17%), Calcium and sodium oxides (11%), Iron and magnesium oxides (10%), Potassium oxides (2%).
**Minerals:** Plagioclase feldspar (oligoclase or andesine); Biotite mica; Amphibole (hornblende); Small amounts of pyroxene (augite), quartz and alkali feldspar (sanidine). Feldspathoid diorite and feldspathoid monzonite: Foids (nepheline) instead of quartz.
**Accessories:** Magnetite, apatite, zircon, titanite, olivine
**Phenocrysts:** Plagioclase feldspar, hornblende
**Formation:** Intrusive: sills, dykes, stocks, bosses, plus xenoliths in granite
**Notable occurrences:** Argyll, Scotland, Jersey (Channel Islands), England; Bavarian Forest, Black Forest, Harz, Odenwald, Germany; Finland; Washington; Massachusetts

## Monzodiorite

This rock is midway between monzonite and diorite in composition. That means most monzonite contains some quartz, and a little more plagioclase than alkali feldspar, and fewer dark minerals than diorite. There is another kind of monzonite – feldspathoid monzodiorite – which contains nepheline or other foids instead of quartz. Monzodiorite used to be called syenodiorite, but IUGS (International Union of Geological Surveys) recommended it should be called monzodiorite to avoid confusion with monzonite and monzosyenite, which also lie in between syenite and diorite in composition, but contain more alkali feldspar.

**Identification:** Monzodiorite has the same 'salt-and-pepper' look as diorite and monzonite, but has slightly more 'pepper' than monzonite and slightly less than diorite.

# Gabbro

**Polished gabbro**: Rarely, gabbro is cut and polished and used as a decorative stone.

Named after a town in Tuscany, Italy, by the great German geologist Christian Leopold von Buch, gabbro is the coarse-grained, intrusive equivalent of basalt and dolerite. It is a dark rock, basically made up of plagioclase and pyroxene. More pyroxene and less plagioclase merges it into peridotite; less pyroxene and more plagioclase blends it into diorite. Gabbro is a very widespread rock, especially in the oceanic crust, where it forms part of the ophiolite sequence. This is the sequence of rocks down through the ocean bed that develops either side of a mid-ocean rift. As pillow lavas and sheeted dykes of erupted basalt form the top of the sequence, so gabbro continually freezes in clumps from molten peridotite on to the magma chamber walls beneath as the walls move apart. Over millions of years, this has created a layer of gabbro underneath all the world's oceans.

Gabbro can also flow into sills and dykes, and occasionally, huge sheet complexes called lopoliths, like that at the Bushveld complex in South Africa, Duluth in Minnesota and Rhum in Scotland. In many places, the sinking of heavier minerals as they crystallized has created distinct layers in the gabbro with dark minerals concentrated at the bottom and light minerals at the top of each layer.

## The Sudbury structure

In places around the world, there are huge, mostly ancient layered intrusions in which mafic magmas have crystallized in layers of different chemical composition. The biggest by far is the Bushveld complex in South Africa, which covers 65,000km²/25,000 sq miles. One of the most fascinating is at Sudbury in Ontario, Canada. The area is one of the world's richest sources of nickel copper, found in association with gabbro, and was once thought to be entirely igneous in origin. Now geologists have realized that it is not actually igneous at all but the huge impact crater of a meteorite that struck the ground here 1,850 million years ago – the biggest ever. This is clear from shatter cones, rocks fractured in a cone shape by the impact (above). What makes this crater unusual, even for a meteor crater, is that it is oval – 200km/124 miles long and only about 100km/62 miles wide. Scientists believe, from mapping the geology of the area and creating various models, that it was created by a meteorite of some 10–19km (six to 12 miles) in width, which exploded on impact with the force of 10 billion Hiroshima bombs, fracturing the Earth's crust and bringing magma rich in mineral ores to the surface. This resulting heat melted the exposed granite and gneiss rocks into a glassy magma that deformed the crater. This mafic magma sits on top of the layered gabbro.

**Identification**: Gabbro can look similar to diorite, but tends to be darker as it contains the darker plagioclases (labradorite and bytownite) rather than the lighter plagioclases (oligoclase and andesine) of diorite. Gabbro is often ophitic (see texture, right), giving it a frosted look.

Gabbro is a very tough rock, which is why it is used widely for railway ballast and road metalling, but it is one of the least attractive of the intrusive igneous rocks, so is much less used as a decorative stone than the granites or syenites. However, it is virtually the only significant source of nickel, chromium and platinum minerals.

**Grain size**: Phaneritic (coarse-grained), occasionally pegmatitic
**Texture**: Even-grained or porphyritic – often close together in the same rock mass. Frequently ophitic, which means long light plagioclase feldspar crystals are enveloped by dark pyroxene (augite) crystals.
**Structure**: Foliation and xenoliths common. Often forms alternating layers, with mostly light minerals at the tops and mostly dark at the bottoms of the layers.
**Colour**: Black and white or grey, occasionally dark greenish or bluish
**Composition**: Silica (58% average), Alumina (17%), Calcium and sodium oxides (10.5%), Iron and magnesium oxides (11%), Potassium oxides (2%)
**Minerals**: Plagioclase feldspar (labradorite or bytownite); Pyroxene (augite); Olivine; Small amounts of amphibole (hornblende) and biotite mica; Very small amounts of quartz and alkali feldspar (sanidine)
**Accessories**: Magnetite, apatite, ilmenite, picotite, garnet
**Phenocrysts**: Plagioclase feldspar, hornblende
**Formation**: Intrusive: batholiths, lopoliths, sills, dykes, stocks, bosses, plus xenoliths in granite
**Notable occurrences**: Shetland, Skye, Rhum, Aberdeen, Argyll, Scotland; Pembroke, Wales; Lake District, Lizard (Cornwall), England; Skaergaard, Greenland; Bergen, Norway; Odenwald, Harz, Black Forest, Germany; Wallis, Switzerland; Bushveld complex, South Africa; Jimberlana, Windimurra, Western Australia; Eastern Canada; Baltimore, Maryland; Peekskill, New York; Stillwater, Montana; Duluth, Minnesota

**Monzogabbro**: Monzogabbro is gabbro with slightly less pyroxene and containing feldspathoids rather than quartz.

# GABBROIC ROCKS

*Gabbros are phaneritic (coarse-grained) rocks made of plagioclase feldspar, pyroxene and olivine. They are divided into various types according to how much of each they contain. Anorthosite is rich in plagioclase; troctolite is rich in plagioclase and olivine but not pyroxene; gabbro is rich in plagioclase and pyroxene but not olivine; essexite is rich in pyroxene. Norite is the midpoint.*

## Norite

Norite is a similar rock to gabbro, based on a mix of plagioclase, pyroxene and olivine, and the two often form in the same large, layered intrusions as the mix separates during crystallization. Norite contains very slightly less plagioclase than gabbro, but the real difference is that gabbro's pyroxene is a clinopyroxene such as augite, while norite's is an orthopyroxene such as hypersthene. Unfortunately, the two can look so alike that they are impossible to distinguish without a microscope. Norite typically occurs in small, separate intrusions, or as layers along with other mafic igneous rocks such as gabbro. Norite also formed in association with ancient basalt intrusions, beneath huge basalt dyke swarms. One famous norite intrusion is at Sudbury in Ontario. Here a cavity 30m/98ft deep has been excavated from solid norite to house the Neutrino Observatory to detect neutrinos, minute particles streaming from the stars. Norite is unusually low in natural radioactivity and acts as a shield to allow scientists to block out unwanted background radiation.

**Identification**: Norite is a dark grey rock with a slightly matted look dominated by quite long, prismatic black hypersthene or enstatite crystals. It looks very like gabbro, but the plagioclase feldspar tends to be sandy coloured, while in gabbro it is whiter.

**Grain size**: Phaneritic (coarse-grained), occasionally pegmatitic
**Texture**: Even-grained or porphyritic
**Structure**: Layering and xenoliths are common
**Colour**: Dark grey, bronze
**Composition**: Silica (58%), Alumina (17%), Calcium and sodium oxides (10.5%), Iron and magnesium oxides (11%), Potassium oxides (2%)
**Minerals**: Plagioclase feldspar (labradorite or bytownite); Pyroxene (hypersthene); Olivine; A little hornblende, biotite mica, quartz and alkali feldspar
**Accessories**: Magnetite, apatite, ilmenite, picotite
**Phenocrysts**: Plagioclase feldspar, hornblende
**Formation**: Intrusive: dykes, stocks, bosses, often with gabbro
**Notable occurrences**: Aberdeen, Banff, Scotland; Norway; Great Dyke, Zimbabwe; Bushveld complex, S Africa; Sudbury, Ontario

## Anorthosite

**Identification**: Anorthosite is the lightest coloured of all the gabbroic rocks. Dark and light minerals are often aligned in long crystals, giving anorthosite a streaky look.

Anorthosite is almost entirely plagioclase feldspar. Over 90 per cent is either bytownite or labradorite. Labradorite crystals may show an iridescence known as labradorescence. Although not as abundant as basalt and granite, anorthosite often occurs in huge formations such as in Labrador in Canada, and in giant complexes such as South Africa's Bushveld along with gabbro and norite. It is also one of the rocks that makes up the Moon's surface. While lunar seas are basalt, highlands are anorthosite. When the Moon was young its surface was melted, not only from heat within but by meteor impacts. Light plagioclase feldspar floated to the top and, when the lunar surface cooled, it solidified to form anorthosite. The Earth has much less anorthosite, but it is found in ancient rocks. On the early Earth, anorthosite may have been as abundant as on the Moon, but Earth's surface is so dynamic that most has long since vanished.

**Grain size**: Phaneritic (coarse-grained)
**Texture**: Long crystals often aligned
**Structure**: Layering common
**Colour**: Light grey
**Composition**: Silica (51%), Alumina (26%), Calcium and sodium oxides (16%), Iron and magnesium oxides (5%)
**Minerals**: Plagioclase feldspar (labradorite or bytownite); Small amounts of pyroxene; olivine; magnetite and ilmenite
**Formation**: Intrusive: dykes (rare), stocks, batholiths, often with gabbro
**Notable occurrences**: Norway; Bushveld complex, South Africa; Sudbury, Ontario; Labrador; Stillwater, Montana; Adirondacks, New York; the Moon

**Bushveld Complex**

South Africa's Bushveld complex in the former Transvaal is one of the world's great geological wonders. It is by far the largest layered intrusion, covering up to 65,000km²/25,097 sq miles and reaching up to 8km/5 miles thick. It is incredibly rich in minerals, containing most of the world's chromium, platinum and vanadium resources, as well as a great deal of iron, titanium, copper and nickel. The whole complex formed in a remarkably short time about 2,060 million years ago, as magmas were poured out on the surface and intruded into the ground to form large, complex layers of gabbroic and mafic rocks such as norite, anorthosite and pyroxenite. Some geologists thought it was created by the hotspot above a mantle plume; others, noting the coincidence of dates with the nearby Vredefort meteor crater, thought it was a meteorite impact feature. A recent theory uses both ideas, suggesting a meteorite impact triggered off a mantle plume to fountain huge amounts of magma up from the mantle – almost as if the meteorite had burst the Earth's crust.

## Essexite

Named after Essex County in Massachusetts where it occurs, essexite is the rock used in Scotland in its porphyritic form to make curling stones. It is the gabbro that forms when there is less silica in the melt. It is less viscous than gabbro and flows into small intrusions near the surface, cooling quickly to form medium- and fine-grained rocks. The lack of silica means that nepheline forms in essexite instead of quartz, so it is actually a foid rock, like foyaite and nephelinite. Essexite is also richer than gabbro in pyroxene, and its pyroxene is titanaugite.

**Grain size**: Medium to fine
**Texture**: Granular, sometimes porphyritic
**Structure**: Layering common
**Colour**: Light grey
**Composition**: Silica (45%), Alumina (15%), Calcium and sodium oxides (17%), Iron and magnesium oxides (18.5%), Potassium oxides (5%)
**Minerals**: Plagioclase feldspar (labradorite or anorthite); Pyroxene (augite); Biotite; Hornblende; plus small amounts of nepheline and alkali feldspar
**Formation**: Small intrusions, dykes, sills, often with gabbro
**Phenocrysts**: Augite
**Notable occurrences**: Lanarkshire, Ayrshire, Scotland; Kaiserstuhl, Baden, Germany; Oslo, Norway; Roztoky, Czech Republic; Tyrol, Italy; Essex Co, MA

**Identification**: Essexite is a fine- to medium-grained grey rock often with slightly larger dark spots of augite. It is attractively evenly mottled.

## Troctolite

This is a gabbroic rock which has almost no pyroxene. Instead it is made of plagioclase feldspar and olivine, midway between anorthosite and peridotite. It very often occurs in layered igneous complexes such as South Africa's Bushveld, and, most famously among geologists, the Isle of Rhum in Scotland's Hebrides. Layered complexes are intrusions that seem a layer-cake of related igneous rocks formed within a single magma chamber in the Earth's crust. The Rhum complex formed some 60 million years ago, during the birth of the North Atlantic Ocean, when ancient north-west Europe and North America began to drift apart, allowing magma to flood on to the surface. The original magma was probably an olivine-rich basalt, but as minerals crystallized in the magma chamber, heavier minerals probably sank to the bottom, creating layers of troctolite on top of layers of peridotite. Troctolites elsewhere probably formed in a similar way.

**Identification**: In German, troctolite is called *Forellenstein*, which means 'trout rock', and the name is apt, for it looks just like the skin of a trout. The medium-grained dark grey plagioclase looks like the trout's scales. Olivine forms black spots within it which, just like a trout's spots, can be red, green or brown when wholly or partly altered to serpentine by exposure to the weather.

**Grain size**: Medium to coarse
**Texture**: Granular
**Structure**: Layering common
**Colour**: Grey studded with black, occasionally red or green
**Composition**: Silica (51%), Alumina (26%), Calcium & sodium oxides (16%), Iron & magnesium oxides (5%)
**Minerals**: Plagioclase feldspar (labradorite or anorthite); Olivine; Small amounts of pyroxene, magnetite and ilmenite
**Formation**: Intrusive: dykes, cone sheets, stocks, laccoliths, often with gabbro
**Notable occurrences**: Rhum, Scotland; Cornwall, England; Oslo, Norway; Harz, Germany; Wolimierz (Silesia), Poland; Niger; Great Dyke, Zimbabwe; Bushveld complex, South Africa; Stillwater, Montana; Oklahoma

# DYKE, SILL AND VEIN ROCK

*Fingers of magma ooze out into the country rock from every intrusion, either cutting across strata as dykes in which lamprophyres may form, or sliding between as sills to form rocks such as dolerites. As the intrusion begins to cool, cracks open in the solidifying rock. Residual fluids ooze into these cracks, altering the surrounding rock to greisens or solidifying to form veins of new rocks such as aplite.*

## Aplite

Aplites are unusually pale igneous rocks with fine, even grains that look just like unrefined sugar. They are closely related to pegmatites, and likewise form veins of crystalline igneous rock. Aplites, though, are fine-grained and tend to be much simpler in composition. In fact, they are basically quartz and potassium feldspar, with no mica, which is why they are so pale in colour. Moreover, while there are often complex zones of different composition in pegmatites, aplites are generally uniform throughout. Aplite veins form in almost every large granitic intrusion, striking like a pale scar across the host rock, and rarely more than a few centimetres across. As the intrusion cools and begins to crack, aplite veins develop when residual magma fills up the cracks. These aplites form at the lowest temperature of any igneous rock and water comes out of the melt as it loses pressure. So they crystallize very rapidly creating a texture that is remarkably fine-grained considering they form deep underground.

**Identification**: With its fine crystalline texture, aplite has a sugary look almost like pale sandstone. Unlike sandstone, though, the grains in aplite interlock, and there is none of the cement that glues sandstone grains together.

**Grain size**: Fine-grained
**Texture**: Even-grained or, occasionally, porphyritic
**Structure**: None
**Colour**: Pale pink or whitish
**Composition**: Silica (75% average), Alumina (14.5%), Calcium and sodium oxides (3.5%), Iron and magnesium oxides (5%)
**Minerals**: Quartz; Potassium feldspar (orthoclase or microperthite)
**Accessories**: Plagioclase feldspar, muscovite, apatite, tourmaline
**Phenocrysts**: Quartz, orthoclase feldspar, tourmaline
**Formation**: Aplite forms dykes in granite and granitic intrusions. It occasionally forms independent bosses, or on the rim of an intrusion
**Notable occurrences**: Wherever there are large granitic intrusions

## Greisen

**Identification**: Greisen almost always occurs within granite, but is pale grey with almost no black mica.

Strictly speaking, greisen is a metamorphic, not igneous, rock, but it is always closely linked to granite, especially in tin-mining districts. In fact, it is granite that has been altered or 'metasomatized' by exposure to hydrothermal fluids or vapours rich in fluorine, lithium, boron and tungsten – just as basalt is metasomatized to spillite. As fluids flood through veins in granite, they alter the composition of the granite in the vein walls, destroying all the feldspar, and leaving just quartz and white mica. Gradually the vein becomes infilled with greisen. There is usually no definite boundary between the greisen and granite, and altered granite merges into unaltered granite imperceptibly. Greisens belong to the quartzolite family, the most quartz-rich of all rocks, with a quartz content of over 90 per cent.

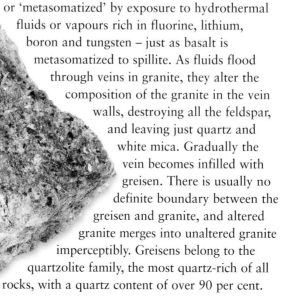

**Grain size**: Medium-grained
**Texture**: Even-grained or, occasionally, foliated
**Structure**: None
**Colour**: Grey or brown
**Composition**: Silica (90% average)
**Minerals**: Quartz; White mica (muscovite, zinnwaldite, lepidolite, sericite)
**Accessories**: Topaz, fluorite, apatite, tourmaline, rutile, cassiterite, wolframite
**Formation**: Short vein infillings no more than a few hundred metres long
**Notable occurrences**: Skiddaw (Lake District), Cornwall, England; Galicia, Spain; Fichtelberg, Erzebirge, Germany; Portugal; Queensland, New South Wales, Tasmania, Australia

## Lamprophyres

**Camptonite**: Named after Campton in New Hampshire, this dark lamprophyre has a hornblende, labradorite feldspar and pyroxene groundmass with phenocrysts of the amphiboles kaersutite and ferrohornblende, along with titanaugite, olivine and biotite.

Lamprophyres get their name from the Greek for 'glistening mixture', and it is apt for these rocks are stuffed with large, gleaming phenocrysts of mica, amphiboles and olivine, giving the rock a very distinctive appearance. Unusually, they have no feldspar phenocrysts whatsoever; all their feldspar is in the fine groundmass. They are dark, or even ultramafic, rocks, and probably form from cool melts of metasomatized (altered) mantle material. They are the classic dyke rocks. Most dyke rocks are simply versions of the same rocks that form larger intrusions. Lamprophyres alone form almost exclusively in dykes – though in recent years small lava flows and plutons have been found. They typically occur in dykes near tonalite and granodiorite plutons. The lamprophyres are a very varied group, and some geologists think they should be called a facies – a diverse group of rocks that simply crystallized under similar conditions. The most widespread form is minette.

**Vosgesite**: Named after the Vosges in Alsace, France, vosgesite has phenocrysts of hornblende along with augite and olivine. It is one of the calc-alkaline lamprophyres normally found along with rhyolites and basalts in island arcs and subduction zones.

**Grain size**: Mixed
**Texture**: Porphyritic
**Colour**: Dark grey with dark, even black phenocrysts
**Composition**: Variable. Minette: Silica (47.5% average), Alumina (9.3%), Calcium and sodium oxides (11.5%), Iron and magnesium oxides (26%).
**Groundmass**: Plagioclase feldspar, feldspathoid, carbonates, monticellite, mellilite, mica, amphibole, pyroxene, olivine, perovskite
**Phenocrysts**: Biotite/phlogopite, amphibole (hornblende, barkevikite, kaersutite), pyroxene (augite), olivine
**Formation**: Mainly dykes
**Notable occurrences**: Cairngorms, Cheviots, Scotland; Lake District; England; Ireland; Vosges, France; Black Forest, Harz, Germany; Wasatch, Utah

**Palisades Sill**
New Jersey's Palisades are a dramatic line of brown cliffs that tower anything from 107m/350ft to 168m/550ft above the west bank of the Hudson River. The cliffs are the exposed margin of a vast sill of diabase (dolerite) rock 305m/1,000ft thick and 72km/45 miles long that dips away westwards. Radiation dating has shown the sill formed between 186 and 192 million years ago in the Early Jurassic, when a fat wedge of magma squeezed between layers of sandstone and shale. As the magma cooled and solidified, it cracked into the columns that characterize the cliff face – and earned the Palisades their name, given by explorers with Verrazano in 1524, who thought the cliffs resembled the forts of wooden stakes built by local Indians. In the 19th century, these rocks were ruthlessly exploited for building stone, and many a New York sidewalk is made of 'Belgian stone' from the Palisades. Eventually, in the 1930s, the area was designated an Interstate Park to halt the destruction.

## Dolerite

A tough stone used for road metal, dolerite is a dark, mafic rock, the medium-grained equivalent of basalt and gabbro. It is known in the United Kingdom as diabase and is typically found in sills, such as New Jersey's vast Palisades sill. The famous bluestones of England's ancient stone circle Stonehenge were carved from dolerite cut from sills in the Prescelly Mountains of Wales. Usually when magmas cool and crystallize, dark minerals such as olivine crystallize first, followed by feldspar and mica, leaving quartz and any other silica to fill in the gaps. Lath-like crystals of feldspar form first, and the dark minerals are forced to fit in between them – often growing right around them in what is called ophitic texture.

**Grain size**: Medium
**Texture**: Often ophitic, with large clinopyroxene (augite) crystals enclosing plagioclases
**Structure**: Vesicles and amygdales common
**Colour**: Dark grey, black, with green tinge when fresh. May be mottled white.
**Composition**: Silica (50%), Alumina (16%), Calcium and sodium oxides (13%), Iron and magnesium oxides (18%)
**Minerals**: Plagioclase feldspar (labradorite); Olivine; Pyroxene; Biotite; Magnetite; Ilmenite; Quartz; Hornblende
**Phenocrysts**: Olivine and/or pyroxene or plagioclase
**Groundmass**: Plagioclase and pyroxene with olivine or quartz
**Formation**: Sills and dykes, often in large dyke swarms; occasionally lava flows
**Notable occurrences**: Whin Sill, NE England; Lake Superior, Canada; Palisades, New Jersey

**Identification**: Dolerite is best identified by its dark, greenish colour and its medium grain size.

# PEGMATITES

*Pegmatites are the cream of igneous rock, the places where all the biggest crystals and rarest minerals are concentrated when an igneous intrusion reaches its final stages of crystallization. Pegmatite formations are typically small pods and lenses no bigger than a house, but they are the source of some of the world's best gems and most valuable minerals.*

## Pegmatite features

**Identification**: Pegmatites are instantly recognizable from their gigantic crystals. What is harder to identify is the particular crystals within them, and so the particular kind. Large creamy or pink crystals are usually feldspar, white sugary crystals may be quartz, brown striped crystals are mica, black may be tourmaline. More colourful crystals are rarer minerals.

*Quartz*

*Pink beryl*

*Amazonite feldspar*

**Lithium pegmatite**: Many pegmatites are enriched with the mineral lithium, turning mica to lepidolite and creating the spodumene gems – lilac kunzite and green kunzite.

*Lepidolite mica*

*Pink tourmaline*

Pegmatites are perhaps the most fascinating bodies of rock in the world. No other rock formation contains such a wealth of large, spectacular crystals. All the world's largest natural crystals have been found in pegmatites. Even the average grains in pegmatites are not just clearly visible, as in coarse-grained granite, but substantial – at least the size of a grapefruit. Some pegmatite crystals are truly gigantic. Tourmaline and beryl crystals the size of a log are often found, while a spodumene crystal found in a pegmatite in South Dakota in the USA was a gigantic 13m/42ft long.

Pegmatites are also the source of an amazing range and variety of minerals. Over 550 different kinds of mineral have been found in pegmatites. Pegmatites are the source of many of the world's gems. Besides fabulous topaz and wonderful garnets, gems of all the beryl varieties (aquamarine, morganite, golden), all the tourmalines (pink, green, and multi-hued elbaite) and all the spodumenes (kunzite and hiddenite) are found in pegmatites. Pegmatites are also sources of rare elements such as beryllium, niobium, tantalum, rubidium, caesium and gallium, as well as tin and tungsten. Because they are so richly concentrated here, pegmatites are even major sources for more common minerals such as feldspar and quartz.

The term pegmatite was originally used in the early 19th century to describe graphic granites, which often occur in pegmatites. Now the term is used to describe any small body of igneous rock with crystals at least 1.3cm/0.5in across. They vary hugely in size and shape. Some are veins. Some are shaped like lenses. Some are shaped like knobbly turnips. The smallest are typically no bigger than a mattress but a few giant pegmatites are 3.2km/2 miles long and 0.5km/0.3 mile wide. Pegmatites are by no means isolated structures. In the famous Black Hills district of South Dakota in the United States, there are an estimated 24,000 pegmatite bodies in an area of 700km²/270 sq miles!

**Grain size**: Very coarse-grained. Crystals are at least 1–2cm/0.5in across, average 8–10cm/3–4in, and can be much bigger.
**Texture**: Hugely varied, with complex zoning and lots of vugs (open cavities)
**Structure**: None
**Colour**: Pale pink or whitish
**Composition**: Silica (75% average), Alumina (14.5%), Calcium and sodium oxides (3.5%), Iron and magnesium oxides (5%)
**Minerals**: Quartz; Potassium feldspar (albite and perthite)
**Accessories**: Plagioclase feldspar, muscovite, apatite, tourmaline, plus minerals containing elements such as tin, tungsten, niobium, tantalum, beryllium, gallium, rubidium and caesium
**Large crystals**: Quartz, feldspar, tourmaline, beryl (aquamarine, morganite, golden), spodumene (kunzite and hiddenite), tourmaline
**Formation**: Dykes, veins, pods, lens around the margins of intrusions, Pegmatites are typically either granite or syenite
**Notable occurrences**: Pegmatites occur all around the world, wherever there are granite and syenite intrusions. Famous examples include those on the Island of Elba in Italy, Madagascar (especially Anjanbonoina), Pakistan and the Mesa Grande, California (notably the Himalaya Mine in Pala County). They are most abundant in mountain chains and stable continental shield areas, such as the Canadian Shield, Greenland and north Russia. Shield pegmatites are usually at least a billion years old. Mountain chain pegmatites such as those in the Himalayas are no more than 5 to 20 million years old.

# Pegmatite formation

Pegmatites usually form at the margins of a large pluton, clustering like currents on its surface, or extending like fingers into the mass, or outwards into the surrounding country rock. Occasionally they are found completely separated from their parent intrusion in pockets in the country rock. It is thought that pegmatites form in the last stages of the crystallization of an intrusion. With the main body of rock formed, the bulk of the common minerals have already crystallized, leaving just a few small pockets to be filled in to create pegmatites. The melt left to create them is rich not just in rarer elements such as boron and fluorine, but also volatile liquids – and a great deal of water. It is this high water content that allows the crystals in pegmatites to grow so big. All this water dramatically increases the mobility of particles within the melt, and this means they can travel farther and faster as they become incorporated into crystals. Normally, large crystals form only when magmas cool very, very slowly from high temperatures, but the water in pegmatites means huge crystals grow rapidly at temperatures of no more than 100–200°C/212–392°F. Pegmatites can form from just about any kind of igneous intrusion including gabbro and diorite – and even in metamorphic gneisses and schists – but most form from granites and syenites and so have the same basic ingredients – quartz and potassium feldspar with a little muscovite mica. Pegmatites can be divided into simple and complex. Simple pegmatites are basically very coarse-grained equivalents of the parent rock, made of the same three basic ingredients, plus a little tourmaline. Complex pegmatites form later and have higher concentrations of rare minerals. Lithium, for instance, is typically found at concentrations of 30ppm (parts per million) but in complex pegmatites, lithium concentrations can reach over 700ppm. Complex pegmatites are typically divided into highly complex zones, with graphic granite in one place, tourmalines in another, and so on. They are often riddled with open cavities. It is the complex pegmatites that are the source of the most valuable and spectacular crystals.

Black tourmaline

**Tourmaline pegmatite**:
Tourmaline is a boron mineral and tourmaline pegmatites are created when the boron content is especially enriched in the last stages of the mix. An increase in fluorine often creates the gem topaz.

**Varieties of pegmatites**:
Pegmatites are very varied. Some are named after the main source rock. Others are named after a mineral or element that is particularly enriched in them.

**Rock source pegmatites**:
Granitic pegmatite
Syenitic pegmatite
Gabbroic pegmatite
Diorite pegmatite

**Mineral- or element-enriched pegmatites**:
Tourmaline pegmatite
Lithium pegmatite
Beryl pegmatite
Emerald pegmatite
Spodumene pegmatite
Albite pegmatite
Quartz-albite pegmatite
LCT pegmatite

**Rock source and element-enriched pegmatites**:
Phosphate granitic pegmatite
Boron granitic pegmatite
LCT granitic pegmatite

**LCT pegmatites**: LCT (Lithium-Caesium-Tantalum) pegmatites are enriched not just with the elements lithium, caesium and tantalum, but also with rubidium, beryllium, gallium and tin. Granitic LCT pegmatites are host to many of the world's most precious gemstones, including emerald, chrysoberyl and topaz from Minas Gerais in Brazil, sapphire and ruby from Afghanistan and Pakistan, and gem tourmaline.

### Isola d'Elba, Italy

The western end of the Island of Elba off the west coast of Italy is riddled with pegmatites that have been one of the world's richest sources of beryls and tourmalines, including the elbaite variety named after the island. In 1805, the first quarries were dug to extract the local granite to build houses and roads. Then in 1820, a local mineralogist called Captain Foresi noticed large, colourful crystals in the rock, later found to be tourmalines. In 1830, Foresi opened the first tourmaline mine at Grotta d'Oggi, or Cave of Today. He then traced the pegmatite zone and discovered many other sources of tourmalines and beryls such as the Masso Foresi (Foresi's Mass), the Fonte del Prete and la Speranza. Scores of quarries and mines were opened up and yielded many thousands of fine tourmalines and beryls. However, these localities existed within around 10 sq km (six sq miles) of each other and, unsurprisingly, by the end of the 19th century, the existing veins – sunk deep into granite rock – had been mined to exhaustion, and the best stones taken away. Many are now on display in mainland Italy, at the Florence Mineral Museum. Visitors to the island do occasionally still find fine elbaite crystals here, and many collectors believe there are countless new pegmatite-rich veins waiting to be discovered. However, with new laws to safeguard the landscape of the island against future mining, it is unlikely that the Isola d'Elba will regain its previous status as a mecca for those seeking pegmatite gems.

Yellow beryl

**Beryl pegmatite**:
This is rich in beryl, and may often contain gems like emeralds, such as in the pegmatites from Minas Gerais in Brazil.

Smoky quartz

Feldspar

# SEDIMENTARY ROCKS: LUTITES

*Sedimentary rocks are made from sediments of loose material that is gradually lithified (consolidated and turned to stone) over millions of years. Many sediments are fragments, or 'clasts', of older rocks broken down by weather. Clasts are mainly silicates (quartz, feldspar, mica). Rocks made from them are described as siliciclastic, and classified according to grain size. The finest grained are lutites or mudrocks, made mainly of clay- and silt-size grains. They include claystone, mudstone, siltstone and shale.*

## Claystone and mudstone

These siliciclastic rocks are the most abundant sediments on Earth. Half of all sedimentary rocks are clays and muds, and beds of clay stripe nearly every sedimentary formation. London and Paris both sit on vast dishes of clay that provide the bricks that built the cities and the rich soils of the farmlands around. Dull, flat and common claystones may be, but they are the most useful of all rocks. Impure clays are used for making bricks and tiles – and their organic content makes many self-firing. Pure clays such as kaolinite are so wonderfully mouldable they still provide the best materials for making pottery as well as fillers for papers.

No rocks are made from tinier grains than these. More than half the grains in claystone are clay-sized – less than 4µm/0.15mil across. Over two-thirds of the grains in mudstones are clay-sized. Tiny grains like these are the last remnants of rocks broken down by weathering. Being so light they are carried farthest from their source. When rivers flow into the sea and drop their sediment load, clays fall last. Many grains float right out into the deep ocean before sinking to become part of the ocean floor ooze.

Most claystones form from clay sediments that settle in shallow waters just off shore, in calm areas below the waves. Clays like these are dotted with fossils of sea creatures, from tiny shellfish to giant marine dinosaurs. Besides these marine sediments, claystones may also form on lake beds and where rivers flood. Some claystones are not sediments at all but 'residuals' developed as rocks are altered in situ to create soils such as laterites. Few claystones are old, however. Buried under later sediments, they are quickly consolidated first into shale and then to slate in a process called diagenesis. So clay tends to appear only in younger geological formations.

Clay minerals are divided into four broad groups: the kandites (such as kaolinite) formed by the breakdown of potassium feldspar; the illites formed from feldspars and mica; the smectites (including montmorillonite) formed from pyroxenes and amphiboles; and the chlorites. Each claystone contains its own mix of these four, with varying proportions of organic material as well. Illites and montmorillonites are most prevalent.

**Claystone**: The particles in clay are so tiny that, when pure, it feels smooth and slippery when wet, like plasticine. Claystones look like earthenware and come in many colours from grey clays rich in plant material to red clays rich in iron oxide.

**Black mudstone**: Mudstones are defined as rocks made of one-third silt grains and two-thirds ultra-fine clay grains. They are basically hardened mud, and like most muds they are often rich with both plant and animal matter. It is this organic matter that often turns them black.

**Grain size**: Over 50% of grains are clay-sized, less than 4µm/0.15mil
**Texture**: Even-grained, with fossils. No grittiness like silt. Can be plastic and often sticky when wet.
**Structure**: No fine layering like shale, but clay beds show larger scale stratification, including originally horizontal topset and bottomset beds formed on the top and beyond a delta, and originally sloping offset beds formed on the delta front. Sun cracks, rain prints etc are common. All clay particles are microscopically layered, which makes clays plastic and slippery when wet as layers slide over each other. Mudstones have a blocky, massive fabric.
**Colour**: Black, grey, white, brown, red, dark green or blue
**Composition**: Mix of detrital quartz, feldspar and mica. Iron oxides turn clays red or brown. Organic matter turns them black.
**Different groups of minerals**: Kandites such as kaolinite; Illites; Smectites such as montmorillonite; Chlorites
**Formation**: From clays and muds settling offshore, on lake beds and on river floodplains. Also as residuals as rock is altered in situ.
**Notable occurrences**: London Clay (London basin), Oxford Clay (Weymouth to Yorkshire), England; Paris basin, France; North German basin, Molasse basin, Upper Rhine, Germany; Kamchatka, Russia; Sydney basin (New South Wales), Australia; Trinity River, Texas; Appalachian Mountains; Newland, Montana; Muldraugh Hill, Kentucky

# Shale

**Gray shale**: Shale is often dark grey or brown with a thin, platy structure and no visible grains.

Like claystone and mudstone, shale is made from the fine particles that settled on the floor of shallow seas and lakes long ago. Yet unlike claystone and mudstone, shale has laminations like the pages of an ancient book, created as it was squeezed by the weight of overlying sediments. As a result, shale looks flaky like slate, and likewise splits easily into thin layers, a tendency called fissility. The layers vary from paper thin to card thick. Unlike slate, though, shale often contains the fossilized remains of sea life, buried in the mud and preserved forever, albeit somewhat flattened, as the mud turned to stone. Shale varies tremendously in colour according to the minerals it contains. Black shales are rich in carbon from organic remains (typically plankton and bacteria), which often turned to kerogen as the rock formed. Oil shales are black shales so rich in kerogen and bitumen (at least 20 per cent) that they yield oil if heated intensely. On average, 1 tonne/0.98 tons of rock can yield 750 litres/ 165 gallons of oil. Scientists have yet to find a way of extracting this oil economically.

**Black shale**: This shale is black because the remains of sea creatures it contains were never oxidized. Some formed in basins in which circulation was restricted. Others may have developed in times when global warming peaked, cutting down circulation of deep ocean currents. Black shales are famous for the extraordinary preservation of fossilized sea creatures. Even soft tissues often leave impressions.

**Grain size**: 50% of grains are clay-sized, less than 4µm/0.15mil
**Texture**: Even-grained, with fossils. No grittiness like silt.
**Structure**: Splits easily into thin layers
**Colour**: Black, grey, white, brown, red, green or blue
**Composition**: Mix of detrital quartz, feldspar and mica. Iron oxides turn shales red or brown. Organic matter turns them black.
**Formation**: From clay sediments settling offshore, on lake beds and on river floodplains then undergoing diagenesis
**Notable occurrences**: Many locations around the world: *Black shale*: Posidonia, Hünsruck, Germany; Chattanooga, TN; New Albany; PA; Great Plains of Kansas, Oklahoma, South Dakota; *Oil shale;* Torbane Hill, Scotland; Estonia; Lithuania; Israel; Tasmania; Green River, Colorado

## Jurassic mud

It was in the remarkable Oxford and London Clays of England that Victorian fossil hunters made many of the great finds that led to the discovery of dinosaurs and many other prehistoric creatures. Both contain a wealth of marine fossils, but the Oxford Clays are especially rich. The sediments they are made from developed some 140–195 million years ago in the Jurassic period. At this time, southern England was entirely covered by the waters of a tropical ocean, teeming with sea creatures. Oxford Clay is full of the fossils of fish and shellfish that swam there then, including the giant Leedsichthys fish, and countless ammonites and belemnites. But it is most famous for its marine dinosaurs, including the plesiosaurs *Cryptoclidus*, saucer-eyed *Opthalmosaurus* (pictured above), and the awesome *Liopleuridon*. At almost 25m/80ft long, *Liopleuridon* was the biggest carnivore that ever lived, with a mouth 3m/10ft long and teeth twice as long as those of the *Tyrannosaurus rex.*

# Siltstone

Siltstones are much less common than clays and muds and rarely form thick beds. At least half the grains in siltstone specimens are coarser, silt-sized grains, 4–60µm/ 0.15–2.5mil across – large enough to be visible with a magnifying glass. They are mostly quartz, making the rock tougher than clay, and giving it a slightly gritty feel. Because the grains are heavier, siltstones form closer to the shore than clays, and often show ripple marks and crossbedding created by the interplay of the river currents and waves in shallow water. As the flow of water changed with the seasons, so sediment deposition varied. So pale siltstones are often found interlayered with darker mudstones.

**Grain size**: Over 50% of grains are silt-sized, in the range 4–60µm/0.15–2.5mil
**Texture**: Even-grained, with fossils. Slightly gritty.
**Structure**: Often laminated. Shows crossbedding and ripple marks.
**Colour**: Pale grey to beige
**Composition**: Mix of detrital quartz, feldspar and mica
**Formation**: From clay sediments settling in river deltas, on lake beds and on river floodplains
**Notable occurrences**: Many locations around the world including south-east England, The Great Plains of North America, China

**Identification**: Siltstone is easily identified by its pale colour, just-visible grains and slightly gritty feel. It is often laminated with bands of dark mudstone.

# MORE MUDROCKS

*Besides claystones, mudstones and siltstones, there is a wide range of other mudrocks, including marls, bentonites and boulder clays. Marls are earthy, crumbly mixtures of lime and silicate fragments. Bentonites are clays formed from volcanic ash that falls on the sea bed. Boulder clays are basically the debris left behind by moving sheets of ice.*

## Marl and marlstone

**Green marl**: Marls are often given a green tinge by the potassium mica mineral glauconite. These green marls are often very rich in fossils. There are extensive deposits in places such as England's Isle of Wight and North America's Atlantic seaboard.

**Red marl**: The lime and clay content of marl means that they are normally white, grey or brown, but some marls are very rich in iron, which turns them red. Strictly speaking, they are not marls, since they have a low lime content, but they have the same earthy texture.

Since many sediments form on sea and river beds, it is inevitable that they become enriched with a fair share of debris of shellfish and other marine life. As the rocks form, this debris turns to carbonates, first to calcite and aragonite, and eventually to calcite and dolomite in older rocks. Limestones and chalks are almost pure calcium carbonate or lime. Mudstones and claystones, however, contain only a little lime. Marlstone lies in between, rich in both lime and silicate fragments of weathered rocks.

Strictly speaking, marlstone is the rock, while marl is the soft, earthy material that forms as this and other rocks are weathered, but geologists often use the word marl as a general term for any hybrid of mudstone and fine-grained limestone. Extra lime turns marls into limestones; less turns them into clays and mudstones.

The mixed lime and clay content makes all marlstones soft and friable, even when they are not actually earths. Many disintegrate in water, and the lime content means they are easily dissolved in dilute hydrochloric acid or even vinegar.

In some marls, called shelly marls, the carbonate material is actual shell fragments. Shelly marls like these are much valued by farmers as a source of lime, because the lime is easy to extract. In others, the lime is a fine powder mixed in completely with the quartz and feldspar grains. Marls that form in freshwater are quite similar to those that form in the sea. They also often contain shell fragments, but most of the organic material usually comes from algae.

In England, there is a group of rocks called New Red marls that form beds up to 300m/1,000ft thick in places, as part of the Keuper system. These are iron-rich clays rather than pure marls, because they contain only a little calcium carbonate. They probably formed in salt lakes in desert conditions, and in places contain thick salt beds, such as those in Cheshire. Some hard slates in Germany are also described as marls, including the important copper-bearing marl-slates of the Mansfeld area.

**Grain size**: Over 50% of grains are clay-sized, less than 4μm/0.15mil
**Texture**: Earthy, even-grained, with fossils. Marl has none of the grittiness of silt, feeling much softer. The lime is sometimes powdery, sometimes in the form of shell fragments.
**Structure**: No fine layering like shale, but clay beds show larger stratification. Sun cracks, rain prints etc are common. All clay particles are microscopically layered, which makes clays plastic and slippery when wet as layers slide over each other. The high lime content makes these rocks very friable and crumbly. The combination of lime and clay makes a very good basis for soil, which is why marl is often added to soils to improve fertility.
**Colour**: Various, including brown, white or grey; may also be red with iron content or green with glauconite
**Composition**: Even mix of carbonates (mainly calcite) from organic sources and detrital quartz, feldspar and mica
**Formation**: From clays and muds settling offshore, on lake beds and on river floodplains
**Notable occurrences**: North Yorkshire, Leicester, Northamptonshire, Oxford, Exmouth, Vale of Eden, England; Valkenburg, Netherlands; Paris basin, France; Mansfeld, Bavaria, Germany; Sydney basin (New South Wales), Australia; Weka Pass, Canterbury Plains, New Zealand; Green River Formation, Wyoming; South Dakota; Atlantic coastal plain (New Jersey, Delaware, Maryland, Virginia)

# Bentonite

Named after a kind of clay found near Fort Benton, Wyoming, in 1890, bentonite is a clay formed by the alteration of volcanic ash that has settled on the sea floor. Similar clays called tonsteins form when ash is weathered in the acidic waters of coal swamps. Bentonites and tonsteins consist of mostly smectite clays, but also contain unchanged volcanic fragments such as quartz grains and mica flakes. They may also contain beads of volcanic glass. There are two kinds of bentonite: sodium bentonite and calcium bentonite. Sodium bentonite is an incredibly useful material because it swells enormously when wet, creating a gelatinous mass that has been used for everything from sealing dams and drilling for oil to cat litter and detergents. Calcium bentonite makes the absorbent clay called fuller's earth. Bentonites are typically found interbedded with shallow marine limestones and shales, and represent a sudden and dramatic event when a volcano showered the sea floor with huge quantities of ash. Although beds up to 15m/45ft thick have been found, most are less than 0.3m/1ft. Although they are frequently altered beyond recognition, they can give a valuable insight into past volcanic events. In the Ordovician period, much of the eastern USA was covered by an immense ashfall 1m/3ft thick, leaving extensive bentonite deposits from Tennessee to Minnesota.

**Bentonite**: Bentonite looks like clay mud, but is generally and buff to olivegreen colour. If it absorbs water it will swell dramatically.

**Grain size**: Over 50% of grains are clay-sized, less than 4μm/0.15mil
**Texture**: Earthy, even-grained. Slippery and plastic when wet. Greasy or waxy feel.
**Colour**: White to light olive green, cream, yellow, earthy red, brown and sky blue. Bentonite turns yellow on exposure to air.
**Composition**: Smectite clay minerals, quartz grains, mica flakes, volcanic glass beads, calcite and gypsum
**Formation**: Bentonite formed by the alteration of volcanic ash falling on the sea bed. Tonstein formed from ash falling in coal swamps.
**Notable occurrences**: Redhill (Surrey), Woburn (Bedfordshire), Bath (Avon), England; Spain; Italy; Poland; Germany; Hungary; Romania; Greece; Cyprus; Turkey; India; Japan; Argentina; Brazil; Mexico; Saskatchewan; Wyoming; Montana; California; Arizona; Colorado; Black Hills, South Dakota

## Marl, the farmer's friend

Farmers have added marl to soil to improve its fertility for thousands of years. When added to acid soils, the lime in marl helps to neutralize the acidity. It also helps to glue sand grains together so that they retain heat and water better. When added to clay soils, wonderfully it has the opposite effect – helping to make the soil more crumbly and friable and allowing air, heat, water and roots to penetrate better. So marl promotes plant growth in a number of ways: it increases the food available for plants, and makes it easier for them to reach it. For centuries until artificial fertilizers began to take over, marl was dug from marlpits in large quantities. In the eastern USA, where marl is abundant, farmers often put 20–30 tonnes/19.7–29.5 tons of it on every 0.4 hectare/ 1 acre of land in the 19th century, giving magnificent potato, tomato, and berry crops. Clover grew especially lush on marled soils.

# Boulder clay

Also known as tills and ground moraine, boulder clays are a legacy of the great ice ages that once covered much of northern Europe and North America in vast ice sheets. Mixed in like a fruit cake are large pebbles and boulders that were swept along beneath the glaciers and fine clay from rocks shattered by frost and stripped by moving ice. The materials in the boulder clay reflect where the ice travelled. Thus in Britain, boulder clays near Triassic and Old Red Sandstone areas are red, while near Silurian rocks they are buff or grey, and those near chalk can be white.
Although the biggest boulder clay deposits were left by past ice ages, they are forming even today under glaciers and ice sheets in polar and mountain regions.

**Grain size**: Mixture of pebbles, boulders and clay-sized grains, less than 4μm/0.15mil. Boulders can weigh up to several tons.
**Texture**: Smooth clay embedded with angular stones
**Colour**: Varies according to original rock – red, white, grey, brown, black
**Composition**: Depends on the original rock
**Formation**: Debris accumulated and swept along beneath glaciers and ice sheets
**Notable occurrences**: All across northern Europe and northern North America, especially East Anglia in England and the North German plain

**Identification**: With large stones and boulders set in a sticky clayey mass, boulder clay is unmistakable. The interesting task is to work out the origin of the material.

# SANDSTONES

*Sandstones are second only to mudrocks in abundance, making up 10–15 per cent of all Earth's sediments,
and because they are so durable, they often form some of the most prominent hills and landmarks,
as well as providing valuable building stone. They are made mostly of sand-sized grains 60µm–2mm/
2.5–80 mil across. At least half the grains must be this size for it to be classed as a sandstone.*

## Sandstone

Sandstone, as its name suggests, is made from grains of
sand – quartz, feldspar, or simply sand-sized
fragments of rock. Sometimes the sand was
piled up by desert winds, and the grains
were worn almost round as they were
buffeted along. Sometimes the sand
was laid down on river beds, beaches
or in shallow seas, and the grains
are a little more angular. The
sharpest sand of all came from glacial
debris or high up in rivers, where it
had not travelled far.

Beach sand is typically yellow, but each
sandstone is stained by the cement that binds the sand.
Limonite cement gives some sandstones a yellowish hue.
Calcite turns them white – perfect for glass. Bitumen turns
them black like the sandstones of Alberta, while iron oxides
stain them red and brown. It is these warm reds and browns
that are seen in New York's famous brownstone fronts, and
the rusty red mesas and buttes of Utah, Colorado and
Arizona. Occasionally, the cement is so weak that the rock
crumbles in your hands. Most of the time, it is much harder,
and sandstones resist erosion to create some of the world's
most dramatic landscapes – high ridges, steep bluffs and
towering tablelands. Sandstone's toughness also makes it the
perfect building stone, more widely
used than any other.

Sandstones can be like a 'book' displaying the history of
their formation. Cracks reveal where sand dried out in the
sun. Ripples show where waves rolled over it. Bedding
marks bear witness to the way sand deposition
changed continually season by season, year by year.
Desert sandstones, like those in Zion Canyon, Utah,
may even capture the shape of ancient wind-
blown sand-dunes. Most sandstones are also
rich in fossils of the creatures that burrowed in
the sand, or lived in the waters above it. In the
brownstone quarries of Portland, Connecticut,
huge footprints have been found that were made
by dinosaurs that walked over these sands long ago.

**Identification**: With their visible
grains of sand, sandstones are
easy to identify but it is much
harder to distinguish the kind of
sandstone. In a fresh surface, you
may be able to identify quartz and
feldspar. Quartz grains are milky
to clear, glassy with no cleavage
marks. Feldspars are usually
white or pinkish, with marked
cleavage planes. They may be
dissolved out leaving holes or
changed to clay.

**Malachite sandstone**: Sandstones are never pure quartz sand
or even quartz and feldspar. Most contain traces of minerals.
This sandstone from the Triassic period is specked with
green malachite.

**Grain size**: Over 95% sand-
sized grains, 60µm–2mm/
2.5–80mil

**Texture**: Gritty texture like
solid sand. Grains well
sorted, often well
rounded. The amount
of cement between
grains varies widely.

**Structure**: Typically
occurs in blanket-shaped
deposits varying from a few
metres to
several hundred metres
thick. Sandstones are
usually interbedded with
mudstones, limestones and
dolomites. They usually
display dramatic cross-
bedding and ripplemarks,
reflecting their formation in
high-energy environments.
Aeolian rocks often show
sand-dune shapes.

**Colour**: Variable – typically
red, brown, greenish, buff,
yellow, grey, white

**Composition**: 40–95%
quartz, with feldspar and rock
fragments. Other
components include mica,
clay, organic fragments, plus
many heavy minerals. Quartz
and calcite cement.

**Formation**: Nearly all
sedimentary environments
from small alluvial fans to
vast deep-sea plains. Some
form in high-energy marine
environments such as
beaches. Some are formed
from aeolian (wind-blown)
sand-seas in deserts, where
there is a ready supply of
sand. A type called ganisters
forms when most other kinds
of grain are leached away,
leaving just quartz sand.

**Notable occurrences**:
Western Highlands, Scotland;
Pennines, England;
Apennines, Italy; Carpathians,
Romania; Nile Valley, Egypt;
India; Appalachian Mountains;
Colorado and Allegheny
plateaux; Montana

# Old Red Sandstone

The Old Red Sandstones are among the most famous and studied of all rock formations. They are a gigantic sequence of rocks that formed from sediments piled up in a vast basin that stretched across what is now north-west Europe in the Devonian period from 408 to 360 million years ago. This was the time in the Earth's history when the first fish swam, the first land plants grew and the first insects crawled. As the massive Caledonian mountain range was slowly worn away, its remnants accumulated in this basin and in time turned to stone. So extensive were these sediments that geologists used to refer to them as the Old Red Sandstone Continent – and included the Catskill Mountains of North America in it, although these actually formed quite separately at roughly the same time. The Devonian sediments are by no means all sandstones, nor did they all form in the same way. Some were laid down by rivers, some in the sea and some in lakes. But the dominant beds are the massive layers of red sandstone. The basin lay in the baking tropics south of the Equator in Devonian times, and these sands piled up in desert sand-seas and alluvial fans. They acquired their distinctive red colour as moisture later rusted iron in them.

**Identification**: Old Red Sandstone formations are best identified by their location and the fossils they contain, such as the famous Devonian fish. These formations include shales and other mudrocks as well as sandstone. The sandstone can be recognized by its visible sand grains, often stained red by iron oxides.

**Grain size**: Over 95% sand-sized grains, 60μm–2mm/2.5–80mil
**Texture**: Gritty texture like solid sand. Grains well sorted, often well rounded. The amount of cement between grains varies widely.
**Structure**: See sandstone
**Colour**: Red, green, grey
**Composition**: See sandstone
**Formation**: Most of the red sandstones formed in vast alluvial fans spilling into desert basins, and in desert sand-seas
**Notable occurrences**: Shetland, Caithness, Midland Valley, Borders, Scotland; Fermanagh, Antrim, Northern Ireland; Mid-Wales; Shropshire, Devon, Somerset, England. North American red sandstones: western Canada; Catskill Mountains

**Brownstone fronts**
In the decades after the American Civil War in the 1860s, it was the fad to clad well-to-do houses in Boston and especially New York with brownstone. Entire districts became characterized by their brownstone fronts. Brownstone is a feldspar-rich sandstone that formed about 200 million years ago in the Triassic period. Iron-oxide cement coloured it a warm chocolate-brown. The most distinctive formation is near Portland in Connecticut, and in the late 1800s, the Portland quarries boomed. Yet the fad for brownstone did not last long – partly because of the coming of concrete, and partly because brownstone, which formed in horizontal layers, was set in buildings vertically face out or 'face-bedded.' Face-bedded like this, the brownstones quickly flaked off as water got in behind the layers and froze. Now these beautiful old buildings are cherished again, and the fronts are being restored with fresh stone from the reopened Portland Quarry and better mortar.

# Greensand

This can be either a sandstone or mudrock turned green by tiny pellets of the clay mineral glauconite, which gets its name from the Greek for 'blue-green'. Some greensands are over 90 per cent glauconite with just a little quartz sand and clay. Glauconite is a potassium iron aluminium silicate and is a useful potash fertilizer and valuable water softener. It forms in shallow seas (50–200m/164–656ft deep) only at times when sediments are piling up slowly, allowing sealife to burrow widely. Pellets form as faeces or the insides of dead foraminifera shells are chemically altered. However, glauconite-rich rock is not always green because it is turned brown or yellow by weathering. Most greensands were laid down in the Jurassic and Cretaceous periods. In England, sandstone beds formed at this time are called greensand whether they contain glauconite or not.

**Grain size**: Clay to sand size
**Texture**: Sometimes gritty and sandy, sometimes smooth like clay
**Structure**: See sandstone
**Colour**: Red, green, grey
**Composition**: Mostly glauconite, with quartz sand and clay
**Formation**: Greensands form on shallow, slowly sedimenting sea beds. They are often the last stage in a sedimentation sequence and typically appear just below an unconformity.
**Notable occurrences**: The Weald, Dorset, Berkshire, Oxfordshire, Bedfordshire, England; Boulonnais, France; New Jersey; Delaware

**Identification**: Unweathered, greensand is coloured pale olive green by glauconite, but this turns brown or yellow when exposed to air, and so is less distinctive.

# ARENITES AND WACKES

*There are two main kinds of sandstone: arenites and wackes. Arenites are all sand-sized grains (60µm–2mm/2.5–80mil) with little cement. Wackes are less sorted, with sand chaotically embedded in silt and clay. Both arenites and wackes may be mostly quartz (like orthoquartzite), a mix of quartz and feldspar (like the arenite arkose), or 'lithic' – that is, made of various rock fragments (like the wacke greywacke).*

## Orthoquartzite (Quartz arenite)

**Identification**: With a bare minimum of cement materials, orthoquartzite looks like solidified sand, which it is. It looks even more like lump sugar because the predominance of quartz makes it very pale in colour.

Orthoquartzites, or quartz arenites, are among the most quartz-rich of all rocks, made almost entirely of sand-sized grains of quartz with a bare minimum of cement. Indeed, the definition of an orthoquartzite is a sandstone consisting of over 95 per cent quartz. There are also a few traces of 'heavy' minerals such as zircon, tourmaline and rutile, but these are fairly scanty.

Orthoquartzites form in high-energy environments. They are created where sand is dropped by waves crashing on beaches and by powerful rivers streaming into the sea. The often dramatic cross-bedding and ripple marks in orthoquartzites are a telling reminder of the way these strong currents tugged the sands to and fro. These sands accumulate above the level where the biggest storm waves start, piling up along the shoreline as beaches, dunes, tidal flats, spits and bars. Look closely at any orthoquartzite formation and you can often see the remnant form of these ancient coastal features.

Not all orthoquartzites form in water. Because they are made of essentially dry sand, they can form from sand-seas in deserts, where sands are piled high by desert winds. Water-formed orthoquartzites tend to be white or pale grey, because they are almost pure quartz. These wind-blown, or 'aeolian', orthoquartzites are often stained red or pink by fine powdered iron oxides, which coat the grains.

About a third of all sandstones are orthoquartzites, but their spread in space and time is patchy. Many formed in a surprisingly narrow time band in the Palaeozoic period (570–245 million years ago). It needed a plentiful supply of continental rock to be weathered, and an unusually long and stable period of weathering to provide all the sand to make them (as well as the removal of other impurities). This is why orthoquartzites are found on the stable margins of ancient continental cratons, such as central Australia, the Russian platform and the St Peters Sandstone of central North America. Some hugely thick orthoquartzites began as deposits where continents rifted slowly and moved apart, which were then folded up into mountain ranges. The Clinch sandstones of the Appalachians and the Tapeats of the Rockies are believed to have been formed by this process.

**Grey orthoquartzite**: Being almost pure quartz, washed by water or scrubbed by the wind over countless years, quartz arenite or orthoquartzite is often a remarkably clean, pale white or grey quartz colour.

**Grain size**: Over 95% sand-sized grains, 60µm–2mm/2.5–80mil

**Texture**: Gritty texture like solid sand. Grains well sorted and well rounded.

**Structure**: Typically occurs in blanket-shaped deposits varying from a few metres to several hundred metres thick. They are usually interbedded with mudstones, limestones and dolomites. They usually display dramatic cross-bedding and ripplemarks reflecting their formation in high-energy environments. Aeolian rocks often show sand-dune shapes.

**Colour**: Water-formed orthoquartzites are typically white or pale grey. Aeolian orthoquartzites are often stained red, pink or brown by iron oxides.

**Composition**: Over 95% quartz, with a smearing of feldspar and carbonate cement. Also chert and metaquartzite, zircon, tourmaline and rutile.

**Formation**: Some form in high-energy marine environments such as beaches and spits around the edges of stable cratons. Some form on the continental shelf between rifting continents. Some are formed from aeolian (wind-blown) sand-seas in deserts, where there is a ready supply of sand.

**Notable occurrences**: Russian steppes; central Australia; St Peter sandstone, mid-west USA; Chilhowee, Tuscarora and Clinch formations in the Appalachian Mountains; Flathead and Tapeats formations in the Rocky Mountains

**Uluru**

Australia's Uluru is the world's largest single block of freestanding rock. Towering to over 345m/1,100ft, Uluru looks like a giant boulder poking out of the sand of the Simpson Desert. In fact, the exposed rock is just the very tip of an ancient outcrop of arkose sandstone extending far under the desert. This outcrop formed when an ancient ocean floor called the Amadeus Basin was uplifted some 550 million years ago, initiating a dramatic period of erosion, and the deposition of arkoses. Later crustal movements have tilted these arkoses almost on end, at 80–85 degrees. Finally, Uluru's arkose was buried beneath the sediments of a shallow sea, and has only re-emerged as wind and water stripped these sediments away. Uluru was long known by its European name, Ayers Rock, but it is a sacred site for Aboriginal peoples, and in 1985 the Australian government gave its custodianship back to the Aboriginals and restored its Aboriginal name, Uluru.

# Greywacke

Often called dirty sandstone, greywackes are tough, dark sandstones made from large, sharp grains of quartz, feldspar and rock fragments set in a mass of clay and silt. This unusually chaotic mix was often piled up by submarine avalanches or 'turbidity currents' that plunged from the continental shelf into the deep in a huge, churning mass of water and debris. Deposits are often thousands of metres thick and include the fossils of all kinds of deep-water creatures and plants caught up in the maelstrom. Greywackes were the main sandstones formed early in Earth's history, because land masses were so small at the time. Sandstones formed more recently are often better sorted.

**Grain size**: Mostly sand, mix of sizes from clay to gravel
**Texture**: Chaotic mix of sand, gravel and silt. Poorly sorted but well graded.
**Structure**: Graded bedding. Beds folded and deformed. No cross-bedding. Forms sequences with laminated sandstones and shale.
**Colour**: Grey, green, brown
**Composition**: Quartz (40–50%), feldspar (40–50%), mica, plus clay and rock
**Formation**: Deposited by turbidity currents, and in other high-energy environments
**Notable occurrences**: All fold mountain belts (except where there is lots of limestone), e.g. Wales; Scottish Uplands, Scotland; Cumbria, England; Schiefergebirge, Harz, Germany; Massif Central, France; Caples, Torlesse and Waipapa terrane, New Zealand; Coast Range, California; West Virginia

**Identification**: The grey colour and chaotic mix of large fragments amid sand and clay make greywacke easy to identify.

# Arkose (Feldspathic arenite)

Arkoses look so much like granite it can be hard to tell them apart. Often bedding marks are the only telltale signs that a rock is sedimentary arkose, not granite. This is because arkose is essentially reconstituted granite, with the same basic ingredients: quartz, feldspar and mica. It is the rock that forms when granite breaks down under particular conditions. What makes it different from other sandstones is that it contains feldspar. Under normal conditions, feldspar is weathered to clay, leaving just clay and quartz. Yet in arkose, feldspar is preserved. It was once thought this meant arkoses could form only in desert environments where there was too little moisture to destroy the feldspar. The Torridonian sandstones of north-west Scotland formed liked this. Now geologists know that feldspar may also be preserved if granite is being eroded and uplifted very rapidly. As a result, many arkoses formed as deltas and alluvial fans, where rivers spill out on to the grabens (depressions) created by the rifting of continents. Others occur along volcanic island arcs. So arkoses are linked with extremes in Earth's past – either extreme climates, or dramatic tectonic movements and high relief.

**Identification**: Arkose can look very like granite, with the same pinkish colour and the same assemblage of coarse-grained quartz, feldspar and mica minerals. The telltale signs are usually the shape of the formation, and evidence of bedding and layering.

**Grain size**: Mostly sand-sized grains, at least 1–2mm/40–80mil across
**Texture**: Grains not as well sorted or rounded as ortho-quartzite, except desert arkoses
**Structure**: In fan-shaped deposits a few metres deep. Less cross-bedding and ripple-marks than orthoquartzites. Aeolian rocks may show sand-dune shapes
**Colour**: White, grey or pink reflecting feldspar content
**Composition**: Quartz (40–50%), feldspar (40–50%), mica. In continental arkoses, orthoclase and microcline are the main feldspars; in island arc arkoses, plagioclase dominates
**Formation**: As deltas and in river bars in areas of high relief and aeolian (wind-blown) deposits in deserts
**Notable occurrences**: Torridon, Scotland; Pennines, England; France; Czech Rep; Uluru, Australia; Fountain Form., CO Calif; eastern USA

# RUDITES

*Sandstones, siltstones, mudstones and claystones are all made of small, fairly evenly sized grains.*
*However, some sedimentary rocks are made from a chaotic jumble of stones of many different sizes.*
*These jumbled, stone-filled rocks are called rudites, and are divided into two types: conglomerates and*
*breccias. In conglomerates, the stones are smooth and rounded. In breccias, they are sharp and angular.*

## Conglomerates

Sometimes called roundstone, conglomerates are basically round stones set in a matrix of finer sand and clay. The stones can be gravel (2–4mm/0.079–0.157in), pebbles (4–64mm/0.157–2.52in), cobbles (64–256mm/2.52–10.08in) and boulders (larger than 256mm/10.08in). Pebbles like these must have been tumbled along beaches or bowled down streams for countless years to round off all the sharp edges – and they had to be tough to survive this battering, so the stones in conglomerate are usually tough materials such as quartz, flint, chert and hard igneous rocks. In time, though, even the hardest stones are reduced to sand and clay. So conglomerates mark an interruption in the slow, steady process of deposition.

There are two kinds of conglomerate – orthoconglomerates and paraconglomerates. Orthoconglomerates are true sedimentary rocks and form where gravel and pebbles are dropped by flash floods in rivers or by storm waves on beaches. The stones in them are quite evenly sized and tightly packed. The spaces in between them are gradually filled up with finer sediment to cement them together, but the rock would be much the same shape with or without it.

Paraconglomerates are formed in one fell swoop and are a jumble of stones of all sizes scattered through a matrix. They are typically formed by landslides, by turbidity currents, and by glaciers – all dramatic events that move material wholesale without any sorting. Take away the matrix and all that is left is a pile of stones. Boulder clay is paraconglomerate.

Conglomerates are widespread, but deposits are usually small and localized. In some, dark pebbles stand out against the light cement like raisins in a pudding, earning them the name puddingstones. The brown puddingstones of Hertfordshire in England and Roxbury in Massachusetts, and the jasper puddingstones of St Joseph Island on Lake Huron in Canada, are all good examples of this.

**Puddingstone**: With their raisin-like pebbles, the puddingstones of Hertfordshire in England are very striking conglomerates. The white is a cement of quartz and feldspar; the pebbles are flints from the nearby chalk hills.

**Petromict conglomerate**: The great majority of conglomerates are described as petromict or polymict. This means they contain a wide mix of different stones from a variety of sources, such as basalts, slates and limestones. They are mainly river deposits washed down from areas of high relief and dumped in alluvial fans.

**Grain size**: Over 2mm/ 0.079in and can be granules, pebbles, cobbles or boulders
**Texture**: Orthoconglomerates are mostly gravel-sized grains nearly touching and less than 15% sand and clay matrix. Paraconglomerates are at least 15% matrix and are really sand- or mudstones scattered with pebbles, cobbles and boulders.
**Structure**: Conglomerates are generally small, poorly stratified deposits with none of the bedding marks of finer sediments
**Colour**: The colours are as varied as the rocks their stones came from. The stones are often markedly different in colour from the matrix. In jasper puddingstone, red stones are set in a pale matrix, like cherries in a cake.
**Composition**: The stones can be pure quartz or feldspar from sources such as pegmatites, but usually they are rock fragments – typically harder rocks such as rhyolite, slate and quartzite. The matrix can be silicates, calcites or iron oxides.
**Formation**: Orthoconglomerates form in fast-moving rivers and in shallow surf. Paraconglomerates are deposited by glaciers, landslides, avalanches and turbidity currents.
**Notable occurrences**: Hertfordshire, England; Kata Tjuta (Northern Territory), Australia; Huron, Ontario; Keeweenaw, Michigan; Ohio; Indiana; Illinois; Bahamas; Crestone (San Luis Valley), Colorado; Roxbury, Mass; Fairburn, S Dakota; Brooks Range, Alaska; Basin and Range, New Mexico; Van Horn, Texas; Death Valley, California

# Breccias

Sometimes called sharpstone, breccia is basically rubble turned into stone. The stones in breccia are jagged, caught up before there was time to round off any rough edges. Unlike conglomerates, breccias can form from almost any rock, soft and hard alike. But they almost always form near to their source and are said to be 'intraformational'. If the stones are washed any further away, they tend to get sorted and so do not form breccias. In mountain areas, breccias often form when screes are cemented together by finer sediment accumulating between the stones. Many breccias are formed rapidly by dramatic events – as when landslides and avalanches come to rest, or when flash floods or storm waves sweep masses of sediment into a beach or bar. Breccias also form when the roofs of limestone caves collapse, burying the floor in rubble. Coral reefs often contain extensive limestone breccias made of fragments broken off the reef. A few breccias are 'extraformational,' swept far from their source before consolidating and so have a very mixed composition.

**Identification**: Breccias are easily recognized by the large, angular stones they contain. It is not so easy to identify what the stones are or where they came from. The best place to start is a comparison with nearby rocks.

**Grain size**: Over 2mm/ 0.079in
**Texture**: Large angular stones in a finer matrix
**Structure**: Breccias are generally small, poorly stratified deposits
**Colour**: The colours are as varied as their source rocks
**Composition**: The stones are usually rock fragments – of almost any rock, including softer rocks such as marble
**Formation**: Some form in fast-flowing rivers, or on storm beaches. Others form from landslides and avalanches, both on land and under the sea.
**Notable occurrences**: Thessaly, Greece; Mexico; Vancouver Island, Midway, British Columbia; Platte Co, Wyoming; San Bernardino Co, California; Makinac Island, Michigan; Zopilote, Texas

## Volcanic, crush and impact breccias

Not all breccias are sedimentary. Volcanic breccias are tuffs that form from fragments blasted out by volcanoes. Crush breccias are formed when rocks are crushed underground by the sheer weight of formations above or by powerful tectonic movements. Some crush breccias are small scale, forming when veins and fissures are squeezed by crustal movements. Others occur on a much larger scale along faults, when the world's tectonic plates crunch past each other, or when layers of rock are folded in mountain building. Meteorite impacts create yet another kind of breccia when the huge force of an impact smashes crustal rocks to bits.

**Grain size**: Over 2mm/ 0.079in
**Texture**: Large angular stones in a finer matrix
**Structure**: Small, poorly stratified deposits
**Colour**: The colours are as varied as their source rocks
**Composition**: The stones are usually rock fragments
**Formation**: Volcanic breccias form from pyroclasts. Crush breccias form underground when rocks are crushed by crustal movement. Impact breccias form from rocks smashed by meteorite impacts.
**Notable occurrences**: Volcanic breccias: Arizona; New Mexico.
Crush breccias: Highlands, Scotland; Alps, Switzerland; Appalachian Mountains.
Impact breccias: Haughton Impact Crater (Devon Island), Nunavut.

**Identification**: Volcanic breccia contains angular pyroclasts at least 2mm/0.079in across. The pyroclasts are often black glass.

### Landslides
Every now and then a hill or cliff collapses suddenly in a landslide. Some landslides, like Black Ven in Dorset, are triggered as waves undercut the coast. Some are set off by a storm, like the thousands all over New Zealand after Cyclone Bola in 1986. Some are set off by volcanoes and earthquakes, like the 1989 Loma Prieta quake in California. Few events re-shape geology and remake rock material quite so quickly and dramatically. Soft rocks such as clays are very prone to landslides, but tougher rocks can also slide under certain conditions. They tend to fail along existing cracks such as joints. A key factor is often the presence of water, which pushes grains apart and reduces their cohesion. Local rains have caused landslides in the coastal town of Ventura, California (above). Very large rock falls can trap enough air to cushion the fragments, allowing them to travel far and fast. The 1970 Huascaran avalanche in Peru hurtled down the mountainside at a speed of over 320kph/200mph, killing 17,000 people in the towns in its path.

# BIOCHEMICAL ROCKS

*Countless creatures are able to extract dissolved chemicals from seawater and use them to make shell and bone. Some use calcium and carbon to make carbonates. Others use dissolved silica to make silicates. When these creatures die, the solid material they created turns into sediments, which form 'biochemical' sedimentary rocks such as chert, flint, chalk and diatomaceous earth.*

## Bedded chert (biochemical chert)

Chert is made of quartz crystals so fine they can be seen only under a microscope. It is an incredibly hard rock, yet when hit with a hammer it cracks almost like glass into sharp conchoidal fragments – a quality that was much appreciated by prehistoric people for making cutting tools. Most beds of chert formed from the ooze that covers much of the deep ocean floor even today. The ooze is built up from the constant rain of plankton remains such as radiolarians, diatoms and microscopic sponges called spicules. Once the ooze is buried it slowly solidifies into chert. Relatively pure silica-rich oozes are known as radiolarian or diatomaceous oozes, depending on which microscopic organism is dominant. Slightly less pure oozes are known as sarls and smarls. Each forms a particular kind of chert. Ocean bed ooze chert is the top layer, above serpentines and basalts, in ophiolite sequences – segments of the sea floor thrown up on to dry land.

**Identification**: Chert is easy to recognize by its very fine-grained, almost glassy texture, and its tendency to break into sharp, conchoidal fragments when hit with a hammer.

**Grain size**: The crystals are cryptocrystalline (too small to be seen with the naked eye)
**Texture**: Almost glassy, with conchoidal fracture
**Structure**: Biochemical cherts form in thin layers 1–10cm/0.4–3.9in thick. Typically massive or finely laminated (reflecting seasonal currents), but can show cross-bedding and scour marks from turbidity currents.
**Colour**: Black, white, red, brown, green, grey, depending on impurities
**Composition**: Mostly pure quartz
**Formation**: Forms when sea floor ooze solidifies
**Notable occurrences**: Aberdeenshire, Scotland; Peaks, England; Bavaria, Harz, Schiefergebirge, Germany; Bohema, Czech Republic; La Salle County, Illinois; Marion Co, Arkansas; Ozarks, Missouri; Minnesota

## Flint (replacement chert)

**Identification**: Flint nodules look like white, knobbly pebbles on the outside, but once broken they look like black or treacle-toffee coloured glass – though they are much harder and break with very sharp edges.

Not all chert is biochemical in origin. Some is simply chemical. In other words, the silica is formed without any organisms, as calcite crystals in limestone are replaced. The best known of these replacement cherts are flints. Flints are nodules of black or toffee-coloured chert that form in limestones, especially the Cretaceous chalks of southern England and northern France. Any chert that is black may also be called flint. Both kinds of flint were widely used by prehistoric peoples for making tools, and also for striking sparks to make fire. Chert formed by replacement can also occur as a fine powder scattered throughout limestone, and it is also very occasionally found as the cement in sandstones.

**Grain size**: The crystals are cryptocrystalline, which means they are too small to be seen with the naked eye
**Texture**: Almost glassy, with conchoidal fracture
**Structure**: Nodules. Sometimes flint forms around a network of burrows like those of *Thalassinoides* (a branching burrow with Y- or T-shaped branches), so flint takes this shape.
**Colour**: Usually black
**Composition**: Nearly pure quartz
**Formation**: Flint forms from the solidification of sea floor ooze
**Notable occurrences**: North Yorkshire Moors, North and South Downs, England; Rugen, Germany; Mon, Denmark; Flint Ridge, Ohio

# Chalk

Chalk is a white rock of almost pure calcite found in Europe and North America. About 100 million years ago in the Cretaceous period, large lowland areas of these continents were covered with tropical seas. Countless tiny floating algae left plate-like remains called coccoliths across the sea bed some 90–600m/300–2,000ft down, along with the shells of almost equally tiny organisms such as foraminifera. These algal plates and shell fragments turned quickly to almost pure white calcite. The sea bed remained undisturbed for a long time, and layer upon layer of these micro-organisms, along with the occasional larger shells such as ammonites, built up into thick layers of chalk, famously exposed in England's White Cliffs of Dover. Chalk is much softer than other limestones, and the vast beds that once covered most of north-west Europe have been stripped away, leaving bands of rounded hills. Chalks are porous rocks, though not very permeable, and these hills are marked both by dry valleys or bournes formed in wetter times, and also combes created by masses of crumbled rock flowing downhill during colder times.

**Red chalk**: Chalk may often be stained red by iron oxides.

**Identification**: Chalk's white colour is unmistakable. It looks like a fine powder, but the coccolith plates and foraminifera shells are clearly visible under a powerful microscope.

**Grain size**: Very fine-grained like mudstone
**Texture**: Powdery grains
**Structure**: Well stratified, with layers often shown up by beds of clays, shell layers and flint nodules. Often has burrow patterns. Occasional layers of crusted material called hardgrounds or Chalk Rock
**Colour**: White, occasionally red
**Composition**: Pure calcite
**Formation**: Forms from the remains of marine algae and microscopic shells
**Notable occurrences**: North Yorkshire Moors, Downs, Chiltern Hills, England; Champagne, France; Rugen, Germany; Mon, Denmark; South Dakota to Texas to Alabama

**Stone axes**
Flints gave our human ancestors their first tools. Chipped to give a sharp edge, they made it possible to cut through tough hides to get at meat, or, later, to cut hide to make clothes and plants to make tools and shelters. The first stone toolmaker was *Homo habilis*, who appeared about 2.3 million years ago, but it was *Homo erectus* (1.8 million years ago) who made the first crafted stone hand axes. Named Acheulian axes after the French village where they were first found, these axes had two cutting edges and a round end for holding. Axes like these were widely used for over a million years, until half a million years ago a technique for creating a long narrow blade was devised. About 50,000 years ago, modern humans, *Homo sapiens*, made another key breakthrough in blade technology, creating stone knives. Getting a good edge from a flint stone, called knapping, was a tremendously skilled job, and there is evidence that factories were set up where the best knappers would work.

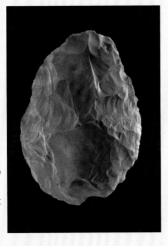

# Diatomaceous earth

Diatoms are among the most abundant of all microscopic marine algae. When they sink to the bottom, their minute shells collect in the ooze and eventually turn to what is called diatomaceous earth. When this occurs in a more compact form as a soft, very light, porous, chalky rock it is called diatomite or kieselguhr. Miners sometimes call it white dirt because in bright sunlight it can look like fresh snow. Diatomaceous earth's remarkable purity and fine grain makes it a perfect filtration material, as well as a filler for paper, paint and ceramics. When sugars and syrups are clarified, diatomaceous earth is usually the filter. It is also used as a mild abrasive in toothpastes and polishes.

**Grain size**: Very fine-grained like mudstone
**Texture**: Powdery grains. Diatom shells can be seen under a powerful microscope
**Structure**: Well stratified, with layers often shown up by beds of clays
**Colour**: White, yellow, greenish grey, sometimes almost black
**Composition**: Silica shells of diatoms
**Formation**: Diatomaceous earth forms from the remains of marine algae and microscopic shells
**Notable occurrences**: Denmark; Lüneburger, Saxony, Halle, Germany; France; Central Italy; Russia; Algeria; Nevada; Oregon; Washington; Santa Barbara, California

**Identification**: Diatomite looks a little like chalk but is so light it almost floats on water like pumice.

# LIMESTONES (CARBONATE ROCKS)

*Made up of at least half calcite (or the similar aragonite), limestones are distinctive whitish, grey or cream rocks. They are the third most abundant sedimentary rocks on Earth, after mudrocks and sandstones, and extend over vast areas of continents and continental shelves, dominating many mountain chains. Limestone 'karst' landscapes can often be very dramatic, with their caverns and gorges.*

## Limestone

**Coral limestone**: Few rocks are richer in fossils than limestones. Very often you can see perfectly preserved remains of sea creatures that swam and crawled in tropical seas long ago, or, like the coral polyps preserved in this rock, simply sat on the sea floor and waited for a meal to pass.

Limestones are a striking testament to the sheer profusion of life on Earth, especially in the sea. They are almost entirely the work of living things. Huge beds of limestone thousands of metres thick may be the accumulated remains of countless sea creatures piled up on the sea bed over millions of years, then slowly changed into rock as their chemistry alters. This accumulation is going on today, notably in places such as the Bahamas, and these remains too will in time turn to rock.

Living things contribute to the creation of limestone in two ways. Sometimes they contribute their 'skeletal' remains, their hard shells and bones, to the rock. Alternatively, like plankton and algae, they change the chemistry of the sea, and encourage the deposit of calcite. The key chemicals in limestones are carbonates – and in particular calcium carbonate in the form of calcite or aragonite. Carbonate sediments may be rich in either calcite or aragonite, but ancient limestones are almost always calcite-rich because aragonite alters over time to calcite.

Limestones form in many places – soils on old rocks, river flood plains, lakes – but most are the creation of shallow, clear tropical waters. Here there is not only an abundance of sea life, but the evaporation of such warm waters boosts the precipitation of calcium carbonates. This does not mean limestones are found only in the tropics, however. The continents have shifted so much through the ages that many places now nearer the Arctic were once in the tropics. During the Carboniferous period around 300 million years ago, much of what is now North America and Europe lay in the tropics, and was inundated by vast tropical seas. Huge beds of limestone, now visible in places such as Texas and the English Pennines, are the legacy of this time. In England, such limestones are called Carboniferous limestones.

**Reef limestone**: Reef limestones are the work of corals, those remarkable sea creatures still building up huge colonies like Australia's Great Barrier Reef. Reef limestones are made partly from their skeletons, built up over the ages, and partly from sediment trapped and bound by mats of microbes living on the reef. Unlike some other limestones, reef limestones contain no visible skeletal remains. They are also harder than other limestones, and are often left protruding as small hills after softer surrounding limestones has been weathered away.

**Grain size**: Varies from clay-sized to gravel-sized

**Texture**: Highly variable, from very fine-grained, porcelain-like look to aggregate of large fossils

**Structure**: Most limestones show the same range of structures as sandstones and mudrocks. Beds often include reef limestones, the fossils of coral reefs. Reef limestones show little bedding, although they preserve the growth pattern of corals and cavities filled by carbonate debris and cement. Patch reefs or 'bioherms' are oval lumps left by small round coral colonies. 'Biostromes' are large long limestone formations left by barrier reefs.

**Colour**: White, grey, cream plus red, brown, black

**Composition**:
Skeletal remains: Algae and microbes (coccoliths and stromatolites); Foraminfera; Corals; Sponges; Byrozoans; Brachiopods; Molluscs; Echinoderms; Arthropods. Carbonate grains (overleaf): Ooids and pisoids; Peloids; Aggregates; Intraclasts. Lime mud: Bone, teeth and scale debris (phosphates); Wood, pollen and kerogen (carbonates); Cement (calcite, aragonite, dolomite).

**Formation**: Forms as carbonates form, mainly on the sea floor, either from the skeletal remains of sea creatures or by the precipitation of calcite

**Notable occurrences**: Burren, Ireland; Pennines, Cotswolds, England; Slovenia; Italy; Swartberg, South Africa; Ratnapura, Sri Lanka; Laos; Thailand; Guilin, China; Victoria, Australia; Paparoa, New Zealand; New Mexico; Kentucky; Texas; South Dakota; Indiana; Onondaga, New York

Lagoon

Ocean

Fringing reef

Bedrock

**Coral reefs**

Coral reefs are one of the wonders of tropical seas, teeming with an astonishing variety of sea creatures. The reefs themselves are made up from tiny sea anemone-like animals called polyps, which stay all their lives fixed in one place attached to a rock or to dead polyps. They take dissolved calcium carbonate from seawater and turn it into the mineral aragonite to build the cup-shaped skeleton or corallite in which they live. The skeleton becomes hard coral when they die. Coral reefs are made from millions of polyps and their skeletons, and can stretch for thousands of kilometres. Fringing coral reefs grow at a particular depth along the shoreline. Barrier reefs form a little way offshore. Coral atolls form around the edge of an island volcano. As the volcano sinks or the sea level rises, so the coral grows up and eventually leaves just a ring or atoll. Corals have been around since Cambrian times, and their reefs and fossils are abundant in limestone rocks of all ages since then.

# Fossiliferous limestone: Bryozoan limestone

Like crinoids, bryozoans were sea creatures that lived in such vast numbers in the tropical oceans of the past that their remains have gone on to make a specific and abundant kind of limestone, bryozoan limestone. Over 15,000 species of bryozoan have been identified, of which 3,500 are alive today, living in many ocean shallows such as the western Pacific. They live in colonies of hundreds of animals or zooids, each secreting a short tube of lime to enclose its soft parts. A ring of about ten tentacles snakes out from the end of the tube to guide food into the animal's mouth. Bryozoan colonies look so like lace, they are also known as sea lace.

**Grain size**: Sand-sized grains with fossil remnants
**Texture**: Highly variable, with sand-sized grains and partial and complete fossils
**Structure**: Marked cross-bedding and ripple-marks. Layering from repeated cycles of sedimentation. Often broken into massive blocks divided by vertical joints and horizontal bedding planes
**Colour**: White, cream
**Composition**: Calcite
**Formation**: From bryozoans in shallow tropical seas
**Notable occurrences**: North Wales; Norfolk, England; Southern Sweden; Stevns Klint (Zealand), Denmark; Moravia, Czech Republic; Torquay and Geelong (Victoria), St Vincent (SA), off Tasmania, Australia; off Otago, Oamaru (South Island), New Zealand; Biscayne, Florida; Indiana

**Identification**: Bryozoan limestone is identified from the lace-like colonies of bryozoans. Individual animals are tubes about 2mm/0.08in long.

# Fossiliferous limestone: Crinoidal limestone

Many limestones consist largely of recognizable fossils of ancient sea creatures. Among the most widespread of these 'fossiliferous' limestones are crinoidal limestones. Sometimes called sea lilies, the crinoids of the past were animals that looked like long-stemmed flowers, with a central 'cup' containing the soft parts of the animal, numerous branching 'arms' and a stem up to 30m/98ft 5in long, which attached the animal to the ocean floor. In the Carboniferous period in particular, crinoid flowers grew in such extraordinary profusion that they created vast 'meadows' on the sea floor. When the animals died, ocean currents broke up most of their skeletal plates into sand-sized grains and rolled them together until they were cemented by calcite into thick deposits of limestone. Dramatic cross-bedding in these rocks bears witness to the shallowness of the seas in which the crinoids grew, and the power of the waves and currents that broke up their remains. Whole fossils are rare. The volume of crinoidal limestones around the world is staggering, and incorporates the remains of a huge number of crinoids. There are estimated to be at least 60,000km$^3$/14,400 cu miles of crinoid remains in the Mission Canyon-Livingstone formation in the Rockies alone.

Crinoid fossil

**Grain size**: Sand-sized grains with fossil remnants
**Texture**: Highly variable, with sand-sized grains and partial and complete fossils
**Structure**: Marked cross-bedding and ripple-marks. Layering from repeated cycles of sedimentation. Often broken into massive blocks divided by vertical joints and horizontal bedding planes.
**Colour**: White, grey
**Composition**: Calcite
**Formation**: From meadows of crinoids in shallow tropical seas
**Notable occurrences**: North Wales; Derbyshire, Durham, Somerset, England; Austria; Nile Valley, Egypt; Timencaline Wells, Libya; Nepal; Namoi, Bingleburra, Australia; Mission Canyon-Livingston (Rocky Mts), Canada–USA; Leadville, Colorado; Redwall, Arizona; Burlington, Iowa to Arkansas

**Identification**: Crinoidal limestone is stuffed full of the fossils of crinoids. Although very few remain intact, there are usually enough of the cups, arms and stems surviving to be recognizable.

# OOLITHS AND DOLOSTONES

*There is a huge variety of carbonate rocks. While some limestones are largely fossiliferous or shelly –*
*made largely of fragments of shell and bone – others consist of grains formed by the precipitation of*
*calcite and aragonite from carbonate-rich sea-water. Like limestones, dolostones are carbonate rocks, but*
*they are made of magnesium carbonate instead of calcium carbonate.*

## Grain limestone (Oolitic and Pisolitic limestone)

Limestones show the same range of grain sizes and
textures as sandstones and mudrocks. Indeed, some
geologists describe them using the same terms
(lutites, arenites and rudites), adding 'calci-' or
'calca' to show they are limestones. So calcilutites are
limestone muds, calcarenites lime sands and
calcirudites gravels. Many calcarenites contain only a
few shellfish remains. Instead, they are made mostly
of calcite or aragonite grains precipitated out of
water. Calcite grains can be washed into deposits just
like sand and mud grains, but most form in situ.
Ooliths or ooids are tiny balls made as layers of calcite
build up on clay grains, kept round as they are rolled by
underwater currents. Pisoids are gravel-sized balls that form
in the same way. They look similar to grains called oncoids,
but oncoids are actually created by microbes. Peloids are
oval grains that usually started life as pellets of snail and
shellfish faeces and were then altered to micrite (fine-grained
calcite). Intraclasts are bits of broken calcite sediment.
Limestones can be classified according to the dominant type
of grain, as shown in the table below. They can also be
classified by their texture (see table opposite).

**Oolitic limestone**: Also known
as roestone because it looks like
fish roe, oolitic limestone is made
of sand-sized grains called ooliths.
Ooliths form in shallow, carbonate-
rich tropical waters such as those
around the Bahamas today,
starting as aragonite and later
changing to calcite. Wherever
oolitic limestones appear, they
are reminders that conditions
were once like this.

**Grain size**: Ooids
(0.2–0.5mm/7.87–19.69mil);
pisoids and oncoids (over
2mm/78.8mil); peloids (over
1mm/39.4mil); intraclasts
(1mm–20mm/0.04in–0.8in)
**Texture**: (see table opposite)
**Structure**: Grain limestones
show the same range of
structures as sandstones
and mudrocks
**Colour**: White, grey,
cream plus red, brown,
and black
**Composition**:
Carbonate grains with
lime mud cement (sparite
and micrite)
**Formation**: Forms by the
precipitation of aragonite in
shallow, carbonate-rich
tropical waters
**Notable occurrences**:
Dorset, Cotswolds, England;
Luxembourg; Harz, Thuringia,
Germany; Ukraine; Kertsch,
Russia; Caucasus,
Georgia; Newfoundland;
Texas; Alabama

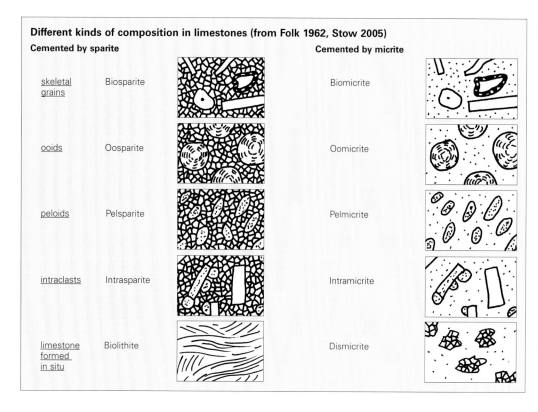

**Different kinds of composition in limestones (from Folk 1962, Stow 2005)**

| Cemented by sparite | | | Cemented by micrite | |
|---|---|---|---|---|
| skeletal grains | Biosparite | | Biomicrite | |
| ooids | Oosparite | | Oomicrite | |
| peloids | Pelsparite | | Pelmicrite | |
| intraclasts | Intrasparite | | Intramicrite | |
| limestone formed in situ | Biolithite | | Dismicrite | |

**Pisolitic limestone**: Oolitic
limestone is made from sand-
sized grains 0.2–0.5mm/
7.07–19.69mil in diameter;
pisolitic limestone is made from
larger, pea-sized grains at least
2mm/78.8mil across.

# Dolostone (Dolomite limestone)

Ever since they were first identified in 1791 by Frenchman Deodat de Dolomieu in the Italian Dolomite mountains named after him, dolostone or dolomite limestone has intrigued geologists. While ordinary limestones are made of calcite or aragonite, dolostones are at least half made of the magnesium carbonate mineral dolomite. Until the 1960s, when it was found forming along the shore in the Arabian Gulf and in the Bahamas and Florida, no one had seen it actually forming directly from seawater. It seemed as if all dolostone formed by the chemical alteration of calcite in limestones by magnesium-rich solutions, a process called dolomitization. This is probably how most dolostones did form, but the process is now better understood. It seems to involve salty brines formed as evaporation concentrates seawater in tropical lagoons. These magnesium-rich briny waters sink seawards through limestones, slowly turning their calcite to dolomite. This process was more prevalent in the past, and most dolostones are Precambrian in origin (at least half a billion years old).

**Identification**: Dolomite is a much tougher rock than limestone and has a sugary white crystalline look. Recrystallization destroys fossils, so there are no visible organic remains.

**Grain size**: Varied – some forms are microcrystalline; others are sand-sized
**Texture**: Dense sugary texture
**Structure**: Stands out from ordinary limestone in rib-like beds because it is so tough. Coarse crystal dolostone shows the same structures as other limestones; fine crystalline dolostone does not.
**Colour**: White, grey, cream but weathers pink or brown
**Composition**: At least half dolomite
**Formation**: Thought to form when calcite in limestone is dolomitized (recrystallized and turned to dolomite)
**Notable occurrences**: Central England; Swabian and Franconian Jura, Rhineland, Germany; Dachstein, Austria; Dolomites, Italy; Niagara, Ontario; Arkansas; Iowa; Ohio; Kentucky

**Karst scenery**
Limestone may have formed in water and yet the calcite it is made of is also quite easily dissolved by water that is slightly acidic. Rain and groundwater take up carbon dioxide from the air and soil, turning them into weak carbonic acid. Wherever limestone is near the surface, this acidic water seeps into cracks and begins to dissolve the rock. After thousands of years, huge cavities can be etched out often creating spectacular scenery, known as Karst after the Kras plateau in Slovenia, one of the many places where such scenery is found. Underground, huge potholes and caverns with stalactites and stalagmites are created. Above ground, cracks around blocks of rock on surfaces are etched out to create striking limestone pavements. Often cavern roofs collapse or potholes grow and merge to create deep gorges. Eventually, so much rock will be dissolved away that only distinctive, towerlike pillars are left, such as these in the famous Guilin Hills of China (above).

**Different kinds of deposit texture in limestones**

**Original components not bound together**

Mudstone (mud-supported, less than 10% grains)

Wackestone (mud-supported, more than 10% grains)

Packstone (grain-supported)

Grainstone (lacks mud and is grain-supported)

**Original components bound together**

Boundstone

**No recognizable deposition texture**

Crystalline

**Original components not organically bound**

Floatstone (matrix-supported, less than 10% sand-sized grains)

Rudstone (sand-supported, less than 10% sand-sized grains)

**Original components organically bound**

Bafflestone (organisms act as baffles)

Bindstone (organisms encrust and bind)
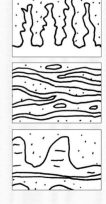

Framestone (organisms build a rigid framework)

This classification was devised by Dunham in 1962, then modified by Embry and Klovan in 1971 and Stow in 2005

# CHEMICAL ROCKS

*Chemical sedimentary rocks form neither from debris nor with the aid of living things, but entirely chemically as minerals precipitated out of water solutions. Many are left behind as solid 'evaporites' when the solution evaporates. Yet precipitation can occur whenever a solution becomes saturated and can no longer retain the minerals dissolved in it, forming rocks such as tufas, travertines and dripstones.*

## Tufa

Tufas are calcite deposits that build up around the rim of calcite-rich springs, rather like the limescale that builds up in baths and taps in areas of hard water. Tufa often builds towers underwater where springs bubble up into lakes or under the sea. If lake levels drop, these towers may be exposed, as in California's famous Mono Lake. Although tufas are chemical rocks, algae and other plant material does play a part in their formation. Tufa is always precipitated on to some surface or other, and quite often the surface is algae or plants. Indeed, algae actively spurs tufa to precipitate, forming algal mats or mounds called stromatolites made of tufa bound together by filaments of algae. Often the algae rots away leaving a sponge-like rock called a sinter. Tufa is sometimes called calcareous sinter to distinguish from siliceous sinter, a sinter that forms by the precipitation of opaline silica. Because it is so full of holes, tufa is light and easy to cut, which is why the Romans used it to line the Aqua Appia, the underground aqueduct they built in 312BC to supply the city of Rome with water.

**Identification**: Full of holes like a sponge, and quite light and soft, tufa is easy to recognize. It is usually white or a buff colour, but iron oxides can turn it red or yellow. Deposits are usually quite thin.

**Grain size**: Powdery
**Texture**: Compact to earthy and friable
**Structure**: Tufa is spongy and full of holes. Structures take the form of the places that they formed. Towers form around underwater springs. Algal colonies often form mounds.
**Colour**: White, buff, yellow, red
**Composition**: Calcium carbonate in the form of calcite, or occasionally aragonite
**Formation**: By precipitation from calcium-rich waters, typically in streams, around springs or algal mounds.
**Notable occurrences**: Glen Avon, Scotland; Ikka Fjord, Greenland; Great Rift Valley, Kenya; Kimberley, Western Australia; Mono Lake, Mojave Desert, California

## Travertine

**Identification**: Denser and more compact than tufa, with fewer holes, travertine looks a little like tofu, and is usually an attractive pale honey colour.

Tufa forms mainly around cool springs, typically when plants take carbon dioxide from the water and make less available to combine with calcium. Around hot springs, calcite is precipitated when hot water loses carbon dioxide as it cools. This leaves dense, hard crusts, such as those around Mammoth Hot Springs in Yellowstone Park, Wyoming. The terms tufa and travertine are sometimes used interchangeably, but geologists usually call the dense variety travertine, and the spongy variety tufa. Travertine is a pale honey colour, often with delicate banding. Many sculptors have used it as an easier-to-carve alternative to marble, and it is also cut into slabs and made into polished floors. The most famous travertine is Roman travertine, which gave the rock its name.

**Grain size**: Powdery
**Texture**: Compact to earthy and friable
**Structure**: Much denser than tufa, with only a few holes. Often banded.
**Colour**: Honey, red, brown
**Composition**: Calcite, or occasionally aragonite
**Formation**: By precipitation from calcium-rich waters around hot springs or in caves (see Dripstone)
**Notable occurrences**: Bohemia, Czech Republic; Aniene River, Italy; Pammukale, Turkey; Algeria; Thebes, Egypt; San Luis, Argentina; Baja, Vera Cruz, Mexico; Yavapai Co, Arizona; Yellowstone, Wyoming; Jemez, New Mexico; San Luis Obispo Co, California

# Evaporite

In arid conditions, salty water may evaporate to leave dissolved minerals as evaporite deposits. Some evaporites form when desert salt lakes dry up. They form on a larger scale when seawater evaporates in lagoons, coastal shallows and salt flats called sabkhas. The scale of some seawater evaporations is staggering. Evaporites are highly soluble, so they are rare on the surface, but there are ancient evaporites thousands of metres thick dating from the Cambrian, Permian, Triassic and Miocene periods. A depth of 1,000m/3,280ft of seawater needs to steam off to form each 15m/49ft of deposit. So, to build up these massive beds, coastal flats must have been flooded by the sea again and again over vast time spans. There are a large number of minerals dissolved in seawater, but only a few are abundant, and they always tend to be deposited in the same sequence, creating a bull's eye pattern of deposits. The sequence starts with the least soluble, dolomite, then goes through gypsum, anhydrite and halite (rock salt) to finish with the most soluble, potassium and magnesium salts called bitterns. The evaporites formed in salt lakes inland are typically dominated by halite, gypsum and anhydrite, but there are also many more minor salts.

**Identification**: Evaporites are usually crystalline, looking like solidified sugar or salt. Crystals can vary hugely in size. On lagoon and lake floors, selenite gypsum crystals can grow up to 1m/3ft 3in.

**Grain size**: Crystal size varies
**Texture**: Coarse/fine, earthy, friable, massive, sugary
**Structure**: Lagoon deposits: cracked. Deep water deposits: laminated. Nodules of anhydrite form in sabhka gypsum, often leaving just a 'chicken wire' mesh of gypsum between them.
**Colour**: White, pink, red
**Composition**: Dolomite, gypsum, anhydrite, halite or bittern
**Formation**: Evaporation of salty waters in coastal salt flats, lagoons and salt lakes
**Notable occurrences**:
*Currently forming*: Caspian Sea, Georgia; Persian Gulf; Dead Sea; Great Salt L, Utah
*Ancient formations:* Lakes: Green River, Wyoming. Sabhka and shallow shelf: northern Europe; Elk Pt, British Columbia; Salina, Michigan; Williston, Montana; Delaware, Texas. Deep sea: Mediterranean.

**The great Mediterranean salt pan**
In 1970, a team drilling in the Mediterranean Sea made an extraordinary discovery. There beneath the sea were the thickest evaporites ever found, many thousands of metres thick. It transpires that at the end of the Miocene epoch, about five million years ago, the movement of the continents greatly narrowed the Straits of Gibraltar. A brief ice age triggered a global drop in sea level, and suddenly the Atlantic stopped flowing into the Mediterranean to keep it topped up. Within a few thousand years, the entire Mediterranean – some 2.5 million km³ (599,782 cubic miles) of water – had evaporated to create one gigantic salt basin, like the Dead Sea but 4,000m/13,123ft deep! Buried in the sediments under the Nile in Africa is a great canyon 2,500m/8,202ft deep dating from this time – indicating that the Mediterranean had dried up entirely. This whole episode is known as the Messinian Event because the best known deposits from the time are under the port of Messina, Sicily (situated just south of the peninsula enclosing the Strait of Messina, shown in the satellite image above).

# Dripstone and flowstone

Although most travertines form around hot springs, the most spectacular and beautiful are often those that form in limestone caverns. Here calcite-rich waters dripping from the ceiling create deposits called dripstones. Dripstones can build up in all kinds of fantastic formations, such as stalactites hanging from the ceiling and stalagmites projecting from the floor (see Calcites and Dolomite). Sliced across, these dripstones usually reveal how they were built up in layers, like the layers of an onion, in darker and lighter bands. Cavern walls and floors continually wet with running water may be coated in sheets of travertine called flowstone.

**Grain size**: Powdery
**Texture**: Compact to earthy and friable
**Structure**: Dense, compact. Stalactites and stalagmites show 'growth rings' caused by variations in precipitation.
**Colour**: Honey-coloured, red, brown
**Composition**:
Calcium carbonate in the form of calcite, or occasionally aragonite
**Formation**: By precipitation from dripping and flowing calcium-rich groundwaters in limestone rock
**Notable occurrences**: Kent's Cavern (Devon), England; Skocjan, Slovenia; Aggtelek, Hungary; Sorek, Israel; Reed Flute (Guilin), China; Philippines; Carlsbad, New Mexico; Mammoth Cave, Kentucky; Luray, Virginia

**Identification**: Dripstones are often markedly layered, revealing variations in the seasonal flow of water down through the limestone.

# ORGANIC ROCK

*Coal is a very unusual sedimentary rock. Not only does it burn, which makes it a very useful fuel, but it is also almost entirely organic. It is made not from grains of minerals, like other sediments, but from the remains of plants that grew in tropical swamps hundreds of millions of years ago, transformed into solid black or brown carbon as they were buried.*

## Coal formation

Most of the coal resources in North America, Europe and northern Asia formed in the Carboniferous and early Permian periods, around 300 million years ago. At this time, these continents lay mostly in the tropics, and vast areas were covered in steamy swamps where giant club mosses and tree ferns grew in profusion. Waters moved through these swamps only sluggishly, so when plants died, their remains piled up on the swamp floor and rotted only slowly in the stagnant, poorly oxygenated water. Microbes began to turn the remains into peat. Peat is about half carbon and is a useful, if smoky, fuel when dried, but to transform peat into coal, it must be deeply buried, to a depth of at least 4km/2.5 miles.

Over millions of years, the peats from the Carboniferous swamp were buried under layers of accumulating sediment until they were not only squeezed completely dry, but began to cook in the heat of the Earth's interior. Cooking did not only destroy plant fibre – it drove out hydrogen, nitrogen and sulphur as gases, and gradually transformed the carbon compounds in the plants to pure carbon. The deeper and longer they were buried and the hotter they got, the more plants turned to carbon. Peat is quite soft and brown and only about 60 per cent carbon; anthracite, the deepest and oldest kind of coal, is hard, black and over 95 per cent carbon. In between come intermediate 'ranks' of coal – brown coal, or lignite (73 per cent carbon), and dull black bituminous coal (85 per cent carbon).

Most black coal dates from the Carboniferous and early Permian. The world's largest resources of these coals are in Russia and the Ukraine, which has almost half the world's entire coal reserves, but there are also huge black coal beds in the USA. Besides black coals, there are brown coals formed more recently, especially in the Tertiary, 1.6 to 64 million years ago. Although less rich in carbon, these coals are widespread, found in China, North America, especially Alaska, as well as southern France, central Europe, Japan and Indonesia.

**Peat**: All coal may have begun as peat. If so, the peat of old must have formed in tropical swamps. Peat today forms only in bogs in cool places. Here decomposition of plant material is so slow that thick layers can build up before the plants totally rot. Microbes do get to work, however, converting at least half of the plant material to carbon as it becomes compacted.

**Lignite**: Once peat is buried deeply, the process of 'coalification' begins. Microbial activity ceases, but pressure and heat begin to turn more of the plant remains to carbon. Lignite or brown coal is the first stage. It crumbles when exposed to the air and has a texture like woody peat. Most lignite is more recent than black coal, dating from the Tertiary. It is found nearer the surface than black coal, but is much less carbon-rich and burns with less heat and more smoke.

**Grain size**: Fine-grained, similar to mudrocks

**Texture**: Varies with coal rank. The lower ranked coals contain many only partly altered plant remains; the highest ranked coals contain very few. Peat contains un-decomposed plants.

**Structure**: Coal occurs as beds or seams interlayered with other sedimentary rocks, often with a thin layer of carbon-affected material called seat-earth beneath. Seams are generally only a few metres thick, but can be several hundred metres. Coals form in stagnant environments so do not show any cross-bedding, but humic coals (see Formation below) contain bands from 1–10mm/ 0.039–0.39in thick. Each seam has its own banding profile, which can help to identify it almost like a fingerprint.

**Colour**: Brown, black

**Formation**: Most coals are 'humic' and form when plant material piles up in situ in tropical coastal swamps and is then buried deep and converted by heat to carbon. Rarer 'sapropelic' coal forms when plant debris, spores, pollen and algae pile up far from their original source.

**Notable occurrences**: Some of the world's biggest coal reserves are in the heart of Siberia in Russia, in Kazakhstan and the Ukraine. There are also major reserves of black coal in northern Europe, the Damodar Valley in India, and Appalachians and Midwest of North America. Germany and China have huge resources of brown coal. Pennsylvania is famous for its anthracite deposits.

# Coal types and components

Plants are made from a wide range of different components including massive, hard trunks, soft leaves and tiny seeds and spores. Once a plant dies and falls into a swamp, oxygen and microbes get to work on each of these components differently. These differences are most significant in the early stages of the coal formation process, when peat forms. Consequently, peats can differ widely in character according to the plant parts involved. Even once peat is buried and coalification proper begins, the variations in plant parts makes a difference to the nature of the coal. The plant components in coal are called 'macerals', and divided into three broad groups: vitrinite, liptinite and inertinite. Vitrinite comes from the woody parts of the plant – trunks, branches, roots. It's tough and shiny and is the major component in a type of coal called vitrain. Liptinite comes from the waxy and resinous parts of the plant – the seeds, spores and sap. It is softer and duller than vitrinite. Mixed with vitrinite, it makes a silky, laminated kind of coal called clarain. Inertinite comes from plant material much altered by oxidation during peat formation, or from parts affected by fungus. Mixed with liptinite, it makes a dull hard coal called durain. By itself it makes the soft, powdery charcoal-like kind of coal called fusain – easy to identify because it leaves your fingers smeared black.

Each coal seam contains varying amounts of these different kinds of coal, but the higher the rank of the coal – the closer to pure carbon anthracite it gets – the more they lose their distinctiveness as a result of the greater degree of 'coalification'.

**Bituminous coal**:
Bituminous or soft coal is second only in rank to anthracite, with a 75–85 per cent carbon content. It is dark brown to black and banded, and usually made of over 95 per cent vitrinite, which comes from plants' woody parts. This is the most widely used type of coal, but its high sulphur content can contribute to the creation of acid rain when it is burned.

**How coal is mined**
The way companies mine coal depends partly on the depth of the seam. With a seam less than 100m/328ft below the surface, the cheapest method is to simply strip off the overlying material with a giant shovel called a dragline. Brown coal tends to occur near the surface, and can often be mined economically by strip mining. The best bituminous and anthracite coal typically lies in narrow layers called seams, far below ground. To get at the coal, mining companies have to sink deep shafts to reach the seam. The Ashton pit in northern England plunged almost 1,000m/3,280ft. With the shaft dug, they then created a maze of horizontal or gently sloping tunnels to get into the seam and extract the coal. The surface of the exposed seam is called the coal face. Mining operations can be hazardous, with the constant danger of roof-falls or of explosions as methane gas forms from the coal. Miners can also suffer lung damage by inhaling coal-dust.

**Anthracite**: Anthracite, or hard coal, is the highest ranked of all the coals – shiny black and over 95 per cent carbon. Temperatures in the ground have to reach over 200°C/392°F to turn bituminous coal to anthracite. It is the rarest, and usually most ancient, of coals but it has a very high energy content and burns almost without smoke.

**Composition**:
*Peat*: Over 75% water by weight; Solid matter: over 50% carbon, under 50% dry mineral-free volatiles.
*Lignite*: 33–75% water by weight; Solid matter: 50–60% carbon, under 50% dry mineral-free volatiles.
*Sub-bituminous*: 10–32% water by weight; Solid matter: 60–75% carbon, 35–42% dry mineral-free volatiles.
*Bituminous*: Under 10% water by weight; Solid matter: 75–85% carbon, 18–37% dry mineral-free volatiles.
*Anthracite*: No water; Solid matter: 75–85% carbon, 18–37% dry mineral-free volatiles.

**Plant components (macerals)**:
*Vitrinite group (50–90%)*: Woody tissue – polymers, cellulose, lignin.
*Liptinite group (5–15%)*: Waxy parts of plant – seeds, spores, resins.
*Inertinite group (5–40%)*: Shiny black plant material highly altered during peat formation.

**Coal types**:
*Vitrain*: Glassy, brittle, bright bands, conchoidal fracture, dominated by vitrinites.
*Clarain*: Finely laminated, silky, bright and dull bands, smooth fracture, mix of vitrinite and liptinites.
*Durain*: Hard, dull, matlike, dull bands, mix of inertinites and liptinites.
*Fusain*: Soft, powdery, charcoal-like, dirties fingers, mostly inertinite.

**Inorganic components**:
Detrital quartz, heavy minerals, sulphates, phosphates, pyrite nodules, marcasite, siderite, dolomite, calcite.

# METAMORPHIC ROCKS: NON-FOLIATED

*Metamorphic rocks are formed from neither melts nor sediments but are created deep underground when other rocks are remade by heat and pressure, sometimes by direct contact with hot magma, sometimes by the tremendous forces present in the Earth's crust. The original rock's minerals are cooked and recrystallized in new forms or even as completely new minerals. Metamorphic rocks are divided into foliated (striped) rocks and non-foliated rocks, which include hornfels, metaquartzite and granofels.*

## Hornfels

Hornfels is a tough, splintery rock that gets its name from the German for 'horn rock' because broken edges are translucent like horn. Making it involves less stress than other kinds of metamorphism. The original rock or protolith is simply cooked by close contact with an intrusion. The heat is tremendous – typically about 750°C/1,350°F – but the rock is neither crushed, twisted nor pulled. So hornfels is free from foliation. Crystals are fine-grained and point in all directions. Indeed, hornfels can easily look like a volcanic rock. Small structures in the protolith are obliterated during metamorphism. The crystals reform in a tight, interlocking pattern like crazy paving called pfiaster structure, visible under a magnifying glass. Some hornfelses may also be distinctively 'spotted' with porphyroblasts (large crystals like phenocrysts in igneous rock), such as andalusite hornfels and cordierite hornfels.

Hornfels is not just a type of rock, though, but helps identify some of the various 'facies' of metamorphic rock – the particular combinations of minerals formed in different pressure and temperature regimes. Hornfels facies include the hornblende hornfels and the pyroxene hornfels facies. These facies are the array of minerals that form when pressure is low but temperatures are high. The exact composition depends on both the original rock and the temperature, often grading through different minerals the nearer to the intrusion the rock forms and the hotter it gets.

Hornfelses are often divided into three groups according to their protolith: those made from shales and clays; those made from impure limestone; and those made from igneous rocks such as dolerite, basalt and andesite. All these are fine-grained.

Shales and clays form biotite hornfelses specked with black biotite mica, though they also contain feldspar and quartz, and a little tourmaline, graphite and iron oxide. Geologists look in these rocks for the aluminium silicates andalusite, kyanite and sillimanite. Each forms at a particular temperature and pressure, so finding one reveals the conditions in which the rock formed.

Impure limestone hornfelses are tough rocks containing calcium-rich silicates such as diopside, epidote, garnet, sphene, vesuvianite and scapolite, as well as feldspars, pyrites, quartz and actinolite. The igneous hornfelses are, like their protoliths, rich in feldspar with brown hornblende and pale pyroxene, but they also contain streaks and patches of new minerals such as aluminium silicates.

**Identification**: Plain hornfels like this is very easily confused with basalt and other dark volcanic rocks. Sometimes, though, hornfels is unmistakably 'spotted' with porphyroblasts of minerals such as andalusite, cordierite, garnet or pyroxene.

**Striped hornfels**: Many hornfels rocks are streaked with crystals of aluminium silicates such as sillimanite and andalusite. These minerals are very characteristic of the hornfels facies, marked by high temperatures and low pressure.

**Rock type**: Non-foliated, contact metamorphic
**Texture**: Even, fine-grained; sometimes contains porphyroblasts (large crystals), or poikiloblasts (large crystals enveloping smaller crystals)
**Structure**: Most small structures are obliterated by metamorphism, though bedding from protolith may be preserved
**Colour**: Black, bluish, greyish, often speckled with dark porphyroblasts
**Composition**: The matrix is too fine-grained for individual minerals to be easily distinguished, but tiny flakes of mica can sometimes be seen under a magnifying glass. Square black or red porphyroblasts of andalusite are visible in andalusite hornfels. If these crystals are cross-shaped, they are known as chiastolite, and the rock is called chiastolite hornfels. In cordierite hornfels, the rock is dotted with rice-grain-like porphyroblasts of dark cordierite. In pyroxene hornfels, there are porphyroblasts of pyroxene, andalusite or cordierite. Other common minerals may be garnets, hypersthene and sillimanite.
**Protolith**: Fine-grained rocks including shales, clays, impure limestones, dolerite, basalt, andesite
**Temperature**: Very high
**Pressure**: Low
**Notable occurrences**: Comrie (Perthshire), Scotland; Cumbria, Dartmoor (Devon), Cornwall, England; Vosges, France; Harz Mountains, Germany; Elba, Italy; Nova Scotia; Sierra Nevada, California

## (Meta)quartzite

(Meta)quartzite is a tough, whitish, sugary-looking rock that looks rather like white marble, but is made from quartz, not calcite. Indeed, it is over 90 per cent quartz. It forms mainly from sandstone. Like the sandstone orthoquartzite, it is often simply called quartzite, and the two often grade into each other, depending on how much the original sandstone has been altered by metamorphism. During metamorphism, the quartz grains in sandstone recrystallize, creating new, larger grains. The cement and open pores in sandstone vanish, leaving only tightly interlocking grains. In fact, the quartz grains become effectively welded together so that when the rock breaks, it fractures right across the crystals, rather than breaking around the grains as sandstone does. Most metaquartzite is non-foliated. However, under extreme heat and pressure, it may be flattened or sheared in such a way that the grains are stretched out in a pancake shape, creating foliated metaquartzite.

**Identification**: (Meta)quartzite is a white rock that looks like marble but is much tougher. Unlike marble, it cannot easily be scratched with a coin or knife. White quartzite is also a little more brown than marble.

**Rock type**: Non-foliated, contact and regional metamorphic
**Texture**: Even, medium-grained; sometimes granoblastic (grains are roughly shaped but even-sized)
**Structure**: Most small structures are obliterated by metamorphism, though bedding from the protolith may be preserved
**Colour**: White, grey, reddish
**Composition**: Tightly interlocking grains of quartz, with a little feldspar and mica
**Protolith**: Sandstones and quartz-rich conglomerates
**Temperature**: High
**Pressure**: Low to high
**Notable occurrences**: Islay, Grampians, Scotland; Anglesey, Wales; Norway; Sweden; Taunus, Harz, Germany; Wallis, Switzerland; Steiermark, Tyrol, Austria; North and South Carolina

**Stone aggregates**
Virtually every construction project in the world, from the simplest house to the biggest suspension bridge, relies on 'aggregate' – the small chunks of rock that are cemented together to make bricks, concrete, asphalt and various other building materials. The average house contains over 50 tonnes/49.2 tons of aggregate. Some aggregates are readymade from sand and gravel deposits. Most are crushed rock – and the choice of rock is crucial. Soft rocks such as shale are really usable only for cement. The main hard rocks are basalt, gabbro and granite, limestone, gritstone and sandstone and the tough metamorphic rocks hornfels, amphibolite and gneiss. Road aggregates must not just be tough; they must be resistant to polishing by tyres, since this makes them slippery when wet, and must allow bitumen to stick to them. This rules out quartz-rich rocks such as granite. As a result road chippings tend to be limestone, basalt, hornfels or amphibolite. A furnace quarry at a stone aggregate mine is shown above.

## Granofels and charnockite

Granofels is one of the few non-foliated rocks to form under relatively high temperatures and pressures. This combination is generated only deep in the crust by tectonic forces that operate on a grand scale, so granofels is a product of regional, rather than contact, metamorphism. It is formed mostly from the granite family of rocks, or occasionally from thoroughly reconstituted clays and shales. Charnockite is a particularly widespread form of granofels. It was named by geologist T H Holland in 1900 after the tomb of Job Charnock, the founder of Calcutta, in St John's Church in Calcutta, India, which is made of this rock. Charnockite was once thought to be igneous, but it is now known to be metamorphic since despite the high temperatures and pressures, the original protolith never actually melted.

**Rock type**: Non-foliated, regional metamorphic
**Texture**: Coarse-grained
**Structure**: Most small structures are obliterated by metamorphism
**Colour**: Dark grey. Feldspar crystals may be dark green, brown or red; quartz may be bluish; hornblende may be brown to green.
**Composition**: Charnockite is made mostly of feldspar and quartz, but also contains the orthopyroxene hypersthene, plus hornblende and often pyrope garnet
**Protolith**: Granitoids and altered shales and clays
**Temperature**: High
**Pressure**: High
**Notable occurrences**: Scotland; Norway; Sweden; France; Madagascar; southern India; Sri Lanka; Brazil; Baffin Island; Labrador; Quebec; Adirondacks, New York

**Identification:** Granofels is a dark grey, coarse-grained rock mottled with brownish feldspar and greenish hornblende crystals.

# MAFIC METAMORPHIC ROCKS

*When mafic igneous rocks such as basalt are subject to regional metamorphism, increasing heat and pressure progressively changes them from greenstone to greenschist, and then to amphibolite and finally to eclogite. This sequence can often be traced in the landscape, at right angles to the direction of the original pressure when the rock was metamorphosed deep underground.*

## Greenstone and greenschist

Greenstones are often very ancient indeed, and bands of greenstone rock called greenstone belts are found wrapped around granite in cratons, the billions-of-years-old cores of continents. Neither greenstone, nor the related greenschist, are single kinds of rock. Instead, greenstone encompasses any metamorphosed mafic igneous rock turned greenish by the presence of chlorite, epidote or actinolite. Greenschist is similar but foliated, marked by schist-like stripes. Under mild pressure, basalt simply recrystallizes to greenstone, leaving structures such as pillows and cavities intact. Further compression breaks these structures down to create the foliation of greenschist. Greenschist is also the name of one of the facies of metamorphic rock, and includes greenstone. The greenschist facies is the assemblage of minerals that is formed by low-grade regional metamorphism – low temperatures (300–500°C/572–932°F) and only moderately high pressure. In greenschist facies, minerals such as albite, epidote, chlorite, actinolite, titanite and pumpellyite totally or partially replace the major minerals in the original igneous rock such as pyroxene and plagioclase.

**Identification**: Greenschist's green colour is its most distinctive feature. Like many metamorphic rocks it has slightly sparkly crystalline appearance. Unlike greenstone, greenschist is slightly foliated, with signs of the banding called schistosity.

**Rock type**: Non-foliated, low-grade regional metamorphic
**Texture**: Very fine-grained
**Structure**: Phenocrysts, cavities and pillow structures from the original volcanic rock may be preserved
**Colour**: Greenish
**Composition**: Mainly actinolite, with other epidote group minerals such as chlorite
**Protolith**: Mafic igneous rocks such as basalt (greenstone), or shale (greenschist)
**Temperature**: Low
**Pressure**: Moderate
**Notable occurrences**: Norway; Atlas, Morocco; Barberton, South Africa; Pilbara, Western Australia; Northwest Territories; Manitoba; Quebec; Ontario; Cascades; Rockies

## Amphibolite

**Identification**: The high pressures and temperatures that form amphibolites mean their texture is distinctively metamorphic. Crystals have a unique contorted form called crystalloblastic, which can be created only by high-grade metamorphism.

This is a coarse-grained rock composed mostly of plagioclase and hornblende. Strictly speaking, it is non-foliated, but geologists may call any plagioclase-hornblende rock amphibolite, whether foliated or not. Amphibolite is also one of the metamorphic facies, encompassing the assemblage of minerals that form in any rock under the huge pressures and moderate temperatures typical deep down during mountain building. Extreme conditions like this turn amphibolites into some of the toughest of all rocks, which is why they are often used for building roads. Some amphibolites are metamorphosed from dykes and sills cutting clean across softer sedimentary rocks. The tremendous pressure and heat that alters these intrusions to amphibolite transforms even the softest surrounding sediments into schists and gneisses. However, amphibolite is so resistant to shear stress that it remains unfoliated and survives intact as fragments within the other metamorphosed rocks.

**Rock type**: Non-foliated, regional metamorphic
**Texture**: Medium- to coarse-grained. Sometimes contains porphyroblasts of garnet.
**Structure**: Hornblende crystals may be aligned, giving weak foliation
**Colour**: Black, dark green, green, streaked white, or red
**Composition**: Hornblende amphibole and plagioclase feldspar, plus mica almandine garnet and pyroxene
**Protolith**: Mafic, intermediate igneous rocks: basalt, andesite, gabbro, diorite
**Temperature**: Medium
**Pressure**: High
**Notable occurrences**: Donegal, Connemara, Ireland; Grampians, Scotland; Thuringia, Saxony, Germany; St Gothard Massif, Switzerland; Hohe Tauern, Austria; Quebec; Arizona; Adirondacks, New York

# Eclogite

Eclogites are among the rarest of metamorphic rocks, but they are also among the most interesting. They are very striking-looking rocks, typically made of red pyrope or almandine garnets embedded in a green pyroxene called omphacite. No other rock is so often full of interesting crystals and minerals.

There is little doubt that they formed under extreme conditions. The assemblage of minerals in eclogite, called the eclogite facies, could have formed only under high temperatures and pressures. They are closely linked with basalts, and a few geologists have argued that they are not metamorphic at all, but formed directly from basalt magmas deep underground in the Earth's mantle. Eclogites are never very large. Although there are instances of isolated blocks measuring 100m/328ft across in metamorphic rocks, most are xenoliths – chunks of foreign stone swept up from the lower depths in magmas. Xenoliths such as this often occur in diamond-bearing kimberlite and lamproites, and the diamonds are usually embedded in the eclogites themselves. It is now thought that there are actually three different types of eclogite, each forming in a different way. There are those that occur as xenoliths in kimberlite and basalt, as in Hawaii's Oahu crater. These formed at extremely high pressures and temperatures at least 100km/ 62 miles down in the mantle. Secondly, there are those that occur in bands and lenses in the midst of the most extremely metamorphosed gneiss, like those in west Norway and the Dabie mountains of China. The third type of eclogite occurs as blocks or bands in subduction zones along with blueschist, as in the Greek islands of the Cyclades. These crustal eclogites formed at lower temperatures and pressures. One theory is that these formed from massive gabbros in conditions where there was little water present; others suggest they formed from deeply subducted basalt crust.

**Identification**: Tough, dense and coarse-grained, eclogite is basically green and can look almost like solid gelatin. Often it is studded with large red porphyroblasts of garnet like this specimen.

**Rock type**: Non-foliated or foliated, regional metamorphic. May also be igneous, forming from basaltic magma.
**Texture**: Medium- to coarse-grained. Often contains porphyroblasts of garnet or pyroxene.
**Structure**: Very high density, massive, occasionally foliated
**Colour**: Greenish, reddish, or green with red spots
**Composition**: Dominantly omphacite pyroxene and almandine-pyrope garnet, with no plagioclase. Also includes quartz, kyanite, orthopyroxene, rutile, pyrite, white mica, zoisite and occasionally coesite. Xenoliths may contain diamonds.
**Protolith**: Basalt or gabbro, marl
**Temperature**: Xenoliths in kimberlites, lamproites and orangeites above 900°C/1,652°F; eclogite lenses and xenoliths in ancient gneiss terranes 550–900°C/932–1,652°F; in blueschists near ocean trenches less than 550°C/932°F
**Pressure**: High
**Notable occurrences**: Glenelg, north-west Scotland; Greenland; West Norway; Saxony, Bavaria, Germany; western Alps, Switzerland; Carinthia, Austria; Apennines, Italy; Cyclades, Greece; DR Congo; South Africa; Botswana; Namibia; India; Borneo; Dabie Mts, central China; Western Australia; north-west Canada; Oahu, Hawaii; California

**The ancient hearts of continents**

Although some rocks forming the continents are quite young geologically, all of them have a very, very ancient core, or several cores. These cores are called cratons, and continents have grown around them over the ages to become the land masses they are today. The rocks in cratons are the oldest on Earth, dating back at least 2.5 billion years. Gneisses metamorphosed from the volcanoes that created the first land masses are the oldest rocks. The Acasta gneiss of northern Canada is almost four billion years old. Almost as old are the distinctive greenstone belts, famous from Barberton in South Africa, from Pilbara in Australia and from northern Canada (above). Between 2.5 and 3.5 billion years old, these are rock islands of twisted greenstone wrapped around granite. Their origins are the subject of debate, but traces of pillow lavas are found in the greenstone, so many geologists think it may be pieces of ancient sea floor pushed up by a granite intrusion in ancient rift.

**Retrograde eclogite:** As eclogite xenoliths are brought nearer the surface, the minerals in them may sometimes be changed by retrograde metamorphism when they are affected by decreasing temperatures and pressures. Minerals such as amphibole may replace garnet and pyroxene.

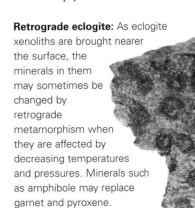

# MARBLE

*Snowy white or cream with an extraordinary inner glow, marble is without doubt the most beautiful of all stones, cherished since the days of Ancient Egypt. For sculptors it is the finest of all stones, carved into shining statues such as Bernini's* Ecstasy of St Theresa *and Michelangelo's* David. *Polished marble slabs have been used to face buildings from the Taj Mahal to the most modern skyscraper.*

## Carrara marble

**Identification**: Pure marble is white but even pure marble can be stained grey by specks of graphite, or diopside like this. However, grey marble may be bleached snow white by contact with a hot intrusion.

**Carrara marble**: Those from the quarries near Carrara in Tuscany, Italy, are the most prized marbles of all. These snow-white rocks are almost pure calcite and were cherished not just by the great sculptor Michelangelo, but also in Roman times. The marbles occur in four main valleys in the Apennine mountains around Carrara.

For builders and sculptors, the word 'marble' covers a wide range of rocks. Limestones, serpentines and even quartzites may be called marble if they are pale in colour and can be carved or polished. For geologists, though, marble is a very specific kind of rock, made metamorphically under specific conditions. Even so, there is ambiguity. Some geologists describe as marble any rock that is metamorphosed from carbonate rocks. This includes metamorphosed dolomite, made from magnesium carbonate. A few geologists suggest that only rocks metamorphosed from pure calcium-rich limestones should be called marble.

This kind of true marble formed when beds of limestone were buried deep in the crust and altered by the heat of the Earth's interior and the pressure of overlying rocks. Marble is often brought up from deep mountain roots and continental collision zones interlayered with other ancient metamorphic rocks such as phyllites, quartzites and schists. Marble can be formed by contact as well as regional metamorphism, and small outcrops develop where hot granite intrusions have pushed their way into pure limestone beds.

Like metaquartzite, marble is made from reformed crystals of the same mineral as its protolith. During metamorphism, the calcite in limestone recrystallizes in larger, formless grains. Pore space between grains disappears, and grain and cement blur into one, leaving a tightly interlocking mass of calcite grains. The grains are odd shapes, and the texture can look sugary or even like the cracked pattern on ancient glazed porcelain. But this dense, uniform texture is just what makes marble so beautifully smooth for sculpture. The stone even seems to glow because it is slightly translucent and allows light to penetrate through the surface grains and reflect off internal grains.

Marble is soft enough to carve, but is tough enough to survive quite well in dry conditions. However, it is easily corroded by acid rain. Large masses of marble can be weathered into the same karst formations as limestone, and marble walls and statuary become pitted over time.

**Rock type**: Either foliated or non-foliated, low-grade regional metamorphic or contact metamorphic

**Texture**: Medium- or coarse-grained, clearly visible to the naked eye. Even-grained, often sugary in appearance. Translucent in slabs up to 30cm/12in thick.

**Structure**: Old bedding structures and even fossils are occasionally preserved. More often, though, marble is evenly massive. Pure marble is rarely foliated, but because it flows under high pressure, coloured minerals may be stretched out to give highly contorted stripes.

**Colour**: Occasionally pure white, but often stained different colours by minerals in the protolith. Pyroxene turns it green; garnet and vesuvianite turn it brown; and sphene, epidote and chondrodite turn it yellow. Other minerals and the process of metamorphism usually add waves, flecks, grains and stripes of colour.

**Composition**: Mainly calcite or, in dolomitic marble, dolomite. Additional minerals include quartz, muscovite and phlogopite mica, graphite, iron oxides, pyrite, diopside and plagioclases such as albite, labradorite and anorthite. Other minerals include scapolite, vesuvianite, forsterite, wollastonite tremolite, talc, chondrodite, brucite, apatite, sphene, grossular garnet, zoisite, tourmaline, epidote, periclase, spinel, pyrrhotite, sphalerite and chalcopyrite.

**Protolith**: Limestone. Carbonate limestone gives pure marble; dolomitic limestone gives dolomitic marble.

**Temperature**: Low to high

**Pressure**: Low to high

# Marble varieties

Pure marble is white, and made mostly of calcite with minor traces of other minerals. The commonest additional minerals are small rounded grains of quartz, scales of pale muscovite and phlogopite mica, dark, shiny plates of graphite, iron oxides and pyrite. Different metamorphic conditions and different minerals in the original limestone can give it all kinds of different colours and patterns. Often these impurities are smudged out into wonderful whirling streaks, like ripple ice cream, as the rock flowed slightly during metamorphism. Common additional minerals are green diopside, pale green actinolite, plagioclase feldspars and many more (see data panel). Sometimes the entire mass of marble may be stained by impurities. Pyroxene turns marbles green. Garnet and vesuvianite turn it brown. Sphene, epidote and chondrodite turn it yellow. Graphite can turn marble grey or even black.

Once formed, marble can often be altered by both chemical and physical stresses. As it is attacked chemically, minerals such as hematite may develop, staining it red, while limonite stains it brown and talc stains it green. A particularly attractive alteration is when the marble is coloured by patches of green or yellow serpentine altered from diopside and forsterite in the original marble. This variety is called ophicalcite or verd antique.

The rock called onyx marble is not actually marble at all. Neither is it onyx, which is banded chalcedony. It is rings of calcite deposited from cold mineral-rich solutions around springs in crevices and caves, often as stalagmites. Onyx marble is also called alabaster and was widely used for carving in the ancient world. Reddish Siena marble from Tuscany is onyx marble, as is the Algerian marble used in the buildings of Carthage and Ancient Rome.

**Dolomite marble**: Dolomite marble is not true marble since it was metamorphosed from doleritic limestone and is made mostly from dolomite (magnesium carbonate) rather than calcite (calcium carbonate). This usually makes it a little greyer.

**Ophicalcite**: This marble gets its name, like 'serpentine', from the classical word for snake, and is basically serpentinized marble. Exposure to chemical attack changes forsterite and diopside to serpentine, giving the rock an appearance of snakeskin.

**The artist's stone**
Because of its softness, glow and beautiful colours, marble has been prized as a stone for sculpture since Egyptian times. Pentelic marble from Attica was the luscious white stone that Ancient Greek sculptors such as Phidias and Praxiteles used to make their wonderful statues, the first lifelike carvings of people. The famous Elgin marbles that once adorned the Parthenon in Athens were made of Greek marble, too. In the Middle Ages, Michelangelo carefully chose a block of pure white marble from the Carrara quarries in Tuscany, Italy, to make his great statue of David. Antonio Canova chose the same white stone for his famous *Three Graces*, and many others. Marble has been used even more widely to face buildings, ever since the Romans discovered how to stick it to walls with cement. So many of the buildings of Ancient Rome were covered in marble that the city shone even at night. Today, buildings such as Washington's National Gallery are clad in marble.

**Notable occurrences**:
Devon, England; Connemara, Ireland; France; Spain; Fichtelberg, Germany; Tyrol, Austria; Tyrol, Tuscany, Italy; Wallis, Switzerland; Talledega County, Alabama; Harford County, Maryland; Vermont; Georgia.

*Pure marble*: Mount Pentelicus (Attica), Greece; Carrara, Massa and Serravezza (Tuscany), Italy; Bergen, Norway; Alabama; Georgia; Maryland; Vermont; Yule, Colorado.

*Dolomite marble*: Glen Tilt, Scotland; Norway; Sweden; Fichtelberg, Germany; Steiermark, Austria; Tyrol, Italy; Karelia, Russia; Utah.

*Ophicalcite*: Sutherland, Scotland; Connemara, Ireland; Mona (Anglesey), Wales; Fichtelberg, Germany; Wallis, Switzerland; Alps, France; Piedmont, Italy; Estramadura, Portugal.

*Onyx and stalagmite marble*: Siena (Tuscany), Italy; Oued-Abdallah, Algeria; Tecali, Mexico; El Marmol, California.

*Black marble (non-metamorphic limestone)*: Kilkenny, Galway, Ireland; Ashford (Derbyshire), Frosterley (Yorkshire), England; Shoreham, Vermont; Glen Falls, New York.

# FOLIATED METAMORPHIC ROCKS

*High or moderately high pressures during metamorphism can create rocks with distinct layers called foliation, including slate, schist and gneiss. Foliation makes some rocks stripy, like mylonite, migmatite and glaucophane schists, and makes others, like phyllite, liable to split into thin sheets. Foliation means either that some minerals have been separated into bands, or that crystals have been aligned in parallel.*

## Mylonite

Sometimes, the huge forces involved in crustal movement literally tear rocks apart and drag the broken edges past each other. Near the surface, rock is shattered into angular fragments along these fault zones and ultimately crushed to powder. Deep down, however, the heat of the Earth's crust makes rock too soft and plastic to break. So when rocks are sheared, they smear out like toffee to form streaky rocks called mylonites. Softer materials recrystallize as minute grains, while a few more robust larger crystals may survive, crushed and reduced within this fine matrix. Because the larger crystals have not recrystallized, they are called porphyroclasts, not porphyroblasts. It was once thought that the fine grains in mylonite were simply pulverized; however, it is now known that they are actually new crystals that form under the strain, in a process called syntectonic recrystallization. The word mylonite was coined by Charles Lapworth in 1885 to describe the streaked rock he found in the Moine Thrust fault zone of the Scottish Highlands. Now it is used to describe any rock with a smeared-out streaky texture like this, and bands can be anything from 1–2cm/ 0.4–0.8in to 2–3km/1.2–1.9 miles thick.

**Identification**: With their streaky, smeared-out texture, mylonites are quite easy to recognize, but there are many kinds of mylonite, including protomylonite in which many of the grains are porphyroclasts – pulverized but not recrystallized – and ultramylonite in which there are no porphyroclasts left at all.

**Rock type**: Foliated, dynamic metamorphic
**Texture**: Smeared-out, streaky texture with larger, but still tiny porphyroclasts in a very fine-grained matrix
**Structure**: Mylonites sometimes but not always split along the direction of the streaks
**Colour**: Varied
**Composition**: Varies with the original rock, but the matrix is typically quartz and carbonate, with feldspar and garnet porphyroclasts
**Protolith**: All kinds of rock
**Temperature**: Low
**Pressure**: High shear
**Notable occurrences**: Moine Thrust, NW Scotland; Alps, Switzerland; Turkey; Deccan Traps, India; Ross Sea, Antarctica; Canadian Shield; Sierra Nevada, California; Blue Ridge, Virginia; Adirondacks, New York

## Migmatite

Migmatites are often the most extremely metamorphosed of all rocks, forming deep down in the continental crust under even greater pressure and heat than gneiss. Indeed, conditions are so hot that the rock partially melts. Minerals that melt at low temperatures liquidize, turning into igneous rock. Migmatites were first identified in 1907 by Finnish geologist J J Sederholm, who named them after the Greek word *migma* for mixture. The name is apt for migmatites are really a mixture of metamorphic and igneous rock. They usually consist of dark gneiss, schist or amphibolite striped by bands of leucocratic (pale-coloured) rock such as granite. At first migmatites were thought to be just pockets within gneiss. Now a few geologists think they may also be the last vestiges of rock that melted to form a granite magma. Some geologists argue that the pale bands have been intruded into the rock from an external source, rather than melting in situ. The gneiss portion is therefore older and called the 'palaeosome'.

**Identification**: With its distinctive humbug stripes of dark metamorphic rock and pale igneous rock, migmatite is usually fairly easy to identify.

**Rock type**: Foliated, regional metamorphic
**Texture**: Medium-grained
**Structure**: Alternating stripes of dark metamorphic and pale (leucocratic) igneous rock
**Colour**: Varied
**Composition**: Typically gneiss with granite. Can also be schist or amphibolite.
**Protolith**: May be all gneiss (or schist or amphibolite) or may be gneiss and granite
**Temperature**: Very high
**Pressure**: High
**Notable occurrences**: Sutherland, Scotland; Scandinavia; Auvergne, France; Black Forest, Bavaria, Germany; Cyclades, Greece; Lake Huron, Ontario; Adirondacks, New York; New Jersey; Washington

# Phyllite

When mudstone and shale are subjected to mild metamorphism, their crystals line up perpendicular to the direction of pressure, and the rocks turn to slate. If the pressure and heat become a little more intense, they turn to phyllite. Even more heat and pressure turns phyllite to schist. Phyllite gets its name from the Latin for 'leaf-stone', and like slate it is characterized by laminations similar to the leaves of a book. Like slate, phyllite is made from very tiny grains of mica, chlorite, graphite and similar minerals, which grow flat at right angles to the pressure. Yet while slate looks dull, phyllite almost glitters because the extra heat and pressure creates thicker flakes of mica, especially the muscovite mica sericite. This silky sheen is called phyllitic lustre. In phyllite, the leaves are so compressed that it does not split into sheets nearly as well as slate, especially in its most highly metamorphosed, protophyllite, form. All the same, it is sometimes used, like slate, as roofing tiles.

**Identification**: Like slate, phyllite is distinctly layered. The layers, though, are not completely flat as in slate, but slightly wrinkled. These 'crenulations' make phyllite look like crepe. Phyllite also has a silky, silver lustre quite unlike slate's drab grey.

**Rock type**: Foliated, regional metamorphic
**Texture**: Fine-grained with porphyroblasts
**Structure**: Marked laminations at right angles to pressure. May have slaty cleavage and split into sheets as thin as 0.1mm/3.9mil. When metamorphism has gone further, the cleavage is only apparent and the rock won't split. May show minor folds and corrugations.
**Colour**: Silver grey, greenish
**Composition**: Mostly sericite mica and quartz
**Protolith**: Shale, mudstone
**Temperature**: Moderate
**Pressure**: Moderate
**Notable occurrences**: Donegal, Ireland; Grampians, Scotland; Anglesey, Wales; Cornwall, England; Scandinavia; Vosges, France; Fichtelberg, Bavaria, Harz Mts, Germany; Alps, Switzerland; Connecticut; New York; Appalachians

**The Moine Thrust**
The discovery of the Moine Thrust along the coast of Sutherland, north-west Scotland, in 1907 was a key moment in the history of geology. Geologists were already familiar with simple thrust faults. These are shallow reverse faults created when the crust is squeezed, forcing one block of rock up over another. But the Moine Thrust is not a single thrust. In fact, it is a complex belt of thrusts. We now know that such belts develop when tectonic plate movement repeatedly forces layers of crust up and over each other, then pulls them back, creating a complex, broken, multi-layered formation. At Moine, this all happened between 410 and 430 million years ago, when Scotland was crushed by opposing tectonic plates, creating a thrust belt stretching 180km/112 miles from the Moine Peninsula to the Isle of Skye. Similar thrust belts have now been discovered along the edges of fold mountain ranges all around the world. They are often characterized by complex bands of mylonite rock.

# Glaucophane schist: blueschist

Glaucophane schist is a rock turned blue by the amphibole mineral glaucophane. It is also called blueschist, but it is one of a variety of rocks that form in similar conditions known as the blueschist facies. Not all blueschist facies rocks are blue, but laboratory experiments have shown they all form when pressures are very high but temperatures are low. This is a surprising combination, since high pressures usually go hand in hand with high temperatures, forming greenschists. Geologists now believe the answer is that blueschists form in subduction zones. The theory is that as a cold basaltic ocean slab is shoved deep into the mantle, a wedge of material, called an accretionary wedge, is scraped off and pushed back to the surface by slab material descending behind. This all happens so quickly in geological terms that the rock in the descending slab is squeezed hard, altered to blueschist then lifted back on the surface before it has time to heat up.

**Identification:** Schistose banding gives away glaucophane as a schistlike rock. A bluish tinge may establish its identity.

**Rock type**: Foliated, regional metamorphic
**Texture**: Fine, medium-grain
**Structure**: Weakly schistose. May show folding.
**Colour**: Bluish, light violet
**Composition**: Mostly glaucophane or lawsonite amphibole or epidote, quartz, or jadeite, with garnet, albite, talc, zoisite, jadeite and chlorite
**Protolith**: Usually basalt or dolerite, but may be mudrock
**Temperature**: Low
**Pressure**: High
**Notable occurrences**: Anglesey, Wales; Channel Islands, England; Spitsbergen, Norway; Calabria, Tuscany, Val d'Aosta, Italy; Alps, Switzerland; California

Schist

Mica

# SLATE

*The word slate is sometimes used to describe any stone that splits into flat slabs and is used as roofing tiles. True slate, however, is a very distinctive dark grey, brittle metamorphic rock that flakes into smooth, flat sheets. It is created when shales and clays are altered by low-grade regional metamorphism at low temperatures and moderate pressures.*

## Slate

Getting its name from the Old German word for break, slate is essentially metamorphosed mudrock that has been strongly compressed deep underground, but in a low-grade regional metamorphic environment, away from the most intense metamorphism. Conditions such as these are found deep at the root of fold mountains, where the convergence of tectonic plates slowly but surely crushed rocks deep down. Most slates occur in old mountain chains, like the Appalachian Mountains of the USA, or Snowdonia in Wales. They tend to be Precambrian or Silurian in age. Occasionally, though, they form in more recent fold mountain chains, like the Alps.

Slate varies enormously in colour, though it is normally dark grey, or purplish or greenish grey. But it is always easy to recognize because of the way it cleaves into the flat sheets that make it so useful for roofing. This distinctive 'slaty' cleavage develops when mudrock is metamorphosed. As the rock is compressed, water is squeezed out and the rock is compacted. All the tiny clay and silt grains are not simply recrystallized as mica and chlorite but are reoriented at right angles to the pressure. This alignment occurs partly because just as the layered nature of clay crystals means they can be moulded, they can also be pressed flat, and partly because new crystals grow in this direction.

Metamorphism usually destroys most of the original sedimentary structures, so the cleavage planes are entirely unrelated to bedding planes and are probably at an entirely different angle. Fossils are usually destroyed by metamorphism, too. Only when the pressure is pretty much at right angles to the bedding are fossils preserved – though often rather dramatically flattened. Because slate's cleavage is produced by the same forces that fold mountains, slate cleavage usually clearly marks out the pattern of folding in the formation and the direction of compression. This makes it a very useful rock when studying the tectonic history and structural geology of an area.

**Identification**: A dull dark, smooth grey, turning shiny black when wet, slate is a distinctive rock, even before it is broken. But its tendency to break into thin, flat sheets marks it out even more clearly. No other rock has such a distinctive cleavage.

**Clayslate**: This is a very mildly metamorphosed rock halfway between shale and phyllite. Some geologists regard it as a sedimentary rock, but it has been metamorphosed enough to prevent it absorbing water and swelling like shale. Clayslates never smell earthy when damp like shale, and rarely have any fossils. They also split like true slates.

**Rock type**: Foliated, low-grade regional metamorphic
**Texture**: Very fine-grained. The grains are so small that it is impossible to identify individual minerals even under a magnifying glass.
**Structure**: Slates are characterized by single, perfect flat, slaty cleavage that allows it to be split easily into sheets. Traces of bedding planes and other original protolith structures are sometimes revealed like a picture on the flat cleavage surfaces. Sometimes fossils are preserved but they are usually squeezed flat.
**Colour**: Grey, black, shades of blue, green, brown and buff. Limonite and hematite colour it brown; chlorite colours it green.
**Composition**: Mainly mica and chlorite, with quartz, pyrite and rutile. Minor minerals include calcite, garnet, epidote, tourmaline, graphite and dark carbonate minerals.
**Protolith**: Mudrocks (mostly shale) and volcanic tuff
**Temperature**: Low
**Pressure**: Moderate
**Notable occurrences**: Wicklow Mts, Ireland; Highland Boundary Fault, Scotland; Snowdonia, North Wales; Cornwall, England; Ardennes, France; Fichtelberg, Thuringia, Germany; South Australia; Brazil ('rusty' slate); New Brunswick; Nova Scotia; Ontario; Martinsburg, Pennsylvania; western Vermont; eastern New York; central Virginia; central Maine; northern Maryland

# Spotted and chiastolite slate

Slate is the first stage in the sequence of rocks that develop when mudrock is progressively metamorphosed on a regional scale. Moderate heat and pressure on mudrock alters it to slate, but if the pressure increases it develops into phyllite. Even more intense pressure turns phyllite to schist. Just like sedimentary and igneous rocks, slate can also be cooked and altered by contact with a hot granite intrusion. Right next to the intrusion, slates lose their distinctive cleavage, and develop into splintery, tough hornfels. Further away, they retain their cleavage but develop dark or light round spots of altered minerals, typically white mica or chlorite. Spotted slates such as these usually contain minerals such as andalusite, garnet or, more rarely, cordierite. Andalusite in the form of chiastolite is especially characteristic of these spotted slates. Chiastolite slates contain distinctive large porphyroblasts of andalusite with dark crosses embedded in a light crystal. These crystals can often be 7–8cm/2.3–3.1in long. Commonly, in exposed slates, though, they are weathered to white mica or kaolin.

**Spotted slate**: Just as shale is metamorphosed to slate by pressure on a regional scale, so slate is metamorphosed locally to form spotted slate by contact with a hot intrusion.

**Chiastolite slate**: Chiastolite slate is a very distinctive rock. Like ordinary slate, though, it is tough yet brittle and breaks easily into flat sheets. Unlike ordinary slate, it is marked with porphyroblasts, created by the heat of contact with an intrusion. The porphyroblasts are pale crystals of andalusite, aligned randomly throughout the rock.

**Rock type**: Foliated, low-grade regional metamorphic
**Texture**: Very fine-grained, but studded with porphyroblasts of minerals such as andalusite and mica
**Structure**: Like ordinary slates, they are characterized by single, perfect, flat, slaty cleavage that allows them to be split easily into sheets
**Colour**: Grey, black, shades of blue, green, brown and buff. Limonite and hematite colour it brown; chlorite colours it green.
**Composition**: Mainly mica and chlorite, with quartz, pyrite and rutile. Minor minerals include calcite, garnet, epidote, tourmaline, graphite and dark carbonate minerals.
**Protolith**: Mudrocks (mostly shale) and volcanic tuff
**Temperature**: Moderate
**Pressure**: Moderate
**Notable occurrences**: Snowdonia, Wales; Skiddaw, Devon, England; Betic Cordilleras, Spain; Halifax, Nova Scotia; California

## The slate industry

Slate may be very brittle and split easily into sheets, but it is actually a tough rock that is very resistant to the weather. This is why it is often seen in craggy outcrops in mountain regions, standing out darkly, almost black when it rains. The combination of slate's weather resistance, and the ease with which it can be broken into flat sheets makes it a superb light and durable roofing material.

Buildings have been roofed with slate for thousands of years. The famous slates of North Wales have been used since at least Roman times. The Roman fort of Segontium (modern Caernarfon) had its tiles replaced with slate in the 4th century, while at nearby Caer Lugwy a fort had a slate roof two centuries earlier.

By the Middle Ages, Welsh slate was being shipped all around the British Isles, and maybe even abroad. When Chester castle was renovated in 1358 under the supervision of Edward the Black Prince, 21,000 slates were shipped from Wales to cover its roof. Many other castles and large houses used slate from the Welsh quarries at Cilgwyn and Penrhyn. Further north in Scotland, a thick, more durable kind of slate was used on the roofs of medieval houses in Edinburgh.

The use of slate remained fairly small-scale, though, until the 19th century and the Industrial Revolution. As cities in both North America and Britain grew rapidly, houses were built in millions, and each one of them had a slate roof. In Britain, the output of slates from the Welsh quarries expanded enormously. By 1832, they were digging out 100,000 tonnes/98,420 tons a year. Half a century later, almost half a million tonnes of slate were coming out of the Welsh quarries alone. In North America, the situation was similar, with huge quantities of slate dug out of the quarries of Vermont and Pennsylvania to cover the roofs of millions of houses.

Demand for slate has declined dramatically since its 19th-century peak, as natural slate has been replaced by cheaper, more regular, mass-produced artificial tiles. The Welsh quarries now produce less than 5 per cent of what they did at their height, and Vermont quarries even less.

Slates are still made today by hand by slaters in the same way they have been for centuries. Large blocks are dug out, then cut with a saw across the grain into sections slightly longer than the finished tile. Then the blocks are 'sculped' or split into slabs with a mallet and a broad-faced chisel. Finally, the slabs are split into tiles using a mallet and two chisels, and trimmed down to exactly the right size and shape. A last touch may be to punch two nail holes in one end. These holes allow the slate to be fixed quickly in place by the roofer. This last task requires some care if the tile is not to split, and relies on the slater's estimate of the particular qualities of the slate.

# SCHISTS

*The resilient rock that provides a firm base for Manhattan's towering skyscrapers, schist is the most extreme form of the regional metamorphism of mudrocks. When pressures on slate and phyllite climb, and temperatures rise above 400°C/752°F, the rocks completely recrystallize and reform as schist. All schists form this way, but there are many kinds, depending on the minerals they contain.*

## Schists

**Folded schist**: Sometimes the layers in schist can be intensely contorted even on a small scale.

Schist is one of the most striking of all rocks, with its distinctive layering or 'schistosity'. Schists mostly develop deep in the roots of mountain ranges as they are being folded. Here pressure and temperatures reach the point where the original clay minerals in mudrocks, slates and phyllites are completely broken down. The chemicals in them then reform as larger crystals of minerals such as mica and chlorite. Schists are therefore usually medium- to coarse-grained rocks, with crystals that, though not as well defined, can be as large as those in granite.

Schistosity develops only partly because the different minerals separate into layers. The main reason is that the continuous squeezing and shearing of the rock during metamorphism allows crystals only to grow in one plane, at right angles to the pressure. Because the crystals that develop are tabular flakes such as mica, or needle-like crystals such as amphiboles, this layering effect is even more marked. Whenever schist is split, it tends to break along layers of mica within the rock, giving the slightly misleading impression that it is entirely made of glistening mica. Quartz is also an important constituent, but the quartz layers tend only to be seen clearly when the rock is cut across the grain.

Although schist breaks into sheets like slate, and is sometimes used as roofing tiles where slate is scarce, it does not cleave quite as easily. The extreme heat and pressure mean the layers are more tightly knitted together. They are often also slightly wrinkled, or 'crenulated', similarly to phyllite but even more so. In some schists, these contortions can become quite dramatic.

Although they develop mainly from mudrocks, they can form from any rock that contains the right constituent minerals to make mica. Like gneiss, they are found primarily in areas of ancient rock. Most date back to at least Precambrian times (older than 570 million years). Schists do also occur in more recent formations, though, such as in the young fold mountain belts of the Alps and Himalayas.

**Garnet schist**: Under fairly intense metamorphism, large porphyroblasts of garnet may develop in mica schist. Garnets 10mm/ 0.4in or more across can sometimes be seen, as in this garnet schist, and may be big enough to chip out and use as gems. The schistose layers tend to bend around the garnet like a stream flows around rocks. The garnets are typically iron-rich, pink almandine metamorphosed from pyroxenes and other minerals.

**Chlorite schist**: In chlorite schist, weakly developed schistosity is created by flaky green chlorite crystals and fine green needles of actinolite which often form radiating clusters. This rock forms under relatively mild, 'greenschist' regional metamorphic conditions.

**Chlorite schist**
**Rock type**: Foliated, regional metamorphic
**Texture**: Fine to medium-grained, sometimes with porphyroblasts of albite or chloritoid. Not as markedly schistose as mica schist. Unlike gneiss, schist's crystal fabric is dominated by long 'planar' crystals. This is a useful clue to identity.
**Structure**: Typically folded, on a small or large scale
**Colour**: Greenish grey
**Composition**: Chlorite, actinolite, epidote, talc, glaucophane and albite feldspar. Little or no mica and quartz.
**Protolith**: Mainly mudrocks such as shale
**Temperature**: Moderate
**Pressure**: Moderate
**Notable occurrences**: Argyll, Scotland; Lake Tauern, Austria; Tyrol, Piedmont, Lombardy, Italy; Sierra Nevada, California

**Garnet schist**
**Rock type**: Foliated, regional metamorphic
**Texture**: Medium- to coarse-grained. Garnet porphyro-blasts common. Well-developed schistosity.
**Structure**: Typically folded, on a small or large scale
**Colour**: Black, brown, reddish
**Composition**: Garnet, plus biotite and muscovite mica and quartz. Garnet schist also contains the same range of other minerals as mica schists.
**Protolith**: Mainly mudrocks such as shale
**Temperature**: Moderate to high
**Pressure**: Moderate to high
**Notable occurrences**: Connemara, Ireland; Scotland; Scandinavia; Alps, Switzerland; Black Forest, Germany; Quebec; Duchess Co, NY; New Hampshire

# Mica schists

The most common schists are mica schists. Flakes of mica give them the most marked schistosity, and a real shine. The flakes are typically about 0.5mm/0.02in thick and can often be prised off with a knife. There is plenty of quartz in mica schist too, often concentrated in mica-poor layers, and a fair amount of albite feldspar. Sometimes red garnet or green chlorite crystals are visible. The mica in mica schists can be

**Biotite schist**: Biotite schist is brown and dark, but still has the mica gleam.

muscovite, sericite or biotite. Biotite is usually brown; muscovite and sericite are pale coloured and called white mica. If a white mica is fine-grained, it is called sericite; if it is coarser it is called muscovite. Most mica schists contain all three, but one usually predominates. Muscovite and sericite schists develop where metamorphism

is of moderate intensity, and are often associated with greenschists and phyllites. Biotite develops partly at the expense of muscovite (and chlorite) when metamorphism becomes more intense. Even more intense metamorphism edges the schist towards garnet schists.

**Muscovite schist**: Muscovite schists, with sericite schists, are the lightest-coloured schists, coloured by white mica. Unlike sericite schist, the grains of mica in muscovite schist are clearly visible to the naked eye.

**Mica (muscovite, sericite or biotite) schist**
**Rock type**: Foliated, regional metamorphic
**Texture**: Medium to coarse-grained, sometimes with porphyroblasts. Thin schistose layering of mica flakes always marked.
**Structure**: Typically folded, on a small or large scale
**Colour**: Light grey, greenish (biotite schist is browner)
**Composition**: Quartz and mica (usually muscovite), plus kyanite, sillimanite, chlorite, graphite, garnet, staurolite
**Protolith**: Mainly mudrocks such as shale
**Temperature**: Moderate
**Pressure**: Moderate
**Notable occurrences**: Connemara, Ireland; Scotland; Scandinavia; Alps, Switzerland; Black Forest, Germany; Quebec; Duchess Co, NY; New Hampshire

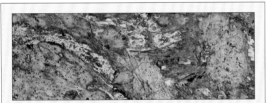

**Metamorphic facies**
It is impossible to tell from a single mineral at what pressure and temperature a metamorphic rock formed, but you can tell from the groupings of minerals known as 'facies' – assemblages that form in certain conditions. These facies include: zeolite, greenschist, amphibolite, blueschist, eclogite, granulite and various hornfelses. Although most facies are named after a rock containing one of these groups of minerals, different rocks can be in the same facies. Amphibolite and hornblende schist both form in amphibolite facies, for instance, and the above thin section shows a greenschist to amphibolite facies in meta-basalt, in which most of the green crystals are in fact hornfels amphibole. Although the link isn't always definite, hornfels, granulite and eclogite are high-grade; greenschist and amphibolite medium-grade; and zeolite and blueschist low-grade. Hornfels facies are linked to high-temperature contact zones; granulite to the high temperatures and moderate pressures typical of mountain roots; amphibolite to moderate temperatures and pressures in mountain roots and continental interiors; greenschists and zeolite to mild conditions under continental interiors; and blueschist to low temperatures and high pressures in accretionary wedges along subduction zones.

# Amphibole schist

Amphibole schist is schistose like mica schist, but the layers are formed not by flakes of mica but by parallel bands of long, thin amphibole crystals. If the crystals are not parallel, the rock is not schistose and is called amphibolite. The amphibole in amphibole schist is usually hornblende, and the rock is called hornblende schist, but it can also be actinolite or tremolite. All amphibole schists are much richer in feldspar than amphibolite. Other minerals in hornblende schist include chlorite, epidote, pyroxene and garnet. Garnet often forms dark red porphyroblasts.

Dark amphibolite crystal

**Amphibole (hornblende) schist**
**Rock type**: Foliated, regional metamorphic
**Texture**: Medium- to coarse-grained, sometimes with porphyroblasts. Thin schistose layering of amphibole needles always marked.
**Structure**: Typically folded, on a small or large scale
**Colour**: Dark black or brown, often streaked or flecked with white or red
**Composition**: Hornblende (or actinolite or tremolite), plagioclase feldspar, quartz and biotite mica, plus pyroxene, epidote, muscovite mica and garnet
**Protolith**: Basalt and dolerite, as well as mudrocks
**Temperature**: Moderate
**Pressure**: Moderate
**Notable occurrences**: Connemara, Ireland; Scotland; Tyrol, Austria/Italy; St Gotthard Massif, Switzerland; Quebec; Mitchell Co, North Carolina

# GNEISS AND GRANULITE

*The word gneiss (pronounced 'nice') comes from an old slavonic word for 'sparkling', and that's exactly what gneiss does. Under a microscope it can be seen to be made of tightly packed, iridescent crystals forged by the most intense metamorphism of all. Gneiss and granulite are incredibly tough rocks and are found together in terranes that are the most ancient rock formations on Earth.*

## Gneiss

**Identification**: Gneiss can often be identified by its humbug stripes of dark and light minerals and its crystal fabric (see Texture, right). It is also incredibly tough, found in the most ancient and time-worn landscapes, such as the vast Canadian Shield and Scotland's Hebridean islands.

Almandine garnet

**Granular gneiss**: Granular gneiss is less distinctly banded than other gneisses. Its composition is often close to granite, and is made from high proportions of quartz, white and pink feldspar and white and dark mica.

Unlike schist, gneiss is not dominated by long, planar crystals. But it can often be the most markedly striped of all rocks, composed of alternating bands of light and dark minerals. In most cases these bands are just 2mm/0.08in thick, but they can be as wide as 1m/39in. The bands in gneiss are not like the layers in schist, which are made from sheets of mica, nor does gneiss split easily in the same way. The high temperatures it takes to create gneiss tend to destroy mica, and the banding is formed in an entirely different way – as minerals separate out and form into distinct bands. The light-coloured bands are formed by light-coloured, typically felsic, minerals such as quartz, feldspar and white mica (usually muscovite). The dark bands are made of dark, typically mafic, minerals like amphibole, pyroxene and biotite mica. Compositional bands like these form only at very high temperatures when minerals almost melt and so can move freely before recrystallizing. Gneisses form deep in the Earth in subduction zones or under the roots of fold mountains, and are bought to the surface only by massive tectonic movements, or the slow erosion of the overlying mountains.

Compositional bands in gneiss can also form when variations in the original rock survive through all the stages of metamorphism. A rock originally made of alternate narrow beds of shale and sandstone may be transformed by metamorphism into gneiss made of alternate bands of quartzite and mica.

Some gneisses, however, derive their bands in an entirely different way. These gneisses get their bands when thin floods of granitoid magma ooze their way in between layers of the protolith, or when there is local melting. These gneisses blend into migmatites, and have led some geologists to conclude that many ancient gneisses formed from granodiorite and tonalite magmas in this way. Such gneisses are closely linked to ancient greenstone belts, and often merge into them.

Gneiss is an incredibly tough rock, perhaps the toughest of all, and vast quantities of it have survived since the very early part of the Earth's history. Large areas of Greenland are made from gneisses at least three billion years old. The world's oldest known rock is Acasta gneiss from northern Canada, which has been dated to 3,900 million years ago.

**Rock type**: Foliated, regional or dynamothermal metamorphic

**Texture**: Medium- to coarse-grained. Marked by striking alternate light and dark bands. The light bands are often coarsely granular. The dark bands are finer-grained and, when they contain biotite mica, may be foliated like schist. Unlike schist and granulite, gneiss has a mix of long 'planar' crystals and 'equant' crystals, crystals that measure much the same in all directions. Schist has more planar crystals and granulite more equant crystals. This difference in crystal fabric is a useful clue to identity.

**Structure**: May be marked by large-scale as well as small-scale dark and light bands. Often folded. Very often criss-crossed with granite and pegmatite veins.

**Colour**: Greyish, pinkish, reddish, brownish, greenish with dark stripes

**Composition**: Varies with protolith, but typically abundant in feldspar and quartz and white mica, which forms the light layers, and biotite and hornblende which forms the dark layers. Other constituents include cordierite, garnet and sillimanite.

**Protolith**: Almost any other rock. Gneiss formed from igneous rocks is called orthogneiss; gneiss made from sedimentary rock is called paragneiss.

**Temperature**: High
**Pressure**: High

**Notable occurrences**: Lewis, Orkneys, Scotland; Greenland; Scandinavia; Vosges, Massif Central, Brittany, France; Bavaria, Erzebirge, Germany; Alps, Switzerland; Southern India; Thailand; Canadian Shield; Appalachians; Idaho

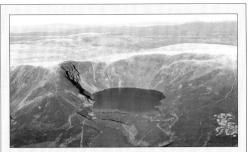

**Mineral identifiers**
About a century ago, geologist George Barrow was investigating the rocks of the Scottish Highlands around Aberdeen (pictured above). Here shale, sandstone, limestone and mafic lava were crushed and folded during a powerful phase of mountain building that created the ancient Caledonian mountains. As he studied these ancient metamorphosed rocks, Barrow noticed how particular minerals appeared in rocks in a sequence across the landscape, reflecting different intensities of the metamorphosis of pelites (metamorphosed mudrocks). These 'index' minerals were, in order: chlorite, biotite, garnet, kyanite and sillimanite. Zones in which these index minerals appear are now called Barrovian metamorphic zones, and the boundary of each is marked by a line on a map called an isograd. Similar zoning was found running through andalusite, cordierite, staurolite and sillimanite. Zones in which these minerals are found are called Buchan zones. The Buchan sequence is thought to be created by lower pressures than Barrovian zones.

# Granulite

Granulite is a tough, coarse-grained rock that, like gneiss, forms at very high temperatures and pressures. It is also the facies of metamorphic minerals that form under these extreme conditions, which tend to destroy mica and replace it with minerals such as pyroxene. The high pressure drives out any water, so the minerals that form are said to be anhydrous. It is thought that granulite formed at the base of the continental crust. Indeed, most of the underside of the continental crust is probably made of granulite. Granulite has mostly reached the surface either as small xenolith chunks in magmas, or when mountain ranges are worn away so far that their very roots are exposed. Most granulites are very ancient, and are found with gneisses in the granulite-gneiss terranes that contain the oldest rocks on Earth, dating back to billions of years ago.

**Rock type**: Mostly non-foliated, regional or dynamothermal metamorphic
**Texture**: Coarse-grained. Often banded like gneiss but granulite has mostly 'equant' crystals (see Gneiss; Texture).
**Structure**: Marked by dark and light bands
**Colour**: Light, almost white
**Composition**: Pyroxene (diopside or hypersthene), quartz and feldspar, plus garnet, biotite, cordierite and sillimanite
**Protolith**: All kinds of rock
**Temperature**: High (>700°C)
**Pressure**: High
**Notable occurrences**: NW Scotland; Greenland; Finland; Aldan shield (Yakut), Siberia; Ukraine; Limpopo, South Africa; Hopeh, Liaoning, China; Yilgarn, Australia; Enderby Land, Antarctica; Canadian Shield; British Columbia; Adirondacks, NY; Beartooth Mts, Montana

**Identification**: Granulite is a hard, sparkling rock made of coarse, rounded interlocking grains of mostly pale minerals.

## Augen gneiss and other gneisses

Gneisses can be distinguished by their protolith, such as granite gneiss and syenite gneiss, or by their characteristic mineral, such as biotite gneiss and garnet gneiss. Some gneisses may be distinguished by their texture, such as platy gneiss and augen gneiss. The word augen comes from the German for 'eye', and refers to large, oval or eye-shaped crystals in the rock. The crystals are typically alkali feldspar, in a matrix of quartz, feldspar and mica, but can be quartz, or garnet (in which case the rock is known as garnet augen gneiss). Each eye, or auge, can be up to 10cm/3.9in across. Feldspar augen typically contain inclusions of minerals such as biotite. The augen in a rock tend to be much the same size and shape, and it is thought that they are survivors from an earlier stage, with a core too big to be affected by the recrystallization that aligned other minerals in bands. The bands flow around them, like a stream around a rock. Sometimes, garnet augen rotate as they grow during metamorphism, creating 'snowball' garnets, containing spiral inclusions of other minerals.

**Identification**: Both schists and gneisses can contain augen, which are large, oval crystals of feldspar, quartz or garnet. Augen gneiss is more common, and the augen are usually surrounded by dark, banded gneiss layers, rather than silvery, flaky schist.

**Rock type**: Foliated, regional or dynamothermal metamorphic
**Texture**: Medium- to coarse-grained. Marked by large pale crystals or augen.
**Structure**: May be marked by large-scale as well as small-scale dark and light bands
**Colour**: Greyish, pinkish, reddish, brownish, greenish with dark stripes
**Composition**: Augen made of alkali feldspar or garnet. Matrix of feldspar and quartz forming light layers, and biotite forming the dark layers.
**Temperature**: High
**Pressure**: High
**Notable occurrences**: Lewis, Orkneys, Scotland; Greenland; Scandinavia; Vosges, Massif Central, Brittany, France; Bavaria, Erzebirge, Germany; Alps, Switzerland; Canadian Shield; Appalachians; Idaho

# ROCKS ALTERED BY FLUIDS AND OTHER MEANS

*Not all metamorphic rocks are formed directly by the heat of contact with an intrusion, or by heat and pressure deep within the crust. Skarns and serpentinites are formed by the interaction of fluids with the country rock – skarns by fluid heated by an intrusion, serpentinites by cold water. Halleflintas are altered volcanic tuffs and fulgurites are rocks formed by the intense heat of lightning strikes.*

## Skarn

Skarns are treasure troves of unusual and valuable minerals such as grossular garnet and ores of iron, copper, lead, tungsten and zinc. They are typically patches of metamorphosed rock around a granite intrusion, but the term 'skarn' covers a wide range of different rocks and mineral deposits that originated in a variety of different ways. Some geologists use the word skarn to describe any calcium- and silicate-rich metamorphic rock containing unusual minerals. Most prefer to describe skarns as only metamorphic rocks that form when limestones and dolomites are altered by contact with hot granite intrusions. Granite intrusions generate hot fluids carrying copious amounts of silicon, iron, aluminium and magnesium either emanating directly from the intrusion or cooked up as the intrusion heats groundwater in the limestone. Infiltrating the limestone, this rich brew alters minerals to calcium, iron and magnesium silicates. This process is really metasomatism, not metamorphism, because the minerals in the rock are replaced by others as they come into contact with the hot fluids.

**Identification**: Skarns are very piebald in appearance. They are characterized by large patches of minerals of different colours, formed as they were concentrated by the hot fluids that oozed through the limestone during metasomatism.

*Apatite*

*Orange calcite*

**Rock type**: Non-foliated, hydrothermal metasomatic
**Texture**: Fine-, medium- or coarse-grained
**Structure**: Occurs in small patches, with minerals concentrated in nodules, lenses and radiating masses
**Colour**: Brown, black or grey but very variable
**Composition**: Pyroxene, garnet, idocrase, wollastonite, actinolite, magnetite, epidote. Skarns host copper, lead, zinc, iron, gold, tungsten, molybdenum and tin ores.
**Protolith**: Mostly limestones and dolomites
**Notable occurrences**: Dartmoor (Devon), England; Central Sweden; Elba, Italy; Trepca, Serbia; Banat, Romania; Arkansas; Crestmore, California

## Halleflinta

**Identification**: No metamorphic rock looks more like flint than halleflinta. It is very fine-grained, almost cryptocrystalline, and splinters like flint when hit with a hammer.

Halleflinta gets its name from the Swedish for 'rock-flint'. It is a very hard, flinty, metamorphic rock so fine-grained that it is hard to identify individual minerals even under a microscope. It is basically a very intimate mix of quartz, feldspar and other silicate minerals. It forms in similar conditions to gneiss and schist, under intense heat and pressure, and often occurs in association with them in Scandinavia, where it was first identified. But it contains none of the banding of gneiss, nor the schistosity of mica. Indeed, it is almost glassy in texture, and breaks into sharp splinters like flint. The reason for this difference is almost certainly due to its protolith. It is probably metamorphosed volcanic tuff, and halleflinta often retains signs of the original layers of volcanic debris as it settled after successive eruptions. Extra silica has usually got into the rock during metamorphism.

**Rock type**: Foliated, regional or dynamothermal metamorphic
**Texture**: Very fine- and even-grained, almost glassy, so that the rock splinters. May contain larger porphyroblasts of quartz.
**Structure**: Layering related to original volcanic deposit, but no schistosity or banding
**Colour**: Grey, buff, pink, green or brown
**Composition**: Quartz, feldspar, mica, iron oxides, apatite, zircon, epidote, hornblende
**Protolith**: Volcanic tuff
**Temperature**: High
**Pressure**: High
**Notable occurrences**: Sweden; Finland; Tyrol, Austria; Bohemia, Czech Republic; Galicia, Poland; Ukraine

## Serpentinite

Serpentinization is a process that alters rocks, but it is not like other forms of metamorphism. It gets its name because it creates a rock flecked like snakeskin called serpentinite. This consists mostly of fibrous serpentine minerals such as chrysotile, antigorite and lizardite. In serpentinization, it is not heat and pressure that alter the minerals but heat and water. It affects mostly ultramafic rocks such as peridotite and dunite, although serpentinite can form from gabbro and dolomitic limestone, as well. What happens is that water infiltrates the rock and alters iron-rich minerals such as olivines and pyroxene to create serpentine minerals. The water is cool but the chemical reaction is exothermic and generates its own heat. It was once thought serpentinite was quite rare, and occurred only above subduction zones, or within small ultramafic intrusions. Now it is realized that serpentinites pretty much underlay the entire ocean floor, forming part of the ophiolite sequence, as olivine-rich magmas oozing up through the mid-ocean rift are serpentinized by sea water. Hydration (the uptake of water) makes serpentinites light so they well up in many places, creating undersea mountains. They also well up in the accretionary wedges above subduction zones.

**Identification**: Serpentinites are dark green to black and look very much like the snakeskin that earned them their name. They are often quite coarse-grained, and green serpentine crystals are usually easy to see.

**Rock type**: Foliated, hydrothermal metamorphic
**Texture**: Medium- to coarse-grained. Compact, dull, waxy. Fractures in splinters.
**Structure**: Often banded. Usually criss-crossed with veins of chrysotile serpentine.
**Colour**: Grey-green to black
**Composition**: Serpentine (chrysotile, lizardite, antigorite), olivine, pyroxene, hornblende, mica, garnet, iron oxides
**Protolith**: Peridotite, dunite, pyroxenite, and occasionally gabbro and dolomite
**Notable occurrences**: Lizard (Cornwall), England; Shetland Islands, Scotland; Pyrenees, Vosges, France; Liguria, Italy; Montana; Oregon; California; Maine; The Lost City, Mid-Atlantic seabed; Izu-Bonin-Marian seamounts, Pacific

**The Lost City**
Geologists have long known about 'black smokers', or hydrothermal vents (above). These are remarkable chimneys on the sea floor in the mid-ocean ridge. They are built up from deposits left by smoky clouds of sulphide-rich water that bubble up through the sea floor, superheated by magma. In 2001, oceanographers discovered an entirely different kind of smoker towering up from the Atlantic ocean floor. Forming what was dubbed the Lost City, these white smokers are made of carbonate, and develop in an entirely different way to black smokers. For a start, they form well away from the central ocean rift. More significantly, they are heated not by magma but by the heat generated from serpentinization reactions in peridotite rocks under the ocean floor surface. As sea-water infiltrates the peridotites, it not only turns them to serpentinite but also generates warm, alkali-rich waters that bubble up in white smokers to form brucite and calcite towers.

## Fulgurite

Fulgurites are the most unusual and rarest of all metamorphic rocks. They get their name from the Latin for 'thunderbolt', and they are natural tubes or crusts of glass that form when lightning strikes. To fuse sand instantly into glass needs temperatures of 1,800°C/3,272°F, and lightning regularly reaches a searing 2,500°C/4,532°F. There are two kinds of fulgurite: sand and rock. Sand fulgurites form in the loose sand on beaches and in deserts. They are branching tubes that look like roots. They average 2.5cm/1in in diameter and can be up to 1m/39in long. Rock fulgurites are crusts or coats of glass that form when lightning strikes solid rock. Typically, they form branching marks across the rock surface, or line pre-existing fractures in the rock. Rock fulgurites are typically found on mountain tops, most famously on Oregon's Mount Thielsen, known as the Cascade's Lightning Rod due to evidence of strikes found there.

**Rock type**: Non-foliated, contact metamorphic
**Texture**: Glassy
**Structure**: Sand fulgurites: branching tubes of glassy sand in loose sand. Rock fulgurites: glassy crusts on solid rock in veins or fractures.
**Colour**: Grey-green to black
**Composition**: The silica mineral lechtalierite
**Protolith**: Sand fulgurites form in loose sand; rock fulgurites can form on any rock
**Notable occurrences**: Sand fulgurites: Sahara Desert, Africa; Namib Desert; Botswana; Lake Michigan, Atlantic coast of North America; Utah deserts. Rock fulgurites: Isle of Arran, Scotland; Mt Blanc (Alps), Pyrenees, France; Mount Ararat, Turkey; Toluca, Mexico; Sierra Nevada, CA; Wasatch Range, UT; Mount Thielsen (Cascade Range), OR; South Amboy, NJ

**Identification**: Sand fulgurites are branching knobbly tubes of glassy sand.

# SPACE ROCKS

*Meteorites are chunks of rock from space, mostly asteroids, that crash into the Earth. Because large meteorites strike the ground with such force that they are instantly vaporized, most meteorites are small – the largest ever, from Grootfontein in Namibia, is no larger than a double bed. But you can also find entirely new rocks and minerals forged by the impact called impactites, which include tektites and suevite.*

## Stony meteorite

Perhaps reflecting Earth's stony mantle and iron core, meteorites are divided into two main kinds, stony and iron, plus a few made from both stone and iron. Nine out of ten meteorites falling to Earth are stony meteorites, made largely of silicates and containing many minerals familiar from Earth rocks such as olivine and pyroxene. Stony meteorites are of two kinds: chondrites and achondrites. Chondrites get their name because most contain little globules called chondrules, typically 1mm/0.04in across. Most achondrites, on the other hand, contain no chondrules. Like grains in sedimentary rock, chondrules in chondrites are set in a matrix of finer material. The theory is that chondrules are droplets of olivine and pyroxene that condensed and crystallized in space while the Solar System was forming, then clustered together to create asteroids. The chondrites are the most jumbled in composition of all meteorites, perhaps little changed since the very earliest days of the Solar System. Minerals in achondrites are less jumbled, reflecting how they have become differentiated over time as asteroids and planets developed crusts and mantles. Most achondrites come from asteroids, but 28 have come from Mars and 20 from the Moon.

**Identification**: A single unusual-looking knobbly stone quite unlike any others in the area could just be a meteorite. Look for a dark outside showing signs of melting, and a light-coloured inside. A very heavy feel is also a good clue. If it is full of holes, it is more likely to be volcanic. Light-grey chondrule spots may be visible in a chondrite.

**Rock type**: Meteoritic
**Texture**: Fine-matrix, possibly with tiny spheres called chondrules, up to pea-size
**Structure**: No obvious internal structure
**Colour**: Light to dark grey, black
**Composition**: Similar to peridotites or gabbros, mostly made of olivine, pyroxene and nickel-iron. Chondrules are olivine, pyroxene, bronzite, diopside or, more rarely, chromite, magnetite, graphite or spinel. The matrix is the same material.
**Origin**: Asteroids and comets
**Notable occurrences**: Bjurbole, Finland (1899); Jillin, China (fell 1976); Hoba Farm, Grootfontein, Namibia (prehistoric times); Norton County, Kansas (1984); Long Island, New York (1948); Paragould, Arkansas (1930)

## Iron and stony-iron meteorites

Iron meteorites are unlike any Earth rock. Thought to come from the cores of asteroids, they are almost pure metal – basically an iron-nickel alloy in the form of the rare minerals kamacite and taenite. Only 1 in 10 meteorites is iron, but they are much easier to spot being large, dark, heavy and odd-shaped. They also survive for a long time in soil. So, despite their rarity, they are found more often than stony meteorites, and all the biggest specimens are iron. They may be divided into three groups according to the structures that appear on their surface when etched with nitric acid: octahedrites, hexahedrites and ataxites. Octahedrites are marked by criss-cross ribbons called Widmanstätten figures and hexadrites by parallel 'Neumann' lines. Ataxites have no clear marks. Each group is characterized by a different mix of kamacite and taenite. The rare stony-iron meteorites are made of iron and silicate minerals. They are thought to come from the core-mantle boundary of large asteroids.

**Identification**: Knobbly, heavy, solid and unbreakably metallic – and magnetic – iron meteorites are easy to identify. Prehistoric people used them as a source of iron, called sky iron.

**Rock type**: Meteoritic
**Texture**: Fine-matrix, possibly with tiny spheres called chondrules, up to pea-size
**Structure**: See text
**Colour**: Brown, grey, black
**Composition**: Iron and nickel as two main minerals: kamacite (nickel-poor) and taenite (nickel-rich). Hexahedrites are mostly kamacite and ataxites mostly taenite. Octahedrites are both kamacite and taenite.
**Origin**: Asteroids and comets
**Notable occurrences**: Sikhote-Alin, Russia (1947); Odessa, Ukraine; Nantan (Guangxi Province), China (fell 1516, found 1958); Antarctica; Campo del Cielo, Argentina; Allende, Mexico; Canyon Diablo, Arizona

# Tektite

Tektites are remarkable dark, glassy lumps, first observed by Charles Darwin in Tasmania. They are clearly made from molten glass, and Darwin thought they were volcanic bombs. Their origins sparked heated debate, but geologists now agree that most, if not all, tektites are solidified splashes of rock melted by the impact of a meteorite. They are usually found only in particular regions, called strewn-fields. Some strewn-fields are linked to known impact craters, like the Bosumtwi crater in Africa's Ivory Coast, and the Ries crater in Germany. With others, the crater has yet to be found. By far the largest field is in Indochina, stretching from Malaysia to Tasmania, where millions of tektites have been found. Particular kinds of tektite are named after a strewn-field, such as australites from Australia and the beautiful green moldavites from the Moldau region in the Czech Republic, used as jewellery in prehistoric times. There are four main kinds of tektite: microtektites are grain-sized balls found only in marine sediments; Muong-Nuong tektites are pea- to truck-sized chunks; australites have been shaped while molten into saucer shapes; and splash-form tektites are dark globs of black or green glass.

**Splash-form tektite**: These tektites are dark globs of black or green glass. They can be round-, teardrop-, disc-, dumbell- and even rod-shaped. Their surface is always marked by pits and furrows created by corrosion.

**Rock type**: Impactite
**Texture**: Glassy
**Structure**: See text
**Colour**: Black to green, occasionally yellowish
**Composition**: Similar to granites, with 70% silica
**Origin**: Meteorite impact melting sandstone and shale
**Notable occurrences**: Ries-Nördlingen, Germany; Moldau, Czech R (linked to the Ries impact); Irghiz, Russian Fed; Bosumtwi, Ivory Coast; Muong-Nong, Laos; Cambodia; Malaysia; Philippines; Mt Darwin (Tasmania), Kalgoorlie (WA), Victoria, Australia; Albion I (Corozal), Belize; Beloc, Haiti; Arroyo el Mimbral, Mexico; Bedias region (Fayette County), Texas; Martha's Vineyard, Massachusetts; Georgia

*Meteorite impact*

*Impact structures in rock*

**Meteorite impact sites**
The Earth is struck by debris from space with remarkable frequency. Although smaller fragments burn up on their way through the atmosphere, at least three million meteorites big enough to create a crater at least 1km/0.65 miles across have crashed into the Earth during its existence. The effect of such impacts is clearly visible on the pitted surface of the Moon, but the Earth is so geologically active that the signs of many impacts have long since been wiped away here. Until recently, scientists believed that Earth was hit by meteorites only early in its history. Now they know it is being hit all the time, and the remnants of even quite ancient craters, or 'astroblemes', are there if you know what to look for – including key minerals such as stishovite. The first firm identification was Meteor Crater in Arizona, initially suggested as an impact crater by Daniel Barringer in 1902, then confirmed by Eugene Shoemaker, Edward Chao and Daniel Milton in 1960. Now, more than 160 major astroblemes have been discovered, including the Sudbury impact in Ontario and the Ries-Nördlingen site in Bavaria in Germany.

# Suevite

Besides sending out splashes of molten rock, the tremendous impact of a meteorite can literally pulverize the rock where it hits creating what is called an impact breccia. One of these breccias, first identified at the Ries crater in Germany, is suevite. Suevite is a jumbled mix of glass melt bombs and fragments of crushed rock. Unlike other impact breccias, it usually forms only when there is plenty of water around. This water is usually in the ground, but the surprisingly large amounts of suevite at the famous Sudbury impact crater in Canada may be explained if the impact was not an asteroid, as most impacts are, but a comet. Comets bring water with them. Thin layers of suevite have proved to be a key piece of evidence supporting the theory that the dinosaurs were wiped out by the effects of a huge meteorite impact 65 million years ago, at Chicxulub in Mexico.

**Rock type**: Impact breccia
**Texture**: Breccia, with powdery matrix containing various-sized angular rock fragments and rounded glassy melt bombs
**Colour**: Buff, light grey with dark stones
**Origin**: Meteorite impact pulverizing country rock
**Notable occurrences**: Ries-Nördlingen, Germany; Popigai, Kara, Siberia; Lonar, India; Vredefort, South Africa; Bosumtwi, Ivory Coast; Woodleigh, Gosses Bluff, Australia; Chicxulub, Mexico; Haughton (Devon I), Nunavut Territory of Canada; Manicougan, Quebec; Sudbury, Ontario; Manson (Des Moines), Iowa; Chesapeake Bay, Maryland and Virginia; Meteor Crater (Painted Desert), Arizona

**Identification**: With its mix of rock powder and glass bombs, suevite looks very much like volcanic breccia but is closely linked to impact sites.

# DIRECTORY OF MINERALS

*The Minerals Directory gives detailed portraits of over 250 species of mineral from around the world. Using the clues on the following page, you can make a rough identification of a mineral, then follow up those clues in the Directory to make a closer identification. The diagrams here show how entries work.*

Minerals are natural, solid chemicals. Most, but not all, are crystalline, and their crystals fit into one of the six or seven major systems of crystal symmetry, although each has its own particular habit or way of growing.

Most minerals are found in rocks, and form part of their chemical make-up, and so are called rock-forming minerals. Minerals valued primarily for their ores are also covered, in the final section of the Directory. 'Rock-formers' are ordered according to the major chemical groups associated with minerals; ore-formers according to their major metal constituent (see Classifying Minerals; Mineral Ores; Understanding Rocks and Minerals).

*Above: Spectacular minerals like these needles of millerite growing in a cavity are very rare indeed.*

In fact, many of the rock-formers profiled in the Directory occur only in very tiny amounts in rocks. There are just a few dozen minerals that are actually major constituents of rocks.

Major minerals in igneous rocks include quartz, feldspars, feldspathoids, micas, augite, hornblende and olivine. Major minerals in sedimentary rocks include salts and clays, plus various carbonates, sulphates and phosphates that occur only in sedimentary rocks as well as quartz and feldspars. Major minerals in metamorphic include many of the same as those in igneous rocks such as quartz, feldspars, mica and hornblende, plus many that are primarily characteristic of metamorphic rocks including: actinolite, andalusite, axinite, chlorite, epidote, the garnet group, graphite, kyanite, prehnite, sillimanite, staurolite, talc and tremolite.

---

**Mineral name**: may be plural if several varieties are profiled

**Chemistry**: The chemical formula and name is given for each mineral.

**Inset detail**: Illustrations of related species and special features.

**Identification**: Notes the most useful clues for identifying specimens found in the field.

**Data panel**: Quick reference tool summarizing standard mineral characteristics.

**Crystal system**: The way in which crystals of the mineral are symmetrical. The line diagram shows the form in which crystals of the mineral commonly grow.

**Crystal habit**: The characteristic way crystals or aggregates grow.

**Colour; Lustre; Streak**: see Optical Properties, Understanding Rocks and Minerals. Streak is particularly useful for identifying a mineral (see Identifying Minerals, Understanding Rocks and Minerals).

**Hardness; Cleavage; Fracture; Specific Gravity (SG)**: see Physical Properties, Understanding Rocks and Minerals. SG is useful for identifying a mineral (see Identifying Minerals).

**Notable locations**: Entries are country by country (except for Canada and the USA which are listed last, state by state) with each site separated by a comma.

## Silver

*Ag Silver*

In Ancient Egypt, silver was called white gold and was valued even more highly than gold itself. There are silver mines in eastern Anatolia (Turkey) that were excavated by the pre-Hittite people of Cappadocia over 5,000 years ago. Today, its high conductivity (better than copper) means that silver is used in electronics, as well as for decoration. When polished, silver is a beautiful, shiny white metal, but it quickly tarnishes with a black coating of silver sulphide (inset). This is why it is hard to identify in nature, even though it grows in distinctive wiry, dendritic (tree-like) masses with the appearance of twisted wood. Like gold, it typically forms in hydrothermal veins, commonly in association with galena (lead ore), zinc and copper. Nuggets or grains rarely form so it is uncommon in placer deposits. Native silver is very rare, and most of the silver used today has been separated out from other minerals, especially in large argentite (silver sulphide) ore deposits in Nevada, Peru and Mexico.

*Dark areas of silver sulphide, or tarnish*

**Identification**: You are unlikely to find any other white, softish metal in its native state. Scraping off a black tarnish to reveal a bright silvery metal confirms the identity. Cubes like that here are rare, and you are more likely to find silver in the form of wiry, branching masses.

*Calcite block*

*Silver*

**Crystal system**: Isometric

**Crystal habit**: Wiry, branching masses or grains, or, rarely, cubic crystals. Wires can form coils like rams' horns.

**Colour**: Silver-white but tarnishing quickly to black

**Lustre**: Metallic

**Streak**: Silver-white

**Hardness**: 2.5–3

**Cleavage**: None

**Fracture**: Hackly

**Specific gravity**: 10–12

**Other characteristics**: Soft enough to stretch into wires and hammer into shapes

**Notable locations**: Kongsberg, Norway; Sankt Andreasberg (Harz Mts), Freiburg (Saxony), Germany; Jachymov, Czech Republic; Chihuahua, Mexico; Great Bear Lake, Northwest Territories; Cobalt, Ontario; Michigan; Creede, Colorado

**Profile**: General information on specimen; its discovery, where it is found, how it forms and its special characteristics. See also data panel, right.

**Specimen photograph**: Some important features may be annotated.

**Caution**: Specimen is poisonous. Handle with care

**Notes on safe handling**: Warnings advocating cautionary usage may appear in the data table, or as a separate panel. See Safe Handling of Specimens, opposite

## MINERAL LOCALITIES

Good mineral specimens are not found scattered evenly around the world but concentrated in a few locations where rare combinations of conditions create particular mineral formations.

Every mineral has a type locality. This is the place where the first formally recognized specimens of a mineral were discovered. Sometimes, a mineral takes its name from the type locality such as Franklinite, after the famous Franklin mines in New Jersey.

Very few type localities are host only to one kind of mineral. Some of the most famous sites are type localities for dozens of other minerals – as well as many other minerals found first elsewhere.

Besides type localities, there are sites famous either for the sheer number of different minerals found there, for the rarity of the species, or simply for the very special nature of the specimens found there. A few sites are famous for the large and spectacular crystals they yield, for instance, or their rare twins, or beautiful gems. Some, of course, are simply famous for the sheer quantity of accessible specimens they provide the collector. A list of the more famous locations appears to the right, some still producing, some now exhausted.

*Right: The Isle of Skye, off the north-west coast of Scotland, offers many excellent opportunities for mineral collecting.*

### FAMOUS MINERAL LOCALITIES

**Europe**
Almaden, Ciudad Real, Spain
Binntal, Switzerland
Black Forest, Germany
Cornwall, England
Cumbria, England
Durham, England
Harz Mountains, Germany
Ilmaussaq, Greenland
Kola Peninsula, Russia
Langban, Varmland, Sweden
Langesundfjord, Norway
Leadhills, Lanarks, Scotland
Lavrion, Greece
Pribram, Czech Republic
Skye, Scotland
Strontian, Argyll, Scotland
Ural Mountains, Russia
Mount Vesuvius, Italy

**Australia and Asia**
Bombay mines, India
Broken Hill, NSW, Australia
Coober Pedy, South Australia
Dundas, Tasmania
Kashmir
Mogok, Myanmar (Burma)
NSW, Australia
Ratnapura, Sri Lanka

**Africa and South America**
Katanga, Congo
Kimberley, South Africa
Kivu, Congo
Transvaal, South Africa
Tsumeb, Namibia
Copiapo and Atacama, Chile
Llallagua, Potosi, Bolivia
Minas Gerais, Brazil

**USA and Canada**
Arizona copper mines
Bancroft Ontario
Black Hills, South Dakota
Boron mines of California
Cobalt, Ontario
Francon, Montreal, Quebec
Franklin & Sterling Hill, NJ
Keeweenaw, Michigan
Magnet Cove, Arkansas
Mississippi Valley region
New Hants phosphate mines
Rapid Crk & Big Fish, Yukon
Mont Saint-Hilaire, Quebec
San Benito Co, California
San Diego Co, California
Sudbury, Ontario
Tristate Mining District,
Kansas-Missouri-Nebraska

## SAFE HANDLING OF SPECIMENS

Handling mineral specimens safely is basically common sense. Only very few minerals are significantly poisonous or radioactive, and even these can be handled safely. You just need to make sure you handle them only in a well-ventilated room to avoid breathing in fumes, and wash your hands carefully afterwards to make sure contamination is not carried to your mouth. Minerals that are especially toxic or radioactive are identified in the directory. Of course, all mineral specimens should be kept out of children's reach, but especially these minerals.

**Handling and storing radioactive minerals**

Certain minerals are mildly radioactive, including carnotite, autunite and torbernite. They are mostly radioactive because of their uranium content. However, their radioactivity is very mild. You would have to hold a large chunk of high-grade uranium ore in your hand for a few hours to get the same dose of radiation as from a chest X-ray. You would have to hold it in your hand continuously for over four days to get the same dose as you get naturally from everyday things around you over a year. All the same it is worth taking a few basic precautions when handling minerals that are classed as naturally radioactive:

**1** Don't carry radioactive minerals in pockets, or bring them close to the reproductive organs.
**2** Keep specimens away from the eyes.
**3** Wash hands properly after handling specimens.
**4** Never crush or grind specimens, since the dust can get in the air.
**5** Wash hands properly after handling specimens.
**6** Store specimens out of children's and pets' reach.
**7** Store specimens in screwtop glass containers in a cabinet in a well-ventilated room not used for everyday living.
**8** Label specimens clearly so that everyone knows what they're touching.

# IDENTIFYING MINERALS

*Of over 4,000 different minerals in existence, a few of them, such as crocoite and malachite, are instantly recognizable. Many of the rest, though, can look very similar to one another. So how do you tell them apart and make a positive identification?*

You might think that you could identify minerals in the same way as flowers by colour and shape alone. Unfortunately, you cannot in all but a few cases. Nearly every mineral is far too variable in colour and shape – and the differences between them either subtle or completely misleading. Fortunately, there are other more reliable clues to identity. There are also a number of simple tests you can conduct to confirm a mineral's identity.

Although a mineral's visual colour is variable, its streak is not, so you can narrow down the range of possibilities by first doing a streak test – scraping the mineral across the back of a white ceramic tile – then Mohs hardness test (see Mineral Properties: Physical in Understanding Rocks and Minerals). Find the streak colour in the table below, then find the mineral's hardness within the group. This should give you at most a dozen or so choices. If you can test its specific gravity (SG), you should be able to narrow the choice even farther.

## Identifying in three steps

### NON–METALLIC LUSTRE — White streak

| Mohs | Mineral | SG |
|---|---|---|
| 1 | Talc | 2.8 |
| 1–2 | Scarbroite | 2 |
| 1–2 | Aluminite | 1.7 |
| 1–2 | Carnallite | 1.6 |
| 1–2.5 | Chlorite | 2.5–2.9 |
| 1.5–2 | Kaolinite | 2.6 |
| 1.5–2 | Nitratine | 2.2–2.3 |
| 1.5–2.5 | Chlorargyrite | 5.5–5.6 |
| 2 | Ulexite | 1.5–2 |
| 2 | Sylvite | 2 |
| 2 | Halite | 2.1 |
| 2 | Sulphur | 2 |
| 2 | Gypsum | 2.3 |
| 2 | Vivianite | 2.6 |
| 2 | Melanterite | 1.9 |
| 2–2.5 | Epsomite | 1.7 |
| 2–2.5 | Muscovite | 2.8 |
| 2–2.5 | Zinnwaldite | 3.0 |
| 2–2.5 | Hydrozincite | 3.7 |
| 2–3 | Gaylussite | 1.9 |
| 2.5 | Lepidolite | 2.8 |
| 2.5 | Jouravskite | 1.95 |
| 2.5–3 | Mendipite | 7–7.5 |
| 2.5–3 | Ferrimolybdite | 4.–4.5 |
| 2.5–3 | Cryolite | 2.95 |
| 2.5–3 | Phlogopite | 2.95 |
| 2.5–3 | Glauberite | 2.7–3 |
| 2.5–3 | Biotite | 3 |
| 2.5–3 | Thenardite | 2.7 |
| 2.5–3 | Gibbsite | 2.4 |
| 3 | Kainite | 2.1 |
| 3 | Calcite | 2.7 |
| 3 | Anglesite | 6.3 |
| 3 | Wulfenite | 6.8 |
| 3 | Vanadinite | 7 |
| 3–3.5 | Polyhalite | 2.8 |
| 3–3.5 | Cerussite | 6.5 |
| 3–3.5 | Celestine | 4 |
| 3–3.5 | Barite | 4.5 |
| 3.5 | Witherite | 4.3 |
| 3.5 | Adamite | 4.3 |
| 3.5 | Kieserite | 2.6 |
| 3–4 | Anhydrite | 2.9 |
| 3–4 | Serpentine | 2.6 |
| 3.5–4 | Pyromorphite | 6.5–7 |
| 3.5–4 | Mimetite | 7.1 |
| 3.5–4 | Strontianite | 3.8 |
| 3.5–4 | Scorodite | 3.1–3.3 |
| 3.5–4 | Magnesite | 3 |
| 3.5–4 | Wavellite | 2.3 |
| 3.5–4 | Dolomite | 2.9 |
| 3.5–4 | Ankerite | 2.9–3.8 |
| 3.5–4 | Aragonite | 2.9 |
| 3.5–4 | Alunite | 2.5–2.8 |
| 3.5–4 | Stilbite | 2.2 |
| 3.5–4 | Heulandite | 2.2 |
| 3.5–4.5 | Siderite | 3.8–3.9 |
| 4 | Fluorite | 3.2 |
| 4 | Rhodochrosite | 3.5 |
| 4 | Kyanite | 3.6 |
| 4–5 | Smithsonite | 4.4 |
| 4–4.5 | Jarlite | 3.87 |
| 4–4.5 | Magnesite | 3 |
| 4.4.5 | Phillipsite | 2.2 |
| 4–5 | Triphyllite | 3.6 |
| 4.5 | Colemanite | 2.4 |
| 4.5 | Chabazite | 2.1 |
| 4.5–5 | Scheelite | 6 |
| 4.5–5 | Stibiconite | 3.5–3.9 |
| 4.5–5 | Wollastonite | 2.8 |
| 4.5–5 | Apophyllite | 2.3 |
| 5 | Apatite | 3.2 |
| 5 | Hemimorphite | 3.4 |
| 5–5.5 | Monazite | 4.9–5.3 |
| 5–5.5 | Sphene | 3.5 |
| 5–5.5 | Analcime | 2.2 |
| 5–5.5 | Natrolite, | |
| | Scolecite | 2.3 |
| 5.5 | Perovskite | 4 |
| 5–6 | Lazurite | 3 |
| 5–6 | Scapolite | 2.6 |
| 5–6 | Turquoise | 2.6–2.8 |
| 5–6 | Bronzite | 3.3 |
| 5.5–6 | Sodalite, | |
| | Hauyne, | |
| | Nosean | 2.4 |
| 5.5–6 | Anatase | 3.8 |
| 5.5–6 | Nephelite | 2.6 |
| 5.5–6 | Leucite | 2.5 |
| 5.5–6 | Rhodonite | 3.5 |
| 5.5–6 | Actinolite | 3.1 |
| 5.5–6 | Nephrite | 3.1 |
| 5.5–6 | Amblygonite | 3–3.1 |
| 5.5–6.5 | Opal | 1.9–2.5 |
| 5.5–6.5 | Diopside | 3.3 |
| 6 | Fassaite | 3.3 |
| 6 | Zoisite | 3.3 |
| 6 | Adularia | 2.5 |
| 6 | Orthoclase, | |
| | Microcline, | |
| | Sanidine | 2.5 |
| 6 | Albite | 2.6 |
| 6–6.5 | Anorthite | 2.76 |
| 6–6.5 | Plagioclase | 2.6–2.8 |
| 6–6.5 | Prehnite | 2.9 |
| 6.5 | Jadeite | 3.2 |
| 6.5 | Vesuvianite | 3.4 |
| 6–7 | Cassiterite | 7 |
| 6–7 | Kyanite | 3.6 |
| 6–7 | Epidote | 3.3–3.5 |
| 6.5–7 | Sillimanite | 3.2 |
| 6.5–7 | Olivine | 3-2–4.3 |
| 6.5–7 | Axinite | 3.3 |
| 6.5–7 | Spodumene | 3.2 |
| 6.5–7 | Diaspore | 3.4 |
| 6.5–7.5 | Garnet family | 4 |
| 7 | Quartz | 2.65 |
| 7–7.5 | Staurolite | 3.7 |
| 7–7.5 | Boracite | 3 |
| 7–7.5 | Cordierite | 2.6 |
| 7–7.5 | Tourmaline | 3.1 |
| 7.5 | Andalusite | 3.1 |
| 7.5 | Zircon | 4.5 |
| 7.5–8 | Beryl | 2.7 |
| 8 | Topaz | 3.5 |
| 8 | Spinel | 3.7 |
| 8.5 | Chrysoberyl | 3.7 |
| 9 | Corundum | 4 |
| 10 | Diamond | 3.52 |

### Yellow to brown streak

| Mohs | Mineral | SG |
|---|---|---|
| 1.5–2 | Orpiment | 3.4 |
| 2 | Sulphur | 2 |
| 2 | Autunite | 3.1 |
| 2 | Carnotite | 4.5 |
| 2.5 | Uranophane | 3.8 |
| 2.5–3 | Vanadinite | 7 |
| 2.5–3 | Crocoite | 6 |
| 2.5–3.5 | Jarosite | 2.9–3.3 |
| 3 | Wulfenite | 6.8 |
| 3–4 | Vanadinite | 6.7–7.1 |
| 3.5–4 | Pentlandite | 4.6–5 |
| 3.5–4 | Sphalerite | 4 |
| 3.5–4 | Copiapite | 2.1 |
| 4 | Zincite | 5.4–5.7 |
| 4–4.5 | Siderite | 3.8 |
| 4.5 | Xenotime | 4.4–5 |
| 4–6 | Pitchblende | |
| | Uraninite | 9–10.5 |
| 5 | Goethite | |
| | Limonite | 4.3 |
| 5–5.5 | Wolframite | 7.3 |
| 5–5.5 | Plattnerite | 9.4+ |
| 5.5 | Chromite | 4–4.8 |
| 5.5–6 | Hornblende | 3.2 |
| 5.5–6 | Brookite | 4 |
| 5.5–6 | Hypersthene | 3.5 |
| 6 | Columbite | 5–8 |
| 6–6.5 | Aegirine | 3.5 |
| 6–6.5 | Rutile | 4.2 |

## Minerals with distinctive colours

Some minerals exhibit particular colours that make them easier to recognize. When noting the outward characteristics of a specimen, be as descriptive as possible – for example, jotting down what the colour reminds you of. Getting into the habit of making acute observations may help you to recognize the mineral on sight the next time you encounter it.

*Scarlet orange: crocoite*

### Yellows and golds
- gold: gold, pyrite, chalcopyrite, pyrrhotite, marcasite
- yellow: sulphur, carnotite
- lemon: adamite
- custard: jarosite
- yellow-green: autunite
- golden syrup: orpiment

### Reds and oranges
- vermillion: cinnabar
- rose red: rhodonite
- scarlet orange: crocoite, vanadinite
- red wine: cuprite
- rosé wine: grossular garnet
- ruby red: ruby
- strawberry jam: proustite; pyrargyrite
- blood red: jasper
- jelly-red: rhodochrosite
- marmalade: citrine

### Purples and blues
- purple: amethyst
- blue: diaboleite, chalcanthite, azurite, cyanotrichite, lazulite, chrysocolla, linarite, labradorite, sodalite
- sky blue: sapphire

### Greens
- opaque green: malachite, varsicite, garnierite
- apple-green: atacamite

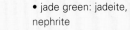

*Opaque green: malachite*

- jade green: jadeite, nephrite
- pale green or cyan: hemimorphite
- clear green: olivine, emerald, dioptase

---

| | | |
|---|---|---|
| 6–7 | Cassiterite | 7 |

**Orange streak**

| | | |
|---|---|---|
| 1.5–2 | Realgar | 3.5–3.6 |
| 2.5–3 | Crocoite | 6 |

**Green streak**

| | | |
|---|---|---|
| 1–2.5 | Chlorite | 2.5–2.9 |
| 1.5–2 | Vivianite | 2.6 |
| 1.5–2.5 | Annabergite | 3 |
| 2–2.5 | Garnierite | 4.6 |
| 2–2.5 | Torbernite | 3.5 |
| 2–2.5 | Autunite | 3.1–3.2 |
| 2.5–3 | Köttigite | 3.3 |
| 3 | Olivenite | 3.9–4.4 |
| 3–3.5 | Mottramite | 5.7–6 |
| 3–3.5 | Millerite | 5.3–5.5 |
| 3–3.5 | Atacamite | 3.75 |
| 3.5 | Antlerite | 3.9 |
| 3.5–4 | Malachite | 4 |
| 4 | Libethenite | 3.6–3.9 |
| 4.5 | Cuprotungstite | 7 |
| 4.5 | Conichalcite | 4.3 |
| 5.5–6 | Hornblende | 3.2 |
| 5.5–6 | Hedenbergite | 3.5 |
| 5.5–6 | Augite | 3.4 |
| 6–6.5 | Aegirine | 3.5 |

**Blue streak**

| | | |
|---|---|---|
| 1–3 | Cyanotrichite | 3.8 |
| 2 | Vivianite | 2.6 |
| 2–2.5 | Proustite | 5.6 |
| 2.5 | Chalcanthite | 2.2–2.3 |
| 2.5 | Linarite | 5.3 |
| 3–3.5 | Boleite | 5 |
| 3.5–4 | Azurite | 3.8 |

| | | |
|---|---|---|
| 5–6 | Glaucophane | 3–3.2 |
| 5.5–6 | Lazulite | 3.1 |

**Red or crimson streak**

| | | |
|---|---|---|
| 1.5 | Realgar | 3.5 |
| 2–2.5 | Proustite | 5.6 |
| 2–2.5 | Cinnabar | 8.1 |
| 2.5 | Pyrargyrite | 5.8 |
| 3–3.5 | Polyhalite | 2.8 |
| 3–3.5 | Greenockite | 4.5–5 |
| 3–3.5 | Descloizite | 5.9 |
| 3.5–4 | Cuprite | 6 |
| 4 | Rhodochrosite | 3.5 |
| 6 | Columbite | 5–8 |
| 6.5 | Hematite | 5.1 |
| 6.5 | Piemontite | 3.4 |

**Grey to black streak**

| | | |
|---|---|---|
| 1.5 | Covellite | 4.7 |
| 2 | Argentite | 7.3 |
| 2.5–3 | Chalcocite | 5.6 |
| 3–3.5 | Cerussite | 6.5 |
| 3–4 | Tetrahedrite | 4.4–5.4 |
| 5–5.5 | Wolframite | 7.3 |
| 5–6 | Psilomelane | 4.5 |
| 5–6 | Ilmenite | 4.7 |
| 5.5–6 | Ilvaite | 4.1 |
| 5.5–6 | Magnetite | 5 |
| 5.5–6 | Hornblende | 3.2 |
| 5.5–6 | Diallage | 3.3 |
| 5.5–6 | Hedenbergite | 3.5 |
| 5.5–6 | Augite | 3.4 |
| 5.5–6 | Hypersthene | 3.5 |
| 5.5–6 | Anthophyllite | 2.8–3.4 |
| 6 | Columbite | 5–8 |
| 6.5 | Thortveitite | 3.5 |
| 6–7 | Epidote | 3.4 |

**METALLIC LUSTRE**

**White streak**

| | | |
|---|---|---|
| 2–2.5 | Muscovite | 2.8 |
| 2.5–3 | Biotite | 3 |
| 5–6 | Bronzite | 3.3 |
| 5.5–6 | Anatase | 3.8 |
| 6–7 | Cassiterite | 7 |

**Yellow to brown streak**

| | | |
|---|---|---|
| 2.5–3 | Gold | 15–19.5 |
| 3 | Baumhauerite | 5.3 |
| 3.5–4 | Sphalerite | 4 |
| 5–5.5 | Niccolite | 7.7 |
| 5–5.5 | Wolframite | 7.3 |
| 5.5 | Chromite | 4–4.8 |
| 5.5–6 | Chloanthite | 6.5 |
| 5.5–6 | Hypersthene | 3.5 |
| 5.5–6 | Brookite | 4 |
| 6–6.5 | Rutile | 4.2 |

**Greenish black streak**

| | | |
|---|---|---|
| 3.5–4 | Chalcopyrite | 4.2 |

**Red streak**

| | | |
|---|---|---|
| 2–2.5 | Cinnabar | 8.1 |
| 2–2.5 | Pyrargyrite | 5.8 |
| 2.5–3 | Native copper | 8.9 |
| 3–4 | Tetrahedrite | 4.4–5.4 |
| 3.5–4 | Cuprite | 6 |
| 5–6 | Hematite | 5.3 |
| 5–6 | Ilmenite | 4.5–5 |

**Grey to black streak**

| | | |
|---|---|---|
| 1 | Graphite | 2.2 |
| 1.5 | Molybdenite | 4.8 |
| 1.5 | Covellite | 4.7 |
| 2 | Stibnite | 4.6 |
| 2 | Argentite | 7.3 |
| 2–3 | Jamesonite | 5.5–6 |
| 2–3 | Pyrolusite | 4.5 |
| 2.5 | Cylindrite | 5.5 |
| 2.5–3 | Chalcocite | 5.6 |
| 2.5–3 | Digenite | 5.6 |
| 2.5–3 | Galena | 7.4 |
| 2.5–3 | Altaite | 8.2 |
| 3 | Bornite | 5.1 |
| 3 | Bournonite | 5.8 |
| 3.5 | Enargite | 4.4 |
| 3–4 | Tetrahedrite | 4.4–5.4 |
| 3.5–4 | Chalcopyrite | 4.2 |
| 4 | Stannite | 4.3–4.5 |
| 4 | Manganite | 4.3 |
| 4 | Pyrrhotite | 4.6 |
| 4.5–5.5 | Carrollite | 4.6 |
| 4.5–5.5 | Safflorite | 7–7.3 |
| 5 | Löllingite | 7.3 |
| 5–5.5 | Wolframite | 7.3 |
| 5–5.5 | Niccolite | 7.7 |
| 5.5 | Cobaltite | 6.2 |
| 5–6 | Ilmenite | 4.7 |
| 5.5–6 | Hypersthene | 3.5 |
| 5.5–6 | Arsenopyrite | 6 |
| 5.5–6 | Magnetite | 5 |
| 5.5–6 | Ilvaite | 4.1 |
| 5.5–6 | Skutterudite | 6.6–7.2 |
| 5.5–6 | Chloanthite, Rammels–bergite | 6.6–7.2 |
| 5.5–6.5 | Franklinite | 5.1 |
| 6–6.5 | Pyrite | 5.1 |
| 6–7 | Iridosmine | 19–21 |
| 6–7 | Sperrylite | 10.6 |
| 6.5 | Hematite | 5.1 |

# IDENTIFYING MINERALS BY SURROUNDINGS

*Where you find a mineral specimen – its location and associations – can often provide many important clues to its identity. Not only are particular minerals characteristic of particular rocks and geological environments, but some minerals are nearly always found together.*

Just as a certain range of animals live in a particular habitat, likewise certain minerals often occur together. Gold, for instance, is often found with milky quartz. Minerals that occur together are said to be associated. Some associations are the minerals that form a particular kind of rock, such as quartz, feldspars and micas in granite. Other associations might form in particular types of mineral-forming environment, such as a vein, or a cavity, or an encrustation.

Sometimes the association is built up in stages, with first one mineral added then another, through time. On a small scale this happens in balls of minerals found in sedimentary rocks called septarian nodules. These begin as mudballs surrounding decomposing

sealife. As they dry out they fill with minerals such as dolomite. These minerals begin to crack, and as they do, the cracks fill with veins of calcite.

On a larger scale, ore deposits in rocks are often altered by watery solutions seeping down through cracks. Chemicals weathered from pyrite ore, for instance, are washed down through the rock and react with minerals lower down. Ferric sulphate reacts with copper, lead and zinc minerals to create sulphates which can, in turn, be dissolved and carried on down by the water. Sulphuric acid dissolves carbonates and as these are washed down, they react with copper minerals to create a layer of minerals such as malachite and azurite. Even farther down in the rock – below the

water table (the level to which the rock is saturated) – the reaction of local minerals to the watery solutions can create a layer of copper minerals such as chalcocite, covellite, bornite and chalcopyrite. Because these minerals are very rich in copper, the process is called secondary enrichment.

## Mineral assemblages

In other situations, mineral associations form at more or less the same time. This is called an assemblage and happens, for example, as igneous rocks form from melts, or when metamorphic or sedimentary rocks form, under particular conditions. In igneous rocks, minerals such as feldspars, quartz and micas form in granite, for example – partly because

## Mineral associations

### Distinctive associations
• Green adamite on orange, earthy limonite.
• Red almandine garnet crystals set in shiny black biotite.
• Green amazonite with smoky quartz.
• Purple amethyst with golden or clear calcite.
• White analcime with pinky serandite.
• Green apatite in orange calcite.
• Green apophyllite or turquoise cavansite with white stilbite.
• Fibrous artinite on masses of green serpentine.
• Vivid blue azurite with green malachite.
• Honey coloured barite on yellow calcite.
• Blue benitoite, brown neptunite with white natrolite.
• Blue boleite forming star-shaped crystals with cumengite.
• Blue celestine with yellow sulphur.
• Blue chrysocolla coated with quartz or patched with green malachite.
• Red copper with silver.

• Pink elbaite tourmaline with mauve lepidolite.
• Purple fluorite with black sphalerite.
• Black hübnerite with clear quartz.
• Deep black neptunite and egg white natrolite.
• Golden pyrite with milky quartz.
• Red ruby with green zoisite.
• Silver galena with yellow anglesite and sparkling cerussite.
• Silver sulphide clusters: polybasite, stephanite and acanthite.
• Grey willemite, white calcite and black franklinite.

### Precious metals
• Gold: calaverite, krennerite, nagyagite, pyrite, quartz, sylvanite.
• Silver: acanthite, pyrargyrite, proustite, galena.

### Typical associations
#### Sulphides and sulphosalts
• Arsenopyrite: gold, cassiterite, scorodite.
• Boulangerite: galena, pyrite, sphalerite, tetrahedrite, tennantite, proustite, quartz, carbonates.
• Bournonite: tetrahedrite, galena, silver, chalcopyrite, siderite, quartz, sphalerite, stibnite.
• Chalcocite: bornite, calcite, chalcopyrite, covellite, galena, quartz, sphalerite.
• Chalcopyrite: pyrrhotite, quartz, calcite, pyrite, sphalerite, galena.
• Cinnabar: pyrite, marcasite and stibnite.
• Enargite: quartz and sulphides such as galena, bornite, sphalerite, pyrite, chalcopyrite.
• Greenockite: prehnite, zeolites.
• Marcasite: lead and zinc minerals.
• Pentlandite: chalcopyrite, pyrrhotite.

*Blue azurite and green malachite*

• Pyrargyrite: calcite, galena, proustite, sphalerite, tetrahedrite.
• Pyrrhotite: pentlandite, pyrite, quartz.
• Realgar: orpiment; other arsenic minerals.
• Sphalerite; galena, dolomite, quartz, pyrite, fluorite, barite, calcites.
• Sylvanite: fluorite, other tellurides, sulphides, gold, tellurium, quartz.
• Sylvanite: gold tellurides calaverite and krennerite.

#### Oxides and hydroxides
• Brookite: rutile, anatase, albite.
• Cassiterite: wolframite, quartz, chalcopyrite, molybdenite, tourmaline, topaz.
• Cuprite: native copper, malachite, azurite, chalcocite, iron oxides.
• Diaspore: corundum, magnetite, spinel, bauxite, dolomite, spinel.
• Goethite: limonite, magnetite, pyrite, siderite.
• Manganite: barite, calcite, siderite, goethite.
• Uraninite: cassiterite, arsenopyrite, pitchblende.

the chemicals that make them occur in the melt. The same melt also contains chemicals that under different conditions combine to make the range of rare minerals associated with pegmatites.

Similarly, shales are made from the assemblage muscovite-kaolin-quartz-dolomite-feldspar. But as shales are metamorphosed to hornfels, the heat alters them to create a new assemblage: garnet-sillimanite-biotite-feldspar. Particular conditions of metamorphism produce particular assemblages of minerals. Called facies, these include blueschists rich in glaucophane and albite, and greenschists rich in chlorite and actinolite.

## Identity links

Because many minerals are likely to be found together, associations can be useful clues to identity. A purple-coated, coppery red mineral found in hydrothermal veins along with chalcopyrite, marcasite, pyrite and quartz is likely to be bornite, for instance. Alternatively, if you find a mineral in a pegmatite you think is vivianite, it might be worth a rethink if there is no triphylite around. Associations can also be useful signposts to particular minerals, such as ores. The lead and zinc ores galena and sphalerite, for instance, are often found in association with calcite and barite. So finding a vein of calcite and barite can often lead to the discovery of galena or sphalerite deposits.

## Mineral environments

Minerals are often linked to particular geological environments and processes, and this can help you in narrowing down identities. You might find thin, pale blue crystals in sedimentary rocks, for example, and guess they are kyanite. If so, you'd probably be wrong because kyanite is forged by the heat of metamorphism. So you are unlikely to find it in sedimentary rocks but very likely to find it in schists and gneisses. Pale blue crystals in sediments are more likely to be celestine.

### Where did you find it?

| Igneous veins | Garnet | Limestone quarry |
|---|---|---|
| Sulphides such as pyrite | Tourmaline | Calcite |
| Coppers such as malachite | **Volcanic vents** | Gypsum |
| and azurite | Sulphur | Fluorite |
| Gold and silver | Sulphates | Galena |
| | Hematite | Sphalerite |
| **Igneous intrusions** | **Hot springs** | Marcasite |
| | Travertine | Hematite |
| Quartz | Gypsum | |
| Feldspar | Selenite | **Metamorphic rocks** |
| Mica | Salts | Sulphides |
| Pyroxenes | | Garnet |
| Amphiboles | **Volcanic debris** | Mica |
| | Pumice | Calcite |
| **Pegmatites and cavities in lava** | Olivine | Chromite |
| | Augite | Quartz |
| Quartz | Obsidian | Spinel |
| Feldspars | | Chlorite |
| Mica | **River sands** | Andalusite |
| Sulphides | Quartz | Sillimanite |
| Siderite | Gold | Kyanite |
| Apatite | Diamond | Antigorite |
| Beryl | Emerald | Feldspars |
| Sapphire | Cassiterite | Chrysotile |
| Topaz | Pyrite | Staurolite |
| | Magnetite | Talc |

---

### Halides
- Atacamite: malachite, azurite, quartz.
- Chlorargyrite: silver, silver sulphides. cerussite, limonite, malachite.
- Fluorite: silver and lead ores, quartz, calcite, dolomite, galena, pyrite, chalcopyrite, sphalerite, barite.
- Halite: anhydrite, gypsum, sylvite.

### Carbonates
- Dolomite: lead, zinc, copper ores.
- Smithsonite: malachite, azurite, pyromorphite, cerussite, hemimorphite.
- Strontianite: galena, sphalerite, chalcopyrite, dolomite, calcite, quartz.
- Trona: halite, gypsum, borax, dolomite, glauberite, sylvite.
- Witherite: quartz, calcite, barite.

### Phosphates, arsenates and vanadates
- Adamite: azurite, smithsonite, mimetite, hemimorphite, scorodite, olivenite, limonite.
- Carnotite: tyuyamunite.
- Mimetite: galena, pyromorphite, vanadinite, arsenopyrite, anglesite.
- Olivenite: malachite, goethite, calcite, dioptase, azurite.
- Pyromorphite: cerussite, smithsonite, vanadinite, galena, limonite.
- Vanadinite: galena, barite, wulfenite, limonite.
- Variscite: apatite, wavellite, chalcedony.
- Xenotime; zircon, anatase, rutile, sillimanite, columbite, monazite, ilmenite.

### Sulphates and relatives
- Anhydrite: dolomite, gypsum, halite, sylvite, calcite.
- Barite: galena, sphalerite, fluorite, calcite.
- Brochantite: azurite, malachite, copper minerals.
- Crocoite: wulfenite, cerussite, pyromorphite, vanadinite.
- Ferberite: cassiterite, hematite, arsenopyrite.
- Hübnerite: quartz, cassiterite, topaz, lepidolite.
- Scheelite: wolframite.
- Wulfenite: cerussite, limonite, vanadinite, galena, pyromorphite, malachite.

*Greeny yellow adamite on orange, earthy limonite*

### Silicates
- Andalusite: corundum, kyanite, cordierite, sillimanite.
- Anorthoclase: augite, apatite, ilmenite.
- Dioptase: limonite, chrysocolla, cerussite, wulfenite.
- Glaucophane: epidote, almandine, chlorite, jadeite.
- Haüyne: leucite, nepheline, nosean.
- Hemimorphite: smithsonite, galena, calcite, anglesite, sphalerite, cerussite, aurichalcite.
- Humite: cassiterite, hematite, mica, tourmaline, quartz, pyrite.
- Kaolinite: clays, quartz, mica, sillimanite, tourmaline, rutile.
- Lepidolite: tourmaline, amblygonite, spodumene.
- Leucite: natrolite, analcime, alkali feldspar.
- Monticellite: forsterite, magnetite, apatite, biotite, vesuvianite, wollastonite.
- Natrolite: other zeolites, apophyllite, quartz, heulandite.
- Nepheline: augite, aegirine, amphiboles.
- Quartz: beryl, calcite, fluorite, gold, hematite, microcline, muscovite, pyrite, rutile, spodumene, topaz, tourmaline, wolframite, zeolite.
- Sillimanite: corundum, kyanite, cordierite.
- Spodumene: feldspar, micas, quartz, columbite-tantalite, beryl, tourmaline, topaz.
- Staurolite: garnet, tourmaline, kyanite or sillimanite.
- Talc: serpentine, tremolite, forsterite.
- Tourmaline: beryl, zircon, quartz, feldspar.
- Vesuvianite: grossular garnet, wollastonite, diopside, calcite.
- Willemite; hemimorphite, smithsonite, franklinite, zincite.
- Wollastonite: brucite, epidote.

# NATIVE ELEMENTS: METALS

*Most minerals occur in combinations of chemicals as compounds. However, 20 or so are 'native elements' that occur in small quantities by themselves in relatively pure form. Most native elements are metals such as gold, which does not readily combine with other materials. Many metals typically occur in conjunction with others in ores, but these less reactive metals are often found alone. Indeed, gold – unusually – is primarily found alone.*

## Silver

*Ag Silver*

Dark areas of silver sulphide, or tarnish

In Ancient Egypt, silver was called white gold and was valued even more highly than gold itself. There are silver mines in eastern Anatolia (Turkey) that were excavated by the pre-Hittite people of Cappadocia over 5,000 years ago. Today, its high conductivity (better than copper) means that silver is used in electronics, as well as for decoration. When polished, silver is a beautiful, shiny white metal, but it quickly tarnishes with a black coating of silver sulphide (inset). This is why it is hard to identify in nature, even though it grows in distinctive wiry, dendritic (tree-like) masses with the appearance of twisted wood. Like gold, it typically forms in hydrothermal veins, commonly in association with galena (lead ore), zinc and copper. Nuggets or grains rarely form so it is uncommon in placer deposits. Native silver is very rare, and most of the silver used today has been separated out from other minerals, especially in large argentite (silver sulphide) ore deposits in Nevada, Peru and Mexico.

**Identification**: You are unlikely to find any other white, softish metal in its native state. Scraping off a black tarnish to reveal a bright silvery metal confirms the identity. Cubes like that here are rare, and you are more likely to find silver in the form of wiry, branching masses.

Calcite block

Silver

**Crystal system**: Isometric
**Crystal habit**: Wiry, branching masses or grains, or, rarely, cubic crystals. Wires can form coils like rams' horns.
**Colour**: Silver-white but tarnishing quickly to black
**Lustre**: Metallic
**Streak**: Silver-white
**Hardness**: 2.5–3
**Cleavage**: None
**Fracture**: Hackly
**Specific gravity**: 10–12
**Other characteristics**: Soft enough to stretch into wires and hammer into shapes
**Notable locations**: Kongsberg, Norway; Sankt Andreasberg (Harz Mts), Freiburg (Saxony), Germany; Jachymov, Czech Republic; Chihuahua, Mexico; Great Bear Lake, Northwest Territories; Cobalt, Ontario; Michigan; Creede, Colorado

## Copper

*Cu Copper*

A warm reddish gold in colour, copper is the most easily recognized of all metals. It is quite soft, and sometimes found pure in native form – which is why it was one of the first metals people learned to use. The oldest knives found, dating back 6,000 years, are made of copper. Pure copper is often found in sulphide-rich veins in warm desert areas, or in cavities in ancient lava flows. Like silver, it often grows in branching masses and tarnishes quickly. Yet the tarnish is bright green, not black, and a copper deposit is often revealed by bright green stains on rocks called copper bloom. As a native element, copper is quite rare, so most of the copper used today comes from ores such as chalcopyrite.

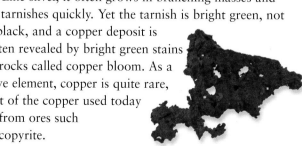

**Identification**: Copper is readily identified by its reddish gold colour. It appears darker when tarnished, as shown opposite.

**Crystal system**: Isometric
**Crystal habit**: Typically wiry, branching masses or clusters
**Colour**: Copper, green tarnish
**Lustre**: Metallic
**Streak**: Red copper colour
**Hardness**: 2.5–3
**Cleavage**: None
**Fracture**: Hackly, ductile
**Specific gravity**: 8.9+
**Other characteristics**: Can be stretched and shaped
**Notable locations**: Chessy, France; Siegerland, Germany; Turinsk, Russia; Namibia; Broken Hill (NSW), Australia; Bolivia; Chile; New Mexico; Keweenaw, Michigan; Arizona

# Gold

*Au Gold*

No metal is quite like gold. Because it rarely forms compounds with other elements, it occurs naturally in almost pure form, and remains shiny and untarnished for thousands of years. It was one of the first metals used by mankind, and some of the world's oldest metal artefacts are gold. So far, about 150,000 tonnes of gold has been taken from the ground; a further 2,500 tonnes or so are mined each year. About a quarter of this is locked up in vaults, primarily in the USA and Europe, to provide the reserves against which the world's currencies are valued according to the Gold Standard. In the past, most gold came from South Africa, but this required costly, deep mines to be sunk, such as that at Savuka in Witwatersrand which is almost 4km/2½ miles deep. In recent years, mining companies have begun to work deposits nearer the surface with opencast mines in places such as China, Russia and Australia. The Grasberg gold mine in Indonesia is now the world's largest. Most gold is still used for jewellery, but the electronics industry is consuming increasing amounts for use in computer and communications technologies.

**Identification**: Shiny and gold in colour, gold is instantly recognizable – but a few other minerals can be mistaken for gold, such as pyrites and other sulphides and some tellurides. Only gold forms gold grains and nuggets.

**Crystal system**: Isometric
**Crystal habit**: Crystals are rare and tiny, typically cubic or octahedral. Usually forms grains and nuggets or wire, branchlike crystal clusters.
**Colour**: Golden yellow
**Lustre**: Metallic
**Streak**: Golden yellow
**Hardness**: 2.5–3
**Cleavage**: None
**Fracture**: Hackly
**Specific gravity**: 19.3+
**Other characteristics**: Ductile, malleable and sectile.
**Notable locations**: Verespatak (Bihar Mountains), Romania; Siberia; Witwatersrand, South Africa; Grasberg, Indonesia; Bendigo & Ballarat (Victoria), Flinders Range (SA), Australia; Yukon; California; Colorado; South Dakota

Gold

Small quartz crystals

**Striking gold**
Gold is found in two major kinds of deposit. It typically forms in volcanic veins or 'lodes' in igneous rocks, where it is often found in association with quartz or with sulphide minerals such as stibnite. All the world's greatest gold mines exploit lodes like these. Yet in the past, many people found gold by searching in rivers for placer deposits. These are small grains or nuggets of gold washed there after the rock in which they formed was broken up by the river. Because gold grains are so dense and resistant to corrosion, they accumulate in shoals in the stream bed. These grains can be recovered by the simple technique of panning. The process is painstaking and rarely produces any reward – yet panning still occurs in countries such as Chile, above. The idea is to scoop shingle from the river bed and gradually swill out all the sand with water. With skill, the lighter sand is discarded, leaving the heavier gold grains behind.

# Platinum

*Pt Elemental platinum*

Platinum is one of the rarest and most precious of all native elements. It typically occurs in thin layers of sulphide metal ores in mafic igneous rocks (dark igneous rocks rich in magnesium and iron). Only very rarely are crystals of platinum found. More usually platinum is found as fine grains or flakes or, occasionally, as grains and nuggets, which, like gold, are found concentrated in placer deposits (see Striking gold, left). Unlike gold, it is rarely pure in nature and tends to be mixed in with other metals such as iridium and iron. It is typically associated with chromite, olivine, pyroxene and magnetite. Nearly all of the world's platinum comes from two very distinct parts of the world – the Urals in Russia and the Bushveld complex in South Africa.

**Crystal system**: Isometric
**Crystal habit**: Crystals rare and tiny, typically cubic. Platinum is usually found as grains and flakes; occasionally nuggets.
**Colour**: Pale silver-grey
**Lustre**: Metallic
**Streak**: Steel grey
**Hardness**: 4–4.5
**Cleavage**: None
**Fracture**: Hackly
**Specific gravity**: 14–19+
**Other characteristics**: Doesn't tarnish, may be weakly magnetic and is ductile, malleable and sectile.
**Notable locations**: Norlisk, Russia; Bushveld complex, S Africa; Colombia; Ontario; Alaska; Stillwater, Montana

**Identification**: Platinum is best identified by its pale, silver-grey colour and its relative softness.

# NATIVE ELEMENTS: METALS AND SEMI-METALS

*It is not just metals that occur as native elements. So too do some semi-metals, such as antimony and bismuth. Semi-metals are metallic in appearance, but not always as shiny as true metals. They are also brittle, shattering when struck with a hammer, and are less conductive than proper metals.*

## Antimony

*Sb Elemental antimony*

Antimony is a silvery grey semi-metal that only rarely occurs as a native element, typically in hydrothermal veins. In fact, its name comes from the Greek words *anti* and *monos*, which mean 'not alone', because it combines so readily with other minerals, such as sulphur. The chemical symbol Sb comes from the Latin word for its most common ore, stibnite. Antimony is found in about 100 minerals, and traces are sometimes extracted from silver, copper and lead ores when they are smelted. Yet the only major ore is stibnite, three-quarters of which comes from China. Antimony was not identified as a separate element until the 17th century, even though the alchemists knew how to purify it from stibnite. Yet in the form of stibnite it has a long history. Powdered to make kohl, it has been used as black eye make-up since the time of the Ancient Egyptians. Today antimony is mainly used to impregnate plastics, rubbers and other materials to make them fireproof. It is also used to toughen up the lead in lead acid batteries.

**Identification**: Antimony is often found as small silvery plate-shaped crystals and masses on quartz. It can easily be confused with bismuth.

*Quartz*

*Antimony*

**Crystal system**: Trigonal
**Crystal habit**: Crystals look cubic but it is typically found in botryoidal, lamellar and radiating masses
**Colour**: Whitish grey but can be darker when tarnished
**Lustre**: Metallic but dull when tarnished
**Streak**: Whitish grey
**Hardness**: 3–3.5
**Cleavage**: Perfect in one direction, basal
**Fracture**: Uneven
**Specific gravity**: 6.6–6.7+
**Other characteristics**: Melts at the relatively low temperature of 630°C/1,166°F
**Notable locations**: Carinthia, Austria; Sala (Vastmanland), Sweden; Auvergne, Brittany, France; Malaga, Spain; Lombardy, Italy; Lavrion, Greece; Wolfe Co, Quebec; Kern Co, California; Arizona
**Caution**: Antimony is mildly poisonous; handle with care

## Bismuth

*Bi Elemental bismuth*

Like antimony, bismuth is a silvery white semi-metal that rarely occurs as a native element. It is found typically in high-temperature veins along with quartz, and minerals formed by metals such as cobalt, silver, iron and lead, or along the edge of granite intrusions where they meet limestone. More commonly, bismuth occurs in its main ore minerals, bismuthinite and bismite. The name bismuth probably comes from the German for 'white mass' – although the famous chemist Paracelsus said it came from the German for 'white meadow', because it was found in the fields of Saxony. Like antimony, bismuth shares with water the rare quality of expanding rather than contracting as it freezes. This property makes it very useful in soldering, because it expands to fill gaps as it solidifies. Because it is non-toxic, bismuth has replaced lead in many uses such as plumbing. Its low melting point makes it the perfect plug for fire-sprinkler systems. It is also used as a medicine for stomach upsets.

**Identification**: Bismuth exhibits a rainbow-coloured iridescent tarnish and has a pink tinge when freshly broken.

**Crystal system**: Trigonal
**Crystal habit**: Crystals are rare. Typically occurs in foliated masses.
**Colour**: Silver-white with an iridescent tarnish
**Lustre**: Metallic
**Streak**: Greenish black
**Hardness**: 2–2.5
**Cleavage**: Perfect in one direction, basal
**Fracture**: Uneven, jagged
**Specific gravity**: 9.7–9.8
**Other characteristics**: Pinkish tint on broken surfaces
**Notable locations**: Devon, England; Saxony, Germany; Wolfram (Queensland), Australia; San Baldomero, Tasna, Bolivia; South Dakota; Colorado; California
**Caution**: Bismuth is mildly poisonous; handle with care

# Arsenic

*As Elemental arsenic*

Arsenic is a silvery grey semi-metal. In nature it occurs as a brittle metallic mineral, but in the laboratory it can be made into a white powder – and this is the kind of arsenic that poisoners have used since the days of the Ancient Greeks. Arsenic rarely occurs as a native element and is more typically found in sulphides and sulphosalts such as arsenopyrite, orpiment, realgar and tennantite. When it is found, native arsenic is usually mixed in with silver and antimony. Arsenic is a common by-product when silver ore is mined. It usually occurs in masses with onion-like layers called 'shelly' arsenic or 'scherbencobalt', or in kidney-like crusts. Very occasionally arsenic crystals are found, typically trigonal in form. However, arsenic exhibits polymorphism (has more than one shape) and in Saxony, Germany, some orthorhombic crystals have been found. These orthorhombic arsenic crystals are called arsenolamprite.

**Identification**: Arsenic gives off a characteristic garlic smell when hit with a hammer. This specimen is a dull black mass of arsenic, containing proustite.

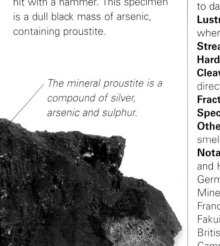

The mineral proustite is a compound of silver, arsenic and sulphur.

**Crystal system**: Trigonal
**Crystal habit**: Typically in round banded or botryoidal masses
**Colour**: Pale grey. Tarnishes to dark grey or black.
**Lustre**: Metallic but dull when tarnished
**Streak**: Black
**Hardness**: 3–4
**Cleavage**: Perfect in one direction, basal
**Fracture**: Uneven
**Specific gravity**: 5.4–5.9+
**Other characteristics**: Garlic smell when hit or crushed
**Notable locations**: Saxony and Harz Mountains, Germany; Sainte-Marie-aux-Mines (Vosges Mountains), France; Kongsberg, Norway; Fakui (Honshu), Japan; Atlin, British Columbia; Washington Camp (Santa Cruz Co), Arizona
**Caution**: Arsenic is very poisonous; handle with care. Wash your hands afterwards.

---

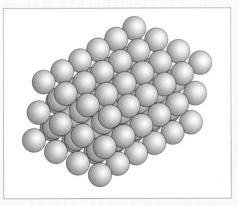

**Metal crystals**
Metals are special because of the way that their crystals form. Unlike other minerals, metals tend not to form separate crystals. Instead, their atoms pack together in simple lattice-like structures, tied together by special chemical bonds called metallic bonds. In a structure like this, the bonds all work together, making metals strong but not brittle, which is why they can typically be hammered, bent and stretched into shape without breaking. The lattice arrangement also leaves electrons (tiny subatomic particles) only loosely attached in the spaces in between the atoms. This results in metals being good conductors of electricity (and heat), because there are plenty of 'free' electrons to transmit it through the lattice. In magnesium and zinc, the lattice is arranged in closely packed hexagons, whereas in aluminium, copper, silver and gold the atoms are arranged in cubes with an atom in the middle of each side of the cube.

# Mercury

*Hg Elemental mercury*

Mercury is one of the few metals that is liquid at room temperature, along with caesium and gallium. In fact, it only freezes at less than -40°C/-40°F. Strictly speaking, it is not a mineral but a mineraloid because it does not normally form crystals. It is the only mineral besides water to occur naturally as a liquid. All the same, it doesn't often form pools but is found as tiny blobs on the mercury ores of cinnabar and calomel, typically lodged in crevices or attached by surface tension. Occasionally, pools of mercury can also be found filling rock cavities, usually in active volcanic regions. It has also been found as a precipitate from hot springs, along with cinnabar and other minerals. Because it is so rare, native mercury is not used as a source of mercury.

**Identification:** Beadlike drops of mercury are instantly recognizable.

**Crystal system**: Hexagonal crystals below -40°C/-40°F
**Crystal habit**: Droplets or pools of mercury liquid
**Colour**: Bright silvery metallic
**Lustre**: Metallic
**Streak**: Liquid, has no streak
**Hardness**: Liquid so does not have hardness
**Cleavage; Fracture**: None
**Specific gravity**: 13.5+
**Other characteristics**: Mercury is a liquid metal
**Notable locations**: Almadén (Ciudad Real), Spain; Idrija, former Yugoslavia; Almaden mine (Santa Clara Co), Socrates mine (Sonoma Co), California
**Caution**: Mercury fumes are poisonous; handle only in a well-ventilated space

Mercury beads

# NATIVE ELEMENTS: NON-METALS

*Only a few non-metals occur as native elements, of which there are really only two: sulphur and carbon. Carbon exists in various forms, including graphite, diamond and chaoite. Carbon and sulphur are among the most interesting and important of all minerals, and carbon compounds play a vital role in the chemistry of every living organism.*

## Sulphur

*S Elemental sulphur*

Sulphur is also known as 'brimstone' or burning stone because it burns easily, giving a blue flame when lit. (Don't do this though; it gives off a poison gas when it burns!) Pure, native sulphur is quickly identified from its bright yellow colour. It typically forms crust-like deposits around the margins of hot volcanic springs and smoky volcanic chimneys called fumaroles. Most of the world's sulphur is mined from beds of limestone and gypsum such as those under the Gulf of Mexico. Extracting the sulphur involves taking advantage of sulphur's low melting point, which is only a little above the boiling point of water. Wells are drilled and superheated water is injected into the sulphur formation, melting the sulphur. The resulting slurry is then pumped to the surface, where the water is evaporated to leave behind the sulphur residue. This is called the Frasch process. Unfortunately, the process destroys the good sulphur crystals that are often found in limestone beds. Around volcanic springs, sulphur typically forms crumbly-looking masses that are full of little bubbles and have a strong smell of rotten eggs.

*Masses of small sulphur crystals*

**Identification**: Sulphur's bright yellow colour, low melting point, rotten egg smell and softness make this an easy mineral to identify.

**Crystal system**: Orthorhombic
**Crystal habit**: Typically massive or powdery forms but chunky crystals are also common. Sometimes found in an acicular (needle-like) form called rosickyite.
**Colour**: Bright yellow colour to yellow-brown
**Lustre**: Vitreous as crystal to greasy or earthy as masses
**Streak**: Whitish or yellow
**Hardness**: 2
**Cleavage**: Very poor
**Fracture**: Conchoidal
**Specific gravity**: 2.0–2.1
**Other characteristics**: Can give off the smell of rotten eggs; very brittle. Has a low melting point and burns readily with a bluish flame. Often associated with the pungent (and poisonous) gas it produces when heated.
**Notable locations**: Sicily; Poland; France; Russia; Japan; Mexico; Yellowstone, Wyoming; Sulphurdale, Utah; Louisiana; Texas

## Graphite

*C Elemental carbon*

Graphite forms as carbon compounds interact in veins, and in metamorphic rocks as organic material in limestone is altered by heat and pressure. It is one of the softest of all minerals, with a value of less than 2 on the Mohs scale of hardness. In fact, its softness along with its black colour make it the perfect material for pencils – which earned its name from *graphein*, the Greek word for 'writing'. Yet despite its softness, graphite, like diamond, the hardest of all minerals, is a form of pure carbon. Graphite breaks into minute, flexible flakes that easily slide over one another. This 'basal cleavage' gives graphite a distinctive greasy feel that makes it a good dry lubricant. In nature, graphite is found in two distinct forms: flake graphite and lump graphite. Lump graphite is compact and lacks graphite's normal flakiness.

**Identification**: Graphite is dark grey, soft and greasy looking. It will leave black smudges on your fingers.

**Crystal system**: Hexagonal
**Crystal habit**: Crystals are rare but typically form as flaky plates or masses in veins
**Colour**: Black-silver
**Lustre**: Metallic, dull
**Streak**: Black to brown-grey
**Hardness**: 1–2
**Cleavage**: Perfect in one direction
**Fracture**: Flaky
**Specific gravity**: 2.2
**Other characteristics**: Leaves black marks on fingers and paper. It also conducts electricity but only very weakly.
**Notable locations**: Borrowdale (Cumbria), England; Pargas, Finland; Mount Vesuvius, Italy; Austria; Galle, Sri Lanka; Korea; Ticonderoga, Bear Mountain, New York; Ogdensburg, New Jersey

# Diamond

*C Elemental carbon*

Diamond is virtually the hardest substance known to man. It gets its name from the Ancient Greek word *adamantos*, meaning 'invincible'. The only mineral that is harder is the very rare lonsdaleite formed in meteorite impacts. Like graphite and lonsdaleite, diamond is pure carbon. It glitters like glass because it has been transformed by enormous pressure underground. It is now possible to make diamonds artificially be squeezing graphite under extreme pressure. But pressures like these are rare in nature, occurring only deep in the Earth's crust and upper mantle. All diamonds found today are extremely old, being formed at least a billion years ago, with some more than three billion years old! They formed at least 145km/90 miles below the Earth's surface and were gradually carried up in pipes of hot magma. These volcanic pipes cooled to form blue rocks called kimberlites and lamproites, which are the source of most of the world's best diamonds. Diamonds can easily be weathered out of kimberlites to be washed away by streams into placer deposits. In their rough state diamonds look dull and it was only when jewellers began to cut them in the Middle Ages that their amazing brilliance was revealed.

— Diamond

*Kimberlite*

**Identification**: Diamond looks non-descript when rough, but its hardness is unmistakable. It is the only clear crystal that will scratch glass deeply and easily.

**Crystal system:** Isometric (cubic)
**Crystal habit:** Typically forms cubes and octahedrons, but very varied
**Colour:** Typically colourless, but also tinged yellow, brown, grey, blue or red
**Lustre:** Adamantine, or greasy when rough
**Streak:** White
**Hardness:** 10
**Cleavage:** Perfect in four ways
**Fracture:** Conchoidal
**Specific gravity:** 3.5
**Other characteristics:** When cut, diamonds show 'fire' – rainbow colours that flash as light is reflected internally at different angles
**Notable locations:** Mir, Yakhutsk, Russia; Kimberley, South Africa; Ellendale, Argyle (WA), Echunga (SA), Australia; Minas Gerais, Mato Grosso, Brazil; Murfreesboro (Pike Co), Arkansas

---

## The alter egos of carbon

Carbon is an extraordinary element. It has a remarkable capacity for forming bonds with other chemicals, which makes it the basis for all the chemicals of life, from simple sugars to complex proteins and enzymes. But even pure elemental carbon is found in a variety of forms, as its atoms have a rare capacity to form either single, double or triple bonds with each other. When the atoms of an element combine to form different-shaped molecules, the varieties are called allotropes. Until recently, carbon was thought to form just two very different allotropes: graphite and carbon. Now scientists know of a third, buckminsterfullerene, and possibly a fourth (carbon nanotubes). When crystals of the same mineral have a different structure, the varieties are called polymorphs. Carbon is found in a range of mineral poly-morphs – not just diamond and graphite, but possibly also lonsdaleite, chaoite and fullerite.

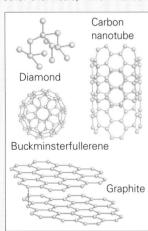

Carbon nanotube

Diamond

Buckminsterfullerene

Graphite

# Chaoite

*C Elemental carbon*

When meteorites strike the ground, they create such extreme pressure and heat that minerals in the impact zone can be transformed into new ones such as suessite and martensite. This process is called shock metamorphism. Impacts are believed to change graphite to a rare kind of extra-hard diamond with a hexagonal crystal system called lonsdaleite. They are also thought to change graphite into carbon polymorphs called carbynes. In 1968, two geologists found a carbyne at the Ries impact crater in Germany. They called it chaoite and identified it as a new polymorph of carbon. Chaoite is recognized as a mineral by the International Mineral Association, but, as so few specimens have been positively identified, some geologists question whether chaoite should be given mineral status.

**Crystal system:** Hexagonal
**Crystal habit:** Forms in flakes and small grains
**Colour:** Dark grey
**Lustre:** Submetallic
**Streak:** Dark grey
**Hardness:** 1–2
**Cleavage:** Unknown
**Fracture:** Unknown
**Specific gravity:** 3.3
**Locations:** Chaoite has been found in only three locations with any certainty: the Ries meteorite crater (Bavaria), Germany, and the Goalpur and Dyalpur meteorite craters, India

**Identification:** Geologists have found it hard to identify chaoite positively, and some insist that elaborate X-ray analyses are necessary to be certain that a sample is chaoite.

# SULPHIDES

*Sulphides are compounds of sulphur with one or two metals, so they usually have a metallic lustre. They include some of the world's most important metal ores (see also Ore-forming minerals in this section for copper, silver, lead, zinc, cobalt and nickel). They are typically brittle and heavy and are formed from magmas or the hot fluids in hydrothermal veins. Acanthite, cobaltite, carrolite and digenite are all what are called simple sulphides because their molecules include just one sulphur atom.*

## Acanthite (and Argentite)

*$Ag_2S$ Silver sulphide*

Acanthite, or 'silver glance', gets its name from the Greek *acantha*, for 'thorn', because of its spiky crystals. It is often listed as the same mineral as argentite, and argentite is often said to be the main ore of silver. In fact, both argentite and acanthite are 87 per cent silver and it is acanthite that is the main silver ore. Argentite and acanthite are simply polymorphs. Acanthite is the form that occurs at normal room temperatures in flat, monoclinic crystals. Argentite only forms at temperatures of over 173°C/343.4°F, forming cubic crystals. When forming from hot magmas, argentite crystallizes first. But as soon as the temperature drops below 173°C, the cubic argentite crystals will change to flatter, monoclinic acanthite. The change is not always so obvious, and some crystals retain argentite's cubic shape, even though their internal structure has changed. They look rather like argentite, but are actually acanthite. These are called 'pseudomorphs' (false shapes).

**Identification**: Shiny, dark grey crystals that tarnish to black on exposure to light. The tarnish on sterling silver is acanthite. It can also be cut with a knife.

**Crystal system:** Monoclinic (acanthite) and isometric (argentite)
**Crystal habit:** Distorted prisms and branching masses. Also cubelike pseudomorphs that look like argentite but are acanthite.
**Colour:** Dark grey to black
**Lustre:** Metallic
**Streak:** Shiny black
**Hardness:** 2–2.5
**Cleavage:** Absent
**Fracture:** Conchoidal
**Specific gravity:** 7.2–7.4
**Other characteristics:** Sectile (can be cut with a knife) and malleable. Surfaces will darken on exposure to light.
**Notable locations:** Kongsberg, Norway; Black Forest, Freiberg, Schneeberg, Germany; Batopilas (Chihuahua), Guanajuato, Mexico; Comstock Lode, Nevada; Butte, Montana; Michigan

## Cobaltite

*CoAsS Cobalt arsenic sulphide*

*Cubic cobaltite crystal*

Cobaltite or cobalt glance is a very uncommon mineral that forms in sulphur-rich veins when the metals cobalt and arsenic join to form a sulphide. The very rarity of cobaltite crystals makes them much sought after by collectors. Cobaltite forms cubic crystals that look very similar to iron pyrite, although the actual structure is slightly different. Fortunately cobaltite is easily distinguished from pyrite by its colour. Pyrite is brassy yellow while cobaltite is silvery white. However, it is much harder to tell cobaltite from one of the other cobalt ores, skutterudite, which is also white and forms cubic crystals. Sometimes, when cobaltite has been exposed to the air, it will become covered with a bright pink or purple crust of other minerals such as erythrite. This colourful crust is called 'cobalt bloom' and is a strong sign of the presence of cobaltite or skutterudite. Cobaltite is one of the important ores of cobalt.

**Identification**: Cobaltite forms silvery cubes (here embedded in pyrrhotite). It may have a slightly sulphurous or garlic smell.

**Crystal system:** Appears isometric
**Crystal habit:** Cubic, pyrite-like shapes. Grains and masses.
**Colour:** Silver-white with pink or purple tinge
**Lustre:** Metallic
**Streak:** Dark grey
**Hardness:** 5.5
**Cleavage:** Breaks into cubes
**Fracture:** Uneven, subconchoidal
**Specific gravity:** 6–6.3
**Other characteristics:** Arsenic (garlic) smell
**Notable locations:** Cornwall, England; Skutterud, Norway; Hankansbö, Tunaberg, Sweden; Siegerland, Rhineland, Germany; Bou Asser, Morocco; DR Congo; New South Wales, Australia; Sonora, Mexico; Cobalt, Ontario; Boulder, Colorado

# Carrollite

*Cu₂S₄ Copper sulphide*

Carrollite is a very rare copper sulphide mineral. It was first discovered in 1852 in the Papasco Mine, Finksburg, and the Mineral Hill Mine, Sykesville. Both of these mines are in Carroll County, Maryland, USA, earning the mineral its name carrollite. It typically forms very small crystals. Indeed, it is often cryptocrystalline – that is, the 'hidden' crystals are too small to be seen except under a microscope. Recently, some wonderful octahedral crystals up to 5cm/2in across were found in the Kambove Mine, Katanga, in the Congo. These were shiny silver and almost mirrorlike in lustre. Typical carrollite crystals are more likely to be dark grey and metallic in lustre, and are commonly intergrown with the minerals sphalerite, bornite and chalcopyrite.

**Identification**: Carrollite so rarely forms good big crystals that it is very hard to recognize, and only an expert can usually make a positive identification.

*Carrollite*

**Crystal system**: Isometric
**Crystal habit**: Typically forms grains. Crystals are usually cubic but can be octahedral
**Colour**: Grey, copper red
**Lustre**: Metallic
**Streak**: Dark grey to black
**Hardness**: 4.5–5.5
**Cleavage**: Poor
**Fracture**: Conchoidal
**Specific gravity**: 4.5–4.8
**Notable locations**: Buskerud, Norway; Siegerland, Germany; Katanga, DR Congo; Hokkaido, Japan; Suan, North Korea; Yukon, Alaska; Carroll County, Maryland; Franklin, New Jersey

**Katanga, Africa's mineral treasure trove**
Ancient metamorphic processes have endowed the gneiss, pelite and psammite rocks of the Katanga plateau in south-east DR Congo with some of the world's richest mineral deposits. There are huge deposits of copper, cobalt, manganese, platinum, silver, uranium and zinc ores here, plus occurrences of hundreds of rare minerals, including digenite, cuprosklodowskite, demesmaekerite, metatorbernite, swamboite, soddyite, stilleite, schoepite, cornetite, fourmarierite, thoreaulite and uranophane. The copper sulphide ores in Katanga's shale beds are among the world's largest copper reserves, and copper was dug here and traded through Africa centuries before European colonization in the 19th century. At its height in 1960, Katanga was producing 10 per cent of the world's copper, 60 per cent of its uranium and 80 per cent of its industrial diamonds. The uranium mines of Katanga were of huge importance to the early development of nuclear weapons in the United States, until alternative Canadian sources began to be exploited. All the 1500 tons of uranium oxide needed to get the Manhattan project up and running came from the Shinkolobwe mine in Katanga. Yet this mineral wealth has meant that Katanga has been fought over ever since the Belgians first began mining there in the 1880s, From 1971 until 1997, Katanga was called Shaba and was a focus of fighting in the civil wars. The political situation means it is now impossible to tell how much ore Katanga produces. In March 2004 the Central Bank of Congo stated that it produced just 783 tonnes of cobalt and yet the country recorded 13,365 tonnes of cobalt in exports. So maybe as much as 90 per cent of the mineral trade from Katanga is illicit.

# Digenite

*Cu₉S₅ Copper sulphide*

Digenite is a rare ore of copper that is very similar to chalcocite. In fact, digenite is sometimes mistaken for chalcocite, and is usually found in association with it. However, the two minerals have distinct but similar chemical compositions. Chalcocite has ten copper atoms to every five sulphur atoms, whereas digenite has only nine copper atoms for every five sulphur atoms. The two are related by the fact that digenite is a high-temperature form of chalcocite that forms cubic crystals. Digenite was named after the Greek word *digenes*, meaning 'two kinds', because it was originally thought to be a mix of two different kinds of copper ore.

**Crystal system**: Isometric
**Crystal habit**: Commonly forms masses or as grains in in sulphide-rich masses in sedimentary rocks. More rarely forms much-prized octahedral crystals.
**Colour**: Blue or black
**Lustre**: Submetallic
**Transparency**: Opaque
**Streak**: Black
**Hardness**: 2.5–3
**Cleavage**: Good
**Fracture**: Conchoidal fracture
**Specific gravity**: 5.6
**Notable locations**: Cornwall, England; Auvergne, Alpes-Maritimes, France; Sangerhausen, Thuringia, Germany; Carinthia, Salzburg, Austria; Katanga, DR Congo; Tsumeb, Namibia; Khingan Mts, China; Queensland, Australia; Kennecott, Alaska; Butte, Montana; Bisbee (Cochise Co), Arizona

*Pyrite*

*Rich mass of digenite*

**Identification**: Digenite is usually identified by its black streak and the blue tinge to its black crystals – and the blue lustre it acquires when polished.

# SIMPLE SULPHIDES

*The simple sulphides are minerals made by a combination of a single sulphur atom with one or two other metal atoms. This group includes the economically important metal-bearing ores of galena (lead), cinnabar (mercury) and sphalerite (zinc) as well as greenockite, covellite, alabandite and millerite. They are typically brittle and heavy and form from magmas or in hydrothermal veins.*

## Greenockite

*CdS Cadmium sulphide*

Greenockite is a rare mineral made of cadmium sulphide, which occurs as small, brilliant honey-yellow crystals. It was first described in 1840 by Jameson and Connell, who found crystals during the cutting of the Bishopton tunnel on the Glasgow and Greenock railway in the United Kingdom. A specimen had been found over 25 years earlier but wrongly identified as sphalerite. The newly discovered mineral was named greenockite after Lord Greenock, on whose land it was discovered. Good crystals of greenockite have been found only around Glasgow, where they formed in amygdaloidal cavities in basaltic lava about 340 million years ago. Greenockite has been discovered elsewhere such as at Joplin in Missouri, but only as a powder or crust dusted over the top of sphalerite and other zinc minerals. Greenockite is actually the only proper ore of the metal cadmium, but it is so rare that all cadmium is obtained by extracting the trace amounts from lead and zinc ores. The only other cadmium-containing mineral is hawleyite, and the two can be hard to distinguish.

**Identification**: Greenockite has a honey colour, but looks very like sphalerite. In the field, the honey-coloured crusting, combined with its orange streak, is the best identifier. This enlarged view shows one of the rare complete crystals. Its absorption of certain wavelengths of white light creates the intense yellow colour.

**Crystal system**: Isometric
**Crystal habit**: Small tapering hexagonal crystals. Also seen as crusts or dustings over zinc and calcite ores.
**Colour**: Honey yellow, orange, red or light to dark brown
**Lustre**: Adamantine to resinous
**Streak**: Red, orange or light brown
**Hardness**: 3–3.5
**Cleavage**: Poor in one direction (basal), good in three others (prismatic)
**Fracture**: Conchoidal
**Specific gravity**: 4.5–5
**Notable locations**: Greenock, Scotland; Przibram (Bohemia), Czech Republic; Lavrion, Greece; Potosi, Bolivia; Silver Standard mine, British Columbia; Paterson, New Jersey; Joplin, Missouri; Kansas; Oklahoma; Illinois; Kentucky

## Covellite

*CuS Copper sulphide*

Sometimes called covelline or indigo copper, covellite is a rare, deep indigo-blue mineral with shimmering iridescence that makes it much sought after by collectors. The blue colour turns to purple when wet, and crystals often have a black or purple tarnish. It was discovered in the early 19th century on Mount Vesuvius in Italy by Italian mineralogist Niccolo Covelli (1790–1829) and it is named after him. Covelli found his specimen in a fumarole where it probably formed directly from volcanic material. Yet it is more commonly found as a secondary mineral, formed by the alteration of other copper minerals in veins. Covellite typically forms in thin, hexagonal plates, and the best examples of crystals like these were found at Butte, Montana, USA, often called the richest hill on Earth. Even more strikingly coloured masses have been found at Kennicott in Alaska, USA.

Covellite

Pyrite

**Identification**: Covellite is usually recognizable from its iridescent indigo-blue colour and the way it breaks into sheets.

**Crystal system**: Hexagonal
**Crystal habit**: Forms platelike, hexagonal crystals, and also occurs as grains and striplike masses
**Colour**: Iridescent indigo blue, tarnishing black or purple
**Lustre**: Metallic
**Streak**: Grey to black
**Hardness**: 1.5–2
**Cleavage**: Breaks into sheets
**Fracture**: Flaky
**Specific gravity**: 4.6–4.8
**Other characteristics**: Sheets of covellite bend like mica. Fuses when heated.
**Notable locations**: Dillenberg, Germany; Calabana, Sardinia; Bor, Serbia; Felsöbanya, Romania; Shikoku, Japan; Moonta, South Australia; Butte, Montana; Kennicott, Alaska

# Alabandite

*MnS Manganese sulphide*

Also known as manganblende and manganese glance, alabandite was first found in south-east Turkey and its name comes from Alabanda, the place where it was first identified. It typically forms in epithermal sulphide deposits (shallow, sulphide-rich vein deposits formed by hot fluids rising through the ground). Alabandite forms in the early stages of vein deposition along with arsenopyrite, pyrite and quartz. In the later stages, alabandite is replaced by rhodochrosite, the carbonate of manganese. Alabandite is also, less commonly, found in stony enstatite-type chrondrite meteorites. In fact, enstatite or E chrondrites are divided into EH (high) and EL (low) chondrites according to their sulphide content. The presence of alabandite identifies a meteorite as an EL chondrite. The presence of the associated mineral niningerite (magnesium manganese sulphide) identifies it as an EH chondrite.

**Identification**: Alabandite is hard to identify except by its dark green streak.

**Crystal system**: Isometric
**Crystal habit**: Small cubic and octahedral crystals in matrix, or in small masses or grains
**Colour**: Iron black, or brown tarnish
**Lustre**: Submetallic
**Streak**: Dark green
**Hardness**: 3.5–4
**Cleavage**: Perfect
**Fracture**: Uneven
**Specific gravity**: 4
**Other characteristics**: Brittle
**Notable locations**: Alabanda, Turkey; Shakotan, Japan; Broken Hill (NSW), Nairne (SA), Australia; Allan Hills meteorite, Antarctica; Pierina, Peru; Mule Mts, Patagonia Mts, Tombstone, Arizona

---

**Unearthly minerals**

Meteorites fascinate mineralogists because they contain a unique mix of minerals that tells us both about other planets, and about the origins of minerals on Earth. The bulk of meteorites is made up from seven minerals that are common on Earth – olivine, pyroxene, plagioclase feldspar, magnetite, hematite, troilite and serpentine – and three minerals that are found only in meteorites – taenite (high-nickel iron), kamacite (low-nickel iron) and schreibersite (iron-nickel phosphide). There are also small amounts of millerite, alabandite and almost 300 other minerals found in meteorites. Of these, over 25 occur only in meteorites and nowhere else on Earth: barringerite; brezinaite: brianite; buchwaldite; carlsbergite; chaoite; daubreelite; farringtonite; gentnerite; haxonite; heidite; kosmochlor; krinovite; lawrencite; lonsdaleite; majorite; merrihueite; niningerite; oldhamite; osbornite; panethite; ringwoodite; roedderite; sinoite; stanfeldtite; yagiite. A thin section of an iron meteorite, showing the rare minerals taenite and kamacite, appears above.

# Millerite

*NiS Nickel sulphide*

Millerite was named after the British mineralogist W H Miller (1801–1880). It is sometimes used as an ore of nickel, but it is best known for its extraordinary acicular (needle-like) yellow crystals. Indeed, these are so distinctive that it is sometimes called 'capillary pyrites'. These typically grow like cobwebs inside cavities in limestone and dolomite, but millerite can form in veins carrying nickel and other sulphide minerals. Millerite needles are so thin that you would never know their crystals are trigonal. Millerite is also one of several minerals found in iron-nickel meteorites.

*Siderite*

**Crystal system**: Trigonal
**Crystal habit**: Typically grows in long, thin, acicular (needle-like) clusters, often in radiating sprays. Also forms fibrous coatings and granular masses.
**Colour**: Brassy yellow
**Lustre**: Metallic
**Transparency**: Opaque
**Streak**: Greenish black
**Hardness**: 3–3.5
**Cleavage**: Perfect, but crystals are so thin this is rarely seen
**Fracture**: Uneven
**Specific gravity**: 5.3–5.5
**Other characteristics**: Crystals inflexible and brittle
**Notable locations**: Glamorgan, Wales; Wissen, Freiberg, Germany; Western Australia; Sherbrooke and Planet mines, Quebec; Ontario; Manitoba; South Central Indiana; Keokuk, Iowa; Sterling Hill, New Jersey; Antwerp, New York; Lancaster Co, Pennsylvania

**Identification:** Millerite is easily identified from its sprays of very thin brassy yellow needles.

# IRON SULPHIDES

*Iron sulphides are by far the most widespread of all the metal sulphide minerals, often found as beautiful, pale gold crystals. They form mostly in veins, where hot fluids bring minerals up through cracks in the ground, and in marine sediments where there is little oxygen present. Iron sulphide grains end up just about everywhere and are among the most common minerals in soil.*

## Pyrite

*$FeS_2$ Iron sulphide*

This shiny, yellow mineral can look so like gold it has fooled many prospectors into thinking they have struck it rich. No wonder, then, it is sometimes known as 'fool's gold'. It is among the most common of all minerals, found in almost every environment. Indeed, any rock that looks a little rusty probably contains pyrite. It comes in a vast number of forms and varieties, but the most common crystal shapes are cubic and octahedral. One sought-after form is flattened nodules found in chalk, siltstone and shale called 'pyrite suns' or 'pyrite dollars'. The nodules are usually made of thin pyrite crystals radiating from the centre. Pyrite gets its name from the Greek for 'fire' because it can give off sparks when struck – which is why it has been used to light fires since prehistoric times. Although it is rich in iron, it has never been used as an iron ore. In the past, though, it was used as a source of sulphur for making sulphuric acid.

**Identification**: Pyrite looks rather like gold, but it gives off sparks if struck hard with a metal hammer. Cubic crystals often have stripy marks or striations, often clearly visible in the larger cubes.

**Crystal system**: Isometric but huge variety of forms
**Crystal habit**: Very varied. Crystals, cubes and pyritohedrons. Forms 'iron cross' interpenetrating twins. Also grains, radiating nodules.
**Colour**: Brassy yellow
**Lustre**: Metallic
**Streak**: Greenish black
**Hardness**: 6–6.5
**Cleavage**: Poor
**Fracture**: Conchoidal
**Specific gravity**: 5.1+
**Other characteristics**: Brittle, striations on cubic faces
**Notable locations**: Elba, Italy; Rio Tinto, Spain; Germany; Berezovsk, Russia; South Africa; Cerro de Pasco, Peru; Chihuahua, Mexico; Bolivia; French Creek, Pennsylvania; Illinois; Missouri; Leadville, Colorado

## Marcasite

*$FeS_2$ Iron sulphide*

Marcasite

Marcasite can be very similar to pyrite. Indeed, it gets its name from the Arabic for 'pyrite'. It is actually a polymorph of pyrite, which means that, just like diamond and graphite, it has the same chemistry but a slightly different crystal structure. Just to cause further confusion, jewellers called pyrite 'marcasite'. It typically forms near the surface where acid solutions percolate down through shale, clay, chalk and limestone. Among the most distinctive marcasite crystals are spear-shaped twins, like those found in the chalk in Kent, England, and 'cockscomb' clusters of curved crystals. Collectors' specimens of marcasite often rust quickly, freeing sulphur to form an acid that speeds the crumbling of the specimen. There seems no way of preventing marcasite eventually turning to dust if it is left exposed to the air for any length of time.

**Identification**: Marcasite looks very, very similar to pyrite, but changes colour when exposed and soon begins to disintegrate.

**Crystal system**: Orthorhombic
**Crystal habit**: Tabular, bladed or prismatic forms. Also massive, botryoidal, stalactitic and nodular.
**Colour**: Pale yellow, with greenish tint
**Lustre**: Metallic
**Streak**: Greenish brown
**Hardness**: 6–6.5
**Cleavage**: Poor in two directions
**Fracture**: Uneven
**Specific gravity**: 4.8+
**Other characteristics**: Sometimes has sulphur smell
**Notable locations**: Pas de Calais, France; Russia; China; Guanajuato, Mexico; Peru; Joplin, Missouri; Wisconsin

# Arsenopyrite

*FeAsS Iron arsenide sulphide*

The name of this mineral comes from the Greek word *arsenikos*, which was the name the Greek philosopher Theophrastus gave to the mineral orpiment, another mineral containing arsenic. While arsenic is a poison, it can also be very useful in medicine (in the drug salvarsan) and in alloys. Arsenopyrite is a major ore of arsenic, yet it is rarely mined just for its arsenic. It is more commonly an unwelcome by-product in mining for other metals, such as in the nickel-silver mines of Freiberg, Germany, and in the tin mines of Cornwall, because it often forms in high temperature veins in association with other metals. The problem is how to dispose of the arsenic safely. In the copper and silver mines of Boliden in Sweden, special silos have been built to avoid spreading contamination.

**Identification**: Arsenopyrite looks very similar to marcasite, but fracturing it with a hammer releases arsenic's garlic smell.

**Caution**: Arsenic in arsenopyrite is poisonous; handle with extreme care and wash hands and surfaces.

*Sphalerite*

*Arsenopyrite*

**Crystal system**: Orthorhombic
**Crystal habit**: Wedge-shaped or prismatic. Often twinned: sometimes cruciform, sometimes multiple.
**Colour**: Brassy white to grey, tarnishes to brown or pink
**Lustre**: Metallic
**Streak**: Dark grey to black
**Hardness**: 5.5–6
**Cleavage**: Distinct in two directions forming prisms
**Fracture**: Uneven
**Specific gravity**: 6.1+
**Other characteristics**: Bitter garlic smell when powdered or broken
**Notable locations**: Cornwall, England; Freiberg, Germany; Valais, Switzerland; Panasqueira, Portugal; Kyushu Island, Iname, Japan; Broken Hill (NSW), Australia; Bolivia; Wawa, Ontario; Edenville, New York; New Hampshire

**Life turned to pyrite**
There are many ways living things can be preserved as fossils, but one of the most common is pyritization. Pyritization is a chemical process that involves the formation of iron sulphide minerals. What happens is that when an organism dies it is buried in sediments and the remains then begin to react chemically with fluids moving through the sediments. If the organism is buried rapidly – before it begins to disintegrate – and there are plenty of dissolved sulphates in the fluids, the organic tissue of the remains can be replaced molecule by molecule with iron sulphide minerals, essentially pyrite. In this way, over millions of years, the organic remains retain their shape but are transformed to pyrite. Pyritization can in this way preserve exquisite detail, even of soft tissues, which are not normally fossilized. Some of the best fossils of insects have been preserved by pyritization, including some wonderful dragonfly-like insects from the Cretaceous period.

# Pyrrhotite

*Fe₁₋ₓS Iron sulphide*

Pyrrhotite gets its name from the Greek word *pyrrhos*, meaning 'reddish', yet it is not always red. In fact, it looks similar to other brassy-coloured sulphides like marcasite and chalcopyrite. It forms mostly in mafic igneous rocks and hydrothermal veins. Pyrrhotite is the only other common magnetic mineral besides magnetite. Not all specimens are strongly magnetic, but you can be sure you have pyrrhotite if it attracts a paper clip suspended from cotton, or moves a compass needle. Unusually, pyrrhotite's sulphur content can vary by up to 20 per cent. When the sulphur content is low, pyrrhotite crystals tend to be hexagonal in shape, whereas when the sulphur content is high, the crystals are usually flat plates.

**Identification**: Pyrrhotite's magnetism is usually enough to distinguish it from similar yellowish metallic minerals. But its slightly reddish tinge, its softness and its hexagonal or flat crystals can help to confirm the identification.

**Crystal system**: Hexagonal
**Crystal habit**: Hexagonal or flat plates, but usually found in masses in rocks
**Colour**: Bronze
**Lustre**: Metallic
**Streak**: Grey-black
**Hardness**: 3.5–4.5
**Cleavage**: None
**Fracture**: Uneven
**Specific gravity**: 4.6
**Other characteristics**: Weakly magnetic, colour will darken with exposure to light
**Notable locations**: Trentino, Italy; Andreasberg (Harz Mts), Germany; Kisbanya, Romania; Trepca, Serbia; Dalnegorsk, Russia; Japan; Kambalda, Western Australia; Morro Velho, Brazil; Chihuahua, Mexico; Sudbury, Ontario; Riondell, British Columbia; Standish, Maine; Ducktown, Tennessee; Pennsylvania; Franklin, New Jersey

*Intergrown hexagonal crystals*

# SULPHOSALTS

*The sulphosalts are sulphide minerals in which a semi-metal – antimony, bismuth or arsenic – combines with a true metal such as lead or silver. Although nearly all these minerals are comparatively rare, they frequently form good crystals, because they crystallize slowly in cool pockets near the Earth's surface. Unfortunately, their very accessibility means that most good samples are hard to find.*

## Cylindrite

*$FePb_3Sn_4Sb_2S_{14}$ Iron lead tin antimony sulphide*

**Crystal system**: Trigonal, but this is disputed
**Crystal habit**: Unique cylindrical crystals that look like tubes or rolls of metallic cloth, but occasionally found in masses
**Colour**: Black to grey
**Lustre**: Metallic
**Streak**: Black
**Hardness**: 2.5
**Cleavage**: None
**Fracture**: Conchoidal
**Specific gravity**: 5.5
**Notable locations**: Only found at Potosi and Mina Santa Cruz (Poopo) in Bolivia and in a few tin sulphide ores

**Identification**: Cylindrite's tube-shaped crystals are unmistakable and impossible to mix up with any other mineral.

Cylindrite is one of the most unusual of all minerals. It owes its name to its almost unique crystal habit, which is cylindrical. Only chrysotile, a variety of serpentine, also forms tubular crystals, but these are microscopically thin with the appearance of tiny hairs. Crystals of cylindrite are actually coiled sheets that grow as if rolled into pipes. Sometimes the sheets can become uncoiled if put under pressure. Cylindrite is occasionally mined as an ore of lead, tin and the rare element indium, which is used by the microelectronics industry in the manufacture of transistors and silicon chips. However, cylindrite is collected primarily for its very unusual crystal habit. The majority of the best specimens of cylindrite crystals come from Bolivia – at Poopo in Oruro and at Potosi. Bolivian specimens are found in tin-rich mineralized veins and are typically associated with similar minerals in the sulphosalt group such as franckeite, incaite, potosiite and tellaite.

## Jamesonite

*$Pb_4FeSb_6S_{14}$ Lead iron antimony sulphide*

*Quartz*

*Jamesonite crystals*

**Identification**: Jamesonite and similar sulphosalts can be identified by the dense, felt-like mats they form.

Jamesonite was named after the Scottish mineralogist Robert Jameson, who identified it in Cornwall, England. It forms in low-temperature lead-rich veins along with galena, sphalerite and pyrite, and in marbles. Jamesonite crystals are dense, felt-like, matted hairs sometimes called 'feather ores'. A number of other sulphosalts, including plagionite, zinkenite, boulangerite and jordanite, form in the same way and look almost identical. Boulangerite crystals can be bent while jamesonite crystals tend to snap, but otherwise almost the only way to tell these minerals apart is by chemical tests that reveal the iron in jamesonite. Jamesonite can also look quite similar to stibnite, but stibnite crystals tend to be better defined and break cleanly along the line of the crystals.

**Crystal system**: Monoclinic
**Crystal habit**: Include loosely matted hairs and feathery masses
**Colour**: Dark grey, tarnishing iridescent
**Lustre**: Metallic and silky
**Streak**: Grey-black
**Hardness**: 2–3
**Cleavage**: Perfect across the crystals at right angles
**Fracture**: Uneven to conchoidal
**Specific gravity**: 5.5–6
**Other characteristics**: Crystals are brittle and snap easily.
**Notable locations**: Cornwall, England; Auvergne, France; Maramures, Romania; Kosovo; Mount Bischoff, Tasmania; Bolivia; Noche Buena mine (Zacatecas), Mexico; Colorado; South Dakota; Arkansas

## Pyrargyrite

*Ag₃SbS₃ Silver antimony sulphide*

Pyrargyrite is a deep red silvery colour giving both its nickname 'ruby silver' and its official name, from the Greek for 'fire' and 'silver'. Proustite is also called 'ruby silver' and the two minerals are very similar. Both are used as ores for silver and are often found together in low-temperature veins along with silver and other silver sulphides. In fact, pyrargyrite and proustite are 'isostructural', which means they have the same structure even though they are chemically slightly different. They both get darker when exposed to light, but pyrargyrite tends to be a deeper red than proustite. Pyrargyrite's tendency to darken on exposure to light means translucent crystals can quickly go opaque in the light, so good specimens are usually stored in a dark place. All the same, the dark coat can usually be cleaned off with a gentle washing in soap and water, or a quick dip in silver polish.

**Identification**: The combination of prismatic crystals and a dark red silvery colour is enough to identify a mineral as either pyrargyrite or proustite. Proustite is usually lighter in colour.

**Crystal system**: Trigonal
**Crystal habit**: Typically prismatic crystals or massive forms
**Colour**: Dark red when translucent but black when opaque
**Lustre**: Adamantine
**Streak**: Purplish red
**Hardness**: 2.5
**Cleavage**: Sometimes distinct in three directions forming rhombohedrons
**Fracture**: Conchoidal, uneven
**Specific gravity**: 5.8
**Other characteristics**: Darkens upon exposure to light, crystals may be striated
**Notable locations**: Harz Mts, Saxony, Germany; Alsace, Isère, France; Colquechaca, Bolivia; Castrovirrenya, Peru; Guanajato, Mexico; Silver City, Idaho; Comstock Lode, Nevada

### Boulangerite

*Pb₅Sb₄S Lead antimony sulphide*

Boulangerite forms pale bluish-grey hairlike fibres and is hard to distinguish from other 'feather ores' with similar crystals such as jamesonite. Unlike jamesonite, which snaps, boulangerite crystals bend. A variety of boulangerite with feathery plumes called plumosite was once thought to be a different mineral. Now it is simply classed as boulangerite.

### Renierite

*Cu(Zn)₁₁As(Ge)₂Fe₄S₁₆ Copper arsenic iron sulphide*

Named after the Belgian geologist who discovered it in 1948, bronze-yellow renierite is found typically in Katanga in the DR Congo. Small grains are often found in granite and other igneous rocks.

### Tetrahedrite

*Cu₁₂Sb₄S₁₃ Copper antimony sulphide*

Tetrahedrite is a minor ore of copper and silver. It gets its name from the tetrahedral (pyramid-shaped) crystals.

## Baumhauerite

*Pb₃As₄S₉ Lead arsenic sulphide*

Baumhauerite is a very rare mineral that is seen embedded in dolomitic marble. It is found primarily in the Lengenbach quarry, Binnetal, in the Valais region of Switzerland. The mineral is named after Heinrich Baumhauer, who discovered it at Lengenbach in 1902. The Lengenbach quarry is famous among mineralogists for its array of rare minerals. Besides baumhauerite, many other rare arsenic sulphide and sulphosalt minerals have been found there, including marrite, bernardite, hatchite, novakite, smythite and many others. There is even a mineral that is named after the quarry, a sulphosalt discovered in 1904 called lengenbachite. Baumhauerite has also been found at Sterling Hill, New Jersey, USA, typically in association with molybdenite, and in massive aggregates at Hemlo, Thunder Bay, Ontario, Canada.

**Identification**: Baumhauerite is best identified by the striped prismatic shape of its crystals, which are typically about 1mm/¹⁄₂₄in long, and also by its density.

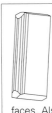

**Crystal system**: Triclinic
**Crystal habit**: Striated prismatic, acicular crystals about 1mm/¹⁄₂₄in long with rounded faces. Also occurs as masses and grains
**Colour**: Grey-black to blue-grey
**Lustre**: Metallic to dull
**Streak**: Dark brown
**Hardness**: 3
**Cleavage**: Indistinct
**Fracture**: Conchoidal
**Specific gravity**: 5.3
**Notable locations**: Lengenbach quarry (Binnetal), Switzerland; Thunder Bay, Ontario; Franklin and Sterling Hill mines, New Jersey

*Realgar appears as red spots*

*Dolomitic marble*

*Baumhauerite*

# TELLURIDES AND ARSENIDES

*The tellurides and arsenides are two small groups of minerals that are very similar to sulphur in chemical make-up – except that with tellurides, the element tellurium takes sulphur's place, and with arsenides, arsenic takes its place. Antimony and selenium can take sulphur's place in the same way, and so form two further small groups, the antimonides and selenides.*

## Tellurobismuthite

*$Bi_2Te_3$ Bismuth telluride*

Tellurium is a semi-metal, like antimony and bismuth. It was discovered in Transylvania in 1782 by Franz von Reichenstein. As an element it exists in two forms – as a silvery white, brittle, metallic-looking solid and as a dark grey powder. It is by no means common, and is usually found only in the tellurides of copper (kostovite), lead (altaite), silver (hessite and empressite), silver and gold (sylvanite, petzite and krennerite) and bismuth (tellurobismuthite). Tellurobismuthite is a rare silver-grey mineral typically found along with other tellurides in quartz-gold veins that form at high temperatures. It is very hard to distinguish from tetradymite, which is also a bismuth telluride but also contains an appreciable amount of sulphur. Like altaite, tellurobismuthite is a semiconducting material (a material like silicon that conducts electricity only under certain conditions). As a result, it is sometimes used in thermoelectric devices that produce electricity when heated.

**Identification**: Tellurobismuthite is typically a silvery white mineral that tarnishes to grey. It forms silvery flakes, as on this specimen, and usually occurs with tellurides.

**Crystal system**: Trigonal hexagonal
**Crystal habit**: Foliated aggregates, irregular plates like mica, fine-grained fibres and masses
**Colour**: Pale silvery grey
**Lustre**: Metallic
**Streak**: Pale lead grey
**Hardness**: 1.5–2
**Cleavage**: Perfect, flat leaves
**Fracture**: Flexible
**Specific gravity**: 7.8
**Notable locations**: Clogau (Dolgellau Gold Belt), Mid Wales; Boliden (Västerbotten), Sweden; Tokke, Norway; Alpes-Maritimes, France; Larga (Metaliferi Mts), Romania; Kamchatka, Russia; Tohoku (Honshu), Kyushu, Japan; Dahlonega (Lumpkin Co), Georgia; Sylvanite (Hidalgo Co), New Mexico; Mule Mts, Arizona; Colorado

## Altaite

*PbTe Lead telluride*

Altaite gets its name from the Altai mountains in southern Siberia where it was discovered in 1854. Like other tellurides, it is frequently found in quartz-gold veins. It is a lead telluride related to another lead compound in the sulphide group, galena (lead sulphide). Like galena, altaite is an ore of lead, although it is much, much less abundant and widely extracted. Like galena it is unusually dense. Indeed, it is one of the few minerals that is actually denser than galena. This means it is often easy to identify by its heavy weight alone. It is distinguished from galena by the yellowish white colour. If the colour is not obvious, it is possible to identify it from the shape of the crystals. Although they are cubic as with galena, altaite crystals do not have the triangular pits in the faces that galena exhibits.

*Altaite*

**Identification**: Altaite and galena can be identified by their heavy weight. Altaite is yellow-white or silvery; galena is dark grey.

**Crystal system**: Isometric
**Crystal habit**: Includes cubic and octahedral crystals, but more commonly found in masses and grains
**Colour**: Tin white to yellowish white; tarnishes bronze yellow
**Lustre**: Metallic
**Streak**: Black
**Hardness**: 2.5–3
**Cleavage**: Perfect in three directions and forms cubes
**Fracture**: Uneven
**Specific gravity**: 8.2–8.3
**Notable locations**: Transylvania, Romania; Przibram, Czech Republic; Altai Mountains, Zyrianovsk, Kazakhstan; Coquimbo, Chile; Moctezuma, Mexico; Greenwood, BC; Mattagami Lake, Quebec; Price County, Wisconsin; California; Arizona

# Rammelsbergite

*NiAs₂ Nickel arsenide*

Rammelsbergite is one of the group of rare minerals called arsenides. The two most common arsenides, niccolite and skutterudite, are both used as metal ores, niccolite for nickel and skutterudite for cobalt. So too is sperrylite, the rare platinum arsenide. Rammelsbergite is rare in itself, but is often found with other more common arsenides, and can be very hard to distinguish from them, especially the other nickel arsenides, niccolite, maucherite, dienerite and oregonite. All the arsenides tend to occur in similar conditions, but different minerals form according to the temperature and oxidization level in the vein. Arsenide minerals crystallize in the following order with increasingly oxidizing conditions: maucherite, niccolite, rammelsbergite, skutterudite, safflorite and löllingite. Rammelsbergite can also be hard to distinguish from nickel sulphides such as gersdorffite, millerite and pentlandite. It has a dimorphic cousin, pararammelsbergite, with the same chemistry but different crystal structure.

**Identification**: Rammelsbergite looks very similar to most arsenides but can sometimes be identified by its red tinge, and its yellowy pink tarnish.

**Crystal system**: Orthorhombic
**Crystal habit**: Masses, grains and radiating fibres. Rarer as flat tablets, stubby prisms or even cockscombs.
**Colour**: Silvery white with reddish tinge. Tarnishes yellow or pink.
**Lustre**: Metallic
**Streak**: Grey
**Hardness**: 5.5–6
**Cleavage**: None
**Fracture**: Uneven
**Specific gravity**: 6.9–7.1
**Notable locations**: Sainte-Marie-aux-Mines (Vosges de Alsace), France; Schneeburg (Harz Mountains), Germany; Lölling, Austria; Kongsberg, Norway; Binnetal, Switzerland; Bou Azzer, Morocco; Batopilas (Chihuahua), Mexico; Great Bear Lake, Northwest Territories; Cobalt, Ontario; Keweenaw, Michigan; New Jersey

**Telluride gold**
Tellurium has a great affinity for gold, and gold tellurides are among the few significant ores of gold, which combines with few other elements but tellurium. The gold tellurides include petzite, coloradoite, melonite, krennerite, kostovite, nagyagite, stützite and montbrayite, but the most common are calaverite and sylvanite. Some gold tellurides are such good sources of gold that they have actually started gold rushes. Although it was not realized at the time, the gold in placer deposits (grains in river gravel) that started the famous Cripple Creek gold rush in the 1860s in Colorado came from telluride veins. When these telluride veins were discovered in the 1890s, it started a second gold rush (the above photograph of mining activity was taken in 1903). In Western Australia, Kalgoorlie's famous Golden Mile is mainly telluride gold. Cripple Creek is known for krennerite, sylvanite and calaverite. Kalgoorlie is known for calaverite, petzite and coloradoite. Chelopech in Bulgaria is known for kostovite.

# Safflorite

*CoAs₂ Cobalt arsenide or, more commonly, CoFeAs₂ Cobalt iron arsenide*

Safflorite is closely related to rammelsbergite and both belong to the löllingite group of arsenide minerals. Safflorite is the cobalt-rich version of the group, rammelsbergite is the nickel-rich version and löllingite is the iron version, but each usually contains traces of the other two metals. In fact, safflorite can contain up to 50 per cent nickel before it becomes rammelsbergite, and contain 50 per cent iron content before it becomes löllingite. Safflorite gets its name from the German word *Safflor*, which means 'dyer's saffron', and may have got its name because trillings (groups of three intergrown crystals) of safflorite can look a little like tiny bunches of white crocuses (saffron flowers). It is often spotted close to erythrite, or 'cobalt bloom', the pinkish grey tinge that some cobalt minerals acquire when exposed to the weather.

*Safflorite*

*Calcite*

**Crystal system**: Orthorhombic
**Crystal habit**: Typically tiny flat tablet-shaped or prismatic crystals. Also in masses, grains, fibres, cockscombs or star-shaped trillings.
**Colour**: Bright white or grey but tarnishes to black
**Lustre**: Metallic
**Streak**: Black
**Hardness**: 4.5–5.5
**Cleavage**: Indistinct
**Fracture**: Conchoidal
**Specific gravity**: 7–7.3
**Other characteristics**: Safflorite often forms twins that grow into groups of star-shaped crystals.
**Notable locations**: Nordmark (Varmland), Sweden; Schneeburg (Harz Mountains), Germany; Javornik, Czech Republic; Great Bear Lake, Northwest Territories; Oregon; Lafayette County, Wisconsin

**Identification**: Safflorite can usually best be identified by its bright colour and black tarnish.

# OXIDES

*Oxygen is so common in the Earth's crust that 90 per cent of all minerals contain it. So all these are, in a way, oxides. To simplify things, geologists describe as oxides only those minerals that are a simple combination of a metal with oxygen, or a metal with oxygen and hydrogen (a hydroxide). Even so, oxides include everything from common ores such as bauxite to precious gems such as sapphires. Rutile, plattnerite, anatase and brookite are four simple oxides.*

## Rutile

*$TiO_2$ Titanium oxide*

Rutile was given its name by the famous 18th-century German mineralogist Abraham Gottlob Werner (1749–1814). It comes from the Latin *rutilus*, meaning 'reddish', from its coppery tinge. It is a minor ingredient in many plutonic rocks and crystalline slates, and of many basic pegmatites such as nelsonite. Famously, it is found alongside quartz, albite, chlorite, siderite, muscovite, ilmenite and apatite in vugs (pockets) in the Swiss Alps, as well as with its polymorphs brookite and anatase. Rutile is the most important ore of titanium, however, and these titanium ores come mainly from gravels and sands. Rutile can be often found as large crystals, but is best known for its presence as tiny needle inclusions in gemstones such as clear quartz, tourmaline, ruby, and sapphire, creating much-valued cat's eye and star effects. Clear quartz is turned into the beautiful ornamental stone rutilated quartz by golden needle rutile inclusions (inset).

*Rutilated quartz*

**Identification**: Rutile can be identified by its copper tinge, bright sparkle and, often, by the long golden needles it forms.

*Rutile*

*Calcite*

*Schist*

**Crystal system**: Tetragonal
**Crystal habit**: Typically stubby eight-sided prisms capped by low pyramids. Masses of long needles. Also inclusions.
**Colour**: Reddish brown in crystals. Yellow in needles and inclusions.
**Lustre**: Adamantine to metallic
**Streak**: Brown
**Hardness**: 6–6.5
**Cleavage**: Good in two directions forming prisms
**Fracture**: Conchoidal, uneven
**Specific gravity**: 4.2+
**Other characteristics**: Stripes on prism-shaped crystals. Very sparkly.
**Notable locations**: Alps, Switzerland; Urals, Russia; Minas Gerais, Brazil; Magnet Cove, Arkansas; Lincoln County, Georgia; Alexander County, North Carolina

## Plattnerite

*$PbO_2$ Lead oxide*

**Identification**: Plattnerite can be identified by its dark, black colour, and unexpected sparkle. It is also extremely heavy.

*Plattnerite may appear as small black needles*

Plattnerite is a black, heavy mineral named after German mineralogist K F Plattner. It belongs to a small, important group of minerals known as rutiles, all of which have chain molecules that give distinctive prismatic crystals. Besides the mineral rutile itself, this includes a number of key ores such as cassiterite (tin ore) and pyrolusite (manganese ore), and also stishovite, which is a key indicator of meteorite impact. Plattnerite has a very high lead content, and this makes it one of the densest of all minerals. It is markedly denser than both galena and altaite. The lead in plattnerite also makes it sparkle. If this sounds odd, remember that lead is added to glass crystal to make it sparkle. Like many oxides, plattnerite is a 'secondary' mineral, and does not form directly in magma, but when other lead-bearing minerals are oxidized by exposure to the atmosphere.

**Crystal system**: Tetragonal
**Crystal habit**: Typically stubby prisms capped with pyramids. More commonly massive. Often forms a dry oxidation crust with tiny sparkling crystals on other lead minerals.
**Colour**: Black
**Lustre**: Adamantine to metallic
**Streak**: Chestnut brown
**Hardness**: 5–5.5
**Cleavage**: Good in two directions forming prisms. Poor basally.
**Fracture**: Conchoidal, uneven
**Specific gravity**: 9.4+
**Notable locations**: Leadhills (Lanarkshire), Dumfries and Galloway, Scotland; Alpes-Maritimes, France; Mapimi, Mexico; Shoshone Co, Idaho; Pima County, Arizona

# Anatase

*TiO₂ Titanium oxide*

Once known as octahedrite, anatase typically forms in low-temperature veins and in alpine fissures. The Binnetal district of the Alps is famous for its anatase. Anatase is the rarest of three titanium oxide minerals, anatase, brookite and rutile. These three are polymorphs, as they are chemically alike but have different crystal structures. Anatase is the version thought to form at the lowest temperatures, and is readily altered to rutile by exposure to higher temperatures. Where good crystals are found, in the quartz veins of the Diamantina district of Brazil, they are often only preserved as anatase where they are encased in quartz. Specimens of anatase like these are usually preserved as discovered, encased in quartz, and are much sought after. They are unmistakable, with blue-grey anatase forming long, double-pyramid-shaped crystals inside the clear or golden quartz.

**Identification**: The blue-grey double pyramid-shaped crystals of anatase are hard to mistake, especially when encased in quartz as shown below.

*Quartz crystal*

*Anatase crystal*

**Crystal system**: Tetragonal
**Crystal habit**: Typically forms stretched double-pyramids
**Colour**: Blue-grey, also brown and yellow
**Lustre**: Adamantine to metallic
**Streak**: White
**Hardness**: 5.5–6
**Cleavage**: Perfect in four directions forming pyramids
**Fracture**: Subconchoidal, uneven
**Specific gravity**: 3.8–3.9
**Notable locations**: Tavistock (Devon), England; Binnatal, Switzerland; Alpes-Maritimes, France; Diamantina, Brazil; Somerville, Massachusetts; Gunnison County, Colorado

**Titanic titanium**
In 1791, William Gregor, a vicar from Cornwall, England, found a magnetic black sand on the local beaches, and named it menachanite, after the nearby village of Menaccan. A few years later, the German chemist M H Klaproth separated a new metal element from the mineral, which he called titanium after the giants of Greek mythology. It wasn't until 1938, though, that German metallurgist W J Kroll developed a method of refining titanium from the ores ilmenite and rutile. Now titanium is becoming something of a miracle metal. It is three times as strong as steel and twice as light, making it ideal for the aerospace industry, where it is now widely used both by itself and in alloys. Titanium alloys are capable of operating at temperatures from sub zero to 600°C, and have been used in fuel tanks for space stations and in blades, shafts and casings in aircraft parts, including front fans and high pressure compressors. Because titanium is very resistant to corrosion, it is also the perfect metal for artificial hip joints, and architects are experimenting with it for building. A great deal of titanium, however, goes to making titanium dioxide, a white pigment for paints. Titanium dioxide paint is unrivalled for brightness and opacity and, unlike lead, which was once used for white paint, it is non-toxic.

# Brookite

*TiO₂ Titanium oxide*

Brookite is one of the titanium oxide mineral trio, with anatase and rutile. It is much more common than anatase, and forms at the higher temperature of 750°C/1,382°F (650°C/1,202°F for anatase and 915°C/1,679°F for rutile). Brookite typically forms in quartz veins, but it can also be found as grains in sandy sediments, where large crystals can form, probably fed by cool solutions percolating through the rock. The best known specimens come from St Gotthard in Switzerland, where very thin, flat crystals are found. The quartz veins at Tremadoc in North Wales are also famous for brookite. In the USA, Arkansas's Magnet Cove quartzite yields very high quality brookite crystals.

*Brookite*

**Crystal system**: Orthorhombic
**Crystal habit**: Flat, platelike crystals – except at Magnet Cove, where they tend to be fatter and more complex in shape
**Colour**: Dark reddish brown to greenish black
**Lustre**: Adamantine to submetallic
**Streak**: Yellow or white grey
**Hardness**: 5.5–6
**Cleavage**: Poorly prismatic
**Fracture**: Subconchoidal, uneven
**Specific gravity**: 3.9–4.1
**Notable locations**: Gwynedd, Wales; Carinthia, Salzburg, Tyrol, Austria; Liguria, Italy; Brittany, Savoie, France; St Gotthard, Switzerland; Urals, Russia; Nova Scotia; Magnet Cove, Arkansas; Somerville, Massachusetts; Ellenville, New York; Franklin, New Jersey; Pima Co, Arizona

**Identification**: Brookite can usually be identified by its long, black, plate-like, roughly hexagonal crystals.

# HYDROXIDES

*Hydroxides are minerals formed from a combination of a metal with oxygen and hydrogen. They form at low temperatures typically in changing mineral-rich waters or in hydrothermal veins. The hydroxide minerals include the iron ore limonite, as well as brucite, gibbsite (an ingredient of the major aluminium ore bauxite), the manganese ore psilomelane and stibiconite.*

## Brucite

*Mg(OH)₂ Magnesium hydroxide*

Brucite is named after American mineralogist A Bruce, who first described it in 1814 in New Jersey, USA. It forms when ultramafic, magnesium-rich rocks and minerals, such as olivine and periclase, are altered during contact with hot, watery solutions – especially during serpentinization, when magnesium silicates are changed to the mineral serpentine. Serpentinization is common on the sea floor where ultramafic rocks come into contact with seawater, but brucite is common wherever there are serpentinized rocks, chlorite and talc schists, phyllites and marbles. Brucite is usually soft and breaks easily into layers because its molecules stack up in sheets of octahedrons of magnesium hydroxide. Brucite layers are often incorporated into crystals of serpentine, dolomite and talc. It was brucite's distinctive layer structure that gave the revolutionary architect Buckminster Fuller the idea for the ingenious octet truss structure now widely used in buildings.

**Identification**: Brucite typically forms soft white masses that flake off in plates when scraped with a fingernail.

*Brucite plates*

**Crystal system**: Trigonal hexagonal
**Crystal habit**: Typically forms ill-defined plates. Also forms fibres and foliated masses.
**Colour**: White or colourless, sometimes with tinges of grey, blue or green
**Lustre**: Vitreous or waxy; pearly lustre on cleavage surfaces
**Streak**: White
**Hardness**: 2–2.5
**Cleavage**: Perfect in one direction, forming plates
**Fracture**: Uneven, sectile (can be cut with a knife)
**Specific gravity**: 2.4
**Notable locations**: Unst (Shetland Islands), Scotland; Filipstad, Nordmark, Jakobsberg, Sweden; Aosta, Italy; Urals, Russia; Asbestos, Quebec; Tilly Foster Mine (Brewster), New York; Lancaster County, Pennsylvania; Wood's Mine, Texas; Gabbs, Nevada

## Gibbsite

*Al(OH)₃ Aluminium hydroxide*

**Identification**: Gibbsite is soft and white and breaks easily into plates. It also has a very distinct clay smell.

Gibbsite is an important ore of aluminium, and one of the main ingredients of bauxite. Bauxite is often mistakenly thought of as consisting of a single mineral; however, it is actually a mixture of various aluminium minerals, one of which is gibbsite. Gibbsite is also one of the main minerals in tropical and subtropical soils. It usually forms when rocks rich in aluminium are weathered in the hot, wet conditions that are typical of the tropics, especially in densely forested regions. Occasionally, crystals of gibbsite form directly in aluminium-rich hydrothermal veins. Like brucite, gibbsite molecules are arranged in octahedral layers, making it soft and liable to break off in plates. Gibbsite also occurs as microscopic layers in the molecules of other minerals, such as illite and kaolinite.

**Crystal system**: Monoclinic
**Crystal habit**: Typically massive but rare flat crystals are found. May form pisolites and other concretions.
**Colour**: White or colourless sometimes with tinges of grey, blue or green
**Lustre**: Vitreous to dull; pearly lustre on cleavage
**Streak**: White
**Hardness**: 2.5–3.5
**Cleavage**: Perfect in one direction, forming plates
**Fracture**: Flexible, tough
**Specific gravity**: 2.4
**Other characteristics**: Has noticeable clay smell
**Notable locations**: Vogelsberg, Germany; Gant, Hungary; Les Baux, France; Lavrion, Greece; Guyana; Dundas, Tasmania; Brazil; Surinam; Saline County, Arkansas; Alabama

# Psilomelane

*Typically Ba(Mn+2)(Mn+4)₈O₁₆(OH)₄ Barium manganese oxide hydroxide*

Psilomelane gets its name from the Greek words for 'smooth' and 'black' because of its tendency to form smooth black knobbly masses. Psilomelane is a general term used to describe various hard, massive mixtures of manganese hydroxides. Psilomelanes are mostly the mineral romanechite (from Romaneche-Thorins in France), which is essentially barium manganese hydroxide. Psilomelanes form when manganese-rich rocks are weathered – typically as concretions deposited by groundwater, or in swamp or lake bed deposits and clays. Psilomelanes also replace other minerals such as manganese carbonates and silicate minerals in limestones. Branchlike growths of psilomelane called manganese dendrites form along bedding planes between rocks. Psilomelane is often intergrown with iron oxides such as hematite and goethite. It also occasionally occurs in alternating black and grey bands with grey pyrolusite, making a very attractive stone when polished. Like pyrolusite, psilomelane is an important ore of manganese.

**Identification**: Psilomelanes are hard to tell from pyrolusite, but pyrolusite is generally shinier and softer, leaving marks on fingers. The key presence of barium is hard for an amateur to ascertain.

 **Crystal system**: Monoclinic
**Crystal habit**: Forms in knobbly masses, nodules, concretions, dendrites, and tufts of hairlike fibres
**Colour**: Metallic black to grey
**Lustre**: Submetallic to dull
**Streak**: Black or brownish black
**Hardness**: 5–5.5
**Cleavage**: None
**Fracture**: Uneven
**Specific gravity**: 4.4–4.5
**Other characteristics**: Sometimes banded with the mineral pyrolusite
**Notable locations**: Cornwall, England; Schneeburg (Harz Mountains), Germany; Romaneche-Thorins (Saône-et-Loire), France; Tekrasni, India; Ouro Prêto (Minas Gerais), Brazil; Wythe County, Virginia; Keweenaw, Michigan; Tucson, Arizona; Sodaville, Nevada

**Knobs and nodules**

Most sedimentary rocks are not all one even mass. Instead, they often contain hard lumps of particular minerals that grew around a tiny nucleus – such as a shell fragment – as the rock was forming. Lumps have a host of common names such as crogs, knots, beetlestones, yolks and countless others. Some geologists call them concretions if they are lozenge-shaped with a smooth surface, and nodules if they are round and knobbly. The smallest concretions are oolites: sand-sized balls of calcite that form the basis of rocks such as oolitic ironstone (above). Gibbsite often forms oolites. Bigger concretions are called pisolites, from the Greek words for pea and stone. Pisolites are typically pea-sized, like the pisolites in bauxite, but can be the size of a pumpkin or bigger. The mineral composition of a concretion usually depends on the nature of the surrounding sediment and the conditions in which the sediment formed. Quite often, there are thin layers of concretions along bedding planes, where they formed when sedimentation was interrupted.

# Stibiconite

*Sb₃O₆(OH) Antimony oxide hydroxide*

Stibiconite is a dirty white to yellowish mineral that forms when antimony-rich minerals such as stibnite are altered by exposure to warm air and oxidized. Stibiconite crystals are often pseudomorphs of stibnite – that is, minerals that adopt the same crystal structure as another as they form. In this case the stibnite crystals are replaced with stibiconite one by one in situ, as oxygen replaces sulphur, so that the shape of the stibnite crystal is retained. Because stibnite often forms spectacular swordlike crystals arranged in radiating clusters, so stibiconite forms matching spiky clusters. The only visible difference is that stibnite is a shiny steel grey whereas stibiconite is a dull dirty white in colour.

 **Crystal system**: Isometric
**Crystal habit**: Typically earthy masses and crust but also as stibnite pseudomorphs in sword-like clusters
**Colour**: White or grey tinged with brown or yellow
**Lustre**: Earthy
**Streak**: White
**Hardness**: 4–5.5
**Cleavage**: None
**Fracture**: Earthy, except as pseudomorphs of stibnite, then brittle
**Specific gravity**: 3.5–5.9
**Notable locations**: Goldkronach, Germany; Oruro, Bolivia; Huaras, Peru; San Luis Potosi, Mexico; Wolfe County, Quebec; Nevada

**Identification:** Stibiconite pseudomorph clusters look like stibnite, but they are a dull, dirty white colour.

*Stibiconite clusters*

# OXIDE GEMS

*Some oxides form deep down within the Earth's crust, in magma, or in very hot mineral veins. Oxides that form in this way include some of the toughest and most beautiful minerals, including corundum and its gem varieties ruby, sapphire and star sapphire. The rare gem taafeite and spinel in all its colour forms are also formed in this way as well as 'cat's eye' chrysoberyl.*

## Corundum

*Al₂O₃ Aluminium oxide*

Corundum is one of the world's hardest minerals – only diamond is harder. Powdered corundum is used to coat paper to make an abrasive paper finer than sandpaper, and blocks of corundum are used

*Tapering corundum crystal set in syenite rock.*

for knife sharpening. The main type of corundum used for abrasive paper and knife sharpeners is called emery, which forms masses underground. When exposed to the atmosphere it erodes and crumbles into a powder called black sand, which derives its colour from traces of iron. Not all industrial 'emery' is mined; some is made from ground-up crystals of pure corundum, or it can be manufactured synthetically. When it forms crystals, pure corundum is brown and translucent. The crystals are typically small, and shaped like two six-sided pyramids joined at the base.

**Identification**: The simplest way to identify corundum is to use the Mohs test to confirm its extreme hardness (9).

*Tablet*
*Spindle*
*Barrel*

**Crystal system**: Hexagonal
**Crystal habit**: Typically double-pyramid hexagons or flat hexagons, often elongated into barrels, or spindles. Also occurs as grains and masses.
**Colour**: Pure corundum is brown or brownish white; emery is black
**Lustre**: Vitreous, adamantine
**Streak**: White
**Hardness**: 9
**Cleavage**: None but splits basally and in two other ways
**Fracture**: Conchoidal, uneven
**Specific gravity**: 4+
**Notable locations**: Myanmar (Burma); Thailand; Sri Lanka; numerous locations in Africa; North Carolina; Montana

## Ruby

*variety of corundum, Al₂O₃ Aluminium oxide*

Dubbed Rajnapurah, the king of gems, by the ancient Hindus, ruby is one of the most sought after of all precious gems. Large transparent rubies are even rarer and more valuable than diamonds. Rubies are a variety of corundum and get their rich red colour from traces of chromium. Traces of iron can make rubies slightly brown. The most sought-after rubies are deep blood red with a slightly purplish hue. These are known as 'Pigeon's blood ruby' or 'Burmese' ruby. For centuries, rubies like these have come from Mogok and Mong Hsu in

*Rubies fluoresce red with long-wave UV*

Myanmar (Burma). Burmese rubies were originally embedded in marble and other metamorphic rock, but because ruby is so hard, the rubies have survived the breakdown of their parent rock and are typically found in river deposits. The majority of the good rubies today are brownish in colour and come from Thailand.

**Identification**: Rubies embedded in schists like this are unmistakable, but they are quite rare.

*Tablet*
*Spindle*
*Barrel*

**Crystal system**: Hexagonal
**Crystal habit**: Found as prisms and double-pyramids
**Colour**: Shades of red, often with a violet or purple tinge.
**Lustre**: Adamantine
**Streak**: None
**Hardness**: 9
**Cleavage**: None
**Specific gravity**: 4
**Notable locations**: Mogok, Mong Hsu, Myanmar (Burma); Thailand; Sri Lanka; Cambodia; India; Pakistan; Tadjikistan; Madagascar; Umba River, Tanzania

# Sapphire

*variety of corundum, Al₂O₃ Aluminium oxide*

Corundum gems come in many colours besides the red of rubies. Geologists call all these non-red, coloured corundums sapphires. For jewellers, though, sapphires are only the most stunning blue corundum gems. These stones are coloured blue by traces of the titanium oxide mineral ilmenite. Different impurities give corundum a whole variety of colours including pink, yellow, orange and green. In the past, these other colours of sapphire were known as 'oriental' versions of other gems of the same colour, so green corundums were known as oriental emeralds, for instance. Nowadays, however, green corundums are simply called green sapphires. Only orange-pink sapphire has its own recognized name, padparadschah. The most famous sapphires are the cornflower-blue stones from Kashmir. Nowadays most sapphires come from Australia, although they also come from Myanmar (Burma), Thailand and Sri Lanka.

**Identification**: Like other corundum gems, sapphires are typically found in river deposits, where they stand out because of their blue colour and hardness.

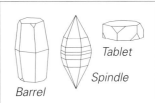

**Crystal system**: Hexagonal
**Crystal habit**: Found as prisms and double-pyramids
**Colour**: Shades of blue
**Lustre**: Adamantine
**Streak**: None
**Hardness**: 9
**Cleavage**: None
**Specific gravity**: 4
**Notable locations**: Kashmir; Mogok, Myanmar (Burma); Thailand; Ratnapura, Sri Lanka; Australia; Judith Basin County, Montana

**Stars and cat's eyes**

Some gemstones display light effects created by light reflecting off the mineral's internal structure, or inclusions of other mineral crystals inside. These light effects show up well only when the stone is cut and polished in the right way. Asterism is the star effect caused by the inclusion of criss-crossing needle-like crystals. It is best known in star sapphires, but also occurs in rubies and diopsides. Another effect seen in some sapphires is chatoyancy, or 'cat's eye'. Here, mineral inclusions create a bright band across the stone that makes the stone look a little like a cat's eye. A number of other minerals exhibit light effects. Opalescence manifests as a milky shimmer, created as light is refracted and reflected by tiny silica spheres under the surface of opals and other minerals. Adularescence is the floating blue cloud effect, as seen in moonstone and some transparent opals. Labradorescence is the shimmering play of colour in labradorite as light is bounced around through lamellae (leaves) in the crystals. It is like the bronzy 'Schiller' effect created by internal plates in orthopyroxene.

# Star sapphire

*variety of corundum, Al₂O₃ Aluminium oxide*

Although flawless, transparent sapphires are the most valuable, jewellers also prize sapphires that contain needle-like crystals of rutile. The rutile crystals often grow in three directions. White or silver light is reflected from these needles in such a way that it looks as if the stones contain a six-pointed (or occasionally twelve-pointed) star. Sapphires like these are known as star sapphires, and the effect is called asterism. In very rare black and gold star sapphires, asterism is caused not by rutile, but by hematite and ilmenite crystals. The sapphires themselves are black or dark brown, while the star is a deep golden colour.

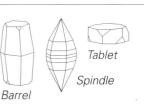

**Crystal system**: Hexagonal
**Crystal habit**: Found as prisms and double-pyramids
**Colour**: Various shades of red
**Lustre**: Adamantine
**Streak**: None
**Hardness**: 9
**Cleavage**: None
**Specific gravity**: 4
**Notable locations**: Mogok, Myanmar (Burma); Tanzania; black and gold star sapphires are found only in Chanthaburi province, eastern Thailand

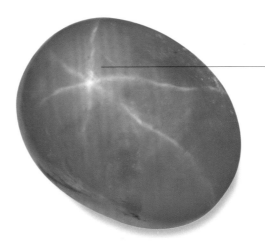

*When reflection of white or silver light produces a six-pointed star like this, the effect is known as asterism*

**Identification:** The star effect is immediately obvious when the stones are polished *en cabochon* – in other words, into a smooth, flat oval shape.

# COMPLEX OXIDES

*While some oxides are simply a combination of a metal and an oxide or hydroxide, a number of other oxides are more varied and complex, including at least two different metals in their chemical make-up. Aluminium, iron, manganese and chromium frequently form minerals containing two other metals in their chemical composition.*

## Perovskite

*CaTiO₃ Calcium titanium oxide*

Perovskite is one of the world's most abundant minerals, since it makes up the bulk of the Earth's mantle, which is 80 per cent of Earth's volume. Perovskite is less abundant in surface rocks, but still common. Here, perovskite is commonly found in mafic igneous rocks low in silica and aluminium, such as nepheline syenites, carbonatites, kimberlites and melilites, and in some schists. It was discovered in the Russian Urals in 1839 by Gustav Rose, who named it after Russian mineralogist Count Lev von Perovski. Mineral collectors look for its apparently cubic crystals. They are only apparently cubic, because although box-shaped, their internal structure is actually orthorhombic (longer in one direction), not isometric (equal length in all directions). Mining engineers seek out the massive variety of perovskite to use as an ore for titanium. It can also be a source of niobium and thorium, and rare earth metals like cerium, lanthanum and neodymium.

**Identification**: The simplest way to identify perovskite is from the nature of the local rocks. Dark-coloured, box-shaped crystals in syenites and carbonatites are likely to be perovskite.

*Calcite*

*Schist rock*

*Perovskite*

**Crystal system**: Orthorhombic (pseudocubic)
**Crystal habit**: Box-shaped crystals, plus blades, grains and masses
**Colour**: Dark grey or brown to black. Occasionally with orange or yellow tinge.
**Lustre**: Submetallic to adamantine, greasy or waxy
**Streak**: White to grey
**Hardness**: 5.5
**Cleavage**: Imperfect
**Fracture**: Subconchoidal, uneven
**Specific gravity**: 4
**Notable locations**: Medelpad, Sweden; Zermatt, Switzerland; Lombardy, Italy; Eifel, Germany; Gardiner complex, Greenland; Zlatoust, Urals, Russia; São Paulo, Brazil; Riverside County, San Benito County, California; Bearpaw Mountains, Montana; Magnet Cove, Arkansas

## Spinel

*MgAl₂O₄ Magnesium aluminium oxide*

**Identification**: Spinel is usually identified by its twinned crystals or, failing that, its hardness in the Mohs test. It gets its name from the crystal's sharp points.

*Spinel crystal*

Spinels are a group of complex oxide minerals, including magnetite, franklinite and chromite, that have a similar structure. The best known is the gem spinel, which commonly forms in metamorphic rocks, especially marbles and calcium-rich gneisses, but can also form in pegmatites and as phenocrysts (spots) in lava. Gem spinel comes in many colours, such as green gahnite and black galaxite, but it is typically red and rivals the colour of ruby. In fact, many gems thought to be rubies have proved to be spinels. The most famous example is the great Black Prince's Ruby, set in the British imperial state crown. Spinel and ruby are chemically quite similar – the former is essentially magnesium aluminium oxide while ruby is aluminium oxide – and both get their red colour from chromium. Spinel typically forms in eight-sided crystals, but it often forms twins in a way no other mineral does, with two mirror-image planes.

**Crystal system**: Isometric
**Crystal habit**: Typically octahedral, but can be found as dodecahedrons (12 sides) and other isometric forms. Also found as rounded grains in river deposits.
**Colour**: Typically red, but also green, blue, purple, brown or black
**Lustre**: Vitreous
**Streak**: White
**Hardness**: 7.5–8
**Cleavage**: None
**Fracture**: Conchoidal to uneven
**Specific gravity**: 3.6–4
**Notable locations**: Sweden; Italy; Madagascar; Turkey; Myanmar (Burma); Sri Lanka; Afghanistan; Pakistan; Lake Baikal, Russia; Brazil; Amity, New York; Franklin mine, New Jersey; Galax, North Carolina

# Franklinite

*(Zn,Fe,Mn)(Fe,Mn)₂O₄ Zinc iron manganese oxide*

Franklinite is a mineral of the spinel group rather similar to magnetite, one of the chief ores of iron. Like magnetite it is magnetic, but franklinite's magnetism is quite weak, and this weak magnetism is a simple way of telling these two similar-looking minerals apart. Franklinite gets its name from the famous Franklin mine in New Jersey, USA, where it was discovered in 1819. It has since been found in neighbouring mines such as the Sterling mine in Ogdensburg, but nowhere else in the world in any quantity. At Sterling and Franklin, it is abundant, commonly occurring in either thick pure beds or mixed in with zinc minerals (zincite and willemite) in crystalline limestone when it is mined as an ore of zinc (with a 5 to 20 per cent zinc content). After the zinc is extracted, the residue is used to make *spiegeleisen*, or 'mirror iron', a manganese-iron alloy important in steelmaking.

**Identification**: The best indicator of franklinite is where it is found, at Franklin, New Jersey, but its dark colour and weak magnetism help to confirm the identity.

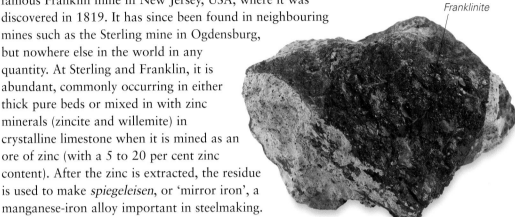

*Franklinite*

**Crystal system**: Isometric
**Crystal habit**: Typically large octahedral crystals with rounded edges, but it has been found with 12 and even 16 sides. It is more commonly found as grains and masses.
**Colour**: Black
**Lustre**: Metallic, submetallic
**Streak**: Brownish black to reddish brown
**Hardness**: 5.5–6.5
**Cleavage**: None
**Fracture**: Conchoidal to uneven
**Specific gravity**: 5–5.2
**Other characteristics**: Slightly magnetic
**Notable locations**: Found only in the Franklin and Sterling Hill mines, Sussex County, New Jersey

## The jewel mine

No other single place in the world can boast such an extraordinary array of rare and fascinating minerals as the famous Franklin and Sterling Hill mines in Sussex County, New Jersey. Over 300 different minerals have been found there, including 60 new ones. Manganese and zinc are the key metals but they were transformed a billion years ago by the cataclysmic tectonic events that threw up the Appalachian Mountains and later by hydrothermal action, creating an astonishing range of minerals. Rare manganese and zinc oxides such as franklinite, and silicates such as willemite, are characteristic of the area. Franklin is especially renowned for its fluorescent minerals such as willmenite, esporite, clinohedrite and hardystonite, which turn the mines into magic caves when lit by ultraviolet light. Visitors to the mine are given a dirt bucket and encouraged to pan for gems, particularly rubies, rhodolites, sapphires and garnets. They get to keep any they find. The mines were first opened in the 18th century, and reached their zenith in the late 19th century. They were mined partly for franklinite, which is an iron ore, but especially for zinc, and played a key part in America's Industrial Revolution. Bright red zincite was often found in large masses and lenses in black franklinite. One spectacular 8-tonne mass found in the 1840s was almost pure zincite, which is 80 per cent zinc metal. This great lump of ore was shipped at great expense to the Great Exhibition in London's Crystal Palace in 1852, where it attracted a great deal of attention and won a prize.The Franklin mine finally closed in 1954 and the Sterling Hill mine in 1986.

# Chrysoberyl

*BeAl₂O₄ Beryllium aluminium oxide*

Chrysoberyl is an extremely hard gemstone typically found in pegmatite dikes, mica schists and where granites meet mica schists, and in river gravels. It looks a little like gem beryl and its name is derived from the Greek *chrysos* meaning 'gold' – that is golden beryl. There are three varieties of chrysoberyl: the less popular greenish clear chrysoberyl, cymophane and the highly sought-after alexandrite. Yellow-green or brown cymophane is the most distinctive of all gems displaying chatoyancy, the cat's eye effect created by inclusions of other minerals. Alexandrite was named in honour of the Russian Tsar Alexander II. It is coloured green under natural light as a result of traces of chromium, but, uniquely, it changes in colour in different lighting conditions, surprisingly changing to crimson in artificial light.

**Crystal system**: Orthorhombic
**Crystal habit**: Often elongated prisms and tablets, or twinned either in v-shapes or more complex forms
**Colour**: Yellow, green or brown. Alexandrite becomes violet-red in artificial light.
**Lustre**: Vitreous
**Streak**: White
**Hardness**: 8.5
**Cleavage**: Fair in one direction, poor in another
**Fracture**: Uneven to conchoidal
**Specific gravity**: 3.7+
**Other characteristics**: Pleochroic (displaying colours from different viewing angles)
**Notable locations**: Urals, Russia (largely worked out); Sri Lanka; Myanmar (Burma); Tanzania; Brazil; Colorado; Connecticut

*Chrysoberyl*

**Identification:** Chrysoberyl can often be identified by its golden colour, its hardness (only slightly less than corundum) and its elaborate crystal twins (not shown in this specimen).

# SALTS

*Halides are minerals that form when a metal combines with one of the five elements called halogens –
fluorine, chlorine, bromine, iodine. (There is another halogen, astatine, but this is never found naturally.)
The best known by far is halite or rock salt. Like rock salt, all the halides, including sylvite,
chlorargyrite, and mendipite, are salts. Salts dissolve easily in water, which is why many halides occur
only in special conditions. However, rock salt is so abundant it is found in huge deposits the world over.*

## Halite

*NaCl Sodium chloride*

Halite is common salt or rock salt and is the source of the salt
we use on our tables. It is forming all the time as water
evaporates from salty lakes. Most salt is mined from thick
underground beds left behind long ago when ancient oceans
evaporated. When halite crystallizes, it usually forms cube-
shaped crystals, but it dissolves so easily in water that large
crystals are rare. Where they do occur, they can be white,
orange and pink. Some colour changes are created by
bacteria and some are created by exposure to natural
radiation. Gamma rays, for instance, turn halite
first amber, then deep blue. The blue colour
comes from specks of sodium metal, created
when radiation knocks electrons towards
sodium ions. When halite does form
crystals, it often takes unusual habits, such
as hopper crystals. Hopper crystals have a
dent in each face that makes them look like the
hoppers on a mine conveyor belt. The indentation
occurs because the edges of the crystal grow faster than the
centres of the faces.

**Identification**: Halite can be
identified by its salty taste,
but there is a risk of
poisoning if you make a
mistake, so it is better to
identify it by its softness and
the cube shape of its crystals.

**Crystal system:**
Isometric
**Crystal habit:**
Mainly cubes or
in massive
sedimentary beds,
but also grains
and fibres. Also forms
hopper crystals
**Colour**: Clear or white, but
can be orange, pink, purple,
yellow or blue
**Lustre**: Vitreous
**Streak**: White
**Hardness**: 2
**Cleavage**: Perfect in three
directions forming cubes
**Fracture**: Conchoidal
**Specific gravity**: 2.1+
**Other characteristics**:
Soluble in water
**Notable locations**: Stassfurt,
Germany; Salzburg, Austria;
Galicia, Poland; Mulhouse,
France; Uyuni, Bolivia;
Bogota, Colombia; Great Salt
Lake, Utah; Searles Lake,
California; Gulf of Mexico;
Retsof, New York

## Sylvite

*KCl Potassium chloride*

**Identification**: Sylvite forms pale
reddish white cubic crystals that
look like halite, but more often
have truncated corners.

Sylvite is chemically a chloride very similar to halite, and
like halite it formed in massive deposits on ancient sea
beds. But while halite is sodium chloride, sylvite is
potassium chloride. Sylvite's potassium
content has long made these ancient
sylvite beds a major source of 'potash'
for fertilizers. A quarter of the
world's sylvite is mined in
Saskatchewan in Canada. Sylvite
crystals do occur, but they are quite
rare. Although basically white, they
often have an attractive reddish tinge.
Sylvite and halite can be so similar that it
can be hard to tell them apart. The corners
of sylvite's cubes are truncated (cut off)
more often than with halite. With massive
beds, another way to tell them apart is to slice them with a
knife: halite powders but sylvite does not.

**Crystal system**:
Isometric
**Crystal habit**:
Cubes or
octahedral (or rather a cube
with flattened corners).
Commonly massive
and granular.
**Colour**: Colourless or white,
tinged red, blue or yellow
**Lustre**: Vitreous
**Streak**: White
**Hardness**: 2
**Cleavage**: Good in three
directions forming cubes
**Fracture**: Uneven
**Specific gravity**: 2
**Other characteristics**:
Crystal corners often cut off.
**Notable locations**: Mount
Vesuvius, Italy; Stassfurt,
Germany; Spain; Kalush,
Russia; Saskatchewan;
New Mexico; Texas; Kern
County, California

# Chlorargyrite

*AgCl Silver chloride*

Chlorargyrite, once called cerargyrite, is a silver mineral that forms when the surface of silver ores is exposed to the air and oxidized. Where there is plenty of chlorine present, such as in desert conditions, the silver in the ores combines to make chlorargyrite, which is silver chloride. Where there is more bromine around, the silver forms bromargyrite, silver bromide. In both cases, the effect is to concentrate the silver in a process called 'supergene enrichment', making the ore much more economically viable than it would otherwise be. As a result, chlorargyrite was once an important ore of silver in places like Mexico, Peru, Chile and Colorado, USA. These deposits have almost been completely worked out, and there are now very few unworked veins close enough to the surface to provide good specimens. Moreover, chlorargyrite rarely forms good crystals, so when they are found, they are much treasured.

**Identification**: Chlorargyrite can usually be identified by its tendency to turn dark when exposed to light and by the ease with which it can be sliced. It can form horn-like masses, which earned it its old name of horn silver.

*Chlorargyrite may appear as brown-grey masses*

**Crystal system**: Isometric
**Crystal habit**: Rare cubes; more commonly massive crusts or columns.
**Colour**: Colourless when pure on fresh surfaces; turns pearly grey, brown or violet-brown on exposure to light
**Lustre**: Resinous or adamantine
**Streak**: White
**Hardness**: 1.5–2.5
**Cleavage**: Poor
**Fracture**: Subconchoidal
**Specific gravity**: 5.5–5.6
**Other characteristics**: Crystals darken on exposure to light. Plastic and sectile.
**Notable locations**: Harz Mountains, Germany; New South Wales, Australia; Atacama, Chile; Peru; Mexico; Treasure Hill, Comstock Lode, Nevada; Colorado; San Bernardino County, California

---

**Underground salt city**
Salt has been a precious commodity for health and a preservative since the earliest times, and salt mines are among the oldest of all mines. The famous Wieliczka mine in southern Poland near Krakow has been worked since the 13th century and has over 200km/124 miles of underground passages, and 2,000 chambers hundreds of metres/yards below the ground in the thick salt beds. Over the centuries, miners have carved churches, altars, bas-reliefs, giant statues – even chandeliers (above) – out of the glistening white salt. Wieliczka is now a World Heritage site, and one of the most popular tourist destinations in southern Poland. Yet salt is very soluble, and even the water vapour in the ventilation air is enough to dissolve the salt. So the amazing features are slowly being lost.

# Mendipite

*Pb₃Cl₂O₂ Lead chlorate*

Discovered in 1839 in the Mendip Hills in south-west England, mendipite combines lead with chlorine and oxygen. It is a rare white, grey or pinkish white mineral that forms around volcanic vents and in hydrothermals. It is commonly found in association with calcite, cerussite, malachite, manganite, pyrolusite and pyromorphite, and masses of white mendipite are often found scattered in black masses of manganese oxide minerals miners call 'wad'. Deposits of mendipite are usually fibrous or column-like masses, often with radiating needles. Mendipite is both soft and dense.

*Wad*

**Crystal system**: Orthorhombic
**Crystal habit**: Typically fibrous masses, in columns, or radiating like a star
**Colour**: Bronze
**Lustre**: Adamantine, pearly
**Streak**: White
**Hardness**: 2.5–3
**Cleavage**: Distinct in two directions
**Fracture**: Uneven fracture giving small, conchoidal fragments
**Specific gravity**: 7–7.2
**Notable locations**: Mendip Hills (Somerset), England; Värmland, Sweden; Lavrion, Greece; Ruhr, Sauerland, Germany; Hampshire County, Massachusetts; Chester County, Pennsylvania

*Pink mendipite mass*

**Identification**: Mendipite can be identified by its pinkish white fibrelike crystals, typically set in manganese oxide. Separate masses are both soft and very heavy.

# HYDROXIDES AND FLUORIDES

*Among the other halides or salts are minerals that contain the halogen element fluorine. These fluorides, many of which were found originally in Greenland, include cryolite and jarlite. Other halides include hydroxides that are made with a halogen element such as chlorine. These include atacamite and boleite, both of which are often strikingly coloured.*

## Cryolite

*$Na_3AlF_6$ Sodium aluminium fluoride*

Cryolite was discovered by Danish geologists in Greenland in 1794, but was long known to the Eskimos, who saw it as a kind of ice because it melts so easily, even in a candle-flame. It was this ice-like quality that earned its name, from the Greek for ice and stone. It is called *Eisstein* (ice-stone) in Germany. It usually occurs in colourless or snow-white masses, often tinged brown or red by iron oxide, and occasionally black. It is normally translucent with a waxy lustre, but becomes virtually transparent when immersed in water. Cryolite is found in pegmatite veins at Ivigtut in south-west Greenland (now exhausted) and only a few other places, but it is vital to the aluminium industry. It is used as a flux when melting the aluminium in bauxite to lower the melting temperature and help draw out impurities. It is also used to make soda, and in the manufacture of very tough glass and enamelled ware. Much cryolite is now made artificially.

**Identification**: Cryolite can often be identified by its pseudocubic crystals.

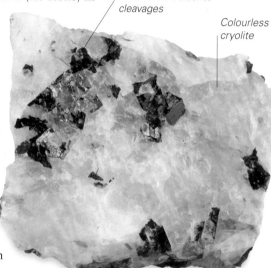

*Small brown siderite cleavages*

*Colourless cryolite*

**Crystal system**: Monoclinic
**Crystal habit**: Usually massive and, rarely, as pseudocubic crystals with deep striations.
**Colour**: Clear or white with red or brown tinges, but can also be black or purple
**Lustre**: Waxy
**Streak**: White
**Hardness**: 2.5–3
**Cleavage**: Good, can break as if into cubes
**Fracture**: Uneven
**Specific gravity**: 2.95
**Other characteristics**: Melts very easily. Normally translucent or transparent. It seems to vanish in water because its refractive index is so close to that of water.
**Notable locations**: Ivigtut, Greenland; Spain; Miyask (Ilmen Mountains), Russia; Mont Saint-Hilaire, Francon Quarry (Montreal) Quebec; Yellowstone, Wyoming; Pikes Peak, Colorado

## Atacamite

*$Cu_2Cl(OH)_3$ Copper chloride hydroxide*

*Atacamite*

*Blue chrysocolla*

**Identification**: Atacamite is typically a distinctive dark green colour that forms thin needle-like crystals or as a coating on other minerals. It forms only in very dry places.

Atacamite is a bright green copper chloride mineral. It gets its name from the Atacama Desert in Chile, where some of the best specimens are found. The Atacama is one of the world's driest places, receiving on average less than 1cm/½in of rain in a year. Atacamite forms only in very dry places where copper sulphide minerals are exposed to the air. Typically, atacamite forms when these copper minerals are oxidized in very arid conditions. It is commonly associated with malachite, cuprite, limonite and azurite, as well as rarer minerals such as chrysocolla, connellite, pseudomalachite, libethenite, cornetite and brochantite. Atacamite has an unusual property in that it absorbs water very rapidly, and in the days before blotting paper was invented, atacamite was often used for drying ink blots.

**Crystal system**: Orthorhombic
**Crystal habit**: Includes slender needles, prisms or tablets and also fibres
**Colour**: Dark green or emerald green
**Lustre**: Vitreous
**Streak**: Light green
**Hardness**: 3–3.5
**Cleavage**: Perfect in one direction
**Fracture**: Conchoidal, brittle
**Specific gravity**: 3.75+
**Other characteristics**: Crystals often have striations
**Notable locations**: Atacama, Chile; Mount Vesuvius, Italy; Wallaroo, South Australia; El Boleo (Baja California), Mexico; Pinal County, Arizona; Tintic, Utah; Majuba Hill Mine, Nevada

## Jarlite

*Na(Sr,Ca)₃Al₃F₁₆ Sodium aluminium fluoride*

A glassy-looking mineral, jarlite is named after Carl Frederik Jarl (1872–1951), once President of the Danish Cryolite Company, who discovered the mineral. It is one of a number of fluoride minerals found at Ivigtut in Greenland besides cryolite, and it typically forms in vugs (pockets) in cryolite deposits along with other fluorides. Jarlite usually occurs in masses, but can also occur as simple, very small monoclinic crystals, typically no bigger than 1mm/¹⁄₂₄in long or so. Sometimes the crystals form in almost flat plates or sheaves. They can also form radiating layers inside druses, where they are intermixed with white barite, brick-red iron stain and, occasionally, the white powdery mineral gearksutite. Jarlite is typically white or pinkish white. A variety of the mineral called metajarlite is more greyish.

**Identification**: Jarlite is perhaps best identified by its glassy lustre and when it forms sheaves of platy white crystals.

**Crystal system**: Monoclinic
**Crystal habit**: Jarlite typically forms flat plate- or sheaflike crystals. It is often also found as round aggregates or in masses.
**Colour**: White to greyish white to pinkish white
**Lustre**: Vitreous or waxy
**Streak**: White
**Hardness**: 4–4.5
**Cleavage**: Poor
**Fracture**: Uneven, with flat surface breaking in an uneven way
**Specific gravity**: 3.87
**Other characteristics**: Forms in cavities in cryolite pegmatite
**Notable locations**: Ivigtut (Arsuk Fjord), Kitaa, Greenland

**Minerals from the frozen north**
The ancient rocks of Greenland have yielded a remarkable number of rare minerals. Although the most famous mines here are now all but exhausted, they have produced some fabulous specimens in the past and many collections contain some beauties from Greenland. The best known of Greenland's mineral sites is Ivigtut on the Arsuk Fjord in Kitaa in south-west Greenland. Hundreds of different minerals have been found here, including rare sulphides and sulphosalts such as eskimoite, matildite, vikingite and gudmundite. Ivigtut is particularly renowned for its halide minerals, found in pegmatites. The area was mined from 1854 until 1987 for its cryolite, which was used as a flux in aluminium smelting. Other halides from Ivigtut include acuminite, böggildite, bøgvadite, cryolithionite, gearksutite, jarlite, pachnolite, prosopite, ralstonite, stenonite and thomsenolite. For each of these, it is the type locality (the source in which the mineral was originally found).

## Boleite

*KPb₂₆Ag₉Cu₂₄Cl₆₂(OH)₄₈ Hydrated lead copper silver chloride hydroxide*

Named after the place it was first discovered – Boleo in Baja California, Mexico – boleite is a rare halide mineral that has a very complex chemistry. Each molecule contains multiple atoms of lead, copper, silver and chlorine as well as numerous hydroxide groups and three molecules of water. Boleite is a very minor ore of copper, silver and lead, but it is valued by collectors because of its distinctive indigo-blue coloured crystals, which are sometimes cut to make gemstones. Boleite crystals are unusual because they look like cubes, but are actually always twinned rectangular crystals that pair in such a way that they look like cubes. Crystals like these are called pseudocubes.

*Boleite*

**Crystal system**: Tetragonal
**Crystal habit**: Rectangular crystals typically form pseudocubes
**Colour**: Indigo blue to deep navy blue
**Lustre**: Vitreous, pearly
**Streak**: Greenish blue
**Hardness**: 3–3.5
**Cleavage**: Perfect in one direction
**Fracture**: Uneven and brittle
**Specific gravity**: 5
**Other characteristics**: Notches or interpenetrating angles can be seen in some specimens, revealing their true twinned nature
**Notable locations**: Broken Hill (New South Wales), Australia; El Boleo (Baja California), Mexico; Mammoth District, Arizona

**Identification**: Boleite is easily identified by its dark indigo-blue cube-shaped crystals.

# FLUORITE

*Fluorite displays a wider range of colours than any other single mineral – varying from the typical purple through to blue, green, yellow, orange, pink, brown and black, with all kinds of pastel shades in between. Yet remarkably, pure fluorite is actually colourless. All fluorite's rainbow of colours comes from traces of impurities of various metals taking the place of calcium in the molecule.*

## Fluorite

*CaF₂ Calcium fluoride*

**Green fluorite (below)**: Green is one of the major fluorite colours. It comes in many hues of green, but they all tend to be an acid or mint green, rather than grass green.

**Purple fluorite (below)**: The mauve cubic crystals displayed here are characteristic of the English fluorite mined in the North Pennines, but purple fluorites are found in many other locations, such as, historically, at Regensburg in Germany, and now in China. Purple fluorites tend to be more fluorescent than the green varieties.

*Fluorite*

*Brown sphalerite masses*

Fluorite is chemically calcium fluoride, a compound of the elements calcium and fluorine. But even though it contains fluorine, its name does not come from its chemical composition. Instead, it was originally named fluorspar by the famous German mineralogist Georg Agricola in 1546. Agricola named it from the Latin word *fluere*, which means 'to flow', because fluorite melts easily. A spar is the name given by mineralogists to any clear or pale crystal that breaks easily. It is this meltability that has made fluorite valued since Roman times in making steel, glass and enamel as a flux – a substance that lowers the melting point of a material and makes it easier to work. Most industrially extracted fluorite, however, goes to making hydrofluoric acid – the basis for all substances containing fluorine (including for dental care).

Fluorite is usually fairly pure, but can have up to a fifth of the calcium replaced with rare-earth metals such as yttrium and cerium. Yttrium-rich fluorite is called yttrofluorite; yttrium- and cerium-rich fluorite is called yttrocerian fluorite. Fluorite is found in many different environments. In southern Illinois, for instance, it is found in thick veins in limestone beds, where it formed at low temperatures and developed into simple, but many-hued, crystals. In other places it is found around hot-springs, in cavities and pegmatites. But by far the most typical fluorite-forming environment is metal-rich veins – especially those with lead or silver. Here the higher temperatures encourage fluorite to crystallize in a whole variety of different forms, varying from octahedral to dodecahedral.

**Cubic crystals (above)**: The barely yellowish tinge of this fluorite specimen indicates that it is relatively pure. In fact, clear fluorite can be so good optically that it is sometimes used for microscope lenses because it eliminates colour distortion.

**Crystal system**: Isometric
**Crystal habit**: Typically forms cubes or octahedrons, or both together. Twins are common, and penetration twins often look like two cubes grown together.
**Colour**: Varies hugely, the widest colour range of any mineral. Colours include intense purple, blue, green, or yellow, reddish orange, pink, white and brown. A single crystal can be multicoloured. Pure, unflawed fluorite crystals are colourless.
**Lustre**: Vitreous
**Streak**: White
**Hardness**: 4
**Cleavage**: Perfect in four directions forming octahedrons
**Fracture**: Flat conchoidal
**Specific gravity**: 3–3.3
**Other characteristics**: Fluorite is translucent or transparent. It is typically fluorescent blue or, more rarely, green, white, red or violet. Fluorite is also thermoluminescent, phosphorescent and triboluminescent.
**Notable locations**: Alston Moor (Cumbria), Weardale (Durham), Castleton (Derbyshire), Cornwall, England; Harz Mountains, Wölsendorf (Bavaria), Germany; Tuscany, Italy; Göschenen, Switzerland; Nerchinsk (Urals), Russia; Maharashtra, India; Hunan, China; Naica, Chihuahua, Mexico; Hastings County, Ontario; Elmwood, Tennessee; Rosiclare and Cave-in-Rock (Hardin County), Illinois; Ottawa County, Ohio; Grant County, New Mexico

## Hardness and colour

Although beautifully coloured, fluorite is only rarely used as a gemstone because it is quite soft and fragile. Some collectors regard it as a worthwhile challenge to cut and polish it. Yet fluorite is so consistent in its relative hardness that Friedrich Mohs used it as the standard number 4 on his hardness scale.

Fluorite gets its extraordinary range of colours because of something called a 'colour centre'. A colour centre is a small region in the crystals where there is a slight defect in the network of atoms. These crystal defects interrupt light in a particular way, absorbing and reflecting only particular wavelengths of light. So fluorite's colour varies according to the pattern of its colour centres. Heat and radiation can both induce the defects that create colour centres – so heat and radiation can change fluorite's colour. The rare earths like yttrium that are found in many fluorites may also influence fluorite's colour – especially under ultraviolet light.

**Octohedral crystals (above):** This green fluorite displays slightly frosted octahedral crystals. These fluorites are less common than those with cubic crystals.

**Botryoidal fluorite (above):** Sometimes fluorite grows in extraordinary lemon-yellow botryoidal (grapelike) balls like this fluorite ball in a cavity from India.

## The best fluorites

The most highly prized fluorites are perhaps the pink to red octahedral fluorites from alpine clefts in the Swiss and French Alps. Here they are often found with smoky quartz, and form from mineral-rich solutions circulating through the rock as it is metamorphosed. Some of the crystals found here are over 10cm/4in long.

The most famous locations for fluorite crystals, however, are in Germany and England. In Germany, small but beautiful fluorite crystals ranging from green to yellow are found in metal-rich veins. In England, the classic locations were the lead and iron mines in Cumbria and the tin mines in Cornwall. The majority of the highest quality English fluorites are purple, and they are among the best at displaying fluorescence. These sources are now largely exhausted. In the USA, the best Illinois fluorites have also been fully exploited, and America's most highly prized fluorites now originate from deposits found in Elmwood, Tennessee.

**Fluorite geode (above):** The best fluoride crystals often grow on the inside of geodes, and are revealed only when the geode is cracked open.

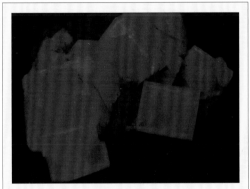

### Fluorite's special glows

Fluorite is not only unique in the range of colours it displays under normal lighting – it also glows in the dark in various different ways. When some minerals are exposed to ultraviolet light, they glow purple, blue or green – no matter what colour they are in normal daylight. This glow is called fluorescence, after fluorite, because it glows like this more readily than any other mineral. Fluorite usually fluoresces blue or green, though it can also glow white, red or violet. Minerals often fluoresce because of tiny impurities they contain. Fluorite is thought to fluoresce because of the traces of uranium and rare-earth metals it contains. Calcite fluoresces bright red when it contains traces of manganese. Fluorite also glows when gently heated – a property called thermoluminescence. And when some fluorites are taken out of direct sunlight and placed in a dark room, they glow – a quality called phosphorescence. Fluorite may even glow when crushed, scratched or rubbed – a quality called triboluminescence – as the pressure distorts colour centres.

**Blue John (left):** Most fluorites are a single colour, but a few have colour bands in line with the mineral's crystals. One of the best known banded fluorites is Blue John, found only in the Peak District, Derbyshire, England. Blue John gets its name from the French description of the rock, Bleu Jaune, which means 'blue yellow'. It was discovered in the 18th century when miners were exploring caves to look for sources of lead.

# CARBONATES

*Carbonates are typically light-coloured, often transparent, soft, brittle minerals that tend to dissolve in acids. They form when metals or semi-metals join with a carbonate – a combination of a carbon atom with three oxygen atoms. Some carbonates are brought to the surface from deep in the Earth by hot fluids. Many more form by the alteration of other minerals on the surface, as they are attacked by the mild acidity of the air. There are 80 kinds, including the aragonites and related minerals.*

## Aragonite

*CaCO₃ Calcium carbonate*

Aragonite is a common white mineral discovered in Aragon, Spain. Many sea creatures secrete it naturally to make their shells. Geologically, it crystallizes from low-temperature solutions in many sediments, metamorphic rocks such as schist and basic igneous rocks such as serpentinite. It is usually the last mineral to form in veins. It is also a product of the weathering of siderite and ultrabasic and magnesium-rich rocks.

Groups of tapering crystals tinged red by hematite inclusions.

Crystals of aragonite also form around hot springs, or in caves, where they may create stalactites and grow in coral-like shapes called 'flos ferri' (flowers of iron). Aragonite is a polymorph of calcite – chemically identical, but with a different crystal structure. Calcite crystals are trigonal, but those of aragonite are orthorhombic. Some calcite and aragonite crystals are too small to see, requiring complex scientific tests to tell them apart. Aragonite changes to calcite if heated above 400°C/725°F.

**Identification**: Aragonite and calcite both fizz in dilute acid. It can be hard to tell their crystal system apart, but each has different crystal habits. This crystal is a triplet of prismatic twins that join to make it look hexagonal. It is said to be pseudohexagonal.

**Crystal system**: Orthorhombic
**Crystal habit**: Prismatic with wedge-shaped ends. Often forms triplets of twins that look hexagonal.
**Colour**: White or colourless. Tinges of red, yellow, orange, brown, green or blue.
**Lustre**: Vitreous to dull
**Streak**: White
**Hardness**: 3.5–4
**Cleavage**: Distinct one way
**Fracture**: Subconchoidal
**Specific gravity**: 2.9–3
**Other characteristics**: Fizzes in cold dilute hydrochloric acid. It is also fluorescent.
**Notable locations**: West Cumbria, England; Aragon, Spain; Mount Vesuvius, Italy; Agrigento, Sicily; Styria, Austria; France; Honshu, Japan; Tazoula, Morocco; Tsumeb, Namibia; Australia; Baja California, Mexico (Mexican onyx); Bisbee (Cochise Co), Arizona; Socorro County, New Mexico; White Pine County, Nevada

## Witherite

*BaCO₃ Barium carbonate*

**Identification**: Witherite is best identified by its triplets of twinned crystals and by its reaction to dilute acid.

Witherite was named after Dr Withering (1741–1799), the Birmingham physician who discovered it in 1784 at Alston Moor in Cumbria, England. It occurs here in low-temperature hydrothermal veins of lead ore or galena, and this is typical. It also forms in masses, deposited in limestone and other calcium-rich sediments. Unusually, witherite crystals are always twinned in groups of three, giving a double-pyramid shape. Although quite rare, witherite is the second most common barium mineral after barite. Because it dissolves easily in sulphuric acid, it is preferred to barite for some manufacturing uses such as making rat poison, in glass, porcelain and steelmaking, and, in the past, for the refining of sugar.

**Crystal system**: Orthorhombic
**Crystal habit**: Triple twins form double-pyramid twin. Also occurs in botryoidal, massive and fibrous forms.
**Colour**: White, colourless, grey, yellowish or greenish
**Lustre**: Vitreous to dull
**Streak**: White
**Hardness**: 3–3.5
**Cleavage**: Distinct one way
**Fracture**: Uneven
**Specific gravity**: 4.3+
**Notable locations**: Alston Moor (Cumbria), Hexham (Northumberland), England; Tsumeb, Namibia; Thunder Bay, Ontario; Rosiclare (Hardin Co), Illinois
**Caution**: Witherite is mildly toxic. Wash hands after use

# Strontianite

*SrCO₃ Strontium carbonate*

Strontianite gets its name from the location of its first discovery, Strontian in Argyll and Bute, Scotland, where it was found in ores mined from the local lead mines in 1764. In 1790, Andrew Crawford separated the substance called strontium from the mineral, and in 1808 Sir Humphrey Davy showed that strontium is an element. Strontianite is almost the only mineral containing strontium; celestite is the only other significant source, which is used for the red in fireworks and signal flares, for refining sugar and as a painkiller. Strontianite typically occurs not as developed crystals but in masses of radiating fibres or tufts, although it can occasionally form twins rather like those of aragonite. These are usually white, but can be pale green, yellow or grey. The crystals are soft and brittle, and are commonly associated with galena and barite in low-temperature hydrothermal veins, or cavities in limestones.

**Identification**: Strontianite is best identified by its radiating needle-like crystals, and its reaction to acid when powdered.

*Barite*

*Strontianite*

**Crystal system**: Orthorhombic
**Crystal habit**: Typically forms in radiating needle-like clusters and tufts, or in concretions. Occasionally forms triplets of twinned crystals like aragonite.
**Colour**: White, colourless, grey, yellowish or greenish
**Lustre**: Vitreous to greasy
**Streak**: White
**Hardness**: 3.5–4
**Cleavage**: Good in one way
**Fracture**: Uneven, brittle
**Specific gravity**: 3.8
**Other characteristics**: Fizzes in warm dilute acid or, when powdered, in cold dilute acid
**Notable locations**: Strontian, Scotland; Yorkshire, England; Drensteinfurt, Black Forest, Harz Mountains, Germany; Styria, Austria; Mifflin Co, Pennsylvania; San Bernadino Co, California; Schoharie, NY

**Mother of pearl**
Aragonite is the main mineral in nacre, or 'mother-of-pearl' – the beautiful, iridescent substance that lines the shells of many shellfish. Many molluscs make mother-of-pearl but the main commercial sources are oyster-like species. In mother-of-pearl, aragonite is chemically mixed and bonded with water and an organic horn substance, known as conchiolin. Conchiolin binds the microcrystals of aragonite together to form the mother-of-pearl. The result is sometimes harder than inorganic aragonite and sometimes softer, depending on the ratio of the mixed chemicals. It can vary in colour depending on the species of mollusc and the character of the water. Colours range from soft white to pink, silver, cream, gold, green, blue or black. It always has the same pearly lustre and iridescent play of colours, which is caused by a film of conchiolin and the way overlapping platelets of aragonite interfere with light.

# Cerussite

*PbCO₃ Lead carbonate*

The name cerussite comes from *cerussa*, the Latin for 'white lead', and cerussite is often called white lead ore. It was once used in white pigments. Queen Elizabeth I of England painted her face with a paste made from cerussite, in keeping with the fashion of the time for pale faces. Unfortunately, it was so poisonous it scarred her face and, without knowing the danger, she put more cerussite on her face to cover the damage. The lead content of cerussite means that in clear form (it is often white) it sparkles like lead crystal glass, and has one of the highest densities of any clear mineral crystal. Like other aragonite group minerals, cerussite forms twins, but those of cerussite are especially spectacular, including spoked star and snowflake shapes, and elbow or chevron-shapes. Cerussite is typically found where lead deposits are exposed to the air, and often forms crusts around galena (lead ore).

**Crystal system**: Orthorhombic
**Crystal habit**: Typically forms needles, plates and spikes. Star-shaped and chevron-shaped twins are very distinctive. Also forms crusts on galena.
**Colour**: Usually colourless or white, also grey, yellow and even blue-green
**Lustre**: Adamantine to greasy
**Streak**: White or colourless
**Hardness**: 3–3.5
**Cleavage**: Good in one direction
**Fracture**: Conchoidal, brittle
**Specific gravity**: 6.5+
**Other characteristics**: Very sparkly when clear
**Notable locations**: Ems, Germany; Montevecchio, Sardinia; Murcia, Spain; Touissit, Morocco; Tsumeb, Namibia; Broken Hill (New South Wales), Dundas (Tasmania), Australia; Oruro, Bolivia; Socorro, New Mexico; Arizona

**Identification**: Cerussite is usually striking for the weight, sparkle and twinning of its crystals. But it can often form white masses of needles as shown here.

# CALCITE GROUP AND DOLOMITE

*The calcite group is an important group of minerals that typically form in large masses, or in pearly, hexagonal crystals. They are formed when a carbonate compound (carbon and oxygen) combines with certain metals, such as calcium, cobalt, iron, magnesium, zinc, cadmium, manganese and nickel. The calcite group includes magnesite, rhodochrosite, siderite and smithsonite, as well as calcite itself.*

## Calcite

*$CaCO_3$ Calcium carbonate*

Calcite is one of the world's most common minerals. It is the main component of limestone, marble, tufa, travertine, chalk and oolites. It may also be mixed in with clay to form marl. Calcite is also the fur deposited in kettles and boiler scale in hard-water districts, and the material from which bones and fossil shells are made. When dissolved in water, it can be deposited in crevices as grains and fibres, or precipitated from drips in limestone caves as stalagmites, stalactites and other speleothems (see Cave Formations, right). Most calcite forms in masses and aggregates, but good crystals do form in hydrothermal veins, alpine fissures, and pockets in basalt and other rocks. There are over 300 kinds of calcite crystal, including Iceland spar, dogtooth spar and nailhead spar. Nailhead spar is a form of calcite beautifully described by its name. The flat-topped crystals look just like the heads of nails. Calcite is trimorphic (same chemistry, different crystal structures) with aragonite and the rare mineral vaterite, often formed by microbes.

**Identification**: Dogtooth spar calcite is very easy to recognize. Each crystal is as big and pointed as a canine tooth. Crystals like this form in clusters in standing pools in limestone caves. The crystal shape is called a scalenohedron, because the sides are scalene triangles – triangles in which each side is a different length.

**Crystal system**: Trigonal
**Crystal habit**: Most calcite is found in masses, but crystals are found in a huge variety of forms, more than any other mineral
**Colour**: Usually white or colourless
**Lustre**: Vitreous to resinous to dull
**Streak**: White
**Hardness**: 3
**Cleavage**: Perfect in three directions
**Fracture**: Subconchoidal, brittle
**Specific gravity**: 2.7
**Other characteristics**: May be phosphorescent, thermoluminescent and triboluminescent
**Notable locations**: Cumbria, Durham, England; Eskifjord, Iceland (Iceland spar or optical calcite); Harz Mountains, Germany; Bombay, India; Tristate, Kansas-Missouri-Oklahoma; Keeweenaw, Michigan; Franklin, New Jersey

## Magnesite

*$MgCO_3$ Magnesium carbonate*

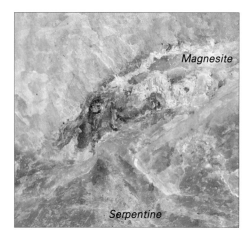

**Identification**: When a whitish porcelain-like mass appears in dolomite or magnesian limestone, it is likely to be magnesite.

Magnesite is thought to have got its name from the region of Magnesia in Turkey. It is the main ore of the metal magnesium, and is also used in making rubber and fertilizers. It typically forms when hot water alters limestone and dolomite rocks rich in magnesium minerals, such as serpentine. When this happens, solid white veins of magnesite are often created in the rock. It can also form when magnesium-rich solutions alter calcite. Magnesite rarely forms crystals, and the magnesite used industrially comes from very fine-grained massive deposits that look a little like porcelain and stick to the tongue when licked because they contain tiny holes. Crystals of magnesite can be hard to tell from calcite or dolomite.

**Crystal system**: Trigonal
**Crystal habit**: Typically fine-grained, porcelain-like masses. Crystals are rare but typically rhombohedral or hexagonal.
**Colour**: White, grey, yellowish brown
**Lustre**: Vitreous
**Streak**: White
**Hardness**: 3.5–4
**Cleavage**: Perfect in three directions forming rhombs
**Fracture**: Conchoidal, brittle
**Specific gravity**: 3
**Other characteristics**: Unlike calcite, does not fizz in cold hydrochloric acid
**Notable locations**: Styria, Austria; Bahia, Brazil; Korea; China; Coast Ranges, California; Staten Island, NY

# Rhodochrosite

*MnCO₃ Manganese carbonate*

Rhodochrosite is one of the most easily recognized minerals. It is nearly always rose pink, although when exposed to air it often develops a coating of dark black manganese dioxide. Indeed, the name comes from the Greek *rhodon* for 'rose' and *chroma* for 'colour'. It typically forms in hydrothermal veins along with sulphide ores of copper, lead and silver, and occasionally in pegmatites. Massive deposits of rhodochrosite provide one of the major ores of the metal manganese. But rhodochrosite commonly forms striking crystals in cavities in veins. The ancient Inca silver mines of Catamarca province in Argentina are famous for stalactites made from rhodochrosite. These pink 'icicles' can be sliced like cucumbers to reveal beautiful rings of rhodochrosite in different shades of pink. They form when manganese minerals (or calcite) are dissolved by groundwater, combine with a carbonate material and then drip off the cave ceiling and from crevices.

**Identification**: Rhodochrosite is instantly recognizable by its rose-pink colour. This is stalactite rhodochrosite sliced to reveal the bands.

**Crystal system**: Trigonal
**Crystal habit**: Can be massive, but crystals are typically rhombohedrons and scalenohedrons with rounded or curved faces. It also forms globules, fills veins and nodules or forms stalactites.
**Colour**: Rose pink
**Lustre**: Vitreous to resinous
**Streak**: White
**Hardness**: 3.5–4
**Cleavage**: Perfect in three directions
**Fracture**: Uneven
**Specific gravity**: 3.5
**Notable locations**: Cornwall, England; Harz Mountains, Germany; Trepca, Serbia; Romania; Russia; Gabon; Hotazel, South Africa; Japan; Catamarca, Argentina; Huaron, Peru; Mont Saint-Hilaire, Quebec; John Reed mine (Lake Co), Sweet Home Mine (Park Co), Colorado; Butte, Montana

**Cave formations**

Many caves in limestone are filled with spectacular rock formations called speleothems. They are created by the slow dripping or ponding of water rich in calcite dissolved from the limestone. The calcite comes out of the water and hardens in all kinds of shapes and forms, made mostly of calcite or aragonite. The best known speleothems are icicle-like stalactites that hang from the cave roof, and post-like stalagmites that grow up from the cave floor. But there are dozens of others, including draperies, which form like curtains from overhanging walls, cave pearls, which grow when calcite forms balls around a grain of sand, helictites (twisted stalactites), mushroom-shaped bell canopies, rimstones, which form around the rims of ponds, and soda straws (early stalactites that look just like drinking straws).

# Dolomite

*CaMg(CO₃)₂ Calcium magnesium carbonate*

Dolomite is named after French mineralogist Deodat de Dolomieu, who discovered it in 1791. Massive beds of the mineral dolomite several hundred feet thick are found around the world. These are called dolomitic limestone, or simply dolostone – and their existence is a bit of a mystery (see Sedimentary Rocks: Dolomite, in the Directory of Rocks). Dolomite crystals form in marbles and hydrothermal veins. They also form in small deposits where water rich in magnesium filters through limestone. The magnesium replaces about half the calcium in calcite or aragonite to form dolomite, a process called dolomitization. Dolomite looks similar to calcite, but does not fizz in cold, dilute acid solutions like calcite.

**Crystal system**: Trigonal
**Crystal habit**: Typically massive, but crystals can be prismatic or rhombohedral. It also forms distinctive saddle-shaped rhombohedral twins.
**Colour**: Colourless, white, pinkish, or light tints
**Lustre**: Vitreous to dull
**Streak**: White
**Hardness**: 3.5–4
**Cleavage**: Perfect in three directions
**Fracture**: Subconchoidal
**Specific gravity**: 2.8
**Notable locations**: Cumbria, England; Binnetal, Switzerland; Styria, Austria; Saxony, Germany; Pamplona, Spain; Trepca, Serbia; Piedmont, Trentino, Italy; Algeria; Namibia; Brazil; Lake Erie, Ontario; Tristate, Kansas-Missouri-Oklahoma

**Identification**: Dolomite typically forms pinkish or colourless rhombohedral crystals rather like calcite. The rhombs may have very slightly curved faces.

# HYDRATED AND COMPOUND CARBONATES

*Hydrated and compound carbonates never form directly in rocks; they are always secondary minerals that form when other minerals are altered. The brightly coloured compound carbonates malachite and azurite form when copper minerals are altered. Hydrated carbonates such as scarbroite and gaylussite form when other minerals are altered by water.*

## Scarbroite

*Al₆(CO₃)(OH)₁₃.5H₂O Hydrated aluminium carbonate hydroxide*

Scarbroite was discovered in 1829 by the English geologist Doctor James H Vernon. He found the mineral on the coast at Scarborough in England, and the mineral is named after the town. Scarbroite is an aluminium carbonate hydroxide mineral that has absorbed plenty of water. It forms in vertical fissures in sandstone, or as nodules. When scarbroite forms crystals, they are hexagonal, although they appear to be rhombohedral. More typically it forms very soft white, earthy masses, only a little harder than talc. In these, the crystals are visible only with a microscope. Scarbroite is also found in a platy sheet form a bit like micas, but this is rare.

**Identification**: Scarbroite is a white knobbly mineral found in clumps in sandstone. It looks a little like cotton wool and is very soft.

**Crystal system**: Triclinic
**Crystal habit**: Scarbroite can be either pseudorhombohedral or hexagonal but is typically found as microcrystalline masses
**Colour**: White
**Lustre**: Earthy
**Streak**: White
**Hardness**: 1–2
**Cleavage**: Poor
**Fracture**: Uneven
**Specific gravity**: 2
**Notable locations**: Scarborough (North Yorkshire), Chipping Sodbury (Gloucestershire), Weston Favell (Northampton); East Harptree (Somerset), England; Pilis Mountains (Pest Co), Hungary; Soria, Spain

## Malachite

*Cu₂(CO₃)(OH)₂ Copper carbonate hydroxide*

**Crystal system**: Monoclinic
**Crystal habit**: Its massive forms are botryoidal, stalactitic or globular. Crystals are typically tufts of needles.
**Colour**: Green
**Lustre**: Vitreous to dull in massive forms and silky as crystals
**Streak**: Pale green
**Hardness**: 3.5–4
**Cleavage**: Good in one direction but rarely seen
**Fracture**: Subconchoidal to uneven, brittle
**Specific gravity**: 4
**Notable locations**: Chessy, France; Sverdlovsk, Urals, Russia; Katanga, DR Congo; Morocco; Tsumeb, Namibia; Burra Burra, South Australia; Greenlee County, Pima County, Arizona

Unusually for a carbonate, malachite is bright green, and gets its name from the Greek for 'mallow leaf'. It is a secondary mineral of copper, which means it forms when copper minerals are altered. It forms, for instance, when carbonated water interacts with copper, or when a copper solution interacts with limestone. Malachite is the tarnish on copper and serves as a bright green signpost to the presence of copper ore deposits. It also forms tufts of needle-like crystals and various other masses. The classic malachite specimens are rounded masses with concentric bands of light and dark green, revealed when a specimen is polished or cut open. Because of its beauty and relative softness, polished, banded malachite has been carved into ornaments and worn as jewellery for thousands of years. Malachite is also popular as an ornamental stone, especially in Russia, where an enormous deposit of rounded malachite was found in the Ural Mountains long ago. This malachite was used to make the columns of St Isaac's Cathedral in St Petersburg.

**Identification**: Malachite's bright green colour is so distinctive it is easy to identify, even when just in velvety crusts like this specimen here. But when a specimen shows concentric internal banding, the identity is established beyond doubt.

# Azurite

*Cu₃(CO₃)₂(OH)₂ Copper carbonate hydroxide*

Azurite, like malachite, is formed by the weathering of other copper minerals. The copper gives its basic colour, but the presence of water in the crystal helps turn it bright blue rather than green. It was this brilliant blue that made it so popular with painters in the Renaissance as a pigment. It probably gets its name from *lazhward*, the ancient Persian word for 'blue', and in the past it was often confused with blue lapis lazuli and lazurite. Azurite is actually 55 per cent copper, and in Arizona and South Australia, large masses were once worked as copper ores. Like green malachite, bright blue stains of azure act as a colourful sign of the presence of copper. Malachite and azurite often occur together, but azurite is the rarer of the two since it is altered to malachite by weathering. Azurite typically forms velvety masses and rosettes of needle-like crystals, or tablet-like masses.

**Identification**: Azurite is immediately recognizable by its bright blue colour, its softness and associated minerals such as malachite.

Azurite coating

Minor malachite

Barite

**Crystal system**: Monoclinic
**Crystal habit**: Crystals are typically stubby prisms and tablets. These often have many faces, often over 45 and sometimes as many as 100. Also found as crusts, tufts and earthy masses.
**Colour**: Deep blue crystals; pale blue masses and crusts
**Lustre**: Vitreous to dull
**Streak**: Sky blue
**Hardness**: 3.5–4
**Cleavage**: Good in one direction
**Fracture**: Conchoidal, brittle
**Specific gravity**: 3.7+
**Notable locations**: Chessy, France; Touissit, Morocco; Tsumeb, Namibia; Katanga, Congo; Sinai, Egypt; Guangdong, China; Burra Burra (SA), Alice Springs (NT), Australia; Lasal, Utah; Bisbee (Cochise Co), Arizona; New Mexico

# Gaylussite

*Na₂Ca(CO₃)₂.5H₂O Hydrated sodium calcium carbonate*

**Ancient colours**

People learned long ago to make coloured pigments by grinding minerals into a paste. It may be that the world's oldest mine is Lion Cavern in Swaziland in southern Africa. Here, over 40,000 years ago, African bushmen mined for specularite, which they then powdered and rubbed on their heads to make them shimmer. By 20,000 years ago, cave painters were using four mineral pigments – red ochre from hematite, yellow ochre from limonite, black from pyrolusite and white china clay from kaolin. These four pigments were popular in many tribal civilizations, like those of the San people of South Africa (including the exquisite paintings above in the Drakensberg Mountains), first discovered by European settlers some 350 years ago. As the first civilizations arose, people learned to exploit other minerals to create a rich range of colours – realgar for red, orpiment for yellow, malachite for green, azurite for blue and precious lapis lazuli for ultramarine. The best pigments were highly coveted.

Gaylussite was first identified in soda deposits at Lagunillas, Venezuela, and is named after the famous 18th-century French chemist and physicist Joseph-Louis Gay-Lussac, who pioneered the study of gases and made many advances in applied chemistry. It is a carbonate mineral, made of hydrated sodium and calcium carbonate, and is one of several carbonate minerals that form as evaporites far away from the sea, typically in soda lakes. It is thought that gaylussite has been forming in California's famous Mono Lake since 1970, when the salinity rose above 80 per cent. Gaylussite looks very much like all the other inland evaporites minerals such as nahcolite, pirssonite, thermonatrite and trona, and often X-rays are the only way to tell them apart.

**Crystal system**: Monoclinic
**Crystal habit**: Includes intricately faceted prism- and tablet-shaped crystals, but also forms masses and crusts
**Colour**: Colourless or white
**Lustre**: Vitreous
**Streak**: White
**Hardness**: 2–3
**Cleavage**: Perfect in two directions
**Fracture**: Conchoidal
**Specific gravity**: 1.9–2
**Notable locations**: Tuscany, Italy; Kola Peninsular, Russia; Guateng, South Africa; Lake Chad, Central Africa; Gobi, Mongolia; Lagunillas (Merida), Venezuela; Deep Spring, Owens Lake, Searles Lake, Borax Lake, Mono Lake, China Lake, California; Soda Lake, Nevada

**Identification**: The best indicator of gaylussite is the environment where it formed – an inland soda lake, like the famous lakes of California.

# NITRATES AND BORATES

*Nitrates, iodates and borates are not actually carbonates, but are grouped with them because their chemical structure is very similar. All three groups form mostly in very dry places – nitrates and iodates such as nitratine are found in the deserts of Chile, and borates such as boracite, colemanite and ulexite in the Mojave Desert and Death Valley in the south-west USA.*

## Nitratine

*$NaNO_3$ Sodium nitrate*

Nitratine, or soda niter, is rare in most places because it is very soluble in water. In fact, nitratine is so easily dissolved that it can turn liquid simply by absorbing moisture from the air, a phenomenon called deliquescence. This is why specimens have to be kept in airtight containers containing a dessicant such as silica gel. Not surprisingly, nitratine forms mostly in desert regions. In the Atacama Desert of northern Chile, it forms under the soil in beds about 2–3m/6½–10ft thick called caliche. Caliche is a hard, cemented mix of nitrates, sulphates, halides and sand that builds up as water rich in dissolved minerals evaporates in the dry conditions. Nitratine also forms as growths on dry cave and mine walls. Nitratine was once an important source of nitrates for fertilizers and explosives, and a century ago, there were over 100 nitrate extraction plants in the Atacama Desert near Antofagasta in Chile. Nowadays, most nitrogen comes from the air.

**Identification**: Nitratine is best identified by its source location. It is found in very dry conditions, and is fairly soft. It also dissolves easily if there is any moisture in the air. A drop of water makes a small chunk seem to vanish.

**Crystal system**: Trigonal
**Crystal habit**: Typically in beds and soil deposits in deserts. Rare rhombohedral crystals are found.
**Colour**: White or grey
**Lustre**: Vitreous
**Streak**: White
**Hardness**: 1.5–2
**Cleavage**: Perfect in three directions forming rhombohedrons
**Fracture**: Conchoidal
**Specific gravity**: 2.2–2.3
**Other characteristics**: Deliquescent
**Notable locations**: Kola Peninsula, Russia; Antofagasta, Atacama, Tarapaca, Chile; Bolivia; Bahamas; Niter Butte, Nevada; Pinal County, Maricopa County, Arizona; San Bernardino County, California; Dona Ana County, Luna County, New Mexico

## Boracite

*$Mg_3B_7O_{13}Cl$ Magnesium borate chloride*

**Identification**: Boracite is best identified by its colour, its relative hardness and its association with other evaporite minerals.

First discovered on Luneberg Heath near Hanover, Germany, in 1789, boracite is rich in the element boron, and so is often used as a source for borax, which is important in everything from a healthy human diet to making fibreglass. Although boracite can form quite attractive crystals, it is rarely used as a gem because it loses its shine very easily in damp conditions. It is an evaporite mineral, which means it is left behind as a deposit when water evaporates. Boracite is therefore often found mixed in with other evaporites such as anhydrite, gypsum, hilgardite, magnesite and halite, and boracite crystals are commonly embedded in the crystals of these other evaporites. Boracite crystals show double refraction, like Iceland spar calcite.

*Surface of small spheres covered with micro-crystals*

**Crystal system**: Orthorhombic
**Crystal habit**: Typically pseudocubic and octahedrons, but also forms masses, fibres and embedded grains
**Colour**: White to colourless, tinges of blue green with increased iron
**Lustre**: Vitreous
**Streak**: White
**Hardness**: 7–7.5
**Cleavage**: None.
**Fracture**: Conchoidal, uneven
**Specific gravity**: 2.9–3
**Other characteristics**: Slightly soluble in water. Piezoelectric and pyroelectric.
**Notable locations**: Boulby (Yorkshire), England; Stassfurt, Germany; Lorraine, France; Inowroclaw, Poland; Kazakhstan; Khorat, Thailand; Tasmania; Cochabamba, Bolivia; Muzo, Colombia; Chactaw Salt Dome, Louisiana; Otis, California

# Colemanite

*$CaB_3O_4(OH)_3.5H_2O$ Hydrated calcium borate hydroxide*

Colemanite is a borate that occurs either as brilliant colourless or white crystals much cherished by collectors, or in large masses. It was discovered in 1882 in Death Valley, Inyo County in California, one of the world's hottest, driest places. Like other borates, it is an evaporite and typically forms in desert lakes called playas, which fill up in the rainy season as water rich in boron runs off nearby mountains. When the rains stop, the lake waters

evaporate, leaving borate evaporites behind. Interestingly, the colemanite does not form directly. Instead, minerals such as ulexite form first in beds. Then groundwater trickling through the ulexite reacts with it to form colemanite, which is deposited in cavities. Colemanite also occurs in large masses in ancient clays and sandstone – from 1–1.6 million years old – and these provide industrial sources of borax.

**Identification**: Colemanite is hard to tell from many other colourless or white minerals, but a specimen found among borates in playa lake deposits is likely to be colemanite.

**Crystal system**: Monoclinic
**Crystal habit**: Include stubby equant crystals and prisms with complex facets. Also occurs as masses, sheets and grains.
**Colour**: White to clear
**Lustre**: Vitreous
**Streak**: White
**Hardness**: 4.5
**Cleavage**: Perfect in one direction, distinct in another
**Fracture**: Uneven to subconchoidal
**Specific gravity**: 2.4
**Other characteristics**: Transparent to translucent
**Notable locations**: Balevats, Serbia; Atyrau, Kazakhstan; Panderma, Turkey; Salinas Grandes, Argentina; Boron, Death Valley (Inyo Co), Daggett (San Bernadino Co), California; Nevada

**Salt flats**
Deserts are not always entirely dry. In fact, from time to time, they contain some of the largest (and shallowest) lakes in the world. These lakes form when heavy rain falls in surrounding mountains and fills them up. Soon, though, the rains stop and the dry conditions steam off all the water in the lake, leaving behind a hard crust of salty minerals. These salt pans, or playas, are probably the world's flattest pieces of land, which is why they are used for land speed record attempts, like Utah's salt lake. They typically slope no more than 20cm/8in over 1km/ 0.6 miles – and when the rain comes, vast areas may be covered with just a few centimetres/ inches of water. The evaporite deposits on the lake bed vary from place to place. In California's Death Valley, they are typically borate minerals. Elsewhere they may be halides or sulphates such as gypsum and epsomite.

# Ulexite

*$NaCaB_5O_6(OH)_6.5H_2O$ Hydrated sodium calcium borate hydroxide*

Ulexite is a borate evaporite that forms in desert playa lakes as boron-rich water evaporates. It is used as a source of borax, and forms in masses as well as tufts of needle-like crystals called 'cotton balls'. Yet it is best known among collectors for the remarkable crystals found at Boron in California, dubbed 'TV rock'. Here huge chunks of ulexite are found in veins of tightly packed fibre-like crystals. When cut about 2.5cm/1in thick and polished, the crystals behave like optical fibres and transmit light, so you see on the crystal surface a stunningly clear picture of what is on the far side of the stone.

**Identification:** With its light-transmitting, straight, fibre-like crystals, 'TV rock' ulexite is unmistakable.

**Crystal system**: Triclinic
**Crystal habit**: Tufts of acicular crystals and masses of straight fibre-like crystals. Also masses.
**Colour**: White to light grey
**Lustre**: Silky
**Streak**: White
**Hardness**: 2
**Cleavage**: Perfect in one direction
**Fracture**: Uneven
**Specific gravity**: 1.6–2
**Notable locations**: Harz Mts, Germany; Balevats, Serbia; Atyrau, Kazakhstan; Chinghai, China; Salinas Grandes, Argentina; Tarapacá, Chile; Arequipa, Peru; Boron, California; Mojave, Nevada

# SULPHATES, CHROMATES AND MOLYBDATES

*Sulphates are a group of over 200 minerals that are made from a combination of one or more metals with a sulphate compound (sulphur and oxygen). They form when sulphides are exposed to air, either in evaporites or in deposits formed by hot volcanic water. All are soft, light coloured and are commonly translucent or transparent. The barite group is a small but important group of sulphates – barite, anglesite, celestine and hashemite. All but hashemite are important ores for the metals they contain.*

## Barite

*$BaSO_4$ Barium sulphate*

A sulphate of the metal barium, barite (or, in industry, barytes) is unusually heavy for a non-metallic mineral. Indeed, it has long been known as 'Heavy spar', and its name comes from *baryos*, the Greek word for 'heavy'. It is this very density that makes it such a useful material. Barite was once used in making asbestos goods. Now millions of tonnes are used in heavy muds pumped into the apparatus for drilling oil wells. Ground barite mud is forced down the drill hole to carry back rock cuttings and prevent water, gas or oil entering the hole before drilling is completed. Powdered barite is also used to help bulk out white paper and give it a smooth finish. Barite is so dense and unreactive it absorbs gamma rays, so special concrete and bricks are made with barite for shielding radioactive sources in hospitals.

Barite occurs along with quartz and fluorite in hydrothermal ore veins – especially those containing lead (galena) and zinc (sphalerite). It is also found as nodules in clay left by the weathering of some limestones and forms the cement that holds many sandstones together. Barite even occurs in massive beds that are thought to have been formed as sediments. Beds like these in China, Morocco and Nevada, USA, are the main sources of the world's industrial barytes. Some of the finest large barite crystals, however, come from igneous rocks in Cumbria in England and Felsöbanya in Romania.

Barite forms a huge variety of crystal shapes. It often forms as large, tablet-shaped crystals, but it also grows as prisms, fans, tufts and many other forms. It sometimes grows in thin blade-like crystals that cluster in a cockscomb formation. These crested barite cockscombs are often mixed with sand and stained red with iron, earning them the name desert rose (see Cherokees' tears, right).

**Identification**: The specimen above is an example of botryoidal, or layered, barite. The crystals form rings like the growth layers seen in a piece of oak. The resemblance can be so striking that, when cut and polished, oakstone barite has even been mistaken for petrified wood.

*Rings of barite crystals*

**Identification**: The largest barite crystals often appear in tabular form, as seen in the specimen shown to the left.

**Crystal system**: Orthorhombic
**Crystal habit**: A huge variety of forms include tablet and prism shapes. Also occurs as grains, plates, cockscombs and rosettes. Masses and fibres are also common. Banded nodules are known as oakstone because of their striking resemblance to oak wood.
**Colour**: Colourless, white, yellow, but also reddish, bluish or multicoloured and banded
**Lustre**: Vitreous
**Streak**: White
**Hardness**: 3–3.5
**Cleavage**: Perfect in one direction
**Fracture**: Uneven
**Specific gravity**: 4.5
**Other characteristics**: In 1604, a cobbler from Bologna, Italy, found that concretions of barite phosphoresced (glowed) when heated. These are called Bologna stones.
**Notable locations**: Many including: Alston Moor (Cumbria), North Pennines, England; Strontian, Scotland; Felsöbanya, Romania; Harz and Black Mountains, Germany; Bologna, Italy; Alps; Ugo, Japan (hokutolite barite); Peitou (Hokuto), Taiwan (hokutolite barite); Morocco; Australia; Norman, Oklahoma; Nevada; Stoneham, Colorado; Elk Creek, South Dakota

# Anglesite

*PbSO₄ Lead sulphate*

Named after the Welsh island of Anglesey, Anglesite is an unusually pure form of lead sulphate, and is a minor ore of lead, sought after in Britain by the Romans long ago. It usually forms when galena is exposed to air, creating a ring-banded mass around a galena core. Cerussite (lead carbonate) often forms at the same time or soon after. Although it was first found in Wales, the best crystals now come from Tsumeb in Namibia and Touissit in Morocco. The brilliant lustre associated with many lead minerals (as in lead crystal glass) is apparent in many anglesite specimens and makes the mineral especially appealing to collectors. Where it occurs in its yellow form, it is particularly attractive. Frequently, though, crystals are turned grey or black by galena impurities. When colourless or white, it can look a little like barite, but its lead content makes it much, much heavier.

**Identification**: The best way to identify anglesite is by its association with galena, its high density and, commonly, the grey colour of the crystals.

**Crystal system**: Orthorhombic
**Crystal habit**: Crystals take a wide variety of forms but are typically tablet- or prism-shaped, sometimes elongated. It also forms crusts, grains and masses.
**Colour**: Usually colourless, white or yellow, but also pale grey, blue or green
**Lustre**: Adamantine
**Streak**: White
**Hardness**: 2.5–3
**Cleavage**: Perfect in one direction
**Fracture**: Conchoidal, brittle
**Specific gravity**: 6.4
**Other characteristics**: Fluoresces yellow
**Notable locations**: Caldbeck (Cumbria), England; Black Forest, Germany; Sardinia; Touissit, Morocco; Tsumeb, Namibia; New South Wales, Australia; Joplin, Missouri

# Celestite

*SrSO₄ Strontium sulphate*

**Red celestite**: Despite its name, celestite may also be red.

Discovered in Pennsylvania in 1791, celestite, or celestine, is popular with collectors for its typical sky-blue, 'celestial' colour, unique in the mineral world. It is often found in colourful combinations with minerals such as yellow sulphur. Although celestite can look similar to barite, it is actually strontium sulphate, and has long been used as a source of strontium, for fireworks, glazes and metal alloys. Like calcite and dolomite, celestite forms in sediments under the sea – not as they are deposited but in pockets and fissures afterwards as water trickles through them. Celestite may also be found in the cavities of fossils. It is known to form, for example, in fossilized ammonites.

**Crystal system**: Orthorhombic
**Crystal habit**: Crystals take a wide variety of forms but are typically tablet-, prism- or plate-shaped. It also forms crusts, nodules, grains and masses.
**Colour**: Usually blue but may be colourless, yellow, reddish, greenish or brownish
**Lustre**: Vitreous
**Streak**: White
**Hardness**: 3–3.5
**Cleavage**: Perfect in one direction
**Fracture**: Uneven
**Specific gravity**: 4
**Other characteristics**: Burns red in flame tests (see below)
**Notable locations**: Gloucestershire, England; Bohemia, Czech Republic; Tarnowitz, Poland; Sicily; Madagascar; San Luis Potosi, Mexico; Ohio, Michigan; NY

**Identification**: Celestite is very easy to recognize when coloured sky blue. Otherwise, to distinguish it from barite, try a flame test. Soak a thin wooden splint in water overnight, then dip the soaked end in a little powdered celestite. Wearing safety goggles, hold it over a gas flame. Celestite burns red; barite burns lime green.

# EVAPORITE SULPHATES

*A range of sulphates form when salty waters evaporate from salt lakes and lagoons near the sea. Typically these form large masses. Alternatively, fascinating crystals can be formed where salty waters evaporate through rocks and soils. These evaporite sulphates include the many forms of gypsum, one of the most common and useful minerals in the world, as well as anhydrite and glauberite.*

## Gypsum

*$CaSO_4.2H_2O$ Hydrated calcium sulphate*

Gypsum is a very common mineral that occurs all over the world in a variety of forms. It is most commonly a soft white mineral that forms in thick beds where salty water evaporates. Most large deposits formed either on the beds of shallow seas, deposited along with anhydrite and halite, or in salt lakes. Gypsum also forms where anhydrite deposits are moistened by surface water. As the gypsum takes up water, it swells, so the beds are commonly contorted. In beds like these, gypsum is massive and fine-grained (see Alabaster, right), and this is the form that, when heated and dried, turns to the powder used as a base for most plasters, including plaster of Paris, and in most cements. It is also used in a wide range of other applications, such as in fertilizers and as a filler in paper.

Gypsum may also form clear or silky white crystals with fibre-like needles. These crystals are called satin spar or 'beef' and are treasured for carving into jewellery and ornaments. (Spar is a word geologists use to describe any white or light-coloured crystals that are easily broken.)

The more common crystalline form of gypsum, however, is selenite. Selenite crystals are transparent, and usually white or yellowish. They are typically tablet-shaped and form spearhead or swallowtail twins. They can also be prism-shaped, and these prisms can be curved or bent. Long thin crystals may twist in spirals known as ram's horn selenite.

In hot deserts, water often evaporates from shallow, salty basins. Under such conditions, gypsum can grow around grains of sand to form flower-like clusters of flat, bladed crystals. These clusters are called desert roses. Cockscomb barite forms similar roses, but the 'petals' in gypsum are usually better defined. Namibia in Africa is famous for its desert roses.

**Selenite (above)**: This form of gypsum gets its name from the Greek word *selene*, which means 'moon', and bladed crystals of selenite do indeed look like half moons.

**Selenite swords (above)**: Selenite may form long prismatic 'swords', most famously in Mexico's spectacular Cave of Swords in Chihuahua, where there are crystals up to 2m/6ft long.

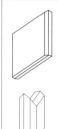

**Crystal system**: Monoclinic
**Crystal habit**: Gypsum occurs in three main forms: crystals of selenite; fibrous satin spar; and fine-grained masses such as alabaster. It also forms elaborate 'daisies' and sand rosettes on various surfaces in dry places. Crystals include tablet, blade or prism shapes. Tabular crystals are often twinned, either as spearheads or swallowtails. Prisms may be bent.
**Colour**: Usually white, colourless or grey, but can also be shades of red, brown or yellow
**Lustre**: Vitreous to pearly
**Streak**: White
**Hardness**: 2
**Cleavage**: Good in one direction and distinct in two others
**Fracture**: Splintery
**Specific gravity**: 2.3+
**Other characteristics**: Thin crystals can be bent slightly. A crystal of gypsum feels warmer than a crystal of quartz.
**Notable locations**: Nottinghamshire, England (satin spar); Thuringia, Bavaria Germany (swallowtail twins); Volterra, Bologna, Pavia, Italy; Montmartre, Paris; Sahara, Africa (desert roses); Whyalia, Tasmania; Pernatty Lagoon, South Australia; Naica (Chihuahua), Mexico (large bladed crystals in Cave of Swords); Nova Scotia; Alfalfa County, Oklahoma; Ellsworth (Mahoning Co), Ohio (isolated whole 'floating' crystals); Mammoth Caves, Kentucky (gypsum flowers); Lockport, New York

*Well-defined, daisy-shaped clusters of evaporite gypsum crystals*

**Daisy gypsum (left)**: When gypsum forms from small pockets of moisture on the surface of rocks, it can often grow in radiating, overlapping patterns of crystals. These 'radiating aggregates' look so much like daisies that they are usually called daisy gypsum.

## Anhydrite

*CaSO₄ Calcium sulphate*

Like gypsum, anhydrite is a white powdery mineral that typically forms in thick beds when water evaporates. In fact, anhydrite is commonly the mineral that forms when gypsum dries out – which is why it is harder – but it was recognized as a mineral in its own right in the 18th century, and can form independently. When concrete is made from gypsum, the gypsum is turned to anhydrite by heating. In nature, the drying-out process makes anhydrite shrink, so layers of anhydrite are often contorted, and sometimes riddled with caverns and smaller cavities. Although anhydrite forms mostly as masses in beds, it can form crystals in hydrothermal veins and alpine fissures or, more commonly, in druses with zeolites in basaltic rocks. Nevertheless, crystals of anhydrite are rare, because contact with water can easily turn them to gypsum. Beautiful lilac blue anhydrite is called angelite, because of its 'angelic' colour.

**Identification**: Anhydrite is best identified by the rectangular way it breaks and by its hardness relative to gypsum. Because they take up water, anhydrite specimens should be kept in an airtight container with silica gel.

 **Crystal system**: Orthorhombic
**Crystal habit**: Usually fine-grained masses. Rare crystals include tablet and prism shapes, typically rectangular.
**Colour**: White, grey or colourless but also bluish or purplish or even reddish
**Lustre**: Vitreous
**Streak**: White
**Hardness**: 3.5
**Cleavage**: Perfect in one direction, good in two others, forming rectangles
**Fracture**: Anhydrite is very, very brittle, breaking conchoidally
**Specific gravity**: 3
**Notable locations**: Lower Saxony, Germany; Pyrenees, France; Switzerland; Tuscany, Italy; Naica (Chihuahua), Mexico; Peru; Nova Scotia; New Mexico; Texas-Louisiana

**Alabaster**
Massive gypsum commonly occurs as the hard white stone alabaster. This beautiful stone has been used since the time of Ancient Egypt for carving and engraving (and trade continues to thrive; see left), and there is a famous sphinx

dating from 1700 BC which is made entirely from alabaster. Alabaster is a wonderful material for carving because it is so soft and easily shaped, although it is also easily damaged. The stone is beautifully translucent, shining through the colours and gilts that were often applied to it in the past. In the Middle Ages, it was widely used for carving in churches across Europe. Another English location, the city of Nottingham, was particularly famous for its alabaster carving in medieval times, exporting altarpieces as far afield as Iceland and Croatia. Italy was another famous medieval source for alabaster, while Roman alabaster originated from Egypt and Algeria. Italian alabaster was often known as Florentine marble while marble from the Middle East was known as Oriental alabaster. Today, alabaster from Mexico is known as Mexican onyx, and is widely used in the carving of ornaments and jewellery.

## Glauberite

*Na₂Ca(SO₄)₂ Sodium calcium sulphate*

Glauberite gets its name from the sodium sulphate salt it contains. This salt, called Glauber's salt, was first made by Johann Rudolf Glauber from Hungarian spring waters to use as a mild laxative. Glauberite typically forms from evaporating salty water in the same places as halite, gypsum and calcite. Although glauberite crystals are rare, their 'ghosts', or pseudomorphs, are common. Because it is soluble in water, glauberite crystals often dissolve away to be replaced in exactly the same shape by other minerals, including opal. Glauberite has a distinctive crystal habit, so the pseudomorphs are easy to identify. Opal pseudomorphs of glauberite in Australia are known as pineapples.

 **Crystal system**: Monoclinic
**Crystal habit**: Includes steeply pointed, inclined, flattened double-pyramid shaped crystals
**Colour**: White, yellow, grey or colourless
**Lustre**: Vitreous, greasy to dull
**Streak**: White
**Hardness**: 2.5–3
**Cleavage**: Perfect in one direction
**Fracture**: Conchoidal
**Specific gravity**: 2.7–2.8
**Other characteristics**: In water, it turns white and partially dissolves.
**Notable locations**: Lorraine, France; Salzburg, Austria; Stassfurt, Germany; Villarrubia (Toledo), Spain; Kenya; Salt Range, Pakistan; India; Atacama, Chile; Gypsumville, Manitoba; Camp Verde, Arizona; Saline Valley (Inyo Co), Searles Lake (San Bernardino Co), California; Great Salt Lake, Utah. Pseudomorphs and casts found notably in Australia and in Paterson and Great Notch, New Jersey, USA.

**Identification**: Glauberite is best identified by the distinctive shape of its crystals – flattened prisms typically marked with grooves.

# HYDROXIDE SULPHATES

*When many sulphates (and other groups of minerals) crystallize, they include water in their structure and are said to be 'hydrated'. Some minerals lose this 'water of crystallization' if heated and become new anhydrous, or 'dry', sulphates, like barite and celestine. The hydroxide sulphates featured here – anterlite, linarite, alunite and jarosite – retain water in the form of OH.*

## Antlerite

*$Cu_3(SO_4)(OH)_4$ Copper sulphate hydroxide*

Antlerite is a copper mineral that was first found in the Antler mine in Mojave County, Arizona, USA. It typically occurs as bright emerald-green, gem-like, stripy crystals, but can also occur as a fine-grained pale green crust on other copper minerals. It is one of a number of minerals that form when copper minerals are oxidized (changed by exposure to oxygen in the air). Where there is plenty of carbon, the minerals formed tend to be copper carbonates such as malachite. If there is less carbon, then copper sulphates such as antlerite and brochantite are formed. These secondary minerals commonly occur in the same place and are quite hard to distinguish. Brochantite can only be definitively distinguished from antlerite by laboratory tests. Antlerite was once thought to be very rare until it was realized that the copper ore being mined in Chile's Chuquicamata is antlerite. Antlerite has since been confirmed at various other copper mines around the world.

*Antlerite*

**Identification**: Antlerite's bright green colour is a clear clue to its identity as a copper mineral. Striations and slightly elongated crystals help to narrow the identity down to antlerite.

**Crystal system**: Orthorhombic
**Crystal habit**: Long slender prisms, or fibre-like crystals in tufts. Also found in veins and as masses, grains and crusts.
**Colour**: Emerald to very dark green
**Lustre**: Vitreous
**Streak**: Pale green
**Hardness**: 3.5
**Cleavage**: Perfect in one direction
**Fracture**: Uneven
**Specific gravity**: 3.9
**Other characteristics**: Crystals are often striated, and it does not fizz in dilute hydrochloric acid
**Notable locations**: Chuquicamata (Antofagasta), Chile; Mexico; Antler mine (Hualpai Mts, Mojave Co), Bisbee (Cochise Co), Arizona; Nevada; California; New Mexico; Utah

## Linarite

*$PbCu(SO_4)(OH)_2$ Lead copper sulphate hydroxide*

**Identification**: The bright blue colour immediately identifies a specimen as linarite or azurite. Linarite does not react to dilute hydrochloric acid but azurite does.

Linarite derives its name from the town of Linares in Spain. Like antlerite, linarite is a copper sulphate mineral, formed by the oxidation of copper minerals such as chalcopyrite – only with linarite there is lead (usually galena) involved as well. It is lead that gives linarite its bright blue colour, so cherished by collectors. In fact, it looks pretty much the same colour as the much better known azurite, and these two bright blue minerals are frequently confused – particularly since they are both found in the same kinds of locations. Sometimes the only way to tell them apart is to test them with dilute hydrochloric acid – azurite reacts, linarite does not. Linarite typically forms as a coating of tiny, bright blue crystals, but can form large masses in association with other copper minerals and is occasionally used as a copper ore.

**Crystal system**: Monoclinic
**Crystal habit**: Tiny tablet-shaped crystals and long prisms. More typically in tiny needle-like layers and crusts. All crystals tend to have multiple facets.
**Colour**: Bright blue
**Lustre**: Subadamantine to earthy
**Streak**: Blue
**Hardness**: 2.5
**Cleavage**: Perfect in one direction, but only in larger crystals
**Fracture**: Conchoidal
**Specific gravity**: 5.3+
**Notable locations**: Cumbria, Cornwall, England; Leadhills (Lanarks), Scotland; Black Forest, Germany; Linares, Spain; Tsumeb, Namibia; Argentina; Chile; Tiger (Mammoth, Pinal Co), Bisbee (Cochise Co), Arizona; Butte, Montana; Juab County, Utah

# Alunite

*KAl₃(SO₄)₂(OH)₆ Potassium aluminium sulphate hydroxide*

Known also as alum stone, alunite has been mined for making alum at Tolfa near Rome since the 15th century. Alum, a sulphate powder, was used in Roman times as a mordant (binder) for dyes and as a medical astringent. Nowadays, alum means just aluminium sulphate, but it is still used for a range of purposes, including water purification. In 1825, alum stone was found to contain a metal that came to be known as aluminium, and alunite is still a minor ore for the metal though much better sources have since been found. Alunite typically occurs as veins and replacement masses in potassium-rich volcanic rocks such as trachyte and rhyolite. In a process called 'alunitization', sulphuric acids in hydrothermal solutions react with metal sulphides in the rocks to create alunite. Large masses of alunite can be created in this way, and the white powdery masses can easily be mistaken for dolomite or limestone rock. Alunite may also form around fumaroles.

**Identification**: Masses of alunite look very like dolomite and limestone rock – but unlike these it does not fizz in dilute acid.

**Crystal system**: Trigonal
**Crystal habit**: Typically forms earthy masses and crusts. Crystals rare and pseudocubic (look like cubes).
**Colour**: White or grey to reddish
**Lustre**: Vitreous to pearly
**Streak**: White
**Hardness**: 3.5–4
**Cleavage**: Most crystals are too small
**Fracture**: Conchoidal, uneven
**Specific gravity**: 2.6–2.8
**Other characteristics**: Some specimens fluoresce orange. Also piezoelectric.
**Notable locations**: Tuscany, Tolfa, Italy; Hungary; Bulladelah (New South Wales), Australia; Marysvale, Utah; Goldfield district, Nevada; Red Mountain (Custer Co), Colorado

---

## Mineral water on Mars?

In March 2004, NASA announced that the Mars rover *Opportunity* had found jarosite. In December of the same year, *Opportunity*'s companion rover *Spirit* found the similar mineral goethite on the far side of the planet in a rock dubbed Clovis. The discovery of both minerals may indicate there was once water on Mars's surface – jarosite because of the way it forms, and goethite because it is a hydrated mineral that can contain up to 10 per cent water. Another of *Opportunity*'s mineral finds was tiny 'blueberries': balls that may be hematite concretions – further evidence of water. The rover took the microscopic image shown above, where the 'berries' appear as dark grey globules on rougher-textured, popcorn-like matter. Known as 'moqui marbles', similar balls are found on Earth in Utah and are thought to develop from groundwater. Earlier Mars missions had found evidence of significant quantities of carbonate minerals on the planet – signs too that there has been water there. However, in 2000 the *Mars Global Surveyor*, which was orbiting the planet, showed at least 2,589,988km²/1,000,000 square miles of the green mineral olivine. Since water reduces olivine quite quickly to clay and serpentine, this suggests that the Martian atmosphere has been dry for a very long time.

# Jarosite

*KFe₃(SO₄)₂(OH)₆ Potassium iron sulphate hydroxide*

Jarosite is a distinctive custard-coloured mineral formed by weathering and as deposits around hot springs, and tends to occur mainly in arid regions. It gets its name from the Barranco del Jaroso (Jaroso Gorge) in the Sierra de la Almagrera region, Spain, where it was first found in 1852 by the German mineralogist August Breithaupt. Like natrojarosite, jarosite has the same trigonal crystal structure as alunite and these minerals form the alunite group. Jarosite occurs only as microscopic crystals, and is popular among collectors who specialize in 'micromounts'. In 2004, jarosite was discovered on Mars by the *Opportunity* rover and scientists think this is further evidence that the planet's surface once had large amounts of liquid water present.

**Crystal system**: Trigonal
**Crystal habit**: Normally occurs as earthy masses or crusts. Crystals are always tiny, and are typically hexagonal or triangular, or sometimes pseudocubic.
**Colour**: Yellow or brown
**Lustre**: Vitreous to resinous
**Streak**: Pale yellow
**Hardness**: 2.5–3.5
**Cleavage**: Good in one direction but only in very rare large crystals
**Fracture**: Uneven
**Specific gravity**: 2.9–3.3
**Notable locations**: Barranco del Jaroso (Sierra Almagrera), Spain; Clara (Black Forest), Germany; Burra Burra, South Australia; Huanani, Bolivia; Sierra Gordo, Chile; Iron Arrow mine (Chaffee Co), Colorado; Maricopa County, Arizona; Custer County, Idaho; Mono County, California

**Identification:** Jarosite is usually best identified by its striking custard colour, tiny crystals and its association with minerals such as hematite, limonite, variscite, pyrite, galena, barite and turquoise.

# HYDRATED SULPHATES

*Hydrated (wet) sulphates that incorporate molecules of water in their structure when they crystallize include colourful minerals such as cyanotrichite, jouravskite and copiapite, as well as the duller-coloured aluminite. Minerals like these tend only to form in damp environments underground. They may lose their water and disintegrate in dry air so need to be kept in airtight containers.*

## Aluminite

*$Al_2(SO_4)(OH)_4 7H_2O$ Hydrated aluminium sulphate hydroxide*

Aluminite is also known as websterite (after geologist Webster) and hallite (from Halle in Germany, where it was discovered in 1730). It is a white or grey mineral that typically forms in bauxite (aluminium ore) deposits and fissures or joints, commonly in association with gypsum, calcite, boehmite, limonite and quartz. Aluminite occurs in knobbly masses or nodules that look a little like cauliflower. These masses consist of fibrous crystals, but the individual crystals are generally too small to see. Consequently, aluminite is sometimes referred to as being a nodular mineral. It is a hydrated sulphate, which means its crystals contain water. In the caves of the Gaudalupe Mountains in New Mexico, aluminite is found as a bright to brilliant white and bluish white, paste-like to powdery, finely crystalline deposit on the cave walls. Milky deposits such as these are thought to form when aluminium-rich fluids crystallize then effloresce (dry out).

**Identification**: Aluminite can often be identified by the white cauliflower-like nodules it forms.

**Crystal system:** Monoclinic
**Crystal habit:** Usually forms masses of tiny fibrous crystals, typically, rounded 'mamillary' form, like cauliflowers, botryoidal (grapelike). Also forms earthy clay-like mass.
**Colour:** White, greyish white
**Lustre:** Earthy
**Streak:** White
**Hardness:** 1–2
**Cleavage:** None
**Fracture:** Irregular, uneven
**Specific gravity:** 1.7
**Other characteristics:** Fluorescent
**Notable locations:** Sussex, England; Halle, Germany; Ile-de-France; Mount Vesuvius, Italy; Zhambyl, Kazakhstan; Kinki (Honshu), Japan; Mount Morgan (Queensland), Australia; Miranda, Venezuela; Tristate, Missouri; Alum Cave, Tennessee; Utah

## Copiapite

*$(Fe,Mg)Fe_4(SO_4)_6(OH)_2 - 20H_2O$ Hydrated iron magnesium sulphate hydroxide*

**Identification**: Yellow encrustations tend to be iron sulphates, particularly on pyrite or pyrrhotite, but it can be hard to specifically identify copiapite.

*Coquimbite*

*Copiapite*

Copiapite gets its name from Copiapo in Chile, where it was first discovered. It is a secondary mineral, forming as an alteration product of other minerals – typically as pyrite, pyrrhotite and other iron sulphide minerals are exposed to the air. Many other hydrated iron sulphate minerals form in the same way – including melanterite, ferricopiapite, rozenite, szomolnokite, fibroferrite, halotrichites and bilinite. It can be very hard to distinguish copiapite from any of these other iron sulphates without X-ray studies. They can all be yellowish crusts, and yellow uranium minerals can even look quite similar but tend to be a darker yellow. Like some other hydrated minerals, copiapite loses water easily and disintegrates to a powder. Specimens should therefore be kept in an airtight container.

**Crystal system**: Triclinic
**Crystal habit:** Typically grainy crusts and scaly masses. Individual crystals are rare
**Colour:** Yellows to olive green
**Lustre:** Pearly to dull
**Streak:** Pale yellow
**Hardness:** 2.5–3
**Cleavage:** Perfect in one direction
**Fracture:** Uneven
**Specific gravity:** 2.1
**Other characteristics:** Dissolves in water, relatively low density
**Notable locations:** France; Spain; Hunsrück, Black Forest, Germany; Elba, Italy; Copiapo (Atacama), Chile; Utah; California; Nevada

# Cyanotrichite

*$Cu_4Al_2(SO_4)(OH)_{12}.2H_2O$ Hydrated copper aluminium sulphate hydroxide*

Cyanotrichite is one of the most strikingly coloured of all minerals and gets its name from its deep 'cyan'-blue colour. The 'trich' part comes from the Greek for 'hair', because it typically occurs as crusts or radiating sprays or balls of fine crystals. The crystals in the sprays are tiny (1mm/$\frac{1}{24}$in long), but may cover an area as big as a postcard. Just as copiapite forms by the oxidation of iron sulphide minerals, so cyanotrichite forms by the oxidation of copper sulphide minerals. Like copiapite, too, it is similar to copper minerals that form in the same way, including other copper sulphates such as antlerite and brochantite, the carbonate mineral malachite and the halide mineral atacamite. Copper gives all these minerals a green colour; the water in cyanotrichite keeps it a vivid blue. It is therefore very important to keep it in an airtight container, to prevent it losing its water and beautiful colour.

**Identification**: Cyanotrichite's sky-blue colour, its velvety look and its association with other copper minerals such as malachite and smithsonite are clear signs of its identity.

**Crystal system**: Orthorhombic
**Crystal habit**: Crusts, as well as radial sprays and balls of tiny needle-like crystals and small tabular crystals
**Colour**: Sky blue
**Lustre**: Vitreous to silky
**Streak**: Blue
**Hardness**: 1–3
**Cleavage**: None
**Fracture**: Uneven
**Specific gravity**: 3.7–3.9+
**Other characteristics**: Transparent to translucent
**Notable locations**: Cornwall, England; Leadhills, Scotland; Black Forest, Germany; Auvergne, France; Romania; Lavrion, Greece; Russia; Broken Hill (New South Wales), Australia; Arizona; Nevada; Utah

**Something in the air**
The oxygen in the air is one of the most reactive of all elements, and whenever metal minerals are exposed to the air, their surface begins to change as the oxygen begins to react with it. Iron rusts like this. This reaction is called oxidation, and it is always linked with a mirror image process called reduction. Oxidation and reduction often involve a swapping of oxygen between substances. As coal burns, for instance, its carbon joins with oxygen in the air to make carbon dioxide. Indeed, oxidation once referred to any chemical reaction in which a substance combines with oxygen. Burning, rusting and corrosion are all reactions like this. But now the definitions have been widened so that oxidation is when a substance loses electrons and reduction is when it gains them. Many new, secondary minerals form as primary minerals are exposed to the air and oxidized. Minerals formed by the oxidation of ores of metals like copper, vanadium, chromium, uranium and manganese are among the most colourful of all minerals.

# Jouravskite

*$Ca_3Mn(SO_4,CO_3)_2(OH)_6.13H_2O$ Hydrated calcium manganese sulphate hydroxide*

Just as copiapite forms by the oxidation of iron minerals and cyanotrichite from copper minerals, jouravskite forms by the oxidation of manganese minerals. It forms distinctive lemon-yellow masses and crusts. It is a rare mineral and was first identified in the famous Tachgagalt manganese mine in Ouarzazate in the Atlas mountains of Morocco only as recently as 1965. It was named in memory of the French geologist Georges Jouravsky, head of the Moroccan geology division, who died the previous year. Jouravskite has been found in only a limited number of other places, also associated with manganese, including the Kalahari manganese fields in South Africa.

**Crystal system**: Hexagonal
**Crystal habit**: Typically forms in grainy masses, but crystals are double-pyramids
**Colour**: Greenish orange, greenish yellow, yellow
**Lustre**: Vitreous
**Streak**: Greenish white
**Hardness**: 2.5
**Cleavage**: Good
**Fracture**: Uneven
**Specific gravity**: 1.95
**Other characteristics**: Translucent
**Notable locations**: Tachgagalt mine (Ouarzazate), Morocco; N'Chwaning mine (Kalahari manganese fields, Northern Cape Province), South Africa

**Identification**: Jouravskite is best identified by its lemon-yellow colour, its sugary texture – as is apparent in this enlarged view of the specimen – and its association with manganese ores.

# WATER-SOLUBLE SULPHATES

*A small number of sulphate minerals dissolve easily in water, including epsomite, chalcanthite, melanterite and thenardite. They are more common than you might think, even in relatively moist parts of the world, but specimens will quickly deteriorate unless kept in airtight containers with a dessicant (drying agent) such as silica gel.*

## Epsomite

*$MgSO_4.7H_2O$ Hydrated magnesium sulphate*

Epsomite is well known from the medicinal Epsom salts, first discovered in mineral waters at Epsom in England. Most Epsom salts are now made artificially, and epsomite dissolves so easily that it is rare in wetter regions. Epsomite does, however, occur as thick sedimentary beds and there is epsomite in sea salt deposits in South Africa. More usually it occurs as an efflorescence – a powdery deposit from mineral waters – in dry limestone caves out of the rain, or in desert regions around playa lakes. Epsomite can also be found growing on the walls of coal and metal mines and on abandoned equipment. Epsomite also occurs around hot springs, and fumaroles such as those on Mount Vesuvius in Italy. Large crystals are extremely rare and very fragile. Specimens are best cleaned with a little alcohol and kept in a sealed container. Yet although moisture is epsomite's main enemy, so too is dryness: losing even a single molecule of its water can change it to another mineral, called hexahydrite, with different monoclinic crystals.

**Identification**: Epsomite is best identified by its often fibrous habit, its location, colour, low density, solubility in water.

**Crystal system**: Orthorhombic
**Crystal habit**: Does not usually form crystals, but occurs as masses, grains, fibres, needles, crusts, grapelike clumps and stalactites, typically as cave efflorescences and in playa lakes
**Colour**: Colourless, white, grey
**Lustre**: Vitreous silky, earthy
**Streak**: White
**Hardness**: 2–2.5
**Cleavage**: Perfect in one way
**Fracture**: Conchoidal
**Specific gravity**: 1.7
**Other characteristics**: Very soluble in water
**Notable locations**: Epsom (Surrey), England; Mount Vesuvius, Italy; Stassfurt, Germany; Herault, France; Sahara, Africa; Central Australia; Kruger Mountain, Washington; Carlsbad, New Mexico; Alameda County, California

## Chalcanthite

*$CuSO_4-5H_2O$ Hydrated copper sulphate*

Chalcanthite comes from the Greek words for 'copper' and 'flower'. Chalcanthite is the basis of the classic copper sulphate solutions often seen in school chemical laboratories and is often used for demonstrations of how crystals grow. Indeed, chalcanthite crystals are so easy to grow that most specimens for sale are artificial. In nature, it forms through the oxidation of copper sulphide minerals such as chalcopyrite, covelite, bornite, chalcocite and enargite. It often forms crusts and stalactites on timbers and walls of copper mines. Chalcanthite is rare in wet regions because it is so soluble in water, but is common enough in arid regions such as the Chilean deserts to be used as a minor ore of copper.

**Caution**: Chalcanthite is poisonous; wash hands after contact.

**Identification**: Chalcanthite is best identified by its bluish 'copper sulphate' colour, a dry environment, and the stalactites and crusts it forms.

*Sandstone rock*

**Crystal system**: Triclinic
**Crystal habit**: Natural crystals are rare but typically stubby prisms and thick tablets. Typically occurs as grapelike and stalactite-like masses, and in veins and crusts.
**Colour**: Bright and deep blue
**Lustre**: Vitreous, silky
**Streak**: Pale blue to colourless
**Hardness**: 2.5
**Cleavage**: Poor (basal)
**Fracture**: Conchoidal
**Specific gravity**: 2.2–2.3
**Other characteristics**: Very soluble
**Notable locations**: Minas de Rio Tinto, Spain; Chuquicamata, El Teniente, Chile; Bingham Canyon, Utah; Ducktown, Tennessee; Imlay (Pershing Co) Nevada; Bisbee (Cochise Co), Ajo, Arizona

# Melanterite

*FeSO₄·7H₂O Hydrated iron sulphate*

Melanterite is a sulphate of iron that is typically formed by the oxidation of iron ore, particularly the iron sulphides pyrite, pyrrhotite, marcasite and the copper ore chalcopyrite. It typically forms white or green powdery deposits, encrustations, stalactites and, occasionally, small clusters of crystals. Miners in iron mines commonly see powdery crusts of melanterite along the walls of the mine's shafts where the ore has been altered. Melanterite is sometimes known as copperas, from the Greek for 'copper water'. It gets this name because when melanterite is dissolved in water, it creates exactly the same iron sulphate solution as when iron is dropped in dissolved chalcanthite (copper sulphate), precipitating metallic copper. Less commonly, melanterite gets a bluey colour from copper impurities – the more copper, the bluer it goes.

**Identification**: Melanterite is best identified by its greenish white colour, and its association with iron and copper sulphide minerals. Specimens lose water and crumble on exposure to air so they should be kept in a sealed container.

**Crystal system**: Monoclinic
**Crystal habit**: Typically forms crusts, but crystals are shaped or prismatic, often twinned, sometimes forming crosses or stars
**Colour**: White, green, or blue-green
**Lustre**: Vitreous to silky
**Streak**: White
**Hardness**: 2
**Cleavage**: Perfect in one direction
**Fracture**: Conchoidal, brittle
**Specific gravity**: 1.9
**Other characteristics**: Soluble in water
**Notable locations**: Minas de Rio Tinto, Spain; Rammelsberg, Harz Mts, Germany; Falun, Sweden; Ducktown, Tennessee; South Dakota; Colorado; Bingham Canyon, Utah; Comstock Lode, Nevada; Butte, Montana

# Thenardite

*Na₂SO₄ Sodium sulphate*

Thenardite is named after the French chemist Louis-Jacques Thenard. It is found in huge deposits near salt lakes and playas throughout the dry regions of south-west USA, Africa, Siberia and Canada, where it has been formed by evaporation. It is also found as a powdery deposit on desert soils and as a crust around fumaroles. Thenardite is natural sodium sulphate, an important chemical vital for making soaps and detergents, paper and glass. Huge amounts of thenardite are dug from the ground to satisfy industrial demand. Searles Lake in California alone contains about 450 million tonnes of thenardite. The Great Salt Lake in Utah contains 400 million tonnes. But some of the biggest deposits are at Hongze in eastern China's Jiangsu province.

**California's dry treasure lake**
Searles Lake in San Bernardino County in California is one of the most famous locations in the world for evaporite minerals. It is a playa lake in the Mojave desert, one of the world's driest regions. It is now mostly dry or shallow, but it formed in the last Ice Age, when rain conditions made it the centre of a large drainage network. It was named after the Searles brothers, John and Dennis, who discovered borax here in 1863, and began working its huge deposits ten years later. So far Searles Lake has yielded a billion dollars' worth of chemicals. Besides borax, there are large deposits here of the evaporite trona or 'natron', naturally occurring sodium bicarbonate, after which the nearby town of Trona is named. It is said that nearly all the 90 or so naturally occurring elements can be found at Searles Lake, and there are deposits of rare minerals such as hanksite and pink halite. The area around Trona is home to over 500 tufa spires, which have been the setting for films such as *Star Trek V*, *Planet of the Apes*, and Disney's *Dinosaur*.

**Crystal system**: Orthorhombic
**Crystal habit**: Typically forms crusts, grains and massive rockbeds. Also forms distorted intergrown clusters of crystals. Rare individual crystals are slender tablet- or prism-shaped.
**Colour**: White, yellowish, grey, brown
**Lustre**: Vitreous
**Streak**: White
**Hardness**: 2.5–3
**Cleavage**: Perfect in one direction
**Fracture**: Splintery like hornblende
**Specific gravity**: 2.7
**Other characteristics**: Soluble in water, and fluoresces white
**Notable locations**: Espartinas, Spain; Mount Etna, Sicily; Bilma Oasis, Niger; Khibiny and Lovozero massifs (Kola Peninsula), Russia; Kazakhstan; Hongze (Jiangsu), China; Pampa Rica, Chile; Searles Lake, California; Great Salt Lake, Utah; Camp Verde (Yavapai Co), Arizona

**Identification**: Thenardite is best identified by its location and its white fluorescence.

# CHROMATES, MOLYBDATES AND TUNGSTATES

*These heavy, soft and brittle minerals have the same chemical structure as sulphates, except that chrome, tungsten and molybdenum replaces the sulphur in the molecule. Besides ores such as wolframite and scheelite, they include some of the most striking of all minerals – crocoite and wulfenite – and two rarities – ferrimolybdite and cuprotungstite.*

## Crocoite

*PbCrO₄ Lead chromate*

Blood red or orange, crocoite is one of the most beautifully coloured of all minerals. It is a chromate, in which chromium replaces sulphur, and it is the chromium that gives it its distinctive colour. It was first found at Berezovsk near Ekaterinburg in the Russian Urals in 1766, and was named crocoite in 1832 from the Greek for 'crocus' or 'saffron', because of its colour. In the Urals, crocoite is found in quartz veins running through granite and gneiss, and is associated with the similar minerals phoenicochroite and vauquelinite. Vauquelinite is named after the French chemist L N Vauquelin, who, in 1797, at the same time as H Klaproth, discovered the element chromium in crocoite. For a while, crocoite was the main ore of chromium. Now it is too rare. The most famous crocoite specimens come from Dundas in Tasmania, where crystals up to 20cm/8in long were once found. Most specimens, though, are made of small crystals like splinters, known as 'jackstraw' crocoite.

**Identification**: Crocoite's blood-red, often splinter-like, crystals are unmistakable. It can be confused with wulfenite but its crystals are prismatic and have a lower specific gravity.

**Crystal system**: Monoclinic
**Crystal habit**: The long, slender, splinter-like crystals are distinctive. Crystal ends are sometimes hollow. Also forms grains and masses in granite and other igneous rocks.
**Colour**: Bright orange-red to yellow
**Lustre**: Adamantine to greasy
**Streak**: Orange-yellow
**Hardness**: 2.5–3
**Cleavage**: Distinct in two directions
**Fracture**: Conchoidal to uneven, brittle
**Specific gravity**: 6.0+
**Other characteristics**: Very high index of refraction
**Notable locations**: Urals, Russia; Umtali, Mashonaland, Zimbabwe; Luzon, Philippines; Dundas, Tasmania; Ouro Prêto, Brazil; Inyo Co, Riverside Co, California

## Wulfenite

*PbMoO₄ Lead molybdate*

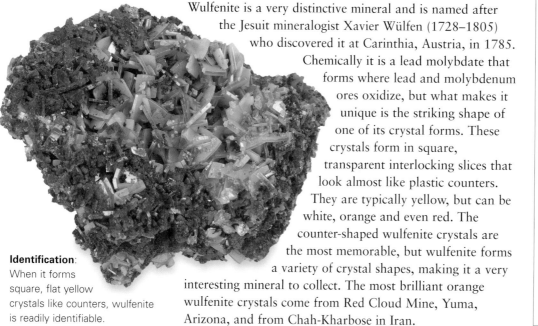

**Identification**: When it forms square, flat yellow crystals like counters, wulfenite is readily identifiable.

Wulfenite is a very distinctive mineral and is named after the Jesuit mineralogist Xavier Wülfen (1728–1805) who discovered it at Carinthia, Austria, in 1785. Chemically it is a lead molybdate that forms where lead and molybdenum ores oxidize, but what makes it unique is the striking shape of one of its crystal forms. These crystals form in square, transparent interlocking slices that look almost like plastic counters. They are typically yellow, but can be white, orange and even red. The counter-shaped wulfenite crystals are the most memorable, but wulfenite forms a variety of crystal shapes, making it a very interesting mineral to collect. The most brilliant orange wulfenite crystals come from Red Cloud Mine, Yuma, Arizona, and from Chah-Kharbose in Iran.

**Crystal system**: Tetragonal
**Crystal habit**: Very thin square crystals like plastic counters, and also grains and hollow masses
**Colour**: Orange-yellow
**Lustre**: Vitreous
**Streak**: White
**Hardness**: 3
**Cleavage**: Perfect in one way
**Fracture**: Subconchoidal to uneven
**Specific gravity**: 6.8
**Other characteristics**: Index of refraction: 2.28–2.40 (high but typical of lead minerals)
**Notable locations**: Carinthia, Austria; Slovenia; Czech Rep; Morocco; Tsumeb, Namibia; Zaïre; Australia; Sonora, Durango, Chihuahua, Mexico; Pinal Co, Yuma Co, Gila Co, Arizona; Stephenson Bennett mine, New Mexico

# Ferrimolybdite

*Fe₂O₃.3MoO₃.8H₂O Hydrated iron and molybdenum oxide*

Like molybdenite, powellite and wulfenite, ferrimolybdite is rich in molybdenum. It typically forms when molybdenite is weathered, especially in quartz veins, and is commonly found in layers in molybdenite. It can also form on spoil heaps. What marks ferrimolybdite out is its iron content, which is why it is commonly found in association with pyrite. Weathered ore deposits are often a mix of red hematite, yellow jarosite and ferrimolybdite, brown goethite and black oxides. Officially, ferrimolybdite was recognized by Pilipenko in 1914 in Khakassiya, eastern Siberia, but the process of discovery goes back much earlier. In 1800, the existence of 'molybdite' was noted in Europe, and German geologists described 'molybdenum ochre' in molybdenum layers. A few years before the Civil War, American geologist David Dale Owen found a specimen in California and noted its iron content. In 1904, Schaller insisted that although there was an iron-rich molybdenum oxide, it had yet to be proved that it occurred naturally, which is what Pilipenko did in 1914.

**Identification**: Ferrimolybdite is best identified by its association with other molybdenites, its yellow colour and its tiny, flat, needle-like or fibrous crystals.

*Ferrimolybdite crust*

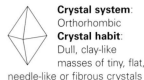

**Crystal system**: Orthorhombic
**Crystal habit**: Dull, clay-like masses of tiny, flat, needle-like or fibrous crystals
**Colour**: Yellow
**Lustre**: Silky
**Streak**: Light yellow
**Hardness**: 2.5–3
**Cleavage**: Good, but natural crystals are too small
**Fracture**: Uneven
**Specific gravity**: 4–4.5
**Notable locations**: Bohemia, Czech Republic; Saxony, Germany; Hohe Tauern Mountains, Austria; Bipsberg, Bastnas, Sweden; Lake Iktul (Khakassiya), Russia; Dundee (New South Wales), Australia; Climax, Colorado; Arizona; Texas; New Mexico

**Dundas mines, Tasmania**
The mines of Dundas, near Zeehan in Tasmania, have long been famous for their magnificent crocoite specimens – like the Red lead mine shown here. Well over 90 per cent of the world's crocoite comes from here, and crocoite is Tasmania's state mineral emblem. Crocoite was first discovered here in 1896 by James Smith and W R Bell, when silver and lead miners dug deep into the ore bodies here and found them honeycombed with cavities full of cerussite and extraordinary blood-orange 'jackstraw' crystals of crocoite. The crocoite was so plentiful here that many beautiful crystals were sent off to be used as flux in smelters. Eventually, though, both the ores and the crocoite were worked out and the mines were largely abandoned. Then in the 1970s and in 2002, new deposits of wonderful crocoite and pyromorphite specimens were found at Dundas in the Platt Mine and the famous Adelaide Mine. Both these mines now harvest crystals for the collectors' market.

# Cuprotungstite

*Cu₂(WO₄)₂(OH)₂ Copper hydroxytungstate*

Cuprotungstite was discovered in 1869 in Chile, and tends to be more common in drier environments such as Baja California, Broken Hill in Australia and Namibia, although good specimens have been found in places such as the Old Gunnislake mine in Cornwall, England. It is a combination of copper and tungsten often found as a tan- or green-coloured coating on copper minerals. It typically forms when scheelite deposits (tungsten ore deposits) contain copper sulphides. Cuprotungstite then forms when these two sets of minerals interact as they are weathered and oxidized.

**Crystal system**: Tetragonal
**Crystal habit**: Typically fine, fibre-like crystals or masses
**Colour**: Emerald green or brown
**Lustre**: Vitreous, waxy
**Streak**: Green
**Hardness**: 4–5
**Fracture**: Conchoidal, brittle
**Specific gravity**: 7
**Notable locations**: Cornwall, Cumbria, England; Black Forest, Germany; Namibia; South Africa; Broken Hill (New South Wales), Australia; Honshu, Japan; China; La Paz (Baja California), Sonora, Mexico; Cochise Co, Maricopa Co and Pima Co, Arizona; Deep Creek Mountains, Utah

*Cuprotungstite*

**Identification**: Cuprotungstite is best identified by its tan or green colour and its association with copper and tungsten ores.

# PHOSPHATES, ARSENATES AND VANADATES

*The phosphates, arsenates and vanadates are a group of interesting and often very distinctive minerals. The phosphates include many minerals rich in rare-earth elements found in few other minerals such as yttrium, caesium, thorium and even less known samarium and gadolinium. The vanadates include some of the most amazing crystals such as those of descloizite and vanidinite. The phosphates featured here are 'primary' (minerals that form directly), and are among the few phosphates that are anhydrous (contain no water).*

## Xenotime

*YPO₄ Yttrium phosphate*

Xenotime is one of a handful of minerals with a name starting with 'x', and its name contains a few historical errors. It comes, supposedly, from the Greek for 'empty honour' – because it was once thought to have the honour of containing a brand new element yttrium. It does contain yttrium, but it was not a new element, and *xenos* is the Greek word for 'strange'; *kenos* is the Greek for 'empty' – so it should really have been called kenotime! However, it remains a very interesting mineral and one of the very few to contain yttrium, which can be replaced by erbium. Xenotime forms brown, glassy crystals in clusters and rosettes in pegmatites within granites and gneisses, just like the very similar mineral monazite. Once the rock it formed in has been weathered away, it sometimes turns up in river sands and beaches, just like monazite, because it is relatively dense. However, it is softer and lighter than monazite and is therefore much rarer in these deposits.

**Identification**: Xenotime is best identified by its hardness and crystal habits.

**Crystal system**: Tetragonal
**Crystal habit**: Crystals are typically prisms ending in slanted double-pyramids. Also forms rosettes and radiating clusters.
**Colour**: Shades of brown; also greyish, greenish or reddish
**Lustre**: Vitreous to resinous
**Streak**: Pale brown
**Hardness**: 4–5
**Cleavage**: Perfect in two ways
**Fracture**: Uneven to splintery
**Specific gravity**: 4.4–5.1
**Other characteristics**: Traces of uranium and other rare-earth elements may make crystals slightly radioactive
**Notable locations**: Arendal, Hittero, Tvedestrand, Norway; Sweden; Madagascar; Brazil; Colorado; California; Georgia; North Carolina
**Caution**: Xenotime is radioactive. Handle with care and store appropriately.

## Monazite

*(Ce,La,Th,Nd,Y)PO₄ Cerium lanthanum thorium neodymium yttrium phosphate*

Monazite is actually a blanket term for a range of phosphates that include varying amounts of rare-earth elements such as cerium, thorium, lanthanum and neodymium, as well as smaller amounts of praseodymium, samarium, gadolinium and yttrium. It forms as small brown or golden crystals in pegmatites within granites and gneisses, like those in Norway and Maine, or in alpine cavities with quartz (a combination called turnerite). When the rock is broken down by weathering and washed seawards, monazite normally settles close to the shore because it is both relatively tough and heavy. Monazite grains are commonly concentrated in beach sands, known as monazite beaches, most famously along India's Malabar Coast. These beach deposits are excavated primarily for thorium, but also for all the other rare earths that monazite contains.

Yellow beryl crystal

Feldspar

Monazite

Smoky quartz

**Identification**: Monazite is best identified by its complex red-brown splintery crystals – though it is hard to identify as sand grains.

**Caution**: Monazite is highly radioactive, so should be handled with care and stored in an appropriate container.

**Crystal system**: Monoclinic
**Crystal habit**: Typically masses or grains. Crystals flat, splinter-like wedges and tablets – complex twinning.
**Colour**: Crystal red-brown or golden; grains yellow-brown
**Lustre**: Resinous, waxy
**Streak**: White, yellow-brown
**Hardness**: 5–5.5
**Cleavage**: Perfect in one way
**Fracture**: Conchoidal **Specific gravity**: 4.9–5.3
**Notable locations**:
Pegmatites: Norway; Finland; Callipampa, Bolivia; Madagascar; Minas Gerais, Brazil; Maine; Connecticut; Amelia, Virginia; Climax, Colorado; New Mexico
Alpine cavities: Switzerland
Sands: Malabar, India; Sri Lanka; Malaysia; Nigeria; Australia; Brazil; Idaho; Florida; North Carolina

# Triphylite

*Li(Fe,Mn)PO₄ Lithium iron manganese phosphate*

Triphylite is a relatively rare phosphate mineral that forms bluish or glassy masses. It gets its name from the Greek for 'family of three' because of the three elements it contains besides phosphate – lithium, iron and manganese. It is very similar to another phosphate mineral, lithiophilite, which contains the same three elements. The only real difference is that lithiophilite contains more manganese, and so is pinker in colour and denser, while triphylite contains more iron, and is bluer in colour and denser. What makes both these minerals interesting is not the minerals themselves but their products of weathering. They both form in phosphate-rich pegmatites within granite. When weathered, they change to various striking minerals such as eosphorite, vivianite, strengite, purpurite, wolfeite and sicklerite. In hydrothermal solutions, they can change to siderite and rhodochrosite.

**Identification**: Triphylite is best identified by its blue-grey colour and its situation in phosphate-rich pegmatites in granite. This triphylite mass has green surface patches of vivianite.

*Vivianite*

*Tryphylite mass*

**Crystal system**: Orthorhombic
**Crystal habit**: Mostly forms glassy masses
**Colour**: Blue or blue-grey
**Lustre**: Vitreous
**Streak**: White to grey-white
**Hardness**: 4–5
**Cleavage**: Near perfect in one direction (basal)
**Fracture**: Uneven
**Specific gravity**: 3.58
**Notable locations**: Verutrask, Sweden; Bavaria, Germany; Mangualde, Portugal; Buckfield, Poland; Karidid District, Namibia; Buranga (pegmatite), Rwanda; Namaqualand, South Africa; Rajasthan, India; Pilbara, Western Australia; Rio Grande do Norte, Brazil; Yellowknife, Northwest Territories; San Diego County, California; Maine; North Groton, New Hamps; Custer, S Dakota; Branchville, Conn't

# Purpurite-Heterosite

*MnPO₄ Manganese phosphate*

**Crystal system**: Orthorhombic
**Crystal habit**: Mostly forms earthy masses, grains or crusts
**Colour**: Purple, brown or red
**Lustre**: Vitreous
**Streak**: Deep red to purple
**Hardness**: 4–4.5
**Cleavage**: Good in one direction (basal)
**Fracture**: Uneven
**Specific gravity**: 3.3
**Notable locations**: Sabugal, Portugal; France; Koralpe Mts, Austria; Namibia; Northern Cape Province, South Africa; Pilbara, Western Australia; Faires Tin mine (Kings Mt, Gaston Co), North Carolina; Portland, Connecticut; Yavapai County, Arizona

Officially discovered in 1905 in Gaston County, purpurite gets its name from its often stunning purple colour. It may have been used as a pigment as long ago as the Renaissance, but it is an extremely rare mineral and even today is used only sparingly by painters. Purpurite forms a series with the phosphate mineral heterosite, with purpurite at the manganese-rich end and heterosite at the iron-rich end. Purpurite is usually no more than a dusty coating or crust on other minerals, because it forms when the primary phosphate minerals that crystallized in granite pegmatites are altered over time by exposure to the air. In fact, it usually forms by the alteration of another rare mineral, lithiophilite, which is why it is itself so rare.

**Identification**: The deep purple colour of purpurite and heterosite usually makes them fairly easy to find in granite pegmatites – but there is no easy way of telling them apart.

**Radioactivity**
The nuclei of some atoms, especially large atoms, are naturally unstable and tend to break down or 'decay' to other more stable atoms. This process results in surplus energy being emitted as radiation, typically as tiny alpha and beta particles, but also as gamma rays (high-energy electromagnetic waves similar to light). This is called radioactivity and is measured with a Geiger counter. Radioactivity was discovered in 1896, and is known for its association with nuclear power and weapons. Yet some rock formations such as granite plutons produce quite high levels of radiation and a number of minerals are also naturally radioactive, including xenotime, monazite and autunite. Radioactive minerals require careful handling and storage, because even low-level radiation is a health hazard. For advice on how to handle radioactive specimens safely, see Handling and storing radioactive minerals at the beginning of the Directory.

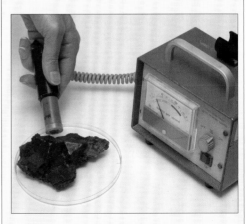

# VIVIANITES

*Vivianite gives its name to a small group of rare hydrated phosphate minerals with very similar crystal structures. Vivianite itself is renowned for its blue colour, but all the members of the group – erythrite, annabergite, köttigite and baricite – are all very colourful. Erythrite is a striking crimson and annabergite is fresh apple green, while köttigite is russet coloured and baricite is baby blue (with occasional yellow patches).*

## Vivianite

*Fe₃(PO₄)₂.8H₂O Hydrated iron phosphate*

$Fe_3(PO_4)_2.8H_2O$ Hydrated iron phosphate

*Blue radiating crystals of vivianite.*

Vivianite was first discovered as a mineral at the famous Wheal Jane tin mine near Truro in Cornwall, England, by J G Vivian, after whom the species was later named. It typically forms in iron ore veins and phosphate-rich pegmatites – either very late in the crystallization process, as in Idaho, Utah and Colorado, or as the original minerals, such as triphylite and manganese oxides, are weathered. Some of the best crystals are found in cavities within tin ore veins in Bolivia. Vivianite also forms concretions in clay, and when minerals are altered in recent sediments, in lignite and peat, and in fossils, such as a mammoth skull in Mexico (see Mammoth turquoise, right). When it first forms, vivianite is almost colourless, but it turns blue as soon as it is exposed to light. Indeed, it gradually turns completely black and also becomes brittle. Specimens should therefore be kept in a dark place.

**Identification**: Vivianite is best identified by its blue colour – and the fact that it gets darker when exposed to light. Vivianite beads become magnetic when heated.

Vivianite

*Ferruginous sandstone*

**Crystal system**: Monoclinic
**Crystal habit**: Radiating clusters of prism-, needle-, or fibre-like crystals. Also forms earthy masses and crusts. May also line fossil shells.
**Colour**: Colourless to green, blue and indigo, darkening on exposure to light
**Lustre**: Vitreous
**Streak**: White or bluish green
**Hardness**: 1.5–2
**Cleavage**: Perfect in one direction
**Fracture**: Uneven
**Specific gravity**: 2.6–2.7
**Other characteristics**: Thin crystals are flexible
**Notable locations**: Wheal Jane mine (Cornwall), England; Trepca, Serbia; Crimea, Ukraine; Japan; Anloua, Cameroon; Bolivia; Brazil; Mullica Hill, New Jersey; Leadville, Colorado; Maryland; Utah; Idaho; Maine

## Erythrite

*Co₃(AsO₄)₂.8H₂O Hydrated cobalt arsenate*

$Co_3(AsO_4)_2.8H_2O$ Hydrated cobalt arsenate

**Identification**: A crust of erythrite is readily identified by its dark pink colour, with the appearance of raspberry jam smeared on toast.

Erythrite is a striking crimson-coloured mineral that is formed by the weathering of cobalt-rich minerals such as cobaltite. Its bright crimson colour is very noticeable and miners used it to help them locate veins of cobalt-, nickel- and silver-bearing ores. Erythrite may occur as radiating crystals and concretions but more commonly forms a crust on cobalt minerals known as 'cobalt bloom'. Just as substances completely intermixed in liquids form liquid solutions, so components of solids can intermix to form solid solutions. A solid solution series is a range of minerals in which components swap around. Erythrite is part of a solid solution series, with annabergite at the other extreme, in which nickel changes place with cobalt. As the nickel content increases, the colour lightens to white, grey or pale green annabergite.

**Crystal system**: Monoclinic
**Crystal habit**: Typically earthy crusts or masses. Rare crystals in slender prisms or clusters of long flat needles.
**Colour**: Crimson to lighter pink in crusts
**Lustre**: Vitreous
**Streak**: Pale red
**Hardness**: 1.5–2.5
**Cleavage**: Perfect in one direction
**Fracture**: Uneven, sectile
**Specific gravity**: 3
**Notable locations**: Cornwall, Cumbria, England; Schneeburg, Germany; Czech Republic; Bou Azzer, Morocco (with skutterudite); Queensland, Australia; Alamos, Mexico; Cobalt, Ontario

# Annabergite

*$Ni_3(AsO_4)_2.8H_2O$ Hydrated nickel arsenate*

Long known as nickel ochre, or 'nickel bloom', annabergite was given its name in 1852 by H J Brooke and W H Miller, after Annaberg in Saxony in Germany, one of the best locations for the mineral. It is the nickel-rich equivalent of erythrite, and the nickel turns annabergite apple green or even white – in marked contrast to erythrite's deep crimson. However, there are so many variations in between that it is not always so easy to distinguish them, except with the aid of laboratory analysis. Annabergite is a rare mineral that forms near the surface of cobalt nickel-silver ore veins, typically forming a thin greenish film as the nickel ore is weathered. Unlike erythrite, annabergite has never been found as large crystals. Even small crystals are rare and treasured. One of the few places they are found is Lavrion in Greece, where the specimen shown here was found. Lavrion annabergite crystals are unofficially known as cabrerite after Sierra Cabrera in Spain, where similar crystals have been found.

**Identification**: Annabergite forms as an apple-green coating and is associated with erythrite and nickel minerals such as skutterudite, niccolite and gersdorffite.

*Annabergite*

*Calcite*

**Crystal system**: Monoclinic
**Crystal habit**: Typically earthy crusts and films. Rare small crystals like tiny straws.
**Colour**: Pale apple green to pink
**Lustre**: Silky, glassy, dull
**Streak**: Pale green or grey
**Hardness**: 1.5–2.5
**Cleavage**: Perfect in one direction
**Fracture**: Flaky
**Specific gravity**: 3
**Notable locations**: Teesdale, England; Lavrion, Greece; Sierra Cabrera (Almeria), Spain; Allemont (Isère), Pyrenees, France; Annaberg (Saxony), Black Forest, Hesse, Germany; Carinthia, Salzburg, Austria; Cobalt, Ontario; Humboldt, Nevada

**Mammoth turquoise**
In the Middle Ages, French Cistercian monks created a turquoise-blue gemstone to use in church decorations. They called the gemstone 'toothstone' because they made it by heating the fossilized tusks of mastodons, which they thought were giant teeth. Mastodons were an elephant-like creature that lived in Europe 13 to 16 million years ago. These fossilized tusks came from ancient sediments near the Pyrenean mountains. The monks thought toothstone was really the semi-precious stone turquoise, because it looked so much like turquoise. In fact, toothstone was a substance now called odontolite, and is chemically quite different from turquoise. It is essentially fluorapatite, with traces of manganese, iron and other metals. It was once thought that odontolite turned blue as it was heated by changing to vivianite. Recently, though, scientists at the Louvre in France subjected odontolite to spectroscopic analysis. No vivianite was found and they now believe that the colour comes from the alteration of manganese particles.

# Köttigite

*$Zn_3(AsO_4)_2-8H_2O$ Hydrated zinc arsenate*

Köttigite is a rare mineral, first found in the Schneeburg region of Saxony, Germany. Like erythrite and annabergite, it is arsenate that forms by the weathering of metal ores. While erythrite is cobalt-rich and annabergite is nickel-rich, köttigite is zinc-rich. However, there is no real gradation among köttigite and either of the other two, as there is between erythrite and annabergite. This is because zinc particles do not exchange places so readily with nickel or cobalt particles as nickel and cobalt do with each other. Köttigite is found in many locations in small quantities, but the best sites are Schneeburg, Germany, and Mapimi in Durango, Mexico.

*Köttigite crystals*

**Crystal system**: Monoclinic
**Crystal habit**: Typically forms crusts or powdery masses. Rare, small crystals are flattened blades or radiating needles.
**Colour**: Reddish or white and grey
**Lustre**: Vitreous
**Streak**: Pale green or grey, in grey specimens
**Hardness**: 2.5–3
**Cleavage**: Perfect in one direction
**Fracture**: Uneven
**Specific gravity**: 3.3
**Other characteristics**: Thin crystals are flexible
**Notable locations**: Black Forest, Harz Mountains, Schneeburg, Germany; Hohe Tauern, Austria; Bohemia, Czech Republic; Lavrion, Greece; Otjikoto, Namibia; Honshu, Japan; Flinders Range, South Australia; Waratah, Tasmania; Mapimi (Durango), Mexico; Franklin, New Jersey; Churchill, Nevada

**Identification**: Köttigite is best identified by its needlelike crystals, its occurrence as a crust and its association with zinc minerals such as smithsonite.

# ANHYDROUS PHOSPHATES WITH HYDROXIDE

*The hydroxide phosphates include apatite – one of the most abundant minerals, but also the white mineral that forms bones and teeth in all animals. Amblygonite is also typically white, but copper and magnesium turn two other hydroxide phosphates, libethenite and lazulite, into rich shades of green and blue, which makes them highly prized by collectors.*

## Apatite

*$Ca_5(PO_4)_3(OH,F,CL)$ Calcium (fluoro, chloro, hydroxyl) phosphate*

Discovered by the famous German geologist Abraham Werner in 1786, apatite gets its name from the Greek *apatan*, which means 'deceive', because it can be confused with beryl, quartz and other hexagonal crystals. It is not actually a mineral species itself, but three similar minerals – fluorapatite, chlorapatite or hydroxyapatite – each of which gets its name from how much fluorine, chlorine or hydroxyl it contains. Together, the apatite trio is incredibly abundant around the world, found mostly in igneous rocks, but in metamorphic and sedimentary rocks as well. It is the main source of phosphorus in soil, which is needed by plants, and apatite and phosphorite are the only natural sources of phosphate minerals used for fertilizer. Although abundant, most apatite is found as tiny grains and crystals. Good, large crystals are rarer, occurring mainly in pegmatites, ore veins and igneous masses. Crystals come in many colours. Asparagus stone is a clear green gem variety of apatite that forms in pegmatites. Beautiful violet apatite forms in the tin veins of Ehrenfriedersdorf in Germany. Big gemlike yellow apatite is found in iron deposits in Durango in Mexico.

**Identification**: With its hexagonal crystals, apatite can look a little like beryl, tourmaline and quartz, but is much softer and often has a 'sucked sweet' (candy) look.

*Apatite crystal*

**Crystal system**: Hexagonal
**Crystal habit**: Crystals are typically hexagonal, but apatite can also form tablet-, column- and globe-shaped masses, or form needles, grains and earths. Most commonly occurs as massive beds.
**Colour**: Typically green but also yellow, blue, reddish brown and purple
**Lustre**: Vitreous to greasy
**Streak**: White
**Hardness**: 5
**Cleavage**: Indistinct
**Fracture**: Conchoidal
**Specific gravity**: 3.1–3.2
**Other characteristics**: Some apatites fluoresce yellow
**Notable locations**: Saxony, Germany; Tyrol, Austria; Panasquiera, Portugal; Kola Peninsula, Russia; Campo Formosa (Bahia), Brazil; Copiapó, Chile; Durango, Mexico; Wilberforce, Ontario; Mount Apatite, Maine

## Libethenite

*$Cu_2PO_4(OH)$ Copper phosphate hydroxide*

**Identification**: Libethenite is olive green, but can be hard to tell from other green copper minerals without complex tests.

Discovered by the famous German mineralogist Friedrich Breithaupt in 1823, libethenite gets its name from Libethen in Romania (now Lubietova in Slovakia), where it was first found. It is a rare copper mineral that is formed by the alteration of other copper minerals. It typically occurs in deeply weathered, concentrated copper sulphide ore bodies. Like many copper minerals it is green, but libethenite is a particularly deep, rich, olive green. It typically occurs in grains, crusts and microscopic crystals, but in 1975 spectacular large crystals were found at the Rokana mine in Zambia's copperbelt. Libethenite is isostructural with olivenite and adamite. This means they both have the same crystal shapes but different properties.

*Above: Close-up view of libethenite crystals*

*Libethenite*

**Crystal system**: Orthorhombic
**Crystal habit**: Crystals typically diamond-shaped. Also forms needles, grains, masses and globules and druses.
**Colour**: Dark olive green
**Lustre**: Resinous to vitreous
**Streak**: Olive green
**Hardness**: 4
**Cleavage**: Good in two directions
**Fracture**: Brittle
**Specific gravity**: 3.6–3.9
**Other characteristics**: Does not fizz like malachite in dilute hydrochloric acid
**Notable locations**: Cornwall, England; Black Forest, Germany; Lubietova (Libethen), Slovakia; Urals, Russia; DR Congo; Zambia; Tintic, Utah; Gila, Pima and Pinal Cos, Arizona; California

# Amblygonite

*(Li, Na)Al(PO₄)(F, OH) Lithium sodium aluminium phosphate fluoride hydroxide*

First discovered in Saxony, Germany, by Friedrich A Breithaupt in 1817, amblygonite has now been found in many places around the world – typically in lithium- and phosphate-rich pegmatites. It usually forms large masses embedded in other constituents of these rocks such as quartz and albite. Because amblygonite looks rather like these minerals, it can make up a rather larger percentage of the rock than is perhaps at first apparent. The difference is that amblygonite contains lithium – although it might need a flame test to prove it. When powdered, amblygonite can be set alight with a gas flame, and the lithium burns bright red. Amblygonite gets its odd-sounding name from the Greek *amblus* for 'blunt' and *gouia* for 'angle' because of the shallow angles of its crystal cleavage. However, because amblygonite is usually found embedded in other minerals, it rarely forms good quality crystals. The exceptions are the gem-quality crystals that come from Minas Gerais in Brazil and those found in Myanmar (Burma).

**Identification**: It is quite difficult to tell amblygonite from other white minerals such as albite without more exhaustive tests, such as the flame test for its lithium content.

**Crystal system**: Triclinic
**Crystal habit**: Typically large masses with irregular outlines, or fine, white crystals including short prisms, tablets and laths
**Colour**: Typically creamy white or colourless, but can be lilac, yellow or grey
**Lustre**: Vitreous
**Streak**: White
**Hardness**: 5.5–6
**Cleavage**: Perfect in one direction, interrupted in others
**Fracture**: Brittle, subconchoidal
**Specific gravity**: 3–3.1
**Other characteristics**: Some specimens fluoresce orange
**Notable locations**: Varutrask, Sweden; Montebras, France; Sakangyi, Myanmar (Burma); W. Australia; Minas Gerais, Brazil; Yellowknife, Northwest Territories; Pala, California; Newry, Maine; Yavapai Co, Arizona; Black Hills, S. Dakota

**Apatite for bones and teeth**

Teeth and bones are white because they are made mostly from calcium phosphate in the form of the mineral apatite. Bones are not solid like rock, of course, but comprise a honeycomb of cavities and criss-crossing struts. This composite structure makes bones both light and strong. The struts are actually a mix of organic materials and minerals – and the main mineral is the form of apatite called hydroxyapatite. Bonemaking cells called osteoblasts are constantly at work inside bones creating molecules of the organic material collagen – to renew old bone destroyed by bone-dissolving cells called osteoclasts. By a process called heterogeneous nucleation or heteronucleation, particles of hydroxyapatite dissolved in the surrounding fluid stick to the collagen particles and build up the bone. For bones to stay healthy and strong, we must eat food containing enough calcium and phosphate to keep the osteoblast supplied with hydroxyapatite.

# Lazulite

*(Mg, Fe)Al₂(PO₄)₂ (OH)₂ Magnesium iron aluminium phosphate hydroxide*

Named for its resemblance to the blue gem lapis lazuli, lazulite is a rare and sometimes beautiful azure-blue mineral prized as an ornamental stone. It typically forms at high temperatures in hydrothermal veins, but can also form in phosphate-rich pegmatites, some metamorphic rocks and quartz-rich veins. Lazulite is closely associated with the mineral scorzalite. In fact, lazulite and scorzalite are simply the opposite extremes of a solid solution series (a gradation of mixtures). Lazulite is at the magnesium-rich end; scorzalite is at the iron-rich end. Most lazulite crystals are smallish and quite dull to look at, although occasionally specimens can be quite spectacular and may be as large as a hazelnut.

**Crystal system**: Monoclinic
**Crystal habit**: Typically small wedge shapes. Also granular and massive.
**Colour**: Pale to deep azure
**Lustre**: Vitreous to dull
**Streak**: Pale blue to white
**Hardness**: 5.5–6
**Cleavage**: Distinct in one direction
**Specific gravity**: 3.1
**Other characteristics**: Clear gemmy crystals show strong pleochroism (yellowish, clear, blue). Crystals are slightly soluble in warm hydrochloric acid.
**Notable locations**: Zermatt, Switzerland; Horrsjøberg, Sweden; Salzburg, Austria; Copiapó, Chile; Diamantina, Minas Gerais, Brazil; Yukon; Graves Mount, Georgia; Death Valley (Inyo Co), California

**Identification**: Lazulite is best identified by its dark blue colour, but it is hard to tell from lazurite, sodalite and other blue minerals.

*Quartz*

*Lazulite crystals*

# HYDRATED PHOSPHATES

*The hydrated phosphates include some fascinating minerals – not only the beautiful blue-green stone turquoise, one of the most ancient and most widely cherished gems, but also wavellite, with its distinctive starburst clusters, and two uranium-rich, radioactive minerals – dark green, blocky torbernite and greenish yellow, fluorescent autunite.*

## Turquoise

*CuAl₆(PO₄)₄(OH)₈.5(H₂O) Hydrated copper aluminium phosphate*

**Identification**: Although often imitated by fakes such as chrysocolla, turquoise is generally very distinctive with its vivid blue-green colour and smooth, waxy appearance.

*Coating of turquoise*

*Quartz*

One of the most beautifully coloured of all stones, turquoise is a phosphate that combines copper and aluminium. The copper causes the exquisite blue-green, but the colour varies from green to yellowish grey. Pale sky blue is the most cherished gem colour – especially when infused with fine veins of impurities that show it is natural, not artificial. Although opaque, solid turquoise is actually crystalline, or rather, cryptocrystalline, since the crystals are too small to be seen by the naked eye. It typically forms in waxy veinlets where groundwater washes over weathered, aluminium-rich rock in the presence of copper. Thus it is often associated with copper deposits as a secondary mineral. Turquoise contains water, but won't form if conditions are wet, so most major deposits are in dry regions. For thousands of years, the best turquoise came from the deserts of Persia and was known as Persian turquoise. In the late 1800s, deposits of turquoise were discovered in the American south-west, and this is now the world's prime source of high-quality 'Persian' turquoise.

**Crystal system**: Triclinic
**Crystal habit**: Typically tiny, cryptocrystalline forms as nodules and veinlets. Also forms crusts.
**Colour**: Shades of blue-green
**Lustre**: Dull to waxy
**Streak**: White with green tint
**Hardness**: 5–6
**Cleavage**: Perfect in two directions, but not often seen
**Fracture**: Conchoidal
**Specific gravity**: 2.6–2.8
**Other characteristics**: Colour can change with exposure to skin oils
**Notable locations**: Neyshabur, Iran; Afghanistan; Sinai; Broken Hill (NSW), Victoria, Australia; Baja California, Mexico; Arizona; Nevada; Colorado; San Bernardino Co, Inyo Co, Imperial Co, California

## Wavellite

*Al₃(PO₄)₂(OH)₃-(H₂O)₅ Hydrated aluminium phosphate hydroxide*

Named after William Wavell, the English country doctor who discovered it in Harwood, Devon, in 1805, wavellite is an aluminium phosphate. It typically forms in hydrothermal veins and crevices and on surfaces in limestone, chert and aluminium-rich metamorphic rocks, and is often associated with limonite, quartz and micas. The classic wavellite specimens are radiating 'starburst' clusters of sparkling yellow-green needle-like crystals. Sometimes called cat's eyes, these clusters typically form as nodules in crevices in limestone and chert, and are revealed when the crevices are split open to show them growing on surfaces like thin coins. If there was room for them to grow freely, they might form half-globes. Although the starburst cluster is best shown when the samples are split, some collectors prefer just a few split, leaving the rest as solid half-globes.

**Identification**: Wavellite's radiating starburst clusters are unmistakable. These clusters often form in globules, or botryoidal masses.

**Crystal system**: Orthorhombic
**Crystal habit**: Radiating needles forming globules or botryoidal masses
**Colour**: Yellow green or white
**Lustre**: Vitreous
**Streak**: White
**Hardness**: 3.5–4
**Cleavage**: Perfect in two directions
**Fracture**: Uneven
**Specific gravity**: 2.3+
**Notable locations**: Devon, Cornwall, England; Zbiroh, Czech Republic; Ronneburg, Germany; Pannece, France; Llallagua, Bolivia; Garland County, Arkansas; Pennsylvania

# Torbernite

*Cu(UO₂)₂(PO₄)₂-10(H₂O) Hydrated copper uranyl phosphate*

Torbernite was first found in 1772 at Johanngeorgenstadt in Saxony, Germany, but is named after 18th-century Swedish scientist Torbern Bergmann. It typically forms small, dark green plates and square crystals embedded in and coating other crystals in cracks in pegmatites and granites. Torbernite is a uranium-rich mineral like autunite and usually forms by alteration of pitchblende, a black, massive form of uraninite, the main ore of uranium. The uranium content makes torbernite radioactive. The radioactivity is unlikely to do any harm, but specimens should be handled with care, and kept well away from children. Most uranium ores produce radioactive dust when handled, so touch specimens as little as possible and wash hands thoroughly afterwards. Keep specimens in an airtight container as well to contain any radon gas emitted, and open only outside. The main problem with torbernite is that samples disintegrate and lose their water easily to become crumbly metatorbernite – another reason why they should be handled infrequently and kept in an airtight container.

**Identification**: Torbernite is best identified by its dark green square crystals and its association with autunite and uraninite.

**Caution**: Torbernite is radioactive, so should be handled with care and stored appropriately.

**Crystal system**: Tetragonal
**Crystal habit**: Typically square, tablet-shaped crystals, often stacked like books. Also forms crusts, micaceous, foliated and scaly aggregates.
**Colour**: Dark to light green
**Lustre**: Vitreous to pearly
**Streak**: Pale green
**Hardness**: 2–2.5
**Cleavage**: Perfect in one direction
**Fracture**: Uneven
**Specific gravity**: 3.2+
**Other characteristics**: Radioactive
**Notable locations**: Gunnislake (Cornwall) England; Trancoso, Portugal; Erzebirge, Germany; Bois Noir, France; Katanga, Zaïre; Mount Painter, South Australia; Mitchell County, North Carolina; Utah

# Autunite

*Ca(UO₂)₂(PO₄)₂-10H₂O Hydrated calcium uranyl phosphate*

Named after Autun in France, autunite is a uranium mineral. It is closely related to torbernite, but is much more common, and therefore is frequently used as a uranium ore. It typically forms by the alteration of the surface of other uranium ores found in pegmatites. By daylight, it can be very difficult to see on the rock faces, but when it is exposed to ultraviolet light at night, it reveals its presence by fluorescing dramatically. Like torbernite, it is radioactive and tends to crumble easily when exposed to air (turning to meta-autunite), so it should always be handled with care and stored in an airtight container well out of the reach of children.

**Crystal system**: Tetragonal
**Crystal habit**: Typically square, tablet-shaped crystals, often stacked like books
**Colour**: Greenish yellow
**Lustre**: Vitreous to pearly
**Streak**: Pale green
**Hardness**: 2–2.5
**Cleavage**: Perfect in one direction
**Fracture**: Uneven
**Specific gravity**: 3.1–3.2
**Other characteristics**: Radioactive and fluorescent
**Notable locations**: Dartmoor, England; Trancoso, Portugal; Saône-et-Loire, Margnac, France; Katanga, DR Congo; Mount Painter, South Australia; Mount Spokane, Washington; Mitchell County, North Carolina
**Caution**: Autunite is radioactive, so should be handled with care and stored appropriately.

**Identification**: Autunite is best identified by its fluorescence, its yellow-green square, tablet-shaped crystals and its association with torbernite and uraninite.

**Ancient turquoise**
Turquoise is probably one of the oldest gems known. The Egyptians cherished it 6,000 years ago, and established the world's oldest mines in hard rock, in the Sinai peninsula. When the tomb of the Egyptian queen Zer was excavated in 1900, she was found to be buried with a gold and turquoise bracelet – one of oldest known surviving pieces of jewellery. In Ancient Persia, where it was mined on Mount Alimersai, now in Iran, it was used as a talisman for good fortune. It probably came to Europe from Persia from the time of the Crusades onwards. The Europeans thought it originated in Turkey and it may have got its name from the French for Turkish. In the Americas, turquoise has been valued since at least 200BC by native peoples in the American south-west such as the Navajo, and by Indian tribes in Mexico. The Navajo made turquoise into beads, carvings and mosaics. The Navajo are said to believe turquoise is a piece of sky that has fallen to Earth, while the Apache think it combines the spirits of sea and sky to help hunters. The Aztecs also cherished turquoise, and the treasure of Montezuma contains a turquoise mosaic serpent.

# ARSENATES

*Arsenates are very similar in make-up to the phosphates and vanadates, with arsenic often simply replacing phosphorus and vanadium in the mix. They include the rare and attractive green and greenish yellow minerals adamite, conichalcite, olivenite, scorodite and bayldonite. When powdered and burned with charcoal, they all give off arsenic's distinctive garlic smell.*

## Adamite

*$Zn_2(AsO_4)(OH)$ Zinc arsenate hydroxide*

Adamite is named after the 19th-century French mineralogist Gilbert-Joseph Adam, who discovered it at Chanarcillo in Chile. Its vividly coloured, lustrous crystals make it popular with collectors. It is a secondary zinc mineral that typically forms where zinc-rich ores are oxidized. Cobalt impurities give it a pink tinge; copper impurities turn it greenish. Pure adamite, uncontaminated by copper, is a distinctive yellow or white, and is also brilliantly fluorescent, glowing lime green under ultraviolet light. Typically, adamite is found lining cavities in limonite, but the classic location for adamite crystals is Mapimi, in the state of Durango, in Mexico. Mapimi is a limestone replacement deposit rich in rare arsenic minerals. Here, adamite is found not with limonite but in yellow straws and sprays with hemimorphite, austinite and rare minerals such as legrandite (see inset) and paradamite. All the best specimens of fluorescent adamite come from this location.

*Legrandite*

**Identification**: The lime-green colour and high lustre of adamite are hard to miss – and the brilliant fluorescence of pure adamite is unmistakable. Crusts of adamite can look like smithsonite.

*Adamite*

**Crystal system**: Orthorhombic
**Crystal habit**: Crystals are typically blunt-end wedge-like prisms, mostly in druses and radiating clusters in wheels and sheaves
**Colour**: Yellow or white when pure, tinged green by copper and pink by cobalt
**Lustre**: Adamantine
**Streak**: White to pale green
**Hardness**: 3.5
**Cleavage**: Perfect in two slanting directions
**Fracture**: Absent
**Specific gravity**: 4.3–4.4
**Other characteristics**: Fluoresces bright green
**Notable locations**: Cumbria, England; Tyrol, Austria; Hyeres, France; Reichenbach, Germany; Tuscany, Italy; Lavrion, Greece; Chanarcillo, Chile; Mapimi, Mexico; Inyo County, California; Gold Hill, Utah; Nevada

## Conichalcite

*$CaCu(AsO_4)(OH)$ Calcium copper arsenate hydroxide*

*Calcite*

*Coating of conichalcite*

**Identification**: Conichalcite's striking grass-green colour and crust-forming habit, seen here on geothite.

Conichalcite gets its name from the Greek for 'powder' (*konis*) and 'lime' (*chalx*). It was first identified in 1849 near Córdoba in southern Spain by the famous German mineralogist Friedrich A Breithaupt. It has a very distinctive grass-green colour unlike any other mineral, making it easy to identify. It coats limonite rock with a crust that looks rather like moss, but is entirely mineral in origin, and the green colour comes from the copper. This copper content means that it is occasionally used as a copper ore. It forms where copper is oxidized when oxygen-rich water reacts with copper sulphide or oxide minerals. Sometimes the limonite is red or yellow, providing a striking colour combination. It is typically found in association with copper and arsenic minerals such as adamite, azurite, bayldonite, linarite, malachite, olivenite and smithsonite.

**Crystal system**: Orthorhombic
**Crystal habit**: Typically forms crusts
**Colour**: Grass green
**Lustre**: Vitreous
**Streak**: Green
**Hardness**: 4.5
**Cleavage**: Absent
**Fracture**: Uneven
**Specific gravity**: 4.3
**Notable locations**: Gunnislake (Cornwall), Cumbria, England; Black Forest, Germany; Poland; Lavrion, Greece; Córdoba, Spain; Guanaco, Chile; Mapimi, Mexico; Lun County, New Mexico; Tintic Mountains (Juab County), Utah; Esmeralda, Eureka and Mineral Counties, Nevada; Cochise, Pima, Pinal, and Yavapai Counties, Arizona

# Olivenite

*Cu₂AsO₄(OH) Copper arsenate hydroxide*

Despite its name, olivenite bears no relation to the mineral olivine. Its name comes entirely from its typical olive-green colour. It is a now rare, secondary mineral that crystallizes in small veins and vugs (pockets), where it forms by the alteration of copper ores and mispickel (arsenopyrite). It was once found in considerable quantities in association with limonite and quartz in mine dumps, and in the upper workings of copper mines, in Cornwall, England, especially near St Day and Redruth. It was in Cornwall, at the Carharrack mine at Gwennap, that olivenite was first identified in 1820. Cornish olivenite occurs as crusts of whitish colour-banded vertical needles that look like wood splinters, earning it the local name 'wood copper'. Wood copper is also found at Tintic in Utah, while the best olivenite crystals come from Tsumeb in Namibia. The arsenic in olivenite is often replaced by a proportion of phosphorus, forming a libethenite that looks like olivenite, as at Lubietova in Slovakia.

**Identification**: Olivenite is best identified by its coating of tiny, needle-like olive-green crystals. Wood copper olivenite forms distinctive wood splinter mineral crusts.

Quartzite            Olivenite

**Crystal system**: Orthorhombic
**Crystal habit**: Tubby, prism-shaped crystals or crusts of needle-like crystals
**Colour**: Dark olive green, yellow, brown, whitish
**Lustre**: Vitreous to greasy
**Streak**: Olive green
**Hardness**: 3
**Cleavage**: Rarely noticed
**Fracture**: Conchoidal
**Specific gravity**: 3.9–4.4
**Other characteristics**: Soluble in hydrochloric acid
**Notable locations**: Cornwall, England; Grube Clara (Black Forest), Germany; Lavrion, Greece; Tsumeb, Namibia; Tintic, Utah; Majuba Hill, Nevada

**Cornish tin mines**
When the South Crofty mine based at Camborne in Cornwall, England, closed in the late 1990s, it marked the end of a tradition of tin mining there dating back to the Bronze Age. At its peak in the 1870s, Cornwall was the world's leading tin mining area, with over 2,000 pits at work. In the end Cornish tin proved uneconomic because it is so hard to access. As Cornwall's granite masses cooled, fissures opened up and were filled with hot molten material, which crystallized to form lodes rich with minerals such as tin, copper, zinc, lead and iron. Each vertical fissure had to be mined with a separate shaft, plunging deep and straight into the ground, often well below the water table – which is why powerful water pumps were needed, especially in mines perched on cliffs right next to the sea, like the Wheal Coates tin mine pictured above. Although the mines are now closed, specimens of rare minerals can be found on the old mine dumps, especially the Penberthy Croft at Wheal Fancy, where natanite, jeanbandyite, segnitite and bayldonite were first found. This site is now protected by law.

# Scorodite and Bayldonite

*Fe₃AsO₄·2H₂O Hydrated zinc arsenate (Scorodite)*

Scorodite is an attractive mineral that forms pale grey-green clusters of crystals, or pale greenish earthy masses. It typically forms as a secondary mineral where zinc minerals in arsenic-rich veins are altered by exposure to oxygen. But it has also been found in crusts around hot springs. Scorodite forms a solid-solution series with mansfieldite in which aluminium replaces iron in the scorodite structure. Bayldonite (inset) is a much rarer, but even more attractive, mineral that forms where copper and lead minerals in arsenic-rich veins are altered by exposure to oxygen. It was first discovered at the Penberthy Croft mine (Wheal Fancy) in Cornwall, England.

*A thin green coating of bayldonite on quartz.*

Scorodite
Bayldonite

**Crystal system**: Orthorhombic
**Crystal habit**: Double pyramids that look like octahedrons. Also forms crusts and earthy masses.
**Colour**: Pale green, grey green, blue, and brown
**Lustre**: Vitreous to sub-adamantine or greasy
**Streak**: White
**Hardness**: 3.5–4
**Cleavage**: Generally poor
**Fracture**: Conchoidal
**Specific gravity**: 3.1–3.3
**Notable locations**: Cornwall, England; Lavrion, Greece; Tsumeb, Namibia; Mapimi, Zacatecas, Mexico; Ouro Prêto, Brazil; Ontario; California; Utah

**Identification**: Scorodite is best identified by its grey-green colour. It can look like zircon, but is not fluorescent.

Scorodite            Quartz

# VANADATES

*The vanadates are a group of minerals formed when vanadium and oxygen combine with various metals to form complex molecules. The conditions in which they form are very particular, so these minerals are quite rare. However, vanadinite and carnotite are often mined as ores of vanadium, radium and uranium, and many vanadates are prized by collectors for their brilliant colours.*

## Mottramite

*PbCu(VO₄)(OH) Lead copper vanadate hydroxide*

Originally named psittacine, mottramite was named in 1876 after the village of Mottram St Andrews in Cheshire, England, in 1876 by Sir Henry Enfield Roscoe (1833–1915). Roscoe was the chemist who first isolated metallic vanadium, then discovered that it occurs naturally in mottramite. Vanadium salts are obtained by 'digesting' mottramite with concentrated hydrochloric acid. Vanadium is now known to occur in vanadinite, descloizite, roscoelite and pucherite as well. Mottramite is a green to black mineral that usually occurs as a drusy crust on other rocks and minerals such as wulfenite and vanadinite. It is usually found in places where copper and lead minerals have been oxidized by contact with air and water, or just water. Large crystals of mottramite up to 2.5cm/1in long have been found in the Otavi triangle, Namibia. Mottramite is typically found in 'green' associations with other copper minerals such as descloizite, malachite and pyromorphite.

**Identification**: Dark, dirty green velvety crusts of mottramite are usually easy to identify, especially if associated with vanadinite, descloizite, malachite and wulfenite.

 **Crystal system**: Orthorhombic
**Crystal habit**: Typically tiny drusy crusts, radiating and stalactitic masses
**Colour**: Typically various shades of green, but also more rarely black
**Lustre**: Resinous
**Streak**: Green
**Hardness**: 3–3.5
**Cleavage**: None
**Fracture**: Conchoidal to uneven
**Specific gravity**: 5.7–6
**Other characteristics**: Nearly always found in association with descloizite
**Notable locations**: Mottram St Andrews, England; Grootfontein, Otavi, Namibia; Bolivia; Chile; Bisbee, Tombstone (Cochise Co), Pinal County, Arizona; Sierra County, New Mexico

## Descloizite

*PbZn(VO₄)(OH) Lead zinc vanadate hydroxide*

**Identification**: Descloizite is best identified by the khaki or black velvety crusts it forms, its high density and its associations with zinc and vanadate minerals.

Dark grey crystals of descloizite

Discovered by A Damour in 1854 near Córdoba in Argentina, descloizite is named after famous French scientist Alfred Louis Oliver Legrand des Cloizeaux. Descloizite and mottramite are at the two opposing ends of a solid solution series – a range of solids in which certain chemical elements are mixed in varying degrees. Descloizite is the zinc-rich end of the range while mottramite is the copper-rich end, but there is a gradation in composition between; most descloizite specimens contain some copper and most mottramite specimens contain some zinc. The more copper thre is in descloizite, the more orange or yellow it is. Descloizite is a secondary mineral and often occurs on the surface of vanadinite. It typically forms small platelike crystals or velvety crusts in the oxidation zone of hydrothermal veins where lead, zinc and copper ores are associated with vanadates and other lead and zinc minerals.

 **Crystal system**: Orthorhombic
**Crystal habit**: Typically forming tiny platelike crystals, arrow-shaped crystals, velvety crusts, 'trees', small drusy crusts and stalactitic masses
**Colour**: Cherry red, brown, khaki, black or yellowish
**Lustre**: Translucent
**Streak**: Orange to brownish red
**Hardness**: 3–3.5
**Cleavage**: None
**Fracture**: Conchoidal to uneven
**Specific gravity**: 5.9
**Notable locations**: Cornwall, England; Carinthia, Austria; Tsumeb, Otavi, Namibia; Córdoba, Argentina; Bisbee, Tombstone (Cochise Co), Pinal County, Arizona; Lake Valley (Sierra Co), Grant County, New Mexico

# Carnotite

*K₂(UO₂)₂(VO₄)₂.3H₂O Hydrated potassium uranyl vanadate*

Named after the French chemist M A Carnot (1839–1920), carnotite is one of the most important sources of the radioactive elements radium and uranium. One hundred years ago, Marie and Pierre Curie, the French husband and wife pioneers of research on radioactivity, used carnotite from Colorado as their experimental material for radium – which is why it must be handled very carefully, like all radioactive minerals. For many years, the carnotite deposits of the American south-west were the world's major source of radium – until even richer sources of radium were found in Katanga, DR Congo, and Radium Hill, South Australia. Today the Colorado and Utah carnotite is a major source of uranium. They are thought to form when uranium and vanadium ores in red-brown sandstones are altered – often replacing fossil wood. Carnotite often forms a brilliant yellow coating on sandstone. It is closely related to tyuyamunite, but carnotite contains potassium while tyuyamunite contains calcium.

**Identification**: Carnotite is bright yellow and can be distinguished from autunite by a lack of fluoresce.

**Caution**: Carnotite is very radioactive, so should be handled and stored with great care.

**Crystal system**: Monoclinic
**Crystal habit**: Includes microscopic platelike crystals, crusts, earthy masses and flaky or grainy aggregates
**Colour**: Bright yellow
**Lustre**: Pearly to dull or earthy
**Streak**: Yellow
**Hardness**: 2
**Cleavage**: Perfect in one direction
**Fracture**: Uneven
**Specific gravity**: 4–5
**Other characteristics**: Strongly radioactive and does not fluoresce
**Notable locations**: Kazakhstan; Kokand, Ferghana, Uzbekistan; Katanga, Zaïre; Morocco; Radium Hill, South Australia; Wyoming, Colorado; Utah; Arizona; Grants County, New Mexico; Mauch Chunk (Carbon County), Pennsylvania

**Namibia's mineral mecca**
Tsumeb in Namibia and the nearby locations of Grootfontein and Otavi are among the world's richest sources of minerals. More than 240 different minerals have been found at Tsumeb alone! Until quite recently, the region's mines were a major source of copper, lead, silver, zinc and cadmium. Even the bushmen found copper here, in a malachite hill, which they bartered for tobacco with the Ovambo people. Now it is more famous for its wonderful crystals of dioptase, mottramite, descloizite, cerussite, aragonite, tennantite, enargite and many more. The mineral deposits centre on a hydrothermal vein, rich with lead, zinc and copper sulphides and arsenides, mixed in with rarer elements such as germanium and gallium. But what makes Tsumeb special is the limestone rock of the region, which allows water to percolate into the vein and oxidize the minerals at many different levels – as far as 1,500m/5,000ft into the ground. Each different level creates cavities containing different secondary minerals.

# Vanadinite

*Pb₅(VO₄)₃Cl Lead chloro-vanadate*

When it was first identified in Mexico in 1801, vanadinite was believed to contain a brand new element that was called erythronium. Only later was this found to be vanadium. In fact, vanadinite is now used as an ore of vanadium, and also a minor ore for lead. It is a secondary mineral that forms mostly in dry and desert regions, such as Namibia, Morocco and the south-west USA. It typically occurs where lead ores are weathered, and is associated with wulfenite, descloizite and cerussite. Sometimes, arsenic replaces some of the vanadium in vanadinite to create the mineral endlichite. When arsenic completely replaces vanadium in the crystal structure, it becomes mimetite.

**Crystal system**: Hexagonal
**Crystal habit**: Typically small, thin six-sided prism-shaped crystals, or globular masses
**Colour**: Mahogany red, brown, brownish yellow or orange
**Lustre**: Resinous, adamantine
**Streak**: Brownish yellow
**Hardness**: 3–4
**Cleavage**: None
**Fractue**: Conchoidal
**Specific gravity**: 6.7–7.1
**Other characteristics**: Very brittle
**Notable locations**: Warlockhead (Dumfries and Galloway), Scotland; Carpathia, Austria; Urals, Russia; Mibladen, Morocco; Otavi, Namibia; Marico, South Africa; Chihuahua, Mexico; Tucson, Arizona; Sierra County, New Mexico

**Identification**: Vanadinite is most easily identified when it occurs in the brown-red form. Association with descloizite, wulfenite and cerussite is a key indicator.

# QUARTZ

*Quartz is the single most common mineral in the Earth's crust and is a major ingredient of many igneous and metamorphic rocks. Because quartz is very tough, it doesn't break down easily and so it is also found as a major constituent of most sedimentary rocks other than those that form biogenically or chemically. Although quartz is basically colourless, impurities cause a huge variety of colours to be seen, ranging from purple amethyst to yellow citrine.*

## Quartz (crystalline and massive)

*SiO₂ Silicon dioxide*

**Rock crystal (below)**: Rock crystal is the clear, colourless variety of quartz. It is one of the least expensive and most popular of all gemstones, simply because it is quite common – although the giant crystals from which fortune tellers' crystal balls were cut are very rare. Some collectors prefer natural clusters of rock crystal with arrays of glittering pinnacles to separate stones.

**Smoky quartz (below)**: This quartz is one of the few brown gemstones. It comes in several varieties, ranging from pale brown to black, and its abundance makes it worth much less than either amethyst or citrine. In Scotland, dark brown quartz is known as Cairngorm, from the Cairngorm mountains, and is a popular ornamental stone, often carved into fireplaces or worn in brooches with Highland costume. Other popular varieties include black morion, and banded black and grey coon tail quartz. The dark colour comes from exposure to natural radiation deep underground. In fact, pale quartz can be artificially turned into smoky quartz by exposure to radiation. But if these artificially coloured stones are heated, they will turn pale again.

Quartz was one of the first mineral crystals known. In fact, the very word crystal comes from *krystallos*, the Ancient Greek word for 'rock crystal', the colourless form of quartz. Rock crystal (clear quartz) looks so much like ice that for a long time it was thought to be a form of ice that wouldn't melt. The word quartz itself is German in origin, but just what it meant is lost in the mists of time. Many varieties of quartz have been known since ancient times, such as carnelian, agate and chalcedony (see following pages). In the Middle Ages, large crystals of clear quartz were carved into balls for fortune tellers and alchemists. In the 16th and 17th centuries, barrel-loads of rock crystal were shipped from Brazil and Madagascar to Europe to be carved into vases, decanters and chandeliers. Now quartz has many uses, from radios and watches (see Electric quartz, right) to machine bearings.

Quartz forms in a huge variety of places. Most originally form when magmas rich in silica and water crystallize to form rocks such as granite. Larger quartz crystals form in pegmatites, but these are typically whitish in colour because they contain minute fluid-filled cavities. When these igneous rocks are broken down by weathering, the toughness of quartz grains ensures they survive to form the basis of most sedimentary rocks. It is these rocks that form the pure quartz sand that is the main source used in glassmaking. Large, collectable crystals of quartz form mainly in crusts, hydrothermal veins and in geodes in sandstone. Indeed, quartz is the dominant mineral in most mineral veins. Some of the best crystals come from cavities in the Swiss Alps known as crystal caves. There are literally hundreds of different varieties and names for quartz. The table opposite covers just the better known ones.

**Crystal system**: Trigonal
**Crystal habit**: Widely variable, but most common is hexagonal prisms ending in six-sided pyramids. Can be cryptocrystalline.
**Colour**: Widely variable but clear is most common, followed by cloudy or milky quartz, purple amethyst and pink agate and brown smoky quartz
**Lustre**: Vitreous or resinous
**Streak**: White
**Hardness**: 7
**Cleavage**: Poor
**Specific gravity**: 2.65
**Other characteristics**: Piezoelectric (see box)
**Notable locations**:
Rock crystal: Aar Massif, Switzerland; Rhine Westphalia, Germany; Salzburg, Austria; Madagascar; South Africa; Brazil; Ouachita Mountains, Arkansas; Lyndhurst, Ontario

Smoky quartz: Scotland; Alps, Switzerland; Brazil; Pikes Peak, Colorado

Amethyst: Kapnik, Hungary; Urals, Russia; Zambia; Namibia; South Africa; Guerrero, Mexico; Bahia, Rio Grande do Sul, Brazil; Uruguay; Thunder Bay, Canada; Maine; Pennsylvania

Chrysoprase: Marlborough (Queensland), Australia

Tiger's Eye: Doorn Mountains, South Africa

Citrine: Salamanca, Spain; Urals, Russia; Dauphine, France; Madagascar

**Citrine (below)**: Citrine is a semi-precious yellow, orange or brown variety of quartz. The name comes from *citrus*, the Latin for 'lemon', and the yellow colour comes from tiny particles of iron oxide suspended within it. It is the most valued quartz gem, but is sometimes thought of as 'imitation' topaz, which it resembles, but is slightly softer than. It can actually be created artificially by heating amethyst, and many of the citrine gems on the market are really heat-treated amethyst from Minas Gerais in Brazil. Heat-treated citrine tends to be more orange than natural citrine, which is typically pale yellow. Natural citrine is found in protruding clusters of small, pyramidal crystals, often in geodes, in places like the Russian Urals, Dauphine in France and Madagascar. Some naturally occurring citrine was once amethyst, but has been turned yellow-orange by exposure to hot magma. In ancient times, citrine was carried as a talisman against snake bites and evil thoughts.

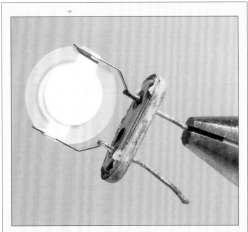

*Citrine*

*Calcite*

*Basalt*

**Amethyst (right)**: Amethyst is one of the most attractive forms of quartz, a favourite with everyone from the pharaohs of Egypt to Catherine the Great of Russia. Tiny traces of iron in the quartz give it a colour varying from pale mauve to deep violet. It is found in most places where granite is exposed on the surface. The name amethyst is said to come from the Ancient Greek myth of the beautiful girl Amethyst. In a drunken rage after a party, so it goes, the god of revelling and drink Dionysus once swore that tigers would eat the next person that came along. When

Amethyst was first to come by, the goddess Athene turned her to white stone to save her. Thoroughly remorseful, Dionysus cried into his drink and poured it over the stone Amethyst, turning it purple. It was later believed that amethyst would ward off drunkenness. Amethyst came to be a symbol of celibacy and piety and a key ornament for Catholics in the Middle Ages, worn by medieval bishops in their rings. Even today, the highest grade of amethyst is known as 'Bishop's Grade'. Leonardo da Vinci wrote that it 'dissipates evil thoughts and quickens the intelligence'. In Tibet, Buddhists make rosaries from it. The largest amethyst crystals come from South American countries such as Brazil and Uruguay, where they are found in gigantic geodes – some big enough to walk into (see How Minerals Form, Understanding Rocks and Minerals). The richest purple amethysts come from African countries such as Namibia and Zambia.

## Electric quartz

Better than any other mineral, quartz demonstrates the phenomenon of piezoelectricity. This means that when pressure is applied to a quartz crystal, a positive electrical charge is created at one end of the crystal and a negative charge at the other. In the same way, if an electric current is applied to a quartz crystal, it bends or changes its shape slightly to and fro. In other words, it vibrates or oscillates, and as it does so it generates little pulses of electricity. This oscillation is so perfectly regular that it can be used as a highly accurate timer in watches, especially if shaped like a tiny tuning fork.

### Crystalline and massive varieties of quartz

| Name | Habit | Colour | Transparency | Cause of colouring, inclusions etc |
|---|---|---|---|---|
| Quartz, common vein quartz | massive crystals | white, grey, yellowish | dull, opaque | gases and liquids, cracks, etc. |
| Rock crystal | crystals | colourless | transparent | — |
| Smoky quartz | crystals | brown | transparent | colouring caused by radiation |
| Morion | crystals | brown to nearly black | translucent | colouring caused by radiation |
| Amethyst | crystals, also massive | purple | transparent | colouring caused by radiation |
| Citrine | crystals | yellow | transparent | traces of very finely divided FeOOH |
| Rose quartz | massive, crystals rare | pink | translucent | minute rutile needles |
| Blue quartz | granular, massive | blue | translucent to transparent | minute rutile needles |
| Prase | massive | leek green | translucent | nickel silicates, actinolite needles |
| Aventurine | massive | iridescent, various colours | opaque | flakes of chromian muscovite or hematite |
| Tiger's eye | fibrous | blue to golden | opaque | silicified crocidolite asbestos |

# CHALCEDONY

*When quartz forms at low temperatures in volcanic cavities, the crystals can be so small that the mineral looks more like porcelain. The general name for this 'cryptocrystalline' quartz is chalcedony. It comes in an astonishing array of colours and patterns, including blood-red carnelian, wine-red jasper, brown-banded agate, green-moss agate, apple-green chrysoprase and black and white onyx.*

## Chalcedony (cryptocrystalline quartz)

*SiO₂ Silicon dioxide*

Chalcedony is a form of chert, and perhaps the most widely used of all gems through the ages. In fact, apart from sticks, bones and plain rocks, chalcedonies may have been the earliest hard materials used by mankind, shaped into arrowheads, knives, tools, cups and bowls. Its natural beauty meant it was also used ceremonially and for decoration long ago. It was a sacred stone for Native Americans, said to promote stability and harmony.

Chalcedony is typically fibrous and splintery and occurs in rounded crusts, rinds or stalactites in both volcanic and sedimentary rocks, precipitating from solutions moving through the ground. It can also form from organic matter. For example, over millions of years, chalcedony can replace the wood in dead trees, preserving the form of the trees in stone. Sometimes, this kind of chalcedony preserves the rings of the original tree, and so is mistaken for agate, the banded form of chalcedony.

**Carnelian (above)**: Carnelian is the orange-red, translucent variety of chalcedony. It gets its reddish colour from traces of hematite (iron oxide) or goethite and its colour can be enhanced by baking and dyeing with iron salts. It was valued long ago by the Greeks and Romans, who used it for signet rings. It is a close relative of russet-coloured sard, which got its name from the ancient Lydian city of Sardis. Together carnelian and sard were known as sardion in the Middle Ages. Sard with bands of white chalcedony is known as sardonyx and was once the most precious of all stones.

**Jasper (below)**: Jasper is the opaque, red, or occasionally green, variety of chalcedony. The red colour comes from traces of iron oxide, while the green comes from microscopic fibres of actinolite or chlorite. Sometimes other minerals can turn jasper brownish or yellow, but its streak is always white. It typically forms as part of agate nodules, but you can often find jasper pebbles on beaches in areas of igneous rock. Although dull when found, jasper takes polishing well, and pebbles glisten red when wet.

There are many varieties of chalcedony, some of which are shown here and on the opposite page. Apart from agate, another strikingly beautiful stone is chrysoprase. This translucent, apple-green stone gets its colour from traces of nickel. It typically occurs in cavities in serpentine. It was once found mainly in Silesia in central Europe. It was a particular favourite of Frederick the Great, and can be seen decorating many buildings in Prague, including the Chapel of St Wenceslas. Now most chrysoprase comes from Australia. Bloodstone or heliotrope is a dark-green stone containing the spots of red jasper that earned it its name. It was highly prized in the Middle Ages, when its 'blood' spots linked it to martyrdom and flagellation. Plasma is a semi-translucent, very fine-grained variety of chalcedony that owes its green colour to silicate particles such as amphibole and chlorite.

**Crystal system**: Trigonal
**Crystal habit**: Cryptocrystalline with a fibrous structure
**Colour**: Widely variable from green chrysoprase and moss agate, through red carnelian and jasper to brown sard and black and white onyx
**Lustre**: Vitreous or resinous
**Streak**: White
**Hardness**: 7
**Cleavage**: Poor
**Fracture**: Brittle and conchoidal
**Specific gravity**: 2.65
**Notable locations**:
Jasper: Urals, Russia; Oregon; Arizona; California

Carnelian: Ratnapura, India; Warwick (Queensland), Australia; Campo de Maia, Brazil

Sard: Ratnapura, India

Bloodstone: Kathiawar Peninsula, India

Onyx: India; Brazil

Plasma: Bavaria, Germany; Egypt; Madagascar; India; China; Australia; Brazil

Agate: Idar-Oberstein, Germany; Salzburg, Austria; Botswana; Madagascar; China; India; Queensland, Australia; Minas Gerais, Rio Grande do Sul, Brazil; Uruguay; Chihuahua, Mexico; Fairburn, South Dakota; Nipomo, California; Oregon; Idaho; Montana; Washington

Thunder egg agate: Jefferson County, Oregon

Fire agate: Mexico; Deer Hill, Arizona

Chrysoprase: Silesia, Poland; Urals, Russia; Australia; Brazil; California

**Agate (left)**: Agate forms when traces of iron, manganese and other chemicals create bands in chalcedony. Although the bands in agate form naturally, agates sold in shops are often stained artificially. Agates come mostly from cavities in basalt. They typically form in frothy basalt lavas that solidify so quickly as they flood on to the surface – especially where they meet water – that they trap gas bubbles. Silicate minerals dissolve from the lava and filter into the gas bubbles. As the lava cools, these dissolved silicate minerals coagulate as a gel inside the bubbles. Then iron and manganese compounds from the surrounding rock infiltrate the gel, creating layers of iron hydroxide. Eventually the whole bubble hardens and crystallizes, forming distinctive nodules of banded agate. The bands are revealed best when the nodule is cut into thin slices. There are scores of varieties of agate, including blue lace agate, with its wavy bands of mauve-blue and white, fire agate, with limonite inclusions, thunder eggs, with star-shaped brown and yellow bands, scenic agate, which looks like a woodland scene, and many more.

*The distinctive brown and white bands of sardonyx make it a popular gem.*

**Onyx (above)**: Onyx is one of the most striking of the banded chalcedonies, known as the agates. Onyx is distinguished by its straight black and white bands but is sometimes confused with the similar-looking building material, striped travertine or 'marble onyx'. It gets its name from the Greek for 'fingernail' and has been popular since Roman times for cameos and other small carvings because a skilful stone cutter can carve out the different coloured bands to create a dramatic contrast between the picture and its background. It is one of the 12 stones mentioned in the famous passage in the Bible (Exodus, 28) where the high priest Aaron's breastplate is described. Onyx forms in the same way as other agates, but near the bottom of agate nodules in horizontal layers. The best natural onyx, as with jasper, is found in river gravels in India, where it was deposited after the breakdown of the basalt rocks of the Deccan. Most onyx specimens are not natural, however, but made by soaking natural agate in sugar water and heating gently for a few weeks – a technique known for 4,000 years. This makes brown onyx; black onyx is made by then treating the stone with sulphuric acid. Carnelian onyx is a form of carnelian with red and white bands; sardonyx (see left) has brown and white bands.

### Idar-Oberstein

The little town of Idar-Oberstein in the Nahe river valley in Germany has been famous since the Middle Ages for its high quality agate work. It was especially famous for its carved agate bowls. Originally the agate came from local river pebbles, or from the nearby Setz quarry, where it was found in cavities in basalt. It was then ground and polished using wheels driven by the river. However, the Setz deposit was largely exhausted by the end of the 19th century, and so the Idar cutters turned to Brazil as a source for agate to cut, and as a result they exploited the other quartz stones there such as amethyst and citrine. Idar-Oberstein is now known throughout the world as a centre for the cutting of all kinds of gemstones.

### Varieties of cryptocrystalline quartz

| Name | Habit | Colour | Transparency | Cause of colouring, inclusions, etc. |
| --- | --- | --- | --- | --- |
| Chalcedony | compact | pale blue, pale grey | translucent | even coloured or slightly banded |
| Carnelian | compact | yellowish to deep red | translucent | very finely divided hematite |
| Sardonyx | compact | brown | translucent | very finely divided iron hydroxide |
| Chrysoprase | compact | apple green | translucent | hydrated nickel silicates |
| Agate | compact | multi-coloured | translucent | finely banded, filling cavities |
| Onyx | compact | grey, black and white | opaque | bands thicker than in agate |
| Enhydros | compact | as chalcedony | translucent | cavities partly filled with water |
| Jasper | compact | multi-coloured | opaque | many impurities of clay, iron, etc. |
| Plasma | compact | leek green | opaque | chlorite, horn-blende and other green minerals |
| Heliotrope | compact | green with red flecks | opaque | red flecks due to hematite |
| Flint | compact | white, grey and other colours | opaque | like jasper, containing some opaline material |

# FELDSPARS

*Together, the two kinds of feldspar, potassium (K) feldspar and plagioclase, make up almost two-thirds of the Earth's crust. K feldspars like orthoclase and sanidine are major ingredients in granite and other 'acidic' igneous rocks, as well as metamorphic rocks such as gneiss and sediments like arkose. Plagioclase feldspars, mostly albite and anorthite, are major ingredients in 'basic' igneous rocks such as gabbro.*

## Orthoclase

*KAlSi₃O₈ Potassium aluminium silicate*

Amazonite, a gem variety of microcline, is also known as amazon jade.

Like all feldspars, orthoclase is basically an aluminium silicate. Orthoclase, microcline and sanidine are all potassium- or K-rich, which is why they are called the potassium feldspars. These three are chemically identical, and the only real difference between them is their crystal structure. In particular, it can be almost impossible to tell microcline and orthoclase apart but by X-ray analysis – except when microcline is in its green form, known as amazonite (inset, top left). Orthoclase is typically white, but can be yellow and forms mainly in granites and syenites, as well as moderate to high grade metamorphic rocks such as gneiss and schist. Although it is incredibly common and a major raw material for the porcelain industry – especially orthoclase from aplite – almost all orthoclase is small grains and masses. Nevertheless, crystals do form in veins and porphyries in dikes. Good size yellow crystals ('noble orthoclase') are found in pegmatites in Madagascar. Colourless orthoclase crystals are named adularia after Adular in Switzerland, where they were first found in cavities in metamorphic rock. Moonstone is a rare and prized gem form of adularia and other feldspars that has a coloured surface sheen called adularescence.

**Identification**: Orthoclase looks like many light-coloured silicates, but it can be distinguished from spodumene by its blocky cleavage and from plagioclases by the lack of striations on the surface.

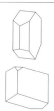

**Crystal system**: Monoclinic
**Crystal habit**: Typically massive and small grained, but crystals are tablet-shaped; adularia forms flattened tablets. Often forms simple twins of the Carlsbad and Baveno type. Twinning common.
**Colour**: Off-white, sometimes yellow or reddish
**Lustre**: Vitreous
**Streak**: White
**Hardness**: 6
**Cleavage**: Good in two directions, forming prisms
**Fracture**: Conchoidal or uneven
**Specific gravity**: 2.53
**Notable locations**: Carlsbad, Czech Republic; Adular, Disentis, Switzerland; Baveno, Italy; Lake Baikal, Siberia; Mount Kilimanjaro, Tanzania; Madagascar; Bernallio County, New Mexico; Robinson, Colorado; Clark County, Nevada

## Sanidine

*KAlSi₃O₈ Potassium aluminium silicate*

**Identification**: Sanidine looks very like orthoclase, but has a glassier, less grainy texture. It looks translucent or even transparent.

Orthoclase and microcline form in magmas that cool only moderately quickly, such as granite and syenite, crystallizing at temperatures between 400°C/750°F and 900°C/1,652°F. Sanidine forms in magmas that reach the surface and cool rapidly from temperatures of over 900°C, like rhyolite and trachyte, and also in rocks that metamorphose at high temperatures, such as gneiss. Rapid cooling means that crystals have little time to grow, and consequently sanidine is almost glassy in texture.

Chemically, sanidine is also the potassium-rich end of a series of feldspars that form at high temperatures and are rich in either potassium or sodium. At the sodium-rich end is the high-temperature form of the plagioclase feldspar albite. Anorthoclase feldspar lies in between the two.

**Crystal system**: Monoclinic
**Crystal habit**: Typically massive, but rare crystals are tablet- or prism-shaped
**Colour**: Off-white or clear or grey; often transparent
**Lustre**: Vitreous
**Streak**: White
**Hardness**: 6
**Cleavage**: Good in two directions, forming prisms
**Fracture**: Conchoidal, uneven
**Specific gravity**: 2.53
**Notable locations**: Elba, Italy; Caucasus Mts, Russia; Ragged Mt (Gunnison Co), Colorado; Grant Co, New Mexico; Bisbee, Arizona

# Albite

*NaAlSi₃O₈ Sodium aluminium silicate*

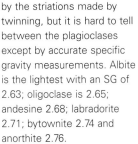

*The green, gold and blue iridescent 'sheen' known as labradorescence is clearly visible in this labradorite specimen.*

Albite commonly occurs in igneous and metamorphic rocks. At high temperatures it mixes with K feldspars and forms a series with sanidine. At low temperatures it separates out as layers inside K feldspar crystals to create a rock called perthite. When albite substitutes orthoclase in granite-like rocks, the rock becomes quartz monzonite. In pegmatites, albite can form bladelike aggregates called clevelandite. Albite is very common, but good crystals are rare, except in pegmatites and lavas called spilites. Albite and anorthite are the only plagioclase feldspars that ever form crystals; labradorite, andesine, bytownite and oligoclase occur only as aggregates. Labradorite exhibits an attractive array of colours called labradorescence (inset). Albite is one of the last feldspars to crystallize from a magma and so is often associated with some rare minerals. Twins are common in all feldspars, but albite crystals in igneous rocks are nearly always twinned.

**Identification**: Plagioclases can be told from K feldspars by the striations made by twinning, but it is hard to tell between the plagioclases except by accurate specific gravity measurements. Albite is the lightest with an SG of 2.63; oligoclase is 2.65; andesine 2.68; labradorite 2.71; bytownite 2.74 and anorthite 2.76.

*Clevelandite*

**Crystal system**: Triclinic
**Crystal habit**: Most albite is grains in rocks but when crystals form they are nearly always twinned. Crystals are typically square in cross-section. Bladelike aggregates (cleavelandite) form in pegmatites.
**Colour**: Off-white, sometimes yellow or reddish
**Lustre**: Vitreous
**Streak**: White
**Hardness**: 6–6.5
**Cleavage**: Good in two directions
**Fracture**: Conchoidal
**Specific gravity**: 2.63
**Notable locations**: Alps, Switzerland; Tyrol, Austria; Minas Gerais, Brazil (cleavelandite); Francon, Mount-St-Hilaire, Quebec; Labrador; Amelia County, Virginia; San Diego County, California

**Perfect pottery**
Porcelain is one of the most remarkable of all synthetic materials, light and strong yet clean and smooth, and wonderfully translucent. In fact, when it was first brought to Europe from China, many assumed it was natural. But the Chinese had discovered how to make it around 1,400 years ago by heating a mixture of a feldspar-rich rock called petuntse and kaolin (china clay). They kept their secret, and many Europeans spent a fortune trying to unravel it, for Chinese porcelain once fetched a higher price than gold. They knew china clay was involved, but they were missing the petuntse, the orthoclase feldspar-rich rock powder that made the clay hard. Some thought the missing ingredient might be ground bone, and around 1800 Josiah Spode added bone to china clay to make bone china. Another successful European equivalent was developed in Meissen in Germany by Johann Böttger and Ehrenfried von Tschirnhaus. Finally, in the 19th century, the role of orthoclase feldspar was revealed.

# Anorthite

*CaAlSi₃O₈ Calcium aluminium silicate*

Each of the plagioclase feldspars has a different proportion of sodium or calcium. Albite has the most sodium; anorthite has the most calcium. The others – oligoclase, andesine, labradorite and bytownite – lie in between. While albite is typical of granite-like rocks that form at low temperatures, anorthite is common in basic rocks such as gabbros that form at high temperatures, and also meteorites and moon rocks. Anorthite crystals are always twinned but quite rare, occurring only in lavas in places such as Miyake-jima, Japan, and near Mount Vesuvius in Italy.

**Identification**: The best ways to identify anorthite are by its occurrence in lavas, its striated twinned crystals and its specific gravity of 2.76.

*Anorthite*

**Crystal system**: Triclinic
**Crystal habit**: Usually massive, but crystals are short prism or tablet shapes and always twinned
**Colour**: Colourless, whitish, grey, pinkish, greenish
**Lustre**: Vitreous
**Streak**: White
**Hardness**: 6–6.5
**Cleavage**: Good in two directions
**Fracture**: Conchoidal
**Specific gravity**: 2.76
**Notable locations**: Mount Somma (Mount Vesuvius), Italy; Miyake-jima, Japan; Franklin, New Jersey; Aleutian Islands, Alaska; Lake Co, Nevada Co, California

# FELDSPATHOIDS

*The feldspathoids is a group of minerals very similar to feldspars, including sodalite, haüyne, nepheline, lazurite, leucite, cancrinite and nosean. They are all minerals that would have become feldspars if there was more silica present when they formed. Feldspars tend to contain three times as much silica. So feldspathoids do not occur in silica-rich rocks such as granite but typically form in volcanic lavas.*

## Sodalite

$Na_8Al_6Si_6O_{24}Cl_2$ Sodium aluminium silicate with chlorine

Sodalite is a feldspathoid mineral that occurs with nepheline and cancrinite in basic igneous rocks such as nepheline syenites, and also in silica-poor dikes and lavas. It gets its name from its sodium content, and generally forms when aluminium silicate-rich rocks are invaded from below by waters rich in sodium chloride. Sodalite's colour ranges from royal blue to light blue and white and makes it very distinctive and likely to be confused only with lazurite and lazulite. Some sodalite is fluorescent and, under longwave UV light, nepheline syenite rock usually shows glowing patches of sodalite. A colourless variety called hackmanite is 'tenebrescent', turning red after exposure to UV then fading to pink. Although crystals are rare, rich blue masses of granular sodalite, big enough for ornamental stone, are found near Bancroft in Ontario, Canada. The Bancroft sodalite was famously excavated in 1906 to decorate Marlborough House in London. Even bigger, bluer masses are found in Bahia, Brazil, while there are thin veins of sodalite at Ice River in British Columbia and smaller masses in Maine. Colourless crystals are found in altered limestone blocks ejected by Mount Vesuvius, Italy.

**Identification**: Sodalite is usually easy to identify by its blue colour, similar only to lazurite and lazulite. Greyer and paler sodalites are typically fluorescent, gaining colour under longwave UV light, before fading again in daylight.

**Crystal system**: Cubic
**Crystal habit**: Rare dodecahedral crystals but usually masses in rock
**Colour**: Blue, white, grey
**Lustre**: Vitreous or greasy
**Streak**: White
**Hardness**: 5.5–6
**Cleavage**: Perfect in one direction
**Fracture**: Uneven
**Specific gravity**: 2.1–2.3
**Other features**: Hackmanite is tenebrescent, briefly changing colour after exposure to longwave UV.
**Notable locations**: Ilimaussaq, Greenland; Mount Vesuvius, Italy; South Africa; Bahia, Brazil; Bancroft, Ontario; Ice River, British Columbia; Litchfield, Maine

## Haüyne

$Na_6Ca_2Al_6Si_6O_{24}(SO_4)_2$ Sodium calcium aluminium silicate sulphate

**Crystal system**: Cubic
**Crystal habit**: Rare rhombo-decahedral crystals but usually masses in rock
**Colour**: Blue, white, gray
**Lustre**: Vitreous or greasy
**Streak**: White
**Hardness**: 5.5–6
**Cleavage**: Perfect in three directions
**Fracture**: Conchoidal
**Specific gravity**: 2.4–2.5
**Notable locations**: Mount Vulture, Mount Somma (Mount Vesuvius), Italy; Niedermendig Mine (Black Forest), Germany; Tasmania

A rare but attractive mineral, haüyne is named after René Just Haüy (1743–1822), the pioneering French crystallographer, who discovered it on Monte Somma, Italy, among the Vesuvian lavas. It is a member of the sodalite group with sodalite and nosean. But unlike sodalite and nosean, haüyne contains calcium. It is usually a striking electric-blue colour, but can be green, red, yellow or even grey. Like all feldspathoids, haüyne usually occurs in igneous rocks low in silica and rich in alkalis such as sodium and calcium, which provide the basic raw materials for it to form. The typical environment for haüyne is silica-poor lavas such as phonolite and trachyte. Apart from Monte Somma, haüyne has been found more generally in the volcanoes of Lazio and notably in Tasmania in Australia. It has also been found at the Niedermendig Mine near Eifel in the Black Forest, Germany, where it occurs in volcanic bombs.

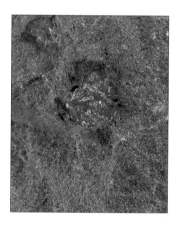

**Identification**: Startling electric blue haüyne crystals stand out clearly from the volcanic bombs or lava flow in which they are usually found.

# Nepheline

*(Na,K)AlSiO₄ Sodium aluminium silicate with chlorine*

Nepheline is by far the most common of the feldspathoids and occurs in many silica-poor, alkali-rich igneous rocks. In fact, the presence of nepheline in a rock is generally taken as an indication that a rock is alkali-rich. In some rocks, nepheline is such a major component that they are named accordingly: nepheline syenite, nepheline monzonite and nephelinite. These rocks are also distinguished by how much of the various feldspars they contain. Although found in masses in rocks around the world, the most notable occurrences of crystals are in plutonic rocks at Bancroft, Ontario in Canada, and Karelskaya (Karelia) in Russia, and in cavities in limestone blocks thrown out by Mount Vesuvius. In recent years, massive nepheline has been used as a source material for soda, silica and alumina for the glass and ceramics industries. Because nepheline-bearing rocks do not contain quartz, they melt well. Nepheline can also be synthesized into a high-temperature mineral called carnegieite.

**Identification**: Distinctive six-sided crystals like these formed in pegmatitic nepheline syenite dikes are rare. More usually, nepheline is seen as white grains in nepheline rock.

**Crystal system**: Hexagonal
**Crystal habit**: Forms column-shaped hexagonal crystals but masses and grains typical
**Colour**: Off-white to grey
**Lustre**: Greasy to dull
**Streak**: White
**Hardness**: 5.5–6
**Cleavage**: Poor
**Fracture**: Conchoidal to uneven
**Specific gravity**: 2.6
**Notable locations**: Monte Somma (Mount Vesuvius), Italy; Karelskaya (Kola peninsular), Russia; Australia; Brazil; Bancroft, Ontario; Ouachita, Arkansas; Kennebec County, Maine; Colfax County, New Mexico

*Hexagonal nepheline crystals*

# Lazurite

*(Na,Ca)₈Al₆Si₆O₂₄(S,SO₄)₂ Sodium calcium aluminium silicate sulphur sulphate*

**Lapis lazuli**

Lapis lazuli is one of the oldest, most treasured of all gemstones. Its name is a combination of the Latin *lapis* for 'stone' and the Arabic *azul* for 'sky' or the ancient Persian *lazhuward* for 'blue'. It usually occurs as lenses and veins in white marble. Consisting largely of lazurite with spots of pyrite, it has a mottled look. Crystals are sometimes found, but more usually it is massive, and is carved to make jewellery, cups and other decorative objects. It was first mined over 6,000 years ago at Sar-e-Sang in the Kokcha valley in Afghanistan, still the source of the world's finest lapis lazuli. The ancient royal tombs of the Sumerian city of Ur contained over 6,000 beautifully carved lapis lazuli statues, and it was a favourite stone of the Ancient Egyptians, much used in the tomb decorations of Tutankhamun. The Roman writer Pliny the Elder described it as 'a fragment of the starry firmament'. Today, lapis lazuli is mined near Lake Baikal in Siberia and at Ovalle in Chile as well as in Afghanistan. Chilean lapis contains flecks of calcite.

Its beautiful, rich blue colour makes lazurite one of the most distinctive and attractive of all minerals. Its chemical make-up is quite complex, but the blue colour comes from the sulphur that takes the place of some silicate atoms. It is soft and brittle and easily ground to make the rich blue pigment ultramarine, but it is most famous as the major ingredient of the gemstone lapis lazuli, famed since the days of Ancient Egypt. Little spots of golden pyrite look like stars in the deep blue lazurite of lapis lazuli. Lazurite is very rare and found in any quantity only in the Kokcha valley of Afghanistan and also high up in the nearby Pamir Mountains by Lake Baikal in Siberia.

**Crystal system**: Cubic
**Crystal habit**: Forms column-shaped hexagonal crystals but masses and grains typical
**Colour**: Off white to grey
**Lustre**: Greasy to dull
**Streak**: White.
**Hardness**: 5.5–6
**Cleavage**: Poor
**Fracture**: Uneven
**Specific gravity**: 2.6
**Notable locations**: Mount Vesuvius, Italy; Lake Baikal, Pamir Mountains, Russia; Kokcha River, Afghanistan; Ovalle, Chile; Sawatch Mountains, Colorado; Cascade Canyon and Ontario Peak, San Gabriel Mountains, San Bernardino County), California

**Identification**: Lazurite is usually easy to identify by its vivid blue colour. It can be distinguished from sodalite by its association with pyrite, and from lazulite by its lower specific gravity.

# ZEOLITES

*Zeolites are a group of 50 or so minerals including heulandite, stilbite, phillipsite, harmotome, natrolite, chabazite and analcime. Popular with collectors for their rarity and beauty, they are also of industrial importance for their ability to act as filters and chemical sponges. Similar to both clay and feldspars, they typically form when the minerals in cavities of volcanic rocks are altered by moderate heat and pressure.*

## Heulandite

*(Ca,Na)$_{2-3}$Al$_3$(Al,Si)$_2$Si$_{13}$O$_{36}$.12H$_2$O Hydrated calcium sodium aluminium silicate*

Heulandite is one of the most common and best known zeolites, named after the English mineral dealer John Henry Heuland, who hunted for it in Iceland. It forms distinctive, cream-coloured, pearly lustred crystals shaped like the coffins in old horror films, with a wide waist. The crystals develop from a hydrothermal solution percolating through magnesium- and iron-rich volcanic rocks, especially basalts, and form in cavities left by gas bubbles trapped as the lava cools. Heulandite forms when the minerals in the bubble left by the solutions are altered by mild metamorphism. It can form in the same way in pegmatites, tuffs, metamorphic rocks and also in deep-sea sediments. It does form in other places, too, but the crystals are generally much smaller. The best specimens are from the basalts of Berufjördhur in Iceland and the Faroe Islands, and the Deccan traps of the Sahyadri mountains near Bombay. Red heulandite crystals have been found on Campsie Fells in Scotland, the Fassathal in the Austrian Tyrol, Gunnedah in New South Wales (Australia) and in eastern Russia.

**Identification**: Heulandite is best identified by its creamy coloured crystals, its pearly sheen and its coffin-shaped crystals.

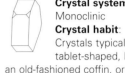

**Crystal system**: Monoclinic
**Crystal habit**: Crystals typically tablet-shaped, like an old-fashioned coffin, or pseudo-orthorhombic
**Colour**: White, pink, red, brown
**Lustre**: Vitreous or pearly
**Streak**: White
**Hardness**: 3.5–4
**Cleavage**: Poor
**Fracture**: Uneven
**Specific gravity**: 2.1–2.3
**Notable locations**: Campsie Fells, Scotland; Berufjördhur, Iceland; Faroe Islands; Fassatal, Austria; Urals, Russia; Sahyadri Mts, India; Gunnedah (NSW), Australia; Partridge Island, Nova Scotia, Canada; Paterson, New Jersey; Idaho; Oregon; Washington

## Stilbite

*NaCa$_2$Al$_5$Si$_{13}$O$_{36}$.14H$_2$O Hydrated sodium calcium aluminium silicate*

**Crystal system**: Monoclinic
**Crystal habit**: Crystals typically thin plates that can aggregate in wheat-sheaf shapes. Cruciform (cross-like) twins common.
**Colour**: White, pink, red, brown, orange
**Lustre**: Vitreous or pearly
**Streak**: White
**Hardness**: 3.5–4
**Cleavage**: Perfect in one direction
**Fracture**: Uneven
**Specific gravity**: 2.1–2.3
**Notable locations**: Kilpatrick, Scotland; Berufjördhur, Iceland; Poona, India; Victoria, Australia; Rio Grande do Sul, Brazil; Bay of Fundy, Nova Scotia; Paterson, New Jersey

Stilbite is another common zeolite very closely related to heulandite. It is very popular among collectors for the extraordinary stilbite crystals that grow in fantastic shapes resembling wheat sheaves or a stack of bow ties. Stilbite crystals are not always shaped like this, but when they are they are almost unique. Only the rare related zeolite stellerite has similar crystals. Crystals are usually whitish, but bright orange examples have been found. Like heulandite, stilbite forms in cavities in basaltic lava, besides ore veins and pegmatites – and so tends to be found wherever there were large floods of basalt lava, such as in the Deccan traps of India. However, it is also the zeolite most likely to form in situations that are not typical for zeolites, such as mineral seams in granite.

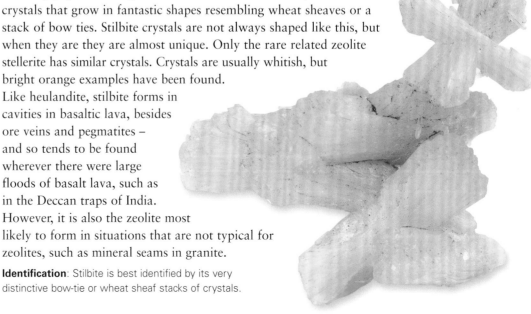

**Identification**: Stilbite is best identified by its very distinctive bow-tie or wheat sheaf stacks of crystals.

# Phillipsite

*(K,Na,Ca)₁₋₂(Si,Al)₈O₁₆.6H₂O Hydrated potassium sodium calcium aluminium silicate*

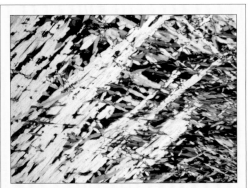

*Harmotome is a glassy mineral whose crystals may form attractive twins.*

Named by Lévy in 1825 after English mineralogist W Phillips (1775–1829), Phillipsite is not one of the most common natural zeolites – though it is often made artificially. Yet it is popular with collectors because, besides crystals, it sometimes forms aggregates of little white balls with a silky surface. These balls form in bubble cavities in lava, like other zeolites, and can be seen in the phonolites near Rome in Italy. Phillipsite can form quite quickly; crystals have actually developed in cavities in the masonry of the hot mineral baths at Plombires in France. It can also form around hot springs. Phillipsite also forms in calcite-rich deep-sea sediments, and in 1951 specimens were dredged by the *Challenger* survey ship from the bottom of the Pacific, where they formed by the alteration of lava. Phillipsite and another rare zeolite, harmotome (inset), are often hard to distinguish.

**Identification**: Phillipsite is most easily identified when it forms silky or rough little balls lining the insides of cavities, but can also form crystals that are not so easy to identify.

**Crystal system**: Monoclinic
**Crystal habit**: Crystals typically twinned in groups of four or more. Often forms aggregates of small balls.
**Colour**: White, clear, yellowish, reddish
**Lustre**: Vitreous, silky
**Streak**: White
**Hardness**: 4–4.5
**Cleavage**: Imperfect in one direction
**Fracture**: Uneven
**Specific gravity**: 2.2
**Notable locations**: Moyle (Antrim), Northern Ireland; Capo di Bove, Mount Vesuvius, Italy; Groschlattengruen, Germany; Cape Grim, Tasmania; Jefferson County, Colorado

# Chabazite

*Ca₂(Al₄Si₈O₂₄).13H₂O Hydrated calcium potassium sodium aluminium silicate*

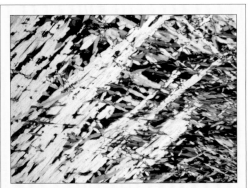

**Zeolite marvels**
Zeolites have been found to be such remarkable minerals that a whole industry has built up around making the most of them. They are aluminium silicates like clay, but unlike clay they have a rigid, honeycomblike crystal structure with networks of tunnels and cages. Water can move freely in and out of these pores without affecting the zeolite framework. The pores are of a uniform size, so the crystal can act like a molecular sieve, filtering out particles of the wrong size. The zeolite can also exchange ions well. The result is that zeolites can act as both microsponges able to retain water, just like the best soil, and as filters able to clean up the tiniest particles. They are so useful that artificial versions are made to take advantage of the properties of particular natural zeolites, especially chabazite, clinoptilolite and phillipsite. Zeolites are used for air filters, water treatment, cleaning oil spills, cleaning up radioactive waste and much more. They are also used as an artificial medium for growing plants.

Getting its name from *chalaza*, the Greek for 'hail', chabazite can look very similar to other zeolites and forms in similar places. Like phillipsite and harmotome, it forms when the bubbles trapped in lava are subjected to gentle metamorphism. The most dramatic chabazite crystals from Poona in India formed like this in the Deccan traps basalt. In these small cavities, chabazite can occur with a huge range of other minerals, especially zeolites such as natrolite, scolecite, heulandite and stilbite. The chabazite crystals are actually rhombohedral, but look like little cubes. Chabazite can also form small crystals around hot springs.

**Crystal system**: Trigonal
**Crystal habit**: Crystals rhombohedral but look like cubes
**Colour**: Usually white or yellowish, can be pink or red
**Lustre**: Vitreous
**Streak**: White
**Hardness**: 4.5
**Cleavage**: Poor
**Fracture**: Uneven
**Specific gravity**: 2–2.1
**Notable locations**: Kilmacolm, Scotland; Berufjördhur, Iceland; Oberstein, Germany; Switzerland; Poona, India; Richmond (Victoria), Table Cape (Tasmania), Australia; New Zealand; Nova Scotia; New Jersey; Yellowstone, Wyoming; Bowie, Arizona

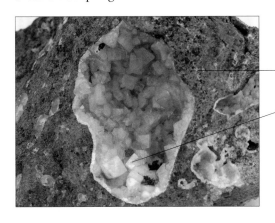

— *Basalt rock*

— *Chabazite*

**Identification**: When found in a bubble cavity, chabazite is clearly a zeolite. Its cubic-looking crystals mark it out as chabazite.

# PYROXENES

*Pyroxenes are present in most igneous and metamorphic rocks, and a major ingredient in darker mafic rocks such as gabbro and basalt. They were given the name 'pyroxene' by French mineralogist R J Haüy from the Greek for 'fire' and 'stranger', because he was surprised to see these dark green crystals ready-formed in lavas. In fact, they simply crystallize at high temperatures, before the lava erupts.*

## Diopside

*$CaMgSi_2O_6$ Calcium magnesium silicate*

**Pyroxenes and amphiboles**
Pyroxenes and amphiboles are closely related silicate minerals that look similar. Pyroxenes form when there is little water present; water turns the same minerals to amphiboles. Pyroxenes form shorter, stubbier, prism-shaped crystals that break almost at right angles, while amphiboles break in a wedge shape – hornblends is a classic example. The difference is usually clear when specimens are viewed through a petrological microscope or sometimes even a very good magnifying glass.

**Identification**: Diopside can usually be identified by its light green colour, and its right-angle cleavage.

Diopside is a silicate that often crystallizes direct from basic magmas, which is why it is a major ingredient in some ultrabasic igneous rocks. It also forms when silicates in dolomitic limestones are metamorphosed and in iron-rich skarns (metamorphosed ore deposits). Most of this diopside is grainy or locked into the rock. Distinct crystals are rarer, but can be attractive, especially green, chrome-rich ones. The name diopside comes from the Greek *dis* and *opsis* for 'double view', because crystals can be strongly birefringent (give a double image). Some display a chatoyancy (cat's eye) effect, and some are chatoyant in two directions, giving a cross. Some ancient civilizations believed spirits observed you through these star crosses.

**Crystal system**: Monoclinic
**Crystal habit**: Usually short, prism-shaped crystals, but also grainy aggregates, columns and masses
**Colour**: Green, khaki, colourless, light blue
**Lustre**: Vitreous, dull
**Streak**: White, light green
**Hardness**: 6
**Cleavage**: Perfect prism
**Fracture**: Brittle, conchoidal
**Specific gravity**: 3.3–3.6
**Notable locations**: Fassa, Ala and Ossola Valleys, Mount Vesuvius, Italy; Binnetal, Switzerland; Zillertal, Austria; Outokumpu, Finland; Baikal, Russia; North Korea; Madagascar; De Kalb, New York; Riverside County, California

## Augite

*$(Ca,Na)(Mg,Fe,Al)(Al,Si)_2O_6$ Calcium sodium magnesium iron aluminium silicate*

**Identification**: Augite is usually recognizable by its dark colour and blocky, prismatic crystals.

Augite is closely related to diopside, but contains a good deal of sodium and aluminium, and much more magnesium. It gets its name from the Greek for 'lustre' because of the sheen it gives to the surface of augite-rich rocks. It is the most common pyroxene mineral, and an important ingredient in many dark-coloured, basic igneous rocks, notably basalts, dolerites, gabbros and peridotites. Some of the best augite crystals are phenocrysts (extra-large, preformed crystals) in basalt. The tuff deposits around some volcanoes are almost entirely augite crystals, and big crystals can be picked out of weathered lavas in the craters of some Italian volcanoes. Augite occurs in rocks metamorphosed at high temperatures, too, such as granulites and gneisses, and also in meteorites rich in basaltic material, which is why augite crystals are found in the Bushveld complex in South Africa (see Gabbroic rocks, Directory of Rocks). Although common, most big augite crystals are quite dull.

**Crystal system**: Monoclinic
**Crystal habit**: Usually short, prism-shaped, rectangular crystals, but also grains, columns and masses
**Colour**: Dark green, brown, black
**Lustre**: Vitreous, dull
**Streak**: Greenish white
**Hardness**: 5–6
**Cleavage**: Perfect prism
**Fracture**: Uneven
**Specific gravity**: 3.2–3.6
**Notable locations**: Mounts Vesuvius, Etna, Stromboli, Lazio, Italy; Auvergne, France; Eifel, Germany; Bushveld complex, South Africa; St Lawrence, Ramapo Mountains, New York

# Spodumene

*LiAlSi₂O₆ Lithium aluminium silicate*

Spodumene gets its name from the Greek for 'burnt to ashes', because of its commonest grey colour. It occurs almost exclusively in lithium-rich granite pegmatites, where it is usually associated with lepidolite mica, elbaite tourmaline, caesium beryl, amblygonite, quartz and albite. Massive spodumene is the main ore of lithium, the lightest of all metals, used in ceramics and lubricants, and a key ingredient in anti-depressive drugs. Rough crystals of spodumene can be huge, and some have been found that are nearly 15m/49ft 3in long and weigh over 90 tonnes. Brilliant, glassy, small gem crystals are quite rare, however. They have never been that popular for jewellery because their colour fades when exposed to sunlight, but they are cherished by collectors and museums. Impurities taking the place of aluminium in the crystal structure give a wide range of colours – iron gives yellow to green spodumene, chromium gives deep green spodumene and manganese gives lilac spodumene. Violet spodumene is known as kunzite, and green spodumene is called hiddenite.

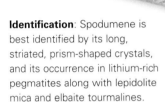

**Identification**: Spodumene is best identified by its long, striated, prism-shaped crystals, and its occurrence in lithium-rich pegmatites along with lepidolite mica and elbaite tourmalines.

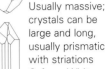

**Crystal system**: Monoclinic
**Crystal habit**: Usually massive; crystals can be large and long, usually prismatic with striations
**Colour**: White or greyish white, also green, pink, yellow, lilac
**Lustre**: Vitreous
**Streak**: White
**Hardness**: 6.5–7
**Cleavage**: Perfect prismatic
**Fracture**: Splintery
**Specific gravity**: 3–3.2
**Notable locations**: Varuträsk, Sweden; Afghanistan; Pakistan; Namibia; Madagascar; Brazil; Black Hills, South Dakota; Dixon, New Mexico; North Carolina

---

**Green jade**
Jade has long been cherished in China, where it was a symbol of royalty and has been carved into jewellery, ornaments and small statues for thousands of years. It is so tough that it was even used to make knives and axes. It has an almost equally long history in South America. Indeed it gets its name from the Spanish *piedra de ijada*, which means 'stone of the side', because the Spaniards who came across it in Central America were told that it cured kidney problems. Europeans applied the name jade to the similar-looking ornamental green stone that came from China and from South America. It was only in 1863 that mineralogists realized there were two minerals involved – 'hard' jadeite and 'soft' nephrite (as in the Maori pendant, above), both of which are found in China and South America. The most highly prized jade is the emerald-green Imperial Jade, produced by traces of chromium. Nephrite can be pale green or white, while jadeite can be green, white, yellow or even violet in colour.

# Jadeite

*Na(Al,Fe)Si₂O₆ Sodium aluminium iron silicate*

Jadeite is one of two minerals called jade. The other is nephrite. Jadeite is the more valued and is very rare. Most jadeite is opaque, and the best translucent stones are rarer still. Jadeite forms at high pressures in rocks subjected to intense metamorphism, which creates this beautiful green stone by altering minerals such as nepheline and albite in sodium-rich rocks. It is associated with the minerals glaucophane and aragonite, but jadeite is very rarely found in situ, as in Guatemala. Instead, it is more normally found as water-worn pebbles, freed from the parent rock by weathering, as is the case in China and Burma. In its pure form, jadeite is pure white in colour, but trace quantities of chrome, iron and titanium give it a green, blue or lavender hue.

**Crystal system**: Monoclinic
**Crystal habit**: Usually massive or granular
**Colour**: Green or white, blue and lavender
**Lustre**: Vitreous, dull
**Streak**: White.
**Hardness**: 6.5–7
**Cleavage**: Good but rarely seen
**Fracture**: Splintery to uneven
**Specific gravity**: 3.25–3.35
**Notable locations**: Urals, Russia; Tawmaw, Myanmar (Burma); China; Kotaki, Japan; Sulawesi; Motagua River, Guatemala; Mexico; San Benito County, California

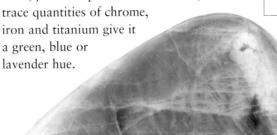

**Identification:** Jadeite is readily identified by its colour and beauty, and by its hardness. It can be distinguished by its specific gravity from nephrite, which is less dense at 2.9–3.3.

# SILICATE GEMS

*The hardness of silica means that when some silica minerals are combined with the right chemical 'colouring agents' they can turn into exquisite gems such as tourmaline, beryl and topaz. Under the headings tourmaline and beryl come a host of other gems, each transformed into unique gems such as elbaite, emerald, aquamarine and morganite by minute traces of particular chemicals.*

## Tourmaline

*$Na(Li,Al)_3Al_6Si_6O_{18}(BO_3)_3.(OH)_4$ Sodium lithium aluminium boro-silicate hydroxide*

**Crystal system**: Trigonal
**Crystal habit**: Typically elongated triangular or six-sided prisms, with striations on the surface. The ends may be of different shapes.
**Colour**: Very variable, but commonly black or bluish black, blue, pink, green
**Lustre**: Vitreous
**Streak**: White
**Hardness**: 7.5
**Cleavage**: Very poor
**Fracture**: Very poor
**Specific gravity**: 3–3.2
**Notable locations**: Elba, Italy; Urals, Russia; Chainpur, Nepal; Afghanistan; Yinniethara, Western Australia; Bahia, Brazil; Maine; San Diego County, California

Tourmaline is the most variably coloured of all gems. The Ancient Egyptians called it rainbow rock, believing it gathered all the colours of the rainbow as it worked its way up through the Earth. Its name comes from the Sri Lankan *tur mali*, meaning 'multi-coloured stone'. Traces of different chemicals transform it into over 100 different colours. Indeed, single specimens can come in a mix of colours. Watermelon tourmaline has a bright pink centre and a vivid green rind. The 19th-century art critic John Ruskin said tourmaline's make-up was 'more like a medieval doctor's prescription than the making of a respectable mineral'. Tourmaline is not a single mineral species, but a group of species including minerals such as schorl (coloured black by iron) and dravite (made brown by magnesium), but most gem tourmaline is lithium-rich elbaite, named after the Italian island of Elba where many good tourmaline crystals were once found. Tourmaline is usually formed in granitic pegmatites, but it is also formed where limestones are metamorphosed by contact with granite magma. Because it is tough, tourmaline can be found in river gravel deposits after its parent rock is broken down by weathering.

**Identification**: Tourmaline is easy to identify when it is multi-coloured, like watermelon tourmaline. Otherwise the best clue to a tourmaline's crystal identity is its triangular cross-section.

## Beryl

*$Be_3Al_2Si_6O_{18}$ Beryllium aluminium silicate*

**Identification**: Beryl's hardness, hexagonal crystals and association with pegmatites mean it can easily be confused only with topaz and quartz. Colour then helps to confirm the identity.

*Yellow beryl*

*Quartz*

Unlike tourmaline, beryl is a single mineral species, yet although pure beryl or goshenite is colourless, impurities give it a colour palette as rich as any other gem mineral. Chromium and vanadium turn it to brilliant emerald. Blue beryl is known as aquamarine, while yellow beryl is heliodor and pink beryl is morganite. The name beryl is reserved for the red and golden variety. Beryl is a tough crystal that forms deep down in the Earth. Most is found in granite pegmatites, typically 'frozen' in masses of quartz-feldspar, but sometimes occurring as free crystals in cavities. It also occurs in skarns, schists intruded by pegmatites and, as in Colombia, introduced by hydro-thermal waters into carbonate-sediments. Most crystals are small, but a few of the Colombian beryls are huge, measuring up to 5.5m/18ft in length. One beryl from Madagascar was recorded as weighing a staggering 36.6 tonnes.

**Crystal system**: Hexagonal
**Crystal habit**: Crystals are long, six-sided prisms, typically with flat pyramid tops and striations on their surfaces
**Colour**: A wide range including green, yellow, gold, red, pink and colourless
**Lustre**: Vitreous
**Streak**: White
**Hardness**: 7.5–8
**Cleavage**: Basal, poor
**Fracture**: Conchoidal
**Specific gravity**: 2.6–2.9
**Notable locations**: Galicia, Spain; Russia; Namibia; Madagascar; Pakistan; Chivor, Muzo, Colombia; Minas Gerais, Brazil; Hiddenite, North Carolina; San Diego County, California

# Opal

*SiO₂.nH₂O Silicon dioxide, with up to 21 per cent water*

Unlike most other minerals, opal never really forms crystals. In fact, it is a hardened silica gel, containing about 5–10 per cent water. It forms when silica-rich fluids solidify in cavities to form nodules, crusts, veinlets and masses. Sometimes opal replaces bones or wood during fossilization. Sometimes it forms around hot springs and in volcanic rocks. Dull yellow, red or black 'potch' opal is incredibly common, and is widely mined for use as an abrasive and filler. Precious opal is much rarer and only forms where minute silica spheres settle completely undisturbed. Potch opal may contain spheres, but they are a varied hotch-potch. Precious opal is made of even-sized spheres, and light is diffracted through these spheres to create opal's distinctive shimmering colours or 'opalescence'. Until the 19th century, most precious opal came from Slovakia, where it was found in andesite. Now 90 per cent of the world's opals come from the sandstones and ironstones of the Australian outback, notably at Coober Pedy.

**Identification**: Opal's silvery sheen and play of colours usually makes this gem easy to identify. However, there are many varieties from dull browns to silvery white. Some are entirely opaque; some are completely transparent.

**Crystal system**: None
**Crystal habit**: Massive, typically kidney-shaped, round, or sheetlike
**Colour**:
Common, potch opal: Various colours, but lacks opalescence
Precious opal: White or black and opalescent
Fire opal: Red and yellow flamelike reflections
Hyalite: Colourless
Hydrophane: Transparent in water
**Lustre**: Vitreous, pearly
**Streak**: White
**Hardness**: 5.5–6
**Cleavage**: None
**Fracture**: Conchoidal
**Specific gravity**: 1.8–2.3
**Notable locations**:
Cervenica, eastern Slovakia; Lightning Ridge (NSW), Coober Pedy (SA), Australia; Ceará, Brazil; Honduras; Mexico; Washington; Idaho; Virgin Valley, Nevada

**The greenest gem**
Emeralds get their name from the Ancient Greek *smaragdos*, meaning 'green'. They are one of the oldest known gems, found with mummies in Egyptian tombs. The oldest Egyptian emerald mines, some 3,500 years old, were rediscovered by the French adventurer Caillaud in 1816. Then in 1900, Cleopatra's mines near the Red Sea were found. The Roman emperor Nero is said to have watched through an emerald as gladiators fought to the death. The best emeralds come from South America, especially the famous Chivor and Muzo mines in Colombia, first mined by the Chibcha Indians long before the Spanish arrived. The Spanish conquistadors pillaged many fine Chivor emeralds from the Aztecs and Incas, and then in 1537 discovered the mine for themselves. Colombia still provides half of the world's emeralds. It was here that the largest gem-quality emerald was found in 1961, weighing 7,025 carats (about 1.4kg/3lb).

# Topaz

*Al₂SiO₄(OH,F)₂ Aluminium fluohydroxisilicate*

Topaz may have got its name from the Sanskrit word *tapaz* meaning 'fire', or from the legendary island of Topazios in the Red Sea, now known as Zebirget. It comes in many colours, including rare pink topazes, and prized yellow topazes from Brazil. Blue topaz can look like aquamarine. Topaz is formed from fluorine-rich solutions and vapours and is typically found in granite pegmatites, or seams in granite altered by fluorine-rich solutions, often accompanied by fluorite, tourmaline, apatite and beryl. It also forms in gas cavities in rhyolite. Because it is so hard, it may be found deposited in river gravels, washed there after its parent rock has been weathered away. Water-worn pebbles of colourless topaz can easily be mistaken for diamonds. In fact, the best known topaz, the 1,649-carat Braganza set in the old crown of Portugal, was once thought to have been a diamond. Most crystals are small and grainy, but gigantic specimens weighing up to 100kg/220lb exist.

**Crystal system**: Orthorhombic
**Crystal habit**: Crystals usually prism-shaped, with two or more long prisms. Also masses and grains.
**Colour**: Colourless, pale yellow, blue, greenish, pink
**Lustre**: Vitreous
**Streak**: White
**Hardness**: 8
**Cleavage**: Perfect basal
**Fracture**: Conchoidal
**Specific gravity**: 3.5–3.6
**Notable locations**:
Erzgebirge, Germany; Sanarka River, Urals, Russia; Pakistan; Minas Gerais, Brazil; San Luis Potosí, Mexico; Thomas Range, Utah; San Diego County, California

**Identification**: Topaz is best identified by its hardness, its high density and its range of pale colours. Its association with fluorite in pegmatites is also a useful indicator.

# GARNETS AND OLIVINES

*Garnets and olivines are dark, dense minerals from deep within the Earth, forming only under conditions of intense heat and pressure. Sometimes, they are brought to the surface when rock formed at these depths is uplifted as a result of tectonic activity; sometimes they are carried to the surface in lava, where garnet and olivine crystals can be seen glistening ready-formed in the newly erupted material.*

## Garnets: Andradite

*$Ca_3Fe_2(SiO_4)_3$ Calcium iron silicate*

Garnet got its name originally because red garnet looks just like seeds of the pomegranate fruit. It is not actually a single mineral but a group of over 20, including uvarovite, grossular and andradite (calcium-rich 'ugrandite' garnets), and pyrope, almandine and spessartine (aluminium-rich 'pyralspite' garnets). All form under extreme conditions, in high-grade metamorphic rocks such as schist and in deep-forming igneous rocks such as peridotite. Garnet can become so concentrated in peridotite that it creates garnet peridotite, a dark rock studded with tiny red or brown garnets, with the appearance of cherries in dark chocolate. Andradite, named after the 18th-century Portuguese mineralogist

*Andradite*

d'Andrada de Silva, can make great gems. It occurs in granite pegmatites, in carbonatites (calcium-rich plugs of deep-formed magma), in metamorphic hornfels and skarns, and on seams and in crusts on serpentinites. It gets its various colours from differing amounts of calcium, iron and other metals in its make-up. Traces of chromium create the green gem demantoid. Demantoid is the most valuable of all the garnets and gets its name from its diamond-like brilliance – though when it was first found in the Russian Urals, it was dubbed 'Uralian emerald' for its green colour. Traces of titanium create black melanite which occurs in igneous rocks such as phonolite and leucitophyre. Topazolite is yellow andradite.

**Crystal system**: Isometric
**Crystal habit**: Crystals are typically 12-faced rhombic shape or 24-faced trapezoid shape, or both
**Colour**: Typically greenish grey to green but also black, yellow and rarely colourless
**Lustre**: Vitreous
**Streak**: White
**Hardness**: 6.5–7.5
**Cleavage**: None
**Fracture**: Conchoidal, brittle
**Specific gravity**: 3.8
**Notable locations**: Northern Italy; Valais, Switzerland; Nizhni-Tagil (Urals), Russia; Gtr Hinggan Mts, China; Korea; Mt St Hilaire, Quebec; San Benito County, California; Arizona; Franklin, New Jersey; Magnet Cove, Arkansas; Chester Co, Pennsylvania

**Identification**: Andradite is best identified by its colour, hardness and association with serpentine, diopside, wollastonite, albite, calcite, orthoclase and micas.

## Garnets: Grossular

*$Ca_3Al_2(SiO_4)_3$ Calcium aluminium silicate*

Grossular is the calcium aluminium garnet. It gets its name from the Latin for 'gooseberry', because one of its colour forms looks like cooked gooseberries. But it comes in a wider range of colours than any other garnet. The most attractive, perhaps, is orange hessonite, sometimes known as cinnamon stone. Tsavorite (from Tsavo in Kenya) is turned green by chromium. African 'jade' is massive veins of opaque green grossular found in the Transvaal, South Africa, that looks rather like jade. Grossular is thought to form in limestones that have been metamorphosed to marble, or in skarns formed when ores in limestone are metamorphosed by contact with magma.

**Identification**: Grossular is best identified by its colour and hardness. The association with calcite, diopside, vesuvianite, and wollastonite is a key indicator.

*Hessonite (cinnamon stone)*

**Crystal system**: Isometric
**Crystal habit**: Crystals are typically 12-faced rhombic shape or 24-faced trapezoid shape, or both
**Colour**: Colourless, yellow, orange, green, red, grey, black
**Lustre**: Vitreous
**Streak**: White
**Hardness**: 6.5–7
**Cleavage**: None
**Fracture**: Conchoidal
**Specific gravity**: 3.5
**Notable locations**: , Scotland; Ala, Italy; Hesse, Germany; Tsavo, Kenya; Transvaal, South Africa; Sri Lanka; Chihuahua, Mexico; Asbestos, Quebec, Canada; Lowell, Vermont

# Garnets: Almandine

*$Fe_3Al_2(SiO_4)_3$ Iron aluminium silicate*

Almandine probably gets its name from Alabanda, an ancient city in Anatolia famous for its gem cutting. With pyrope and spessartine, it is one of the three aluminium-based garnets, but while pyrope is magnesium-rich and spessartine is manganese-rich, almandine is iron-rich, and the most common of the three. The distinction between them is not always that clear, though – rhodolite, for instance, is an almandine with a fair amount of pyrope. All three tend to be reddish or brownish in colour. Pyrope is often the deep ruby red that earned its name from the Greek for 'fire', while spessartine is more peach coloured. Almandine tends towards brown or even black. Pyrope typically occurs embedded in igneous rocks such as dunite and peridotite, whereas spessartine is more usually found in mineralized pockets in rhyolite, pegmatites and marbles. Almandine typically forms in medium- to high-grade regional metamorphic rocks such as mica schists and gneisses. In the garnet-rich rock garnet schist, the garnet is usually almandine.

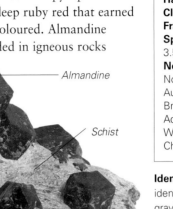

*Almandine*

*Schist*

| | |
|---|---|
| | **Crystal system**: Isometric |
| | **Crystal habit**: 12-faced rhombic or 24-faced trapezoid, or both |

**Colour**: Typically red to brown, or reddish black
**Lustre**: Vitreous
**Streak**: White
**Hardness**: 6.5–7.5
**Cleavage**: None
**Fracture**: Subconchoidal
**Specific gravity**: 4.3 (Pyrope 3.5; Spessartine 4.2)
**Notable locations**: Telemark, Norway; Zillertal (Tyrol), Austria; India; Sri Lanka; Broken Hill (NSW), Australia; Adirondacks Mts, New York; Wrangell Island, Alaska; Chaffee County, Colorado

**Identification**: Almandine is best identified by its colour, specific gravity, occurrence in schists and with micas, staurolite, quartz, magnetite and andalusite.

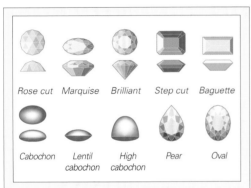

*Rose cut*   *Marquise*   *Brilliant*   *Step cut*   *Baguette*

*Cabochon*   *Lentil cabochon*   *High cabochon*   *Pear*   *Oval*

## Gemstone cuts

Until the late Middle Ages, most gemstones were simply polished along natural breaks. Jewellers then realized that they could produce brilliant effects by grinding or 'cutting' them into very specific shapes. Different styles of cutting are used to bring out a stone's best qualities. Opaque or translucent gemstones such as opals, jade and lapis lazuli are typically cut into a smooth oval, rounded on the top surface and flat underneath. This is called *en cabochon*. Clear precious gemstones, though, are typically cut with a series of mirrorlike facets to make them sparkle. Diamonds are 'brilliant-cut' with multiple triangular facets to make them glitter. Coloured stones, such as emeralds and rubies, are 'step-cut' to bring out the rich hues in the stone. All other cuts are variations of these basic two. Pear cuts are pear-shaped brilliants with a large flat top. Rose cuts or rosettes are brilliants without a 'pavilion' – a deep point at the back. Rose cuts were very popular for diamonds and garnets in Victorian times (1837–1901) but are less favoured today.

# Olivine

*(Mg,Fe)₂SiO₄ Magnesium iron silicate*

*(Mg,Fe)$_2$SiO$_4$ Magnesium iron silicate*

Named for their olive-green colour, olivines are minerals rich in iron and magnesium that form at high temperatures. Olivine with a high magnesium content is forsterite; olivine with a high iron content is fayalite. Olivine is common in mafic rocks such as basalt and gabbro, while ultramafic rocks such as peridotite and dunite are almost pure olivine. Peridotites are what the Earth's mantle is made from, so olivines are among Earth's most common minerals. However, in the crust, they typically occur only as tiny grains. Rare large gems, called peridots, are much sought after. Basalts sometimes hold nodules containing olivine dredged from the mantle as they erupted that give geologists a window inside the Earth. Olivine does not survive weathering long; the higher the temperature a silicate mineral was formed at, the quicker it weathers. Olivine is prone to alteration to serpentine which extends snakelike veins into olivine as it forms.

**Crystal system**: Orthorhombic
**Crystal habit**: Short prisms
**Colour**: Olive green; redder when weathered
**Lustre**: Vitreous
**Streak**: White
**Hardness**: 6.5–7
**Cleavage**: Indistinct
**Fracture**: Conchoidal
**Specific gravity**: Forsterite 3.2; Fayalite 4.3
**Notable locations**: Møre, Snarum, Norway; Eifel, Germany; Mount Vesuvius, Italy; Zebirget (St Johns) Island, Egypt; Burma (Myanmar); Holbrook, Gila County, Arizona
Fayalite: Mourne Mountains, Ireland; Fayal, Azores; Yellowstone, Wyoming

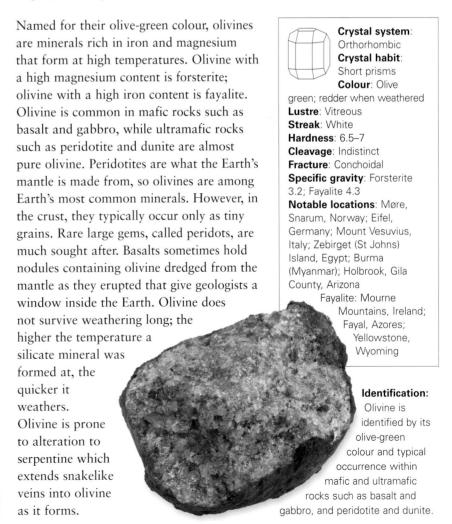

**Identification**: Olivine is identified by its olive-green colour and typical occurrence within mafic and ultramafic rocks such as basalt and gabbro, and peridotite and dunite.

# NESO- AND SOROSILICATES

*Silicates are all built up from the same basic SiO₄ atom groups, called silicate units, but can be classified by how these groups link up. Neso- and sorosilicates generally have the simplest arrangement – nesosilicates are built up from single SiO₄ units and sorosilicates from pairs (Si₂O₇). Nesosilicates include andalusite and sphene, as well as garnet and olivine. Sorosilicates include epidote and vesuvianite.*

## Andalusite, Sillimanite, Kyanite

*Al₂SiO₅ Aluminium silicate*

*Sillimanite, named after American chemist B Silliman*

Andalusite, sillimanite and kyanite are simple aluminium silicates found in metamorphic schists and gneisses, or loose as waterworn pebbles. They are chemically identical but have different crystal structures. Andalusite forms at low temperatures and pressures, kyanite at high ones. The presence of each of these minerals helps geologists tell under which conditions the rocks formed. All may be used as gems, but good crystals are rare, and it is in their massive forms they are useful, because they are so heat-resistant. Turned into mullite fibre, kyanite is used to make everything from insulators for car spark plugs to containers for molten steel. Andalusite, named after Andalusia in Spain, is the most common and widely used of the three. Under a microscope, its crystals may look orangey brown from one angle and yellowish green from another. Kyanite's French name is 'disthene', which means 'double hardness', because crystals have a hardness of 5 lengthways and 7 across.

**Identification**: The bluish blades of kyanite are very distinctive, while the square cross-section of andalusite crystals help to identify them clearly.

*Andalusite*

*Kyanite*

**Crystal system**: Andalusite (A), sillimanite (S): orthorhombic; kyanite (K): triclinic
**Crystal habit**: A: square prisms; S: long prisms; K: flat blades. Also massive and granular.
**Colour**: A: russet, green, gold; S: yellow, white; K: blue to white
**Lustre**: Vitreous
**Streak**: White
**Hardness**: 7.5
**Cleavage**: A: Good, prismatic; S: Perfect, prismatic; K: Perfect, prismatic
**Fracture**: Splintery
**Specific gravity**: A: 3.1–3.2; S: 3.2–3.3; K: 3.5–3.7
**Notable locations**: Tyrol, Austria; Bihar, Assam, India; Sri Lanka (K); Mogok, Burma; Xinjiang, China (A); Bimbowrie, Australia (A); Minas Gerais, Brazil; California; Yancey, North Carolina

## Sphene

*CaTiSiO₅ Calcium titanium silicate*

*Sphene*

**Identification**: Sphene is best identified by its wedge-shaped crystals and its brown, green or yellow colour.

Sphene gets its name from the Greek word for 'wedge', because of its typical wedge-shaped crystals. It is also called titanite, because of its titanium content. Sometimes, mineralogists call titanite 'common sphene', and reserve the name sphene for especially well-developed or twinned crystals. Common sphene is a minor ingredient of deep-forming igneous rocks such as granites, granodiorites and syenites, as well as gneisses, schists, pegmatites and crystalline limestones, where it commonly occurs in association with diopside, garnet and epidote. Beautiful yellow or pale green crystals of sphene with tremendous fire are found in fissures in schist, especially in the Swiss and Austrian Alps. These are cut as gemstones, although they are really too soft.

**Crystal system**: Monoclinic
**Crystal habit**: Crystals typically flattened or wedge-shaped. Usually massive.
**Colour**: Brown, green or yellow, or white, or black
**Lustre**: Adamantine
**Streak**: White
**Hardness**: 5–5.5
**Cleavage**: Indistinct in two directions
**Fracture**: Conchoidal
**Specific gravity**: 3.3–3.6
**Other characteristics**: Pleochroic if strongly coloured
**Notable locations**: Alps, Switzerland; Tyrol, Austria; Madagascar; Minas Gerais, Brazil; Renfrew, Ontario

# Epidote

*Ca₂(Al,Fe)₃(SiO₄)₃(OH) Calcium aluminium iron silicate hydroxide*

*Zircon is a nesosilicate but has a lot in common with epidote.*

The epidote group includes a dozen or so silicate hydroxide minerals, but epidote is the only common one. Best known for its pistachio-green colour – though it can also occur in yellow-green and even black – epidote gets its name from the Greek word *epidosis* which means 'increase', because one side of the crystal is longer than the other. Epidote is a major ingredient of many metamorphic rocks, and typically forms when plagioclase feldspar, pyroxenes and amphiboles are altered by contact metamorphism – though usually only in the presence of hot solutions. It can also be found in association with vesuvianite, garnets and other minerals in contact with metamorphosed limestones and skarns (metamorphosed ores). Epidote sometimes occurs in cavities in basalt, too, or in the seams that form when granite cools and shrinks, allowing gases to escape.

**Identification**: Epidote is best identified by its pistachio green colour, its single cleavage direction, and its association with vesuvianite and garnets in metamorphosed rocks.

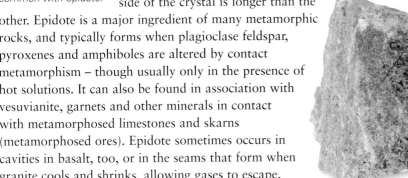

*Epidote*

**Crystal system**: Monoclinic
**Crystal habit**: Crystals prism-shaped with striations; also forms crusts, masses, grains
**Colour**: 'pistachio' green, yellow-green, brown, black
**Lustre**: Vitreous
**Streak**: White to grey
**Hardness**: 6–7
**Cleavage**: Good in only one direction
**Fracture**: Uneven to conchoidal
**Specific gravity**: 3.3–3.5
**Notable locations**: Untersulzbachtal (Tyrol), Austria; Namibia; Afghanistan; Baja California, Mexico; Prince of Wales Island, Alaska

# Vesuvianite

*Ca₁₀(Mg,Fe)₂Al₄(SiO₄)₅(Si₂O₇)₂(OH)₄ Calcium magnesium iron aluminium silicate hydroxide*

**Crystal system**: Tetragonal
**Crystal habit**: Prism-shaped crystals with square cross-section. Occasionally massive.
**Colour**: Normally green, but can also be brown, yellow, blue and/or purple
**Lustre**: Vitreous or greasy to resinous
**Streak**: White
**Hardness**: 6.5
**Cleavage**: Poor in one direction
**Fracture**: Conchoidal to uneven
**Specific gravity**: 3.3–3.5
**Notable locations**: Vala Ala, Mount Vesuvius, Italy; Pitkäranta, Yakutia (Siberia), Russia; Asbestos, Quebec; Eden Mills, Vermont

**Identification**: Vesuvianite is recognized by its greenish colour, and the square cross-section of its crystals, typically completely embedded in limestone calcite.

Vesuvianite was named in 1795 after Mount Vesuvius in Italy by the famous German mineralogist Abraham Werner, who found crystals of it in limestone blocks that had been ejected from the volcano. It was once also called idocrase, from the Greek for 'mixed form', because its chemistry includes elements of both neso- and sorosilicates. It typically forms when limestones are metamorphosed by contact with hot magma. Here it is typically associated with garnet (grossular and andradite), diopside and wollastonite. It can also occur in metasomatic seams and lenses of serpentinized ultramafic rocks, associated with the same minerals and with chlorite. Very occasionally it is also found in pegmatites. It is usually crystalline, but, when massive, it can look a little like jadeite.

**Special twins**
Twinning occurs during crystallization. Instead of a normal single crystal, twins double and seem to grow out of each other like Siamese twins. This is not random but follows rules called twin laws. There are two kinds of twins: contact and penetration. In contact twins, like those in sphene, there is a distinct boundary between the crystals so they look like mirror images. In penetration twins, it looks as if the two crystals grow right across each other. Staurolite shows one of the most amazing examples of twinning. In staurolite, two crystals interpenetrate so completely that it looks as if they grew out of each other. There are two kinds – one in which the crystals cross at 60 degrees to each other, and another, highly sought-after, version in which the crystals cross at right angles (above). The right-angle cross gave the mineral its name, from the Greek for 'cross'. It also gave the mineral its Christian associations with the Maltese cross, and its reputation as a good luck 'Fairy Cross'. Staurolite forms in metamorphic rock, and over a third of crystals found are twinned.

# AMPHIBOLES

*The amphiboles are a large and complex group of nearly 60 minerals that typically form wedge-shaped crystals quite similar to pyroxenes, but longer. Amphiboles occur in many igneous rocks, and many metamorphic rocks – especially those altered from dolomites and mafic igneous rocks. They vary hugely in chemical make-up and appearance, but can be hard to tell apart without the aid of laboratory tests.*

## Tremolite, Actinolite

*$Ca_2Mg_5Si_8O_{22}(OH)_2$ Calcium magnesium silicate hydroxide (Tremolite)*
*$Ca_2(Mg,Fe)_5Si_8O_{22}(OH)_2$ Calcium magnesium iron silicate hydroxide (Actinolite)*

*White tremolite fibres in green chlorite*

Tremolite and actinolite belong to a series of silicate hydroxide minerals in which iron and magnesium swap places. Tremolite is at the magnesium-rich end, and ferro-actinolite is at the iron-rich end, with actinolite in between. Tremolite is clear to white; as little as 2 per cent iron in place of some of its magnesium can change it to green actinolite. Although normally crystalline, they occur in a fibrous form, being the first minerals to be called asbestos, a term now applied to similar fibrous amphiboles. One peculiar fibrous variety of tremolite is called 'mountain leather' and looks just like felt. One kind of actinolite is the tough, smooth green nephrite, one of the two jade minerals. Both tremolite and actinolite form at moderately high pressures and temperatures in a watery environment. Tremolite often forms when dolomites are metamorphosed by contact with hot magma. Actinolites may form when basalt and diabase are metamorphosed to schists. Both may also form when pyroxenes are altered in igneous rocks.

**Identification**: In crystal form actinolite and tremolite can easily be confused with pyroxenes such as wollastonite, but when it forms green fibres actinolite is quite distinctive.

*Long, finely fibrous actinolite crystals in calcite*

**Crystal system**: Monoclinic
**Crystal habit**: Usually long-bladed or prismatic crystals; may be fibrous or massive
**Colour**: White or grey (tremolite), green (actinolite)
**Lustre**: Vitreous or silky
**Streak**: White
**Hardness**: 5–6
**Cleavage**: Perfect in two directions
**Fracture**: Uneven
**Specific gravity**: 2.9–3.4
**Notable locations**: Tremolite: Piemonte, Italy; Tremola V, Switzerland; Haliburton Co, Ontario; St Lawrence Co, New York. Actinolite: Tyrol, Austria; Baikal, Russia; Moonta, Wallaroo, Western Australia; Mont Saint Hilaire, Quebec; Windsor Co, Vermont
**Caution**: Tremolite and actinolite often form asbestos fibres. Keep away from nose and mouth and wash hands carefully.

## Glaucophane

*$Na_2(Mg,Fe)_3Al_2Si_8O_{22}(OH)_2$ Sodium magnesium iron aluminium silicate hydroxide*

*Epidote*          *Glaucophane*

Glaucophane gets its name from the Greek *glaukos*, which means 'blue', and *fanos*, which means 'appearing', because of its typical colour. It is found in rocks such as schist, marble and eclogite, and is generally formed in metamorphic zones known as blueschist facies. Blueschist facies typically occur along continental margins underthrust by shifting oceanic plates and in areas of high volcanic and seismic activity. Some of the best-known examples are in Japan, California, the Mediterranean and the Alps. Glaucophane gives these rocks a bluish hue.

**Identification**: Glaucophane is best identified by its colour, fibrous crystals, location near plate margins, and its association with minerals such chlorite, epidote, aragonite, jadeite, muscovite and garnet.

**Crystal system**: Monoclinic
**Crystal habit**: Rare prism and needle-shaped crystals; usually fibres, grains or masses
**Colour**: Blue to dull grey
**Lustre**: Vitreous to pearly
**Streak**: Pale grey to blue
**Hardness**: 5–6
**Cleavage**: Imperfect in two directions
**Fracture**: Conchoidal to splintery
**Specific gravity**: 3–3.2
**Notable locations**: Anglesey, Wales; Valais, Switzerland; Val d'Aosta, Italy; Syra Is, Greece; Orange River, South Africa; Ishigaki, Japan; Flinders River, S Australia; Coast Range, California; Kodiak Is, Alaska
**Caution**: Glaucophane may form asbestos fibres. Keep well away from nose and mouth; wash hands carefully.

# Hornblende

*Ca₂(Mg,Fe,Al)₅(Si,Al)₈O₂₂(OH)₂ Calcium magnesium iron aluminium silicate hydroxide*

Hornblende gets its name from the German for 'horn', because of its dark colour, and *blenden*, which means 'to dazzle'. The term 'blende' was often used to refer to a shiny non-metal. It is a common ingredient in igneous rocks, especially intrusive rocks such as granites and granodiorites, diorite and syenites. Medium-grade metamorphic gneisses and schists can also be rich in hornblende. Rocks with a predominance of amphiboles (essentially hornblende) are called amphibolites. In rocks such as diorite, the hornblende grows into the space between plagioclase crystals. In granites and granodiorites, hornblende forms tiny, well-formed crystals. Large crystals are rare but are usually stubby and prism-shaped. Hornblende has a large and varied chemical make-up, in which the mix of calcium and sodium, or magnesium and iron, varies. Hornblende with less than 5 per cent iron oxides is grey or white and called edenite, after Edenville, New York, where it was identified.

**Identification**: Hornblende can often be identified as an amphibole by the way it breaks into wedge-shapes, and as hornblende by its very dark colour.

**Crystal system**: Monoclinic
**Crystal habit**: Stubby, prism-shaped crystals; mostly masses, grains, fibres
**Colour**: Black to dark green
**Lustre**: Vitreous to dull
**Streak**: Brown to grey
**Hardness**: 5–6
**Cleavage**: Prismatic, good
**Fracture**: Uneven
**Specific gravity**: 3–3.5
**Notable locations**: Arendal, Norway; Bilina (Bohemia), Czech Republic; Falkenberg (Urals), Russia; Mt Vesuvius, Italy; Murcia, Spain; Bancroft, Ontario; Edenville, New York; Franklin, New Jersey

**The hazards of asbestos**
Remarkable fibres called asbestos are made by the serpentine mineral chrysotile and many amphiboles, notably actinolite, tremolite, anthophyllite, amosite, crocidolite and riebeckite. *Asbestos* is Greek for 'indestructible', and the Greeks and Romans knew of its fire-resistant properties, using it in lamp wicks and in napkins that could be cleaned by throwing them into the fire. They also knew of its health hazards. But it was only in the 1880s that the modern use of asbestos began – when huge deposits of chrysotile were mined in Canada (an abandoned mine appears above) and Russia – and only after World War II that its use became widespread. By the 1970s, the USA was producing around 300 million tonnes of asbestos a year for making everything from car brake pads to fireproof roofs. In the 1980s, however, the terrible long-term health effects of asbestos fibres – especially on the lungs – became clearer, and its use was banned in America and Europe. It is still widely used elsewhere, as in China.

# Anthophyllite

*(Mg,Fe)₇Si₈O₂₂(OH)₂ Magnesium iron silicate hydroxide*

Anthophyllite gets its name from the Latin for 'clove' because of its distinctive clove-brown colour. It is usually confused only with similar amphiboles such as cummingtonite. Anthophyllite is formed by metamorphism and found in gneisses and schists derived by the alteration of magnesium-rich igneous or dolomitic sedimentary rocks. It also forms from metamorphic rocks, and by the alteration of minerals such as olivine by water. Under different conditions (if there were more water), serpentine would be the mineral produced from the alteration of olivine. Well-formed crystals of anthophyllite are rare, but some aggregates can be impressive.

**Identification**: Anthophyllite is best identified by its colour and fibrous masses.

*Fibrous sheaves of anthophyllite on schist*

**Crystal system**: Orthorhombic
**Crystal habit**: Rare, prism-shaped crystals and fibrous, asbestos masses
**Colour**: Brown, off-white grey
**Lustre**: Vitreous or silky in fibrous forms
**Streak**: Grey
**Hardness**: 5.5–6
**Cleavage**: Good in two directions
**Fracture**: Easy, splintery
**Specific gravity**: 2.8–3.4
**Notable locations**: Nuuk, Greenland; Elba, Italy; Kongsberg, Norway; Butte, Montana; Franklin, North Carolina; Tallapoosa, Alabama; Cummington, Massachusetts (Cummingtonite)
**Caution**: Anthophyllite often contains asbestos fibres, which are a major health hazard. Keep well away from nose and mouth and wash hands carefully.

# CLAYS

*The term clay can describe any kind of fine particle, but also specifically a large group of minerals such as chlorite, kaolinite, talc and serpentine. Clay minerals are aluminium and magnesium silicates, and occur as fine particles that form when other minerals are broken down by weathering, water and heat. Their sheet-like molecular structure means that they absorb or lose water easily, making them very useful.*

## Chlorite

*(Fe,Mg,Al)$_6$(Si,Al)$_4$O$_{10}$(OH)$_8$ Iron aluminium magnesium silicate hydroxide*

The chlorites get their name from the Greek word for 'green', and they are a group of mainly pale green minerals, although they can be white, yellow or brown. They form when minerals such as pyroxene, amphibole, biotite mica and garnets are broken down by weathering or by exposure to hot solutions. Sometimes they literally take the place of these minerals within the rock, giving many igneous and metamorphic rocks a green look. Indeed, chlorite is a major ingredient in many schists and phyllites, especially the green chlorite schists. Sometimes they create earth-filled cavities and crevices. Eventually the whole rock might break down to create soil, and chlorite is a major ingredient of soils such as podzols. Occasionally, chlorite forms good, wedge-shaped crystals in cavities, but more typically it is massive and earthy. Chlorite can also form scaly flakes like mica, but they contain more water and no alkalis, making them much softer and lighter, and less well defined.

**Identification**: Chlorite is best identified by its green colour, its softness (almost as soft as talc) and in many specimens its scaly flakes.

**Crystal system**: Monoclinic
**Crystal habit**: Rare crystals are tablet- or prism-shaped hexagons, but more usually earthy aggregates or scaly flakes
**Colour**: Usually green, also white, yellow, brown
**Lustre**: Vitreous, dull or pearly
**Streak**: Pale green to greyish
**Hardness**: 2–3
**Cleavage**: Breaks into slightly flexible flakes
**Fracture**: Lamellar (sheetlike)
**Specific gravity**: 2.6–3.4
**Notable locations**: Carinthia, Austria; Zermatt, Switzerland; Piedmont, Italy; Guleman, Turkey; Renfrew County, Ontario; Brewster, New York; San Benito County, California

## Kaolinite

*Al$_2$Si$_2$O$_5$(OH)$_4$ Aluminium silicate hydroxide*

**Crystal system**: Triclinic; or monoclinic
**Crystal habit**: Foliated and earthy masses. Crystals rare.
**Colour**: White, colourless, greenish or yellow
**Lustre**: Earthy
**Streak**: White
**Hardness**: 1.5–2
**Cleavage**: Perfect basal
**Fracture**: Earthy
**Specific gravity**: 2.6
**Other characteristics**: Mouldable when wet
**Notable locations**: Many including Cornwall, England; Dresden, Germany; Donets River, Ukraine; Kaolin, China

**Identification**: Kaolinite minerals are typically white, soft (if scratched) and powdery.

The mineral kaolinite gives its name to the group of minerals from which kaolin (see China clay, right) comes and includes nacrite, dickite and halloysite as well as kaolinite – all with identical chemistry but differing crystal form. Most clay contains at least some kaolinite, and some clay beds are entirely kaolinite. Indeed, kaolinite is found almost everywhere – in soils, in stream beds, in rocks and many other places. Some kaolinites form as aluminium silicates in rocks and soils that are weathered and broken down. Others are formed in rocks such as granites and pegmatites when feldspars are altered by hot solutions. Kaolin formed from feldspar is often extracted from pegmatites, while in the china clay quarries of Cornwall, England, it comes from kaolinite formed from potassium feldspar in granite.

*Kaolinized granite*

# Talc

*Mg₃Si₄O₁₀(OH)₂ Magnesium silicate hydroxide*

Talc is the softest of all minerals, rating 1 on the Mohs scale. The softness, whiteness and ability of pure talc to hold fragrances has long made it popular when ground into powder for cosmetics and babies. Talc is also used as a filler in paints, in rubber and in plastic. It typically occurs in magnesium-rich rocks affected by low-grade metamorphism – especially rocks such as peridotites and gabbros. It forms when magnesium silicate minerals such as olivine and pyroxene are altered by hydrothermal fluids forced through cracks in the rocks, often along fault lines. Talc also occurs in schists made from metamorphosed magnesian limestone. It typically occurs in association with serpentine, and may be compacted into a mass called soapstone, used since ancient times for carving and, because it becomes hard when heated, for heat-resistant utensils and insulators. Steatite is a particularly dense soapstone made from almost pure, white talc.

*Talc*

*Magnesite*

**Identification**: Talc is best identified by its extreme softness – you can scratch it with a fingernail – its soapy feel and its white or light grey or almond colour. It is often mixed with green chlorite.

**Crystal system**: Monoclinic
**Crystal habit**: Crystals rare; usually forms grains of flaky masses
**Colour**: White, greenish, grey
**Lustre**: Dull, pearly, greasy
**Streak**: White
**Hardness**: 1
**Cleavage**: Perfect in one direction, basal
**Fracture**: Uneven to lameller (sheetlike)
**Specific gravity**: 2.7–2.8
**Other characteristics**: Soapy texture to surface
**Notable locations**: Shetland, Scotland; Florence, Italy; Tyrol, Austria; Transvaal, South Africa; Appalachian Mountains, Vermont; Connecticut; New York; Virginia; California; Texas

**China clay**

Although it is often taken for granted, kaolin, or china clay, is one of the most beautiful and useful of mineral products. It gets its name from Kao-ling hill in China, where it has been quarried for 1,400 years to make porcelain. It is a soft, white, very fine-grained clay made mainly from the mineral kaolinite. It forms from feldspars when soft soda feldspar-rich granites are broken down, and also when gneisses and porphyritic rocks crumble. In its natural state it is often stained yellow by iron hydroxides, and contaminated by micas and quartz. These contaminants can be washed out, and the kaolin bleached pure, shining white. It is this whiteness that makes it the perfect base material for paper, tied together with cellulose fibres from wood. When it is mixed with a quarter to a third water, it becomes 'plastic' – that is, mouldable – and once moulded and fired it retains its shape and white colour. This is what makes it so good for porcelainware. Besides China, the best known sources are Cornwall in England (pictured above; mining began here in the 18th century); Saxony, Germany; Sévres, France; and Georgia, USA.

# Serpentine

*Mg₃Si₂O₅(OH)₄ Magnesium iron silicate hydroxide (Lizardite)*

Named after the green flecks said to make it look like snakeskin, serpentine forms when magnesium silicates in rocks like peridotite and dolomites are altered by hot fluids. The same process makes talc, veins of which are often found in serpentine. A rock entirely made from serpentine is called serpentinite. Serpentine also forms spidery veins in other minerals when they are altered by moisture, a process called serpentinization. Serpentine is not a single mineral but a group of minerals including chrysotile, antigorite and lizardite. Chrysotile is a fibrous, asbestos mineral, like crocidolite and anthophyllite. Antigorite is a corrugated kind of serpentine. Lizardite, named after the Lizard peninsular in Cornwall, England, is a fine-grained, platy variety.

**Lizardite Crystal system**: Trigonal and hexagonal; (Antigorite, Clinocrysotile monoclinic; Ortho- and Parachrysotile orthorhombic)
**Crystal habit**: Usually forms fine-grained platy masses
**Colour**: Green, blue, yellow, white
**Lustre**: Waxy or greasy
**Streak**: White
**Hardness**: 2.5
**Cleavage**: Perfect, basal
**Fracture**: Conchoidal (Lizardite, Antigorite); Splintery (Crysotiles)
**Specific gravity**: 2.5–2.6
**Notable locations**: Lizard (Cornwall), England; Salzburg, Austria; Liguria, Italy; Auvergne, France; Urals, Russia; Asbestos, Quebec; Hoboken, New Jersey; Eden Mills, Vermont

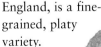

**Identification**: Lizardite can be identified by its yellow-green colour, softness (as hard as fingernail), platy texture and association with talc in rocks like peridotite and dolomite.

# MICAS

*Micas are among the most instantly recognizable of minerals, with their flaky, almost transparent layers. These aluminium silicates are also among the most common of all the rock-forming minerals and major ingredients in all three rock types. There are 30 or so different kinds of mica altogether, but the most important ones are biotite, muscovite, phlogopite and lepidolite. Other important micas are glauconite and paragonite.*

## Biotite

*K(Fe,Mg)₃AlSi₃O₁₀(OH,F)₂ Potassium iron magnesium aluminium silicate hydroxide fluoride*

Biotite is a black, iron-rich mica. It is named after Jean Baptiste Biot, the French physicist who first described the optical effects of micas. It occurs in varying percentages in almost every kind of igneous and metamorphic rock, but is especially prominent in granites, diorites and andesites and schists, gneisses and hornfels. It adds glitter to schists, the black 'pepper' grains in granite and darkness to sandstones. Its iron content makes it the darkest of the micas. It is also one of the softest – scratchable with a fingernail – which is why good crystals are rarely found. All the same, single large plates or 'books' of biotite can grow to quite a size, especially in granite pegmatites. Biotite is part of a series with phlogopite, with denser, black biotite at the iron-rich end, and less dense, brown phlogopite at the iron-poor end. Weathered crystals of biotite can turn golden yellow and sparkle, fooling people into thinking they are gold. Biotite is easily altered; in the presence of seawater, for instance, it quickly turns into the mica mineral glauconite.

**Identification**: Biotite is usually easy to recognize by its dark colour and its soft flakes. It can look like phlogopite but is darker and denser because of its iron content.

**Crystal system**: Monoclinic
**Crystal habit**: Hexagonal tablet-shaped crystals; more often flakes, often in 'books', or grains in rock
**Colour**: Black to brown and yellow with weathering
**Lustre**: Vitreous to pearly
**Streak**: White
**Hardness**: 2.5
**Cleavage**: Perfect in one direction, giving thin sheets or flakes
**Fracture**: Not often visible but uneven when seen
**Specific gravity**: 2.9–3.4
**Other characteristics**: Flakes bend and spring back flat
**Notable locations**: Norway; Monte Somma (Mount Vesuvius), Italy; Sicily; Russia; Bancroft, Ontario, and many other locations

## Phlogopite

*KMg₃AlSi₃O₁₀(OH)₂ Potassium magnesium aluminium silicate hydroxide*

Phlogopite is very similar to biotite, but contains little if any iron and so is lighter in colour, and less dense. It can sometimes have the red-brown hue that earned its name from the Greek *phlogopos*, meaning 'fire-like'. It often occurs with biotite, but whereas biotite is common in granite and other acidic igneous rocks, phlogopite is common only in ultramafic rocks such as pyroxenites and peridotites, and in metamorphosed limestones, notably magnesium-rich marbles. Its low iron content means phlogopite is a good electrical insulator, and is so valued by the electrical industry that there have been a number of attempts to synthesize. Synthetic phlogopite has so far proved too costly, however. When a thin flake of phlogopite is held up to the light, it will sometimes show asterism – a six-rayed star – due to small inclusions in the crystal.

**Identification**: Phlogopite is usually easy to recognize by its reddish brown colour and its soft flakes. It can look like biotite but is lighter in colour and less dense.

**Crystal system**: Monoclinic
**Crystal habit**: Hexagonal tablet-shaped crystals; more often flakes, often in 'books', or grains in rock
**Colour**: Brown, reddish brown, maybe coppery
**Lustre**: Vitreous to pearly
**Streak**: White
**Hardness**: 2.5–3
**Cleavage**: Perfect in one direction, giving thin sheets or flakes
**Fracture**: Uneven
**Specific gravity**: approximately 2.9
**Other characteristics**: Flakes bend and spring back flat
**Notable locations**: Norway; Kovdor (Kola Peninsula), Russia; Madagascar; Bancroft, Ontario

# Muscovite

*KAl₂(Si₃Al)O₁₀(OH,F)₂ Potassium aluminium silicate hydroxide fluoride*

Muscovite is the most common mica, and is found nearly everywhere that intrusive igneous and metamorphic rocks occur. It is particularly abundant in granites and pegmatites, gneisses, schists and phyllites. It also forms when feldspars are altered. Microscopic-grained muscovite or sericite is what gives phyllite its silky sheen. In pegmatites, muscovite often occurs in giant sheets which are commercially valuable, and also in cavities, where the best crystals occur. Most muscovite in igneous rocks forms late as the magma solidifies. It is resistant to weathering, so is abundant in soils over muscovite-rich rocks, and in sands formed from them. Like all micas, muscovite breaks into flakes and can be almost transparent. In old Russia, sheets of muscovite were used for windows, being known as Muscovy glass, after the old name for Russia. It is very heat-resistant and it is still used for the windows in stoves. It is also a superb electrical insulator, and is used as artificial snow for Christmas trees.

**Identification**: Muscovite's thin flakes identify it clearly as a mica. It is much lighter in colour than either biotite or phlogopite mica.

*Intergrowth crystals of muscovite*

**Crystal system**: Monoclinic
**Crystal habit**: Hexagonal tablet-shaped crystals; more often flakes, often in 'books', or grains in rock
**Colour**: White, silver, yellow, green and brown
**Lustre**: Vitreous to pearly
**Streak**: White
**Hardness**: 2–2.5
**Cleavage**: Perfect in one direction, giving thin sheets or flakes
**Specific gravity**: 2.8
**Other characteristics**: Flakes bend and spring back flat
**Notable locations**: Mursinka (Urals), Russia; Inikurti (Nellore), India; Brazil; Amelia County, Virginia, and many other locations

**Marvellous mica**

Micas occur in two forms: flake mica, which occurs naturally in small flakes, and sheet mica which occurs in large sheets that can be cut into particular shapes. Sheet mica is much rarer, but large sheets of muscovite can occur in pegmatites, and these were used for the Muscovy glass once used in Russian windows. Because it is quite rare, sheet mica is often synthesized from flake or scrap mica. The high electrical and heat resistance of sheet mica means it is perfect for use as electrical insulators, for heat insulation, for the windows in stoves, and much more besides. Phlogopite is used as the insulation between the copper and steel in electric motors because it wears at exactly the same rate as the copper. Ground-up mica is also useful, and is added to plasterboard as a filler that prevents cracking. It is also used in paint to make it dry smoothly, and in oil well drills as a lubricant.

# Lepidolite

*K(Li,Al)₃(Si,Al)₄O₁₀(F,OH)₂ Potassium lithium aluminium silicate hydroxide fluoride*

Pinky purple in colour, with a vitreous to pearly lustre, lepidolite is perhaps the most attractive of all the micas. However, it is relatively rare and forms only in granite pegmatites. Indeed, it pretty much only forms in complex pegmatites where there is plenty of lithium present, and where minerals have been replaced with other minerals repeatedly through time. It sometimes forms when lithium minerals alter muscovite, creating beautiful lace-like rims. It was once used as an ore of lithium, but the lithium content varies so much that most lithium is now taken from alkali lake brines. Some specimens are triboluminescent – that is, they will flash colours when pressed.

**Crystal system**: Monoclinic
**Crystal habit**: Hexagonal tablet-shaped crystals; more often flakes, often in 'books', or grains in rock
**Colour**: Violet to pale pink or white and rarely grey or yellow
**Lustre**: Vitreous to pearly
**Streak**: White
**Hardness**: 2.5
**Cleavage**: Perfect in one direction, giving thin sheets or flakes
**Specific gravity**: approximately 2.8+ (average)
**Other characteristics**: Flakes bend and spring back flat. May show triboluminescence.
**Notable locations**: Varuträsk, Sweden; Penig (Saxony), Germany; Urals, Russia; Alto Ligonha (Zambesi), Mozambique; Madagascar; Pakistan; Londonderry, Western Australia; Minas Gerais, Brazil; Maine; Portland, Connecticut; San Diego County, California

**Identification:** Flakes clearly identify lepidolite as a mica, but it is only likely to be lepidolite if found in complex dike rock along with lithium minerals.

# MINERALOIDS

*A few solid substances that occur naturally in the Earth do not quite conform with the basic properties of minerals. They fit into none of the chemical families, rarely form crystals and are typically organic in origin, evolving from fossilized or compacted living matter. Such substances are called mineraloids. Amber is fossilized pine tree resin. Jet, like coal, forms from the remains of trees. Pearl is formed by certain shellfish as a coating around irritant debris inside their shells. Whewellite forms from organic acids.*

## Amber

*Approximately $C_{10}H_{16}O$ Succinic acid*

Although it is often regarded as a gem, amber is not a mineral at all but a solid organic material. It is a form of tree resin that was exuded to protect the tree against disease and insect infestation. This then hardened and was preserved for millions of years. Amber slowly oxidizes and degrades when exposed to oxygen, so it survives only under special conditions. It is almost always found in dense, wet sediments, such as clay and sand formed in ancient lagoon or river delta beds. It is typically found embedded in shale or washed up on beaches. Most amber deposits contain only fragments of amber, but a few contain enough to make it worth mining, such as those found along the shores of Baltic seas where amber formed in sands 40–60 million years ago, and those from the Dominican Republic. Amber can form nodules, rods and droplets in various shades of orange and brown. Milky-white varieties are called bone amber. Modern analysis techniques are beginning to identify the detailed composition of ambers and link them to modern resin-making trees. Mexican amber, for instance, is linked to the *Hymenea* tree.

**Crystal system**: Usually amorphous
**Crystal habit**: Nodules, rods, droplets
**Colour**: Amber, brown, yellow
**Lustre**: Resinous
**Streak**: White
**Hardness**: 2+
**Cleavage**: None
**Specific gravity**: 1.1 (will float in salty water)
**Other characteristics**: Can be burned, fluorescent
**Notable locations**: Kaliningrad, Russia; Lithuania; Latvia; Estonia; Poland; Romania; Germany; Lebanon; Sicily; Dominican Republic; Mexico; Canada

**Identification**: Amber is easy to identify from its amber colour, resinous lustre and smooth, round shape.

## Jet

*C Carbon*

Like amber, jet comes from ancient trees and forests that grew hundreds of millions of years ago. It is sometimes thought of as a type of shiny black lignite coal, because it forms in a similar way, from compacted remains of trees. (Lignite is a less compressed brown coal which retains the structure of the original wood.) However, while coal formed in fresh water from swampy tropical forests that grew in the Carboniferous Age (354–290 million years ago), hard jet probably formed in many periods from logs that floated down river and out to sea to sink on to the sea bed. Despite its black colour, jet is not as rich in carbon as either anthracite or bituminous coal – as its brown streak reveals. The famous Whitby jet from the beaches of Whitby, in Yorkshire, England, has been used in jewellery since prehistoric times. It is found as lenses embedded in hard shales known as jet-rock.

**Identification**: Jet is easily identified by its jet-black colour. It can look like vulcanite, obsidian and black onyx, but has a brown streak.

**Crystal system**: Does not form crystals
**Crystal habit**: Lumps with microscopic wood texture
**Colour**: Black
**Lustre**: Glassy
**Streak**: Brown
**Hardness**: 2–2.5
**Specific gravity**: 1.1–1.3
**Other characteristics**: Breaks with conchoidal fracture
**Notable locations**: Whitby (North Yorkshire), England; Württemberg, Germany; Asturias, Spain; Aude, France; Pictou, Nova Scotia; Wayne Co, Garfield Co, Utah; San Juan Co, Guadalupe Co, Cibola Co, New Mexico; Custer Co, Colorado

# Pearl

Over 6,000 years ago, people around the Persian Gulf were buried with a pierced pearl in their right hand, and pearls featured in all the major cultures of the ancient world. Despite their beauty, pearls are not gemstones: they are organic materials formed by bivalve molluscs such as oysters and mussels. All these shellfish build up their shells with a hard, brown, hornlike protein called conchiolin, then line it with a smooth, shiny mother-of-pearl. Mother-of-pearl, a substance secreted from the outer membrane of the mollusc, is made from a material called nacre, built up from thin alternating layers of colourless conchiolin and the mineral aragonite. Pearls form when an irritant gets in the shell, such as a food particle. To stop it irritating, the mollusc gradually coats it in layers of mother-of-pearl. The longer this process goes on, the bigger the pearl will be. The biggest pearls come from marine oysters, but freshwater molluscs also make pearls. When pearls are cultured on oyster farms, an irritant is deliberately introduced into the oyster to stimulate the growth of a pearl.

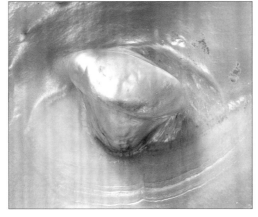

**Crystal system**: Does not form crystals
**Crystal habit**: Forms microscopic alternating layers of aragonite and conchiolin
**Colour**: Iridescent pearly white
**Lustre**: Pearly
**Streak**: White
**Hardness**: 3.5–4
**Cleavage**: None
**Specific gravity**: 2.9–3
**Notable locations**: Freshwater pearls: rivers across northern Europe, Asia and North America (notably Muscatine, Iowa, on the Mississippi River)
Marine pearls: Venezuela, Persian Gulf

**Identification**: The white aragonite in mother-of-pearl is visible through the translucent conchiolin, which gives the lining of the shell, and the resulting pearl, its famous lustre.

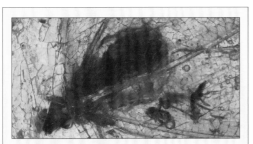

**Amber time capsules**
Perhaps the most amazing thing about amber is the way it perfectly preserves organisms, such as insects, trapped in it when it was liquid resin. Compounds called terpenes link up as the resin hardens, dehydrating the organisms and killing off bacteria that would make them decay. Amazingly, dehydration does not make the organism shrink, so its cell structure is preserved intact. Amber from the Cretaceous period (65–140 million years ago) offers a unique glimpse of insect life at a time when the dinosaurs flourished, not preserved in any other way. The oldest known bee, *Trigona prisca*, for instance, was found in 65–80 million-year-old amber from New Jersey. The oldest known mushroom, 90–94 million-year-old *Archaeomarasmius*, was also found here in amber. Amber preserves things so perfectly that scientists still hold out the possibility suggested in the film *Jurassic Park* of recreating dinosaurs from DNA in blood sucked from them by mosquitoes preserved in amber. The best Cretaceous amber comes from northern Russia, but the oldest is from the Middle East. Early forms of animal life are also trapped in copal, a less mature resin often mistaken for amber.

# Whewellite

*$CaC_2O_4.H_2O$ Hydrated calcium oxalate*

Whewellite is named after the famous Victorian geologist William Whewell (1794–1866). Whewellite forms stones in human kidneys and mineralogists argue over whether it is a mineral or not. It is calcium oxalate, an organic chemical, and it forms from oxalic acid derived from organic sources such as coal and rotting vegetation. In the Arizona desert, whewellite forms on dead agave plants, which has lead some mineralogists to say that it is not a mineral. However, it forms crystals, concretions and crusts, and occurs in septarian nodules. Moreover, oxalic acid forms whewellite by reacting with calcium hydroxide, which occurs in ordinary groundwater and hydrothermal fluids. Whewellite typically forms where these fluids meet carbon-rich rocks, such as graphitic schists and anthracite coal.

 **Crystal system**: Monoclinic
**Crystal habit**: Tiny needles (slender prisms) and crusts
**Colour**: Colourless, white, yellow, brown
**Lustre**: Vitreous to pearly
**Streak**: White
**Hardness**: 2.5–3
**Cleavage**: Good in three directions
**Specific gravity**: 2.2
**Other characteristics**: Very brittle, breaking in conchoidal fragments
**Notable locations**: Freital, Burgk (Saxony), Gera (Thuringia), Germany; Alsace, Rhône-Alps, France; Kladno, Czech Republic; Yakutia, Russia; San Juan Co, Arizona; Havre (Hill Co), Montana

**Identification**: Whewellite is best identified by the environment in which it forms, its tiny needle-like crystals and its very low density.

# PRECIOUS METALS

*Although traces of valuable metals may be found in a number of minerals, only those containing a relatively substantial amount – ore minerals – are of interest to prospectors. Silver, scandium and members of the platinum group of metals such as platinum and osmium are rare and precious metals, found in only a small number of places around the world. Where they are discovered, it is usually very expensive to extract them; however, their value and usefulness make the effort and cost worthwhile.*

## Silver ore: Proustite

*$Ag_3AsS_3$ Silver arsenic sulphide*

Silver is a rare and precious metal that sometimes occurs in pure form as a native element. It also occurs in no less than 248 other mineral species, such as argentite, eskimoite and uchucchacuaite, but only a few are common. Most silver tends to be recovered as a by-product from galena (lead ore), or tetrahedrite and chalcopyrite (copper ores). Silver compounds typically form near the Earth's surface when complex compounds lose their sulphur. Deeper down, silver occurs where hydrothermal veins create sulphides, antimonides and arsenides. Proustite is one of these silver sulphides. Named after the French chemist J L Proust (1755–1826), it is one of the few sulphides that is neither metallic nor opaque, and has beautiful red crystals that are highly sought after by collectors. However, the crystals quickly darken when exposed to light. Massive proustite is a commercial silver ore called ruby silver, but it occurs on only a small scale. Proustite is closely related to pyrargyrite, which substitutes antimony in place of proustite's arsenic.

Dark red proustite

**Crystal system**: Trigonal
**Crystal habit**: Prism-shaped with rhombohedral or scalenohedral ends, resembling calcite dog-tooth spar. Also forms masses.
**Colour**: Scarlet to vermillion
**Lustre**: Adamantine
**Streak**: Scarlet
**Hardness**: 2–2.5
**Cleavage**: Distinct forming rhombohedrons
**Fracture**: Conchoidal
**Specific gravity**: 5.6
**Notable locations**: Markirch (Alsace), France; Freiburg, Marienberg (Saxony), Germany; Joachimstal (Bohemia), Czech Republic; Chanarcillo, Chile; Chihuahua, Mexico; Lorrain, Ontario; Poorman Mine, Idaho

**Identification**: Proustite's red colour and red streak help to identify it. It can be mistaken for its close relative pyrargyrite, but is generally lighter in colour.

## Scandium ore: Thortveitite

*$(Sc,Y)_2Si_2O_7$ Scandium yttrium silicate*

**Crystal system**: Monoclinic
**Crystal habit**: Typically prism-shaped crystals but also occurs in massive and granular forms
**Colour**: Brown, greyish black, greyish green
**Lustre**: Vitreous – adamantine
**Streak**: Grey
**Hardness**: 6.5
**Cleavage**: Perfect
**Fracture**: Conchoidal
**Specific gravity**: 3.5
**Notable locations**: Setesdalen (Aust-Agder), Norway; Ytterby, Sweden; Saxony, Germany; Ankazone, Madagascar; Kinki, Japan; Sterling, New Jersey

Scandium is a rare metal first identified in the minerals euxenite and gadolinite in 1876, but not properly prepared until 1937. It is a soft, light, blue-white metal. Scandium oxide is used in high-intensity light, because it has a high melting point, and scandium iodide is added to the mercury vapour lights used for night-time filming. In the Sun, it is the twenty-third most common element, but on Earth, it ranks fiftieth. Traces of scandium can be found in about 800 minerals, but only wolframite, wiikite, bazzite and thortveitite are useful sources. Thortveitite is a rare silicate mineral found mainly in Scandinavia and Madagascar, typically with uranium ores in granite pegmatites. Scandium is often a by-product of uranium ore processing.

**Identification**: Thortveitite is best identified by its brown colour and its association with rare earth minerals in granite pegmatites. A thortveitite crystal in feldspar is shown above.

## Osmium ore: Iridosmine

*Os,Ir Osmium, Iridium*

Discovered by English chemist Smithson Tennant in 1804 after dissolving platinum in acid, osmium is the densest naturally occurring element. It is the hardest of all the metals, and stands pressure better than diamond. It also has the highest melting point of all the platinum metals. Pure osmium never occurs naturally. Instead, it is found in natural alloys with iridium in siserskite (about four-fifths osmium), iridosmine (about a third osmium) and aurosmiridium (about a quarter osmium). Iridosmine is the most common of these, but is as rare as gold. It occurs in gravels and sands left by the weathering of platinum-rich ultrabasic rocks, such as in the Urals or in gold-bearing conglomerates, as in Witwatersrand, South Africa. This tough, non-corrosive alloy is used as it is, or synthesized to make pen nibs, surgical needles and spark points for cars. However, a significant amount of osmium is derived from other ores, such as the nickel ores of Sudbury, Ontario.

**Identification**: Iridosmine is best identified by its steel-grey colour. Its association with other platinum group metals or with gold is also a key indicator. Shown here are small grains.

**Crystal system**: Hexagonal
**Crystal habit**: Typically tiny crystals in matrix, but forms tablet-shaped hexagonal crystals
**Colour**: Steel grey
**Lustre**: Metallic
**Streak**: Grey
**Hardness**: 6–7
**Cleavage**: Perfect
**Fracture**: Uneven
**Specific gravity**: 19–21
**Notable locations**: Bulgaria; Sverdlovskaya (Urals), Kamchatka, Russia; Hunan, China; Witwatersrand, South Africa; Goodnews Bay, Alaska
**Caution**: Handle iridosmine with care and keep in an airtight container. Osmium powder and vapour are very poisonous.

**The platinum group**
The platinum group of elements represents some of the rarest elements in the Earth's crust – ruthenium, rhodium, palladium, osmium and iridium. Together they are known as the platinum group metals, or PGM. Only two of them, platinum and palladium, occur naturally in pure form, as fine grains or flakes scattered throughout dark silicate rocks rich in iron and magnesium. The remainder occur as natural alloys with gold and platinum. Even platinum usually occurs mixed in with iridium. Most PGMs come from the Urals in Russia and the Bushveld complex in South Africa. All the platinum group metals are very dense with high melting points, which makes them extremely useful despite their rarity. Most of the commercially mined platinum group metals are used in catalytic car exhaust converters to cut down on the emission of smog-creating gases. They work by lowering the energy needed to convert these gases to harmless nitrogen and oxygen. Platinum group metals also have a number of medical uses. For example, they are used in dentistry, in chemotherapy to fight leukaemia, and in heart replacement valves.

## Platinum ore: Sperrylite

*PtAs₂ Platinum arsenide*

Platinum is usually found as a native element, alloyed to similar metals – iridium, osmium, palladium, rhodium and ruthenium. Sperrylite (platinum arsenide), is the only known naturally occurring compound of platinum and the only ore. It was identified in 1889 and named after the American chemist F L Sperry, who found samples of it near Sudbury in Ontario, Canada. Sudbury remains the only major source of sperrylite, although good specimens have been found in places such as the Tarnak deposit near Yakut and in Kamchatka, Russia. It has also been found in the Bushveld complex in South Africa. It is a pyrite group mineral of basic pegmatites, often found concentrated in placer deposits.

**Crystal system**: Isometric
**Crystal habit**: Typically tiny crystals in matrix. Crystals rounded with mix of cubic, octahedral and other shapes.
**Colour**: Tin white
**Lustre**: Metallic
**Streak**: Black
**Hardness**: 6–7
**Cleavage**: Indistinct
**Fracture**: Conchoidal
**Specific gravity**: 10.6
**Other characteristics**: Brittle
**Notable locations**: Finnmark, Norway; Sakha, Kamchatka, Russia; Bushveld complex, South Africa; Sichuan, China; Sudbury, Ontario; Goodnews Bay, Alaska

**Identification**: Sperrylite has a similar crystal shape to pyrite, but is tin white to pyrite's gold. Sperrylite can also be identified by its association with chalcopyrite, pyrrhotite and pentlandite.

# IRON ORES

*Iron is the most common element in the Earth, making up a third of its mass. Most of this iron is buried deep in the Earth's core, but it is still abundant in rocks near the surface – here it is found mixed with other minerals in the form of ores – hematite, magnetite, siderite, goethite and limonite. It is only rarely found near the surface in pure form, such as in the basaltic rocks of Greenland.*

## Hematite

*$Fe_2O_3$ Iron oxide*

Hematite is the most important ore of iron, containing 70 per cent of the metal. It gets its name from the Ancient Greek word for 'blood', because it gives rocks a reddish tinge. If soils or sedimentary rocks have a

*Massive hematite* reddish colour, it is usually due to hematite, and this is what makes the planet Mars red. It occurs in other colours such as grey, brown and orange, but red is typical. Hematite often occurs in an earthy form called red ochre, but it can also occur as steel-grey crystals, in kidney-shaped lumps called kidney ore, and in pockets called iron roses. Most industrial sources of hematite come from massive layers in sedimentary rocks, such as those near Lake Superior in North America, or as beds of 'Clinton-type' ooliths laid down on the bed of shallow seas long ago. Sometimes it occurs in metamorphosed sediments such as those at Minas Gerais in Brazil.

**Identification**: The best clue to hematite's identity is its distinctive red streak.

*Quartz*  *Hematite crystals*

*Massive hematite*

**Crystal system**: Trigonal
**Crystal habit**: Typically earth or sheetlike masses. Also reniform (kidney shapes), or tablet-shaped crystals.
**Colour**: Steel grey to black as crystals and red to brown in earthy and massive forms
**Lustre**: Metallic, or dull in earthy forms
**Streak**: Red
**Hardness**: 5–6
**Cleavage**: None
**Fracture**: Uneven
**Specific gravity**: 5.3
**Notable locations**: Cumbria, England; Gotthard Massif, Switzerland; Elba, Italy; Australia; Minas Gerais, Brazil; Lake Superior, Canada

## Magnetite

*$FeFe_2O_4$ Iron oxide*

**Crystal system**: Isometric
**Crystal habit**: Usually massive or grains. Crystals typically octahedral and dodecahedral.
**Colour**: Black
**Lustre**: Metallic to dull
**Streak**: Black
**Hardness**: 5.5–6.5
**Cleavage**: None
**Fracture**: Conchoidal
**Specific gravity**: 5.1
**Other characteristics**: Magnetism is strong in massive specimens
**Notable locations**: Binnatal, Zermatt, Switzerland; Zillertal, Austria; Traversella, Italy; Nordmark, Sweden; Russia; South Africa; Magnet Cove, Arkansas; Brewster, New York

Magnetite is one of the few naturally magnetic minerals. Its name is thought to come from the region of Magnesia in Ancient Macedonia, where, according to legend, the shepherd Magnes discovered magnetism when the iron nails in his shoes stuck to the rock. Some specimens, called lodestones, are magnetic enough to pick up iron. Ships carried lodestones to magnetize their compass needles until the 18th century. Nowadays, geologists are able to trace the past movement of continents using magnetite crystals frozen in rock in alignment with the North Pole as they formed, a technique called paleomagnetism. Magnetite has over 72 per cent iron content, and is the most important iron ore after hematite. It occurs as grains in a huge variety of rocks, but especially igneous rocks and the sands that form from them as they are weathered. These are the main ores. But magnetite may also form crystals in hydrothermal veins and alpine fissures. In sands, magnetite is often associated with gold, but also forms black beaches of sand in its own right.

**Identification**: Magnetite's dark colour, black streak and magnetism will distinguish it clearly from most other iron-bearing minerals.

*Quartz*

*Massive magnetite*

# Siderite

*FeCO₃ Iron carbonate*

*Curved blades of siderite*

Siderite gets its name from *sideros*, the Ancient Greek for 'iron'. It is similar to calcite, but with iron replacing calcium, often when limestone is altered by iron-bearing solutions. Siderite is widespread in sedimentary rocks, and forms iron-rich clay beds known as clay ironstone. Clay ironstone can form nodules with a nucleus of hematite, and a surface altered to limonite or goethite. Fossils of plants, millipedes or clams are sometimes found in the nodules. Siderite also forms in cool hydrothermal veins. The great iron deposits that gave birth to the European and North American iron industry were the 'Minette' ores, made of siderite ooliths laid down on seabeds hundreds of millions of years ago. Crystals of siderite are attractive but rare.

**Identification**: Siderite's softness (the ease with which it can be scratched) indicates that it is a carbonate. Its dark brown surface colour and white streak show it to be iron carbonate.

**Crystal system**: Trigonal
**Crystal habit**: Crystals curved blades. More often earthy masses or nodules.
**Colour**: Dark brown, grey; surface may be iridescent goethite
**Lustre**: Vitreous
**Streak**: White
**Hardness**: 3.5–4.5
**Cleavage**: Perfect in three directions forming rhombs
**Fracture**: Conchoidal, uneven
**Specific gravity**: 3.9+
**Other characteristics**: Magnetic when heated
**Notable locations**: Cornwall, England; Allevard, France; Erzberg, Austria; Panasquiera, Portugal; Minas Gerais, Brazil

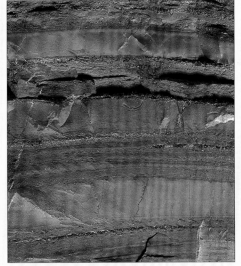

**Banded iron formations**
Some of the world's largest iron ore deposits are remarkable formations of sedimentary rock called banded iron formations (BIFs). BIFs are rock beds some 50–600m/164–1,970ft thick consisting of minutely alternating layers of iron minerals, chert and jasper, each no more than 1cm/½in or so thick. Nearly all of these formations are at least 1.7 billion years old, and some are much older. It is thought that early in Earth's history, huge amounts of iron were dissolved in the oceans – so conditions must have been very different, since iron will not dissolve easily in water now. The remarkable theory is that as primitive plantlike bacteria in the oceans released oxygen, the oxygen combined with the iron and sank to the sea bed as insoluble iron oxides. The banding is thought to mark seasonal peaks in oxygen production. The most famous BIFs are near Lake Superior, USA and in Western Australia's Hammersley Trough.

# Limonite and goethite

*FeO(OH).nH₂O (Limonite) HFeO(OH) (Goethite) Hydrated iron oxide*

*Kidney-form goethite*

Limonite and goethite are basically the same mineral, hydrated iron oxide, but goethite forms crystals, often silky and fibrous in appearance, while limonite is basically amorphous, forming earthy masses and nodules. Named after the German poet Goethe, goethite forms, along with hematite, fluorite and barite, when iron minerals are altered in hydrothermal veins, or as 'bog iron ore' made in lakes and marshes by iron-depositing bacteria. It contains 63 per cent iron and is the second most important iron ore after hematite. Limonite is essentially natural rust, and gives many soils and rocks their yellow-brown colour. It also stains many agates and jaspers. Limonite forms when the surface of iron minerals is altered by weathering and itself alters to hematite as it dries out. It is one of the oldest known pigments, called yellow ochre, and was used in many prehistoric cave paintings.

**Identification**: Limonite can be identified by a yellow stain on a darker brown mass, and its yellowish streak. Fibrous-looking masses are probably goethite.

**Crystal system**: None for limonite; goethite is orthorhombic
**Crystal habit**: Limonite forms earthy masses or kidney-shaped crusts; goethite forms prismatic and platy crystals
**Colour**: Yellow, brown
**Lustre**: Earthy to dull
**Streak**: Brown to yellow
**Hardness**: 4–5.5
**Cleavage**: None
**Fracture**: Crumbly (Limonite); splintery (Goethite)
**Specific gravity**: 2.9–4.3
**Notable locations**: Limonite is found widely; goethite vein specimens common in England, France, Germany; pegmatite goethite crystals found in Florissant, Colorado; goethite fibres are found in the iron mines of Michigan and Minnesota

# ALUMINIUM AND MANGANESE

*Aluminium is the most abundant metal in the Earth's crust, and makes up 8 per cent of the crust by weight. Its compounds are spread throughout almost every rock, plant and animal on the planet. It is primarily extracted from bauxite. Although not quite so widespread as aluminium, manganese is also common and is recovered not just from native manganese, but from ores such as manganite.*

## Aluminium ore: Bauxite

*Al(OH)₃ Aluminium hydroxide (Gibbsite)*

**Bauxite (below)**
Named after the French town of Les Baux, where it was first discovered in 1821, bauxite is found on just about every continent in the world. It is typically buff or white, but can be red, yellow, pink or brown, or a mix of all of them. It can be as hard as rock or soft as clay, and can occur as compacted earth, small balls called pisolites, or hollow, twig-like tubules. Bauxite ore is bauxite with high enough levels of alumina (aluminium oxide) and low enough levels of iron oxide and silica to be worth extracting.

**Gibbsite (below)**
Bauxite is a mixture of three aluminium hydroxide minerals – gibbsite, diaspore and boehmite. Diaspore and boehmite have the same composition, but diaspore is denser and harder. Boehmite is abundant in European bauxites, but rare in America. Diaspore is common in American bauxites. Gibbsite is the dominant mineral in tropical bauxites.

Brown limonite coating

Gibbsite

Remarkably, despite its abundance, aluminium was not discovered until 1808. This is because it is so reactive that it almost never occurs as a pure native element. The only exceptions are microscopic inclusions and as nodules in volcanic mud. It can make gems and corundum, and related rubies and sapphires are all aluminium oxides. Topaz, garnet and chrysoberyl also all contain aluminium. Typically, aluminium occurs in igneous rocks in the form of aluminosilicate minerals such as feldspars, feldspathoids and micas. It also occurs in clay soils that are made from the breakdown of these igneous rocks. However, the most significant occurrence of aluminium is in bauxite. Bauxite is not a mineral, nor even a solid rock like some ores, but a kind of laterite. Laterite is a loose weathered material that forms deep layers in the tropics and subtropics. As rocks rich in aluminosilicates are weathered in the warm, wet climates typical of tropical rainforests, only iron and aluminium oxides and hydroxides are left behind, and everything else is washed away. Bauxite is the residue.

Bauxite is the source of 99 per cent of the world's aluminium, and is excavated in gigantic quarries. Over 40 per cent comes from the huge Australian reserves dug out in places such as Weipa (Queensland), Gove (Northern Territory) and the Darling Range (Western Australia). But Guinea, Brazil, Jamaica and India also have substantial reserves. Aluminium could be obtained from aluminous shales and slates, aluminium phosphate rocks and high alumina clays, but there is so much easily extractable bauxite, it makes no economic sense yet to use these sources.

**Native Aluminium**
**Crystal system**: Isometric
**Crystal habit**: Microscopic inclusions and as nodules in volcanic muds
**Colour**: Silvery white
**Lustre**: Metallic
**Streak**: White
**Hardness**: 1.5
**Cleavage**: Absent
**Fracture**: Jagged
**Specific gravity**: 2.72
**Notable locations**: Russia; DR Congo; Baku, Azerbaijan

**Diaspore**
Diaspore gets its name from the Greek for 'to scatter' because it splits violently when heated.

**Gibbsite**
**Crystal system**: Monoclinic
**Crystal habit**: Typically plates or sheets, or grains. Maybe tablet-shaped crystals.
**Colour**: White, greenish grey, greyish brown, colourless
**Lustre**: Vitreous to pearly
**Streak**: White
**Hardness**: 6.5–7
**Cleavage**: Perfect in one direction, forming plates
**Fracture**: Brittle, conchoidal
**Specific gravity**: 3.4
**Other characteristics**: When heated it splits violently into white pearly scales.
**Notable locations**: Les Baux, France; Larvik, Norway; Tyrol, Austria; Northern Cape, South Africa; Arizona; Nevada

# Manganese ore: Manganite, Psilomelane, Pyrolusite

*MnO(OH) Manganese oxide hydroxide (Manganite)*

A hard, brittle, grey-white metal, manganese gets its name from the same root as magnetite, because when alloyed with other metals such as copper, antimony and aluminium it can be magnetic. It was discovered in 1774 by the Swedish scientist Johan Gahn while heating the mineral pyrolusite in a charcoal fire. In fact, pyrolusite is manganese oxide, and it simply lost its oxygen to the charcoal to leave the metal. Tiny traces of manganese are vital for health, helping the body absorb Vitamin B1 and promoting the action of enzymes. But too much manganese can be toxic. Nowadays, manganese is used for making dry-cell batteries, and for adding to steel to make it harder. Manganese has never been found in pure form, but it combines readily with other elements and is a common but minor ingredient of many rocks.

**Deep sea manganese**
On the surface of the ocean bed, nodules of manganese and other metals are scattered across the ooze like countless marbles. They form when the hot waters from black smokers (undersea volcanic hot springs) meet the cold, deep ocean water. Because the waters are rich in manganese, manganese is deposited in nodules around the smokers, often accumulating on the surface of a grain such as a tiny piece of bone. Once started, each nodule grows slowly, by 1cm/½in in diameter in about 1 million years. As the ocean floor spreads wider, so these nodules are scattered over a vast area. Though rich in manganese, these nodules are too deep in the ocean and too costly to gather at the moment. But some fields of nodules, particularly in the Eastern Pacific, may one day be 'harvested' (mined) commercially as land sources diminish and cost-effective deep-sea mining methods are developed. The photo above was taken at a depth of 5,350m/17,550ft in the Atlantic Oceans.

**Manganite (below)**
Manganite is the mineral richest in manganese, and was once a major manganese ore. It is now too rare to be a significant source, but is often sought after for its distinctive crystals, which resemble only a few other metallic minerals such as enargite. It forms bundles of prismatic crystals or fibrous masses deposited from circulating waters and in low-temperature hydrothermal veins.

It is the manganese oxides pyrolusite and psilomelane and the hydroxide manganite that provide most of the ores for manganese. Manganese silicates such as rhodonite and braunite are less important. Psilomelane gets its name from the Greek *psilos* for 'bald' and *melas* for 'black' because of the smooth, black, botryoidal masses it can form. It is now a general name for all the hard, dark, barium-rich manganese oxides, such as hollandite and romanechite. Like pyrolusite, it typically forms when rocks are weathered, and can often form large masses when other weathered materials are washed away. Wad, or 'bog manganese', is a soft, earthy mixture of manganese ores such as pyrolusite and psilomelane with water. It is often found around marshes and springs.

**Wad (right)**
Wad is a shapeless, dark earthy mass of wet manganese ores that often forms in marshes, which is why it is also called bog manganese.

**Manganite**
**Crystal system**: Monoclinic
**Crystal habit**: Prisms in bundles, or fibrous masses
**Colour**: Black to steel grey
**Lustre**: Submetallic to dull
**Streak**: Reddish to black
**Hardness**: 4
**Cleavage**: Perfect lengthwise
**Fracture**: Uneven
**Specific gravity**: 4.2–4.4
**Other characteristics**: Alters to give dull coat of pyrolusite fibres
**Notable locations**: Cornwall, England; Ilfeld (Harz Mountains), Germany; Ukraine; Negaunee, Michigan

**Psilomelane group**
**Crystal system**: Monoclinic
**Crystal habit**: Massive botryoidal, stalactites
**Colour**: Black to dark grey
**Lustre**: Submetallic
**Streak**: Brown to black
**Hardness**: 5–7
**Cleavage**: None
**Fracture**: Conchoidal to uneven
**Specific gravity**: 3.3–4.7
**Notable locations**: Cornwall, England; Schneeburg, Germany; Ouro Prêto (Minas Gerais), Brazil; Tucson, Arizona; Austinville, Virginia; Michigan

# MOLYBDENUM AND TUNGSTEN

*Molybdenum and tungsten melt only at very high temperatures. Molybdenum melts at 2,610°C/4,730°F, 1,000 degrees above most steels. Tungsten's melting point is even higher at 3,410°C/6,170°F. Both metals are used where heat-resistance is essential. Molybdenite is mainly extracted from molybdenite ores, but also from wulfenite and powellite; tungsten comes from the wolframite minerals, and from scheelite.*

## Molybdenum ore: Molybdenite

*MoS$_2$ Molybdenum sulphide*

**Crystal system**: Hexagonal
**Crystal habit**: Rare crystals are thin hexagonal tablets. Typically forms soft sheetlike masses and crusts.
**Colour**: Bluish lead grey
**Lustre**: Metallic
**Streak**: Greenish grey
**Hardness**: 1–1.5
**Cleavage**: Perfect, basal, forming thin sheets
**Fracture**: Flaky
**Specific gravity**: 4.6–4.8
**Other characteristics**: Leaves marks on fingers
**Notable locations**: Cornwall, England; Raade, Norway; Hirase (Honshu), Japan; Kingsgate and Deepwater, New South Wales; Pontiac County; Quebec; Wilberforce, Ontario; Climax, Colorado; Lake Chelan, Washington

Molybdenite gets its name from the ancient Greek word for 'lead', because its softness and dark grey colour made people wrongly think it contained lead. Molybdenite is widely distributed but rarely occurs in large quantities. There are an estimated 12 million tonnes of molybdenum in molybdenite around the world. Its molybdenum content means it forms mostly in high-temperature environments, typically in granite pegmatites and quartz veins. It also occurs in contact metamorphic deposits and skarns along with scheelite, pyrite and wolframite. It is one of the softest of all minerals, and is rather like graphite. As with graphite, it is soft because it has a sheetlike structure, with the molybdenum and sulphur in alternating layers that slide easily over one another. It also has a greasy feel and leaves dark marks on your fingers in the same way that graphite does. In fact, molybdenite and graphite are often hard to tell apart.

*Hexagonal molybdenite crystal in quartz*

*Molybdenite*

*Feldspar*

**Identification**: Soft, flexible flakes of molybdenum can only really be confused with graphite. Graphite leaves darker marks.

## Molybdenum ore: Powellite

*CaMoO$_4$ Calcium molybdate*

Powellite is named after the American geologist John Wesley Powell (1834–1902), who led the first expedition down the Colorado River through the Grand Canyon. It is one of the few fairly common molybdenum minerals. Most powellite probably forms when hot hydrothermal solutions interact with molybdenite, so it occurs in many of the same places. In fact, powellite often mimics the shape of molybdenite, forming pseudomorphs as the atoms of molybdenite are replaced one by one. Powellite also forms directly in quartz veins. Good crystals are rare, and most come from the Deccan basalts of India, particularly from Nasik in Maharashtra. Powellite forms part of a series with scheelite, in which molybdenum replaces scheelite's tungsten. Both minerals are fluorescent, but scheelite glows bluish white while powellite glows golden yellow.

**Identification**: Powellite is identified by its colour, pyramidal cleavage, association with molybdenite and yellow fluorescent glow under UV.

**Crystal system**: Tetragonal
**Crystal habit**: Rare, small, four-sided pyramids, or crusts on molybdenite
**Colour**: White, yellowish brown, blue
**Lustre**: Adamantine to greasy
**Streak**: White
**Hardness**: 3.5–4
**Cleavage**: Pyramidal
**Fracture**: Uneven
**Specific gravity**: 4.2
**Other characteristics**: Brittle, fluoresces golden yellow
**Notable locations**: Cumbria, England; Telemark, Norway; Black Forest, Germany; Altai Mountains, Russia; Maharashtra, India; Sonora, Mexico; Arizona; Nevada; Seven Devils, Idaho; Keewenaw Peninsula, Michigan

# Tungsten ore: Scheelite

*CaWO₄ Calcium tungstate*

**Crystal system**: Tetragonal
**Crystal habit**: Double pyramids that look octahedral. Masses, grains.
**Colour**: White, clove brown, greenish grey (cuproscheelite)
**Lustre**: Adamantine
**Streak**: White
**Hardness**: 4.5–5
**Cleavage**: Pyramidal
**Fracture**: Conchoidal
**Specific gravity**: 5.9–6.1
**Other characteristics**: Fluoresces blue-white
**Notable locations**: Cumbria, England; Saxony, Germany; Slavkov, Czech Republic; Tong Wha, South Korea; Mill City, Nevada; Atolia, California; Cochise County, Arizona

Named after Karl Scheele, the 18th-century Swedish scientist who discovered tungsten, scheelite is an important ore of tungsten. Although most tungsten comes from wolframite found in Russia and China, scheelite provides the United States with most of its home-produced tungsten. It is found most often in skarns called tactites, where granitic magma intrudes into limestone. Scheelite forms here in association with garnet, epidote, vesuvianite and wolframite. Scheelite can also form in high-temperature, quartz-rich hydrothermal veins, along with cassiterite, topaz, fluorite, apatite and wolframite. Collectors treasure scheelite crystals for their distinctive double-pyramid crystals, with side facets that make them look octahedral. They are also cherished for their bright blue-white fluorescent glow, which can help miners discover the crystals in the dark with ultraviolet lamps. Scheelite is occasionally used as a gem.

**Identification**: Scheelite can be recognized by its distinctive eight-sided double-pyramid crystals and blue-white fluorescent glow in shortwave UV light.

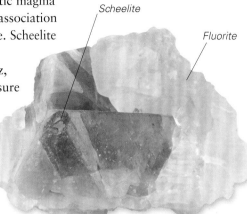

*Scheelite*

*Fluorite*

# Tungsten ore: Wolframite

*(Fe,Mn)WO₄ Iron manganese tungstate*

**Crystal system**: Monoclinic
**Crystal habit**: Flat tablets forming bladed, sheetlike groups. Also masses, grains.
**Colour**: Grey-black to brownish black
**Lustre**: Submetallic
**Streak**: Brownish black
**Hardness**: 5–5.5
**Cleavage**: Perfect in one direction
**Fracture**: Uneven
**Specific gravity**: 7–7.5
**Notable locations**: Cornwall, England; Erzebirge, Harz Mts, Germany; Panasquiera, Portugal; Caucasus Mts, Lake Baikal, Russia; Tong Wha, South Korea; Nanling Mts, China; Llallagua, Bolivia; Northwest Territories; Boulder Co, Colorado

Legend has it that miners in medieval Saxony gave this mineral the name of 'the wolf' because it interfered with tin smelting. Now it is recognized as the major ore of tungsten. Wolframite is not a mineral in its own right but a mix of varying proportions of iron and manganese tungstate minerals. The iron-rich variety is called ferberite; the manganese-rich variety is hübnerite. Wolframite occurs typically in high-temperature quartz veins, pegmatites in granitelike rocks and skarns, often associated with cassiterite, galena and scheelite. It is also found concentrated in alluvial placer deposits. The mineral ore is extracted from opencast mines in Australia and Northwest Territories, Canada, but the largest deposits are in the Nanling Mountains, China, which need to be deep mined. Tungsten is used as a filament in lightbulbs and as a carbide in drilling equipment.

**Identification**: The wolframite minerals can best be identified by their black-brown colour and their distinctive sheetlike groups of flat crystals.

**WSkarns**
When a limestone or marble is invaded by hot magma, it can create remarkable deposits called skarns, which are sources of some of the world's most valuable ores. Hot, slightly acid solutions circulate through the rocks and react with the carbonates in the limestone to create a host of new minerals. The limestone supplies calcium, magnesium and carbon dioxide; the magma supplies silicon, aluminium, iron, sodium, potassium and other elements. The magma's silicon and iron, for instance, combine with the limestone's calcium and magnesium to form silicate minerals such as diopside, tremolite, wollastonite (as in the skarn shown above) and andradite. The hydrothermal solutions may also deposit ore minerals of iron, copper, zinc, tungsten or molybdenum. Tungsten skarns supply much of the world's tungsten from deposits such as those at Sangdong in Korea, King Island, off Tasmania in Australia, and Pine Creek in California, USA.

# NICKEL

*Nickel is a shiny, silvery white metal that is slightly magnetic. It is alloyed to iron in both the Earth's core and in many meteorites and was clearly an important element in the early solar system. It is rarely found in pure form in the Earth's crust, and industry extracts it either from the igneous sulphide ores pentlandite, nickeline and chloanthite or from ores in laterites such as garnierite.*

## Nickel sulphide ore: Nickeline (Niccolite)

*NiAs Nickel arsenide*

**Crystal system:** Hexagonal
**Crystal habit:** Usually massive, though also forms in columnlike groups
**Colour:** Copper red
**Lustre:** Metallic
**Streak:** Pale brownish black
**Hardness:** 5–5.5
**Cleavage:** Poor
**Fracture:** Uneven
**Specific gravity:** 7.8
**Notable locations:** Black Forest, Harz Mountains, Germany; Jachymov, Czech Republic; Anarak, Iran; Natsume, Japan; Great Slave Lake, Northwest Territories; Sudbury, Cobalt, Ontario; Franklin, New Jersey

The mineral nickeline, or niccolite, was known long before anyone identified the element nickel. Copper miners during the Middle Ages in Germany found copper-coloured niccolite deposits when they were looking for copper, but on processing it found only what looked like a white slag. Thinking it bewitched, they named the mineral *Kupfernickel* (copper nickel) after the Old Nick's (the Devil's) impish 'nickels' (little helpers) underground. It was in nickeline that Swedish chemist Axel Cronstedt finally identified nickel in 1751. Nickeline is not common, but it is mined together with other more important nickel and cobalt sulphide ores. It typically occurs in igneous rocks such as norite and gabbro, in association with pyrrhotite and chalcopyrite as well as pentlandite and nickel skutterudite. It also forms in hydrothermal veins along with silver, arsenic and cobalt minerals. On exposure to air, it alters to pale green annabergite, or 'nickel bloom'.

**Identification:** Nickeline's coppery colour is very distinctive and only really looks like breithauptite (nickel antimony).

*Nickeline*

## Nickel sulphide ore: Pentlandite

*(Fe,Ni)₉S₈ Iron nickel sulphide*

The main nickel ore, pentlandite, is usually found intertwined with pyrrhotite (iron sulphide). The two can rarely be physically separated, though pyrrhotite is magnetic while pentlandite is not. They tend to form together when sulphides separate out of molten ultramafic magmas, notably norite and rare komatites. As the magma cools, metal sulphides crystallize and fall to the base of the magma to collect in a rich mass. But the famous nickel sulphide deposits at Sudbury, Ontario, Canada, were probably concentrated by the impact of a giant meteorite. Pentlandite – named after J B Pentland, who discovered it – is here embedded along with sperrylite and chalcopyrite in a huge mass of pyrrhotite in a trough of norite and gabbro rock 60km/ 40 miles long. Pentlandite has also been found in nickel-iron meteorites. Wherever it forms, pentlandite rarely makes good crystals, and is usually found only in the massive form.

**Crystal system:** Isometric
**Crystal habit:** Mostly minute grains and masses
**Colour:** Brassy yellow
**Lustre:** Metallic
**Streak:** Tan
**Hardness:** 3.5–4
**Cleavage:** None
**Fracture:** Conchoidal
**Specific gravity:** 4.6–5
**Notable locations:** Iveland, Norway; Styria, Austria; Noril'sk-Talnakh, Russia; Bushveld complex, S Africa; Kambalda, Western Australia; Lynn Lake, Manitoba; Malartic, Quebec; Sudbury, Ontario; Ducktown, Tennessee; San Diego Co, California

**Identification:** Pentlandite is best identified by its brassy colour and its association with pyrrhotite and chalcopyrite.

# Nickel sulphide ore: Chloanthite (Nickel skutterudite)

*NiAs$_{2-3}$ Nickel arsenide*

Native arsenic

Skutterudite, chloanthite, safflorite and rammelsbergite are rare nickel and cobalt arsenides that merge so closely they are hard to tell apart, and mineralogists argue over which is a proper mineral species. All are tin white, and have a bright metallic lustre and black streak. All were once nickel and cobalt ores, but the good veins are now all but used up. They are basically a pair of solid solution series: one running from skutterudite to chloanthite, the other from safflorite to rammelsbergite. Skutterudite and safflorite are at the cobalt-rich end and chloanthite and rammelsbergite at the nickel-rich end. Sometimes exposure to air helps distinguish them, as the cobalt-rich minerals get coated in red erythrite and the nickel-rich minerals get coated in green annabergite. In fact, *chloanthes* is Greek for 'green flowering'. Many mineralogists no longer recognize chloanthite as a separate species. They now prefer to call the nickel-rich end of the skutterudite-chloanthite series 'nickel skutterudite' and describe chloanthite simply as an arsenic-deficient version of this.

**Crystal system:** Isometric
**Crystal habit:** Massive, grains
**Colour:** Tin white
**Lustre:** Metallic
**Streak:** Yellowish white
**Hardness:** 5.5–6
**Cleavage:** None, crumbly
**Fracture:** Very brittle, conchoidal
**Specific gravity:** 6.5
**Notable locations:** Annaberg, Schneeberg (Saxony), Andreasberg (Harz Mountains), Germany; Cobalt, Ontario

**Identification:** Chloanthite and other cobalt and nickel arsenides all look tin white and are hard to tell apart, except when they are coated green with annabergite.

# Nickel laterite ore: Garnierite, Népouite

*(Ni,Mg)$_3$Si$_2$O$_5$.(OH)$_4$ Hydrated nickel magnesium silicate*

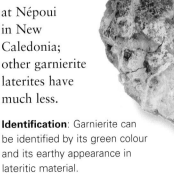

**Crystal habit:** Orthorhombic
**Crystal habit:** Massive, earthy
**Colour:** Pale green
**Lustre:** Vitreous, pearly
**Streak:** Greenish white
**Hardness:** 2–2.5
**Cleavage:** None
**Fracture:** Uneven
**Specific gravity:** 4.6
**Notable locations:** Limpopo, Mpumalanga, South Africa; Népoui, New Caledonia; Australia; Cuba; Washington; Nevada

Garnierite is not a mineral species, but a blanket term for a range of different earthy nickel minerals, including népouite, pimelite and willemsite. Garnierite forms as gabbro, and peridotite rock rich in nickel is deeply weathered in warm climates to form a laterite. Weathering removes much of the original rock, but dissolved nickel may percolate down and collect in sufficient concentrations in the weathered material to create an ore. Garnierites are the 'nickeliferous' laterites richest in nickel, but limonites can contain a fair amount of nickel, too, and are far more widespread. Some garnierite laterites can contain almost 10 per cent nickel, such as in the népouite first excavated at Népoui in New Caledonia; other garnierite laterites have much less.

**Identification:** Garnierite can be identified by its green colour and its earthy appearance in lateritic material.

## Laterites: tropical metal banks

Rocks weather quickly in warm, wet tropical climates to create incredibly deep soil-like layers called laterites. There are deep laterites beneath the Amazon basin, for instance. There are also ancient laterites in North America, and Europe, formed when they were in the tropics long ago. Yet although laterites are deep, they are not good soils, for heavy tropical rains ensure that just about all the useful minerals are quickly washed out. There isn't even much organic matter, since it decays rapidly in the tropical heat. Rainforest trees grow by continually recycling nutrients; when forests are cleared for farming, the soils lose all fertility in just a few years. But though laterites make poor soils, they do hold on to those iron, aluminium and nickel minerals that won't dissolve, and these often become concentrated by percolating water into valuable mineral deposits. Iron-rich laterites such as limonite are not exploited much, because banded iron formations provide a better source of iron. But aluminium-rich laterites are bauxites, the main sources of aluminium, and nickel-rich laterites are garnierites, which can yield nickel.

# CHROMIUM, COBALT, VANADIUM AND TITANIUM

*Chromium and titanium are both tough, light metals that have found an increasing range of uses in the modern world, especially when alloyed with metals such as steel. Cobalt and vanadium, though soft as pure metals, also really toughen up steel and other metals when alloyed with them.*

## Chromium ore: Chromite

*FeCr₂O₄ Iron chromium oxide*

**Crystal habit**: Isometric
**Crystal habit**: Crystals rare, octahedral. Mostly grainy masses.
**Colour**: Black, brownish black
**Lustre**: Metallic
**Streak**: Brown
**Hardness**: 5.5
**Cleavage**: None
**Fracture**: Conchoidal
**Specific gravity**: 4.1–5.1
**Notable locations**: Outokumpu, Finland; Kempirsay Massif, Kazakhstan; Sarany (Urals), Russia; Guleman, Turkey; Luzon, Philippines; Andhra Pradesh, India; Camagüey, Cuba; Maryland

Chromium derives its name from the Greek *chroma* for 'colour', because many minerals get their special colour from its presence, such as green emeralds. Yet although there are small amounts of chromium in many minerals – notably crocoite, in which it was discovered in 1797 – there is only one real ore: chromite. Chromite crystals are sometimes found in veins and scattered through serpentine. But most ore chromite forms as lens-shaped masses in ultramafic magmas, such as peridotites. Chromite has a high melting point and is one of the few ores to form directly from liquid magma. It crystallizes early in the cooling magma, then sinks to create these lenses. It may then stay unaltered when the host rocks are metamorphosed to serpentinites. Most commercial chromite comes from South Africa, Russia, Albania, the Philippines, Zimbabwe, Turkey, Brazil, Cuba, India and Finland.

**Identification**: Chromite is best identified by its association with serpentines. It looks like magnetite but is not magnetic. In the specimen below, all the black is chromite.

## Cobalt ore: Cobaltite

*CoAsS Cobalt arsenic sulphide*

*Skutterudite, a minor cobalt ore*

The Ancient civilizations of Egypt and Mesopotamia used cobalt minerals to make deep blue glass, but it was not until 1735 that it was identified as an element. Now it is known as a widespread natural element found in small quantities in many different minerals. Most commercially mined cobalt is taken from ores of copper, nickel or copper-nickel, where cobalt occurs in sulphide minerals such as carrollite, linnaeite and slegenite, oxides such as heterogenite and asbolite and the carbonate sphaerocobaltite. Much of the world's cobalt comes from copper ores in the Congo and Russia, nickel ores from New Caledonia, Cuba and Celebes, and copper-nickel sulphide ores in Canada, Australia and Russia. Very few ores are mined purely for their cobalt, except notably in Morocco. These include skutterudite, smaltite and cobaltite, noted for its remarkably pyrite-like crystals.

**Identification**: Cobaltite is usually grainy masses but can form either cubes, like galena, or pyrite-shape crystals, but cobaltite's silver white colour usually makes its identity clear.

**Crystal habit**: Isometric
**Crystal habit**: Crystals are typically cubes and pyritohedrons (pyrite shapes), but typically grainy masses
**Colour**: Silver-white with red tinge
**Lustre**: Metallic
**Streak**: Grey-black
**Hardness**: 5.5
**Cleavage**: Perfect like cubes
**Cleavage**: Uneven to subconchoidal
**Specific gravity**: 6–6.3
**Other characteristics**: On cube faces, there are often striations
**Notable locations**: Cumbria, England; Tunaberg, Sweden; Skutterud, Norway; Siegerland, Germany; DR Congo; Sonora, Mexico; Cobalt, Ontario; Boulder, Colorado

# Vanadium ore; Vanadinite

*Pb₅(VO₄)₃Cl Lead chlorovanadate*

Vanadium was named by 19th-century Swedish chemist Nils Seftsrom after Vanadis, the Norse goddess of beauty, because of the colours it forms in solutions, and vanadinite also often lives up to the name. Even in crust form, as seen here, it is an attractive deep red, but when it forms crystals it can be striking, although they tend to fade with time. Vanadinite crystals can even be multicoloured, like tourmaline. Vanadinite is almost always found where lead sulphide ores such as galena are weathered in arid climates, along with minerals such as pyromorphite, mimetite, wulfenite, cerussite and descloizite. Although vanadinite is the mineral with the highest vanadium content, it is too rare to be the only ore. Roscoelite, patronite and carnotite all provide ores, but most vanadium is recovered as a by-product of processing other ores, notably titanium-rich magnetite. It is also found in the ash from ships' smokestacks.

**Identification**: With its sharp, hexagonal prism crystals, vanadinite looks a little like pyromorphite and mimetite, but its blood-orange colour marks it out clearly.

**Crystal system**: Hexagonal
**Crystal habit**: Small prisms
**Colour**: Red, brown, yellow or orange
**Lustre**: Resinous, adamantine
**Streak**: Brownish yellow
**Hardness**: 3–4
**Cleavage**: None
**Fracture**: Conchoidal
**Specific gravity**: 6.7–7.1
**Notable locations**: Dumfries and Galloway, Scotland; Carpathia, Austria; Urals, Russia; Mibladen, Morocco; Otavi, Namibia; Marico, South Africa; Chihuahua, Mexico; Tucson, Arizona; Sierra County, New Mexico

---

## Minerals in iron and steel

Extracting iron out of ore means smelting it in a blast furnace – heating it until the molten metal runs out, leaving the other minerals behind. Yet even then the iron is not pure. Pig iron from the blast furnace is only 93 per cent iron, with 4 per cent carbon, and traces of numerous other substances. Further refining turns it into cast iron, with 2–3 per cent carbon and 1–3 per cent silicon. All the carbon and silicon make iron too brittle to be beaten into shape, though it can be cast (poured into sand moulds). Wrought iron is almost pure iron with most of the carbon taken out so it can be bent and shaped into things like railings. Interestingly, though, pure iron can be toughened by adding the right 'impurities', including carbon, to make steel, a material first discovered in India 2,000 years ago. The most widely used kind of steel is carbon steel, which is 1 per cent carbon. Mild steel for car bodies may be 0.25 per cent carbon. High carbon steel for tools is 1.2 per cent carbon. Other steel alloys may be made by adding traces of other metals to give particular qualities. Chromium makes stainless steel (which clads the famous Gateway Arch of St Louis in the USA, above). Manganese, cobalt and vanadium give strength; molybdenum heat resistance and nickel corrosion resistance.

# Titanium ore: Ilmenite, rutile

*FeTiO₃ Iron titanium trioxide (Ilmenite)*

Titanium was discovered first in black magnetic sands, then in rutile by German chemist M H Klaproth who named it after the Titans, the giants of Greek mythology, because of its strength. Titanium metal is used as a very strong lightweight material, but titanium dioxides such as rutile are used as the basic white pigment in paints, replacing toxic lead. Titanium is sometimes thought of as an exotic metal, but it is the fourth most abundant after aluminium, iron and magnesium, and ilmenite and rutile ores are abundant. Grains of ilmenite occur in rocks such as gabbro and diorite, and as the rocks ares weathered these grains can become concentrated in mineable sands, or as waterworn pebbles. Occasionally, good crystals form in pegmatites.

**Crystal system**: Trigonal
**Crystal habit**: Thick tablet-shaped crystals, but usually grains and masses
**Colour**: Black
**Lustre**: Submetallic
**Streak**: Dark brownish red
**Hardness**: 5–6
**Cleavage**: None
**Fracture**: Conchoidal or uneven
**Specific gravity**: 4.5–5
**Notable locations**: Kragerø, Norway; Sweden; Lake Ilmen (Urals), Russia; Gilgit, Pakistan; Sri Lanka; Australia; Brazil; Lake Allard, Quebec; Bancroft, Ontario; Orange County, New York

*Ilmenite*

**Identification**: Ilmenite looks like many black sulphosalts, but is harder. It can be easily distinguished from hematite by its streak and from magnetite by its lack of magnetism.

# COPPER

*As well as being one of the most distinctive metals, with its red-gold colour, copper is also one of the most widely available, and has long played a part in human culture. It is found worldwide as both a pure native element in basaltic lavas and also in ores such as chalcocite, chalcopyrite, bornite, cuprite, enargite and covellite. It can even be found in seaweed ash, sea corals, molluscs and the human liver.*

## Chalcopyrite

*CuFeS₂ Copper iron sulphide*

**Crystal system**: Tetragonal
**Crystal habit**: Crystals appear tetrahedral; usually massive
**Colour**: Brassy yellow, tarnishes to iridescent blues, greens and purples
**Lustre**: Metallic
**Streak**: Dark green
**Hardness**: 3.5–4
**Cleavage**: Poor
**Fracture**: Conchoidal, brittle
**Specific gravity**: 4.2
**Notable locations**: Cornwall, England; Russia; Kinshasa, DR Congo; Zambia; Ugo, Japan; Olympic Dam, South Australia; Chihuahua, Naica, Mexico; El Teniente, Chile; Bingham, Utah; Ely, Nevada; Ajo, Arizona; Joplin, Missouri

Most of the world's big copper deposits are 'porphyry' coppers, in which the copper minerals are scattered in veinlets evenly throughout the rock, which is typically porphyritic diorite, or schist. The copper ores of the gigantic Chilean deposits are porphyry coppers, as are those of the American south-west. Massive and vein deposits, while more concentrated, are far less extensive. Typically, the upper deposits in porphyries are copper oxides such as cuprite; the deeper deposits are sulphides such as chalcopyrite. Containing less than a third copper, chalcopyrite is the main source of copper, because it is found in such large quantities. It gets its name because it is the same gold colour as pyrite, although slightly yellower. Like pyrite, it has been mistaken for gold. Its surface is often coated with a dark greeny, purplish iridescent tarnish, earning it the name 'peacock copper'. As well as porphyries, it forms in hydrothermal veins and pegmatites, often with pyrite, sphalerite and galena.

**Identification**: Chalcopyrite looks like pyrite, but is more yellow. Like pyrite it also looks like gold, but is brittle and harder.

*Chalcopyrite*

*Calcite*

## Cuprite

*Cu₂O Copper oxide*

**Identification**: A deep red mass with a coat altered to bright green malachite is likely to be cuprite. It is harder than cinnabar.

Cuprite is over two-thirds copper and is a widespread ore that forms by the alteration of other copper minerals. It tends to occur near the surface wherever there are copper sulphide deposits lower down, and forms as they are oxidized. It is typically found mixed in with iron oxides in earthy, porous masses. Some giant cuprite-dominated masses weighing several tonnes have been found. But cuprite can also form wonderful crystals in association with pure native copper and an array of other secondary copper minerals such as malachite, brochantite and azurite. Cuprite crystals range in colour from cochineal red through ruby red to purplish and even black. Fine hairlike masses of cuprite are called chalcotrichite. Tile ore is an earthy mix of the three minerals cuprite, limonite and hematite.

*Cuprite*

**Crystal system**: Isometric
**Crystal habit**: Crystals usually octahedral, but can be other shapes; also acicular, massive, granular
**Colour**: Red to very dark red
**Lustre**: Adamantine to dull
**Streak**: Brick red
**Hardness**: 3.5–4
**Cleavage**: Fair in four directions forming octahedrons
**Fracture**: Conchoidal
**Specific gravity**: Approximately 6
**Notable locations**: Wheal Gorland (Cornwall), England; Chessy, France; Bogoslovsk (Urals), Russia; Ongonja, Namibia; Broken Hill (NSW), Wallaroo (SA), Australia; Bisbee, Arizona

# Chalcocite

*Cu₂S Copper sulphide*

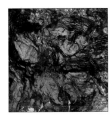

*Covellite is a copper sulphide with a deep indigo iridescence.*

Chalcocite is the most copper-rich of all the copper ores, with a copper content of up to 80 per cent by weight. It is only less important as an ore than chalcopyrite because it is scarce, and most good deposits have been mined out. It can form as a primary mineral direct from magma as 'digenite'. But chalcocite more often forms by a process called secondary, or 'supergene' enrichment. In this, copper sulphide minerals that have been altered by oxidation in surface layers are washed downwards. As coppery solutions percolate down to the lower primary copper ores, they dissolve iron away. Iron-rich chalcopyrite ores are altered to copper-rich chalcocite along the levels of water tables in layers called chalcocite blankets. Typically, as iron is lost, the chalcopyrite alters first to bornite, then to covellite and finally to chalcocite.

**Identification**: Chalcocite is almost always associated with other copper sulphide minerals such as covellite and chalcopyrite. It can be distinguished from them by its dark grey colour.

*Chalcocite coating*

**Crystal system**: Orthorhombic below 105°C/ 221°F and hexagonal above 105°C
**Crystal habit**: Prismatic or tabular crystals, rare; usually massive, or as powdery coat
**Colour**: Dark grey to black
**Lustre**: Metallic
**Streak**: Shiny black to grey
**Hardness**: 2.5–3
**Cleavage**: Prismatic, indistinct
**Fracture**: Conchoidal
**Specific gravity**: 5.5–5.8
**Notable locations**: Cornwall, England; Isère, Belfort, Alsace, France; Rio Tinto, Spain; Sardinia; Messina, South Africa; Butte, Montana; Bristol, Connecticut; Bisbee (Cochise Co), Arizona

**Arizona Copper**

Arizona is sometimes known as 'The Copper State' because of the huge deposits of copper found there in beds of porphyry copper ore. The copper ores here originated 200–100 million years ago when intrusions of porphyry copper ore pushed up into the country rock, and were then concentrated by supergene enrichment (see Chalcocite above). What makes the deposits especially valuable is the presence of many other ores, such as uranium and vanadium. Two-thirds of all America's copper is hacked out of the ground in Arizona – a landscape shaped by strip (or surface) mining is shown above. If Arizona were a country, it would be the world's second largest producer of copper, after Chile. Towns such as Bisbee, Jerome, Globe and Clifton live in the shadow of vast plateaux of tailings piled up here since mining began in earnest in the late 19th century. The industry is now in decline, with copper reserves partly exhausted, and prices around the world falling. But the mines produced an astonishing amount in their heyday. Bisbee alone produced over 4 million tonnes of copper ores between 1877, when copper was first found here, and 1975, when the Phelps Dodge company ceased mining.

# Bornite

*Cu₂FeS₄ Copper iron sulphide*

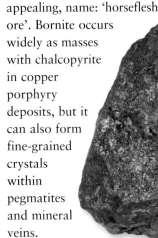

*Enargite: Copper arsenic sulphide copper ore*

Like chalcopyrite, bornite is often known as 'peacock ore' or 'peacock copper'. This is because its surface is often coated with a dark, greeny, purplish, iridescent tarnish made up of the oxides and hydroxides of copper. Peacock ore sold to collectors as bornite is often chalcopyrite with its iridescence enhanced by treatment with acid. To distinguish it from peacock chalcopyrite, you will need to scratch away the tarnish to reveal bornite's true pink copper colour. This pink gives bornite another, slightly less appealing, name: 'horseflesh ore'. Bornite occurs widely as masses with chalcopyrite in copper porphyry deposits, but it can also form fine-grained crystals within pegmatites and mineral veins.

*Bornite*

**Crystal system**: Isometric
**Crystal habit**: Crystals rare but rough, pseudo-cubic and rhomb-dodecahedral; usually massive
**Colour**: Reddish bronze with iridescent peacock tarnish
**Lustre**: Metallic
**Streak**: Grey-black
**Hardness**: 3
**Cleavage**: Very poor, octahedral
**Fracture**: Conchoidal
**Specific gravity**: 4.9–5.3
**Other characteristics**: Tarnishes in hours
**Notable locations**: Cornwall, England; Dzhezkazgan, Kazakhstan; Texada Island, British Columbia; Butte, Montana; Arizona

**Identification:** Bornite tarnishes in hours to peacock ore. To tell it from peacock chalcopyrite, you have to scratch the surface to reveal the true bruised pink colour of bornite beneath.

# LEAD

*Easily shaped and resistant to corrosion, lead has been used since antiquity for items such as pipes and roofing, although, in recent years, the discovery of its toxicity has reduced its use. It is rarely found as a native element, but occurs in compound form in more than 60 minerals, including its main ores galena, cerussite and anglesite, as well as a number of minor ores such as mimetite, pyromorphite and minium.*

## Galena

*PbS Lead sulphide*

Made of 86.6 per cent lead, galena, or lead glance, has been the main lead ore since ancient times, described by Aristotle as the 'Itmid' stone. Its cube-shaped crystals and high density make it among the most distinctive of all minerals. It typically forms in hydrothermal veins, along with sphalerite, pyrite and chalcopyrite, as well as unwanted gangue minerals such as quartz, calcite and barite. Sometimes the hot fluids that deposit galena are trapped in branching cracks beneath the surface; in limestones, these fluids may ooze into cavities to create rich but patchy replacement deposits. Fluids may also well up in undersea volcanic activity to create 'volcanogenic' galena. Ores are often found when partially exposed at the surface by erosion, as in the famous Broken Hill and Mount Isa deposits of Australia. As these surface deposits are exhausted, mining companies are having to probe deeper. Galena usually contains only traces of silver, but so much galena is mined that it is the world's main ore of silver as well as lead.

*Cubic crystals of galena*

**Identification**: Galena crystals are easy to identify by their cubic shape, dark grey colour and high density. Its metallic lustre is usually hidden by a dull film, formed on contact with air.

*Galena*

*Massive quartz*

**Crystal system**: Isometric
**Crystal habit**: Crystals typically cubic. Also forms masses and grains.
**Colour**: Dark grey sometimes with a bluish tinge
**Lustre**: Metallic to dull
**Streak**: Lead grey
**Hardness**: 2.5+
**Cleavage**: Perfect in four directions forming cubes
**Fracture**: Uneven
**Specific gravity**: 7.5–7.6
**Notable locations**: Weardale, England; Black Forest, Harz Mountains, Germany; Sardinia; Trepca, Kosovo; Broken Hill (NSW), Mt Isa (QLD), Australia; Naica, Mexico; Tristate, Kansas-Missouri-Oklahoma

## Mimetite

*Pb₅(AsO₄)₃Cl Lead chloroarsenate*

$Pb_5(AsO_4)_3Cl$ Lead chloroarsenate

*Small wulfenite crystal*

*Mimetite*

**Identification**: Slender yellow mimetite crystals and cauliflower crusts are usually easy to identify by their associations with lead minerals.

Mimetite's name comes from the Greek for 'imitator', as it resembles pyromorphite. Like pyromorphite, it occurs in association with galena, anglesite and hemimorphite, and is one of various lead ores that develop where galena is altered by exposure to air. Mimetite forms where arsenic is present too. It is quite rare and striking crystals like those from Tsumeb, Namibia, are rarer still. It is typically found as botryoidal or cauliflower-like crusts. It can also form barrel-shaped crystals called 'campylite'. Mimetite forms a series with pyromorphite, in which phosphorus replaces mimetite's arsenic, and another with vanadinite, in which arsenic is replaced by vanadium. Vandinite and mimetite look very different, but green mimetite crystals look like pyromorphite.

**Crystal system**: Hexagonal
**Crystal habit**: Slender hexagonal prism-shaped crystals or barrel-shapes (campylite); usually botryoidal or 'cauliflower' crusts
**Colour**: Yellow, brown, green
**Lustre**: Resinous
**Streak**: Off-white
**Hardness**: 3.5–4
**Cleavage**: Rarely noticed
**Fracture**: Subconchoidal
**Specific gravity**: 7.1
**Other characteristics**: Garlic smell when heated
**Notable locations**: Johanngeorgenstadt (Saxony), Germany; Pribam, Czech Republic; Tsumeb, Namibia; Mount Bonnie (Northern Territory), Australia; Durango, Sonora, Chihuahua, Mexico; Gila County, Maricopa County, Arizona

# Pyromorphite

*Pb₅(PO₄)₃Cl Lead chlorophosphate*

Pyromorphite gets its name from the Greek for 'fire form' because of the way its crystals reform when heated and left to cool. It is a secondary mineral that forms where lead ores are oxidized by exposure to air, typically where there is phosphorus available in the apatite of local rocks. It is much less abundant than galena, cerussite or anglesite, but because it typically occurs in the surface layers, it was often used as an ore of lead in the past, notably at Broken Hill in Australia, Caldbeck Fells (Cumbria) in England and Leadville in Colorado, USA. Although it typically forms crusts and masses, pyromorphite is best known for its striking slender, hollow green crystals. It is often indistinguishable from mimetite, and like mimetite can sometimes form barrel-shaped crystals called campylite. Pyromorphite is much more common than mimetite, and good crystals are frequently found, such as in Spain, Idaho, France and now China.

**Identification**: Pyromorphite is best identified by its yellow-green colour, associations with other lead minerals and slender, hollow-ended crystals.

**Crystal system**: Hexagonal
**Crystal habit**: Slender prism-shaped, often hollow-ended, crystals or barrel-shapes (campylite); also crusts and masses
**Colour**: Green, yellow, brown
**Lustre**: Resinous to greasy
**Streak**: Off-white
**Hardness**: 3.5–4
**Cleavage**: Imperfect
**Fracture**: Uneven
**Specific gravity**: 7+
**Notable locations**: Cumbria, England; Auvergne, France; Nassau, Germany; El Horcajo, Spain; Guilin, China; Broken Hill (NSW), Australia; Durango, Mexico; Chester Co, Pennsylvania

**Poisoned by lead**
Lead has been used for at least 7,000 years. Water pipes in ancient Rome, some of which still carry water today, were made of lead. The English word 'plumbing' is from the Latin word for 'lead', *plumbum*. Because it is so widely available and so resistant to corrosion, people went on using lead for water pipes until quite recently, and until the 1970s most homes were painted with lead-based paint. Motor fuel was often rich in lead because it made fuel burn in a more controlled way, protecting engines. But lead has proved to be a quiet killer, inflicting its damage for thousands of years unnoticed, poisoning the digestive system and causing brain damage in children. Some people attribute the downfall of the Roman empire to slow poisoning by lead. England's 16th-century Queen Elizabeth I and many of her ladies had their faces ruined by painting them with 'white lead' in the fashion of the time. Lead pipes are being replaced, paint no longer contains lead and cars are now required to run on unleaded fuel (above), but there is still plenty of lead around.

# Bindheimite

*Pb₂Sb₂O₆(O,OH) Lead antimony oxide hydroxide*

Bindheimite is a minor ore of lead and antimony. It is an earthy yellow mineral that forms as lead and antimony minerals such as jamesonite and boulangerite are altered. As it forms, it often adopts the form of the original mineral and so becomes its pseudomorph. Bindheimite was named after the German mineralogist J J Bindheim (1750–1825) and was officially recognized as a mineral in 1868. However, it was known long before that. In fact, the Ancient Egyptians used it to give coloured glass a brilliant yellow hue. They mixed bindheimite with melted silica and soda ash to create yellow lead pyroantimonite which spread throughout the glass. This has since been used widely as a pigment, sometimes known as 'Naples yellow', in either synthetic or natural form.

**Crystal system**: Isometric
**Crystal habit**: Typically cryptocrystalline masses or crusts but also pseudomorphs of lead antimony sulphides such as jamesonite
**Colour**: Yellow to red-brown or greenish to white
**Lustre**: Light greenish-yellow to brown
**Hardness**: 4–4.5
**Cleavage**: None
**Fracture**: Earthy, conchoidal
**Specific gravity**: 7.3–7.5
**Notable locations**: Cardigan, Wales; Cornwall, England; Saxony, Black Forest, Germany; Carinthia, Austria; Auvergne, France; Nerchinsk, Siberia; Australia; Cochise and Pima Counties, Arizona; Black Hills, South Dakota; San Bernardino County, California

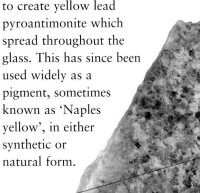

Bindheimite

Quartz

**Identification**: Bindheimite is best identified by its yellow colour, its earthy habit and its association with stibiconite, jamesonite, cerussite, tetrahedrite, lewisite and partzite.

# ZINC

*Used since ancient times with copper in the alloy brass, zinc is a blue-grey, quite brittle metal, and is commonly used to coat iron and steel to stop them rusting in a process called galvanizing. Zinc is rarely found in pure native form, but it is widespread as a compound in rocks, and is extracted from a small number of ores. The chief ore is sphalerite, but smithsonite, zincite and hemimorphite are also important.*

## Smithsonite

*ZnCO₃ Zinc carbonate*

*Yellow smithsonite is sometimes called turkey fat ore*

Named after James Smithson, the English benefactor who founded the Smithsonian Institution, smithsonite is still sometimes known, incorrectly, as calamine (see hemimorphite). It is a secondary mineral that forms in surface layers when zinc minerals like sphalerite are altered by weathering, particularly in limestones, which provide the carbonate. Until the 1880s, when it was replaced by sphalerite, it was the main source of zinc. Smithsonite is a surprisingly attractive mineral. Although it doesn't often form sparkling crystals, it instead forms grapelike or teardrop-shape masses with an extraordinary pearly lustre in a range of colours. Traces of copper give green to blue colours; cobalt, pink to purple; cadmium, yellow; iron, brown to reddish brown. The best known colour is apple-green, but the most sought after are the rarer lavenders. The best specimens come from Tsumeb, Namibia, from Broken Hill in Zambia, and the Kelly Mine in Magdalena, New Mexico.

**Identification**: Smithsonite's pearly, waxlike lustre is very distinctive and only really looks like hemimorphite – but unlike hemimorphite, it looks like plastic at the broken edges.

*Smithsonite*

**Crystal system**: Trigonal
**Crystal habit**: Crystals rare; usually botryoidal or globular crusts; also massive
**Colour**: Green, purple, yellow, white, brown, blue, orange, peach, colourless, grey, pink or red
**Lustre**: Pearly to vitreous
**Streak**: White
**Hardness**: 4–4.5
**Cleavage**: Perfect, forming rhombohedrons
**Fracture**: Uneven
**Specific gravity**: 4.4
**Notable locations**: Cumbria, England; Moresnet, Belgium; Bytom, Poland; Sardinia; Santander, Spain; Lavrion, Greece; Tsumeb, Namibia; Broken Hill, Zambia; Kelly Mine (Magdalena District, Socorro County), New Mexico; Leadville, Colorado; Idaho; Arizona

## Sphalerite

*(Zn,Fe)S Zinc iron sulphide*

**Identification**: In banded schalenblende, sphalerite is often intergrown with wurzite and the two are always hard to tell apart. The best clue is in sphalerite's buff-coloured streak.

Until the 19th century, sphalerite could not be smelted, so smithsonite was the main zinc ore. Now sphalerite is the most important zinc ore by far. It gets its name from the Greek for 'treacherous' because it is so easily mistaken for other minerals, especially galena and siderite. One of the problems with identification is that sphalerite tends to occur in exactly the same hydrothermal veins as galena, and the two are often intergrown. The German miners of old called sphalerite *blende*, which means 'blind', because it looked like galena but did not yield lead. Iron-rich varieties of sphalerite are known as marmatite, reddish ones as ruby-blende or ruby jack, and massive banded ones as schalenblende, in which the sphalerite is often intergrown with galena. Almost uniquely, sphalerite will cleave in six directions, although a single crystal rarely does.

**Crystal system**: Isometric
**Crystal habit**: Include tetrahedrons or dodecahedrons with cube faces. Often twinned. Also granular, fibrous, botryoidal.
**Colour**: Black, brown, yellow, reddish, green or white
**Lustre**: Adamantine, resinous
**Streak**: Buff
**Hardness**: 3.5–4
**Cleavage**: Very good parallel to faces of rhomb dodecahedrons
**Fracture**: Conchoidal rarely seen
**Specific gravity**: 4.0
**Other characteristics**: Triboluminescent
**Notable locations**: Cumbria, England; Trepca, Kosovo; Binnetal, Switzerland; Santander, Spain; Broken Hill (NSW), Australia; St Lawrence County, New York; Tristate, Kansas-Missouri-Oklahoma

# Zincite

*ZnO Zinc oxide*

Zincite is a rare secondary mineral that develops in surface layers of rock when zinc minerals such as sphalerite are weathered and oxidized. It is usually found in platy or granular masses, typically in association with smithsonite, franklinite, gahnite, willemite and calcite. There is only one place in the world where it is found in any quantity – the famous Franklin and Sterling Hill mines in New Jersey. It is found here as red grains and masses in a white, highly fluorescent calcite, typically associated with black franklinite and green willemite. There is so much zincite at Franklin and Sterling Hill that it is a major zinc ore. Good crystals, though, are exceptionally rare. When they are found, typically lying sideways in a calcite vein, they are hemimorphic – that is, they are different shapes at each end with a flat base and a hexagonal pyramid top.

**Identification**: Zincite is usually identified as in New Jersey, as a red mineral in association with white calcite, black franklinite and green willemite.

*Franklinite (black)*

*Zincite (red)*

**Crystal system**: Hexagonal
**Crystal habit**: Usually massive, foliated, granular
**Colour**: Orange-yellow to deep red or brown
**Lustre**: Adamantine
**Streak**: Orange-yellow
**Hardness**: 4
**Cleavage**: Perfect, basal
**Fracture**: Conchoidal
**Specific gravity**: 5.4–5.7
**Notable locations**: Tuscany, Italy; Sardinia; Siegerland, Germany; Tasmania; Franklin and Sterling Hill, New Jersey

## Old Brass

Long before zinc was identified as an element, it was used with copper to make brass. At least 3,000 years ago, people in the Middle East discovered how to make brass by heating native copper and calamine (smithsonite) with glowing charcoal in a clay crucible. This was the method used to make brass right up until the 19th century, and 'calamine brass' is still often considered superior to other kinds. The great thing about brass was that it not only looked like gold, but was tougher, lighter, and cheaper – and corroded much less than any pure metal known except gold. It could also be beaten into shape as well as moulded (unlike bronze). The higher the zinc content, though, the less malleable brass is. Brass has a long history of continuous use in India. In Europe, it was used widely by the Romans for lamps, bowls, plates and other household items – a practice which continued for many centuries. In the Middle Ages, monumental brass plates were used to commemorate the dead. This important alloy has also been used throughout history on a vast number of items connected with time, navigation and observation, such as clocks, compasses, sundials and nautical instruments such as sextants. The latter is a small telescope mounted on an arc, which can help to determine latitude and longitude in relation to the position of celestial bodies.

# Hemimorphite

*Zn₄Si₂O₇(OH)₂.H₂O Hydrated zinc silicate hydroxide*

Like smithsonite, hemimorphite was once called calamine and used as a powder in a lotion to soothe skin irritations. In America, calamine was hemimorphite; in Europe it was smithsonite. To avoid confusion, mineralogists no longer use the term calamine. The name hemimorphite means 'half form' – an illusion to its crystals, which means they are not symmetrical but blunt at one end and pointed like a pyramid at the other. Sometimes, though, in clusters, this hemimorphism is not apparent, because the crystals are attached at the base, hiding the blunt end. Occasionally, hemimorphite is found as clear, bladed crystals arranged in fan shapes; sometimes, it appears as a botryoidal crust similar to smithsonite but duller in lustre and a more acid green.

**Crystal system**: Orthorhombic
**Crystal habit**: Hemimorphic flat based pyramids or arranged in fans; or botryoidal crusts
**Colour**: Blue-green, green, white, clear, brown and yellow
**Lustre**: Vitreous crystals, dull crusts
**Streak**: White
**Hardness**: 4.5–5
**Cleavage**: Perfect in one direction
**Fracture**: Conchoidal to subconchoidal
**Specific gravity**: 3.4
**Other characteristics**: Strongly pyroelectric and piezoelectric
**Notable locations**: Black Forest, Germany; Sardinia; Broken Hill, Zambia; Durango, Chihuahua, Mexico; Leadville, Colorado; Franklin, New Jersey

**Identification**: Hemimorphite forms knobbly crusts like smithsonite but these are a bluer blue-green and duller. Crystals are flat at one end and pointed at the other.

# TIN, BISMUTH AND MERCURY

*Tin, bismuth and mercury are all useful metals known since ancient times. Tin comes from the ores cassiterite and stannite, found mainly in river gravels and veins around granite intrusions. Bismuth comes mainly from bismuthinite, as well as bismite and bismutite, which are found in many of the same places as tin ores. Mercury comes almost entirely from the striking red mineral cinnabar.*

## Tin ore: Cassiterite

*SnO₂ Tin oxide*

Cassiterite gets its name from the Greek word for 'tin', which in turn came from the Sanskrit word *kastira*. Although a small amount of tin comes from sulphide minerals such as stannite, cassiterite is the only significant tin ore. It forms deposits mostly in granites and pegmatites, and in veins and skarns around granite intrusions where tin-bearing fluids from the granite magma have penetrated. Because it is very tough, it survives weathering to collect in river gravels, as gold does, in rounded grains (pebble tin). It was in these placer deposits that people first found tin thousands of years ago, and they still provide 80 per cent of all tin ore. Over half the world's tin now comes from placer deposits formed in river beds that have been submerged under the sea off the coasts of Malaysia, Indonesia and Thailand and are mined by dredging the seabed. Cassiterite has also long been mined from veins in Saxony and Bohemia, and, most famously, Cornwall, where tin mines date back to the Bronze Age. Cornish tin is now uneconomic to mine and most mined ore comes from Tasmania and Bolivia. Wood tin is cassiterite that looks like wood and is formed in high-temperature veins.

**Identification**: Cassiterite is best identified by its black colour, its hardness and its prism or pyramid-shaped crystals. Its high refractive index also gives crystals a tremendous adamantine lustre.

**Crystal system**: Tetragonal
**Crystal habit**: Crystals pyramids or short prisms; also massive, granular
**Colour**: Black or reddish brown or yellow
**Lustre**: Adamantine or greasy
**Streak**: White, or brownish
**Hardness**: 6–7
**Cleavage**: Good in two directions; indistinct in another
**Fracture**: Irregular
**Specific gravity**: 6.6–7.0
**Other characteristics**: High refractive index – approximately 2.0
**Notable locations**: Cornwall, England; Erzgebirge (Saxony), Germany; Zinnwald (Bohemia), Czech Republic; Spain; Fundào, Portugal; Tasmania, Greenbushes (WA), Australia; China; Malaysia; Indonesia; Thailand; Lallagua (Potosi), Araca, Oruro, Bolivia; Durango, Mexico (wood tin)

## Tin ore: Stannite

*Cu₂FeSnS₄ Copper iron tin sulphide*

**Identification**: Stannite is best identified by its iron-black colour, with tinges of bronze yellow, and its association with sulphides.

Stannite

Wolfram

Stannite is a comparatively rare tin sulphide mineral that also contains copper and iron, and was one of the ores once mined in Cornwall and Saxony. It forms grains in granite, or crystals and masses in hydrothermal veins near granite in association with other sulphide minerals. Its pure colour is iron black, but it is often turned bronze yellow by tarnishing or the presence of chalcopyrite. This is why miners sometimes call it bell-metal ore, or tin pyrites. In Bolivia, stannite occurs with silver ores; in Bohemia, it occurs with the minerals galena and sphalerite. The stannite group is also the name of a group of copper sulphides which includes luzonite, kësterite and velikite as well as stannite itself.

**Crystal habit**: Tetragonal
**Crystal habit**: Typically occurs as grains or masses in granite, but can form minute pyramid-shaped crystals
**Colour**: Grey, black
**Lustre**: Metallic
**Streak**: Black
**Hardness**: 4
**Cleavage**: Imperfect
**Fracture**: Uneven
**Specific gravity**: 4.3–4.5
**Notable locations**: Cornwall, England; Auvergne, Brittany, France; Erzgebirge (Saxony), Germany; Carinthia, Austria; Zinnwald (Bohemia), Czech Republic; Kamchatcka, Russia; Zeehan, Tasmania; Oruro, Llallagua (Potosi), Bolivia; Nova Scotia

# Bismuth ore: Bismuthinite

*Bi₂S₃ Bismuth sulphide*

Bismuth does occur naturally in native form but is only about as common as native silver. As a result, bismuth is often extracted from bismuthinite, and occasionally the oxide bismite and carbonate bismutite, which often forms pseudomorphs of bismuthinite when it is exposed to the air. Bismuthinite, or bismuth glance, typically forms when native bismuth is altered by hot fluids in hydrothermal veins and tourmaline-rich pegmatites. Minute, ribbonlike crystals have been found around fumaroles in the Lipari Islands, Italy. When it forms larger crystals in veins, they are often radiating sprays like those of stibnite (and its pseudomorph stibiconite), and the two can be hard to tell apart. Bismuthinite is heavier than stibnite, and its crystals have straighter, flatter sides. Bismuthinite is also commonly associated with tin ores, while stibnite is usually found with antimony and arsenic minerals.

**Identification**: Bismuthinite can usually be identified by its yellowish, slightly iridescent tarnish. Long crystals can be identified by bending them slightly.

Bismuthinite

Quartz

**Crystal system**: Orthorhombic
**Crystal habit**: Usually massive, fibrous; rarely as sprays of long thin crystals
**Colour**: Steel grey to white
**Lustre**: Metallic
**Streak**: Grey
**Hardness**: 2
**Cleavage**: Perfect in one direction
**Fracture**: Uneven
**Specific gravity**: 6.8–7.2
**Other characteristics**: Thin crystals bend a little. Crystals may have a slight yellow or iridescent tarnish.
**Notable locations**: Cornwall, England; Siegerland, Vogtland, Germany; Lipari Island, Italy; Lllallagua (Potosi), Huanani (Oruro), Bolivia; Kingsgate (New South Wales), Australia; Guanajuato, Mexico; Timiskaming, Ontario; Haddam, Connecticut; Beaver County, Utah

**Bronze Age**
Bronze is an alloy, usually of copper and tin. The discovery of this alloy in the Middle East about 5,300 years ago was one of the great milestones in the human story. People had been fashioning native metals such as copper and gold into ornaments and even tools and weapons since about 8000BC. But copper is too soft to keep its shape and stay sharp when made into blades. Yet by adding just a little tin (later found to be ideally 10 per cent), copper could be made into bronze. Bronze was not only more malleable than copper, it was much tougher. The first swords were bronze. So were the first suits of armour, the first metal ploughs and the first metal cooking pots. The illustration of bronze age implements above indicates how the alloy might be adapted to meet differing requirements, both in the prehistoric home and on the battlefield. It is hard to overestimate the impact of bronze on ancient technology. When the Ancient Greeks attacked Troy, they probably did so because it was a focus of the bronze trade. Initially, bronze was brought to Europe by traders from Mycenae. But to supply the smithies that sprang up, ore-hunters ranged across Europe. From 2300BC, tin mining and bronzemaking spread west from Unetice in Hungary and Mittelburg in Germany to Almaden in Spain and Cornwall in England.

# Mercury ore: Cinnabar

*HgS Mercury sulphide*

Getting its name from the ancient Persian for 'dragon's blood', cinnabar is one of the most striking of all minerals. It is a brilliant scarlet colour and was once powdered to make the coveted paint pigment vermillion. Because mercury is liquid at room temperature, it is rarely found in nature except in tiny blobs in crevices, and cinnabar is the main source of mercury, as it has been since Roman times – the cinnabar mines at Almaden in Spain date back 2,500 years. It crystallizes in hydrothermal veins in sedimentary rocks only once the temperature has dropped quite low, so it is typically found fairly near the surface, or even around hot springs.

**Crystal system**: Trigonal
**Crystal habit**: Crystals rhombohedral or thick tabular, sometimes short prisms or needles. Also grains and masses.
**Colour**: Scarlet to brick red. Darkens on exposure to light.
**Lustre**: Adamantine to submetallic
**Streak**: Red
**Hardness**: 2–2.5
**Cleavage**: Perfect in three directions, forming prisms
**Fracture**: Uneven to splintery
**Specific gravity**: 8.1
**Notable locations**: Almaden, Spain; Mount Avala (Idria), Serbia; Slovenia; Hunan, China; San Luis Potosi, Mexico; Cahill Mine (Humboldt Co), Nevada; Sonoma Co, San Benito Co, Santa Clara Co, California; Red Devil Mine (Sleetmute), Alaska
**Caution**: Wash your hands carefully after handling cinnabar; mercury is poisonous.

**Identification**: Cinnabar is identifiable by its bright red colour.

# ARSENIC AND ANTIMONY

*Arsenic and antimony minerals are often found together along with silver. Although both are poisonous, arsenic is still used in making some kinds of bronze, in alloys designed to resist high temperatures and pyrotechnics, while antimony is used as a flame retardant in everything from plastics to textiles, added to tin to make pewter, and as a yellow pigment. The main arsenic ores are orpiment and realgar; ores for antimony include stibnite and bournonite.*

## Arsenic ore: Realgar

*AsS Arsenic sulphide*

**Löllingite**: A minor ore of arsenic, iron arsenide

Realgar got its name in the days of alchemy from the Arabic *rahj al ghar*, which means 'powder of the mine'. The name is apt, because it is liable to crumble as soon as it is exposed to light, slowly but surely. Attracted by its startling orange-red colour, the Ancient Chinese used it to make carvings – and these carvings are now badly deteriorated. As it crumbles, realgar changes to yellow orange pararealgar. It was once used as a red paint pigment, and in many old paintings the original red has decayed to yellow or orange. Collectors are advised to keep realgar specimens in complete darkness. Realgar usually forms late in the cooler parts of hydrothermal veins and around hot springs and fumaroles, nearly always in association with orpiment, and calcite, and also with the mercury ore cinnabar and the antimony ore stibnite. Good crystals can be found in druses and cavities in China and Nevada.

**Identification**: Realgar is easily identified by its orange-red colour, softness and association with orpiment, calcite and stibnite.

**Caution**: Wash your hands carefully after handling realgar; arsenic is poisonous.

**Crystal system**: Monoclinic
**Crystal habit**: Short, striated prisms, terminated by a wedge-like dome. Also found as grains, crusts and earthy masses.
**Colour**: Orange to red
**Lustre**: Resinous, adamantine to submetallic
**Streak**: Orange to orange-yellow
**Hardness**: 1.5–2
**Cleavage**: Good in one direction
**Fracture**: Subconchoidal
**Specific gravity**: 3.5–3.6
**Other characteristics**: Unstable in light
**Notable locations**: Carrara, Italy; Binnental, Switzerland; Tajowa, Hungary; Kresevo, Bosnia; Alsar, Macedonia; Transylvania, Romania; Turkey; Hunan, China; Mercur, Utah; Getchell, Nevada; King County, Washington

## Orpiment

*As₂S₃ Arsenic sulphide*

Orpiment got its name from a corruption of the Latin *auripigmentum*, 'golden coloured', and was long ago used as a pigment called 'king's yellow' and as a cosmetic by women unaware of its dangers. In Ancient China, it was used for gilding silk. Like realgar, orpiment usually forms late in the cooler parts of hydrothermal veins and around hot springs and fumaroles, nearly always in association with realgar and calcite, and also with cinnabar and stibnite. It is often found in mica-like foliated masses, but many fine crystals have been found in Hunan in China, Quiruvilca in Peru and, more recently, at the Twin Peaks gold mine in Humboldt County, Nevada. Like realgar, only less so, orpiment deteriorates on exposure to light, developing a white surface film.

**Caution**: Wash your hands carefully after handling orpiment; arsenic is poisonous.

**Identification**: Orpiment is easily recognized by its golden-yellow colour, softness, garlic smell and often its mica-like flakes.

**Crystal system**: Monoclinic
**Crystal habit**: Usually foliated or columnlike masses and crusts, also tiny tablet-shaped 'orthorhombic' crystals
**Colour**: Orange-yellow to yellow
**Lustre**: Resinous to pearly
**Streak**: Yellow
**Hardness**: 1.5–2
**Cleavage**: Perfect in one direction giving bendable flakes
**Fracture**: Flaky
**Specific gravity**: 3.5
**Other characteristics**: Unstable in light. Arsenic gives it a garlic smell.
**Notable locations**: Tuscany, Campi Fliegri, Italy; Binnental, Switzerland; Maramures County, Romania; Alsar, Macedonia; Hunan, China; Quiruvilca, Peru; Bolivia; Getchell Mine, Twin Peaks Mine, Nevada; Mercur, Utah; Green River Gorge, Washington

# Bournonite

*CuPbSbS₃ Copper lead antimony sulphide*

Named after the French mineralogist Count J L de Bournon (1751–1825), who made the first complete chemical analysis of it in 1804, bournonite is one of the most common sulphosalts. It is an ore of antimony that forms in hydrothermal veins, and also as a secondary mineral associated with copper ores. It is about 42 per cent lead, 24 per cent antimony, 21 per cent sulphur and 13 per cent copper. There are often vugs (open cavities) in the veins where good crystals of bournonite often form. Bournonite is famous for its twinned crystals, especially the groups of repeated twins that look rather like a chunky cogwheel. Many of these 'cog-wheel ores', or *Radelerz*, have been found in mines at Neudorf and Andreasberg in Germany and Cavnic and Baia Mare in Romania. The most spectacular specimens have come from the Herodsfoot mine near Liskeard in Cornwall, England, which was dug for its silver-bearing lead ores.

**Identification**: Bournonite is very easy to identify when the crystals are twinned, especially in the cogwheel pattern; otherwise it can easily be mistaken for many other dark, metallic minerals.

**Caution**: Wash hands after handling bournonite; antimony is poisonous.

*Bournonite*

*Pyrite*

 **Crystal system**: Orthorhombic
**Crystal habit**: Tablet- to prism-shaped crystals. Twins common, often repeated in shapes like cogwheels. Also grains and masses.
**Colour**: Silver-grey or black
**Lustre**: Metallic
**Streak**: Black
**Hardness**: 2.5–3
**Cleavage**: Poor
**Fracture**: Subconchoidal
**Specific gravity**: 5.7–5.9
**Other characteristics**: Often gets a dull tarnish
**Notable locations**: Endellion, Herodsfoot (Cornwall), England; Neudorf, Andreasburg, Germany; Baia Mare, Cavnic, Romania; Pribram, Czech Republic; Chichibu (Saitama), Japan; Quiruvilca, Peru; Park City, Utah

---

**Arsenic poisoning**
Arsenic was used with copper to make the first bronze, but its toxicity as a poison was learned quite early on and it has been a popular poison for murderers for thousands of years. In low doses, though, it was used to treat diseases such as syphilis. In recent years, however, scientists have begun to appreciate that long-term exposure to even low doses may be dangerous – and arsenic is so common in the environment that many people are unwittingly ingesting arsenic in drinking water. Arsenic poisoning may manifest on the hands and feet as keratosis: hard, cornlike spots and callouses (above). Severe lethargy is another common symptom of drinking contaminated water. Some scientists are talking of potential catastrophes in certain parts of the world. Some of the danger is from the leaking of arsenic from mining waste into drinking water, as in parts of Australia and the UK. But the worst danger may be where wells have been sunk into groundwater contaminated by naturally occurring arsenic minerals, especially in Bangladesh, West Bengal and the Ganges plain. Some experts now fear that 330 million people in India and 150 million people in Bangladesh may be at serious risk.

# Stibnite

*Sb₂S₃ Antimony sulphide*

Stibnite gets its name from the Latin for the metal antimony for which it is the main ore. Legend has it that antimony got its name when a monk called Valentinus put stibnite in his fellow monks' food to fatten them up – but, of course, it killed them, so was called *anti-monachium*, 'against monks'. Stibnite typically occurs along with quartz in low-temperature hydrothermal veins, or as replacements in limestone, and around hot springs. It is famous for its radiating sprays of long, thin, bladed or needlelike crystals. The planes within the crystal structure slide over each other, allowing the crystals to bend and droop, without fracturing.

**Crystal system**: Orthorhombic
**Crystal habit**: Forms sprays of bladed or needle-like crystals often bent or curved. Also grains or masses.
**Colour**: Steel grey to silver
**Lustre**: Metallic
**Streak**: Dark grey
**Hardness**: 2
**Cleavage**: Perfect lengthways
**Fracture**: Irregular
**Specific gravity**: 4.5–4.6
**Other characteristics**: Striated lengthwise; crystals slightly flexible
**Notable locations**: Tuscany, Italy; Zajaca, Serbia; Alcar, Macedonia; Baie Mare, Cavnic, Romania; Xikuangshan (Hunan), China; Ichinokawa (Shikoku), Japan; Huaras, Peru; Nye County, Nevada
**Caution**: Wash your hands carefully after handling stibnite; antimony is poisonous.

**Identification**: Stibnite is best identified by its very distinctive spray of long, thin crystals – similar only to bismuthinite and stibiconite.

# GLOSSARY

Terms for mineral optical effects are glossed on p48; lustre on p49; crystal system on p44; and crystal form and habit on p45

**accessory** any mineral not essential to the rock's character.

**accreted terrane** belt of rock welded to the edge of a continent by subduction.

**accretion** various meanings, including gradual growth of a body such as a grain by addition of new material to the surface.

**acidic rock** rock rich in silica.

**aggregate** mass of rock or mineral particles.

**allochromatic** owing its colour to impurities.

**alloy** a manmade combination of two metals.

**alluvial** deposited by rivers.

**alpine cleft** mineral-rich fissure typical of the Alps.

**anion** negatively charged ion.

**aphanitic** of grains too fine to see with the naked eye.

**arenite** sedimentary rock with sand-size grains.

**assemblage zone** strata dated by a group of fossils

**association** minerals that commonly occur together.

**asthenosphere** hot, partially molten layer of the Earth directly below the lithosphere.

**astrobleme** eroded remains of a meteorite impact crater.

**banded iron formation** narrow iron-rich layers of rock.

**batholith** large mass of usually granite plutons at least 100 sq km (39 sq miles) in area.

**bedding plane** the boundary

between layers of sedimentary rock formed at different times.

**bedrock** solid rock that lies beneath loose deposits of soil and other matter.

**Benioff-Wadati zone** sloping zone of earthquake centres in a subduction zone.

**biogenic** formed by living things.

**biostratigraphy** dating layers of rocks with fossils.

**carat** unit of weight for gems, equivalent to 200 milligrams.

**cation** positively charged ion.

**cementation** the stage in lithification when cement glues the sediment particles together.

**chalcophile** of elements such as copper and zinc that have an affinity for sulphur.

**clast** fragment of broken rock.

**clastic sediment** sedimentary rock made mainly of broken rock fragments.

**cleavage** the way a mineral breaks along certain planes.

**compaction** stage in lithification when water and air is squeezed out of buried sediments by the weight of overlying deposits.

**concretion** distinct nodules of materials in sedimentary rocks.

**contact metamorphism** when rocks are metamorphosed by contact with hot magma.

**contact twin** twinned crystals in which each crystal is distinct.

**continental drift** the slow movement of the continents.

**country rock** the rock that surrounds a mineral deposit or igneous intrusion.

**core** the centre of the Earth.

**craton** ancient part of a continent unaltered for at least one billion years.

**crust** the top layer of the earth, attached to the upper mantle.

**cryptocrystalline** with crystals so small that they cannot be seen even under an ordinary microscope.

**crystal form** the way in which the different faces of the crystals are arranged.

**crystal habit** the typical shape in which a crystal or cluster of crystals grows.

**crystal system** one of the different groups into which crystals can be placed according to how they are symmetrical.

**cuesta** low ridge with one steep side and one gently sloping.

**D" or D double prime** the transition zone between the Earth's mantle and core.

**Dana number** number assigned to each mineral according to the classification system devised by James Dwight Dana.

**detrital** made of rock fragments.

**diagenesis** all the processes that affect sediments after deposition including compaction and lithification.

**diaphaneity** the degree to which a mineral is transparent.

**disseminated deposit** mineral deposit created by infilling pores and cracks in igneous rock.

**drift geology** the geology of loose surface deposits.

**dyke** sheetlike igneous intrusion, either near vertical, or cutting across existing structures.

**Ediacaran** the geological period lasting from about 600 to 542 million years ago. This was added to the system in 2004.

**effusive volcano** volcano that erupts easily flowing lava.

**element** the simplest most basic substances, such as gold, each with its own unique atom.

**Era** vast portion of geological time lasting hundreds of millions of years.

**evaporite** a natural salt or mineral left behind after the water it is in has dried up.

**exposure** where a rock outcrop is exposed at the surface.

**extrusive igneous rock** type of rock that forms when volcanic lava cools and solidifies.

**facies** assemblage of mineral, rock or fossil features reflecting the conditions they formed in.

**fault** a long fracture in rock along

which rock masses move.

**feldspathic** rock containing feldspar.

**felsic** rock rich in feldspar and silica, typically light in colour.

**fissure volcano** volcano which erupts through a long crack.

**flood basalt** plateau formed from huge eruption of basalt lava from fissure.

**foid** abbreviation of feldspathoid.

**foliation** flat layers of minerals in metamorphic rock formed as minerals recrystallize under pressure.

**forearc basin** region on the trench side of an island arc in a subduction zone.

**fossil correlation** cross-checking of fossils between separate rock outcrops, used in rock dating.

**fractionation** the way in which the composition of a magma changes as crystals separate out when it melts and refreezes.

**fracture** the way in which a mineral breaks when it does not break along planes of cleavage.

**geode** hollow globe of minerals that can develop in limestone or lava, often lined with quartz.

**geological column** diagram showing the successive layers of strata that have formed over geological time, with the oldest at the bottom, youngest at top.

**glacial** a period in an Ice Age when ice sheets spread, or anything related to glaciers.

**graded bedding** layers of rocks which show a decrease of grain size, from coarse at the bottom to fine at the top.

**granular texture** of rock with visible, similar-sized grains.

**groundwater** water existing below ground. See also *phreatic water.*

**hydrothermal** related to water heated by magma.

**hydrothermal deposit** mineral deposit formed from mineral-rich hydrothermal fluids.

**hypabyssal** igneous rocks in small intrusions such as dykes.

**idiochromatic** mineral getting its colour from its main ingredients.

**igneous rock** rock that has solidified from molten magma.

**impact crater** crater formed by the impact of a meteorite.

**index fossil** key fossil used for correlating strata.

**index mineral** mineral that typifies a metamorphic facies.

**intraclast** any sedimentary rock fragment that originated within the area of the rock's formation.

**intrusion** emplacement of magma into existing rock.

**ion** atom given an electrical charge by gaining or losing electrons.

**island arc** curved chain of volcanic islands in a subduction zone, eg the Aleutians.

**isostasy** the natural buoyancy of the Earth's crust, making it rise and sink as its weight changes.

**isotope** variety of atom of an element that has a different number of neutrons (uncharged particles in its nucleus).

**joint** crack in rock created without any appreciable movement on either side, often at right angles to the bedding.

**karst** typical limestone scenery characterized by caverns, gorges and potholes.

**kimberlite** igneous rocks rich in volatiles, normally forming pipes.

**Large Igneous Province** Vast outflow of lava, typically on the ocean bed.

**laterite** weathered, soil-like material in the tropics rich in iron and aluminium oxides.

**lava** erupted magma.

**leucocratic** of light-coloured igneous rocks.

**lithification** change of loose sediments into solid rock.

**lithosphere** the rigid outer shell of the Earth containing the crust and upper mantle, broken into tectonic plates.

**lode** cluster of disseminated deposits.

**lutite** sedimentary rock made mainly of clay-sized grains.

**mafic** of rocks rich in magnesium and ferric (iron) compounds, equivalent to basic.

**magma** molten rock.

**magma chamber** underground reservoir of magma beneath a volcano.

**mantle** the zone of the Earth's interior between the crust and the core, made of hot, partially molten rock.

**mantle convection** circulation of material in the magma driven by the Earth's interior heat.

**mantle plume** long-lasting column of rising magma in the mantle.

**massive** of rocks with even texture, or a body of a mineral without any distinct crystals.

**melt** a mass of liquid rock.

**metamorphism** the process in which minerals in rocks are transformed by heat and pressure to create a new rock.

**metasomatism** metamorphic process in which minerals are transformed by hot solutions penetrating rock.

**meteoric water** water that comes from the air, typically in reference to groundwater.

**meteorite** a chunk of rock from space that reaches the Earth's surface.

**Mohs scale** the scale of relative hardness of minerals devised by Friedrich Mohs.

**MVT** Mississippi Valley Type mineral deposits, formed as limestone is altered by hot solutions.

**native element** element that occurs naturally uncombined with any other element.

**nodule** rounded concretion.

**nuée ardente** fast-moving clod of scorching ash and gases created by a volcanic eruption.

**ocean spreading** the process in which oceans widen as new rock is brought up at the mid-ocean ridge.

**oolith** small, usually calcareous accretions in a rock.

**oolitic** made mostly of ooliths.

**ophiolite** grouping of mafic and ultramafic igneous rocks, including pillow lavas, that were once part of the sea floor.

**ore** natural material from which useful metals can be extracted.

**orogeny** mountain-building.

**outcrop** area of rocks occurring at the surface.

**oxidation zone** upper layer of mineral deposit where minerals are altered by oxygen and acids in water.

**pegmatite** very coarse-grained igneous rock, usually found in veins and pockets around large plutons and rich in rare minerals.

**penetration twin** mineral crystal twin in which the crystals have grown into each other.

**Period** major portion of geological time lasting tens of millions of years.

**permeable** of rock that lets fluid or gas to seep through it easily.

**phaneritic** of grains visible with the naked eye.

**phenocryst** relatively large crystal in igneous rock.

**phreatic water** groundwater in the saturation zone of rock below the water table.

**pillow lava** lava formed on the sea bed consisting of pillow-shaped blobs.

**pisolith** pea-sized, usually calcareous accretions.

**pisolitic** made mostly of pisoliths.

**placer** deposit of valuable minerals washed into loose sediments such as river gravels.

**pluton** any large intrusion.

**polymorphs** different minerals created by different crystal structures of the same chemical compound.

**porous** full of voids (holes).

**porphyritic** of an igneous rock containing lots of phenocrysts

**primary mineral** mineral that forms at the same time as the rock containing it.

**protolith** the original rock forming a metamorphic rock.

**pseudomorph** mineral that takes the outer form of another.

**pyroclast** fragment of solid magma plug ejected during a volcanic eruption

**radiometric dating** the dating of rocks from radioactive isotopes within it.

**regional metamorphism** metamorphism over a wide area typical of fold mountain belts.

**rift valley** trough-shaped valley bounded by parallel faults.

**rudite** sedimentary rock consisting mostly of at least gravel-sized grains.

**schistosity** banding of minerals in schists created by parallel growth of mineral crystals.

**secondary mineral** mineral formed by alteration of primary minerals.

**sediment** solid grains that have settled out of water.

**seismology** study of earthquakes.

**serpentinization** alteration of ultramafic rocks to serpentine by hydrothermal fluids.

**siderophile** of elements such as cobalt and nickel that have an affinity for iron.

**silicic** of igneous rock such as granite rich in silica, making it acidic.

**sill** sheetlike igneous intrusion, either near horizontal, or following existing structures.

**skarn** typically mineral deposit created by the alteration of limestones by metasomatism.

**streak** mark made by a mineral rubbed on unglazed porcelain.

**strike** direction of fold or fault.

**subduction zone** boundary between two tectonic plates where one plate descends into the mantle beneath the other.

**tectonic plate** one of the 20 or so giant slabs into which the Earth's rigid surface is split.

**tenacity** how a mineral deforms.

**turbidity current** swirling undersea current.

**twin** paired mineral crystals growing together.

**vein** thin deposit of minerals formed in cracks.

**vesicle** small cavity formed by gas bubbles in lava flow.

**water table** level below which rock is saturated by groundwater.

# INDEX